10,000

GARDEN QUESTIONS

Answered By 20 Experts

10,000 garde

uestions

ANSWERED BY 20 EXPERTS

NEW, REVISED EDITION

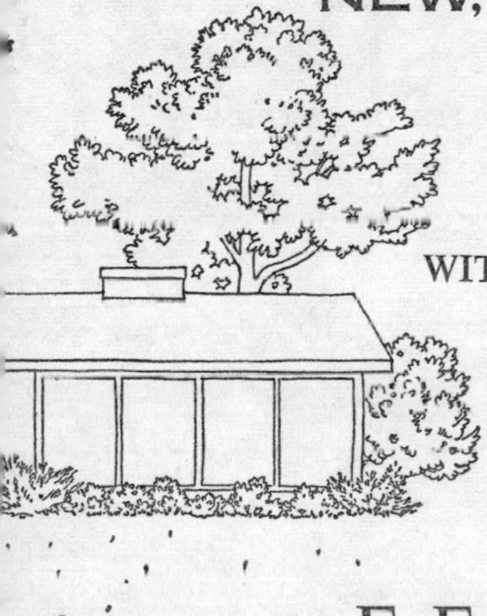

WITH OVER 400 ILLUSTRATIONS
AND TEMPERATURE AND
PLANTING MAPS

F. F. Rockwell

EDITOR

ASSOCIATE EDITORS

Montague Free, T. H. Everett
Esther C. Grayson

VOLUME 1

AN AMERICAN GARDEN GUILD BOOK

Published by

DOUBLEDAY & COMPANY, INC., Garden City, New York

The Editors of
10,000 Garden Questions Answered

THE HORTICULTURAL authorities who have planned and guided the preparation of *10,000 Garden Questions Answered* are well known to the American gardening public. Their combined experience covers pretty much the entire range of gardening activities. In the preparation of this book they have had, in addition to their own broad backgrounds of knowledge upon which to draw, the services of a score of specialists in certain lines.

F. F. ROCKWELL, editor in chief of the American Garden Guild Book Club, and senior editor of *Flower Grower—The Home Garden Magazine,* has long been familiar to this country's amateur gardeners through more than a score of books and his lectures, articles and natural-color photographs. At GrayRock, the country home of the Rockwells, extensive experiments and tests are carried on. Mr. Rockwell is a past president of the Men's Garden Clubs of America, and the 1955 recipient of its gold medal for horticultural achievement.

MONTAGUE FREE, for more than twenty-five years was horticulturist of the great Brooklyn Botanic Garden and is now senior editor and staff horticulturist of *Flower Grower—The Home Garden Magazine* and editor of the American Garden Guild Book Club. He is the author of many garden books and nationally known as an authority on all phases of gardening and a leading figure among garden writers.

T. H. EVERETT, well known lecturer and author of many books, has long been horticulturist of the New York Botanical Garden, a post which has brought him exceptionally broad contacts with the problems of amateur gardeners. His organization and direction of the Garden's courses in practical horticulture have been highlights in his career.

R. C. ALLEN, Ph.D., formerly secretary of the American Rose Society and on the staff of the Department of Floriculture and Ornamental Horticulture at Cornell University, and now Director of Kingswood Center, is a well known specialist in flowering plants, especially roses and delphiniums.

R. S. LEMMON, formerly published *Real Gardening,* and is one of the country's most widely and favorably known garden editors and lecturers. He has specialized in the field of native plants and wild-flowers, and was one of the organizers of the American Rock Garden Society.

P. J. McKENNA, was for many years assistant horticulturist of the world-famous New York Botanical Garden, and later chairman of horticulture for the Federated Garden Clubs of New York State, Inc. He lectured on and taught many horticultural subjects and was a president of the Men's Garden Club of New York.

W. E. THWING, is well known for his work with wildflowers, and his natural-color motion pictures of wild plants have won him wide recognition in the field of photography.

ALEX LAURIE, Ph.D., formerly professor of floriculture at Ohio State University is internationally famous as an authority on the soil and its fertility, plant feeding, and related subjects which have to do with the practical phases of plant growth.

C. H. CONNORS, Ph.D., heads the Department of Ornamental Horticulture at Rutgers University, besides being ornamental horti-culturist of the New Jersey Agricultural Experiment Station; an all-round authority of long and varied experience.

DONALD WYMAN, Ph.D., is horticulturist of the world-renowned Arnold Arboretum of Harvard University where he has earned a national reputation in the field of trees, shrubs and other woody plants.

T. A. WESTON, was the author of the famous newspaper column *One Man's Garden,* and one of America's leading authorities on growing all types of bulbs, corms and tubers; and on the principles and practices of most other phases of flower gardening.

CYNTHIA WESTCOTT, D.Sc., best known to many gardening readers as "The Plant Doctor", is a foremost authority on the pre-vention and control of plant insect pests and diseases. Of her many successful books *The Gardeners' Bug Book* and the *Plant Disease Handbook* are the most outstanding. She is always in close personal contact with the actual practice of what she preaches.

ESTHER C. GRAYSON (Mrs. F. F. Rockwell), is known to gardeners the country over as an expert on flower arrangement, house plants and the growing and use of herbs. Of equal importance is her wide knowledge and experience in the growing of vegetables and garden flowers.

HELEN VAN PELT WILSON, author of numerous garden books and a favorite writer on many phases of home gardening, is especially conversant with plants for the house and herbaceous perennials.

HELEN S. HULL, ex-president of the National Council of State Garden Clubs, Inc., and author of *Wild Flowers for Your Garden,* operates large gardens of her own and knows every plant in them.

LOUIS PYENSON, Ph.D., Professor and Chairman of the Biology Division of the State of New York Agricultural and Technical Institute at Farmingdale, Long Island, N.Y., is the author of books on pest controls, and a well known writer, lecturer and photographer in this field.

O. WESLEY DAVIDSON, Ph.D., is Professor and Research Specialist in Ornamental Horticulture at Rutgers University and the New Jersey Agricultural Experiment Station.

GEORGE L. SLATE, M.S., Professor of Pomology, Cornell University, New York State Agricultural Experiment Station, Geneva, N.Y., is a noted authority on lilies and fruits. He is editor of the Lily Year Book of the North American Lily Society, and his best-known book, *Lilies for American Gardens,* is recognized as a leading work in its field.

Other well-known authorities who have assisted in answering questions are:

MILTON CARLETON, Ph.D., Director of Research of the Vaughan Seed Company in Chicago, is known to gardeners throughout the country as a writer and speaker on horticultural subjects. **FRANCIS C. COULTER,** formerly an executive of one of the country's largest seed concerns, has written many articles and several books which are erudite as well as informative. **ALEX CUMMING,** who was widely known as a specialist in the breeding of fine chrysanthemums and author of a successful book on these popular plants, long headed a New England nursery which has served the gardening public for many years. **HENRY E. DOWNER** has practiced and taught horticulture in this country for a quarter century. He is horticulturist and superintendent of grounds at Vassar College.

KATHLEEN N. MARRIAGE is a widely known authority on rock gardening and the native flora of the Western highlands. **JOHN MELADY** is a noted specialist on lawns and all that goes into their establishment and maintenance. **H. DEWEY MOHR,** a specialist on dahlias, has developed many outstanding new varieties.

H. STUART ORTLOFF, landscape architect and co-author with H. B. Raymore of several excellent books and numerous articles on garden design, planting and maintenance, combines the artistic and practical angles of his profession with unusual success. To him "Will it work?" is really the acid test. **HILDEGARD SCHNEIDER,** head gardener at The Cloisters in New York, is an all-round plantswoman of long experience. **P. J. VAN MELLE** had a particular flair for native plants and rock gardening, and an accurate knowledge of plant histories and types. **THOMAS A. WILLIAMS** was known to hundreds of thousands of radio fans as "The Old Dirt Dobber" on his nationally heard C.B.S. program. **PROFESSOR PAUL WORK,** of the Department of Vegetable Crops, New York State Agricultural Experiment Station, "knows his onions" literally as well as figuratively. **DR. J. H. CLARK,** associate pomologist of the New Jersey State Agricultural Experiment Station, had a prominent part in the extensive fruit-testing and experiment program at that institution.

Other specialists and gardeners who have contributed valuable experience and knowledge to the preparation of this volume are: John H. Beale, George A. Buchanan, George E. Burkhardt, L. C. Chadwick, Dr. A. S. Colby, Charles F. Doney, Professor E. V. Hardenburg, D. C. Kiplinger, Stuart Longmuir, Harriet K. Morse, George D. Oberle, E. L. Reber, Roy P. Rogers, Kenneth D. Smith, Nancy Ruzicka Smith, John V. Watkins, Robert E. Weidner, Natalie Gomez and John Wingert.

Artists who have prepared illustrations are: George L. Hollrock, Pauline W. Kreutzfeldt, Helen Reddy, Carl Sigman, William Ward, Eva Melady, Tabea Hofmann, H. B. Raymore, Natalie Harlan Davis, Frederick Rockwell, Esther C. Grayson, Katharine Burton, Laurence Blair and Russell J. Walrath, who did the temperature and frost maps, adapted from data by the U. S. Department of Agriculture.

Contents

Introduction
To the New, Revised Edition

IT IS of course gratifying to the publishers and editors when any work, after a dozen years, is still sufficiently in demand to justify the expense and work involved in getting out a revised edition. For more than a decade now *10,000 Garden Questions Answered* has been, for hundreds of thousands of home gardeners, the family bible of garden information. This new edition, redesigned and reset, brings it completely up to date, making it even more helpful than in the past.

The preparation of 10,000 Garden Questions Answered was originally undertaken in response to numerous requests from readers of *The Home Garden Magazine*. It seemed worth while to present, in some organized and permanent form, the wealth of information which the answers to these questions convey.

Our purpose was to make this data available to the reader in a form that would enable him to refer to it quickly, and find readily, all the information on any particular subject. The most practical method of obtaining this objective, it seemed to us—after carefully studying several plans which suggested themselves—was to arrange this widely diversified mass of material in ten general categories that would cover the whole field. In the present edition these sections or divisions are:

I	Soils and Fertilizers
II	Landscaping
III	Ornamental Plants and Their Culture
	Trees and Shrubs
	Bulbs, Tubers, and Corms
	Roses
	Perennials
	Annuals and Biennials
IV	Lawns and Turf Areas
V	The Home Vegetable Garden
VI	Home Grown Fruits
VII	House Plants
VIII	Plant Troubles and Their Control
IX	Regional Garden Problems

THE "INTRODUCTIONS"

For each of these sections an introduction which gives general information on the subject covered has been prepared. The introductions are *based upon the questions most generally asked* concerning the subject discussed. In other words, these questions, instead of being answered individually, have been answered in a composite reply that presents the general principles involved and provides a background for the more specific questions which follow.

This treatment has two distinct advantages. In the first place, it enables the reader to get much more from the answers to the individual questions; in the second, it has saved a great amount of space. Actually, the *answers* to more than 13,000 questions are contained in the present volume.

The advantages of having questions answered by experts widely experienced in many lines are obvious. Too often such answers are compiled from outdated reference books. The answers in this volume are by persons who are actually *doing* the things they write about. Many of them are recognized internationally as authorities in their respective fields. At the same time, with few exceptions, their daily work brings them into direct contact with the problems of amateur gardeners the country over.

AN ADVANCE WORD TO CRITICS

With some fifty different persons contributing information of one sort or another, it is inevitable that many differences of opinion have arisen. In so far as possible, the recommendations and suggestions made on any specific subject have been brought into harmony by correspondence or discussion. There are cases where this has not been possible. The result is honest differences of opinion such as would be forthcoming on almost any garden question that might be asked of any group of experts—differences similar to those that would be found in every field of human endeavor, in any science or art, and horticulture partakes of both.

Unfortunately, too, we have in this country no generally recognized single authority in the realm of plant nomenclature. An attempt in this direction has been made in the publication of *Standardized Plant Names*. Botanists in general have been unwilling to follow all the recommendations of the hard-working committee which for many years unselfishly struggled with this perplexing problem. Excellent as has been the intention of this committee, many of its recommendations—particularly in abolishing, changing, and creating new common or English names—have not seemed acceptable even to the non-botanist. Nevertheless, those authorities who will not recognize *Standardized Plant Names* as the last word cannot agree among themselves on any other single authority. Thus this entire subject still remains in a chaotic state.

Even the least-informed beginner can imagine, with this condition existing, and with half a hundred contributors, each with his or her own ideas on the subject, what a problem we have faced in regard to nomenclature. In general, *Standardized Plant Names* has been followed; but in many instances—where it seemed that following its recommendations could only make "confusion worse confounded"— it has not.

The result, we realize, will leave the door wide open to the critics. However, our primary concern has been for the amateur reader; and where he can get the *meaning* of a question or an answer, we are content to let the scientists and botanists wrangle with us—and with each other—as to names, spelling, precedents, and authorities.

The botanically minded critic, too, will find some gall for his ink when it comes to botanical terms. For the most part the questions have been left in the dirt gardener's terminology in which they were written, and often the answers are in kind. Where the questioner has asked about how to plant a dahlia "tuber," for instance, it has not been deemed necessary to instruct him that he should have said "root" (or, more accurately, "bulbous root"). A too-strict adherence to botanical terminology often tends to confuse the beginner rather than to enlighten him, and this volume is primarily for beginners.

I wish to take this opportunity, also, to express my appreciation for the co-operation we have had from the group of contributors who have made possible this volume, and especially to the assistant editors, Montague Free, T. H. Everett, and Esther C. Grayson for the untiring effort they have put into the work of handling the thousands of details involved in its preparation.

Our aim has been to present the amateur gardener with *practical* information in readily available form, concerning his own personal problems. To the extent that this has been accomplished, we will have succeeded in making the kind of book we set out to create.

F.F.R.

What Is YOUR Question?

(Suggestions as to how to use this book most effectively)

To GET from these pages the information you wish, most completely and in the shortest time, read carefully the following paragraphs. They explain, first, how this book is put together; and, second, the definite steps to take in finding the answer to a specific problem, or to one so general in character that it might not be possible to locate it through the Index.

ORGANIZATION PLAN

As you know, there are ten main divisions or sections, covering Soils and Fertilizers, Ornamental Plants and Their Culture, Lawn and Turf Areas, Landscaping, Home Vegetable Gardening, Home Grown Fruits, House Plants, Plant Troubles and Their Control, Regional Problems, and Miscellaneous Lists of Agricultural Experiment Stations, Flower, Fruit and Tree Societies, Garden Centers, and Books and Bulletins on Special Subjects.

Each of these sections is organized along the following lines:

1. A general introduction, giving basic information about the subject concerned. (The introduction for Soils and Fertilizers, for instance, describes the function of the soil in connection with plant growth, different types of soil, soil acidity, the various nutrients essential to plant growth, the part which humus plays in the soil, and so on.)
2. Following the introduction, the questions, in most sections, are arranged in the following order:

What to Grow	Winter Protection
Soils	Propagation
Fertilizers	Varieties
Planting and Transplanting	Specific Plants
Culture	(In Alphabetical Order)

USE OF INDEX

In most instances any specific question can be located through the use of the Index.

1. Formulate your question in your own mind as definitely as possible. (It will be helpful to write it down on paper.)
2. Pick out the KEY WORD in the question. (For instance, it might be "How should I train *tomatoes?*" "How can I *graft* a good variety of apple on a wild tree?" or "What is a good *perennial* to grow in the *shade?*"
3. Then look up the key word ("tomato," "graft," "perennial" or "shade") in the Index. Under this item, in the Index, you will probably find several references. One of these (example: "tomato, staking") may indicate exactly what you are looking for, and you can then turn at once to the specific question you have in mind.

MORE GENERAL QUESTIONS

The question in your mind may, however, be of such a nature that you do not know what to look for in the Index to locate it. Suppose, for example, that you have seen somewhere, growing high on a wall, a vine-like plant with hydrangea-like flowers, and you would like to know what it is. A search through the section on "Vines—Perennial" would quickly reveal that it is the Climbing Hydrangea (*Hydrangea petiolaris*).

It is recommended that, in looking up questions on any general subject—such as fertilizers, lawns, vegetables, fruits—*the introduction be read in full first*. Here you will find in text form the answers to many questions, some of which may not reappear in the questions and answers. Familiarity with the introduction will also help materially in augmenting the information to be gained from the answers to specific questions.

In the answers to some questions the reader is referred to his State Experiment Station. A list of these stations is given on page 1318, and a list of Garden Centers is given on page 1321. Frost maps (showing dates of last killing frost in spring, and first in fall) are on pages 1326 to 1329.

The list of books and bulletins (page 1309) will guide the reader to full and detailed information on many different garden subjects.

10,000
GARDEN QUESTIONS

Answered By 20 Experts

Soils and Fertilizers

INTRODUCTION

BY ALEX LAURIE

AND O. WESLEY DAVIDSON

THE SOIL in which we garden is a product of physical, chemical, and biological forces acting on mineral materials and organic residues. It is teeming with life—up to 3 percent of the weight of a good composted soil is that of the microorganisms present in it—supported by the plant and animal residues. This biological activity makes possible some of the most important processes in our soil:

(1) It makes nutrients available by decomposing complex or insoluble substances containing them.

(2) It produces nutrients by reaction with air.

(3) It produces substances that improve the structure of soils and thus increases the amounts of oxygen available to plant roots.

(4) It transforms some organic materials into substances that bind nutrients to the soil in such a manner that they are available to plant roots but resistant to being washed out.

(5) It produces antibiotic substances that control or limit the development of disease organisms.

Your garden soil, therefore, is not a mass of "dirt" (i.e. "matter out of place," or "filthy substance"). Rather, it is an amazingly complex medium in which processes of inestimable value to society occur. Our care of a soil may drastically influence not only its supply of nutrients to plant roots, but also its very structure and its microbial activity.

Soil Types

Soils vary in texture (size of the individual particles of which they are made up), in structure (the arrangement of the particles), in organic matter content, in water-holding capacity, in heat retention, and in the supply of plant nutrients they contain. According to their texture, soils are classed as sand, silt, and clay.

Loam is an intermediate between any two of these. Thus we have sandy loam, silt loam, or clay loam. The best structure is "crumb," which means granular. This is dependent upon the presence of humus, without which granular structure is hard to obtain. It tends to hold small particles together. Freezing and thawing, cultivation, and the action of roots also help to produce granular structure.

Humus is a dark-brown substance resulting from the decomposition of plant or animal residues. Soil organisms are needed in this process of decomposition. Humus is an important component of soils. It modifies the soil color, texture, structure, water-holding capacity, and air-holding capacity. Likewise, it serves as a source of energy for the minute organisms. In speaking of humus and its action it should be remembered that humus is not synonymous with *undecomposed* organic matter. Organic matter such as manure, straw, or green manure (crops grown to be turned into the soil), becomes humus *only when it has reached an advanced stage of decomposition.*

Other Soil Factors

Soil Aeration. Air is important in the soil. It circulates through the space around the soil particles, making it possible for roots to grow. Furthermore, air is necessary for the existence of certain important soil organisms. It is known that carbon dioxide is given off in the decomposition of organic matter. An accumulation of this gas is injurious to the roots; consequently its removal from the soil by entrance of fresh air is desirable. Poorly granulated soils and wet soils lack aeration. Additions of organic matter help, together with the incorporation of fine sand or fine cinders. In general, *most plants grow best when the soil is well aerated.* Many of our troubles come from lack of appreciation of this fact.

During the past 10 years a number of soil conditioning agents have been developed. Some of these have been offered for sale to gardeners. The function of these materials has been to improve the structure of the soil by cementing clay and silt particles into larger units called aggregates or granules. The spaces between the aggregates are much larger than those between the unaggregated clay and silt particles. Such spaces, in fact, are large enough to permit rapid exchange of carbon dioxide and oxygen in the soil, thereby improving root growth. The aggregated particles, moreover, are relatively resistant to erosion.

Synthetic conditioning agents function in the same manner as do the cementing by-products of microorganisms that decompose organic matter in soils. Although some of the synthetic agents are capable of developing somewhat more stable aggregates than are formed by soil microbes, the differences, nevertheless, have been greatly exaggerated in advertising claims. In many good garden soils aggregation is already adequate, and synthetic conditioning agents fail to improve crop growth, even though they may give the soil a better "feel."

These synthetic conditioners are most effective on silty and clayey soils, especially when the latter are low in organic matter.

Soil Water. The water in the soil most essential to plant growth is capillary water—the water which surrounds and clings to the soil particles. The amount of this water in the soil depends on the size of the particles and upon their structure. The smaller the particles, as in clay, the greater the water content. Sands, because of their relatively large-sized particles, have comparatively low moisture-holding capacity. Clays, on the other hand, comprising extremely small particles, have high moisture-holding capacity. Organic matter tends to improve the moisture-holding capacity of the sands and the drainage and aeration of the clays.

Heavy rains and forcible application of water cause greater losses of water into drainage channels. Hence, in practice, even when heavy watering is required, it should be applied so gradually that it will not run off the surface.

Control of Moisture. Water loss from the soil may be reduced by good tillage, mulching, and additions of organic matter and fertilizers.

Good tillage means plowing or spading at the proper time and to a suitable depth. In regions where fall and winter rainfall is light, fall spading is preferred. The resulting loose surface absorbs any available moisture instead of allowing it to run off. Heavy soils should be spaded deeper than sandy soils unless the latter are well supplied with humus.

The texture of the soil should be considered at the time of spading. If heavy soils are spaded when wet, clods will form. Sandy soils may be worked when relatively wet. Cultivation is also part of tillage. Its chief function is to keep down weeds which draw moisture and nutrients from the soil; its secondary function is to reduce evaporation from the soil by breaking the crust. In heavy soils this secondary function may be advantageous; in sandy soils it may do more harm than good by causing the top to dry out more quickly, without sufficient capillarity to bring up the stored moisture from below.

Mulching is a method of covering the surface of the soil with some organic or inert material which prevents evaporation and yet admits air. Manures, peats, straw, hay, alfalfa or clover chaff, cottonseed hulls, ground corncobs, leaves, mulch paper, may all be used for the mulching purposes.

The gradual decomposition of organic mulches adds humus to soils, improving both the structure of the soil and its capacity to retain added nutrients. The latter effect is one of the most important functions of organic matter in soils. It protects nutrients from loss by leaching.

Soil and Plant Nutrients

Soil Composition. The soil forms a comparatively thin layer over the earth's surface. Its chief constituent is mineral matter; but organic matter, bacteria, soil, air, and water are also essential constituents. The plant derives most of its essential elements from this mineral matter. These elements form only a small percentage of the composition of the plant tissues, and their importance varies. Phosphorus and potassium are two important elements derived from mineral matter that are lacking in the average soil, or exist in forms that are made available too slowly to meet the needs of most cultivated crops. Other essential elements derived from mineral matter are calcium, magnesium, sulfur, iron, manganese, boron, zinc, copper, molybdenum, chlorine, and perhaps sodium.

Nitrogen is one of the most essential elements and is almost universally limited. In nature, nitrogen is added to the soil by means of decaying organic matter and by bacteria found in nodules on the roots of many plants, chiefly the legumes. A small but appreciable amount of nitrogen is added to soils as ammonia carried down with rainfall.

Carbon, hydrogen, and oxygen (which in different combinations form carbohydrates and water) make up the bulk of the plant. These elements are derived from the air and from the soil moisture. Because of the universal presence of each they are not considered as problems to the gardener, although water is often deficient and carbon dioxide may not be present in sufficient quantity for optimum growth.

The Functions and Sources of the Nutrient Elements

Nitrogen forms a part of *all* proteins. Protein makes up the bulk of the protoplasm which is the living matter. Nitrogen is an essential constituent of chlorophyll (the green colored bodies in the leaves and stems of plants). Chlorophyll is essential for the manufacture of sugars. Nitrogen is also a constituent of amino acids, alkaloids, and aromatic compounds within the plant. Nitrogen stimulates the vegetative growth, and size of foliage, and color in flowers.

> *Because of the importance of nitrogen in plant growth it is essential to have an available supply. Since nature cannot provide nitrogen in sufficient quantities, other sources are essential; namely, commercial fertilizers and manures. Nitrate of soda, sulfate of ammonia, dried blood, cottonseed meal, and the various manures are some of the materials used for supplying extra nitrogen when it is needed in greater amounts than the soil seems able to provide.*

Phosphorus is an essential constituent of the proteins. It occurs abundantly in the nucleus and, to a less extent, in the cytoplasm (body cells). It is also essential to cell division. Phosphorus is associated with reproduction: seeds are rich in phosphorus. It is helpful in root development and in balancing nitrogen. Excessive amounts of phosphorus, however, make iron and zinc unavailable, and cause chlorosis —the yellowing of foliage—and stunting of growth.

The phosphorus problem is a nationwide one. Most soils are naturally low in this element and most of the phosphorus present is in the form of tricalcium phosphate—a form that is only slightly available to most garden crops.

> *To enrich the soil with phosphorus, a commercial fertilizer is applied. Superphosphate (20 per cent phosphorus) or treble phosphate (45 per cent phosphorus) are the most effective materials for building up available phosphorus. Bone meal carries about 23 per cent phosphorus, but in less available form.*

Potassium is an element required by plants in relatively large amounts, even though it does not become a part of the cell walls nor any solid portion of a plant. This element functions in association with enzymes, the organic "catalysts" which regulate the digestion and translocation of foods and of some nutrients. Potassium plays an important role in the activity of lateral meristems which are associated with growth in diameter, such as the thickening of beets, potatoes, and dahlia tubers. Potassium also plays an important part in adapting plants to withstand low temperatures.

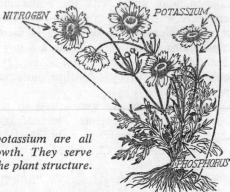

Nitrogen, phosphorus, and potassium are all essential to normal plant growth. They serve different purposes in building the plant structure.

Most soils are deficient in potassium in an available form. Many soils with an apparent potassium deficiency contain as high as 50,000 lbs. per acre, but it exists in chemical combinations, forming compounds which cannot be used by the plant. A heavy soil well supplied with organic matter usually has enough available potassium for plant use. *A soil deficient in organic matter is usually deficient in potassium.*

The organic matter favors beneficial bacterial action, and organic acids render the combined potassium available.

> *Potassium may be added to the soil in the form of potassium chloride or potassium sulfate (muriate or sulfate of potash), or in hardwood ashes and manures.*

Calcium and magnesium are both found in most limestones, and in many fertilizers. Calcium is required by plants for the development of cell walls of all new tissues. It is also essential for the utilization of nitrates in some plants. Magnesium is necessary for the formation of chlorophyll and for the functioning of a number of plant enzymes.

Sulfur is a common constituent of most, but not all, commercial fertilizers. It is also a constituent of some amino acids, proteins, and hormones in plants.

Minor, or trace, elements (iron, manganese, boron, zinc, copper, and molybdenum) have been given considerable attention lately by agricultural research workers and by fertilizer manufacturers. These elements all play very important roles in the growth and development of plants. The fact that each of them is required by the plant in minute quantities has relegated them to the category of "minor elements."

Many years ago, the relatively unrefined fertilizers of the time contained most of these minor elements, and in significant amounts. Manures and various organic fertilizers show traces, or even appreciable amounts, of the minor elements.

In contrast, most of the modern inorganic fertilizer materials are free of minor elements. As a consequence of the continued tillage of a given land, along with the replacement of manure and organic fertilizers with refined chemical fertilizers, the need for the addition of minor elements to fertilizers is increasing. In general, separate applications of minor elements are not warranted. Such a practice should be followed only when advised by the county agricultural extension service, or by a fertilizer authority familiar with the soils of the area.

Some fertilizers are guaranteed to provide small but significant amounts of minor elements. The amounts thus provided are not usually adequate to correct an established deficiency of a minor element in a reasonable time. Continued use of the fertilizer on a given area, however, will provide amounts adequate to prevent the occurrence of a deficiency. Soft glasses, or "frits," are being manufactured to provide the minor elements in slowly soluble forms. One application will furnish enough of these nutrients to see a crop through two or more seasons.

Manures

Barnyard manure has, until recently, been the mainstay in maintaining soil fertility. This type of fertilizer has its advantages in that in addition to supplying some plant nutrients, humus and desirable bacteria are also added. These improve the physical condition of the soil, increase the moisture-holding capacity, provide better aeration, and render unavailable nutrient elements more available.

As far as the *actual value of the chemical nutrients* is concerned, manure is expensive. Some nitrogen and potassium are returned to the soil by adding manure. The quantity of potassium is small; the amount of phosphorus is so little that manure is valueless as a phosphorus fertilizer. The nitrogen content varies greatly with the type of manure and the way it is handled. If this manure is properly cared for while accumulating, so as to prevent leaching and burning, considerable nitrogen as well as potassium can be returned to the soil through its application. But the average manure is handled in such a way that little nitrogen and potassium is retained.

Synthetic Manure. Due to the growing scarcity of manure, the practice of making synthetic manure has increased. Such manure, or, more accurately, compost, made from straw, leaves, weeds, and other garden refuse, is equal in value to manure. The compost pile

Into the compost heap may go anything that will decay. Soil and peatmoss are added to garden refuse. Lime and chemicals hasten decomposition, enrich the compost.

should be 4 to 6 ft. high. The straw or leaves are arranged in 6-inch layers and the reagent (fertilizer) scattered over the surface of each layer. The top of the compost pile should be flat to retain the water. Fermentation starts immediately and within 3 or 4 months, under favorable conditions, decomposition is sufficiently complete for much of the material to be utilized in place of manure. (Portions not entirely decomposed can be used to start a new heap.) The following formula has been worked out for an inexpensive and effective reagent for use in making the compost:

Sulfate of ammonia	60 lbs.
Superphosphate	30 lbs.
Potassium chloride	25 lbs.
Ground limestone	50 lbs.

These materials, when mixed with 1 ton of dry straw, will make 2 or 3 tons of artificial manure. If the heap is made in the spring, with sufficient water applied during the season, good manure may be had by early fall.

Green manures are crops grown for the purpose of being plowed or dug into the soil. Cowpeas, buckwheat, soybeans, oats, rye, clovers, and alfalfa have long been used for this purpose, and are valuable in maintaining the humus content of the soil, preventing excessive leaching of soluble nutrients, increasing bacterial content, aeration, and drainage, and in making certain elements more available. Legumes add nitrogen to the soil. The use of green manures has become more popular with the increasing scarcity of barnyard manure.

Commercial Fertilizers

It has required long experience for the gardener to place his faith in maintaining the fertility of his soil through the use of commercial fertilizers. Many gardeners are still not convinced that commercial fertilizers are all that their advocates claim them to be. This is only to be expected. The confidence in any new thing is not gained until after it has passed the period of experimentation. The value of commercial fertilizers has been definitely proven, and when they are used as recommended, there is little danger of damage. It must be remembered that this type of fertilizer is in an extremely concentrated form and that there is always danger of overdosage, *especially if the humus content of the soil is not maintained.*

Commercial fertilizers may be obtained in a "complete" form, or as fertilizers containing one or more of the individual elements. A complete fertilizer contains nitrogen, phosphorus, and potassium, mixed in various proportions, such as 4–12–4, 5–10–5, or 8–8–8. The first figure represents the percentage of nitrogen, the second of phosphorus, and the third of potassium. Some of the commercial fertilizers offered for sale in certain areas may contain magnesium, as well as some or all of the minor elements. Dealers in fertilizers and garden supplies usually stock the fertilizers recommended for their particular areas.

Soil Acidity

The degree of acidity in the soil is another factor which influences the growth of plants. Practically all the vegetables, and the great majority of ornamental plants, grow well in a slightly acid soil. With some plants, however, a soil too acid or too alkaline will seriously retard growth, or may even prove fatal.

The symbol pH is a means of expressing the acidity or alkalinity of the soil. In technical terms it stands for the hydrogen-ion con-

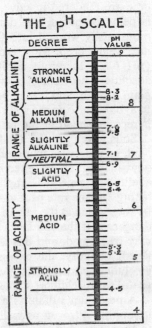

The degree of acidity or alkalinity of the soil is indicated by the pH scale, which ranges from 1 to 10, with 7 as the neutral point. Practically all vegetables, and the great majority of other plants, thrive in neutral to moderately acid soil, with a pH of 6 to 7.

centration. This is measured by means of a potentiometer; or, more commonly, by special synthetic dyes, used as indicators. The colors of the dyes change with the increase or decrease of the hydrogen-ion concentration, and the symbold pH is used as the indicator. The pH scale is graded from 1, which is extremely acid, to 10, which is extremely alkaline. The gradations between 1 and 10 are not exactly uniform, however. The neutral point is, accordingly, 7. The majority of garden plants do best at a pH of 6.0 to 6.5, or slightly acid. Plants requiring acid conditions (such as rhododendrons, azalea, and laurel) generally do best in a soil with a pH of 5.0 to 5.5.

Acid soils are usually common in humid sections. This condition arises through the lack of certain active bases, and, when excessive, is detrimental to many plants in three main ways—(1) unfavorable hydrogen-ion concentration; (2) presence of substances harmful to plant growth, as active aluminum, iron, and manganese; (3) improper nutrition from the lack of calcium.

The most common method of rectifying a soil that is too acid is by the application of lime. Other bases could be used, but lime has its advantages in that it is cheap; it is an essential element; it is easily handled; an excess is not detrimental; and it is an agent which aids in maintaining other nutrients in available form. When lime is applied, it neutralizes the free acids; and the toxic aluminum, iron, and manganese are rendered inactive. Lime is usually applied when the seedbed is being prepared, but during the dry season in the fall the lime is more easily worked into the soil and will be more beneficial to the next year's crop. Most crops do best in soils which are slightly acid (pH 6.5); therefore additions of lime should be made only when absolutely necessary. However, calcium is an important element in plant growth, and it may be lacking in the soil. In such cases, in order to avoid changing the soil reaction (acidity) gypsum (calcium sulfate) is recommended at the rate of 2 to 4 lbs. to 100 sq. ft.

Soils which are too alkaline (above pH 7) usually have to be acidified, as otherwise many of the elements of plant growth may become unavailable. To be effective over a long period sulfur is the best acidifying agent. It is applied—in the fall, preferably, since it is slow acting—at the rate of 2 to 4 lbs. per 100 sq. ft. Aluminum sulfate may be substituted at the rate of 1 lb. per 100 sq. ft. It is quick acting, but is dangerous if the soil lacks phosphorus. In such a case free aluminum may be formed, and this is injurious. If phosphorus is present in sufficient quantity, the excess aluminum combines with it to form an insoluble and harmless aluminum phosphate. Iron sulfate likewise is useful as an acidifier; it is used at the same rate as aluminum sulfate.

Ammonium sulfate is a particularly useful acidifying agent, since it supplies nitrogen as well as acidity. When used in proper amounts to supply needed nitrogen, each pound of ammonium sulfate develops more than enough acidity to neutralize a pound of limestone. Pound for pound, ammonium sulfate develops more than twice as much acid in a soil as does iron sulfate or aluminum sulfate.

Building Up the Fertility of Home Grounds

To summarize the procedures involved, it is best, first of all, to have your soil tested by your State Experiment Station for its acidity and the available elements present. The next step is to be sure that proper drainage exists. After that, to be on the safe side, organic matter, preferably in the form of a 2-in. layer of manure or compost, should be spaded into the soil in the fall. The soil is best left rough and uneven over winter, as this increases the pulverizing action of alternate freezing and thawing. If needed, lime may also be added at the same time. It is well to add phosphorus, too, in the form of super-phosphate, to make sure that this material is worked down into the soil deep enough to do the most good. Further additions of complete fertilizers should be made in the spring and during the growing season.

Peatmoss is rapidly taking the place of manure in suburban gardening, because animal manure is not readily available. Peatmoss can be incorporated into a garden soil at any time, since it does not need to be composted. It has very high capacity to retain fertilizer nutrients and to prevent their loss by leaching but, at the same time, it keeps them available to the plant. In acid soils the addition of a cup of pulverized limestone to each bushel of peatmoss, before the latter is mixed with the soil, helps prevent a further increase in acidity and so may lead to maximum plant growth. In soils that are neutral or alkaline, no limestone need be added with peatmoss.

TYPES OF SOIL

What are the different kinds of soil? How are they prepared for planting? *Sandy soil:* contains less than 20 per cent clay and silt; water lost quickly; fertilizer elements leach quickly; contains too much air; absorbs too much heat. Add as much organic matter as possible. *Clay soil:* contains very fine particles; holds too much water; lacks air; sticky after rain; "puddles"—i.e., runs together in thick mud. Add organic matter and fine cinders or sand. *Loam:* intermediate, between sand and clay, and the most satisfactory for general use.

How do you recognize the value of natural soil? How do you improve it? The nutritional value of soil is hard to determine by casual inspection. A test must be made to determine it. However, dark soils usually have organic matter. To determine good structure use a trowel: loams when lifted will fall apart in small crumbs; sandy soils break up into individual particles; clay soils can be broken apart only by force, and then into clods.

Are there special kinds of soil for different plants? Root crops require friable, light soils for best development. Crops with fine roots do better in coarse open soil, while coarse-rooted plants grow better in more dense soils composed of finer particles.

SANDY SOIL

We have a sandy lot and wish to enjoy good results. Should we put black topsoil on? Yes. Extremely sandy soil needs loam.

What depth of topsoil should we use on sandy ground? Add 3 ins. loam and spade to a depth of 6 ins.

What kind of fertilizer is best for sandy soil? Use a complete fertilizer, such as a 5–10–5, and manure or peatmoss. Fertilizer is best applied frequently, in small amounts.

To build up sandy soil, I have used straw as a mulch and spaded in manure and peatmoss. Still I cannot get many plants to grow. Why? Add loam, plus more manure and peat, and fertilizers in small amounts frequently.

Our soil is very sandy. Results are poor. Can chicken manure be used for improvement? Yes. Apply poultry manure at the rate of 10 to 20 pounds per 100 sq. ft. Use dried, pulverized poultry manure according to the recommendations on the package. To balance the fertilizer value of this, add a pound of 0–14–14 fertilizer per 100 sq. ft. Results will be greatly improved if peatmoss is used at the rate of 5 or 6 bushels per 100 sq. ft.

How can I fertilize a very sandy soil that has little top soil? Incorporate one or more green-manure crops. Add a commercial fertilizer suitable for the crop to be grown.

Can fallen leaves be used to improve a gravelly soil, and how? Yes. Let them decompose first.

I have a very sandy soil that is very rocky. What should I do with it? At present soil seems dead; plants grow, but soon die. Remove surface rocks. Add soil and manure and work in. Add a complete fertilizer several times each year.

How do you loosen a sandy loam that packs? Add manure, peatmoss, or leafmold, and incorporate in the top 6 ins. of soil.

I have a steep gravel bank which I have terraced and planted, but which still looks barren. It is hot, dry, and steep. What will encourage plants to grow? Dig holes in the bank; fill with compost of soil and manure. Gradually the plants set out in this fashion will cover the bank.

How can light sandy soil with gravel base be made productive for LAWN and for FLOWER and VEGETABLE garden? By heavy applications of organic matter—manure, etc.

What plants and GRASS do you recommend where the soil is essentially sandy, and where plants such as wild Mountain Laurel, huckleberry, sumach, etc., flourish extremely well? Have soil tested yearly and apply correct amount of lime. Then plants will grow. Kentucky Blue Grass is most satisfactory.

How can I improve the soil for CACTI? (West Virginia.) The requirements of cacti are simple. Well-drained, sandy soil with little if any fertilizer added. Hot, dry, infertile conditions are best.

What shall be added to soil in FLOWER bed that packs after rain and forms hard crust on top? Soil is of sandy nature. Add 3 ins. of manure, peatmoss, or leafmold, and spade to a depth of 6 ins.

My front yard is mostly sand. What FLOWERS would be best to plant? Portulaca, California poppy, annual phlox, calliopsis, cockscomb, morningglory, anthemis, milkweed, aster, babiesbreath, liatris, yucca. To remedy situation, add manure and fertilizer.

Our soil is sandy. How can we grow good ROSES? Add manure or peatmoss. Keep soil fertilized and water heavily when necessary.

Our soil (on river front) is solid sand. Would surfacing it with black dirt be sufficient for planting FRUIT TREES? No. A very large hole should be dug for each tree, and filled with good soil in which to plant.

What would you suggest for a HOME GARDEN at the seashore where there is a lot of sand? Additions of animal manure will help, although it would be better to mix some loam with the sand. Also dig under green cover crops.

I have a piece of very sandy land and wish to grow excellent CORN. Can it be done? Yes, manure heavily; also apply a complete fertilizer several times during growing season.

Our soil is all gravel. How can I adjust this for growing VEGE-TABLES? Add mixture of loam and manure to a depth of 3 ins. and spade to a depth of 6 ins.

What is the best way of keeping land in shape for VEGETABLES? The soil is light and sandy but well drained. Spade in manure every fall. Keep well fertilized and properly cultivated.

Our soil is very sandy and is acid. What can we do so we can grow a VEGETABLE garden? Increase the organic content of the soil by incorporating green-manure crops, farm manures, or other non-acid materials such as leaves, straw, plant refuse, or non-acid peat. Apply lime as needed to modify the acidity.

Our Long Island soil is very sandy; my VEGETABLES are never much of a success. Is this because of the soil? No matter how much topsoil we put on, it sinks in. Add loam and plenty of manure. A 3-in. layer should be spaded to a depth of 6 ins. Any vegetable can be grown if well watered and fertilized.

Our soil is sandy; fertilizer seems to cause worms in the underground VEGETABLES. Is this due to the soil? The soil is infested with wireworms. Apply 2 pounds of a 5 per cent chlordane dust per 1,000 sq. ft. of soil surface in Eastern States. In Western States, apply 2 pounds of a 10 per cent DDT dust per 1,000 sq. ft. about 6 weeks before planting. In both cases dusts should be worked thoroughly into the upper 6 or 8 inches of soil.

My ground is sandy. What is the best VEGETABLE to plant? Any vegetable will grow in sandy soil if fertilized frequently. Apply fertilizer high in phosphorus and potash.

For sandy soil plant material see also Sandy Environment, Section III.

CLAY SOIL

What makes clay so sticky?   Clay is composed of very minute particles which have a large surface to absorb water. High water content causes the stickiness.

Should clay soil be worked when wet?   No; never. It puddles and makes a poor environment for roots. Digging too soon in spring may make it practically useless for the season.

How much wood ashes is it safe to use on heavy clay soil?   At least 10 lbs. per 100 sq. ft.

My garden plot is heavy clay soil and produces well, but it is hard to work up. Would well-rotted manure and wood ashes be of benefit? Yes. Fine cinders would also be beneficial.

Should coal ashes be sifted before using them on clay soil?   In general, no. Large cinders or lumps should be broken or removed.

How coarse should the coal ashes be for use on clay soil?   One fourth in. or finer.

What proportion of sifted coal ashes should be mixed with clay to make it good for flowers?   A 2-in. layer of sifted ashes spaded in will be safe.

Are sifted coal ashes in clay soil better than sand?   Yes; they are of more help in opening it up and admitting air.

Does it make any difference what kind of sand is mixed with clay soil to lighten it? To what depth should the sand be spread on before spading in?   Yes. Coarse or ungraded sands, containing a large proportion of $\frac{1}{16}$- to $\frac{1}{8}$-inch particles, will bring about the greatest improvement when added to a clay soil. Incorporate a 2-inch layer of such sand.

What shall I do to keep ground loosened? It gets sticky and lumpy. I mixed in sand and ashes but they did not help.   Probably too little sand was used. Manure and/or peatmoss should improve such a soil.

My ground gets hard and dry on the surface, so that it is difficult for the young shoots to break through. It is soft enough beneath the surface. What can I do?   Incorporate sand, and, if possible, well-rotted manure, in the upper surface.

My garden soil is mostly clay. I dug under quite a few leaves in an effort to add humus to the soil. Will leaves tend to make the soil acid?   Usually not; but it would be advisable, in any case, to test the soil for acidity, which see.

Is chemical fertilizer harmful to clay soil?   No. Often necessary to furnish mineral elements so plants will grow.

What can be added to a clay soil to increase root growth? It is slightly acid, and in partial shade.   If wet, soil must be drained by use of tile. Add manure or peatmoss. Slight acidity is all right for vegetables and for most ornamental plants. (See Acidity, this section.)

What kind of fertilizer is best for inert clay soil? Incorporation of organic matter and lime will probably benefit such a soil. The fertilizer to apply will depend upon the crop to be grown.

How may I improve a heavy, extremely wet clay soil? Pine trees thrive on it. The physical condition of an extremely wet clay soil can be improved by using 4 in. agricultural drain tile (see Drainage) and the incorporation of liberal amounts of screened cinders or sand. Add ground limestone, as necessary, to lower the acidity.

Will adding ashes and dry leaves to thin clay soil bring it to the consistency of loam? Yes, if you add enough, and wait long enough. Apply manure, peatmoss, or both, to hasten the process.

The soil in the garden is very clayey and needs conditioning. How can I do that with all the SHRUBBERY and perennials in? Remove perennials after hard frost and spade in 3 ins. of manure and 2–3 ins. of coarse sand. Replant perennials at once.

What are the best materials to mix with a heavy soil of BLUE CLAY? Peatmoss, manure, and fine cinders.

What crops would help to break up soil of blue clay? Shallow-rooted ones, such as rye and oats.

Is lime helpful to soil of blue clay? Have soil tested to determine if lime is needed; usually it is helpful. (See Lime, this section.)

How does GRAY CLAY differ from red clay? Depends on kinds of minerals the clay is composed of and amount of air present when clay was formed. Red clay usually contains iron.

Is gray clay fertile? Yes, but probably would be better for plants if it is fertilized.

What can be done with gray clay soil to make it produce? Add humus first, then apply fertilizers as crop growth may indicate the need for them.

Is it best to grow a green-manure crop in gray clay soil over winter, or dig it up in the fall and leave it so? Fertilize soil, grow a winter cover crop, and plow under in spring.

What will darken light-colored (gray) clay soil? How many years will it take to make such soil black in color? Organic matter— manure, etc. It would require several years of constant applications, but it is not at all necessary to make the soil black in order to have it productive.

Is PIPE-CLAY soil acid? Clay soils vary in their degree of acidity. To determine the reaction of the particular soil in mind, test it or send a sample to your State Agricultural College. (See Acidity, this section.)

I have a patch of heavy RED CLAY soil to condition. Is there an easy way to do it? I've used peatmoss, sand, leafmold, and well-rotted manure. Use more of the same. Sorry; no easy way.

My tract of land has heavy, tough red clay base, with only light topsoil covering. What is best treatment? Grow cover crops of soybeans plowed under before beans are ripe. Follow with crop of rye to be plowed under the following spring.

Will peatmoss make a red clay soil heavier? No. It loosens it up and makes it easier to handle.

What green-manure crop is best for ROCKY CLAY soil, and when should it be sown? Grow soybeans planted in spring, and plow under before beans are ripe. Follow with rye or oats, to be plowed under the following spring.

I have a rocky clay soil that has never been used except to grow grass. Should it be exposed to the winter, or put to cover crop? For a small area, remove surface rocks, add 3 ins. of manure or peatmoss with some sand or ashes, and plow under. Do not disk or harrow until spring.

What does a WHITE CLAY soil need, when it becomes baked hard after a rain? In the early spring it is loose and mellow. Needs organic matter in the form of peatmoss, manure, or leafmold. Apply a 3-in. layer and spade in.

How can a very heavy YELLOW CLAY soil around the foundation of a house be improved so that plants will grow in it? Incorporate 2 ins. of coal ashes screened through ¼-in. mesh, and 2 ins. of manure, straw, or peat, preferably in the fall.

What is the best way to prepare heavy clay for FRUIT TREES? Drainage must be good for fruit trees in heavy soils. Spade or plow under a liberal quantity of manure. Sod spaded under is likewise good.

The soil of my garden consists mostly of clay. Would it be suitable for planting trees such as apples, pears, and cherries? Yes, if well drained.

How can I prepare clay soil in full sun for growing LILIES? All varieties will grow in moderately heavy soil. Add 3 ins. of manure and spade to a depth of 6 ins. Soil must be well drained for satisfactory results with lilies.

What ornamental PLANTS will grow in clay soil? If well prepared—organic matter added, well drained, fertilized—clay soils will grow almost all plants.

What SHRUBS, FLOWERS, and TREES grow best in red clay soil? If soil is well drained, most shrubs and trees will grow. For flowers, add manure or peatmoss along with fine cinders or ashes.

We have clay ground and must prepare it inexpensively. What

VEGETABLES will be successful? Spade in a 3-in. layer of manure. Any vegetable will grow. However, root crops will do better in lighter soils.

Is it practical to begin a VEGETABLE garden on a rocky clay soil of poor color and texture? Probably not, unless no other soil is available. Remove surface rocks and add large quantities of manure or peatmoss each year. Fertilizer will be needed.

SOIL PROBLEMS

What kind of soil is most adaptable for general gardening? Any well-conditioned soil which would grow a crop of corn.

Is there any way to change the condition of a poor soil? Unless the soil condition is extremely unfavorable, it can be improved to the extent that it will produce good crops.

I am planning my first garden. How do I go about preparing the land for it? Manure it (600 lbs. per 1,000 sq. ft.); or 5 bales peatmoss (50 bushels) per 1,000 sq. ft.; fertilizer it (5–10–5), 30 lbs. per 1,000 sq. ft.; lime it (if test shows need). (See also Handling of Soil.)

Is it advisable to apply lime and commercial fertilizer through the winter on the snows for early melting and absorption? Lime and commercial fertilizers, for some crops, can be applied in the fall, but in most cases they are more economically applied in the spring. Nothing is to be gained by making the applications in winter.

Can soil for a garden be improved during the winter? Spade manure or straw in in the fall. Allow to lie in the rough over winter.

Are wood ashes as good or better than coal ashes for the garden? Under what conditions should each be used? Wood ashes and coal ashes serve two distinct purposes—the former adds potash, the latter improves mechanical condition of soil.

If annuals are cut off at the ground in fall, instead of being pulled out, will the soil benefit by decomposition of the roots? Yes.

In clearing off my vegetable plot, I burned the old tomato vines. Does this in any way injure the soil for next year's crop? No. It really should be of benefit.

What can I do to improve tough, gummy black virgin soil? I have added sand. Not enough added. Apply a 3-in. layer of manure or peatmoss. Fertilizer will also help.

What is best treatment for a soil that does not produce root crops? It probably is too heavy; lighten with manure and cinders. It may lack phosphorus and potassium, which may be added in the form of superphosphate and potassium chloride. (See Introduction.)

Our soil is a heavy black gumbo and bakes badly. Should I use manure, sand, sawdust, or peatmoss? For long-lasting improvement, incorporate 2 to 3 inches of peatmoss, a mixture of half peatmoss and half coarse sawdust, plus 2 inches of coarse sand many of whose particles are $\frac{1}{16}$- to $\frac{1}{8}$-inch in diameter.

How can I make a hard-packed, black alkali soil friable and productive? (Nevada.) Sulfur must be added to neutralize the alkali. If not, soil must be drained by use of tile. Add manure or peatmoss to loosen soil.

DEPLETED SOIL

What is the quickest way to bring an old used garden spot back into quick production? Spade in manure in the fall. In the spring, apply superphosphate, hoe, rake, and plant. Add complete fertilizer just before planting, and again during summer.

I have been raising flowers on the same ground for some time. What can I use to keep it in shape? Incorporate organic matter such as leaves, well-rotted manure, or peatmoss in the soil between the plants. Apply a 4–12–4 fertilizer as needed.

Can bulbs and annuals be planted every year in the same soil without using fertilizer, except manure once a year? No. It would be better to use the manure when preparing the soil, and then apply a complete fertilizer to bulbs just as flower buds begin to form; and to annuals during the season of most active growth.

I have planted flowers in the same spot for the last 15 years, using only a commercial fertilizer. My flowers do not have as large blossoms as they used to, but bloom very well. Should I add anything more, or do as I am doing? Unless the soil is very rich, it would be beneficial to add manure or leafmold, or some other form of humus.

ERODED SOIL

What causes erosion? Erosion—the washing away of soil on slopes by the runoff of surface water—results when the soil is left more or less bare and is so handled that it lacks humus to absorb mosisture.

Please tell me how to handle a lot that is very sandy and slopes. The water washes the soil off as fast as it is replaced. I had thought of making about 3 different elevations (terraces). Is this too many for a garden about 50 ft. deep? If the slope is not too steep, the trouble may be overcome by increasing the organic content of the soil through the use of green manures, farm manure, or peatmoss. On steep slopes handle the situation by strip-working the lot, or by terracing. Two terraces should be sufficient on a 50-ft. lot unless the grade is very steep.

How do you keep sharp slopes from opening and washing out? Avoid cultivation near and in these areas. If practical, plant black locust trees (small) to hold soil. If possible, grade off sharp slopes.

What suggestions do you have for hillside soil that is mostly decomposed granite? Prepare small pockets or local areas of good soil by using manure or peatmoss, and use plants which root as they spread.

How can one improve clay soil on a hillside to make it good garden soil? Add manure, spade under, and plant ground covers (ornamental) to hold soil in place. If wanted for vegetables, arrange the slope in terraces.

I have a 10-ft. hill, about 30 ft. from the house, where I am going to build a rock garden. What can I do to prevent the sand from washing down? Use plants that spread and root: sedum, ajuga, *Ranunculus acris,* some creeping phlox (*P. subulata*), pachysandra, ivy, myrtle, arabis, ceratostigma, etc.

FOR FLOWERS

What type of soil is best for a mixed flower border? A sandy loam, slightly acid (pH 6.5) in reaction, with manure worked in.

My annuals and perennials grow tall and spindly. Could this be due to overfertilization, lack of sun, or lack of some fertilizer element? The garden site receives sunlight half the day. The spindling growth of annuals and perennials may be due to lack of sunlight, improper fertilization, or other factors; or to any combination of them. Give as much sunlight as possible; improve the drainage and aeration of the soil; increase the phosphorus and potash in relation to nitrogen in the fertilizer used. A 2–10–10 fertilizer may be best in this case for a few years.

Why do plants grow thin and scraggly? What is lacking in soils that produce such growth? Lack of balanced nutrition. Usually an addition of complete fertilizer (4–12–4 or 5–10–5) will help. Drainage should be good. Calcium (lime or gypsum) may be needed to make good roots. Test your soil.

My flowers grow very poorly, and usually die before long. What causes this? The chances are your soil lacks fertility, moisture-holding capacity, and aeration. Additions of humus and fertilizers should correct these handicaps.

How can you keep soil sweet and in good condition in the grimy atmosphere of New York City? Adequate drainage should be provided. A periodic soil test will determine the amount of lime necessary to maintain the correct soil reaction.

Do soil conditions cause double cosmos to be single? Doubling of flowers is a hereditary tendency. Soil conditions rarely have any effect. Improper selection of seed is the usual cause. Many flowers never come 100 per cent double from seed.

Are angleworms harmful or beneficial in the garden? I find in a short time they eat up all humus in the soil the same as they do when they get into flower pots. Angleworms are not harmful in outdoor soils, unless present in very unusual numbers. In the greenhouse or in pot plants they are a nuisance. If too numerous, apply 5 lbs. of arsenate of lead to 1,000 sq. ft. and water in.

LAKE-SHORE SOIL

Would a garden plot laid out on the edge of a lake be satisfactory? And how would one get it in condition? Yes. Add manure at rate of 600 lbs. per 1,000 sq. ft. Humus content is likely to be low.

NEGLECTED SOIL

Why is soil that has lain idle for years so deficient in plant food? When grass, weeds, leaves, etc., are continually decaying on it, wouldn't natural compost be made? The weeds which grow on poor soils may not require the same proportions of elements for growth as cultivated plants. When these weeds die down, they fail to change these proportions. Besides, insufficient aeration, due to lack of turning the land, may cause trouble.

How can I restore the fertility of an old garden? Soil is sand, with a clay subsoil. I've tried manure, lime, and commercial fertilizer. The predominance of sand seems the difficulty. Try heavy applications of humus—manure, straw, alfalfa, hay, or the use of green manure. (See Index.)

Last year was the first time my garden was plowed in 30 years. I think I need lime, as the ground showed green moss. How much should I use? The best way to tell lime need is to test soil. Green moss is not an indication of acidity. More likely drainage is poor, or nutrients are lacking.

I had a ½-acre vegetable garden last year; plot had been uncultivated for 15 years. Applied a ton of lime after plowing and 2 truckloads of manure direct to plants. Seeded the plot to rye and Perennial Rye Grass last fall, and it looks all right. What, if anything, would you suggest adding this season before and after plowing? Apply 40 to 50 lbs. of 20% superphosphate per 1,000 sq. ft.

I recently bought a 171-acre farm which has not been worked for about 9 years. How can I determine what to plant? Have your soil tested. Insure proper drainage. Consult your county agent.

Have just bought a 3-acre place which has not been worked for 4 years, but annual crop of hay has been cut. Can I bring this into cultivation in a year? Yes. Plow in the fall. Fertilize heavily in the spring.

The plot I expect to use as a vegetable garden is a vacant lot infested with weeds. Will turning the weeds under with a plow be sufficient preparation of the soil? The plowing under of weeds will add humus to the soil. However, it may be too acid or alkaline: test for this. It may be poorly drained. It may need fertilization.

Our back yard is full of wild grass and weeds. Will soil be suitable for anything after condition is changed? If the soil is heavily contaminated with weed seeds, the best practice would be to let it lie fallow (unplanted) for 1 year before planting the desired crops. The chances are good that the soil can be modified to produce the common vegetables and garden flowers satisfactorily.

If the soil produces a vigorous crop of weeds, is it a sign that it will grow desirable things well? Usually, yes. If the desired crops are adapted to the soil type supporting the weed growth, they should do well.

What is the best way to handle soil which has been allowed to grow with bracken and creeping berry vines and has lain idle for years? Mow or cut off and remove all undesired plants. (They may be put into compost heap.) Remove undesired woody material such as limbs and small trees. Plow or dig and leave in rough condition through winter. In spring, redig, fertilize heavily, and plant.

POOR SOIL

How can subsoil fill be converted so that vegetables can be grown? Takes too long—not worth doing unless topsoil is hauled to a depth of 6 to 8 ins.

How can I build up soil that is mostly cinders? In the upper 8 to 10 ins. incorporate manure and haul in soil. The final proportion of cinders should be not more than ¼ of the total volume in top 6 ins.

My garden plot is mostly brown dirt and not too fertile. How can I make it fertile? Apply manure and a complete fertilizer.

My soil is very poor. How can I improve it? Add 3 ins. manure or peatmoss; spade to a depth of 6 ins. Before raking add 4–12–4 or 5–10–5 fertilizer at 4 lbs. per 100 sq. ft.

What garden truck will grow on soil that has just been dug out for a basement 8 ft. deep and is left 3 ft. deep on garden plot? Would you lime and fertilize soil? Only the top 6 ins. of that soil may be expected to be good. If the topsoil was not separated from subsoil, additions of manure and fertilizers would be needed; but even under such a treatment, not much should be expected the first year.

Are flowers or vegetables likely to grow in soil from which the top 18 ins. has been removed? Usually not. By manuring the subsoil and planting green-manure crops, the soil may be made fairly good after 2 or 3 years.

How much topsoil do you advise using over fill in order to grow flowers and vegetables? At least 6 ins.; preferably more.

I am planning to make a garden where the sod is rather heavy. How can I destroy this? Plow or spade in the fall or spring. Apply complete fertilizer before spading to hasten decomposition. Sod land makes the finest of soils.

I have a brand-new home; the builder put in very little loam, and the soil itself is very poor. How can I improve it? Without adding topsoil, the process of improvement will be very slow. Heavy additions of manure would have to be substituted. This should be worked in in the fall or spring. Soil should be tested for acidity and proper corrections made. Fertilizers should be added, and green-manure crops planted—rye in the fall (2 to 3 lbs. per 1,000 sq. ft.), followed by soybeans next spring (after plowing rye under). After plowing the soybeans under, soil should be in fair shape.

I used topsoil from the farm to enrich my soil, but results were poor. How can I determine what is wrong? Drainage may be poor. May need fertilizer. Add 4–12–4 or 5–10–5 at 4 lbs. per 100 sq. ft. Consult your local county agricultural agent.

What is the quickest, cheapest, and best way to rebuild "stripped" land, where loam was scraped off? By use of manure, fertilizers, and green-manure crops.

Will it be necessary to add extra fertilizer to the topsoil we have just put on? Add a fertilizer high in phosphorus and potash.

STONY SOIL

To produce a good crop of the common vegetables, what fertilizer is best for shale ground that has not been farmed for several years? Any complete fertilizer, such as 4–12–4 or 5–10–5, applied at 4 lbs. per 100 sq. ft., twice or three times a year.

Do stones continually work to the surface? If so, why? Yes, small ones do. Alternate freezing and thawing in winter, digging and cultivation, and also wetting and drying in spring, summer, and fall, bring stones to surface.

What shall I do for stony land? I continually rake stones off, but more appear. There is no remedy other than to keep on removing surface rocks.

WET SOIL

Will you explain the terms "well-drained soil" and "waterlogged soil"? A well-drained soil is one in which surplus water runs off quickly and which dries out readily after a rain or watering. A waterlogged soil is the opposite and contains too much water and little air.

Can a low, wet area be used for general gardening? Only if it can be drained.

What vegetables will stand a wet, soggy soil best? Beets seem to like wet sour spots, but carrots won't even come up in these spots. Beets usually do not do well in poorly drained soil. This is true of practically all vegetables. Cabbage will suffer as little as any vegetable in such a soil.

Our soil is in the shade and has too much moisture. What can we do for it? Improve the drainage by the installation of 3- or 4-in. agricultural tile, 12 to 15 ins. deep, with lines 12 to 15 ft. apart, and incorporate liberal amounts of organic matter.

What can be done to eliminate excess water at the foot of a terraced hill? The water always stands in the garden at the foot of the hill. Provide a shallow grass-covered or stone-paved ditch to carry off the excess water, or install a tile drain.

The earth in back of my home is wet and mossy. Is there anything I can do about fertilizing it for a garden? At present nothing will grow. Soil must be drained by use of agricultural tile. Apply 4–12–4 or 5–10–5 fertilizer at 4 lbs. per 100 sq. ft.

My garden is on a slope and the lower end is wet, with heavy soil. Is there any simple way to drain this ground and loosen the soil? Incorporate sand or cinders. If this does not rectify the situation, tile drain.

My garden plot is low and level, the soil moist and heavy in the spring. Will leaves and grass cuttings help, or should I use sand? Soil should be drained by use of tile. The addition of humus will help the soil but will not correct poor drainage.

How much lime should be used to correct soil in wet condition? Lime is not a corrective for wet soils. Add lime only if the soil is too acid for crops to be grown. Improve drainage first.

A sewer pipe backed up last fall and overflowed in a small plot where vegetables were planted. What can I do to purify the ground? Dig it up, and leave in rough, open condition. In a very short time the ground will "purify" itself.

Will waste water from a sand-washing plant damage land where it settles? (Texas.) Since sand-washing plants differ greatly in their practices, this is a difficult question to answer. Have the soil tested for acidity, nitrogen, phosphorus, potash, soluble salts, and organic matter. Consult your county agent.

MOSSY SOIL

The soil turns green in one of my perennial garden beds. What is the best way to remedy this condition? As it is probably caused by poor drainage and lack of aeration, improve the drainage by one of the methods previously suggested.

What kind of fertilizer should be used when the soil is heavy and has a green top coating? Plowing under a green-manure crop will add humus and improve the aeration of heavy soils. The best kind of fertilizer to use under such conditions will depend upon the requirements of the crop to be grown. In general, a 4–12–4 fertilizer will be satisfactory. Addition of lime may be beneficial.

What is the cause, and what the remedy, for soil that has a green mosslike formation over the top? Moss grows on moist soil and often indicates poor drainage. Install tile drains, or incorporate 40 to 50 lbs. agricultural gypsum per 1,000 sq. ft. every 3 to 5 years.

Does green moss growing on the soil in the borders indicate an acid condition of the ground? No. It usually indicates poor drainage or lack of fertility. If it is a green scum (algae), excess nitrogen (especially if from organic sources) and poor aeration may be responsible.

How can I overcome excessive moss on slope? Usual reasons for the excessive growth of moss are poor underdrainage and infertile soil. Rake out as much moss as possible, apply a ½-in. layer of dehydrated manure, and maintain fertility by applying fertilizer rich in nitrogen (10–5–5) in spring and fall.

What is the best type of fertilizer for soil which has not had previous nourishment and which contains a large percentage of clay? Although sunny it tends to become mossy. Tile drain the garden plot; incorporate farm manures or green manures; add commercial fertilizer suitable to the crop to be grown.

Will you tell us what to do for garden soil that packs and turns greenish, even after fertilizer and manure have been added? Too much algae present due, probably, to poor aeration and excess nitrogen. Addition of manure may make it worse. Digging in rotted straw should be helpful.

I have a strip of soil a few feet wide where everything dies that is planted. Why? Maybe due to packing of soil by constant walking. Try aerating by adding screened cinders or fine sand. The trouble may also be caused by the application of some toxic weed killer.

WOODLAND AND SHADED SOIL

What is the quickest, cheapest, and best way to convert a former wood lot into usable land? Remove stumps by hand, tractor, or dynamite, then plow and disk.

Does a garden of vegetables and flowers do well in soil which has just been cleared of hickory, oak, and wild cherry trees? There is a great deal of leafmold in the soil. It will do better in subsequent years, when aeration changes the structure of the soil. When well rotted, leafmold is a good soil conditioner.

Is acid woodland soil in any way beneficial as fertilizer? Woodland soil is not a fertilizer but may serve as a soil conditioner. It may be used as a satisfactory mulch, containing a high percentage of organic matter, and later worked into the soil.

In red virgin soil under and near CEDAR would oak leafmold and chicken fertilizer, mixed with sand, produce good vegetables? Only if the trees do not shade the garden spot.

What can I do with soil surrounded by FIR trees to make it suitable for flowers? Deep spading and incorporation of a 2-in. layer of finely screened cinders should help.

What attention must be given soil from which OAK trees have been cleared? Through the years many layers of oak leaves have rotted and naturally form a part of this soil. Such a soil may be somewhat acid. It should be tested and, if necessary, lime applied.

What is the best treatment of soil under PINE trees for the growth of roses and old-fashioned annuals? If the shade is dense, despite soil preparation neither will grow.

A WILLOW tree shades my yard; the roots mat the soil for yards around. Is there any way to make flowers grow beneath it? Not satisfactorily.

My soil receives sun from noon on. The few things which grow taste like wood (tomatoes, strawberries, etc.). Why? Soil tested poor, but 5–10–5 was added, plus sheep manure. Not enough sun. No fertilizer can substitute for sunlight.

How should I treat the ground where no sun ever shines? The ground packs. Outside of ferns and shade-loving plants, nothing should be grown under such conditions. The packing of the ground may be reduced by working in leafmold or peatmoss.

How can damp, cold, shady soil be fertilized to substitute for sunshine? There is no substitute for sunshine. Additions of nitrogen are helpful if trees take all the nourishment. Flowering plants and vegetables should not be planted in such localities.

What is deficient in soil when plants run to slender stems instead of branching? May not have enough sun. Add a fertilizer low in nitrogen (2–10–10 or 0–12–12), 5 lbs. per 100 sq. ft.

HANDLING OF SOIL

(See also General Culture, Section III.)

PLOWING; DIGGING

When should soil be plowed? Any time of year when not so wet as to roll in large clods, or so dry as to be a powdery dust.

Does it harm soil to work it while wet? Yes, especially if the soil is heavy. Plowing compacts such soils, and clods and unbreakable lumps will result.

What is the result of turning soil while it is wet? Heavy soils will puddle and bake and will be difficult to work into a friable state.

What makes soil break up into large, hard lumps after it is plowed? The structure is bad—too clayey. Add manure and cinders, or sand. Do not plow or dig while soil is wet.

Is it better to plow gardens in the fall or spring? Fall plowing is better, especially when there is sod to be turned under. It reduces erosion, exposes heavy soils to frost, kills exposed insects, brings about decay of organic matter, and makes for earlier planting. In the South, however, where little or no freezing occurs, fall plowing is apt to cause leaching.

Why is it best to plow in the fall? If done early enough, the organic matter decays partially before planting in the spring; the action of freezing and thawing improves the soil structure; some insect pests are killed when exposed; earlier planting (in spring) is made possible.

We had land plowed which has not been cultivated for about 40 years. What is the best time to put lime and fertilizer on soil? Plow early in the fall. Add lime at 2 lbs. or more per 100 sq. ft. (as test indicates) and a complete fertilizer at the same rate (or preferably a week or two later) and cultivate in. In the spring, hoe, apply fertilizer, rake, and seed.

I have a field that hasn't been plowed for years. I would like to have a vegetable garden. Is it best to plow in fall? Fall plowing is best in such cases.

How can soil be best prepared to yield plentifully when it has not been used for over 15 years? Plow in the fall; keep rough during winter; add fertilizers in spring. (See preceding question.)

Last year I made a new garden by filling in about 10 to 18 ins. deep with loam. What should be done with this ground to put in proper shape for this year's home garden? Manure and plow, preferably in the fall.

We plan to make a garden on a city lot infested with poison ivy, wild honeysuckle, and blackberry vines. Can you make any suggestions as to how we can rid soil of these? Will the roots from these vines ruin such root crops as potatoes? Should be plowed, disked, and harrowed in spring. Plant vegetables and remove, by frequent hand hoeing, shoots of weeds that appear. Roots of the vines will decompose and not injure vegetables.

Should ground be tilled or loosened up each year before planting, or only a little hole dug to put in bulbs or seeds? Always plow or spade soil before planting each crop.

Is it necessary to turn over the soil in a truck garden both in the fall and in the spring? Plowing or digging in the fall and disking or cultivating deeply in the spring are the common practices.

Is it undesirable to leave soil barren after plowing, or after crops have been harvested? It should either be kept cultivated, or mulched. If there is time (before the plot will be needed for future use) grow a green-manure crop.

Does burning weeds on vacant lots in any way harm the soil for growing vegetables? The lots have lain idle for a great many years. No. A certain amount of minerals is added and weed seeds are killed. Where there is a choice in the fall, between burning or plowing, it is better to plow.

Should I burn off the garden in the fall, or should stalks be plowed under? If your old stalks are disease free, it is better to plow under than burn. Diseased material should be burned.

In plowing cleared ground that had a growth of wild berries and brush, what should the procedure be? If necessary, tile for drainage (which see), plow, disk, and harrow to prepare land for crop.

How can I loosen up hardpan soil on 40-acre field? Use a sub-soil plow.

How do you prepare soil in the fall for spring flower beds? Spade in a 2-in. layer of manure (600 lbs. per 1,000 sq. ft.). Apply bone meal or superphosphate (30 lbs. per 1,000 sq. ft.). After spading, leave ground surface rough.

Will you please define spading and trenching? See Section V.

After spading in fall, how does one proceed in spring? If manure is dug in at time of spring spading, can lime also be used? How? When spading in the fall, leave soil rough. In the spring, cultivate or hoe if the soil packed then rake and plant. Lime may be used either in spring or fall, but use it only after the soil is tested. Don't guess.

CULTIVATING

What is meant by the term "in good tilth"? Soil which has suitable crumbly structure, sufficient humus, and is well drained. To secure good tilth, use manure; tile if necessary.

Soil is ready to be dug when a handful, firmly compressed, crumbles apart readily. If it remains in a sticky mass, with moisture on the surface, it is still too wet.

How can I determine when to begin to work the soil in early spring?   A soil is in good mechanical condition for working when after being compacted in your hand it gradually crumbles when the pressure is released. If the form is retained, it's too wet.

How fine should soil be prepared for planting?   For seedbeds fine enough so that few lumps remain, else seed covering will be difficult. For large plants, coarse soil is better than fine.

How can I know that my soil is right for growing vegetables and flowers?   If the structure is crumbly, the soil is dark; if manure and a complete fertilizer are added, good crops will grow. To make sure, have a soil test made.

The double-edged Dutch or scuffle hoe, used with a back-and-forth sliding motion, is one of the garden's most useful tools.

Is it possible to grow a vegetable garden in soil which had been treated a year ago with arsenate of lead?   Yes, unless the application was extremely heavy. Five to 10 lbs. of arsenate of lead to 1,000 sq. ft. will do no harm. Higher amounts may.

Is cultivating—stirring the soil—necessary except to control weeds and grass in such crops as corn and potatoes?   Yes, cultivation aids in holding moisture in the soil and in admitting air. (See Introduction.)

Are the rotating types of hand garden cultivators efficient?   When the soil is in good condition and weeds are under control, the rotating type of cultivator will maintain that condition better than any other. This tool is useless in the preparation of a seedbed or the fitting of the soil and is very inefficient in lumpy, cloddy, or strong land.

What is the best way to tell if soil is in condition to cultivate? Put a *clean trowel* or spade into your soil. If, when you pull the tool out of the soil, many particles cling to the clean surface, the soil is too wet to be cultivated.

FALLOWING

What is meant by "fallow"? Fallow means plowing the land and allowing it to stand idle with no crop. May be plowed more than once a season.

What is the purpose of fallowing? For the control of weeds by plowing them under. Soil standing idle 1 year stores moisture for next year's crop. For this reason, it is used mostly in arid regions.

DRAINAGE

How can I properly drain a garden that stays wet too long? If the situation cannot be corrected by incorporation of 3 to 4 ins. of

Wet soils are improved by laying tiles to increase drainage—a very simple operation.

sand or cinders, install 3- or 4-in. agricultural drain tile. Set the tile 15 to 18 ins. deep, with the lines 15 to 18 ft. apart. Carry the lines to an open ditch or storm sewer.

What is best way to drain off a 1-acre garden that is too wet? Would some kind of furrow arrangement be sufficient? Would it be better tiled, or drained to storm-water sewer? Installation of tile drains would be the more satisfactory and in the end more economical on such a large plot.

We have so much subsoil water that in winter our ground in spots is continually water-soaked. What can I do to counteract this in spring? Tile drain the lot. (See previous questions.)

How can we provide drainage economically at low end of lot? Water forms in pool during heavy rains. If the situation cannot be corrected by slight modification of the grade, or shallow ditching, install 3- to 4-in. agricultural drain tile.

Our lot is wide, but slopes. At this spot (at the end of the lot) we have "soggy" soil for days after a rain. Is there anything we can do about it? Tile drain the lower end of the lot. Carry the tile to an open ditch or storm sewer if possible. Drain into sump holes if the water cannot be carried off.

I plan a combination vegetable garden and orchard on a very poor site. Since drainage would be expensive to install, would you advise against the project? If drainage is the only drawback, the project should be entirely practical.

COAL ASHES

Will coal ashes help to break up a heavy clay soil? Yes. (See also Clay Soil, this section.)

Can hard-coal stoker cinders be plowed into heavy soil to lighten it without bad effect? Yes; but if any clinkers are present sift them to get fine ashes for use. Clinkers may be used for drainage deep under topsoil.

Are sifted coal ashes good for the flower garden? Sifted coal ashes help, but the particles must be fine; otherwise they do more harm than good.

Will too much coal ashes harm a flower border? We have been covering beds as we take ashes from grate. It is well to let ashes lie out and be washed by rain and weathered for several weeks before use.

Soil in home vegetable garden packs hard when dry. Would coal ashes benefit this condition? Yes, use 1 in. incorporated into top 6 ins. of soil. Screen through a ¼-in. mesh before applying.

What are the benefits from the fine siftings of coal ashes applied to a vegetable garden and mixed with the soil? The mechanical condition is improved, more air is admitted, bacteria work more efficiently, and roots grow faster.

Are sifted coal ashes of any help to a lawn? Doubtful value if applied to surface. If incorporated in lower portion of soil, they would help drainage.

Can coal ashes be used in the garden at the same time bone meal is worked into the soil? Yes, they can be used at the same time, but they should be fine enough to lighten soil.

Do coal ashes affect manures? No. When added to heavy soils a combination of well-rotted manure and screened ashes greatly helps the mechanical condition.

Are coal ashes of any use as a chemical fertilizer? Coal ashes have very little, if any, fertilizer value. They do improve the mechanical condition of most soils.

Do coal ashes help prevent cutworms? To a degree. If a 1-in. layer is placed about bases of plants, cutworms will have difficulty in attacking them.

A couple of years ago I noticed that an acquaintance had dumped his winter's coke ashes in a low spot in back of his yard. In spring he smoothed them out and set his tomato plants there, and they bore a heavy crop of fruit. Is there any plant food in coke ashes that is good for tomatoes? Or was that just an accident that the plants did so well in the ashes? The coke ashes improved the soil aeration, and thus helped produce better growth.

What would you suggest as the best way to reclaim a back yard that has been filled with coal ashes 8 to 10 ins. deep? Topsoil is worth its weight in gold, and hard to get. The dirt near by is acid woodland soil. Remove at least half the ashes and fork in the balance. Then add half-and-half mixture of your woodland soil and *good* topsoil. Apply lime, as needed, to decrease excessive acidity.

Are briquette ashes good for entire garden? I burn briquettes in the fireplace. Yes; for mechanical betterment of the soil, improving its texture.

Will ashes from fireplace, in which some cannel coal has been used, be harmful in garden use? No; but it is better not to use them fresh from the grate.

Can the fine white ash of cannel coal be used to lighten a heavy soil? Yes. (See previous question.)

I understand cannel-coal ashes are strong in phosphorus and potash. Are they suitable to be added to the flowers and vegetable garden? As mechanical aids mostly; they have but little nutrient value.

SOIL ACIDITY

pH

What is the meaning of the symbol pH? See Introduction.

I have several books on flower growing, but none gives the types of soils (acid or alkaline) in which all plants thrive best. Can you give

me this information? No *complete* list has ever been worked out. Of the vast number of plants grown, comparatively few show marked preferences for decidedly acid or alkaline soils. The vast majority exhibit a wide tolerance. (See following questions.)

What plants grow well on acid soils of fair to good fertility (pH 5 to 5.5)?

Arbutus	Ferns	Raspberry
Azalea	Fir	Red Top
Beans	Hemlock	Rhubarb
Bent Grasses	Huckleberry	Rhododendron
Birch, White	Hydrangea (Blue)	Rye
Blackberry	Lily	Serradella
Blueberry	Millet	Soybean
Brussels Sprouts	Oak, Scrub	Spruce
Buckwheat	Oak, Red	Squash
Carrot	Oats	Strawberry
Cabbage	Orchard Grass	Sweet Potato
Cedar, White	Orchid	Tobacco
Cineraria	Parsley	Tomato
Clover, Crimson	Pea	Turnip
Cowpea	Peanut	Vetch, Hairy
Corn	Pepper	Violet
Cranberry	Pine	Watermelon
Cucumber	Plantain	Wintergreen
Cyclamen	Potato	Wheat
Dewberry	Pumpkin	Zinnia
Endive	Radish	

What plants grow better on slightly acid or neutral soils (pH 5.6 to 6.5)?

Beans	Oats	Soybean
Blackberry	Orchard Grass	Squash
Buckwheat	Parsley	Strawberry
Carrot	Pea	Sweet Potato
Cabbage	Pepper	Tobacco
Clover, Crimson	Pumpkin	Tomato
Corn	Radish	Turnip
Cowpea	Red Top	Wintergreen
Cucumber	Rhubarb	Wheat
Endive	Rye	

What plants do not grow well on strongly acid soils, but prefer slightly acid or slightly alkaline soils (pH 6.5 to 7)?

Alfalfa	Aster	Babiesbreath
Apple	Aurora Flower	Barley
Asparagus	Avens	Balsam

Beets	Fescue, Sheep's	Oak, White
Beggar Weed	Fescue, Tall	Onion
Berseem	Flax	Pansy
Blue Grass	Foxglove	Parsnip
Bokhara	Foxtail	Peach
Broccoli	Gladiolus	Pear
Brome Grass	Gooseberry	Peppermint
Camomile	Grape	Petunia
Candytuft	Helianthus	Phlox
Carnation	Hemp	Plum
Cauliflower	Horseradish	Poppy
Celery	Hops	Quince, Orange
Chard	Hydrangea (Pink)	Rape
Cherry	Iris	Salsify
Chicory	Kale	Sorghum
Chrysanthemum	Kohlrabi	Spearmint
Clover, Alsike	Lady's Finger	Speltz
Clover, Hungarian	Larkspur	Spinach
Clover, Japanese	Leek	Stock
Clover, Mammoth	Lentil	Sunflower
Clover, Red	Lettuce	Sweet Alyssum
Clover, White	Linden, American	Sweetpea
Clover, Yellow	Lobelia	Sweet Vernal
Collards	Lupine	Sweetwilliam
Columbine	Mangel Wurzels	Timothy
Cosmos	Maple	Vetch
Cotton	Marigold	Walnut
Currant	Meadow Grass	Watercress
Dahlia	Meadow Oat	Willow
Eggplant	Mignonette	Wisteria
Elm, American	Muskmelon	Witchazel
Everlasting Pea	Nasturtium	Woodbine

ACID

What makes the soil acid? Soil acidity is common in many regions where rainfall is sufficient to leach large proportions of calcium and magnesium out of the soil. The loss of these salts results in a preponderance of acid-forming ions in the soil.

Soils also become acid due to the use of acid-forming fertilizers, such as sulfate of ammonia and ammonium phosphates. The following table shows the relative acidifying or alkalinizing power of various fertilizing, liming, or acidifying materials, rated in terms of commercial limestone (calcium carbonate) as 1.0:

Material	Acidifying	Alkalinizing
Dolomitic Limestone	— —	1.1
Hydrated Lime (Calcite)	— —	1.4
Hydrated Lime (Dolomitic)	— —	1.7
Sodium Nitrate	— —	0.3
Calcium Nitrate	— —	0.2
Potassium Nitrate	— —	0.2
Ammonium Nitrate	0.6	— —
Ammonium Sulfate	1.1	— —
Monoammonium Phosphate	0.6	— —
Diammonium Phosphate	1.1	— —
Urea	0.8	— —
Sulfur	3.1	— —
Ferrous Sulfate	0.4	— —
Aluminum Sulfate	0.5	— —

What is the chemistry involved in the gradual acidification of soils: when lying fallow? When becoming part of the forest floor? In humid regions removal of calcium and magnesium may cause a high concentration of hydrogen ions which results in acidity. This is more apt to happen on the forest floor, because of a greater amount of organic matter and thus greater generation of carbon dioxide.

Where can soil be sent to have its acidity determined? To your State Agricultural Experiment Station, college or university. (See list of Stations, page 1318).

What simple means can be used to detect acid soil? The litmus-paper test is probably the simplest means of detecting soil acidity. A Soil-tex test (with a testing kit made for the purpose) is easily made and more valuable and reliable.

Is moss an indication of acidity? Moss may result as often from a poorly drained condition of the soil, or from heavy shade, as it does from an acid condition.

Testing the soil for acidity is a simple job which any amateur can do with a test kit. Testing for nutrients is more complicated.

Are toadstools an indication of soil acidity? No, they are not.

What will an acid soil produce? Notable among the plants that do best in an acid soil are those of the Ericaceae family, which includes such plants as azalea, rhododendron, leucothoe, pieris, mountain laurel, and others. (See previous question under pH.)

How can an acid soil be neutralized? An acid soil can be neutralized by adding ground limestone. The amount required can be determined by a soil analysis. (See Introduction.)

What is "sour" soil? A "sour" soil is a term sometimes used to denote the condition that develops in a poorly drained soil. More often, as the term is used, it is synonymous with an acid soil.

How can sour soil be sweetened? If by "sour" soil is meant an acid soil, it can be sweetened by adding agricultural ground limestone or other forms of lime.

What can I do to counteract sour soil in seed boxes? The "sour" soil condition in seed flats can be prevented or corrected by providing sufficient drainage. Separate the boards on the bottom of the flat ¼ in., or bore a few holes in the bottom. Raise the flats on bricks or wood strips. "Sourness," in these cases, generally does not mean acidity.

How can a sour soil be treated to produce? If the "sour" soil condition is being caused by poor drainage, it can be corrected by improving drainage. If the sour soil is an acid soil, with a reaction so low that it will not produce satisfactory crops, the condition can be corrected by adding ground limestone.

How may I improve a dry, acid, heavy clay soil? Incorporate a liberal amount of peatmoss, but first mix 10 to 15 pounds of pulverized limestone with each bale of peat before the latter is worked into the soil. Apply additional limestone to the soil if needed.

I am making a vegetable garden on a piece of lawn; the soil is very acid. Will it be worth trying? Since most vegetables will do well on a slightly acid soil, this very acid soil could be changed without undue expense to grow vegetables.

How should I treat a very acid soil in order to grow vegetables? Apply agricultural ground limestone, preferably in the fall, before planting in the spring. Make a second application if necessary. Most vegetables prefer soil that is slightly acid, so there is danger in using too much lime.

What type of fertilizer is used in planting vegetables in acid soil? If the soil is too acid to produce the vegetable crop in mind, apply lime. In addition apply a fertilizer best suited to the particular crop. A 2–10–10 is recommended for most root crops; a 4–12–4 for others.

Is acidity favorable or unfavorable to crabgrass? A highly acid soil is unfavorable to crabgrass. It is difficult to maintain a sufficiently high degree of acidity to discourage crabgrass on the average lawn.

My soil is neutral. Is there any chemical I can add to the soil to make it acid? I wish to try acorns from red oaks, and other things. Finely ground sulfur or aluminum sulfate can be used to make the soil more acid. Red oaks, however, will do well on a neutral soil.

Can the soil in a garden in a limestone country be made permanently acid? No. An acid soil made under such conditions can be maintained only by periodic treatment.

What use is sulfur for soil? How do you use it? Sulfur is used to increase the acidity of the soil. One to 2 lbs. to 100 sq. ft. are needed to lower the soil each ½ pH.

What materials should be used in maintaining an acid-soil garden in a limestone country? Acid peatmoss or oak leafmold, flowers of sulfur and aluminum sulfate.

How should acidifying materials be handled in the development and maintenance of an acid-soil garden in a limestone country? Make provision for perfect drainage of the area. Incorporate a liberal application of peatmoss. Add flowers of sulfur in the quantity, and as often, as soil tests (made at least once a year) indicate that it is necessary.

What are the best kinds of leaves for producing an acid condition in the soil? Leafmold from oak leaves has long been considered the ideal acidifying material for plants requiring an acid soil, such as rhododendrons, azaleas, and laurel. Recent experiments, however, indicate that this assumption is incorrect. Oak-leaf compost increased the pH temporarily, but after 45 days the pH value was higher (*less acid*) than before the application. However, there is no doubt that oak leafmold is beneficial to the growth of the acid-loving plants.

Will you please tell me how to prepare a soil mixture using oak leafmold for growing blueberries? Dig a hole 3 to 4 ft. wide for each plant; incorporate 3 ins. of leafmold in the bottom; mix the soil for filling with ⅓ its bulk of leafmold, and pack tightly around the roots. Keep the surface over the roots mulched heavily with the oak leafmold, or with sawdust.

ALKALINITY

What is the best method for soil reconstruction? Our soil is of a lime structure (moderately alkaline). Our water is hard and slightly chlorinated. Well-rotted manure at the rate of 1 lb. to a sq. ft. and 2½ lbs. of superphosphate for each 100 sq. ft. This should be thoroughly mixed with the soil. Sow green-manure crops in the fall. Use an acid commercial fertilizer for plants.

What is the best way to counteract highly alkaline soil? Sulfur or aluminum sulfate is used for the purpose. A soil with pH 8 (alkaline) will require 4 lbs. of sulfur to 100 sq. ft. to make it slightly acid (pH 6), or 10 lbs. of aluminum sulfate for the same area. Aluminum sulfate acts much more quickly than sulfur, but in acid soils may do damage unless phosphates are present in sufficient quantity. See question "what makes the soil acid."

Would like to know what grows best in alkaline soil. What will counteract too much alkali? Very few plants do well in strongly alkaline soil. Use sulfur or aluminum sulfate for acidification.

What plants like slightly alkaline soil? See question under pH.

Our soil and water are alkaline. How can I keep a small bed for fringed gentians acid? An acid-soil condition may be maintained by the periodic application of flowers of sulfur or aluminum sulfate.

We have alkaline soil. I succeed with most flowers but not with gladiolus. The bulbs rot. What is the reason? (Washington.) Gladiolus plants do better in slightly acid soil—acidify it with sulfur and use acid-forming fertilizer.

Our soil has considerable alkali in it. For that reason I have hesitated about trying to raise ladyslippers. What can I do to grow these? Leafmold acidified with sulfur will produce satisfactory growth. Acid peatmoss mixed with leafmold will also do.

What will improve an alkaline soil for growing garden peas (early spring)? The use of sulfur of aluminum sulfate will reduce alkalinity.

What vegetables will grow in alkali ground? No vegetables grow well in highly alkaline soil. The most tolerant of alkalinity are asparagus, beet, lima bean, cauliflower, muskmelon, parsnip, and spinach. (See question under pH.)

Can any chemical be used to correct alkali in soil? My soil is heavy and moist. The best methods of control for such conditions consist of (1) providing a soil mulch to retard evaporation, and (2) applications of gypsum if the soil needs calcium; or sulfur, if it need to be acidified.

I have had much difficulty in growing flowers and plants, as many turn yellow. (Soil has been diagnosed by county agent as highly alkaline.) Why? Poor drainage may cause accumulation of alkaline salts. Apply iron sulfate at 1 to 2 lbs. per 100 sq. ft. More than 1 application may be necessary.

What can one add to alkali water to make it suitable for irrigation on a small garden plot? (Kansas.) Water may be acidified by sulfuric, phosphoric acid, or other acids. This should be done, however, only on the advice of your Agricultural Experiment Station.

LIME

What are the functions of lime in soil improvement? Lime furnishes calcium which is needed for root development, strengthening of cell walls, and for formation of protoplasm and proteins; counteracts acidity; hastens decomposition of organic matter; aids in development of nitrogen-fixing bacteria; reduces toxicity of certain compounds.

What type of lime should be used in the garden? Agricultural lime is the slowest but the most lasting. Several weeks may pass before its effect on soil is noticed. Hydrated and burned lime are much quicker in action, but tend to destroy humus. One hundred lbs. of ground limestone is equivalent in action to 74 lbs. of hydrated lime, or 56 lbs. of burned lime. The amounts to use will vary with the acidity of the soil. Usually 2 lbs. of agricultural limestone per 100 sq. ft. is sufficient, unless soils are extremely acid.

What is raw ground limestone? Raw ground limestone is calcium carbonate, and is the material most commonly used for counteracting acidity.

What is agricultural lime? Raw ground limestone.

What is hydrated lime? Hydrated or slaked lime is formed from burned or quicklime (calcium oxide) and water. Hydrated and burned or quicklime are quicker acting than ground limestone (calcium carbonate).

What is "slaked" lime? This is the same as hydrated lime.

What is quicklime? This is another term used for burned lime (calcium oxide). This form of lime should *not* be used in the garden, as it destroys humus, and is toxic when in contact with roots.

Is lime the only material with which to sweeten an acid soil? Some form of lime is usually used to correct soil acidity. The most commonly used forms are ground limestone, dolomitic limestone, and hydrated lime. Other materials that may be used are calcium cyanamide and wood ashes.

Can dry lime, left over from plastering a room, be used in any way as a fertilizer? It may be used to alkalize acid soil, but is apt to be too coarse and lumpy. If lime is needed, apply it in the fall.

Would lime, such as I can purchase at the hardware store, be good for acid soil? Yes. Use a pulverized limestone for this purpose.

Can marl be used in the place of lime, with the same, or as good, results? Marl (a natural deposit of calcium-bearing clay) is coarse, and its effect is very gradual and slow. Ordinarily, lime is both less expensive and much more satisfactory.

What is "overliming" injury? Too much calcium (lime) in the soil causes the soil to become alkaline. Some elements as boron, manganese, zinc, etc., are not soluble in an alkaline solution, and because they are needed in small amounts by plants, poor growth develops. Usually the growth is chlorotic (yellow). Overliming can be corrected by applying sulfur to the soil at 1 lb. per 100 sq. ft. More than one application may be necessary to bring about the desired acidity.

When and under what conditions should lime be added to the soil? Only when the soil is too acid for plants, and when calcium is low.

When, and when not, should lime be used around flowers and shrubs? Use lime only if the soil is so acid as to require correction. Use lime if calcium is lacking and the soil is acid. Use gypsum (calcium sulfate) when calcium is lacking and the soil is alkaline.

What is gypsum? A mineral composed of calcium sulfate which contains 2 molecules of water. Used in horticulture to add needed calcium to the soil when it is not necessary to decrease acidity. It is also used to improve the physical condition of soils and, under some conditions, to improve drainage and soil aeration.

Is lime needed to improve a gravelly soil? Have soil tested; it may not need it.

How can lime benefit clay soil, if the soil is originally composed of disintegrated limestone? As stated by some authorities, benefit is obtained by cementing finer particles into larger ones. The flocculation (cementing of particles) of clay soils as a result of liming has been questioned.

When lightening clay soil with coal ashes, should pH be corrected by addition of lime? In any case low pH (acid) can be corrected by additions of lime.

Should a garden be treated with lime in the fall or spring? If ground limestone is used, it is best applied in the fall, but may be applied in spring. Hydrated lime should be mixed in the spring.

How much lime should be used (for one application)? Two lbs. per 100 sq. ft.

Is it necessary to put lime on the garden every year? Lime should be used only on acid soils. If needed, apply agricultural lime in the fall; hydrated lime in the spring. Usually 2 lbs. per 100 sq. ft. is sufficient.

Can lime be strewn over the ground in winter with the snow? Yes, although it is better to apply early in the fall.

When rotted manure is put on garden in spring, will a coat of ground limestone affect the manure in any way? Not if pulverized limestone is used.

Why is it harmful to put Vigoro and lime into the soil at the same time? What chemical reaction takes place? If lime is allowed to come into contact with superphosphate of fertilizer, the solubility, and hence the availability, of the latter may be reduced, especially in a non-acid or slightly acid soil. In soils that are acid, there is no objection to the application of fertilizer and lime at the same time, providing they are well incorporated into the soil.

When leaves are spaded in, in the fall, should lime be used in the spring?   Most leaves do not produce an acid reaction, so that liming is not necessary unless your soil is naturally acid.

What crops need lime in the soil, and which do better without it? *Legumes* do better in neutral or slightly alkaline soils, hence lime additions are often necessary. *Acid-tolerant plants* like azaleas, rhododendrons, etc., need no lime although they need calcium. (See questions under pH.) For most plants lime should be applied only when the soil is very acid, since they do best in *slightly* acid soil (6. to 6.5 pH.).

Instead of sand, I put very fine limestone on my soil, which has a preponderance of gumbo. It has made soil nice to work with. Will this small amount be apt to affect garden annuals and perennials? I have also added a great deal of barnyard fertilizer.   Small amounts of lime can do no harm. The change in the soil structure was probably due to the manure rather than to the lime.

In foundation planting, if cedars (which require acid soil) are used I assume it is possible that lime coming loose from building and washing into soil may have disastrous effect on such acid-loving plants as azaleas and rhododendrons. Is this so?   There is rarely much lime in the soil from this source. However, any chunks of plaster should be removed. If soil seems alkaline, apply flowers of sulfur at 2 to 4 lbs. per 100 sq. ft. Sulfur is an acidifying agent.

Should I sprinkle my lawn with lime in the fall?   If soil needs lime, it will be most effective when applied in the fall. In acid soil areas, periodic applications of limestone are recommended.

Will lime put on lawn on which oak and dogwood trees are growing injuriously affect such trees?   Not unless excessive amounts are used. Have the soil tested and apply limestone only when needed.

My soil is covered with white-pine needles from adjacent trees. Should this make additional liming or other treatment advisable? Pine needles produce acidity, hence constant use of lime may be required to counteract this condition.

Sewage sludge is very acid from aluminum sulfate. Is lime the proper neutralizer, or does it leave the valuable plant and soil bacteria elements in a non-desirable form?   Sewage sludge does not necessarily contain aluminum sulfate. If it does, lime is a good corrective; or superphosphate may be used.

When vegetable soil is too acid, as ascertained by laboratory test, how much lime should be applied to overcome a state of hyperacidity? The amount of lime required will vary with the degree of acidity and with the texture of the soil. In general, the following amounts will be required, per 1,000 sq. ft., to raise the soil from pH 5.5 to 6.5:

	Sandy Loams	Loams	Clay Loams
Pulverized Limestone	40 lbs.	85 lbs.	125 lbs.
Hydrated Lime	25 lbs.	60 lbs.	90 lbs.

I am planning to plant a small vegetable plot. Can one add too much lime? Lime should not be added, unless a test shows it is needed. Decidedly it can be overdone.

SOIL TESTING

What is the best method of determining the treatment a given soil requires? Test your soil; or have it tested. Your county agent or State Agricultural or Experiment Station will do this for you.

What is the approximate cost of having soil analyzed? It varies. A few states make no charge, but most charge $0.75 to $1.00.

What is the difference between soil analysis and a soil test? A *complete soil analysis* includes the total elements—those available to plants, and the reserve held in the soil in unavailable forms. A *microchemical soil test* gives an approximation of *available* elements only.

Does the test, or the analysis, give more information? The test is more practical than the complete analysis. It is valuable as indicator of needs, but does not tell the exact amounts to apply. However, an experienced soil tester is able to indicate what to apply, and how much.

Are the chemistry sets on the market practical? Many of the soil-testing kits are satisfactory and practical if intelligently used.

Are there any tests available for amateurs to make which will determine soil acidity and alkalinity without sending samples away? Yes, there are several outfits on the market which are simple to use. Write your Agricultural Experiment Station for information covering them.

Could you please tell me how to make an inexpensive soil-test kit? It would be safer, and probably cheaper, to buy a soil-testing kit.

Can I learn the true nature of the soil from a test? Yes. A good soil-testing kit will give acidity, nitrates, phosphates, potassium, calcium, etc.

Where can soil tests be made? What fee charged? What size sample desired? Your Agricultural Experiment Station will test your soil— usually for a small fee. Send ½ pint of soil, taken from at least 10 places. Sample the soil to a depth of at least 6 inches in each of the

10 places. Mix the various samples together in a bucket and send about ½ pint of this composite soil in a tight container.

How can I obtain information on soil analysis without the necessity of taking a course in chemistry? Write to your Agricultural Experiment Station for information on soil testing. Several stations have published bulletins on this subject.

After testing, how can I know what to add to soil, in what quantities, and when? Without experience in testing, one cannot tell from a soil test just what kinds of quantities of fertilizers to use. Send your sample to your Agricultural Experiment Station. All fertilizers contain analysis on each bag.

Which soil should I send for analysis? Soil screened last fall and stored in cellar, or fresh soil as soon as frost is out of it? Send stored soil, or else wait until outdoor soil warms up, before taking sample.

How can we determine what vegetable or fruit a soil is best suited to produce? The best procedure is to consult your local county agricultural agent.

Should untilled soil be analyzed to determine its fertility? Yes.

Should I have my soil tested to determine its acidity? If plants grown do well, it is not necessary. It is desirable to have periodic tests of soils which are used to grow plants that require specific soil reactions, such as rhododendrons and azaleas.

If the ground is poor, how can one tell what is lacking in the soil? By having a soil sample analyzed.

Can soil condition be determined by what is found growing on it, such as wild blueberries and sour-grass? Can soil with fine shell stone be good? Yes. For example, blueberries indicate acid soil; dandelions alkaline soil. Too much lime from shells may be detrimental to some plants.

PLANT NUTRIENTS

ELEMENTS OF PLANT NUTRITION

What are the various elements of plant nutrition; and their uses? The 3 most important essential elements for plant growth, and their effect on plant growth, are as follows: *Nitrogen:* this element enters into the structure of protoplasm, chlorophyll, and various plant foods; it is needed for both the vegetative and reproductive stages of growth; its use is usually manifested by an increase in vegetative growth. *Phosphorus:* it is essential to cell division and for the formation of nucleoproteins; it aids root development; hastens maturity, or stiffens tissues; and stimulates flower and seed production. *Potash:* this element is necessary for the manufacture and translocation of starches and sugar; it is a general conditioner, overcoming succulence and brittleness, hastening maturity and seed production, and aiding in root development.

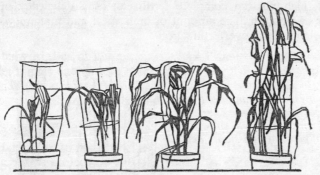

Nitrogen, phosphorus, and potassium are all needed for normal plant growth. Of the four pots of corn above, the first (left) lacked nitrogen; the second, phosphorus; the third, potassium. The one on the right was supplied with all three.

NITROGEN

How can I recognize nitrogen deficiency? The whole plant is dwarfed and the older leaves turn from green to yellow, and then to brown, and remain attached to the plant. Stalks are slender, and few new stalks develop.

How can nitrogen deficiency be corrected? Apply ammonium sulfate at ¾ lb. or sodium nitrate at 1 lb. per 100 sq. ft. A complete fertilizer (as 4 12–4, or 5–10–5) will correct the deficiency of nitrogen as well as supply phosphorus and potash.

What is lacking in my garden soil, since the carrots I raise, though of good size, are almost tasteless and colorless? Nitrogen is lacking; a complete fertilizer (4–12–4, or 5–10–5) at 4 lbs. per 100 sq. ft. will correct this.

What causes yellowing of foliage? It may be due to poor drainage, or to lack of nitrogen.

What shall I do for soil that grows annuals and perennials too large and weedy, but weak-stemmed? Probably too much nitrogen in the soil and not enough phosphorus and potassium. Use a 0–10–10 fertilizer, or something similar, 2 lbs. per 100 sq. ft.

All foliage and few flowers is my trouble. What is wrong? Too much nitrogen and probably not enough phosphorus and potash; add both in the form of a 0–10–10 fertilizer (or similar) at rate of 2 lbs. per 100 sq. ft.

What causes an excess of nitrogen in the soil? Have added 10 lbs. of

bone meal in a 35-sq.-ft. bed for annuals, and some Bovung (100 lbs.) for spring. Excess nitrogen, or the symptoms of excess nitrogen, may be brought about through the excessive use of nitrogenous fertilizers, high-nitrogen complete fertilizers, or a deficiency of phosphorus and potash. The amount of bone meal and manure you have applied constitutes overfertilization.

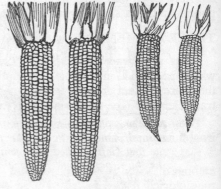

Potash is especially important for fruit and grain crops. The two ears of corn at the right show the result of potash (potassium) deficiency.

PHOSPHORUS

How can I recognize phosphorus deficiency?   The whole plant is dwarfed, but the foliage is a dark, dull green; leaf stem (petiole) often turns purple. Areas between veins on leaf sometimes turn purple, and leaf margins often turn yellow. Loss of lower foliage follows.

How can phosphorus deficiency be corrected?   Apply treble superphosphate or superphosphate, at 5 lbs. per 100 sq. ft. Bone meal is too slow acting to be of immediate benefit.

POTASH

How can I recognize potash (potassium) deficiency?   Lower foliage begins to turn yellow at leaf margin; leaf often mottled yellow and green in between veins; margins of leaves turn brown and foliage drops from plant; plant generally stunted.

How can potash (potassium) deficiency be corrected?   Apply muriate of potash or sulfate of potash, 1 lb. per 100 sq. ft.

What fertilizer should I use to encourage fruits and vegetable roots? Plants grow all to tops.   Withhold nitrogen and increase the proportion of phosphorus and potash in the mixture. Use a 2–10–10 fertilizer for a few years, adding additional nitrogen only where, and as, needed.

Some soils tend to develop barren vines. What is lacking?   This is usually the result of too little phosphorus and potash.

What does soil lack that produces an abundant crop of any vegetable above ground, but no root vegetables such as potatoes, beets, turnips, or salsify? Phosphorus and potassium are probably deficient in this soil. (See previous questions.)

My garden is made of filled earth and has a large amount of street sweepings in it, high in leafmold. All root crops fail; beans and corn are only crops that succeed. Why? Have soil tested; lack of phosphorus and potassium may cause the trouble.

TRACE ELEMENTS

What are "trace" elements? Elements (present in most soils) which are needed in very small amounts, for plant nutrition. Some of these are present in such small quantities that they are known as trace elements (see discussion page 6).

What are the principal trace elements? Boron, chlorine, copper, iron, manganese, zinc, and molybdenum.

Is boron a necessary ingredient in all types of soils? A small amount of boron is essential for plant growth, and to prevent various physiological disorders. It is present in most soils in sufficient quantity. It is most apt to be deficient in soils low in organic matter.

How should boron be used in the soil? Boron is commonly applied in the form of borax, at the rate of 10 to 15 lbs. *per acre.* This is only 4 to 5 ozs. per 1,000 sq. ft.

How can I be sure that my soil will have enough sodium for good growth of beets? Use ½ to 1 lb. nitrate of soda, or ½ lb. table salt, per 100 sq. ft.

My garden soil turns a red color on top when dry; why? The red color probably is due to a surface growth of red algae. These minute plants do no harm and are often found on moist soils. They go unnoticed until the soil surface dries and their red color is then apparent by contrast.

Are iron or steel filings beneficial in darkening colors of perennials, especially roses and lilacs? No. Iron sulfate (copperas) is beneficial where iron in soil is low; chiefly useful in greening foliage, not darkening flower color.

Do the nutrients in dolomite and basic slag leach from the soil? Magnesium from dolomite and phosphorus from basic slag move very slowly in the soil, so there is little loss from leaching.

HUMUS

What is humus? For practical purposes, humus may be defined as the resultant brown or dark-brown substance that develops following the breakdown of organic materials by various soil organisms.

How does one recognize the different types of humus, such as peat, leafmold, muck, etc?   *Peat:* soft, brown, spongy, semigranular material; domestic peats, unless kiln dried, contain more water than the imported type. *Muck:* black, represents further state of decay than peat—not so useful. *Bacterized Peat:* supposedly treated; usually no better than muck. *Leafmold:* brownish-black material with some undecomposed leaves and twigs present; useful soil conditioner. *Wood soil:* usually leafmold, but further decomposed; useless without additions of fertilizer.

In what forms is humus available to the average amateur home gardener?   See previous question. Manure, straw, peatmoss, kitchen waste, hay—all these must decompose before becoming humus. The compost pile (which see) is probably the best of all sources of humus for the home garden.

What is the function of humus in the soil?   Among the important functions of humus are to effect granulation of the soil, thereby improving drainage and soil aeration; to increase its water-holding capacity; to increase the bacterial activity; to increase the percentage of such essential elements as nitrogen and sulfur; and to help in transforming essential elements from non-available to available forms.

Is humus important to soil fertility?   Yes; by increasing moisture absorption and the activity of several of the essential elements, especially nitrogen.

How is humus incorporated into the soil?   By spading or plowing.

Is spring or fall the best time to add humus to soil?   In the fall preferably, but it may be added at any time.

Our soil is rich but hard to work. What is the best source of humus? Manure, peatmoss, or a compost heap.

What method do you recommend to maintain humus and bacteria in soils?   Keep soils aerated by the addition of manures. Use greenmanure crops (which see) wherever possible.

What is to be done when humus keeps the earth too moist?   Incorporate sand or cinders.

What would you recommend to keep a very rich black soil from caking? It forms a hard crust about an inch deep.   Add humus— manure, peat, alfalfa hay. Incorporate fine cinders in the top 6 ins.

What causes soil to become very hard?   Lack of organic matter.

A bog was dug up to make a lake; stuff removed looks like excellent humus. How can this material be converted to garden use?   The material should make an excellent mulch, or to mix with soil. Unless soil on which this is used is very acid, the acidity of the humus will have no detrimental effect. If the material is lumpy, place in small piles to dry; pulverize before applying.

Do commercial fertilizers supply humus? The application of organic fertilizers such as soybean and cottonseed meals supplies a very small amount of humus. The inorganic fertilizers do not supply humus.

PEATMOSS

What is the difference in value between peatmoss and peat? Between domestic and imported peat? Peatmoss is moss (usually sphagnum) in an advanced state of disintegration; peat is a product of some kind of vegetation (not necessarily moss) largely decomposed. Domestic peat is usually of sedge origin, although we have some sphagnum peat in this country. Imported peat is usually sphagnum peat.

What is peatmoss good for? Is manure good to mix with it? Peatmoss makes an excellent mulch. It adds acidity to soils, holds moisture, adds organic matter. When it breaks down, it adds nitrogen. Peat and manure make an excellent combination.

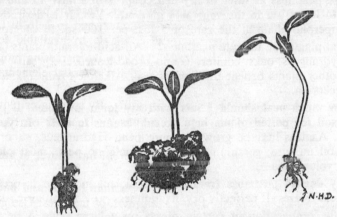

Humus in the soil absorbs and holds moisture, encouraging fibrous root growth. Center seedling above was grown in a half-soil, half-peatmoss mixture; the others in plain soil.

Does peat have any value as a fertilizer? Yes. Domestic sedge peat contains up to 3 per cent nitrogen, which becomes available slowly. Sphagnum peat ("peatmoss") contains less than 1 per cent nitrogen. It is slower in availability than the sedge peat.

Is peatmoss good for flower gardens in general? Yes. When dug into the soil, it helps retain moisture, and in other ways increases productiveness.

When is the best time to use peatmoss—spring or autumn? Apply the peat as a mulch in the fall, and work into the soil in the spring.

Is it true that peatmoss worked into the soil will make a heavy soil lighter and will cause a light soil to hold more moisture? Yes. In this respect its action is similar to that of manure.

As a winter protection is peatmoss considered as good as straw or leaves? This depends upon what is to be mulched. It mats down too much for some plants, such as delphiniums, foxgloves, campanulas, etc. For roses and most shrubs, and especially for rhododendrons and azaleas, it is excellent. The cost is much higher than for leaves, straw, or similar materials.

What is the best way to use peatmoss in flower gardens and on old lawns? In flower gardens apply as a mulch, and later work it into the bed. A thin covering on lawns is beneficial in the fall.

Is putting peatmoss around flowers in the fall harmful? My chrysanthemums seem to be dying. Not if applied only 1 to 2 ins. deep, unless continuous rains make such an application undesirable. Peat holds moisture.

I use peatmoss as litter in my hen coop. Will I have to add anything to it for use in the vegetable garden? Yes. It is desirable to add superphosphate at the rate of 5 lbs. per 100 sq. ft. of ground.

What plants can tolerate peatmoss? All acid-tolerant plants (azaleas, hydrangeas, oaks, coniferous and broad-leaved evergreens, etc.). Most other plants benefit through its use. Alkaline-loving plants are the exception.

How much peat should I mix with my loam and sand to get a good soil for potted plants in a greenhouse? Depends on type of plants. Azaleas may be grown in pure peat. Hydrangeas, ½ of the total soil mixture; geraniums, no peat; cacti, no peat; most plants, ¼ by volume.

Why doesn't peatmoss freeze? If sufficient moisture is present, peatmoss freezes. If perfectly dry, its fluffiness provides an air cushion.

In the propagation of certain plants on a large scale, I need to have about ¼ of my soil mixture consist of peatmoss. Is there any suitable substitute that could be found in the South Carolina low country? Shredded sugar cane, shredded redwood bark, or decomposed pine needles.

What is the best substitute for peatmoss? Sedge peat, bagasse (sugar cane pulp), leafmold, pine needles, shredded redwood bark, ground barks of most trees, and sawdust used in smaller amounts than peat.

MANURES

What does a ton of manure mean in terms of yards? A ton of manure is approximately a cubic yard, and will cover about 2,000 sq. ft., 2 ins. thick. However, the weight per yard varies greatly with the moisture content.

When purchasing manure, should it be bought dry, damp, or wet? If it is in good shape, the drier the better; otherwise you are paying for water.

How is it possible to store well-rotted manure without losing valuable properties by leaching? Keep under cover, on a concrete

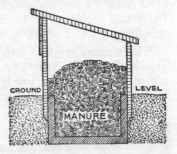

Manure keeps best under cover. A concrete or brick-lined pit, with protecting board roof, will prevent loss of valuable nutrients which manure heap rots down for garden use.

floor. Add superphosphate to it, and keep moist. If no cover is available, stack in piles 4 ft. deep with perpendicular sides. To secure even decomposition, turn the manure pile 2 or 3 times during year.

Where and how should manure be stored to rot? Preferably in a pit of concrete, or on a concrete floor, with a roof over it. Keep moist to prevent firing. Turn every 2 or 3 months.

If there is a roof over a manure pit, will the fresh manure heat up and perhaps cause a fire from spontaneous combustion? I am told the manure is better if roofed over. A roof over a manure pit is desirable. The manure will not burn if kept moist. If there is any sign of its heating badly, turn it "inside out." (It will not start a fire, though the manure itself may "burn out.")

How long should manure be rotted before use? Depends entirely upon the temperature and other conditions. Usually 6 months.

Are pine shavings harmful when mixed in manure? No; but they should be thoroughly decomposed.

I have cow, horse, sheep, and chicken manure. Could you tell me the best way to use them, on vegetables, shrubs, and flowers? Mix the cow and horse manure, allow to decay, and use in the spring. If fresh, plow under in the fall. The sheep and poultry manure (which see) may better be handled separately, because of their high nitrogen content.

Should garden soil be fertilized with barnyard manure every year? Yes, if the manure is available.

How much manure should be spread over the garden each year? A coating about 2 ins. thick.

How is manure applied to the unplanted garden? Apply at the rate of 600 lbs. per 1,000 sq. ft. and plow or dig under in the fall.

Should fresh or half-rotted manure be dug into the ground in the fall, or should the ground be dug first and then the fresh or half-rotted manure spread on the ground for the winter and dug under in the spring? Spread over the surface and spade it under in the fall.

Is the middle of March a good time to put manure on a vegetable plot? Should I use dry pulverized (Bovung) or fresh stable manure? Pulverized manure may be used in the spring. Fresh stable manure should be plowed under in the fall.

Will manure worked into the ground this fall help beyond one growing season? Yes. The residual effect of manure may remain for many seasons. A yearly application is advisable nevertheless.

What is the best fertilizer to put over a vegetable garden during the winter, for turning under in the spring? Manure. Withhold the commercial fertilizers until spring.

I am told that old garden soils are often deficient in minerals, resulting in the same lack of minerals in vegetables grown in same. Does barnyard manure supply minerals? Not in sufficient amounts. A complete fertilizer should be used in addition to the manure.

I made a new garden, size 50 × 12. As fertilizer I used about 10 bu. of chicken manure and 16 bu. of mushroom manure. Do you think this is enough fertilizer for this plot? Yes; in fact, you have overfertilized. You have applied considerably more nitrogen and potash but less phosphorus than would be incorporated if a 4–12–4 fertilizer was applied.

Is manure necessary for FLOWER gardens if a complete fertilizer is added to the soil several times a year? Yes. Manure has other properties besides fertilizer value. If manure is not available, add humus or green manure (which see) yearly.

I fertilize my GARDEN with Vigoro, and continually add humus in form of oak leaves, vegetable tops, and peelings. Is manure also necessary? Weeds are so much worse when I use manure, but I want to keep the soil built up. If you maintain the humus content without manure, its application is unnecessary.

Can barnyard manure be put on young GRASS in the fall without injury? Do not use manure on lawns, except when preparing soil for seeding, or unless it is dried and pulverized.

Should barnyard fertilizer be used in ROSE beds? Yes. Use when making the beds originally, and as a mulch each winter. The mulch is worked into the ground in the spring.

Should manure, used to fertilize single PLANTS or BULBS, be placed in the holes where they are to be planted? In such cases use well-rotted manure only. Place in the hole, cover with 2 ins. of soil, then plant.

CAT AND DOG MANURE

Are cat and dog manure helpful to soil, or the opposite? They have some fertilizing value, but are best when composted with other materials.

I expect to have a dog kennel soon. Could I use dog manure for fertilizing a flower garden? Yes. (See previous question.)

CHICKEN MANURE

Is chicken manure harmful to plants? No. On the contrary, it is very beneficial, as it is high in available nitrogen. It should be used sparingly.

How can chicken droppings be used as fertilizer? Allow to dry for a few weeks, under cover, and thus lose some of the quick-acting ammonium. Mixed with peat or litter, chicken manure is safe to use; but apply in small quantities.

Will you tell me how to use chicken fertilizer? How to determine when it is old? Mix with soil or peat, half and half. When odor of ammonium is dissipated, *unmixed* chicken manure is safe to use in small quantities.

In using chicken manure for fertilizer, how is it applied? Ten to 20 lbs. of dried or well-rotted chicken manure per 100 sq. ft. if broadcast just before, or at time of, planting. Or a half trowelful or so, mixed in the planting hole, for setting out individual plants.

When can one use chicken manure most effectively for results in gardening? See previous question. If at all fresh, apply to the soil several weeks before planting.

Can you please give me a formula for a well-balanced fertilizer, using poultry manure to supply nitrogen? It is difficult, mechanically, to mix animal manures with chemical fertilizers. Better apply separately. The following may be used: to 100 sq. ft. apply 15 lbs. poultry manure, 3 lbs. superphosphate, ½ lb. potassium chloride.

Have 15 hens and clean the dropping-board every day, then spread superphosphate over dropping-board. Is it proper to save the manure in iron barrel? Yes, saving in a container will reduce leaching. Keep dry.

Is it necessary to use commercial fertilizer if I use manure from 200 chickens? Yes. You would have to add superphosphate and potash, unless very large amounts of manure were used, in which case there would be an excess of nitrogen.

I am collecting quite a bit of chicken manure, mixed with sawdust,

and keeping it piled throughout the winter. **What way can I get the best use of it for my lawn and garden? What value has it?** This should make an excellent fertilizer for the garden, but not for the lawn—the sawdust would be objectionable. Apply in the spring or fall at the rate of 5 to 10 lbs. per 100 sq. ft.

Is it good practice to use poultry manure and goat manure, mixed with wood shavings, as litter? There is no objection to the use of wood shavings for litter. They decay slowly, and because of that are not so satisfactory for soil improvement as other forms of litter mixed with manures.

Is a mixture of chicken manure and peatmoss all right to topdress a lawn in winter? (New Jersey.) Yes, very satisfactory; but it would be better not to apply until March.

Can chicken manure be mixed with wood ashes? Do not use together if manure is fresh. Otherwise, the combination is good.

What proportion of chicken manure should be mixed with wood ashes? Mix ashes and chicken manure at 3-to-1 ratio.

How can leaves and poultry manure be prepared for fertilizer in the flower garden? Layer of leaves 12 ins. deep; layer of poultry manure 1 in. deep; sprinkling of complete fertilizer; water well. Repeat until heap is 4 ft. high; water frequently. In 3 months turn "inside out."

Is compost containing chicken manure too strong for most plants? Not if it is well decomposed.

Is chicken manure containing approximately 30 per cent screened sand, 50 per cent ground sugar cane, and 20 per cent droppings suitable for young APPLE trees (not in bearing) on a sandy loam? Yes, excellent.

Would hen manure used on CORN and TOMATOES force them into bearing early, and then cause them to die? The high nitrogen of poultry manure would produce heavy vegetative growth at first, which would affect the corn and would make tomatoes late in setting fruit. It should not hasten death of the plants.

Is chicken manure a good fertilizer for the FLOWER garden? If so, if a year old is it still O.K. to use? It is safer when a year old than when fresh. Very satisfactory for the flower garden. Use at rate of 10 to 20 lbs. per 100 sq. ft.

Can poultry manure be used to good effect on GARDEN ground, especially where potatoes are to be grown? Poultry manure cannot be applied so heavily as barnyard manure. It would be too costly, and would contain too much nitrogen. For potatoes, on a small scale, it would probably be best to apply as a side dressing, when plants are a few inches high, at rate of 8 to 10 lbs. per 100 ft. of row.

I am using old chicken manure on ROSEBUSHES. Can you tell me how much of it to put on each bush? If it is well rotted, 1 to 2 shovelfuls per plant.

Can poultry compost be used on anything other than ROSES and PANSIES? Yes, in small quantities it may be used on any crop. It is especially good for leaf crops, such as lettuce or cabbage.

What can I do for my garden soil that has had too much chicken droppings put on it for several years? Now nothing grows. Apply lime at 5 lbs. per 100 sq. ft. and then water heavily several times. Then spade and add superphosphate at 5 lbs. per 100 sq. ft.

COW MANURE

What is the best all-purpose manure for the garden? Well-rotted cow manure.

Is horse manure or cow manure better for gardens? Fresh horse manure contains more ammonium than cow manure and is apt to "burn out" more readily. Well-rotted cow manure is usually not so badly leached and burned as horse manure. So in general cow manure is preferred. If both are available, the horse manure could be used for earliest spring crops.

Which is the best dressing for flowers, hen manure or cow manure? Cow manure is safer; hen manure is richer, especially in nitrogen.

How can you test cow manure for strength? There is no simple test for this purpose. Manure that has become well decomposed under cover will contain the most nutrients per ton—it has become concentrated. When stored outside and leached by rains, it will lose much of its nutrient value.

How should cow manure be treated to be applied to a garden? Keep under cover and on cement floor to prevent leaching. Do not allow to dry out. It makes better fertilizer when well rotted.

Is cow or horse manure preferred to commercial fertilizers? If so, why? Manures are not balanced fertilizers. Usually additions of phosphates are needed with manures. One ton of manure contains 10 lbs. nitrogen, 5 lbs. phosphate, 10 lbs. potassium. These become available slowly. A complete commercial fertilizer is more quickly available, and 110 lbs. of it would give as much nutrition as a ton of manure. However, manure is valuable because of organic matter, water-holding capacity, addition of bacteria and other organisms to soil, help in changing unavailable materials to available, earlier warming of soil in spring. Thus best results are had when both manure and fertilizers are employed.

Should I use cow manure and oak leaves for my entire garden? Yes; this will prove a good general fertilizer for most plants. It would, however, be still better if supplemented by chemicals. (See previous question.)

On what, and when, should cow manure be used? On almost any plants. Dig under in the fall. Use as a mulch in the fall. Use as a mulch during summer if you don't mind appearance.

Is it better to leave cattle manure on the ground all winter, or should it be turned under and the ground plowed or spaded up again the following spring? Plow the manure under in the fall. Disk or hoe the ground in spring.

If I plow under fresh cow manure in the spring and then plant, is there any danger of crops burning? No, but for a period there will be stoppage of growth. This is due to the fact that while manure is decomposing the bacteria causing this action deplete the soil of nitrogen at the expense of the plants. This can be offset, however, by applying a side dressing of nitrate of soda, chicken manure, or some other quick-acting, high-nitrogen fertilizer.

When fresh cow manure is put on the land, is there any material to add to it so it will rot faster? Use lime on it.

Will cow manure be helpful to EVERGREENS? Yes. Apply when well rotted only. The best time is fall, so that the manure will serve a double purpose—mulch and nutrition. Can be worked into the soil in the spring.

Is cow manure (if well rotted) safe to put around RHODODEN-DRONS? Yes, but if worked into the soil, sulfur or aluminum sulfate may have to be added.

Is cow manure suitable for SHRUBS and LAWNS? For trees and shrubs, yes. For lawns, no. It is likely to infest the lawns with weeds.

Is it advisable to spread rotted manure over a planted TULIP bed, or over a perennial bed after frost? It is better not to use manure on a tulip bed. For mulching purposes, well-rotted manure is too costly and is apt to pack. If used, 4 ins. in depth is needed. Straw or corn fodder will answer the mulching purpose better.

DRIED MANURE

I planted a small vegetable garden of about 2,000 sq. ft. I plan to enrich soil with a compost and Bovung (dried rotted cow manure) this year. How much should be used? At least 100 lbs. of dried cow manure should be used to 1,000 sq. ft. If you can afford it, triple the amount.

I am no longer able to get barnyard fertilizer for my garden plot. Is there a commercial fertilizer that I can procure? "Commercial" (dried and ground) cow manure and sheep manure are available. Incorporate green manures, and, in addition, apply a 4–12–4 fertilizer.

Under what conditions can dried manure be used in place of rotted manure? Only when well-rotted stable manure cannot be obtained.

GOAT MANURE

Can a garden have too much goat manure? Goat manure is reasonably strong in nitrogen. It should be used in about the same way as described for sheep manure.

Should goat manure and straw be put on frozen ground, or put in compost heap until spring? Better in compost heap, if mixed with other materials, otherwise, it would be better to spread the manure and straw on the ground. If left in a pile, some leaching will take place, and not on the spot where wanted.

GUANO

What is guano? Guano is old seafowl, turtle, seal, or bat manure. It is now difficult to obtain, and seldom used in this country. Large deposits of seafowl guano are found in such localities as the Peruvian Islands. Bat guano is found to some extent in bat caverns of the southern United States.

HORSE MANURE

Got fresh horse manure but find it difficult to keep it from burning. Can leaves be mixed with it? When horse manure is "burned," it loses most of its nitrogen, but it is still good as a soil conditioner. Mixing peat or leaves or chopped straw with horse manure and keeping it wet will reduce burning.

Will wood shavings harm horse manure? No. Apply to soil in the fall.

Is horse stable manure harmful to roses and delphiniums? No.

LIQUID MANURE

Is there any fertilizer that can be used as a liquid for the small home garden? Soak fresh animal manure in water, and use the liquid. (See Section VII.) Five teaspoons of a regular 5–10–5, 5–10–10, 7–7–7, or similar grade of complete fertilizer per gallon of water will make a satisfactory liquid fertilizer. Such fertilizers are about 75 per cent soluble. Do not use premium grades of fertilizers containing much organic materials. Apply 1 gal. to 5 sq. ft.

How can you make liquid fertilizer, using chemical ingredients which are cheap to buy? A liquid fertilizer containing 1 teaspoonful each of saltpeter (potassium nitrate), superphosphate (monocalcium phosphate), and Epsom salts (magnesium sulfate) is satisfactory.

PIGEON MANURE

Will it be feasible and practical to scatter pigeon droppings on soil in the fall, which will be sown to lawn in the spring? Yes.

What is the value of pigeon manure as a fertilizer, mixed with hard coal ashes? Any animal manure may be used to advantage, particularly when at least partially decomposed. Mixed with fine cinders, soil condition is improved. Pigeon manure is as good as chicken manure.

PIG MANURE

Is pig manure as good as any other manure? What would be best to use it for in growing vegetables? In nutrient content, pig manure does not differ essentially from cow manure, except that it is higher in potash. It is, however, more difficult to handle, and to break down into a crumbly condition.

Should pig manure be mixed with something else? Mix with straw or hay.

When is pig manure best applied? Apply in the fall.

Will pig manure that has been stored under cover all winter be good for flowers in the spring, or will it burn them? Use pig manure only after it has rotted down.

RABBIT MANURE

What value has rabbit manure in a vegetable garden? How should it be used? It is valuable for its high nitrogen content. Mix with peatmoss or straw, and allow to lie exposed for several weeks before applying to soil. 5 to 10 lbs. per 100 sq. ft. is enough.

Is rabbit manure too strong for use on a vegetable garden? If fresh and applied in the spring, it may do damage unless used as a very light covering. If applied in the fall, rabbit manure is one of our strongest animal manures. When well rotted, especially if mixed with peatmoss, it can be used freely and safely.

SHEEP MANURE

How does sheep manure, as a fertilizer, compare with cow manure or horse manure? Sheep manure contains about twice as much nitrogen, and 1½ times as much phosphate and potassium as cow manure.

One hundred lbs. of pulverized sheep manure is equivalent in fertilizer value to what quantity of rotted cow dressing? From the standpoint of nitrogen content it would take 500 lbs. of dried cow manure to equal 100 lbs. of sheep manure, but the bulkiness of the cow manure makes it a more desirable soil conditioner.

Is sheep litter good to fertilize holly trees with? If allowed to decompose, yes.

GREEN MANURES

GREEN-MANURE CROPS

What is a green-manure crop? A cover crop? The term "green-manure crop" refers to any crop that may be turned into the soil in an undecomposed, green-tissue stage. In contrast, a cover crop refers to a more or less permanent crop used for the purpose of preventing erosion.

How are green-manure crops planted? For small areas, seeds of the green-manure crops can be broadcast. For large areas a drill is used. Seeds should not be covered too deeply—approximately twice their diameter is sufficient.

What are several good summer green-manure crops? The crops most commonly used for summer green manure are alfalfa, cowpeas, Crimson Clover, Red Clover, Sweet Clover, crotalaria, lespedeza, soybeans, and Sudangrass.

Legumes—such as clover, vetch, and soybeans—increase the soil's nitrogen supply.

What green-manure crop can be left on the ground over winter, to be turned under in spring? The most common winter green-manure crops are rye, Perennial Rye Grass, and oats.

What quantity of seed should be sown, per 1,000 sq. ft., of green-manure crops? Alfalfa, ½ lb.; cowpeas, 2½ to 3 lbs.; Crimson Clover and Red Clover, ½ lb.; Sweet Clover, ½ to ¾ lb.; crotalaria, ½ to ¾ lb.; lespedeza, ½ lb.; soybeans, 2–3 lbs.; Sudangrass, ½ to ¾ lb.; rye, 2 to 3 lbs.; rye grass, 1 to 2 lbs.; buckwheat, 1½ lbs. These are approximate amounts. For thick and quick coverage, on small areas, they can be increased up to double these quantities.

I cannot obtain cow manure. What do you suggest as a substitute? Old, partly rotted straw, or alfalfa hay, together with a complete fertilizer, may be used as substitutes. Plow in early in the fall and add fertilizer at time of plowing. Or use a green-manure crop.

How tall should a green-manure crop be before it is turned under?
In general, it is best to turn under green crops when their succulence
is near the maximum, yet at a time when abundant tops have been
produced. This stage occurs when they are about, or a little beyond,
half mature.

Are clover and buckwheat good for soil? Clover and buckwheat
are good green-manure crops, but soybeans and rye are better and
quicker. Sow soybeans in the spring and plow under in early fall.
Sow rye in September and plow under in the spring. Use 2 lbs. per
1,000 sq. ft.

**Where a green-manure crop is plowed under in fall, is it advisable
to follow with a winter crop?** Yes, this is an advisable practice,
especially where there is possibility of soil erosion.

**What winter green-manure crops can be used following the turning
under of Red Clover?** Rye, rye grass, or oats.

*Green manures, such as rye, are dug under
(while still in an immature state) to add
humus to the soil.*

**How soon after the summer green-manure crop is turned under
can the fall crop be sown?** It is advisable to delay the sowing of the
second crop 2 weeks, if possible; but follow the specific planting
dates recommended for the winter crop used.

When should winter green-manure crops be sown? Late August
or early September. Rye can be sown as late as first week of October.

**If soil is respaded in spring, following turning under of green
manure (clover) in fall, will the crop come to the top?** If the green-
manure crop is turned under at the proper time, it will be sufficiently
decomposed by spring so that respading can be done.

When land is cleared, and winter rye sown, what should be done

in spring to prepare for vegetables? Plow the rye under in April. Apply 5–10–5 fertilizer at 3 to 4 lbs. per 100 sq. ft.

How can organics and nitrogen be supplied in city gardens without manure or chemical fertilizer? Peatmoss and dried manures may be used. Soybean meal and cottonseed meal will add nitrogen.

Should turf and large roots be removed from virgin soil or turned under to make humus? It is advisable to turn under as much organic matter as possible in preparing soil for planting. Turf and roots of annual and herbaceous plants should be turned under. Remove the large roots of woody plants.

Can a green-manure crop be planted which will raise the pH and sweeten the soil? No, green-manure crops in themselves exert very little influence on the degree of acidity of the soil.

When there is a shortage of animal fertilizer, what kind and proportion of other fertilizer are suggested for garden use? Incorporate green manures. Apply 4–12–4 or 2–10–10, 30 to 40 lbs. per 1,000 sq. ft. in the spring.

Do any plants, other than legumes and green-manure crops, supply any nutrients to soil? Any plant which is turned under supplies a certain amount of nutrients. The proportions vary with the type of plant.

RYE

Does planting rye in fall and plowing under in spring keep up fertility of the soil? The use of rye as a green-manure crop will do little toward increasing the nitrogen content of the soil; in fact, it may even decrease it temporarily. It does, however, add humus, and thus help to increase crop production.

Should green-manure crops such as rye be used every year? In gardens devoted to the production of vegetables or annual flowers, it is advisable to sow a winter green-manure crop each autumn.

At what stage should rye be turned under? When it is 18 to 24 ins. tall.

Should rye be completely covered when it is turned under? Yes, but the green-manure crop should be incorporated with the upper 8 to 12 ins. of soil instead of being plowed or dug under in a layer. If a few of the stems are not covered, it is all right.

LEGUMES

What is a legume? All leguminous plants belong to the Pea family, recognizable by the formation of their flowers. Peas, beans, and clovers are legumes. They all attract bacteria which collect nitrogen and store it on the roots. The small nodules on the roots, when they decay, add nitrogen to the soil.

What is the special advantage of using a leguminous green-manure crop? The advantage of a legume (as compared to a non-legume) is that the nitrogen content of the soil will be increased by the root-nodule organisms. However, the legume crops take longer to grow. For a small garden, rye or Perennial Rye Grass is usually more practical.

Are inoculant powders for use on legumes really helpful? Yes. These inoculant powders are listed under various trade names (such as Legume Aid, Nod-O-Gen, etc.) and are obtainable in local seed stores. They are used to assist in the development of nitrogen-fixing bacteria on the roots of leguminous plants. They are applied when seeds are planted. The mixtures vary with the crop to be planted, so the crop should always be mentioned when buying these products.

Is it advisable to try to grow ALFALFA for soil improvement in southern part of Maine? Yes. But plant early (mid-August) to avoid heaving out and winter killing. Sow 12 to 15 lbs. per acre.

How is the land prepared for growing ALFALFA? Same as for any other crop. It may be necessary to add lime.

When is it best to plant CRIMSON CLOVER and expect results from it in improving the soil for a garden? Crimson Clover is usually seeded in July or August, or at least 6 weeks before normal date of the first killing frost in fall. It may be turned under the following spring or early summer.

Do you plow CRIMSON CLOVER under when it is in bloom? It is best to turn it under when in bloom, or shortly after this stage. It can, however, be turned under at any stage; but the less growth has been made, the less humus will be produced.

Are Austrian PEAS good to use as a green-manure crop? Yes, they are a good winter crop. Use soybeans as a summer crop. Plow both under to add organic matter to the soil.

At what rate should SOYBEANS be sown for a green-manure crop? Three lbs. per 1,000 sq. ft.

COMPOST

What is "compost"? Compost is the term applied to organic matter—such as leaves, weeds, grass clippings, and the like—which has been sufficiently decayed to form a light, crumbly mold. In making compost in a compost heap, soil and manure are often mixed with the vegetable matter.

Should the average home gardener have a compost heap? Yes, by all means.

COMPOST HEAPS

What materials are used in making a compost heap? Plant refuse: cornstalks, cabbage stems, dead foliage, and discarded vegetables; leaves, grass cuttings, garbage, soil, manure (in fact, any vegetable matter that will decay), plus lime and complete fertilizers. Weeds, even when seeding, may be used if the heap is to be remade at the end of each 3 months, turning it inside out so that every part of the heap is completely decomposed before use. A heap treated in this way is so well rotted that most seeds and insect eggs are destroyed.

How is a compost heap constructed? Heaps 4 ft. wide and 6 ft. long are a convenient size for the small place. Dig out this area to a depth of from 12 to 18 ins. and throw the soil to one side. The bottom layer should be cornstalks, cabbage stems, and other coarse material, tamped down. Over this lay 2 or 3 ins. of soil, and then 2 or 3 ins. of manure, if available. Peatmoss can be used if manure cannot be had. Sprinkle raw ground limestone over each layer at the rate of a pint to a wheelbarrowload of compost material. Add layers of leaves, cuttings, weeds, etc., with a layer of soil, manure, or peatmoss every 12 to 18 ins. Sprinkle soil layers with complete fertilizer containing at least 4 per cent nitrogen thickly enough to whiten the surface like a light snowfall. Keep sides even but sloping very gradually inward toward top. When all material has been placed in layers, soak thoroughly with hose and cover entirely with 3 ins. soil, well firmed down. The top is left saucer-shaped to receive and absorb rainfall. Do not let heap dry out at any time. At end of 3 months remake entire heap, turning inside out, if rapid decomposition is desired.

What length of time is required for a well-made compost heap to rot? Four months to a year, depending on its composition and whether or not ingredients have been added to hasten decay; usually about 9 months.

What is a good formula for making a compost pile rot quickly? I understand lime should not be used as it causes loss of nitrogen. Lime should be used. (For formula, see Introduction, this section.)

Do you advise the use of a chemical such as Adco for the compost heap? Adco is an inoculum used to hasten decomposition. It gives good results, but it is not a substitute for the rather large amounts of fertilizer also needed for the composting process. For instance, a 4–12–4 or 5–10–5 fertilizer (150 lbs.) and 50 lbs. of hydrated lime are sufficient for the decomposition of a one-ton pile of straw.

How often should a new compost heap be started? To maintain a constant supply of compost, a new heap should be started every 6 months.

How is rotted compost used in gardening? It should be sieved through a coarse (1-in.) screen and then diluted with 3 or 4 parts of garden soil. It can be worked into the garden by applying a 1½ in. layer and cultivating it into the upper 6 inches of soil. For a lawn dressing, apply the sieved compost without dilution with soil.

How should decomposed compost be removed from the heap? Cut sections down vertically with a spade, leaving straight, clean sides where it has been removed. Sift through a 1-in. sifter and save coarse siftings for a new compost heap.

GARBAGE

Are these any good for the compost heap: orange peels, banana peels, tea and coffee grounds, and green corn shucks? Yes, any vegetable refuse free of disease is all right. Even weeds with seeds are all right if properly fermented.

Can fresh table refuse and garbage be applied to the garden? I have been putting everything through a meat chopper and this makes a fine lot of refuse. The problem is how to apply it. Are orange skins of much fertilizing value? The materials mentioned, by themselves, do not constitute fertilizers, but when rotted in a compost pile they are valuable.

The refuse from my incinerator consists mostly of ashes and unburned garbage, such as grapefruit, orange peels, etc. Is this O.K. to bury in soil having a large clay content? Yes; but better to make a compost heap with 6-in. alternate layers of soil, garbage, grass cuttings, etc. It would take a year to make a good compost, but it's worth the trouble.

After apples have been crushed and squeezed for cider, would it be advisable to use the apple pomace in the compost pile? Yes, apple pomace is all right to add to compost; cover with soil.

What is the case for, and against, adding garbage to the compost heap? Garbage is a most desirable source of compost. Each layer of garbage must, however, be immediately covered with soil to prevent odors. If dogs run loose in your community, unsorted table garbage will attract them unless the heap is fenced in. Garbage also attracts rodents. Garbage can be placed in a pit, at a distance from house, each layer being sprinkled with a layer of soil and of raw ground limestone. When the contents of the pit are decomposed, it can be added in layers to a new compost heap when one is being built. In this way rodents are kept out of the compost heap and garbage is decomposed underground without odor.

GRASS CLIPPINGS

What good are grass cuttings? How fast do they decay? Clippings make satisfactory compost. If layered with soil in thin layers (4 ins. of soil and 2 ins. of clippings), or added to a mixed heap, a compost will be ready in less than a year.

Is it a real advantage, economical or otherwise, to accumulate grass clippings and convert them into "organic manure" by the use of chemicals such as Adco? Yes.

HICKORY HULLS

Do the hulls (not shells) from hickory nuts cause soil acidity? We have 3 hickory trees on a double lot and don't know whether to put the hulls into the compost pile or burn them? Hickory hulls may be composted satisfactorily with layers of soil.

LEAVES

Should the leaves for compost be rotted? It is best to have them at least partly rotted before placing them in compost heap. If not, it is likely to take a full year for them to decompose, unless manure or peatmoss is also used in the compost pile.

Are elm leaves good to use on the compost heap? Yes.

How do you make fertilizer out of maple leaves? Add to compost heap in the same way as other leaves.

LEAF COMPOSTS

Should anything be used with leaves for compost? Manure or peatmoss, lime, and complete fertilizers. (See page 61)

What can be added to accumulated leaves in the fall to hasten decomposition? Make a pile 4 ft. wide and any desired length. Each layer of leaves 12 ins. deep should be sprinkled with a complete commercial fertilizer (4–12–4) at the rate of 150 lbs. to each ton of leaves. Lime should be added at 50 lbs. to the ton.

Is soil put on the compost pile (made largely of leaves) to help decomposition? Yes.

Will this fall's leaves be fertilizer by next spring? Can anything be done to hurry the process? Not that soon. It will take about a year. Leaves saved from fall and composted in the spring may make good leafmold by fall.

Much has been said about the value of a compost of rotted leaves. I understand that some leaves, due to high acid content, have practically no value as manure. Which should be burned and which should be saved? The leaves of a few kinds of trees, notably oaks, form an acid leafmold. Leafmold from most trees, however, is only slightly, if at all, acid. This reference is to leaves of deciduous trees. Evergreens, however, will produce acid leafmold. The use of lime is an easy way to correct any such acidity.

Are the ashes from burned leaves and grass cuttings of any benefit, or of as much benefit, as those same leaves and cuttings if they were permitted to decay? No. If leaves and clippings are made into a compost, they serve a much better purpose than when burned.

MANURE

In rotting down the compost heap, would it be wise to add hen manure, or would there be a loss of plant food? Hen manure is satisfactory; but superphosphate, potassium chloride, and lime should likewise be added.

MUSHROOM COMPOST

Is it possible for me to get compost from a mushroom farm? How should such compost be used? Is it suitable for garden use? Yes, very satisfactory. Use as a mulch 2 ins. deep, or mix in the soil. Unless a mushroom farm is fairly near by, transportation costs of the material may be too high.

SPECIAL PROBLEMS

What can the home gardener make from refuse, etc., to take the place of 5–10–5 and nitrate of soda? Make a compost pile of straw, weeds, grass clippings, leaves, and other plant parts. (See Compost, Introduction, this section.)
(Or, as a substitute for the above, apply 150 lbs. of cyanamid to a ton of plant refuse.) Keep the pile moist and decomposition will be rapid.

All the refuse from our lawns and vegetables and flower gardens has gone into our compost pile. This includes corn and dahlia stalks, peonies, etc. The entire pile has been covered with clay subsoil (topsoil being scarce). A little fertilizer has been added and some leaves. It is our intention to use this pile, accumulated during summer and fall, by digging it into the vegetable gardens. Is this good practice? A better method would have been to make alternate layers of soil and refuse together, with a definite amount of commercial fertilizer and lime. The only thing to do now is to turn the pile several times, mixing all the ingredients together.

Is composted fertilizer, testing 2 per cent nitrogen, 2 per cent phosphoric acid, and 2 per cent potash, homemade from organic materials, as good as the $60 per ton stuff of the same test from chemical materials? $60 a ton for a 2–2–2 fertilizer is entirely too high. The organic fertilizer will do just as well as the one made of chemicals, but it will be much slower in action, though of longer lasting quality.

Will you give me an idea of the fertilizer value of compost, with inorganic chemicals added, as compared to that made of organic matter only? Organic fertilizers are less satisfactory to add to composts than inorganic, largely because of their slower action. Once decomposed, there should be little difference between the two. Inorganic fertilizers and lime are added to the compost heap both to hasten decomposition and to supply nutrients otherwise low or lacking.

In making a compost pile, is it more advisable to pile up on top of ground, or to dig pit and gradually fill in? Either method is satisfactory. In a pit, however, the pile is less likely to dry out, which is undesirable.

How do you keep a compost pile from smelling? Use lime and cover it with a layer of soil. A well-made heap is not likely to give off any objectionable odor.

What is a good substitute for city dwellers for the objectionable compost pile? A compost pile, when properly made, is not objectionable.

Does the compost lose any of its elements when kept in the house all winter and dried up? The mechanical structure of such soils is affected more than its nutritional value. If stored inside, keep moist.

Compost pits are sometimes thickly inhabited by very large, fat earthworms. Are these harmful, or should they be left in the decomposing material? Worms do no damage in the compost; in fact, they assist in the decomposition of vegetable matter. When compost is sifted for use, they will be eliminated.

PESTS AND DISEASES

In making a compost heap, how can we avoid carrying over diseases of previous year, as tomato and potato blight, etc.? Do not use diseased tops, vines, or fruits for composting, unless special care is taken in "turning" heap. (See next question.)

Some of the waste vegetable matter I put in my compost heap had a lot of aphids or similar insects on it. I put lime and superphosphate with the compost. Will the aphids be killed during the winter? The adults will probably die, but the eggs may carry over. At the time of making the compost the vegetable matter should have been sprayed with Black Leaf 40. However, if the heap is turned "inside out" every 3 months and if every part is thus thoroughly fermented, most insects and diseases will be destroyed.

Does it do any harm to put moldy fruit, vegetables, or mildewed shrubs and leaves into the compost? Any vegetable matter which is not infected with disease or infested with insects may be used safely for composting. Molds resulting from decay do no harm.

Explain the chemistry of the compost heap. Would the pests it might harbor outweigh the advantages for a small (50 × 100 ft.) garden? A compost heap is a mixture of soil, fertilizer, and organic matter. In decomposing, the combination does not always get rid of all diseases and pests. To save organic matter, a compost pile is worth having.

ORGANIC FERTILIZERS

What is organic fertilizer? An organic fertilizer is one which is derived from organic materials—plant or animal substances. All are compounds of carbon. Some of these materials, such as cottonseed meal, bone meal, tankage, and castor pomace, may add small amounts of humus as well as nutrients to the soil. Others, such as urea or urea-form, may not add humus.

What is best for vegetable garden, stable manure or chemicals? Use both. They complement each other. Stable manure is organic but is not a balanced fertilizer, while a chemical fertilizer contains no organic matter to supply humus.

What fertilizers are best for loose soil? Loose soil will be benefited by the incorporation of organic matter, to increase the humus. The use of commercial fertilizer does not depend upon the soil structure.

What causes soil to crack in dry weather? Heavy soils will crack unless sufficient organic matter is present to prevent cohesion of the fine particles.

BONE MEAL

What types of bone meal are available, and for what purpose is each used? Coarse, raw, ground bone releases phosphorus slowly into the soil. Fine bone flower is used for quicker fertilization. Raw bone meal contains 2 to 4 per cent nitrogen and 20 to 25 per cent phosphoric acid. It is less dangerous than quicker-acting fertilizers for such plants as daffodils, tulips, roses, etc., and is often used as a top-dressing in the greenhouse. It is applied at the rate of 30 to 60 lbs. per 1,000 sq. ft. Steamed bone meal contains 1.65 to 2.50 per cent nitrogen and 20 to 30 per cent phosphoric acid, and is more quickly available as fertilizer material than raw bone meal.

When should bone meal be applied for best results? Early in the spring, when the soil is prepared. Work it into the upper 3 to 5 ins. of the soil.

Is bone meal a good fertilizer for all plants? No. Bone meal is a safe fertilizer to use, but it contains no potash. Based on amount of essential ingredients contained, it is more expensive than some chemical fertilizers. However, gardeners use it for many purposes.

Does bone meal act as a complete fertilizer on grass and garden? Bone meal is *not* a complete fertilizer, since it does not contain potash, only a small amount of nitrogen, and considerable phosphorus.

Would bone meal mixed with a small amount of soil, kept in cellar

during winter, and moistened occasionally, work faster when used in the spring than new bone meal? Its activity will be hastened to some extent, but not sufficiently to make the practice worth while.

Will bone meal ever turn soil acid? Bone meal exerts little effect on the soil reaction. If there is any change, it is to make the soil more alkaline.

What percentage of nitrogen is there in ground bone meal? Raw bone meal contains 2 to 4 per cent nitrogen and 22 to 25 per cent phosphoric acid. Steamed bone meal contains 1 to 2 per cent nitrogen and 22 to 30 per cent phosphoric acid.

Will the use of bone meal as a fertilizer harm plants that like acid soil, such as hydrangeas, wildflowers, etc.? No; bone meal exerts little influence on soil reaction.

What is a good application of bone meal? Three to 5 lbs. per 100 sq. ft.

What would the analysis be of 100 lbs. of bone meal? Approximately 3–22–0.

Are the effects of bone meal spread over a greater period in the soil than phosphate? The phosphorus in bone meal penetrates the soil very slowly and becomes available very slowly.

Is bone meal good for pot plants? If soils are not too acid and deficient in phosphorus, bone meal is a satisfactory fertilizer for pot plants.

COTTONSEED MEAL

What nutrients does cottonseed meal contain? Cottonseed meal contains approximately 7 per cent nitrogen, 2.5 per cent phosphoric acid, and 1.5 per cent potash.

How long does it take for cottonseed meal to mix with soil? Part of the nitrogen and other essential elements of cottonseed meal are readily available; the remainder becomes available more slowly.

On what plants can cottonseed meal be used, and in combination with what other fertilizer? It may be used on nearly all plants as it contains about 7 per cent nitrogen, which becomes available slowly; also 3 per cent phosphorus, and 2 per cent potash. It can be used with superphosphate.

DRIED BLOOD

Is blood meal a fertilizer? Dried blood is a complete but unbalanced fertilizer containing approximately 12 per cent nitrogen, 1 per cent phosphoric acid, and .75 per cent potash.

LEAFMOLD

In using leafmold as a fertilizer should it be used liberally or spar-

ingly? Leafmold is not a very high-grade fertilizer. It is a good conditioner, and as such can be used liberally—a covering 4 ins. deep is all right.

What effect do pine needles have on soil? They acidify it, and help improve condition.

When should fallen leaves be used? After decomposition; apply to soil at any time of the year.

Last fall I spaded my garden a foot deep and on the bottom I put a heavy layer of maple leaves. This was covered over with a foot of earth. Was this worth while? It would be better to spade leaves into the soil in the fall; or let them decay first and add to soil later.

How do hard maple tree leaves affect the soil if left where they fall over winter? It is better to compost them. Little value if left on top of soil.

Do large quantities of mixed leaves (elm, maple, oak, beech) make good fertilizer when rotted? They make a good soil conditioner but are of comparatively little fertilizer value; not nearly so effective as manures unless a heavy dosage of fertilizer is added in rotting them.

Is it true that the leaves of Silver Leaf and other poplars, spaded into the soil, are toxic or poison to the growth of flowers? No.

Will oak leaves make the ground sour? No. When decomposed, they make an excellent soil conditioner. Used in quantity, they will make the ground acid but only temporarily. They are frequently employed for this purpose.

SLUDGE

The dried and pulverized sludge from sewage-disposal plants is used as a fertilizer not only for lawns and flowers but vegetables as well. Therefore, would not the liquid and sludge from septic tanks, after it has passed from the first compartment and just before it passes into the third or final compartment, be a good fertilizer? How would it compare with the liquid manure used by farmers? Such sludge should be satisfactory as a fertilizer. It should compare favorably with liquid manure.

The local sewage disposal sells sewage settlings at 55¢ per 100 lbs. Nothing has been added to this. How does this compare in value with barnyard manure and with other commercial fertilizers, for use on lawn and garden? (I have sandy soil.) If sewage sludge can be obtained for 55¢ per 100 lbs. it should be a fairly good buy. It contains nearly twice the essential nutrients found in average manure. Be sure the sludge contains no toxic substances. Sewage sludge at 55¢ per 100 lbs. is expensive when compared with commercial fertilizer, such as 4–12–4.

What is the value of sludge from sanitary district beds? At what rate

should it be applied for flower or vegetable gardens? Recent reports from the Ohio Agricultural Experiment Station indicate that the analysis of sewage sludge from 10 different cities varied as follows: nitrogen, 0.88 to 2.98 per cent; phosphoric acid, 0.42 to 2.10 per cent; potash, 0.05 to 1.6 per cent. The report further showed that the nitrogen in sewage sludge was not more than 10 to 15 per cent as effective as the nitrogen in nitrate of soda.

TANKAGE

What is tankage? Tankage is a by-product of slaughterhouses, which contains such refuse as lungs, intestines, bones, etc. These are processed, dried, and ground to produce a material used in stock feeds and for fertilizer.

What is the value of tankage? It contains about 4 to 10 per cent nitrogen and 7 to 14 phosphoric acid. It is lacking in potash content.

How is tankage applied? About 4 lbs. per 100 sq. ft.; usually as a top- or side-dressing to growing plants, hoed or cultivated into the soil. It is often employed in place of nitrate of soda, which is quicker acting. It must be kept *perfectly dry* in storage, or it will quickly decay.

WOOD ASHES

Are wood or leaf ashes good for the garden? Yes. They contain potash and lime.

How do wood ashes affect manures? Wood ashes containing lime have a tendency to hasten the decomposition of manure.

Where can I use wood ashes and chicken manure to the best advantage? Do *not* use together, if chicken manure is fresh. Otherwise the combination is good. Mix ashes and chicken manure at 3 to 1 ratio.

Is it unwise to use wood ashes and horse manure at the same time? Yes. Horse manure, unless well rotted, contains quickly given off ammonium. Wood ashes are apt to hasten the process and "burning" of plants may result.

What lilies may have wood ashes? What is the best way to apply wood ashes to roses? Since the majority of lilies do better in somewhat acid soils, wood ashes should not be used. Apply wood ashes to roses in the spring; about ½ to 1 lb. around each plant.

What is the best way to use wood ashes in acid soil? Wood ashes tend to reduce acidity because of lime content. Apply to the soil in fall or spring; 4 to 6 lbs. per 100 sq. ft.

What plants and trees benefit by an application of wood ashes? Almost all plants. Those that need potash—fruit trees, vegetable root crops, hydrangeas, carnations, roses, peonies, etc.—are especially benefited.

How can we use to the best advantage, on vegetables, flowers, shrubs, and trees, our accumulation of wood ashes? Work into the soil after growth starts in the spring.

Will the action of wood ashes and cinders destroy alkali on irrigated land? (Washington.) Neither wood ashes nor cinders would have any effect. If the soil is alkaline, sulphur is needed.

Every year I burn a considerable amount of brush. Are the ashes good fertilizer? Wood ashes are especially good for their potash content.

Do oak wood ashes have any value as fertilizer for flowers or vegetables? Yes. They contain potash, and are always safe to use.

If I put wood ashes from our fireplace on the vegetable and flower beds, will the oil from the coal ashes mixed with them harm the plants? No; not unless you use fresh coal ashes.

Is there any value in wood coke from bonfires if applied to garden in fall? Applied in fall, it would be partly wasted. Better to save it under cover and apply in the spring.

Should I spread the wood ashes from my fireplace around as they are available during the winter; or must I store and use during the growing season? Store your ashes under cover to prevent leaching of potash. Leached wood ashes contain little potash, though still of some value.

Are the ashes of burned leaves, twigs, and winter-killed dry stalks of vegetation of any material value if burned on the garden plot? Yes; but the ashes would have more value if stored under cover and scattered in the spring.

OTHER MATERIALS

Is CRAB MEAL a good fertilizer? Fresh crab contains 2 to 3 per cent nitrogen and 2 to 3 per cent phosphoric acid. Its immediate efficiency is relatively low. Mixed fertilizer made with dried and ground king crab may contain 9 to 12 per cent nitrogen.

Can CRAB MEAL be used on most garden plants with benefit? Yes. Its cost will govern the extent of its use.

Is CHARCOAL good to add to soil to help plants? Yes, it adds a small amount of phosphorus and considerable potash and lime. These materials, however, as found in charcoal, become available very slowly.

Are rotted CRANBERRIES good as a fertilizer? They would add a small amount of organic matter, but very small quantities of the essential elements for plant growth.

What effect is caused on soil by a daily application of COFFEE GROUNDS? Coffee grounds may be considered as a soil conditioner if applied in sufficient quantities. Little value would accrue from the daily application of grounds from the family table.

Would water from old COFFEE GROUNDS keep soil acid, or would it kill the plants? The incorporation of coffee grounds with the soil will result in little change in soil reaction. Excessive amounts may be toxic.

Some people say that COFFEE GROUNDS, SOAP WATER, etc., are beneficial to soil and growth of vegetation. Is this so? Coffee grounds help in making the mechanical condition of the soil better if sufficient quantities are applied. Soapy water is not beneficial, and sometimes injurious if large amounts are poured in one spot, particularly where soap contains naphtha.

Are COFFEE GROUNDS and TEA LEAVES good for the soil? Coffee grounds, tea leaves, and any other vegetable refuse, when rotted, serve an excellent use as humus. Do not apply to house plants. They are unsightly and do not serve any purpose.

What fertiilzer value is there in EGGSHELLS? Eggshells contain a considerable quantity of calcium, and a very small amount of nitrogen. Crush or grind them.

What about burying FISH TRIMMINGS deep in the earth? Fish remains make an excellent fertilizer. Bury them just deep enough to avoid objectionable odors.

I'm burying all my GARBAGE around the plants. Do you think this will be sufficient fertilizer? No; garbage at its best is a very low-grade fertilizer; it is excellent to add humus, but should be supplemented by a complete fertilizer.

Can LEATHER DUST be used as a garden fertilizer? Leather dust contains some nitrogen, but it decomposes *very* slowly, so that quick results should not be expected.

Is SAWDUST good to put on a garden? It can be used to lighten soil and as a mulch. Use lightly.

I have some very fine SAWDUST, of white pine. What would be its effect if worked into soil in which vegetables or flowers are planted? It should help lighten your soil if it's heavy. Do not use thicker than 1 in.

How does one prepare kelp and other common SEAWEEDS (which wash up on beaches along Long Island Sound) for fertilizer? If conditions are such that it can be done, the kelp can be handled as a green manure or plowed or spaded under. Otherwise, it can be composted and applied at an opportune time.

What value is SEA KELP as a fertilizer? Sea kelp is high in potash, will compare favorably with farm manure in nitrogen, but is low in phosphorus.

Where can I buy SEA KELP in Iowa for fertilizer? Most of the sea kelp is processed for fertilizer on the West coast. In its natural state it is too bulky to be shipped any distance.

Can SEA KELP be used immediately, or must it be stored? Sea kelp is used fresh as a green manure by farmers and gardeners near the seashore. For shipping, it is dried, then burned to an ash. In this state it can be used at once, or stored. The ash contains about 30 per cent potash.

Are other SEAWEEDS as valuable as a fertilizer as sea kelp? Seaweeds vary considerably in nutritive value. They are worth using if readily available.

Will you please tell me if SEAWEED is any good to use as a fertilizer. If so, how can I use it for best results, as I live on the seashore? I can get all the seaweed I need. Seaweed is a good fertilizer. For one who can get the material fresh it is best used as a green manure spread on the land and turned under.

What soil-conditioning property has chimney SOOT? When is it applied? Soot possesses very little or no soil-conditioning value. It does contain about .5 per cent nitrogen.

Is SOOT taken from an oil burner any use whatever in a garden? Soot contains some nitrogen and may be applied to the soil as a side dressing.

INORGANIC FERTILIZERS

What is inorganic fertilizer? An inorganic fertilizer is one derived from mineral or chemical substances, such as phosphate rock, potash salts, nitrate salts (nitrate of soda).

What is a chemical fertilizer? A chemical fertilizer is one derived from chemically processed or manufactured materials, rather than from natural organic substances. The term is somewhat misleading in that organic fertilizers also may be treated with chemicals to increase their rate of availability. Many fertilizers contain both types of materials.

Are chemicals injurious to future plant growth? Not if they are used correctly. They do not, however, add humus to the soil.

Why don't we use stone dust as a natural fertilizer, which it really is? Pulverized granite (granite meal) is used as a source of potash in some areas. It contains about 5 to 10 per cent potash, along with a wide assortment of other elements. It is applied at rates of ½ to 2 tons per acre, and lasts for a long time. On acid soils pulverized phosphate rock is usually a satisfactory source of phosphate when used liberally. Some rocks are nearly devoid of fertilizer elements.

When preparing the soil in the spring for a garden of either flowers or vegetables, is it necessary to apply a chemical for better results? Usually additions of chemical fertilizers decidedly help production.

What is the fertilizer value of calcium carbonate? Calcium carbonate in itself is of no value as a fertilizer, since it is insoluable in water. It must be converted into the bicarbonate form, or some other soluble calcium salt, before calcium becomes available to the plant. It may also beneficially modify the structure of the soil.

NITRATE OF SODA

For what purpose is nitrate of soda used? Nitrate of soda furnishes a readily available source of nitrogen. Nitrogen stimulates the vegetative growth of the plant and is also essential for the reproductive phases.

What can we use in place of nitrate of soda? Ammonium sulfate, ammo-phos, cottonseed, soybean meal, or tankage.

SULFATE OF AMMONIA

What is sulfate of ammonia used for? This is used as a source of nitrogen. It contains about 20 per cent nitrogen.

When should sulfate of ammonia be used? How much? This is a good fertilizer to use when nitrogen is required. Apply about 5 to 10 lbs. per 1,000 sq. ft.

Is ammonium sulfate best spread on ground when soil is being dug, or later, and raked in? Ammonium sulfate is best applied after the soil is spaded and raked into the upper 2 to 4 ins. of the surface soil.

UREA

What is urea? Urea is a water-soluble organic compound containing 45 to 46 per cent nitrogen. In soil urea almost immediately decomposes to ammonium nitrogen and carbon dioxide.

Does urea leave an acid residue? Yes, but only a slight amount of acidity is left—about a third as much as would be left from a similar amount of nitrogen from sulfate of ammonia.

Can urea be used for foliar fertilization? Yes, but be sure to obtain a grade of urea suitable for that purpose. Urea for foliar fertilization is readily available in many areas. Unlike fertilizer urea, that intended for foliar application should contain less than 0.25 per cent biuret. A safe rate of application is usually 5 to 8 pounds per 100 gallons of water.

SUPERPHOSPHATE

Is there any way to add phosphorus to soil without using com-

mercial fertilizer? Yes, in the form of pulverized phosphate rock, bone meal, or basic slag.

Are the effects of superphosphate somewhat similar to those of bone meal? Yes, the effects are similar. Bone meal contains a low percentage of nitrogen not found in superphosphate. The phosphorus in bone meal, however, becomes available much more slowly.

How should one use agricultural lime and acid phosphate? They should not be mixed. If so, the phosphates are made unavailable.

Is there any advantage in applying superphosphate to perennial border or rock gardens? Many soils are deficient in phosphorus. If perennials or rock plants are planted in such a soil, they will be benefited by applications of superphosphate.

How should phosphate be used? I have some and do not know how to apply it to flowers. Phosphate is best applied when the flower beds are first prepared, by working it into the upper 4 to 6 ins. of soil. If plants are already in the bed, apply the phosphate between the plants and work it into the soil as deep as possible (down 6 to 8 ins.) without disturbing or injuring the roots. Apply 30 to 40 lbs. per 1,000 sq. ft.

When and how often should superphosphate be applied to perennials and rock plants? In addition to the use of superphosphate at the time the beds are prepared, yearly applications of phosphorus are advisable, especially in soils tending to be deficient in this element, by an application of a complete fertilizer in the spring.

Will superphosphate take the place of commercial fertilizer when mixed with manure? Farm manures fortified with superphosphate will make a good general garden fertilizer. Additional nitrogen may be needed for some crops.

MURIATE OF POTASH

What is the best time and method to apply muriate of potash to a vegetable garden? If the amount of potash applied in the complete fertilizer recommended for vegetable gardens is not sufficient, apply an additional quantity (1 lb. per 100 sq. ft.) and incorporate it in the surface 2 to 3 ins.

How often should muriate of potash be applied? Usually one application a year is sufficient. Soil tests will show if additional quantities are needed.

My soil is deficient in phosphorus and potash. What shall I apply to correct this condition? Apply commercial fertilizers such as 2–10–10 or 0–10–10; or superphosphate and muriate of potash.

COMPLETE COMMERCIAL FERTILIZERS

What are the principles of fertilization? Stated briefly, fertilization is practiced to supply the necessary essental elements to secure a normal growth of the plant.

What is commercial fertilizer? The term "commercial fertilizer" applies to any carrier of essential nutrient elements, that is sold (by itself or mixed with other such carriers) commercially.

How can an amateur tell what formulas—such as 10–6–4 and 8–5–3—mean? Formulas such as 10–6–4, 8–5–3, etc., are used to express the percentages of the major ingredients in fertilizers; namely, nitrogen, phosphorus, and potash. A 10–6–4 fertilizer denotes 10 per cent nitrogen, 6 per cent phosphorus, and 4 per cent potash.

Do commercial fertilizers aid or destroy existing bacteria and humus in the soil? Commercial fertilizers aid the beneficial bacteria of the soil. At the same time they may hasten the decomposition of humus.

Does commercial fertilizer burn the minerals out of the ground? No; it adds essential minerals to the soil.

Will commercial fertilizer restore a worn-out soil? Commercial fertilizers will furnish the necessary essential elements and can restore the soil in this respect. To restore humus and to improve the physical condition of the soil, incorporate farm or green manures. (See Introduction.)

What are some substitutes for fertilizer? There are no substitutes for fertilizer. Manure is used for its organic value, but there is little fertilizer value in manure, unless applied in very heavy quantities (at least 20 tons per acre).

Is there a fertilizer generally good as an all-plant fertilizer, for shrubs, perennials, vegetables, rhododendrons, trees, and grass lawns? There is no one fertilizer that would be considered best for all these groups of plants. A 4–12–4 or 5–10–5 comes as near being a general-purpose fertilizer as we have. Recommended for shrubs, 4–12–4 and 10–6–4; for perennials, 4–12–4 and 2–10–10; for vegetables, 4–12–4 and 2–10–10; for azaleas and rhododendrons 4–12–4 with at least 25 per cent of the nitrogen of an organic source such as soybean meal; for lawns, 10–6–4 or 11–48–0.

How can one tell just what kind of fertilizer is best to use? Soil tests will give a partial answer; the habit of growth of the plant is also a determining factor. Ornamental plants normally showing vigorous top growth respond best to a low-nitrogen fertilizer, and vice versa. Fleshy-rooted plants respond best to a fertilizer similar to a 2–10–10.

Can one add certain chemicals to the soil of the garden vegetable patch, in order to get bigger and better crop yields? A 2–10–10 is advocated for root crops. Use a 4–12–4 for other vegetables. Side dressings of a nitrogen fertilizer may be advisable for the leafy vegetables.

How long does it take for organic or inorganic fertilizers to become available to plants?   Inorganic nitrogenous fertilizers are readily available. The insoluble organic nitrogenous fertilizers are slowly available. Phosphorus from superphosphate penetrates the soil slowly, but is readily available in the monocalcium form. Potash is readily available.

How can minerals be supplied to old garden soils?   By using a 4–12–4 or 5–10–5 fertilizer, applied at 4 lbs. per 100 sq. ft.

What is the best fertilizer for a new vegetable garden?   In general, a 4–12–4 or 5–10–5 fertilizer. For root or tuber crops a 2–10–10 is satisfactory.

What fertilizers should be added to the soil to make vegetables yield bountifully?   See previous question. For leafy vegetables, follow the spring application with a side dressing of ammonium sulfate when the tops are half grown.

What is the best fertilizer to use in spring?   In general, a 4–12–4 or a 5–10–5 fertilizer. For root or tuber crops, a 2–10–10 is usually satisfactory.

What is the best fertilizer to use in midsummer?   For leafy crops, ammonium sulfate or nitrate of soda. For other common vegetables, a 4–12–4, if needed.

Is it possible to mix one's own fertilizer for a successful home garden?   To make your own fertilizer, several separate ingredients are needed. It is usually much more satisfactory to buy a ready-mixed fertilizer.

What is the best and simplest method of making chemical fertilizers for the vegetable garden?   Generally, it does not pay for the average gardener to mix his own fertilizer. Buy it already mixed. If it is advisable to mix your own fertilizer, use the following ingredients to make 100 lbs. of 4–12–4 fertilizer: 20 lbs. ammonium sulfate, 60 lbs. superphosphate, 8 lbs. muriate of potash, 12 lbs. sand.

Are there garden fertilizers that are good, and more reasonable in price than the highly advertised brands?   In general the regular 4–12–4, 5–10–5, and 7–7–7 farm fertilizers are the least expensive. They are good fertilizers.

Is a commercial fertilizer, such as Agrico, enough to use for the garden? Or should something be used in the fall and left through the winter?   Agrico is a complete fertilizer and should be sufficient in itself. Additional nitrogen may be required for some crops; if so, it should be applied in the spring or when its need is obvious. Green manures are needed in addition.

I have on hand a 100-lb. bag of Agrico lawn fertilizer; also 100-lb. bag of bone meal. Can these be used? In what proportions? Rather than attempt to mix these fertilizers, use the Agrico fertilizer for the lawn and most flower and vegetable crops. Use the bone meal for plants with fleshy and tuberous roots.

Have been using a fertilizer called Emseco. Is this a good product? The Thomas W. Emerson Co. of Boston puts out a number of trade-name "Emseco" fertilizers. Some of these are 4-8-4, 5-8-7, and 7-7-7; not all of these are garden fertilizers. A 4-8-4 should be the most satisfactory for general garden fertilization.

What is the chemical analysis of the trade fertilizer called Loma? A 5-10-4.

Is Sacco 4-12-4 considered a fertilizer? Yes, it is the trade name of a commercial fertilizer.

What is the phosphorous, nitrogen, and potash content of Vigoro? Vigoro contains 5 per cent nitrogen, 10 per cent phosphorus, and 5 per cent potash, plus small amounts of trace elements.

Is commercial 5-10-5 fertilizer comparable to fertilizers like Vigoro, Armour's garden and lawn fertilizer, and Scott's turf builder? Trade-name fertilizers such as Vigoro and others are usually somewhat better than commercial grades of similar analysis, due to the use of better materials, better mixing, and sometimes the addition of trace elements. The standard formula fertilizers, however, are used with success by commercial growers.

Does the continuous use of Vigoro leave a deposit on the soil which eventually ruins the soil? No, Vigoro may be used continuously without detrimental effects.

What are the relative merits of cottonseed meal, 5-7-5 commercial fertilizer, nitrate of soda, bone meal, Vigoro, rotted oak and woods dirt, as fertilizer for fruit trees, dogwood, holly, grapes, and flowers? Vigoro or a 5-7-5 commercial fertilizer would be generally satisfactory as a fertilizer for these plants. Cottonseed meal contains about 7.5 per cent nitrogen, 2.5 per cent phosphoric acid, and 1.5 per cent potash. It is not a balanced fertilizer but is a good source of organic nitrogen. Nitrate of soda is a good inorganic nitrogen fertilizer. Bone meal is a source of phosphorus and also contains a small amount of nitrogen. Rotted oak or woods dirt has little value as a fertilizer but does act as a soil corrective.

What garden fertilizer such as Vigoro, hydrated lime, nitrate of soda, etc., can be kept several seasons? Which should be used the season it is bought? Practically all garden fertilizers can be kept for several years *if* they are kept dry. Some, such as ammonium sulfate, cake on standing and should be crushed before applying.

Are fertilizers in tablet form recommended? Plant tablets have long been used and they are effective and easily applied, especially to house plants.

What plant tablets are best? There are several kinds on the market that are effective. Avoid the ones that have extravagant claims made about them. No plant tablets will work "miracles." Vitamin B_1 usually has little or no effect.

What commercial fertilizers are reliable for garden use? A 4–12–4, or 5–10–5. Other complete fertilizers, and also carriers of nitrogen, phosphorus, and potash. (See Introduction.)

What quantity of commercial fertilizer is the minimum essential for a vegetable garden 80 × 30? Fifty lbs. of a 4–12–4.

I have a plot 20 × 20 ft., just covered with 6 ins. of sandy loam. What kind of fertilizer could I use to make good soil for raising FLOWERS of various kinds? Incorporate 12 to 16 lbs. of a 4–12–4 fertilizer in the upper 3 to 5 ins. of the soil.

What formula, in a commercial-type fertilizer, gives best results for growth of ANNUALS, PERENNIALS, and SHRUBS in a mixed border? Use a 4–12–4 or 5–10–5 fertilizer applied at the rate of 3 to 4 lbs. per 100 sq. ft.

What type of fertilizer should be used on PLANTS IN WINTER to have blooms and good color in foliage? Poor results in winter are often due to lack of light or presence of illuminating gas. A 4–12–4 or 5–10–5 are good fertilizers; they should be used sparingly, when light conditions are unfavorable.

What commercial fertilizers are suitable for FRUIT TREES? Complete fertilizers; also ammonium sulfate, cyanamide, nitrate of soda, superphosphate, muriate of potash, and several others.

What kind of fertilizer can one obtain to take the place of horse manure for ROSES and VEGETABLES? Where horse manure or other animal manures are not available, other types of organic matter, plus commercial fertilizer, can be substituted. For roses use peatmoss, plus a 4–12–4 fertilizer as needed. For vegetable gardens, incorporate green manures, and add a 4–12–4 or a 2–10–10 fertilizer as required.

APPLYING FERTILIZERS

When should one fertilize the garden—fall or spring? For lawns, permanent plantings of shrubs, evergreens, and flowers, fertilizers may be applied in the fall or spring with equal success. It is best to apply fertilizers to annual crops at, or just previous to, planting time.

Is it better to place fertilizer on the garden in the fall and turn it over in the spring? Or turn the soil first, and then apply the fertilizer? Commercial fertilizers for the most part are best applied after spading or plowing, a week or 10 days before planting, and raked into the upper 2 to 3 ins. of the soil. Superphosphate may be spaded in in either fall or spring.

Should I plant first, and then fertilize? Or vice versa? Fertilizer can be applied and worked into the soil just before planting, or at planting time. One or more subsequent applications may be necessary during the growing season. (See Side Dressing.)

For a new garden, do I have to fertilize the ground before I plant? Usually it is necessary to fertilize. A soil analysis will indicate what is needed.

At what time of the year should fertilizer be applied to the garden? If manure is used, apply it in the fall, unless it is very well rotted. If well rotted, or if commercial fertilizer is used, apply in spring when preparing ground for planting.

Are better blooms obtained when fertilizer is used at time of setting out plants, or at time buds form? For best results apply the fertilizer at the time the plants are set. Make a subsequent application at or previous to bud formation. (See Side Dressing.)

Do you advocate putting fertilizer in the rows under the seed; or between the rows? Recent experiments show that it is best to apply the fertilizer 2 to 3 ins. to the side and 1 to 2 ins. below the seed, rather than to place it in the row beneath the seed.

My soil is very rich but no fertilizer added since last fall. Is it necessary to apply any when ground is so good? No. Except to make sure the soil is maintained in that condition.

What is the best fertilizer to use for soil that has been cleared of trees and in which it is desired to make a vegetable garden? A 4–12–4, unless a soil analysis shows otherwise.

How do you fertilize plants that remain in the same spot in the garden? Apply the fertilizer between the plants and hoe it into the upper few inches of soil without disturbing or injuring the roots of the plants. If soil is dry, water thoroughly.

How often during the season should the flower garden be fertilized? When? Once or twice a season. Apply fertilizer in the spring as growth starts, and again in midsummer if growth is not satisfactory.

What kind of fertilizer is best for peat soil which is turning acid? Peat soils usually becomes *less* acid as they are cultivated. A soil test would be advisable. If soil is acid, use a non-acid fertilizer. (See Introduction.)

Is it good practice to use a commercial fertilizer on acid-loving plants? Yes, if it is needed. A 4–12–4 fertilizer with ¼ to ⅓ of the nitrogen furnished by an organic source is satisfactory.

We are plowing a field that has never been productive. What is the

best fertilizer?   The productivity of this soil may not be due to a lack of essential elements for growth. Be sure the drainage and the organic matter content of the soil are satisfactory. The best fertilizer to use will depend upon the crops to be grown. Consult your county agricultural agent.

Am draining cedar swamp for garden. Soil is black swamp muck, highly nitrogenous, about 2 ft. thick; white sand subsoil. What fertilizer should be used?   The fertilizer to apply will depend upon the nutrient test of the soil and the crops to be grown. In general a 2–10–10 should be satisfactory.

How much water should be applied to garden after fertilizing? Soil is sandy and both commercial and fresh manures are used. Water garden when needed as indicated by tendency of plants to wilt. (See Watering.) Make several applications during the year of a 4–12–4 or 5–10–5 fertilizer at 4 lbs. per 100 sq. ft.

MISCELLANEOUS

SOIL STERILIZATION

What are the different ways to sterilize soil for seeds?   Steam, very hot water, and chemicals, such as tear gas (chloropicrin), methyl bromide and vapam.

How does the gardener sterilize soil with steam?   Make a soil pile 12 ins. deep. Place 4 ins. agricultural tile 2 ft. apart in center of pile and running full length. Plug tile at one end. Insert steam pipe or hose in the other end. Cover entire pile with building paper or canvas. Inject steam for 2 hrs.; remove cloth; allow to cool. Remove tile, and continue the process. Steam sterilization makes structure better. Its effects are entirely beneficial. This is usually impractical for a gardener to do. Small quantities of soil for pot plants may be sterilized in a pressure cooker, without closing the steam valve.

What is an easy and efficient method of sterilizing soil for growing seedlings in small greenhouse where steam is not used?   Boiling hot water should be poured over the soil and, in addition, the seeds should be dusted with Cuprocide, Spergon, Terrachlor (PCNB) or similar compounds.

What is Larvacide?   It is a gas which is packaged in bottles or cylinders as a liquid (chloropicrin, or tear gas) and is applied to the soil with a special applicator. The soil should be 60° F. or warmer, and medium moist. Three c.c. of liquid (a small teaspoonful) is injected about 3 to 6 ins. deep, spaced 10 ins. each way. A heavy watering is applied immediately. Follow with two other applications on successive days. The treatment controls soil diseases, insects, and weeds.

How are small quantities of soil sterilized with Larvacide?   (1) In boxes: Have soil moist and loose; make holes 4 ins. deep and 10 ins. apart; insert 1 medicine dropper full of Larvacide. Cover with soil and immediately lay several thicknesses of newspapers over the surface. Keep tight and wet for 3 days. Then uncover; loosen up the soil. After a week, planting can be safely done. The same process may be employed in outdoor beds, but the temperature of the soil should be 60° F. or higher. Watering the soil 3 days in succession will take the place of wet newspapers. (2) In bins: Allow ¾ lb. Larvacide for each cubic yard. Make a layer of soil 6 ins. deep; pour ⅓ of the Larvacide over it; cover with 6 ins. of soil; add another third of the Larvacide and cover again. The final third may be poured into holes in the top layer and the whole wet down and covered with wet newspapers. This material is tear gas, so do not breathe it. It will make the eyes smart badly.

When is manure added to soil to be sterilized?   Apply manure *before* sterilization to avoid infection later. Commercial fertilizers may be added before or after. Generally, superphosphate and bone meal are best added before—others after, as needed.

How do you sterilize soil with formaldehyde?   Where steam is not available, formaldehyde may be used. Use commercial formalin— 1 gal. to 50 gals. of water. One gal. of the solution is used to 1 sq. ft. of soil 6 ins. deep. Pour solution on, cover for 24 hours, then uncover and permit to dry for 2 weeks before using.

How do you sterilize soil for potted plants?   Use steam, hot water, or chemicals. A pressure cooker may be used satisfactorily.

An easy way to sterilize soil or compost for starting seeds; place in flat and drench thoroughly with boiling water.

How is sand, used as a rooting medium, best sterilized?   If small quantities are wanted, place sand in shallow flat or box, and pour boiling water through it.

How do you sterilize soil in a perennial bed?   This cannot be done satisfactorily unless chemicals are used—formaldehyde, chloropicrin, or mercuric compounds. Beds must be free of plants before chemicals are applied.

PLANT STIMULANTS

How is Vitamin B₁ used in garden?   Don't waste your time with Vitamin B₁; it has proved a failure under most conditions.

What plants do not need to be fertilized with Vitamin B₁?   No plants need to be fertilized with Vitamin B₁. Under normal conditions, plants make B₁ in their leaves; soil bacteria make it; all types of organic matter have some. The plants have a normal supply without being fed pills containing it.

Can Vitamin B₁ be used on all growing plants regardless of their soil requirements?   Almost all plants make enough B₁ in their leaves for their own use. Any B₁ added is superfluous. Fertilizer is much more important.

When my lawn shrubs and evergreens need watering I slip 5 or 6 B₁ tablets into the hose. The results seem to be good. Do you consider this a good practice? Should the B₁ be applied to the foliage, or only to the soil?   Results are due to water only. Almost all plants make enough B₁ in their leaves for their own use; if soil contains no humus, B₁ additions may be helpful.

What is gibberellic acid? How does it affect plants?   Gibberellic acid is a growth-stimulating substance produced by a fungus that attacks rice plants and causes them to grow rapidly for some time before the fungus finally injures too much of the tissue. When applied to some plants, a 10 part per million solution of gibberellic acid in water will stimulate a marked increase in rate of growth—especially in the length of stems and petioles. This stimulated growth is sometimes attractive and sometimes not. Gibberellic acid often hastens flower maturity and, in some instances, it increases flower size. Dwarf varieties of a given species usually respond most markedly to gibberellic acid. Standard sorts respond less, and giants are generally unresponsive. One of the interesting and perhaps most valuable properties of gibberellic acid is that of overcoming the dormancy effect in some plants and seeds.

What is colchicine, and how is it used?   An alkaloid from colchicum is used by plant breeders in attempts to change inherited characteristics of plants by doubling the chromosomes.

Where can I acquire colchicine?   From drugstore or local chemical supply house. It is a very poisonous substance; must be used with caution. Comes in paste or solution, which is applied to top buds of shoots of plants. Of some use to plant breeders, not to average gardener.

Are there any recent new developments in chemical gardening or use of hormones and vitamins for plants?   See gibberellic acid discussion.

Perhaps one of the most interesting developments in chemical gardening is the use of plastic forms of nitrogen and glass forms of potash and minor elements. (These are called frits.) Urea-formalde-hyde plastic may be manufactured with 38 per cent of nitrogen, one quarter of which is readily available, whereas the remainder is slowly released over a period of 2 to 5 months, depending on soil temperatures. An application of 2½ to 4 pounds of urea-form (urea-formaldehyde), worked into 100 sq. ft. of soil will usually furnish enough nitrogen to supply most crops through the summer months.

Potassium can be used to make a glass that dissolves rapidly enough, when ground to a coarse powder, to supply liberal amounts of potash to growing crops for 4 to 12 months despite the leaching effect of rain. One such potassium glass available on the West coast is known as Dura-K.

Minor elements are also furnished in slowly available, long-lasting sources in various glasses or frits. See discussion on page 6.

I desire information concerning "hormones." Hormones (more properly called root-inducing substances) are useful for reducing the time required for some cuttings to root. Most all of them are dusts in which the cutting is dipped. Some are sprayed on developing fruits to prevent drop. Some are sprayed on flowers and thus produce fruits without pollination (tomatoes, holly, etc.). Some are used to increase keeping quality of fruits and vegetables in storage.

Is there anything to the theory of enrichment of the soil with chemicals to include all those needed by the body? Yes. Plant and animal nutrition studies conducted by the various agricultural experiment stations show that an animal that obtains all its food and water from a given area will make a normal or an abnormal growth response, according to the adequacy of the composition of the plants and water fed to it. We should consider ourselves fortunate perhaps, that modern transportation facilities make it possible for Americans to have a daily diet of foods not only from various parts of our large country, but from other countries also.

SOIL DETRIMENTS

Have soapsuds or soapy water from washing clothes any value as fertilizer? The amount of material added in washing water will have very little effect on the nutrient content of the soil. Grease tends to clog the soil, and is objectionable. Naphtha is detrimental.

Is baking powder (double-action) of any use as fertilizer? If so, how is it used? Under the usual soil conditions it has no fertilizer value, and it might even be detrimental.

Is castor oil good for soil around plants? No.

Is cod-liver oil a good plant food for flowers? No. Use a 4–12–4 or 5–10–5 fertilizer.

Do castor beans and sumac sap the soil much? Yes, the very luxuriant foliage depletes soils of nitrogen in particular.

SOILLESS CULTURE

What is water culture? Growth of plants in a watertight container filled with a weak solution of fertilizer salts.

What is sand culture? Growth of plants in a container of sand through which a weak fertilizer solution either drips continually, or is poured on at intervals.

What house plants can be grown in sand culture? With care, almost any house plants.

What is gravel culture? Growth of plants in a watertight container filled with some inert medium, preferably slightly acid, which is flooded, manually or mechanically, from below with a weak fertilizer solution.

What flowering crops may be grown in gravel culture if a green-house is available? Any crop which can be grown in soil. Roses, carnations, chrysanthemums, snapdragons, calendula, annuals, orchids, are all successfully grown.

What vegetable crops may be grown by an amateur in gravel or water culture? It is not practical to attempt to grow vegetables unless a greenhouse is available. Tomatoes, lettuce, cucumbers, radishes, spinach, kale, etc., can be grown.

What type of soilless culture is best suited for the home? Sand culture; it requires less equipment than gravel culture, and is more foolproof than water culture.

What type soilless culture is best suited for commercial use? Gravel culture. Less troublesome than water culture; requires less labor than sand culture.

Will chemical gardening (soilless culture) succeed commercially? Probably not. Good soil has many advantages over soilless culture, not the least of which is the former's adaptation to the use of large-scale equipment. When people realize that good soil is clean and very responsive to proper enrichment with all necessary nutrient elements, soilless culture will become a by-gone fad, except where it is used as a valuable research method.

Has the experiment with tank farming contributed much to general practices and knowledge in general gardening? Tank farming (which is water culture) has not contributed much; but gravel and sand culture have been very helpful in the study of general garden problems, particularly from the standpoint of plant nutrition. However, much has been learned about the needs of minor elements from studies in water culture.

In chemical gardening, which containers are best? Under any conditions for commercial use, concrete is best. In the home, wood can be used.

What chemicals are the best to buy for a water chemical garden, especially tomatoes? I have been told Vigoro is all that is needed to put in the water; is that correct? Vigoro will not be satisfactory for water culture. Obtain the following chemicals from your druggist and use the formula herewith: (The numerals indicate ounces.)

Monobasic potassium phosphate	0.5
Potassium nitrate	2.0
Calcium nitrate	3.0
Magnesium sulfate	1.5
Iron sulfate	1 tsp.
Water	25 gals.

What is a "nutrient solution," for soilless gardens? It is composed of fertilizer elements completely soluble in water. Obtain chemicals from your druggist and use the following formula for water, sand, or gravel cultures:

Potassium nitrate	1.0 oz.
Monocalcium phosphate	0.5 "
Magnesium sulfate	0.75 "
Water	5 gals.
Iron sulfate	1 tsp.

SECTION II

Landscaping

INTRODUCTION

BY DONALD WYMAN

FEW OWNERS of small places can have all the landscaping done at one time. Usually it is extended over several years, a tree or two being added one season; a group of shrubs the next; a perennial border later; and so on.

But if a well-conceived plan—no matter how rough a one—is made in advance, many mistakes are avoided, and the result finally attained is lasting and more pleasing. This will save much time and money later on. Trees and shrubs are permanent fixtures, and should be given their place in the landscape plan only after careful thought and study.

Usefulness and beauty should be considered in that order. Think for a moment of the new house on a bare lot, with no planting whatsoever. Of course it looks bare, if not actually ugly. Trees, shrubs, and flowers, placed in the right situations, will make the house blend into the land, and at the same time fulfill many other desirable purposes. The trees will give shade in the summer and, if properly placed, help keep the building cool. Evergreens will help in the screening of objectionable views and aid in keeping the building warmer in the winter by shielding it from high winds.

Shrubs can be used for beauty and also for the necessary function of screening and hedgemaking, protecting the property from unwanted trespassers. Vines can be added for softening the harsh lines of buildings and to help beautify hard wall surfaces. Annuals, perennials, and bulbs can be planted for beauty and usefulness as well.

The reasons for placing trees, shrubs, and flower borders in definite areas, and in definite relation to each other, should be thought out *in advance of planting*. It is expensive and very time-consuming to "try" a tree for a year or two in a certain situation and then, later on, move it to another. If a specimen tree is wanted, and the Siberian Elm is selected, it is most disheartening to have this tree split from top to bottom by heavy winds or by snow and ice after it has been thriving for a number of years. It would have been far better to take more time at the beginning, when the plan for the landscaping was being made, to select a sturdy tree rather than a fast-growing but weak-wooded one.

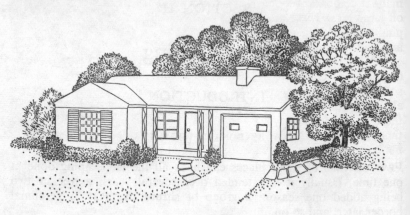

The ideal around-the-house planting provides over-head shade and "ties the house to the ground" without obscuring walls or obstructing windows.

With the great exodus of city dwellers to the country, many families have come to live on small properties in the open, but know little about growing plants. As a result there is an increase of interest in gardening and horticulture. Classes are being formed in many communities, more and more are joining horticultural organizations, more horticultural books are being read, and many commercial nurseries are enjoying some of their best sales' periods.

A very important factor calling for an interest in low-growing plants is the popularity of the picture window. The use of such plants has many advantages. One of these is that the owner may enjoy, to a much fuller extent, all plantings in his garden. The most inexperienced gardener who has a picture window must realize that he will benefit by so arranging his plantings that the garden view from his particular window is as interesting and beautiful as he can possibly make it at all times of the year.

With gardens being forced into smaller and smaller lots, many accessories are being used to make them more interesting and to eliminate as much labor as possible. For instance, there are several types of stripping and metal edgings which are being recommended for edging garden beds and lawn areas to prevent lawn grasses from encroaching on walks or flowers. These certainly make for trim looking beds.

Various types of modern lawn furniture are appearing. Some of it is made of redwood or other substantial material, but some is constructed of light aluminum—in fact so light that the smallest breeze often carries these new chairs over the hill and into the shrubs! Stepping stones are of course still in vogue, but the chain saw has made it comparatively easy and inexpensive to cut thin cross sections off large logs. These are now becoming available as long-lasting stepping "stones" in garden walks, and their use is proving most effective and naturalistic.

Garden labor is being made to look disagreeable by the appearance of all the mechanized garden machinery to mow the lawn, dig the soil, saw the trees, prune off the branches and clip the hedges. After all, a certain amount of muscular work is good for most of us, and there is no better way to obtain just the right amount at the ideal time, than in the garden. Hence, the active gardener might well shun many of these new extras and plan to spend a small amount of his time working at the age-old garden chores. It will do him good physically, and certainly he will become better acquainted with his plants.

Plastics are finding a very important place in the garden in the form of hoses, tools and especially the polythene film. A black type is now being made that is being placed on the ground to smother weeds and to prevent overly rapid water evaporation from the soil. The transparent type of polythene has many uses, for wrapping all kinds of flowers and plants, either for shipping abroad or for delivery to a neighbor down the street. Polythene bags are made for collecting cut flowers and cut branches and for keeping them turgid a day or so.

Also, this same film is being used as a means of winter protection for certain shrubs that might otherwise winter-kill or be burned from excessive winter winds. Plants are not completely enclosed with the film, for if this were done, temperatures might be raised greatly on sunny days, thus resulting in burning of the foliage. However, it is used as a windbreak or shield (with the top open) about plants to protect them from high winter winds and resulting windburn.

Polythene is being used on an increasingly large scale as the covering for small greenhouses, for it is much less expensive than glass; many commercial growers are using it for plant forcing houses. One of its many good properties seems to be its ability to retain heat in any enclosure about which it is securely and tightly fastened.

The selection of the right kind of plant material for the right place does take time, but pays in the end. In making the plan, the trees should be located first, then the evergreens, then the flower borders, shrubs, and vines—in about that order. A typical plan of this sort is shown on page 90. In order to make such a plan intelligently, the gardener must have some knowledge of the different groups of plants, how they can be used, and the types of material available in each. In the following pages these groups are discussed.

Trees

Trees should be considered first because they are the largest and usually the most costly items on the home grounds, and because they require the most time to grow to the desired size. It may take years

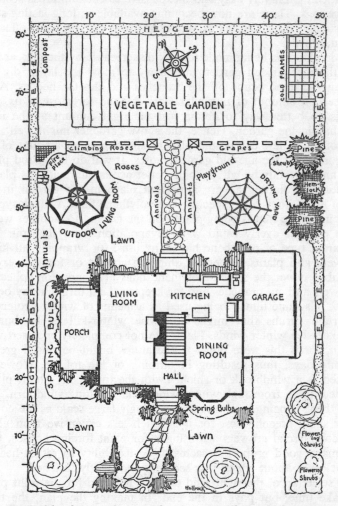

Typical landscape planting plan for a small place, showing the general layout of the entire plot. Detail plans for the different areas can be worked out later.

for a tree to become sufficiently large to give the effect we expect from it. First and foremost, the tree gives shade, either to the house or to the terrace in the garden. It can be planted to obscure some objectionable view, or to aid in giving privacy to the garden. Plenty of room should be given for its full development at maturity (some grow a hundred feet tall, others only twenty-five feet)—a fact not always realized at the time of planting. When trees are well placed they can be beautiful as well as useful.

Sturdy trees should always be selected for permanence, for although many weak-wooded trees do make a good showing in a short time, they are easily broken by wind, snow, and ice. They should never be given a place on the small property unless this fact is well understood. If planted for quick results, it is well to plan to remove or replace them at some future date.

If a tree is to be located where the branches may interfere with service wires, as is frequently necessary, select a tree, such as the wide-arching elm or the wide-spreading oak, for open spaces in the branching of these trees freely permit a pathway for wires, whereas the close-branching habit of a Norway Maple is such that branches must be cut from it to permit a pathway for the wires. Trees should be given plenty of good soil in which to grow. They should not be planted too near flower or vegetable gardens, where their roots undoubtedly will take much nourishment away from the smaller plants.

Small trees, such as the dogwoods, crabapples, and magnolias, are primarily planted for their beauty but can be useful for screening purposes also. Large trees, such as maples, oaks, and lindens, are primarily shade trees but can be counted upon for brilliant autumn color. In planting dig the hole comfortably larger than the roots of the young tree, remembering always that it is far better to put a fifty-cent tree in a two-dollar hole than a two-dollar tree in a fifty-cent hole.

The average house is becoming smaller and the property on which it is situated is becoming smaller. Both these factors are bringing about a change in the type of plants that are being grown on the home grounds. With the size of the average home reduced frequently to one story, there is no need for the continued planting of large 50 to 75 foot shade trees on small properties. Rather there is an increasing interest in trees that mature at about 35 feet, or even less, in height. Many of the once little known maples and crabapples are becoming very popular for this purpose, as well as other trees in this lower class. Because of the wide-spread troubles from the Dutch elm disease, elms are being planted in diminishing numbers. Oaks are still popular but even these are being avoided on the smaller properties. Small trees for small properties seems to be very much the mode at present.

There are many ornamental trees that seldom grow more than 25 to 30 ft. tall. This is well to remember, for frequently there is a place for a small ornamental tree—a crabapple, magnolia, or Oriental cherry, for instance—where a mighty oak or stately elm would dwarf everything else in the planting.

Evergreens

These very useful trees, shrubs, and ground covers are used because of their winter appearance, keeping some of Nature's green foliage color the year 'round. Because of their dense habit of growth, they are especially valued as screening and windbreak plants, and the smaller ones as foundation plants next to the house. They require little attention when soil and climate are to their liking, and are available in a wide assortment of sizes and varieties.

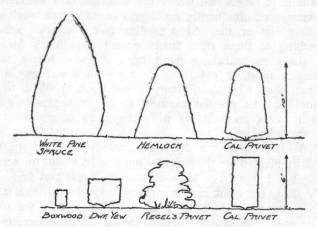

WHITE PINE SPRUCE   HEMLOCK   CAL. PRIVET

BOXWOOD   DWF. YEW   REGEL'S PRIVET   CAL. PRIVET

In selecting shrubs and evergreens, for hedges especially, it is important to consider habit of growth and ultimate height.

Some of the evergreens—hemlocks, pines, and spruces—are big trees. Many others are small trees, bushes, or even low, creeping ground covers. As a group they are more difficult to grow than deciduous plants, so they should be selected with care. Before purchasing an evergreen one should ascertain the soil and climatic requirements of the particular kind desired. In the hot, dry, windswept areas of the Midwest only a very few evergreens survive. They need much more moisture in the summer than conditions prevalent in those areas permit.

In the eastern part of the country there is a wide selection from which to choose. Not only many species and varieties of the narrow-leaved, cone-bearing evergreens do well, but also the many bright-flowering, shrubby rhododendrons and evergreen azaleas. These are truly worth while even though they need especially prepared acid soil in which to grow. It should be remembered that some are decidedly hardier than others, and in areas where high winter winds and very low temperatures prevail only the most rugged types should be selected, for many of the more tender types may be injured by adverse weather conditions and show it by the browning of their foliage. High and dry winds in early spring are especially hard on all evergreens.

Shrubs

Shrubs ranging in height from 1 to 20 ft. make up the bulk of the permanent planting after the trees and the evergreens have been properly placed. They are the plants that do the real bordering or hedging, or those which supply the flowers and fruits to make the grounds colorful. Three very important questions should be asked about every shrub used on the small home grounds, namely:

1. *Are the flowers and fruits ornamental?*
2. *When do they appear, and how long are they effective?*
3. *What is the autumn color of the foliage; and is the plant of interest in the winter?*

Some plants, such as the viburnums and the dogwoods, are colorful in flower and fruit and in their autumn hues, and may even have some interest in the winter. Their color can be enjoyed, during three different seasons, for a total of 6 to 8 weeks at least. On the other hand, there are other plants, such as the lilacs, mockoranges, and weigelas, which are colorful only for a 2-week period when they are in flower, and have no interesting fruits or autumn color. When only a small amount of space is available, it is of the utmost importance to select shrubs which are colorful for several seasons, and so are of interest for a much longer time. Hence it pays well to find out the seasons of interest for the different shrubs, and to select the ones that have interest for several periods each year.

With smaller houses and gardens, we are becoming more anxious to use smaller shrubs too. The tall growing lilac and the once popular, vigorous growing, *Euonymus europaea,* are giving over in popularity to lower growing shrubs not over three to four feet in height. Nurserymen are continually looking for even smaller types of new plants for foundation plantings about the house. Some gardeners are going to the extreme trouble of growing espaliered fruit trees on walls and fences, as well as becoming interested in the ancient Japanese art of Bonsai, in an effort to grow more plants in a smaller space.

The ultimate size of the shrubs is very important; the taller ones should be used for backgrounds and screening purposes, while the smaller ones can be used as specimens in the foreground. Locating single-specimen plants is very difficult, even for the trained landscape architect. The most common mistake is to plant a specimen in the dead center of some lawn area. Usually this is absolutely wrong, for open lawn areas lend beauty and increase the apparent size of any property. So it is desirable to place specimens off center or at the side of lawn areas, leaving as long and clear a sweep of unobstructed lawn as possible.

Dense-growing shrubs, such as the barberries, privets, most of the shrub roses, yews, etc., are used as hedges. In fact, almost any shrub can be clipped enough to make it usable as a hedge plant, but the denser-growing types prove best and easiest to trim. Since there are more than one hundred kinds of plants that make good hedges, it is advisable to define clearly at first the exact reasons why a hedge is needed, then to select the plant material that most closely fills the bill. In this way you will be assured of a serviceable hedge, while at the same time you can select some material out of the ordinary which will lend considerable interest to the general appearance of the place. In placing a hedge, never put it on the exact center of a property line, for some future disgruntled neighbor would have the full right to dig up the half on his property. Prune hedges so that they are wider at the bottom than at the top, thus insuring sturdy branches from the ground up.

Vines

Vines are used either for beauty or for screening purposes, or both. They can be divided into two large groups, those that climb by clinging to a wall or support by means of small rootlike holdfasts (as the English Ivy), and those that climb by twining, like the bittersweets and honeysuckles. Never plant a clinging vine on a wooden house, for it will have to be removed every time the house is painted (and usually cannot be replaced), and the small holdfasts will injure the wood, aiding in its decay. Such vines are for stone and brick walls and tree trunks.

Twining vines can be used on wooden houses provided they have a trellis of some sort, or merely a single wire on which to twine. These supports may be made removable, at least at the top, so that the vine can be taken down and put up again at will, without seriously injuring the vine itself. The supports should be held 4 to 6 ins. away from the wooden boards. Or vines such as bittersweet, honeysuckle, and the Fiveleaf Akebia can be trained to twine around rainspouts. An established vigorous twiner will grow 2 stories high in 2 or 3 years, so that if twining on a rainspout it would not be a serious handicap to cut the vine to the ground when painting and repairs are necessary. Wisteria is frequently used, but often it proves too vigorous for the small home.

Clematis vines, like the Sweetautumn Clematis and the Jackman Clematis, and grapes, really belong to the twining group, for they climb by means of tendrils or modified tendrils. Some of the large-flowered clematis are difficult to grow, requiring just the right kind of limestone soil. Many annual vines, too, are available, some of which make a remarkable growth in one season. For a permanent screen, however, the perennial vines are best; but for flowers, it is difficult to surpass some of the annuals.

Basic Principles

In this section of the book, information has been included concerning the basic principles of landscaping for the small home and about special types of gardens.

Needless to say, these particular topics cannot be fully covered in question-and-answer form; but the number of questions received indicates a very widespread interest in them. Readers who seek further information are urged to procure, or to obtain from libraries, the books referred to in the following pages.

A careful study of the illustrations herewith will give the beginner definite suggestions as to how to attain pleasing results with his plantings and to solve some of the simpler problems of construction in laying out his place.

LANDSCAPE DESIGN AND PLANTING

DESIGN

Why should home grounds be "designed"? To get the most efficient use out of them. Hit-or-miss planting never results in full or efficient use of the land, and it is pictorially ineffective.

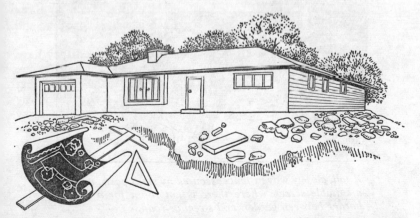

What relationship has planting design to garden design? Garden design has to be carried out largely in terms of planting. This is to say that any plant used should be chosen because it has a definite place *in the design,* rather than merely because we like its flowers or foliage.

Which is the more important, the artistic or the practical, in designing a small property? Neither; one supplements the other. Any garden, no matter how artistic its design may be, will be ineffective unless the layout is practical. If practical matters only are considered, however, the garden is unlikely to be an artistic success.

Is it necessary to make a plan of a garden? For any but the very simplest of gardens a plan will be found to be a great help in carrying out your intentions. Only by planning ahead of time can you be sure that desirable color combinations will actually be achieved. Changes and rearrangements are more easily made on paper than in the garden itself. A plan is also most useful in estimating quantities; if the planting is not to be done all at once, it is essential.

Why should a garden be "balanced"? Balance, whether symmetrical or irregular, gives a garden picture a feeling of stability and restfulness. A garden that lacks it will be less pleasing, although it may not be immediately apparent what the trouble is, particularly in a naturalistic composition.

What is the "garden axis" we read about? Why is it important? A garden axis is the center line of the composition. It is the basic line on which a design is built. Without it balance and symmetry, which give the garden a pleasing, restful appearance, are hard to develop.

A tall, closely woven fence, secured by stout posts, makes a suitable screen where there is not room for a shrub border between garden and street or road.

What is a "terminal feature"? This is a feature placed at the end of an axis in an oblong composition. It terminates the axis and turns one's attention back to the detail within the garden. A garden house, seat, pool, wall fountain, or group planting make suitable terminal features.

What is meant by the term "focal point"? A focal point is a point of highest interest in the development of the design, such as a pool, garden house, or a group of particularly striking plants. It serves as a center around which the design is built up.

In a square garden, where should the focal point be? In the center, usually. In a square design the important lines lead to or from the center.

What is a vista? A vista is a narrow view framed between masses of foliage. It tends to concentrate the observer's attention, rather than allowing it to spread over a wide panorama.

Must a flower garden be level? A geometrical garden need not be level, but the slope should be away from the principal point from which the garden is seen, rather than from side to side. A naturalistic garden should have, if possible, a natural grade, irregular rather than level or smoothly sloping.

How do you decide on the size of a garden? How large a garden can you take care of? Don't lay out more plantations than you can properly care for. A garden should be in scale with its surroundings, not too big for the house; nor so small as to seem insignificant. If the size of the property is limited, it is well to have the garden occupy the whole space instead of leaving a fringe of unusable space around it.

What is the rule for good proportion in the size of a garden? There is no hard-and-fast rule. Oblong areas are most effective when they are about one and a half times as long as they are wide; but the method of treating them and the surrounding foliage masses affect this considerably. Generally an oblong is better than a square; and an oval (on account of perspective) more effective than a circle.

How can you accent a planting? Is it necessary? Plantings made up of all one kind of plant, or of a few similar varieties, are likely to be monotonous and uninteresting. By using an occasional plant of a different sort an accent is created that makes the planting more interesting. For example, a pointed evergreen in a group of flowering shrubs.

FORMAL AND INFORMAL GARDENS

What is the difference between a formal and a naturalistic garden? Formal design uses straight lines and circular curves or arcs. Informal design uses long, free-flowing curves. Formality emphasizes *lines;* informality emphasizes *space.*

What is required in a formal garden? A formal garden is essentially a composition in geometric lines—squares, oblongs, circles, or parts thereof. It need not be large, elaborate, or filled with architectural embellishment. Most gardens, on account of space limitations, are basically formal.

Which is the better suited to a small place, a formal or an informal garden? Topography controls the type of design. On flat ground in proximity to buildings the rectangular (formal) type of design is easier to adapt. On rough land greater informality is desirable, particularly on slopes and in wooded areas.

PLANNING

What are the steps necessary to develop a small property? Rough grading; staking out walks, drives, and garden area; plan for drainage, if necessary; installation of utilities (water, gas, sewage, etc.); preparation of planting areas; finish grading (top-soil); planting trees, shrubs, and perennials; making the lawn, are of importance in this order.

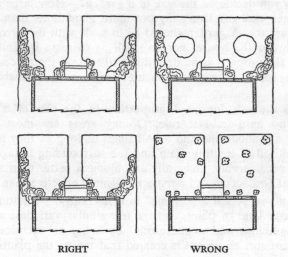

RIGHT   WRONG

Mistakes to avoid in planting. (Top) Leave lawn areas open, free from beds or borders in center of grass plots. (Below) Shrubs planted in polka-dot pattern, and better arrangement of massing them in borders.

Is there anything that can be done in advance of building on a lot that would improve the land or save time later on? The lot is 100 × 100 ft., with trees, bushes, weeds, etc. Clear out undesirable wild growths and trees where they are too thick. Avoid destroying attractive native shrub masses in locations near the property lines where they may be valuable as part of future shrub borders. Plow and harrow the land. Get rid of roots and stones and plant a cover crop, such as winter rye, until you are ready to use the land.

We have a new home to garden completely, and very little money to put into it. What do you advise concerning first plantings in our garden, to take away the bare, new look? Shade trees come first. Then important screen and background plantings of shrubs, flowering trees, and evergreens. These are the framework of the landscape picture. Add details later.

I have just built a new home, with a large front yard, in a country town. What would be best to set out or plant? Shade trees are important. Plant a few in such a way that they will throw their shade where it is most needed, and where they will compose best with the mass of the house. Shrub borders along the side property lines will help frame the picture. Avoid too much planting against the house, also isolated flower beds.

How would you go about designing a town-house garden area about 18 × 25 ft.? It is shady half the day. In such a garden you will have to depend largely upon the pattern of the design and upon architectural accessories. The planting should be mostly specimen evergreens, vines, and spring bulbs. For the summer, a few annuals, either in pots or beds, will give color.

Can you suggest economical landscaping for a small temporary home? Maintain extreme simplicity. Use the minimum of planting next to the house and in the area facing the street. In the rear, if possible, have a compact vegetable garden bordered with annual and perennial flowers.

What sort of garden would you plant in a plot 60 × 30 ft.? An area of this sort is usually most effectively developed by having an open grass panel in the center, with herbaceous borders along the sides backed up by shrub borders, or hedges, and a strong terminal feature at the end. This last could be a pool or garden house backed up by a heavy planting.

How can one arrange flowers in the garden properly? They are best arranged in groups; the size of the groups to conform to the size of the border, 3 to 5 plants of medium and low kinds, 3 of tall kinds. Space the tall plants 18 to 24 ins. apart, and others 9 to 12 ins. apart. Keep the very tall ones to the rear, with an occasional tall group toward the center. Irregularity of outline, irregularity in size of groups, and the avoidance of straight lines are among some of the things to be observed in arranging plants in a border.

What is the best way to arrange plants in a flower bed or border?

Plants in a flower border should be arranged according to height. Keep the low ones near the front edge and the tallest ones at the back. Occasionally, for accent, a tall plant can be brought farther forward than it normally would be. Of course in beds with a path on *both* sides of it, the tall plants would be placed in the center.

In arranging the mixed flower border, tall-growing subjects (such as delphiniums, hollyhocks, and digitalis) are kept to the rear.

How wide should a flower border be?   To provide succession of bloom throughout the season a border 10 to 14 ft. wide is none too much. Narrower borders can be treated effectively for seasonal bloom, but there will be times when few if any flowers will be present. A width of 4 ft. is about the least that can be effectively planted.

How should I plan a perennial flower garden?   Consult one or two good books that carry plans of such gardens. Select a plan that can be fitted easily into your scheme, and of a size you can manage. Consult a table of perennials that gives height, season of bloom and color. Study the arrangement well the first year after planting. Then is the time to do the final replanting. (See other questions.)

Will you give suggestions for a practical mixed perennial and annual flower border?   Two plans can be followed when combining annuals with perennials. One is to leave spaces in the border where annuals can be sown or plants set out early. The other is to raise annual plants for filling in bare spots as they occur. The former plan requires less work since by using this plan one can sow annual seeds directly in place and not go to the trouble of setting out individual plants. Annuals generally are used to pick up the blooming period, which begins in July. In May, sow seeds of *Phlox drummondi*, alyssum, cosmos (early), marigold, zinnia, directly in the border. Obtain plants, or sow seeds in April, of lobelia, nicotiana, petunia, *Salvia farinacea*. Verbenas should be sown early in March. Annuals should, where possible, be planted near those perennials which do not bloom in summer.

I should like a mixed bed of irises, phlox, and chrysanthemums. How can I have blooms spring, summer, and fall? Is this possible? If so, how big a bed? How many plants, and how far apart should they be to make an effective planting? The size of the bed must depend upon how much time you have to devote to it. Time and labor are involved in maintaining a perennial planting. It takes a lot of each. (See questions about size.) Using irises, phlox, and chrysanthemums, so place them in the bed that at their particular season there is a good distribution of bloom. Don't use too much iris, or too large groups. Distribute in the same way a few varieties of the novae-angliae and novibelgi hardy asters for September bloom. Tie all these together with such perennials as *Achillea ptarmica,* anthemis, aquilegia, *Campanula persicifolia,* coreopsis, dictamnus, gypsophila. Plant in groups of 3, placing plants 15 ins. apart. Toward the edge use *Anemone japonica* varieties, dwarf asters (hardy), *Campanula carpatica, Dianthus deltoides* and *D. latifolius,* and geums. Plant in groups of 3, 6 to 12 ins. apart. For early spring, use tulips and narcissi interplanted in groups throughout the planting. Along the edge, plant arabis, aubrieta, *Alyssum saxatile* and *A. saxatile citrinum, Phlox subulata* varieties, and pansies. (See Chrysanthemums for other suggestions.)

Which perennial flowers are most satisfactory for a small garden? Any whose habit of growth and size of flower are not out of scale for a small area. A list of such are *Alyssum argenteum; Arabis albida;* aquilegia, various; dianthus, various; *Aster subcoeruleus* (Himalayan Daisy); bleedingheart; *Campanula carpatica* and *C. persicifolia;* lily-of-the-valley; *Delphinium chinense,* dwarf; candytuft; forget-me-not; chrysanthemum, dwarf; *Geum borisi;* Gypsophila Rosy Veil; heuchera, various; Hemerocallis Goldena; *Lychnis floscuculi; Nepeta mussini; Plumbago larpentae;* primula, various; pyrethrum; *Lilium tenuifolium, L. concolor,* and *L. flavum;* Iceland Poppy; peonies—*P. tenuifolia* and *P. latifolia, Phlox divaricata* and *P. decussata; Veronica incana* and *V. amethystina.*

How can I plan for a continuous succession of bloom from early spring until late fall? First by having a wide planting space, at least 10 or 12 ft. in width, and by so planning that you have a few plants for each season in each part of the border.

Is it all right to plant roses and flowers together? Hybrid tea roses do not do well with other plants, but the floribundas, polyanthas, and hybrid perpetuals can be so used.

Backed by peonies and climbing roses, we have a rectangular bed 15 × 18 ft. What do you advise for a front planting? Interplant Regal Lily and *L. speciosum* among peonies. Enrich soil, plant solid with phlox, such as Africa, Charles Curtis, Columbia, Mary

Louise, Pinkette, Salmon Beauty. Edge with cushion chrysanthemums. For early color you could interplant between the phlox with small groups of cottage tulips and an edging of pansies.

BACKGROUNDS

Should a small garden be enclosed? Yes. Any garden picture is more effective if the flowers can be seen against a background of shrubs, hedge, wall, or fence. Furthermore, views out of a garden tend to distract attention from the garden itself.

The charm of the half-hidden: an enclosing wall leads the imagination to beauty beyond.

Should flower borders and beds have a background? Isolated flower beds with no background are rarely effective. Borders in front of shrubs, hedges, or walls make better places for color compositions.

What makes the best background hedge for a flower garden? Evergreens are probably better than deciduous shrubs because they do not grow so fast or provide such serious root competition. They are also effective in winter. Arborvitae, cedar, hemlocks, or Japanese Yew are suitable. (See also Hedges—Section II.)

I should like to plant a hedge for a background around my garden and have flowers in front. Would the hedge roots interfere with the

flowers? Yes, unless the flowers were planted at least 3 or 4 ft. away from the hedge. To prevent root interference, dig a trench about 3 ft. down, between the hedge and the flower border, and put in a thin wall of concrete to discourage the hedge roots from occupying the border.

I have a square area, about 40 ft. on a side, that I can enclose with a hedge and shrubbery, and which I would like to use for a flower garden. What arrangement of beds would you suggest? In such a definitely circumscribed area a geometrical pattern is almost mandatory. But it can be either a pattern of beds, planted with low bedding plants, or an open-center pattern where taller flowers and some shrubs are used in wide borders around the sides.

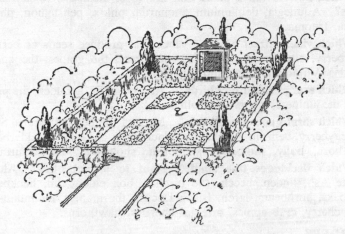

Typical enclosed formal garden of symmetrical design.

FLOWER BEDS

Our flower beds are best viewed from our porch. We use the porch more in July and August. What flowers should be used to give lots of color in these months? Among the perennials: phlox, hollyhock, gaillardia, daylily, coreopsis, heliopsis, rudbeckia, penstemon, stokesia, and plantainlily are all good. Satisfactory annuals are zinnia, marigold, cosmos, salvia, ageratum, calliopsis, calendula, celosia, and cornflower.

What are "bedding" plants; and how are they used? Bedding plants are low, compact annuals set out each year to form a definite pattern. They are most effective when used in a garden that is viewed from above.

Which type of plant makes the best edging for a flower bed?

Low, compact evergreens, such as boxwood or Dwarf Teucrium give the most finished effect. Low, compact perennials, such as dwarf asters, armeria, and heuchera, give a softer effect. Perennials that can be sheared after flowering, such as candytuft and dianthus, can be used.

TO ATTRACT BIRDS

Which flowers attract birds? Birds are attracted by the seed of the plants and then only seed-eating birds. Sunflowers, *Eryngium amethystinum,* rudbeckia, coreopsis, poke, lily-of-the-valley, wild and species roses, partridge-berry, wild strawberry, wintergreen.

Which flowers can I plant that are most attractive to hummingbirds? Aquilegia, delphinium, monarda, phlox, penstemon, physostegia, tritoma.

Which vines attract birds? Vines that produce seeds or berries: bearberry, bittersweet, cranberry, dewberry, the grapes, the honeysuckles. Virginia creeper, morningglories.

Which evergreens attract birds? Redcedar, fir, hemlock, the pines, yew, the junipers, arborvitae, hollies.

Which shrubs encourage birds? Most of the berried shrubs. Some are bayberry, benzoin, blackalder, blackberry, chokeberry, elderberry, hawthorn, holly, mulberry, shadbush, snowberry, the viburnums.

Which deciduous tree shall I plant to attract birds? Alders, White Ash, linden, beech, the birches, box elder, elm, hackberry, the oaks, hornbeam, larch, Black Locust, the maples, mountain-ash, wild cherry, crab apples, oriental cherries, hawthorns.

BORDERS

Will you list a few low plants for edging or the front of a border of perennials? Aethionema (Persian Stonecress); *Ajuga genevensis* (Geneva Bugle); *Alyssum citrinum; Arabis alpina* fl. pl. (Double Rockcress); *Artemisia abrotanum* (Southernwood); dianthus in variety; *Globularia trichosantha* (globedaisy); heuchera in variety; *Jasione perennis* (Shepherd's Scabiosa); *Nepeta mussini; Phlox divaricata* (Canada Blue Phlox); *Polemonium reptans* (Greek Valerian); *Scutellaria baicalensis* (Azure Skullcap); *Silene schafta* (Autumn Catchfly); *Armeria maritima* (thrift); *Stokesia laevis* (Stokes Aster); *Veronica incana* (Woolly Speedwell); viola in variety.

Please give explicit plans for an effective border, mostly of perennials. I have a border on either side of a concrete walk in my back yard, 72 ft. long and 4 ft. wide. I should like to follow a well-planned design that would look well and furnish cutting flowers. How close together can plants in a border be placed? Plan and design your border, including such reliable cut-flower selections as peonies, irises, delphiniums, Regal and Madonna Lilies, together with hardy chrysanthemums for fall cutting. Toward the front of the border you should include such reliable bulbs as tulips, Dutch irises, and narcissi. All of the things mentioned are almost necessary to any good perennial border, but there are many other excellent perennials listed in flower catalogues from which to choose. For constant cutting it will be necessary for you to add some of your favorite annuals each year. The best rule for determining the distance between plants is to visalize them at their blooming season and give them sufficient space so that they will not be crowded by their neighbors. (See also Planning, this section.)

What are good companion plants for tall-bearded irises in a narrow border along driveway? Lupine, pink, veronica, doronicum, *Phlox suffruticosa,* geum, and delphinium.

FOR COLOR

Should a garden have a "color scheme"? If so, how do you make one? Restricted color schemes for small gardens have been overdone. Color harmony is important, and plants should be so placed that interesting color combinations result and violent clashes do not occur. Sometimes it is wise to rule out certain "difficult" colors, such as red and purple.

How important is good foliage in a color scheme? Are the flowers only to be considered? Good foliage should be considered because it creates a background for the flowers. Use strong-foliaged plants near or among weak-foliaged ones, or those whose foliage disappears. Often the foliage itself (which may be gray-green, yellow-green, or bluish-green) plays an important part in the color scheme.

How can I plan lovely color combinations in my garden? Effective color combinations in the garden must be thoughtfully worked out on paper beforehand. Make lists of plants according to color, and also time of bloom. Then with a large-scale plan of the garden and a set of colored crayons indicate their proposed position on paper before you start to plant.

Can you suggest some other BLUE FLOWERS besides larkspur and cornflowers? Ageratum, lobelia, browallia, torenia, Swanriver-daisy (brachycome), linaria, nigella, morningglory, scabiosa, *Aconitum fischeri,* forget-me-nots, aquilegia, aster, companula, catananche, delphinium, clematis, echinops, mistflower, polemonium, *Salvia farinacea,* anchusa, cynoglossum, pulmonaria, ajuga. Bulbs: scilla, grapehyacinth, chionodoxa, hyacinth.

I plan to have a garden of primarily bright RED PLANTS. Can you name some? Zinnia, marigold, poppy, mallow, salvia, geranium, celosia, cardinalflower, nicotiana, hollyhock, penstemon, peony, beebalm, geum, Gaillardia Ruby, dahlia, rose, nasturtium, Heuchera Queen of Hearts, semperflorens begonia. Bulbs: tulip, tigridia, nerine.

Can you suggest some RED FLOWERS for a circular bed around my flagpole? I have planned to use dwarf blue ageratum with white sweet alyssum, but can find no bright red flower with dwarf and free-flowering habits.   Try dwarf scarlet sage (salvia), dwarf red zinnia, cockscomb (celosia), red geranium, or verbena.

I have heard that gardens planted with only WHITE FLOWERS are effective. Are they?   All-white gardens are often effective if one has room for background material such as evergreens and shrubs. They give a feeling of spaciousness and quiet. However, an all-white garden is likely to become tiresome unless one has space enough for other types of gardens and for borders of colorful plants.

What plants would you suggest for an all-white garden?   Phlox, arabis, asters, chrysanthemum, larkspur, babysbreath, iberis, peony, platycodon, scabiosa, stokesia, yucca, veronica, alyssum, saponaria, petunia, poppy, nicotiana, sweetpea, morningglory, moonflower, arctotis. Bulbs: snowdrop, crocus, hyacinth, tulip, narcissus.

Will you suggest some bright YELLOW FLOWERS for the garden?   Potentilla, thalictrum, oenothera, daylily, sunflower, zinnia, marigold, snapdragon, doronicum, chrysanthemum, dahlias, California Poppy, coreopsis, baptisia, *Alyssum saxatile,* anthemis, gaillardia, cosmos, celosia, calendula, nasturtium. Bulbs: snowdrop, crocus, daffodil, tulip, sternbergia.

FLOWERS FOR CUTTING

What are some desirable perennials for cut flowers, blooming in May and June, besides iris, etc.?   *Doronicum caucasicum, Dicentra eximia, Dianthus plumarius* and varieties, *Delphinium belladonna, Alyssum saxatile citrinum, Saponaria ocymoides splendens, Pulmonaria saccharata, Phlox suffruticosa* and varieties, *Phlox divaricata,* Geum Fire Opal, *Anchusa myostidiflora,* Peony and Oriental Poppy.

Can you tell me how to have cut flowers as early as possible, and for as long a time as possible?   Tall-bearded iris, Siberian iris, coreopsis, Delphinium Belladonna, *Eupatorium coelestinum,* gaillardia, geum, gypsophila, helenium, penstemon, physostegia, aster, chrysanthemum; spring bulbs.

Which flowers are best suited for show and cutting purposes?   Tritoma, antirrhinum, aster, campanula, gaillardia, coreopsis, *Anemone japonica,* artemisia, chrysanthemum, and doronicum. Roses, delphinium, daffodil, tulip, peony, gladiolus, iris.

Which garden flowers are best for cutting, and last longest after

being cut? Aster, tritoma, chrysanthemum, helianthus, scabiosa, zinnia, aquilegia, *Stokesia lilacina, Verbena bonariensis,* celosia, and marigold.

Anticipating an August wedding, which white or pastel-colored flowers can we plant with which to decorate the church? White Shastadaisy, delphinium, chrysanthemum, phlox, aster, stock, scabiosa, gladiolus, and gypsophila.

FOR EDGING

What is a desirable perennial edging between lawn and border? Dwarf Teucrium (*T. chamaedrys*), *Iberis sempervirens* Little Gem, *Dianthus caesius.*

I have a formal garden with 100 tulips and phlox at end. Which flowers are best to plant for edging and gradual build-up in size to height of phlox? *Doronicum caucasicum, Phlox arendsi, Phlox divaricata, Dianthus plumarius, Anchusa myosotidiflora, Ajuga genevensis, Alyssum saxatile compactum, Anemone hupehensis, Anemone magellanica, Veronica spicata, Veronica incana,* dwarf asters, dwarf chrysanthemums.

Can you suggest some low edging plants with white flowers (not sweet alyssum) to plant where tulips have finished blooming? Dwarf petunia; annual phlox; dwarf verbena.

I want to lay out a colonial garden using beds in some design. What shall I edge the beds with? Dwarf box edging is typical. Dwarf teucrium and clipped English Ivy can be substituted.

PLANNING FOUNDATION PLANTINGS

(See also Foundation Material—Section III.)

What kind of shrubbery would you plant in front of a new house with a 30-ft. frontage? Use tall, upright-growing plants at the corners and low-growing, rounded masses between. Avoid too much planting. If the house foundation is low enough, leave some spaces bare to give the house the effect of standing solidly on the ground. Either deciduous or evergreen material is suitable.

We have large trees (oak, Gray Birch, maple, and ironwood). What should be planted near the house? The yard slopes toward the south and the house is new, so we are starting from scratch. Let the trees constitute the principal landscape feature. Use a minimum of planting near the house—vines on the foundation, a few shade-loving shrubs at the corners or either side of the entrance.

What is the best method of foundation planting for an "unbalanced" house—one with the door not in the center? An unbalanced composition for a foundation planting can be made extremely attractive. The fact that the door is not in the center will make it even more interesting. Naturally the doorway should be the point of interest, and your maximum height should begin on either side, tapering irregularly to the corners of the house where a specimen shrub or evergreen may go a little higher in order to break the sharp lines of the house corner. These corner accents should not be so tall as the main planting on either side of the doorway.

A symmetrical balanced entrance planting.

What is best for planting around a small house on a small acreage? Everyone has evergreens. Can't we have simplicity and still be different? Deciduous shrubs can be just as interesting throughout much of the year although it is the evergreens which lend interest in the winter. Why not use both deciduous shrubs with a few evergreens as a background?

I want to plant flowers along the base of our house. Will you suggest what kind of flowers to plant? Unless the house is an architectural jewel which should not be hidden, shrubs or vines, or both, as a background, with flowers planted in front of them, give a better effect than flowers which, alone, are apt to look too small and inadequate near a house foundation. Flowers to plant in front of shrubs by house: tulip, narcissus, crocus, *Scilla sibirica,* followed by dictamnus, polyantha roses, and *Phlox decussata.* Or use long drifts of one variety of annual, limited to one or two colors, such as Petunias Elks Pride and Snowdrift, or Heavenly Blue or Rosy Gem; or for a gay effect a good mixture of marigolds.

CAPE COD

How shall I landscape the front of our Cape Cod house? It was built about 1810 and during the 6½ years we have owned it every minute has been spent in restoring the old pine paneling within doors and developing the flower and vegetable gardens outside. There is the main house with front door in the center, an ell, and a long shed-garage combination. What treatment all along the front would you suggest? Planting for a Cape Cod house should be very simple. A suitable planting is shown in the accompanying sketch. Shade trees are important and should be carefully placed. A small dooryard enclosed by a low picket fence often adds to the charm if the house sets far enough back from the highway to permit its being used.

The Cape Cod type of home calls for a low foundation planting, in keeping with its architectural lines.

We have a small home, Cape Cod. Which shrubs can be planted that would not be too expensive or difficult to grow? Among the "sure-fire" shrubs are *Amorpha nana;* berberis, various (barberry); *Caragana aurantiaca; Cotoneaster horizontalis; Deutzia gracilis; Euonymus alatus; Genista tinctoria;* broom; *Hypericum patulum* and *H. frondosum* (St. Johnswort); Philadelphus Mt. Blanc and P. Norma; wild roses; lilac; spirea.

COLONIAL

What can be done with a narrow front lawn between an old-fashioned house with a high porch and the street—which is lined with large, old maples? Grass will probably not be very successful in such a place. Use *Vinca minor* or *Pachysandra terminalis* in place of it, and hide the porch foundation with a planting of laurel (*Kalmia latifolia*), rhododendron, or other shade-loving shrubs. Such a planting will require heavy applications of acid, humus-making fertilizer and frequent watering.

ENGLISH

Could you tell me what kind of foundation planting I could use for an English-type home? The English style, being informal, calls for informal planting. Avoid symmetrically balanced groups of planting, or too much planting. Accent the doorways, the corners, and leave the rest open. Vines are important to soften brickwork or stone.

FARMHOUSES

Do you suggest landscaping a plot around a farmhouse? A farm home needs planting, but it does not need the intensive landscape development that characterizes the average suburban home. Use a few well-placed clumps of hardy shrubs and small-flowering trees.

What native material can be collected in Maine that would be suitable for landscape use around a farmhouse? Hemlock, witch-hazel, winterberry, birch, Sugar Maples, Red Maples, pines, larch, arborvitae, Virginia Rose, blueberries, and many other shrubs. Take a walk through the woods there and see for yourself.

FRENCH

What sort of foundation planting is appropriate to an informal French house? An informal house should have informal planting.

A small home calls for simplicity of design in landscaping.

Avoid rigid balance, and hold the planting down to the minimum. Use a few choice things rather than many ordinary plants. Clumps of broad-leaved evergreens are particularly effective.

MODERN

What plants should be used around a modern ranch-type house in front of a large rock outcrop? Make use of the natural rock by all means, planting rock plants and creeping junipers around it. Low yews, azaleas and pieris might be in the foundation planting with a dogwood and crabapples used as the trees.

RUSTIC

We have a cabin among trees and woodland. We would like to make the immediate grounds of the cottage look much nicer than they now are. How could we go about it? Underplant the area with various kinds of native ferns and woodland wildflowers.

FOR HEDGES

See page 391.

HILLSIDE PLANTING

How could a rather steep hillside, partly wooded, be planted to make it more attractive? Such a wooded hillside could be underplanted with native shrubs, evergreens, ferns, and woodland wildflowers. An interesting system of trails leading through the area would add to its interest.

SCREENS

How can I disguise my chicken house and yard so that they will not injure the appearance of my property? If the wire of the chicken run is strong enough, you might plant a vine such as honeysuckle on it. The house itself can be made less conspicuous by planting a group of pines and spruces around it. Or the whole thing can be hidden behind a dense hedge.

Would a mixture of plants with various colored leaves or blossoms be satisfactory in an informal screening for enclosing a yard? Usually a suitable boundary screen consists of one variety of shrub. Too varied a planting competes with the interest inside the garden instead of merely framing it. Variety in leaf, flower, and fruit may be inside the boundary screen or in foundation plantings of buildings.

What are some fast growing vines that would make good screens? Bower Actinidia, Dutchman's Pipe, Virginia Creeper, Kudzu Vine and grape species.

What type of shrubs make good informal screening for enclosing yard? Choice is determined by size of area to be enclosed and height of objects to be "screened out." Persian Lilac is excellent for areas of a quarter acre and larger. Smaller gardens may use *Rosa hugonis, Rosa rubrifolia,* Truehedge Columnberry, or privet, untrimmed.

SHRUBS

Should shrubs and small trees be used in a flower garden? Yes, an occasional compact-growing tree or shrub in the garden relieves the monotony of perennial and annual planting.

We plan to landscape a 3-acre tract. Will you name flowering shrubs that give a succession of bloom throughout the year? For spring: azalea, forsythia, lonicera, *Viburnum carlesi*. For summer: hydrangea, buddleia, roses, abelia, heather, rose-of-sharon. For fall: abelia, witch-hazel. For autumn color: Euonymus alatus, dogwoods, viburnums, Japanese barberry, sumacs and spice bush.

Can you suggest hardy shrubbery for a small country home? Standard varieties of deciduous shrubs, such as spirea, lilac, deutzia, philadelphus, and weigela, can always be relied upon to thrive with the minimum amount of care. Interest can be added to the planting by using some of the rarer varieties, such as *Philadelphus virginalis*, hybrid lilacs, and a few of the small-flowering trees, such as Tatarian honeysuckle, flowering crab, dogwood, and redbud.

FOR SHADE

See also Shady Environment—Section III.

There is no sun in my garden from September until May. What is the best way to treat a garden of this kind? Since the floral display in this garden will be effective only from late spring to early fall, make sure the garden background is interesting enough to make the garden attractive during the rest of the year. Use evergreen, berry-bearing shrubs and ones that have good, full color. Then for flowers select only those plants that bloom during the time when sunlight is available.

Will you suggest plants for a garden in an all-shade yard? Aconitum, ajuga, aquilegia, campanula, cimicifuga, dicentra, digitalis, ferns, hosta, hemerocallis, hesperis, lily-of-the-valley, thalictrum, tradescantia, trillium, valeriana, and viola are the principal shade-loving kinds of garden flowers. There are many varieties of most.

Which flowers are best for part shade? Perennials for part shade: *Achillea filipendulina,* aconite, cimicifuga, digitalis, *Anemone japonica, Lobelia cardinalis,* mertensia, hosta, helleborus, daylily, trollius, primrose, Virginia-cowslip, may-apple, Showy Ladyslipper.

Which perennial flowers, tall, medium, low, may I use in a garden shaded by oak trees? What soil improvements should be made to overcome acidity from oaks? Most perennial plants are not particular as to the acidity or alkalinity of soil. If there is overacidity from the leaves of your oak tree this may be corrected by an annual sprinkling of ground limestone worked shallowly into the topsoil. Your location should be ideal without treatment for all of your native wildflowers.

The low-growing group would include cypripediums, woods ferns, etc. (See Woodland Wildflowers.) For taller plants you have a wide choice from such things as holly, mountain laurel, azalea, blueberries, and rhododendron. The combination of these should be an attractive planting.

Please name a few plants that will grow in dense shade, around base of large tree. Must I put them in pots on account of roots of tree? Few plants will subsist on what's left in the soil after the roots of a large tree have filled the surface and used all available food. Try digging out pockets, filling them with good loam, and planting one of the following: *Viola canadensis, Mahonia repens, Vinca minor,* Kenilworth Ivy, pachysandra. Potted plants would be of only temporary value.

Which flower is the best to plant under a big maple tree where there are lots of roots and practically no sun? Altitude is 6,600 ft. Norway Maple (*Acer platanoides*) foliage is so dense that few plants can survive both shade and the fight for root space and food. Deep watering of all maples encourages the development of deeper rooting, thus freeing the surface from this strangling network. Ground covers that accept the challenge of most maples are *Vinca minor, Mahonia repens,* pachysandra, *Sedum stoloniferum.*

Which plants would grow well along a shady wall? *Euonymus radicans vegetus,* aquilegia, ladyslipper, hepatica, *Epimedium niveum, Plumbago larpentae,* dicentra, digitalis, sanguinaria, ferns, mertensia, anemone, primula, pulmonaria, aconitum, dodecatheon, thalictrum, *Anchusa myosotidiflora.* Trees which provide shade for plants in nature also supply abundant humus in the soil by their decayed leaves. Shade plants in the garden appreciate humus too.

SLOPES AND BANKS

See also Section III.

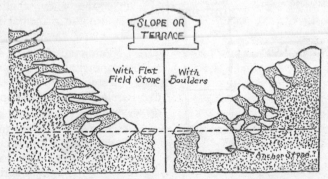

Method of placing stones to hold a slope or a terrace, without a wall.

Will you suggest some shrubs or trees for the sloping terrace in front of my house? Roses such as Max Graf and *Rosa wichuraiana, Jasminum nudiflorum,* lonicera, bearberry, or dwarf, spreading evergreens.

How should a sloping area (15 × 3 ft.) along a driveway be planted? Fence or wall would be unsuitable. The location is sunny. Such a place is best treated by planting the slope with some easy-to-take-care-of, low, trailing shrub or perennial. *Phlox subulata alba, Teucrium chamaedrys, Juniperus chinensis sargenti,* or *Euonymus fortunei vegetus* would be suitable.

How fast does the Memorial Rose grow? And how far apart should it be planted? This is one of the best shrubs for bank planting, rooting all along its stems which can grow 4′ a year. A new planting should have the plants spaced about 4′ apart.

SURFACE DRAINAGE

What is a dry well, and what is it used for? A dry well is a pit dug 5 or 6 ft. deep, filled with stones and gravel. A pipe or sewer leading either from the house or from a poorly drained area leads into this, and provides drainage for difficult situations.

What can be done to prevent rain water from draining off the highway onto a sloping property, causing erosion? A low bank along the highway should be constructed, and at the lowest point in the gutter so created a catch basin can be installed to gather the water and lead it, through a pipe, to a place where it will do no harm. Such a catch basin can be simply 2 18-in. sewer tiles, one on top of the other, with a grating fitted into the top and a 4-in. side outlet about 1 ft. below the top. If there is a great deal of water, it may have to be a brick, concrete, or stone basin.

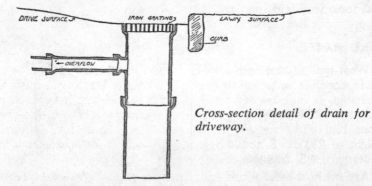

Cross-section detail of drain for driveway.

How can I construct a catch basin to take off surplus rain water from the drive? Two pieces of 18-in. sewer tile, set one on top of the other, and with an iron grating fitted into the top, make a good, cheap catch basin. Smaller tile are too difficult to clean; larger are seldom needed. If the amount of water to be taken care of is large, a 4-in. or 6-in. tile pipe can be taken from the top catch-basin tile (which can be obtained with a side outlet) and carried some distance away to a low point where the water will do no harm, or to the storm sewer.

TREES

Should trees be removed from gardens? Not necessarily. If the trees are fine old specimens, they should be left, and the garden designed around them using plants that will withstand shade; otherwise they should be taken out. Often trees form an important part of the garden's design.

Many American elms are being removed in our town because they have succumbed to the Dutch elm disease. What are some good large shade trees to use as substitutes? Maples, hackberry, yellow-wood, beech, ash, honey-locust, especially the "Moraine" and the yellow leaved "Sunburst" locusts, sweet gum, cucumber tree, Amur cork tree, Buttonball, Sargent cherry, various oaks, sophora, lindens and zelkova.

Can you suggest desirable evergreens and deciduous trees for use in landscaping a suburban home? See Section III.

GARDEN FEATURES AND ACCESSORIES

ARBORS

I want to buy an arbor for my garden on which to train roses. What type is best? White-painted wooden arbors are inexpensive and look well. Get one that is sturdy and well designed. Rustic arbors, made from cedar or redwood, are also suitable.

BIRD BATHS

What type of bird bath is good for the small garden? Any well-made concrete, marble, clay, wood, or stone bird baths that are available, as long as they are well designed and unobtrusive. Select a design which fits your garden plan. Homemade cement-and-field-stone bird baths are not usually desirable. For a small garden a height of 2½ ft. is about right. If the bath is detached from the pedestal, it will facilitate cleaning.

Are the bird baths which are set on the ground without a pedestal practical? Yes, they are very effective if well designed. Handmade ceramic or metal basins are interesting, or a hollowed stone may be used. They are usually placed in a sheltered spot surrounded by ivy or other ground cover, evergreens, or shrubs. It must be remembered, however, that this type bird bath can be used only where no cats are around to harm the birds when they use it.

How often should you clean bird baths?   As often as they look dirty or stained, which is usually 2 or 3 times a week at least in warm weather. It will help to have a special scrubbing brush for the bird bath for removing scum around the edges.

What can be used to remove algae from a bird bath?   Usually water or soapy water and a scrubbing brush are all that is necessary. Borax may be added, or a bleaching disinfectant. These, however, must be well rinsed off before filling the bath with water for the birds.

CURBINGS

Would you recommend brick or stone edging for a driveway or path?   For a driveway, brick edging is somewhat too fragile unless the bricks are set in a heavy foundation of concrete. Then they are likely to be ugly. Granite paving blocks (Belgian blocks) are better because they are heavy enough to stay put without cement. For pathways, brick is ideal. Small rounded stones are useless for either purpose.

What sort of edging should I use for a brick walk?   There are 3 standard sorts of edging: sawtooth, rowlock, and stretcher. For garden paths where there are no grass edges, sawtooth looks well, and it uses less brick than does rowlock. Against a lawn or grass edge rowlock is better because the mower can be run up on it and there is less hand clipping. Stretcher edging uses the least brick of all, but, since the bricks do not go down into the ground any farther than the bricks of the walk itself, it provides less stability for the walk.

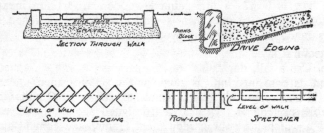

Types of edging for walks and drives.

What can I use to edge a driveway that will look well, but also make a strong, permanent edge?   Granite paving blocks are ideal for this. They are so heavy they will stay in place without concrete to hold them. Do not let them stick up above the lawn area. Set them on end, with the short dimension parallel to the line of the driveway.

Should flower beds be edged with stones, brick, or plants? Stone edgings are a nuisance, since the grass around them has to be hand clipped. Brick edgings have the same fault but in connection with gravel paths give a prim, quaint effect. In most cases edgings of flowering plants are more suitable.

DOORWAYS

The doorway of my house is a reproduction of an old colonial door, with leaded side lights and fanlight. How should I plant this so as to enhance rather than detract from its beauty? For an elaborate doorway, which is sufficiently interesting in itself, elaborate planting is unnecessary. Possibly the most effective thing would be to plant a big old lilac on either side of the door, train a light vine, possibly a large-flowered clematis, over the door itself, and leave it at that.

Suggestion for planting a colonial doorway.

Should planting either side of the front door always be alike on both sides? Certainly not. If the house is in an informal or picturesque architectural style, the planting should also be informal and picturesque. Use a tall, dark plant on one side, with a few smaller things around its base, and on the other side use something lighter, more graceful and spreading. Don't use too many kinds of plants and too many sorts of foliage.

My colonial house seems to me to have a very plain doorway. How can I plant it to make it seem more important? Where the doorway is formal, but very plain, interest must be created through the planting. Use identical groups on either side, but select the various plants carefully for form texture and foliage color. Evergreens give great dignity and are less likely to get too large in a short time. Tall masses to accent the lines of the doorway, with more spreading plants around them, usually make the most effective arrangement.

A nicely balanced, but not symmetrical, front-door planting.

DRIVEWAYS

What material do you recommend for the building of a driveway?
Many materials make satisfactory driveways, but much depends on
whether the drive is straight or curved, flat or sloping, in cold country
or warm. A good, cheap driveway for a level drive in the New York
area can be made of either cinders mixed with loam and sand or
bank-run gravel. Either can be finished with grits or bluestone screenings. If there are curves or grades, crushed stone with a tar binder is
practically mandatory.

**How would you build a driveway on a steep slope to prevent wash-
ing? What material should be used?**   For a short driveway on a steep
slope, granite paving blocks set in sand make an ideal material. They
are rough enough to give good traction in icy weather, they need no
maintenance, they are good-looking. For a long driveway, they may be
too uneven for comfortable riding, and concrete, heavily scored to
provide traction, may be better. But it is a hard, uncompromising-
looking material.

**I am building a driveway for my home. What sort of parking space
for visiting cars do you recommend, and where should it be located?**
Parking space for at least one guest car should be provided right at the
front door or the path leading to it, so arranged that the use of the
driveway by other cars is not prevented. (See next question.) Parking
for a larger number of cars should be located at a distance from the
front entrance of the house. It should be constructed of the same
material as the driveway.

**When guests come to the house and leave their cars before the
front door, it is impossible for anyone else to use the driveway from
the garage to the street. How can I avoid this situation?**   Construct
a pass court in front of the door wide enough so that a car can stand
at the door and another pass it on the outside. The court should be

about 30 ft. long and 16 ft. wide. Any interesting shape can be given
it to make it a pleasing part of the landscape picture.

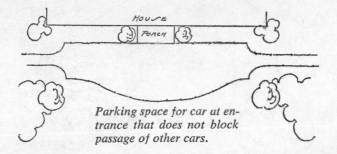

*Parking space for car at en-
trance that does not block
passage of other cars.*

**What is the most practical shape for a turn court at the garage on
a small property?** The so-called Y-turn takes up the least space and
yet provides for easy turning, either for your own car coming out of
the garage, or for other cars using the driveway. The radius of the
curves in the accompanying sketch should be 15 ft. to 20 ft., and it is
important that the space into which the cars back be at least 14 ft.
wide.

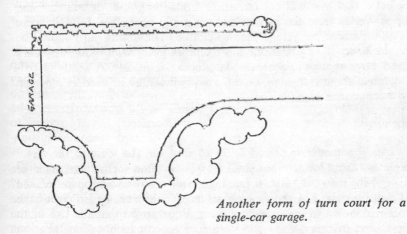

*Another form of turn court for a
single-car garage.*

How large should a turn-around in front of the house be? The
largest cars require a turning space about 60 ft. in diameter for making
a complete turn without backing. An area of bluestone or gravel that
large is often out of proportion to the house. It can be broken up with
a grass island (but this should not have anything else planted in it).
To make arrival at the house door easy, it is wise to distort the shape
of the turn-around somewhat, making it more of an apple shape
instead of a true circle.

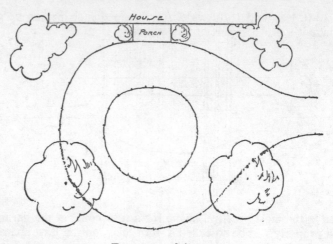

Turn-around for car.

DRYING YARD

How can one go about making a drying yard on the home grounds? Select a spot that will not be visible from the house, or one that can be separated from the garden and yet easily accessible. Usually there is an area near the garage that is suitable. The drying yard should be about 20 sq. ft. in size if one has a clothes pole, or, if clotheslines are used, large enough to accommodate them adequately. A wattle or paling fence about 6 ft. high, or tall evergreens, may be used as a screen to enclose the area.

FENCES

I need a moderate-priced fence to shut out the view of the street from my front lawn. What shall I use? A fence of palings made of 1×4 in. redwood, 5 ft. 6 ins. high, will answer your purpose. The sketch on page 124 shows such a fence. The back, or inside, of the fence is shown to indicate how the palings are supported. Use stout posts and stringers, since wind pressure against such a fence may be very great.

Is a wattle fence appropriate for the home garden? A woven wattle fence made of saplings or thin split logs is expensive, and because of this is not recommended for the small garden unless there is an objectionable view to be blocked or sturdy protection from animals to be provided. Wattle fences are excellent for such purposes as enclosing a drying yard, screening a highway, or to give privacy in a courtyard, small flower or herb garden.

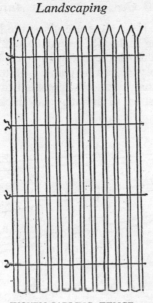

WOVEN-SAPLING FENCE

Where can I get a design for a picket fence? The accompanying sketch shows a typical picket fence such as used to be seen often on village streets. Many modern picket fences are less substantially built, and hence tend to look flimsy. The effectiveness of such a fence depends largely on delicacy of detail, but it must also be, and look, strong.

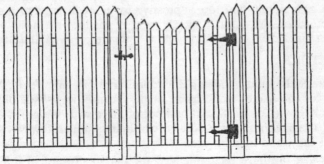

PICKET FENCE

Shall I use perennials or annuals (a) for trellis fence; and (b) for chimney? How fast growing? (a) Ipomoea "Heavenly Blue"—annual, fast-growing; *Lathyrus latifolius*—perennial, fast-growing; *Clematis montana rubens*—perennial, strong grower. (b) *Euonymus fortunei vegetus*—perennial, fast-growing; *Ampelopsis lowi*—perennial, slow-growing; *Hedera helix baltica*—slow-growing, for north or northwest side only.

What sort of fence is best for use along the highway in front of a farm where something elaborate would be out of place? A simple post-and-rail fence, such as the one in the accompanying sketch, has proved very satisfactory. It can be painted white, or, if made of dead chestnut, cypress, or redwood, left unpainted to weather. If it has to be made proof against small animals and chickens, wire can be attached to the inside.

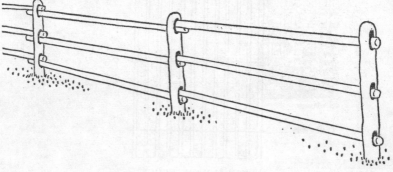

POST AND RAIL FENCE

A post-and-rail fence is excellent support for climbing roses or vines of moderate growth.

FOUNTAINS

Do you recommend putting a fountain into a small home garden? Elaborate fountains throwing large streams of water are rather expensive to maintain and too impressive for a small garden. A small fountain which drips water slowly over a shallow basin or a wall fountain that runs a tiny stream into a bowl are pleasing and in scale.

FURNITURE

Is it better to paint wooden garden furniture white or green? White is good for colonial or white frame homes. Almost any shade of green paint is likely to look artificial and out of place with the green of the garden. Clear varnish, or a soft brownish stain which brings out the grain of the wood may be used.

Is garden furniture recommended for the small garden? Yes. It must be of good design, however, and suit the type of the house. It should be comfortable, light weight (or heavy enough to be placed permanently), resistant to weather, and preferably of a color which will become part of the garden scene.

What kinds of garden furniture are best? The rustic type, made of cedar or other water-resistant wood, if comfortable, usually blends well with any type garden. Being inconspicuous, it does not dominate the garden scene. White-painted wooden furniture is desirable in some gardens, especially if the house is also white. Metal furniture is comfortable, and good for outdoor living rooms or terraces. Stone benches and tables are suitable for the large garden. Cane or woven chairs may be used if not subjected to bad weather. Canvas chairs are comfortable and easy to move about, but also must be protected from rain.

Garden seats should be placed where they will invite use—not stuck out in the middle of a lawn.

GARDEN HOUSES

What kind of garden house is most suitable for the small garden? A very simple house which fits the architecture of the house and the landscape plan of the garden. The English style, with a sloping tiled or thatched roof, is fitting for an English-type garden. Rustic styles are good in a natural setting, out of sight of the main house. Avoid fantastic or baroque styles.

GAME AREAS

How can I lay out a badminton court? Allow about 30 by 60 ft. of lawn space for a badminton court. (See also Lawns.)

I want to make part of my garden into an area for a bowling green and for horseshoe pitching. How much room is necessary? For a bowling green you should have a smooth grass area about 128 ft. sq. A gutter of sand 1½ ft. wide and about 6 ins. deep should surround this strip. For horseshoes, you will need an area 10 × 50 ft. The sand pit at either end should be 6 ft. sq., with a stout wooden or iron stake in the center.

How much room does a croquet lawn require? About 30 × 60 ft. A level, well-mowed area is essential for this game. (See Lawns.)

What games or equipment would be suitable for a children's game area? A wading pool, sandbox or sand pit, swings, seesaw, sliding board, ball court.

My children want a tennis court. What is the most practical type; and how should it be constructed? Clay courts are most satisfactory. See that the drainage of the area is good. Lay down tile lines across the area if necessary. Put in 6 ins. of good clay, tamped and rolled smooth. Let the whole court slope about 6 ins. from one end to the other, or 3 ins. from each end to a low point at the net line. Surface with an inch or less of fine sifted clay with a little sand mixed in.

What area is needed for a tennis court?   The playing space of a double court is 38 × 78 ft., but at least 66 × 138 ft. is needed to give room at sides and ends for free play.

I would like to build a little shelter near our playground area for storing equipment and for spectators. Have you any suggestion?   A simple 3-sided building of white clapboards, or of rustic logs or siding with an open front, might be constructed at the end of the area. The floor can be of stone or concrete. Closets could be built along one wall for storing tennis rackets, croquet mallets, etc. Allow one closet for sweaters, shoes, and other equipment. Comfortable lounging chairs should be at hand for spectators.

GATES

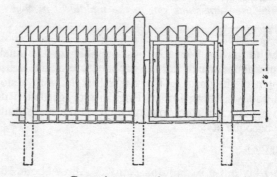

Gate for a picket fence.

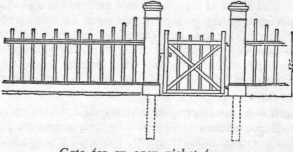

Gate for an open picket fence.

What kind of garden gate do you recommend?   Wrought iron or wood (either rustic or painted). A paling gate would look well with a fence of the same material.

What kind of gate is best to use with a clipped privet hedge?   A well-designed gate of stained, weathered, or painted wood, or wrought iron.

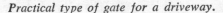

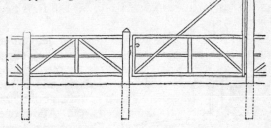

Practical type of gate for a driveway.

Do you recommend wire gates for gardens? Wire gates are not usually so decorative as wooden or iron gates. They are suitable for vegetable areas or dog runs.

To be correct, must the planting either side of a garden gate or entrance be the same? A symmetrically balanced arrangement is the usual thing, but it is often less interesting than an unsymmetrical treatment such as the one in the accompanying sketch. Here 3 elements

Example of a balanced (but not symmetrical) gateway planting.

—the vine on the wall, the urn filled with flowers, and the low, rounded shrub—have been balanced by the tall, dark evergreen on the other side. Such a treatment is easier to arrange when the position of the entrance, or conditions of shade, etc., make a symmetrical arrangement difficult. It is more lively and striking.

LAWNS

Should a garden have a lawn space in the middle? Not all gardens should be so designed, but there are many advantages to this type of layout. A grass panel serves as a foreground to the floral displays in the beds and as a space for chairs and tables. Such a garden is easier to maintain than one made up of many small beds.

Where the house is below the street level, water may be drained away by sloping grade down from both house and street to form slight depression at a low point.

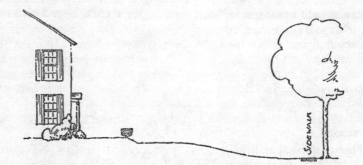

Grading: a flat terrace with a step, and curved slope to sidewalk is more attractive than a uniform grade from door to street.

How would you grade a front lawn where the house is small and is several feet below the highway level? A gradual slope from the house up to the street is usually more pleasing than abrupt terraces. To prevent water draining toward the house, however, the grade should be carried down from the house slightly, to a low point from which the water can drain off to the sides before the slope up to the street begins. (See Section IV, Lawn and Turf Areas.)

PATHS

What materials are suitable for making paths? For an average flower garden, grass paths are usually best, for they present a green foreground for the garden picture. They need no maintenance other than what the lawn receives. Gravel or blue stone paths in the flower garden are likely to be a nuisance to take care of. Where a path must be dry, or at least passable in all sorts of weather, brick and flagstone are serviceable. Often it is possible to make a grass path more practical by laying a line of stepping-stones down its middle, or along either edge.

Should a path be laid out in a straight line or with a curve? Generally speaking, a path should be as direct as possible, because the purpose of it is to provide a passage between two points. However, a natural-looking path should follow the contour of the garden, curving around trees or shrubs that are in a direct line. Sharp curves are to be avoided, and all unnecessary turns. When a curve is to be made, it should have a long, gentle sweep. For very small paths, a straight line, with no curves at all, is advisable.

BRICK AND STONE

How should I construct a brick walk? Brick walks look best when laid in sand rather than cement mortar. Provide a gravel or cinder bed about 6 ins. thick, then put down a layer of fine sand, set the edge courses, and fill in the field brick in whatever pattern you wish. Fill the cracks between the bricks with fine sand, wash it well, and tamp thoroughly. In tamping, lay a heavy board on the walk and pound that rather than the bricks themselves. The walk will be smoother if you do this and you will break fewer bricks. (See curbings, this section.)

What pattern should be used in laying a brick walk? There are two standard patterns, basket and herringbone. Either may be varied

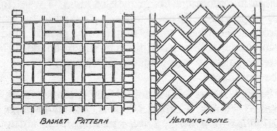

BASKET PATTERN HERRING-BONE

Two "patterns" for laying bricks for a walk.

somewhat according to taste. The basket pattern is more economical, since there is no cutting of brick. The accompanying sketch shows basket pattern with a rowlock edge and herringbone with a sawtooth edge. In laying out the walk, set only one edge course first. Lay out a section of the field to see how the pattern is working out, then set the other edge. Do not decide on a predetermined width for the walk and then try to fit the pattern into it.

FLAGSTONE

The front of my garage is about 50 ft. from street, joined to house; driveway level on one side; 4-ft. slope on other; no walk to house as yet. Would you suggest shrubs, rock garden, stone wall with flagstone walk, or low flowers? A stone wall with flagstone walk to the front door would make the most dignified treatment. The front yard is usually no place for a rock garden or flowers of any sort.

GRAVEL

I have been thinking of putting in a gravel path. Is it commonly used in the garden? Gravel paths are often used. They are inclined to look a bit formal and cold, however, and they are not so comfortable to walk upon as grass or tanbark.

STEPPINGSTONES

What sort of stones are suitable for a path of steppingstones? Water-washed flat stones with rounded edges are the most effective. If these are unobtainable, other flat stones or random slates or flagstones can be used, which are thick enough to bear the weight of traffic.

Are sections of tree trunks practical and long lasting as stepping "stones"? Yes, the chain saw has made it simple and inexpensive to cut flat cross sections of any sized tree trunk, 4–6″ thick. These can be treated with some wood preservative or used in their natural state as stepping stones in the garden and be expected to have a long life.

Is it possible to encourage the growth of moss? I want to put some between steppingstones. Moss can be started only by transplanting sods of it from some place where it naturally grows. Find a variety that is growing under similar conditions of sun or shade. Probably you will get better results by using plants of *Arenaria verna caespitosa,* which can be purchased.

Will you suggest some plants for placing between steppingstones? Various thymes, sedums, *Veronica repens, Mazus reptans, Potentilla tridentata, Achillea tomentosa, Tunica saxifraga.*

TANBARK

Do you recommend a tanbark path? Tanbark paths are expensive and do not adapt themselves to the small garden so well as several other types of path. They are suitable for woodland, rose, or rock gardens.

PATIOS

Which plants are suitable for a patio? In the northeast or north a patio might include a permanent planting of broad-leaved evergreens, an espaliered fruit tree (if there is a sunny wall), and a wisteria vine. Potted foliage plants (monstera, *Nephthytis afzelli,* dracaena, dieffenbachia, etc.) and potted geraniums, fuchsias, lantanas, begonias, and caladiums; crown-of-thorns and other succulents (such as crassulas) could be set out in warm weather. Patios in warm climates have a wider choice of plants, including such shrubs as oleanders, camellias, and gardenias; also bougainvillea and passiflora vines and other semitropical plant material.

I would like to have a patio garden. Would this be suitable with a colonial house? Patio gardens are usually made within a courtyard or similar enclosure. They are of Spanish origin and suited to this type of dwelling. However, if you have or can arrange a suitable protected terrace or courtyard adjacent to your colonial house, you might use flat stones or flagging to pave the area, put potted plants in white containers instead of Spanish pottery ones and, by using colonial ornaments and furniture, arrange a fitting outdoor living room which would serve the same purpose as a patio.

PERGOLAS

What is a pergola? A pergola is a passageway covered by an arbor which supports grapevines or large flowering vines. The structure is usually somewhat elaborate, with decorative columns and crosspieces. It is of Latin origin and is suitable to only a limited number of American gardens.

Is a pergola recommended for the small garden? A pergola can be useful in the small garden for supporting a grapevine over a path and provide a practical as well as ornamental accessory. It is sometimes effective to put a pergola over the path to the garage, thus softening the harsh effect of the building and providing a place for vines. Whenever it is used, the pergola should provide a passageway from one place to another.

POOLS

How should a small pool be constructed? The accompanying sketch shows a simple concrete pool and the necessary plumbing connections. For the successful growing of aquatics the deep part of the pool should be 1½ ft., and if it is to be used at all by birds, some part of it should be shallow enough for them. They do not like water more than 2 ins. deep.

How shall I go about building a small pool?   Excavate the ground about 6 ins. deeper on bottom and wider at the sides than you wish the pool to be. Insert drainage if pool is to be large enough to require it (see accompanying sketch); if it is very small, this will not be necessary. Fill hole with gravel layer, tamp down firm, or line with chicken wire. Pour cement, 1 part cement to 3 parts mixed sand and gravel. Add water enough so that mixture will spread evenly. Layer should be about 4 or 5 ins. thick. Next day finish with a coat of cement mortar, 1 part cement to 2 parts sand, applied with a trowel.

Cross-section detail of inflow and overflow for small pool.

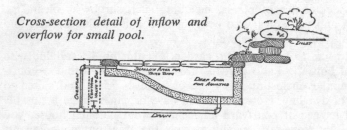

How thick should the concrete walls of a garden pool be?   The thickness of the walls of a pool depends on its size. A large pool naturally has to have thicker walls. For the average small pool (6 ft. or so in diameter) walls 6 ins. thick are sufficient. Some reinforcement in the form of wire or steel rods should be used.

How soon after finishing the construction of a small pool can plants be put in?   Leave the pool filled with water for about 2 weeks, flushing occasionally, before planting or putting in fish.

Are Plastic Pools feasible? I do not want to go to the expense of putting in a concrete pool, but would like to have a small pool for a few years' trial.   Plastic pools are now available in small sizes and are quite inexpensive when compared with concrete pools. Various types are frequently advertised in the garden magazines. They can be easily installed by any gardener.

I want to paint my pool blue. What kind of paint shall I use? There is a special paint available from seed or department stores for just this purpose.

I want to get some complete information on the construction of a small pool. Can you suggest some publication?   A book entitled "Garden Pools, Fountains, Recreation Areas" by R. H. Hawkins and C. H. Abbe, published by Van Nostrand of Princeton, N.J. contains excellent information on this subject.

What shape should a small pool be?   It depends on your location and general garden design. If your garden is informal, an informally shaped pool would be best. This should be basically circular or "egg-shaped" with gently curving, irregular contours. By using the garden hose to lay out the shape of the pool, good curves may be attained. Avoid sharp curves and too many irregularities. Simplicity is the keynote.

I want to build a small informal pool. About what size should I make it? A good-looking small pool might be about 25 sq. ft. in size.

I want to build a small formal pool with a fountain and statue at the back. What shape would be best for the pool? A round or oblong formal pool is always good. If your garden is very formal, you could have a rectangular pool.

Will gold fish live over winter in my pool? That depends on how deep and how large the pool is. Goldfish can live over in large pools that do not freeze solid in the winter, but will not live over winter in small pools that either freeze solid, or have only a few inches of water under the ice in winter. Under such conditions the fish actually smother to death.

STATUARY

I want to have some statuary in my garden. Can you suggest some types? In the small garden, care must be taken not to overdo use of statuary. One well-designed piece, not too large, used as a center of interest, is sufficient. A statue is usually placed at the end of a vista or in a niche formed of evergreens. It needs a background of green plant material to fit it into the garden picture. Avoid use of pottery figures of gnomes, ducks, etc., and other novelties.

A simple treatment of steps in a steep bank—English Ivy for year-round greenery.

STEPS

Of what shall I build my garden steps? Steps of stone with brick or flagstone treads harmonize well in many gardens. All-brick steps often look too harsh and formal. Field stone is all right if you can find enough flat ones. Concrete is much too unyielding.

Grass steps held in place by steel bands imbedded in the turf are beautiful but hard to make and to maintain. For very informal situations, sod, gravel, or tanbark steps held up by field-stone or log risers are most effective. Sometimes the steps themselves are made of squared sections of cypress or Black Locust logs.

SUNDIALS

Do you recommend using a sundial in the garden? A sundial is very effective in the right setting as the center of interest in a rose garden, or formal garden. It must, of course, be placed where the sun will hit it all day. The base can be planted with vines or low-blooming flowers. A sundial is usually placed at the axis where four paths meet, though a sunny position in a border or bed past which a path runs, is also good. Or it may occupy the center of a section of lawn.

TERRACES

How should I construct a flag terrace, and the steps down from it to the lawn? The flagstone, 2 ins. or so thick, can be laid on a bed of cinders or gravel covered with a thin layer of fine sand. No mortar is needed if the flags are heavy enough to stay in place. Slate cannot be used so easily. Brick can be substituted for flag. Steps should have treads with at least 1 in. overhang, and there should be a solid concrete foundation under them. Ramps, parapets, or wing walls should be substantial and have copings with the same overhang as the step treads. Steps and walls should be laid in cement mortar.

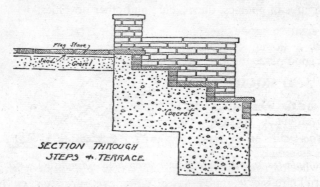

Cross-section detail for concrete and brick steps.

Which flowers will grow on a very windy terrace? Dwarf phlox, astilbe, dianthus, *Eupatorum coelestinum, Gypsophila repens,* hemerocallis, iberis, lavandula, *Anchusa myosotidiflora.*

Will you suggest a plant giving a long period of bloom for the

narrow border around my flagged lounging terrace? Lantana. Purchase young blossoming plants from a florist or seed store and plant 18 ins. apart. They will grow into sturdy shrubs by midsummer; not winter hardy. Try an edging of lobelia on the inside.

TOOL HOUSE

I want to fix up some space in my garage as a tool house and potting shed. How can I arrange this? Build a long bench, at convenient height for standing, to be used for potting plants, mixing sprays, etc. Under this have drawers or shelves for pots, labels, and baskets, and bins for fertilizers and mulching materials. Over the bench, racks may be built for holding vases, and strips of wood nailed close to the wall will be convenient holders for small tools such as trowels, dibbers, and hand cultivators. A space against one wall should be left for the wheelbarrow and lawn mower. Wooden racks for rakes, hoes, and other long-handled tools (which are hung handle down) can be made by nailing a strip of wood on the wall, about 6 ft. above the floor. Pairs of tenpenny nails protruding from this hold the tools. Or an overhead hanging shelf may be notched on both sides to accommodate tool handles. Heads of tools are placed above the shelf. The garden hose needs a special rack where it will not be damaged by sharp tools. A stout 2-ft. bracket jutting out from the wall will be convenient for this purpose.

Where and how can I provide a convenient storage place for my vegetable garden tools and equipment? A small addition to the garage, opening out into the vegetable garden, makes an ideal tool house. If the garden is fairly large and the garage not conveniently near, a small separate building, disguised as a garden house, will serve. On a sloping lot, enclosed space under a rear porch often makes a good place for this equipment.

TOOLS AND EQUIPMENT

What are the most essential tools for the gardener to have? Rake, hoe, shovel, spade, spading fork, trowel, lawn mower.

Will you name other desirable tools for the garden in addition to the main essentials? Onion hoe, hedge shears, grass shears, pruning shears, wheelbarrow, hose, hand cultivator, scuffle hoe, pruning saw, sharp knife, sickle, dibber, lawn roller, lawn sprinklers, cultivator and wheel hoe, manure fork, watering can, lawn weeder, lawn edger, bamboo or steel grass rake.

What is an onion hoe? An onion hoe has a very shallow blade which cultivates only the upper surface of the soil without cutting into the soil or "hacking." It is convenient for cultivating close to plant rows.

What is a scuffle or Dutch hoe?   A scuffle or Dutch hoe has a flat, sharp cutting blade which cultivates the upper part of the soil. It is efficient for making a dust mulch and for weeding.

What is a dibber?   A dibber is a small rounded piece of wood about 6 ins. in length and 1 to 2 ins. in diameter shaped to a rounded point, used for making holes in which to set plants or bulbs. Sometimes dibbers are made of metal or have the point cased in brass. They may be bought, but they are easily made at home from broken tool handles. The dibber should not have a sharp point. This causes a small air space in the bottom of the plant hole.

I want to buy a complete set of garden tools. Do you have any suggestions?   Never buy cheap tools; it doesn't pay. Buy good-quality tools from a reliable company. Avoid "novelties." Standard-type tools, suited to your needs, will usually give better results.

Should tools be cleaned after using?   Yes, decidedly. Wipe them off thoroughly, with a piece of burlap or an old rag each time after using. Rub occasionally with a cloth dipped in oil.

I want to store my tools through the winter. What shall I clean them with first?   Clean off all dirt and spots with an oily cloth.

Will plastic hose (set in the ground) last any appreciable time?   Yes; but plastic *pipe* is much better. This will last for years and makes it possible for gardeners to pipe water underground to all parts of the garden at very little cost. It is best to drain the hose or pipe in winter, but not absolutely essential since it will not crack or break when the water it contains freezes.

What accessories or equipment is necessary for gardening?   A line and reel, stakes, measuring rod (8 to 10 ft.), labels, basket, sprayers, dusters, tying material (twine and patent twisters), flowerpots, plant bands, bulb pans, seed sowers, flats, plant supports.

I have heard of "plant bands" but do not know what they are. Can you describe them?   Plant bands are used, in place of flowerpots, for potting young plants and seedlings. They are made of very thin wood, and are square, thus taking up less room than ordinary flowerpots and making them easy to fit into a flat for carrying. They will collapse when empty, so are easily stored. More important, they are deep enough to allow ample room for root development and are easily removed so that a large ball of earth may be left on the plant when transplanting.

Are there such things as pots that will disintegrate when set in the soil?   Yes, they are made of either heavy paper or a mixture of pressed manure or wood pulp and peat. Plants can be started in them in the greenhouse and then pot and all are planted out in the soil.

What are "canned plants"?   This probably refers to plants grown in tin cans or tubs so that they can be moved anytime during the spring, summer and fall. More and more small plants are being grown in this fashion throughout the entire country, making transplanting possible anytime during the growing season.

LABELS

What kind of labels do you suggest for seedling flats? Plain wooden labels, available in your local dime or seed store. Dip a corner of a clean rag in white paint and rub over the label. Then, while it is still wet, letter with an ordinary lead pencil.

What type label is best for greenhouse plants? Small border-type labels that fit down into the soil of the pot; or pointed wooden labels, in several lengths, like those recommended for flats.

What kind of label is best for the perennial border? Although border labels, similar to rock-garden labels, are sometimes recommended, they are inclined to heave during winter. Best results are usually obtained with wired labels fastened to garden stakes. These should be weather proof and copper-wired.

What type labels would you suggest for a rock garden? Four- or 5-in. weatherproof markers that are plunged into the soil and provide an oblong space for writing. One type has a blank space for marking which slides into a glassine pane; another need only be marked with a pencil on the outside and will remain legible.

I want to buy some labels for my rose garden. What kind would be best? Most permanent are of metal with the lettering pressed in. These are wired to the plant. If these are not available, get waterproof wired wooden ones, mark in waterproof ink, and wire to the plant.

TOPIARY WORK

What is topiary work? Pruning of hedges, shrubs, or trees in specific shapes, as of animals, houses, balls, spools, figures, or geometric forms. Used only in formal gardens and primarily associated with medieval landscape design. Practiced today more in Europe than in America. Boxwood and yew, and less frequently, privet, are employed for this purpose.

VIEWS

I have read that a garden should not "compete with a view." Why? How is it prevented? The intimate detail of a garden suffers by comparison with a wide view into the surrounding landscape. It is usually wiser to surround the garden with an enclosure to shut off outside views, but if these are worth-while, provision should be made to take advantage of them from some point outside the garden.

My house is surrounded by trees, but there is a fine view now ob-

scured by foliage. What should I do?   Do not hesitate to cut out trees to form a vista so that the view can be seen from some vantage point in the house or on the terrace. Often this can be achieved by removing lower branches rather than whole trees.

WALLS

Would a field-stone wall be satisfactory for fencing off a small garden?   In some localities it would be appropriate. A field-stone wall is suited to a country property rather than a city or suburban plot.

How should I construct a retaining wall, to be built of field stones? Since it may be called upon to withstand considerable pressure, a dry wall must have an adequate foundation, and the stones must be firmly bedded. The accompanying sketch shows that the foundation is as wide or wider than the wall and goes down below frost level. The face of the wall slopes back slightly, and all the stones are set with the long dimension horizontal. Use squarish rather than rounded stones, and use as large ones as you can get. Avoid "chinking" with small stones.

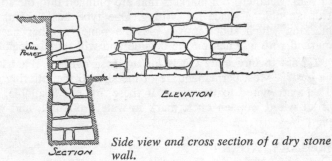

Side view and cross section of a dry stone wall.

How do you make soil pockets in a dry wall?   As the wall is being laid up, leave gaps all the way through it, about 4 ins. in diameter. Be sure these openings slope downward toward the back of the wall to keep soil and plants from being washed out. See that the soil is continuous from the face of the wall to the soil back of the wall to permit moisture to penetrate to it constantly. Fill the holes thus made with rich soil. Be sure the stones above them make solid bridges over the holes.

WEATHER VANES

Should weather vanes be used on small properties?   The use of weather vanes has been overdone in some sections. They are best used in the country, on barns, tool sheds, or other outbuildings. For a small place, get a simple style, not too large, to be used on the garage or garden house.

SPECIAL TYPES OF GARDENS

HERB GARDENS

WHAT TO GROW

Which herbs are annuals and which perennials? I am confused which ones to expect to come up a second year. The annual herbs most widely used are anise, dill, summer savory, fennel, coriander, and borage. The perennial herbs include horse-radish, lemon balm, winter savory, pot marjoram, sage, horehound, mint, tarragon, and beebalm. Parsley and caraway are, technically, biennials, but are grown as annuals. All of these grow in full sun and like a well-drained garden soil. Sow annuals as early in spring as weather permits, either in rows or broadcast.

Which herbs are the best to plant—annuals or perennials? This depends entirely upon your needs and garden facilities. A reasonably good selection of herbs includes both annuals and perennials.

Will you list 6 annual herbs for the kitchen garden? Basil, borage, chervil, parsley (really biennial but treated as an annual), Summer Savory, and Sweet Marjoram.

Sweet Marjoram and Summer Savory—two of the most popular annual herbs.

Which 6 perennial herbs do you suggest for the kitchen herb garden? Chives, horse-radish, mint, sage, tarragon, and thyme.

Which herbs do you suggest for a fragrant herb garden? Bergamot, lavender, lemonverbena, rosemary, scented geraniums, southernwood, sweet wormwood, lovage, valerian, lemon balm, sweetcicely, thyme, and costmary.

What herbs may be grown successfully at home, and preserved for winter use? Try the mints (if there is a moist spot in the garden, and care is taken to prevent the plants from overrunning their space); also sage, thyme, parsley, caraway, dill, and anise.

What are the best combinations of herbs for tea (as a beverage)? For flavoring tea, try mints or lemonverbena. In combination, one authority suggests equal parts of elder flowers and peppermint; another, peppermint and lemonverbena. Sage and chamomile, each used alone, make tasty beverages. Never use a metal container.

How should I start a small herb garden of a half-dozen varieties of herbs? Plant informally in little groups, taller plants more or less in back.

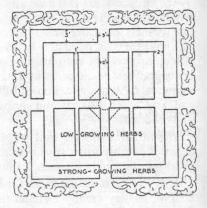

Design for a small formal herb garden.

Can you give some information on herbs—some to eat and some to smell? Good herbs for flavoring: basil (sweet) for salads, soups, and tomato sauces; chives for salads and pot cheese; dill for pickles; fennel to eat like celery, or cooked; sweet marjoram, seasoning for stuffings, etc.; mints for teas and sauces; rosemary for seasoning roasts and chicken; sage for dressing; savory (summer) for flavoring vegetables, particularly string beans; thyme, seasoning for foods and salads; tarragon, to flavor vinegar, and in salads. Herbs for scent: beebalm, lavender, lemonverbena, mints, and scented geraniums.

Which herbs grow successfully in the house? Basil, dittany of Crete, lemonverbena, parsley, rosemary, sweet marjoram, tarragon, and perhaps peppermint, if the room is cool and has plenty of light.

Which herbs do you suggest for an herbaceous border? Some of them grow too tall and scraggly. Lavender, calendula, marjoram, rosemary, rue, sage, thyme, hyssop, and the gray artemisias.

Which herbs are particularly attractive to bees? Thyme, lavender, germander, beebalm, lovage, hyssop, lemon balm, sweetcicely, borage, and marjoram.

Can you name some herbs suitable for low hedges? Hyssop, lavender, santolina, germander, southernwood, and rue. In fairly mild climates—rosemary.

Can you suggest herbs for a usable kitchen garden for the novice? Where can I get information as to their culture, preservation, and use? The following are particularly good for a beginner's garden: sage, tarragon, parsley, chives, shallots, basil, dill, rosemary, some of the thymes, and sweet marjoram. For further information write The Herb Society of America, 300 Massachusetts Ave., Boston, Massachusetts.

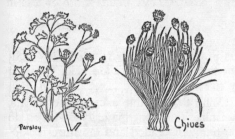

Parsley

Chives

Two of the most useful culinary herbs—Parsley and Chives—often grown in the vegetable plot.

Which geraniums are particularly suited for planting (in summer) in an herb garden? These geraniums are botanically *Pelargonium*. The lemon-scented, peppermint-scented, apple-scented, and rose-scented are all good. (See Fragrant Gardens.)

Do any herbs endure shade? Many medicinal herbs grow well in shade, among them bloodroot, digitalis, ginseng, goldenseal, selfheal, and snakeroot.

Which herbs will tolerate part shade? Balm, bergamot, chervil, sweet fennel, tarragon, sweet woodruff, mints, angelica, sweetcicely, parsley, comfrey, and costmary.

Can you give me information on herbs suitable for an herb rock garden? The garden should be well drained and sunny; the soil on the lean side rather than overrich. Almost any of the lower-growing herbs can be used effectively, with a few taller ones for accents.

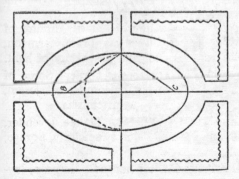

Method of laying out ellipses for a small herb garden. String is secured to stakes at B and C.

Of the varieties of herbs formerly imported, which ones can be grown in northern and central New York? Some of them are coriander, anise, fennel, dill, cumin, and sage.

What is ironweed? Several different plants have been shown me, but

I want to be sure, as I wish to use it in an old-time medical recipe. The ironweed of eastern United States is *Vernonia noveboracensis*. It usually grows in moist places, is 3 to 6 ft. high, and has open-branched cymes with many purple flowers. A full description is given in Gray's *Manual of Botany*.

SOIL

What general type of soil is preferred by herbs? Ordinary well-drained garden soil, lean rather than rich, and not too acid, suits the majority. Mints prefer a fairly rich, moist soil.

Do herbs like sandy soils? With the possible exception of mints, which require considerable moisture, the great majority of herbs do very well in sandy soil if some humus is added and moisture is supplied in very dry weather.

I understand that most herbs need dry soil conditions. Can you suggest some for a moist, but not waterlogged, place? Angelica, bergamot, sweetcicely, sweetflag, yellow-stripe sweetflag, lovage, mints, parsley, English pennyroyal, snakeroot, valerian, and violets.

PLANTING

What is the best exposure for an herb garden? A southeast exposure is ideal, but any location that gets full sunshine during the growing season will do. The soil and cultural practices, which include winter protection, are equally important.

A decorative herb garden at the kitchen door.

Must herbs be grown in an herb garden? No. They will thrive anywhere where soil and exposure are right: in the vegetable garden, by the kitchen door, in a dry wall (certain kinds), and good-looking ones in the flower border.

CULTURE

What are the general cultural requirements for herbs? A rather poor, well-drained sweet soil, warmth, sunlight, and a free circulation of air. Space the plants adequately, according to kind. Keep weeds down and surface soil tilled. This is a generalization; a number of herbs require distinctly different conditions.

What is the most practical arrangement of annual and perennial herbs—to interplant them, or to keep them separate? Plant the perennial kinds together and the annual kinds together. The area devoted to annuals can then readily be prepared afresh each spring and the perennial area is disturbed only every few years, when replanting becomes necessary.

Is it necessary to make more than one sowing of the various annual herbs each season? Yes, if it is desired to pick them fresh throughout the summer. About 3 sowings of most are desirable, the last made in late June or early July.

Is watering important in the herb garden? A few herbs (as mints) need generous supplies of moisture, but the majority develop their fragrances and flavors best when they are subjected to rather dry conditions; therefore, apply water with discrimination. Newly transplanted herbs and young plants need more attention in this respect than established plantings.

Should herbs be fertilized during the summer? The majority of true herbs require no fertilization. Feeding induces rank growth but does not favor the production of the essential oils which give to them their flavor and fragrance.

Can any non-hardy herbs be over-wintered successfully in a cold frame? Thyme, lavender, sage, and other "hardy" herbs which are often susceptible to winter killing can be kept over winter in a cold frame. Really tender subjects, like rosemary, pineapple sage, scented geraniums, and lemonverbena, must be kept in a temperature safely above freezing.

HARVESTING, CURING, AND STORING

Should herbs be washed before drying, and what is the appropriate time needed for this? What is a safe insecticide to use on these plants? Washing is not needed unless foliage is mud spattered. Time needed for drying varies according to kind and environment. A rotenone or pyrethrum insecticide is recommended.

How shall I cure herbs properly so as to retain their flavor? Dry as quickly as possible in a warm, airy, well-ventilated place, *without exposure to sun*.

How does one cure herb leaves for drying? Pick them just before the plants begin to flower, any time in the day after the dew has disappeared. Tie in bundles, each of a dozen stems or so. Hang in an airy, warm, but not sunny place. When they are completely dry and crisp, strip off leaves and put in tight jars. The leaves may also be stripped fresh, right after cutting, and placed in shallow screen-bottomed trays until dry.

When should herb seeds be harvested? When they have matured, and before they fall naturally from the plants.

How should herb seeds be dried? Collect the heads or seed pods and spread them in a tray made of screening, or in a thin layer on a cloth in a warm, well-ventilated room. Turn them frequently. At the end of a week or so they will be dry enough for threshing.

What is the best method of storing dried herbs? In airtight containers.

How can seeds in quantity, such as caraway, be best separated from stems and chaff? Remove as much of the stems as possible. Rub the heads or pods between the palms of the hands. If possible, do this outdoors where a breeze will help carry away the chaff. A kitchen strainer or screen is useful in the final cleaning.

GENERAL

What are "simples"? Herbs that possess, or are supposed to possess, medicinal virtues.

What is the "Doctrine of Signatures"? An ancient belief that plants, by the shape or form of their parts, indicated to man their medicinal uses. The spotted leaves of the lungwort showed that this plant was a cure for diseases of the lungs; the "seal" on the roots of Solomonseal promised the virtue of sealing or closing broken bones and wounds; and so on.

Can you recommend a good book on herbs and herb culture? *Herbs, How to Grow Them,* by Helen N. Webster; *Herbs, Their Culture and Uses,* by R. E. Clarkson; *Gardening with Herbs for Flavor and Fragrance,* by H. M. Fox; and *Old Time Herbs for Northern Gardens,* by M. W. Kamm, are all excellent.

Am interested in medicinal herbs. Are there any books on same? *Try Growing Herbs,* by Helen M. Whitman, published by The Tool Shed Press, Bedford, New York; and *Medicinal Plants,* by Crooks and Sievers, published by the United States Department of Agriculture.

COMMERCIAL GROWING

Where can I obtain information on commercial herb growing? The following bulletins give information on this subject: *Circular 157,*

New York State Agricultural Experiment Station, Geneva, New York; *Circular 83*, Vermont State College of Agriculture, Rutland, Vermont; *Circular 104*, Michigan State College of Agriculture, East Lansing, Michigan; *Bulletin 461*, Indiana College of Agriculture, Purdue, Indiana; *Circular 149*, Connecticut Agricultural Experiment Station, New Haven, Connecticut; and *Extension Circular 64*, Minnesota Agricultural College, University Farm, Minnesota. Also *Miscellaneous Publication 77, Circular 581*, and *Farmers' Bulletins Nos. 1184* and *1555*, all obtainable from Office of Publications, United States Department of Agriculture, Washington, D.C.

HERB WHEELS

I would like to put plants around the spokes of an old wagon wheel that I have. How would you suggest doing this? A wagon wheel or oxcart wheel can be made the central feature of a small, formal herb garden. Select a level, sunny spot in the garden with enriched, well-prepared soil. Place the hub down into the ground and put a few plants of each variety in between the spokes. A narrow path edged with thyme can surround the wheel. Low-growing, compact plants are better for a wheel-planting than tall, straggly ones.

What culinary herbs would be best in a "wheel garden"? Thyme, chives, sage, parsley, mint, lemon balm, French tarragon, winter savory, sweet basil, sweet marjoram, chervil. Or the wheel can be planted exclusively with low-growing varieties of thyme.

Would you suggest some fragrant herbs that would look well planted in an oxcart wheel? Lemonverbena, mint, southernwood, rosemary, Rose Geranium, santolina, sweetcicely. (See Herbs.)

I want to plant some small, bright-blooming flowers in a wagon wheel. What would you suggest? Dwarf marigolds, zinnias, linaria, alyssum, lobelia, portulaca, ageratum, dwarf anchusas.

SPECIFIC HERBS

ANGELICA

How do you grow angelica and what is it used for? Sow in fall as soon as seed is ripe, thin out seedlings, and transplant following spring. Soil should be moist and fairly rich. Light shade is beneficial. The seeds are slow to germinate. The plant is biennial under some conditions, so it is better to sow a few seeds each year to maintain a supply. The stems and leafstalks are used for salads and candied to decorate confections; the seeds for flavoring and for oil.

ANISE

Can you give some information on growing anise? It is an annual, so it must be sown each year. The seeds should be fresh because old seed will not germinate. Sow when the soil has warmed a little (about beginning of May) in rows where the plants are to stand (anise does not transplant readily). Prepare the soil deeply and make it very fine. Sow in rows 15 ins. apart and thin the plants out to 9 ins. apart in the rows. Water in very dry weather.

BALM

Is balm difficult to grow? Is it a useful herb?   Lemon balm or sweet balm (*Mellisa officinalis*) is a hardy perennial of easy culture. It can be grown from seeds sown in prepared soil in July or August; the seedlings are transplanted, when large enough, to their flowering quarters. Balm can also be propagated by division in spring. Any ordinary garden soil is satisfactory. The leaves of balm are used for seasoning, particularly liqueurs. They are also used for salads and for potpourris.

Sweet Basil

BASIL

Can you give me information on growing basil? When should I sow the seeds?   Seeds are sown outdoors after settled warm weather has arrived; or they are started indoors in April and the seedlings transplanted outdoors later. Allow 12 ins. apart between plants. Basil yields abundantly. When cut, it repeatedly sends out new growth. Plants can be lifted in the fall and potted for winter use if desired.

BORAGE

Is borage annual or perennial? Can it be grown from seed?   An annual, easily grown from seed in any good garden soil. Sow in spring when all danger of frost is past. The seedlings can be transplanted if care is exercised, but the plants are better if grown undisturbed. About 15 ins. should be allowed between plants.

CARAWAY

How is caraway grown?   From seeds sown outdoors in late May in rows 2 ft. apart. The plants are thinned to about 9 ins. apart. The first year low-growing plants are formed; the second year seeds are produced; then the plants die. Seed is most abundantly produced if the soil is not too rich. Do not water much, as this tends to keep the stems soft and causes the blossoms to fall before setting seed. Dry, sunny weather favors this crop.

CHERVIL

How is chervil grown? From seeds sown in spring where the plants are to grow. Thin plants to stand 9 ins. apart. Light shade is beneficial. Chervil is an annual.

CHIVES

Can chives be grown from seeds or must I buy plants? They can be grown from seeds sown outdoors early in spring. Thin the little plants out to about ½ in. apart. They are hardy perennials, multiply rapidly, and need little attention. Divide every second year. They like a moderately moist soil.

CLARY

Clary dies out with me. Is it difficult to grow? Clary is a biennial and dies after flowering. Sow seeds in early spring; thin out to 6 ins. apart; as the plants develop pull out every other one. Those removed can be dried for use. The plants bloom and set seeds the second year. A rich soil is advantageous.

CORIANDER

Is it easy to grow coriander seed? Yes. Sow (thinly) in spring in well-drained, average soil and in sunny position. Thin out to stand 9 or 10 ins. apart. Plants and fresh seeds are unpleasantly scented, but ripe seeds become very fragrant as they dry.

COSTMARY

How is costmary grown? Propagate it from seeds or by root division. Plant in full sun or very light shade. Space plants about 3 ft. apart. Lift and replant every third year. A freely drained soil is needed.

Dill

DILL

How do you grow dill? Dill is a fast-growing annual that matures in about 70 days. Sow in early spring in well-prepared soil, in rows

2 ft. apart, where the plants are to stand. The plants grow about 3 ft. tall and make a good-sized bush. Thin out the seedlings to 3 or 4 ins. apart at first; later give a final thinning so that they stand a foot apart.

DITTANY OF CRETE

What is dittany of Crete and how is it grown in the herb garden? It is *Origanum dictamnus*. Increase it by seeds or cuttings. It is not hardy where winters are cold and must be wintered indoors in pots. A sandy soil, perfect drainage, and full sun are cultural desiderata.

FENNEL

Have you data on perennial fennel that grows 10 ft. tall?   The common fennel (*Foeniculum vulgare*) has escaped to the wild down South and grows 8 ft. in height. In colder climates, fennel is less tall, rarely reaching 4 ft.

How is Florence fennel grown?   As an annual. Seeds are sown in spring where the plants are to mature. The seedlings are thinned out to 6 ins. apart. The plants mature in about 60 days.

GINGER

Can ginger root be grown in New York State?   Common ginger (*Zingiber officinale*) is a tropical plant adapted for culture only in warm climates. The wildginger (*Asarum canadense*) is a native of our own rich woodlands. It responds to cultivation if given a rich, rather moist soil.

DIGITALIS

Is the foxglove (digitalis) a perennial?   No, a biennial, although occasionally a plant will persist for 3 years. Sow seeds each June. They like a well-drained soil that is deep and fairly moist.

Can digitalis (foxglove) be grown in partial shade?   Yes, if you are growing it for its decorative effect; but when raised commercially for drug purposes it must be grown in full sun, as the valuable alkaloid does not develop satisfactorily in shade-grown plants.

HORSE-RADISH

See Section V.

HYSSOP

What are the cultural requirements of hyssop?   Give this perennial full sun or light shade, and a warm, freely drained well-limed soil. Allow about a foot between plants. Trim plants back after flowering. Easily propagated by seeds, cuttings, or root division.

LAVENDER

What is the care and use of lavender? Grows well in any well-drained soil, not too acid, in a dry, sunny place. Protect in winter with evergreen boughs; but, even with protection, plants 3 years old or more have a way of dying back in winter. Cut dead branches back in spring after new growth near base is fairly strong. It is best propagated from cuttings of the season's growth taken in the late fall or early spring. The plants are grown for ornament and fragrance. The flowers are used in perfumes, aromatic vinegar, sachets, and are tied into bundles for use in linen closets, etc.

How can I make lavender plants bloom? They give much more prolific bloom, with better fragrance, if grown in a light, well-drained soil high in lime content. Rich or heavy soils encourage foliage growth rather than bloom.

When should lavender flowers be harvested? Just as soon as they are fully open.

Can sweet lavender grow and live over winter as far North as Boston? *Lavandula officinalis* should, if given good winter protection.

Do you have to protect thyme and lavender in winter, and how? The true lavender, *Lavandula officinalis,* is hardier than others of its kind. However, it prefers a sheltered spot. Both lavender and thyme die during the winter because of excessive moisture rather than of cold. Salt hay or evergreen boughs are good mulches. It is safer, if there is any question about the drainage, to winter both of these plants, in the North, in a cold frame.

How can I start lavender from seed? Seeds are rather slow to germinate, and the tiny plants grow slowly. Start seeds indoors in early spring, and set out the new plants after all danger of frost is past. Do not allow them to bloom the first year. Protect through first winter by placing them in a cold frame, if possible. A well-drained soil is essential to success.

Can I propagate lavender from cuttings? Take 2-in. shoots off the main stems and branches in late fall or early spring, each with a "heel" (or portion of older wood) attached to its base. Cut the heel clean. Remove lower leaves for about 1 in. from base. Insert in well-packed sand in a cool greenhouse, and keep the sand moist. Slight bottom heat will help rooting. While roots are not more than ½ in. long, put up in small pots in a mixture of ½ sand, ½ soil. Keep in cool greenhouse for winter if fall-made cuttings, or in a cold frame if spring made.

LEMONVERBENA

How is lemonverbena grown? Lemonverbena is a tender shrub which, in cold climates, must be taken in for the winter. Cut plants back in fall; water just enough to keep them from drying out. In February bring into the light, in a cool temperature. Repot and set out again in the garden when danger of frost is past.

When should cuttings of lemonverbena be made? In fall, when the plants are trimmed back before being brought inside; or in spring, when new growth is made. Give same treatment as advised for cuttings of lavender.

LOVAGE

Is lovage suitable for a tiny herb garden? Hardly. It is a perennial 6 or 7 ft. tall, and plants need to be spaced about a yard apart.

What soil and culture for the herb lovage that has flavor of celery? Propagate by seeds sown in early fall, or by root division in spring. Provide a rich, moist soil in full sun or light shade.

MARJORAM

Can you winter over in the house a plant of marjoram dug up from the herb garden? If you refer to sweet marjoram, this is the only way to keep it for another year. It is a tender perennial, sensitive to frost. Pot the plant in September, before there is any danger of frost, and let it get accustomed to its new quarters before bringing it indoors. Cuttings can be rooted in September, keeping the young plants indoors also. Pot marjoram is a hardy perennial.

In what soil and situation, and how far apart, should sweet marjoram plants be set? Give light, well-drained, non-acid soil; full sun; space 9 or 10 ins. apart. This is a tender perennial that may be grown as an annual. Sow seed in spring. It is slow to germinate.

Are there any hardy perennial kinds of marjoram? Yes. Pot marjoram, showy marjoram, and wild marjoram. Of these, pot marjoram is the best known for culinary purposes.

MINT

Would like a list of all mints that can be grown, and is there a sale for them and where? The mints are very numerous. Write The Herb Society of America, 300 Massachusetts Ave., Boston, Massachusetts, with regard to these and to their marketability.

What is the culture of peppermint? How is oil extracted from it? Grows best in deep, rich, humusy soil which is open and well drained. The runners are planted in spring, 2 to 3 ft. apart, in shallow trenches. Keep well cultivated and free from weeds. When in full bloom the plants are cut and cured like hay. The oil is extracted by distillation with steam. For information concerning commercial cultivation ask the Department of Agriculture, Washington, D.C.

Why can't I start a successful mint patch? Mints are usually easy and very weedy. They like rich, humusy soil and plenty of moisture. Cultivate and weed them well. They should grow.

POTMARIGOLD

What is potmarigold? What is it used for? Is it hard to grow? *Calendula officinalis*—one of our most useful decorative annuals. As an herb, the flower heads are used for seasoning and coloring butter. It thrives best in cool weather. Sow outdoors in spring, or indoors in March for spring planting. Transplant 12 ins. apart. Sow again about July 1 for fall crop. The plants from this sowing will grow on into late fall and will survive light frost.

Rosemary

ROSEMARY

What is the best way to grow rosemary? Rosemary is a tender shrub, not hardy in the North; but it may be plunged outdoors in a sunny, sheltered spot during the summer, and carried over winter in a cool, light room. Pot in well-drained soil to which a sprinkling of lime has been added. Propagate by cuttings.

What is the best protection for rosemary in this location? (Illinois.) It is a tender shrub and must be brought in for the winter in cold climates. If there is not space for so large a plant, make a few cuttings, which will root readily in moist sand and be ready to set out in the spring.

RUE

Is rue hardy in Northern gardens? Could you give its culture? Rue is hardy to Long Island, N.Y. It will not winter over outdoors in very severe climates, so it is much safer to keep it indoors during winter. It is easily grown from seeds sown early in spring in rows 18 ins. apart. Thin seedlings to 8 ins. apart, and again remove every other one. Keep the soil well cultivated. The leaves can be used whenever they are large enough. Any ordinary garden soil is satisfactory.

SAGE

Which variety of sage is used for culinary use? *Salvia officinalis.*

I have been unsuccessful in growing sage. What are its needs? Sage enjoys best a sweet, well-drained, light sandy soil. Sow seeds in very early spring, or in August; or set out good-sized plants in early spring. Sage is not difficult. Give very little water; cultivate during the early part of the season. In spring give a light dressing of bone meal. Easily propagated by means of cuttings.

What are the methods of cultivating sage? See preceding question. Transplant to permanent position when seedlings are 3 to 4 ins. high. Plant in rows 2 ft. apart with 12 ins. between the plants in the row. Cut back established plants in spring to let new growth develop. Do not overwater.

Can sage planted from seed be used and dried first year it is planted? Yes. Don't strip the whole plant bare, however. Take only the largest leaves, or a branch here and there.

When is the best time to "pick" sage; and what is the best method of curing it? Harvest in late summer. Cut shoots before they bloom, tie into bundles, and hang up; or strip leaves and place loosely in shallow trays in a warm, airy place, not exposed to sun.

How does one gather sage? Shoots may be cut twice or three times during summer and early fall.

SAVORY

What kind of soil and culture does savory need? There are 2 kinds of savory: summer savory (annual) and winter savory (perennial). Both grow best in a rather poor but well-limed soil, in an exposed sunny site. The annual kind is considered better than the perennial. The seeds are very small and are best sown indoors in pots and barely covered. Watering is done by immersing the pot in water, as the seeds wash out easily. Seedlings are set out when all danger of frost is over. Set seedlings in rows, 8 ins. between plants, 15 ins. between rows. The perennial sort can be handled in the same way.

SWEETCICELY

What are the garden requirements for growing sweetcicely? Sow seed in early fall, in well-drained average soil, and in light shade. When plants are mature they should stand 18 to 20 ins. apart. It is a hardy perennial and may be increased by root division.

SWEETFLAG

I want to grow sweetflag in my herb garden. Does it need full sun?

Full sun is not necessary, but it must have moist soil. It is really a waterside plant. Propagated by division of rhizomes.

SWEET WOODRUFF

What conditions in the garden does sweet woodruff need? An open, rather moist soil, where drainage is good, and shade or partial shade. A fine perennial ground-cover plant in the right location.

TARRAGON

What soil for tarragon? Shade or sun? Almost any well-drained garden soil. Sun preferred, but will endure light shade.

Will you give me all information possible to grow tarragon? When to plant? Tarragon, a hardy perennial, needs a well-drained soil, moderately rich, with considerable lime. It does best in a lightly shaded location. This plant, since it seeds but little, is propagated by stem or root cuttings, or by division. Stem cuttings are taken any time during the summer, rooted in sand, and planted out. Root cuttings or divisions can be set out in early spring, 12 ins. apart. Do not use chemical fertilizer to force growth, as the quality of the leaves is affected by a too-rich diet.

THYME

I would like to grow thyme for seasoning. Will it stand our severe winters? (Western New York.) There are many varieties of the common thyme that may be used in the herb garden. The greatest menace to thymes during the winter is not so much cold as wetness. Wet crowns, caused by snow, will winter kill. One of the means of preventing this is to grow on rather poor soil, containing gravel or screened cinders. Do not feed in summer to force growth, and do not cut tops after September 1. A cold frame is an excellent place to keep thyme over the winter, where it will be dry. Otherwise, covering the plants with boxes to keep the snow off will help materially. Be certain their position is well drained to begin with. Seeds and plants are available from most houses listing herbs.

How can I grow common thyme? What soil? Shade? Sun? (Massachusetts.) It is best grown on a light, well-drained soil. If the soil is inclined to heaviness, work in screened cinders or gravel. Seeds can be sown in early spring outdoors, or earlier in pots indoors. Transplant seedlings 6 ins. apart. When growth is advanced, do not water much; omit fertilizer, as this tends to force soft growth that will winter kill. Do not cut foliage after September 1, as this depletes vitality. Winter protection is given by covering with light evergreen boughs, or by using brushwood with a light covering of marsh or salt hay. Lift and divide every 2 or 3 years. Grow in full sun.

Will you name several creeping thymes for planting in steps and paths?   Mother-of-thyme (*Thymus serpyllum* and its variety *lanuginosus*); Caraway Thyme (*T. herba-barona*); British Thyme (*T. britannicus*).

WATERCRESS

How could I grow watercress for table use in my home garden that has no water?   Watercress is a plant of running water, growing in the edge of clear, fresh streams. It may be grown, after a fashion, in a moist spot in the garden, and the plants will last for a time in such a location if it is shady, but they will not live through the winter unless covered with water. They become true perennials only when grown in running water. As an alternative, you can grow the garden cress, or peppergrass. This is an annual, and furnishes salad in 3 to 4 weeks. Sow seed thickly in shallow drills 12 ins. apart. Make 2 sowings, 2 weeks apart in spring, and 2 sowings in August.

POTPOURRIS

Would you please tell me where I may obtain information for formulas for making rose jars, potpourris, and sachets?   A good book containing complete information on this subject is *Magic Gardens,* by Rosetta E. Clarkson, published by the Macmillan Company.

What leaves and petals can be used for making potpourri?   Any leaves or petals that have a pleasing fragrance may be used. Some of the best are rose, lavender, lemonverbena, jasmine, marigold, stock, mignonette, heliotrope, violet, geranium, rosemary, lemon balm, mint, southernwood, santolina, pink, wallflower, thyme.

I want to make a potpourri of rose petals from my garden. How can I do this?   Pick the rose petals (red holds its color best) when the flowers are in full bud but not completely blown. Spread them carefully on sheets of paper or strips of cheesecloth in a dry, airy room, away from the sun. Turn daily. Let them dry completely. This will take from a few days to a week. To each quart of petals add 1 oz. of orrisroot. Spices such as cloves, cinnamon, coriander, and mace may be added, if desired, ½ teaspoon of each. Keep in an airtight earthen jar.

What is "wet potpourri" and how is it made?   Potpourri made by the wet method contains rose petals and the petals of any other fragrant flowers that are available. These are spread on cloths or papers to dry out partially. They are then packed in an earthenware jar with layers of table salt or coarse salt between. Add a layer of petals, then a sprinkling of salt, until the jar is filled. One oz. of orrisroot or violet powder is added, and, if desired, some cloves, allspice, and cinnamon. Put a weight on the petals and let them stand in the jar, covered, for several weeks before mixing. In addition to rose petals, lavender, lemonverbena leaves, and geranium leaves are the most commonly used ingredients.

What is a "fixative," and for what is it used in potpourris? A fixative is used to retain the natural scent of leaves or petals and aids in preserving them. Orrisroot, violet powder, ambergris, and gum storax are common fixatives.

In making a sweet jar of flower petals, what can be used to keep the natural color of such flowers as delphinium, pansy, aconitum, and other colorful blooms? If the flowers are carefully dried, out of direct sunlight, they partially retain their color naturally. Orrisroot also seems to have a color-fixing effect.

ROCK GARDENS

PLANNING

To build, or not to build, a rock garden is the question with us. Answerman, what counsel? Can you fit this kind of garden properly into your home landscape without the effect being unnatural? Is there a bank or slope that could be utilized in making the garden? Have you access to natural rock material that could be used? If the area is all level, is there a section where low, natural rock outcrops could be simulated? The extent of the garden will be determined by the time, labor, and money that can be spent on it. A rock garden is costly to build and costly to maintain. These are the facts that need to be considered in deciding to build—or not to build.

Outcropping ledges of rock make an ideal setting for a rock garden. Where such a site is not available, every effort should be made to simulate the same effect.

Will I have as much in a rock garden as in other kinds of gardens? The floral display will be concentrated between early spring and mid-June. From then on your enjoyment will come mostly from pleasing mats and mounds and spreading foliage effects; these are decidedly worth-while.

Can I have flowers in a rock garden all summer long? Yes, by introducing a variety of small annuals and summer- and autumn-flowering bulbs. The use of these may relieve monotony; but it may easily be overdone and spoil the illusion of a mountain garden, which has but one main, brilliant burst of blossom, in the spring.

How can I best fit a rock garden into my place? Use, if you have it, a somewhat steep slope, not overhung by foliage. A natural ledge of porous rock, of acceptable, weathered appearance, and provided with deep fissures, is ideal. Where such a ledge lies buried, it pays to expose and use it.

What exposure is best for a rock garden? For easy-to-grow, sun-loving plants, such as many sedums, pinks and rockcresses, any exposure but a north one. For gardens containing also more finicky, choicer plants, if along a building or a fence, an east exposure; otherwise, an open slope facing east or northeast. As between south and north slopes, choose the latter.

Is there a rock-garden organization? Yes, the American Rock Garden Society, Secretary, 238 Sheridan Avenue, Ho-Ho-Kus, New Jersey.

SOIL AND FERTILIZER

Should the rock-garden soil mixture be acid or alkaline? Some rock plants insist upon acid, some on alkaline soil. But most will do with an approximately neutral soil; it is, therefore, best to provide this kind of mixture throughout, and then to acidify or alkalize special areas for particular plants.

Do all rock-garden plants need a specially prepared soil? No. Many robust, easy-to-grow plants, such as most sedums, pinks, and rockcresses, will thrive in soil that would suit other garden plants. But in sharply drained places even these will be helped by an admixture of some peatmoss, to help retain moisture in summer.

What is a good average rock-garden mixture? Approximately 1 part each of good garden loam, fine leafmold, peatmoss, sand, and fine gravel (preferably ⅛-in. screen). The mixture should be gritty. It should let surface water penetrate promptly, but should be retentive enough to hold a reasonable supply of moisture.

What depth of prepared soil is desirable in a rock garden? About 1 ft. For gardens made above the surrounding grade, there should be, underneath, another foot of a coarse mixture of rubble and retentive ingredients, such as peatmoss or sphagnum moss, to act as a sponge.

In a rock garden is it necessary to provide the great depth of drainage that I read about in books? For gardens laid above the grade—no. In sunken gardens or in low-lying parts, unfailing provision must be made to prevent stagnant moisture below. In our dry summer climate we must think of drainage in reverse as well— of retaining some moisture below, which later will find its way back to the surface.

I have a rock garden at the side of my house and would like to rearrange it. Can you make any suggestions concerning soil preparation and enrichment? It should be deeply dug, and a liberal amount of peatmoss added. Also incorporate cinders, leafmold, well rotted manure, a little bone meal, and a little tankage.

What is the best fertilizer to use for rock-garden plants, and when should I put it on? The majority of rock-garden plants should not be heavily fed; rich feeding causes soft growth which invites disease and leaves the plants subject to winter killing. Mix in fine bone meal and leafmold with the soil when preparing it, and in early spring dress established plantings with a top-dressing containing bone meal mixed with soil and leafmold.

CONSTRUCTION

What type of rock is best for rock gardens? Any porous, weathered rock that will look natural in place. It is all the better if it is deep fissured. Use only one kind of rock throughout the garden.

What about tufa rock? No rock is more acceptable to a wide diversity of plants than a soft, porous grade of tufa. But because of its glaring, bony color in sunny places it is not an attractive-looking material. In shade, and moisture, it quickly accumulates mosses and then becomes very beautiful.

Are large rocks desirable, or will small ones do as well? Construction should simulate Nature. She works with massive rocks. Therefore, in gardens large or small use rocks as large as you can handle; or match smaller ones together in such manner that they will create an effect of large masses.

Can you give me a few pointers on the placing of rocks? Embed the rockwork deeply enough to create an effect of natural outcroppings. Leave no lower edges exposed to betray superficial placing. Have the several rock masses extend in parallel directions, and carry out this principle even with the lesser rocks. Match joints and stratifications carefully. Try to get the rhythm of natural ledges and outcroppings.

How shall I build a rockery in a corner of my level lawn? In the foreground of corner shrubbery create the effect of a smoothish, shelved outcropping with several broad, low shelves. Push this arrangement back far enough for the shrubs to mask the sheer drop behind.

How should I arrange a rock garden and pool in the center of a small lawn without natural elevation of rock? Create the effect of one large, flattish, or somewhat humped rock, broken, so as to provide two or more broad crevices for planting. Locate the pool, somewhat off-center, immediately against this rock effect.

Have you any suggestions for a little rock garden, of slight elevation, with shrubbery as a background? Place or simulate the effect of one large, flattish outcropping, with fissures or wide joints for planting. Place the pool immediately against this rock mass. Your idea of a background of shrubs is excellent.

PLANTING

When is the best time to plant rock gardens? If pot-grown plants are available and you can arrange to water and shade them carefully, planting may be done almost any time from spring to early autumn. Spring is a proper season everywhere. In moderately cold climates (as in lower New York State), September and October are also good months.

What rock-garden plants should one set out in early spring? (New Mexico.) Any of the sedums, pinks (dianthus), dwarf phlox, primroses, painted daisies, bellflowers, and saponarias as well as most any other rock plants.

I am planting a rock garden. What distance between the plants will be necessary? Much will depend upon the kind of plants you are using. If they are spreading kinds, such as cerastium, phlox, helianthemum, sedums, thyme, and dianthus, set the plants about 12 ins. apart. Plants that spread more slowly, such as primulas, sempervivums, saxifragas, candytufts, arenarias, aubrietas, douglasia, anemones, pulsatillas, and the dwarf achilleas, plant 6 to 8 ins. apart.

How deep should rock plants be set in the ground? Most form a spreading top that either roots as it spreads or grows directly from a central root system. The crown of the plant must not be covered. Dig a hole with a trowel; gather the loose tops in the hand; hold the plant at the side of the hole, the crown resting on the surface, the roots extending into the hole while held in position; firm the soil around the roots. When the hole is filled, the crown should be resting on the surface. A good watering will then help establish it.

The soil on the slopes in my rock garden keeps washing out, especially after planting. How can I prevent this? If a considerable stretch is exposed, set in a few good-sized rocks at irregular intervals and tilt them so that their upper surfaces slope downward into the hill. Into the surface 2 ins. incorporate screened cinders mixed with peat or leafmold. Set the plants in groups 9 to 12 ins. apart (depending on their size) and cover the spaces between the groups with peat or leafmold until the plants effect a covering.

CULTURE

What are the main items of upkeep in a rock garden? Weeding; thinning; repressing too-rampant growths; removal of old flower stalks; occasional division of robust plants; watering; winter covering.

For the choicer, high-mountain plants, maintain a gravel mulch about their base and top-dress with compost on steep slopes each spring.

When is the best time to trim and thin plants that begin to overrun a rockery? Cut back the running kinds any time during their growing period.

Will you please discuss spring work in the rock garden? Remove winter covering when all danger of frost is over. If there is danger of cold winds and some plants have started to grow, uncover gradually. Firm back into the soil any plants that have been loosened. Replant as may be necessary. Top-dress with a mixture of 3 parts good soil, 1 part old, rotted manure, leafmold, or peatmoss, and 1 part coarse sand or screened cinders, with a 6-in. potful of fine bone meal added to each wheelbarrowload. When top-dressing, work this down around the crowns of the plants and over the roots of spreading kinds by hand. If a dry spell occurs in spring, give a good watering.

WATERING

How should the rock garden be watered and how often? With a fine sprinkler, so as to avoid washing the soil off the roots. Frequency of watering depends upon type of soil, amount of slope, kind of plants, and whether they are established or are newly planted, amount of shade, exposure, and of course weather. If dry spells occur in spring and early autumn, watering should be done in a very thorough fashion; toward late summer, unless a very prolonged dry spell occurs, watering should be confined to such plants as primulas, globeflowers, and other moisture-lovers. Ripening and hardening of most rock plants are necessary if they are to winter over properly.

WINTER PROTECTION

What is the best winter cover? When applied and when removed? A single thickness of pine boughs or any narrow leaved evergreen that will hold its leaves all winter after being cut. It is more quickly applied and removed than salt hay. Apply after the surface has frozen solid. It is needed, not as a protection against frost, but against thawing of the soil. Remove when danger of very hard frost seems past. Just when is always something of a gamble.

Is salt hay a good winter cover? Yes, but it is not quickly removable in the spring. Use it lightly, lest you invite mice and kindred vermin.

WHAT TO GROW

Will you please name a dozen foolproof rock-garden plants, stating flower color and season? *Alyssum saxatile citrinum* (lemon-yellow; May), *Arabis albida* (double-flowered, white; April to May), *Arabis procurrens* (white, April to May), *Campanula carpatica* (blue; July),

Ceratostigma plumbaginoides (blue; September to October), *Dianthus plumarius* (white and varicolored; June), *Phlox subulata* varieties (white, rose, dark rose, pink; May), *Sedum sieboldi* (rose; September to October), *Sedum album* (white; June), *Sedum ellacombianum* (yellow; July), *Thymus serpyllum coccineum* (deep rose; July), and *T. s. album* (white; June to July).

Can you give a list of some of the best rock plants for spring flowers? *Alyssum saxatile, Anemone pulsatilla, Arabis albida* (double-flowered), *Aubrieta deltoides, Corydalis halleri, Crocus* species, *Epimedium niveum, Scilla sibirica* and *S. bifolia,* and *Tulipa kaufmanniana.*

What are the best plants for a rockery for early spring and midsummer bloom? For early spring: *Tulipa kaufmanniana, Crocus* species, snowdrops, *Scilla sibirica,* and grapehyacinths. Non-bulbous plants: *Arabis albida, Aubrieta deltoides, Viola odorata,* primulas, *Anemone pulsatilla, Armeria caespitosa, Alyssum saxatile* and *A. saxatile luteum,* drabas, epimediums, *Erysimum ruprestre,* and *Phlox subulata.* For midsummer bloom: *Dianthus plumarius, Campanula carpatica, Antirrhinum asarina, Bellium bellidioides, Campanula cochlearifolia, Carlina acaulis, Globularia cordifolia, Lotus corniculatus, Dianthus knappi, Linum alpinum, Linaria alpina, Nierembergia caerulea,* penstemons, *Rosa rouletti, Santolina viridis, Silene achafta,* and *Ceratostigma plumbaginoides.*

Will you list a few of the best rock plants to flower from about May 15 to early June? *Dianthus neglectus, D. plumarius, D. strictus, D. arenaria, Cymbalaria pallida, Dodecatheon* species, *Gentiana acalis, Saxifraga* (encrusted species), and *Veronica teucrium rupestris.*

Can you name 12 good perennials suitable for rock gardens, which bloom at different periods? *Phlox subulata* and varities (April to May), *Aubrieta deltoides* (May), *Alyssum saxatile* and its variety *luteum* (May), *Primula polyanthus* (May), *Dianthus plumaris* (June), *Campanula carpatica* (June), *Lotus corniculatus* (July), *Veronica spicata alba* (June to July), *Thymus serpyllum* and its varieties (July), *Calluna vulgaris* (August to September), *Ceratostigma plumbaginoides* (September to October).

Will you list late-flowering rock plants? *Ceratostigma plumbaginoides, Allium pulchellum, A. flavum, antirrhinum asarina, Calluna vulgaris* and its varieties, *Chrysogonum virgineanum,* Clochicums, autumn crocuses, *Silene achafta, Saxifraga cortusaefolia,* and *Sedum sieboldi.*

What are the fastest-growing plants and vines for a rock garden? *Cerastium tomentosum, Ajuga reptans, Thymus serpyllum* and its varieties, *Lamium maculatum, L. m. album, Phlox subulata* and its varieties, *Arabis albida,* sedums, *Saponaria ocymoides, Lotus corniculatus, Campanula carpatica,* and *Asperula odorata.*

Should I try to furnish my new rock garden quickly with fast-growing plants, or do it gradually, with smaller plants? By all means the latter. Most people come to regret their first impatience, and wind up by rooting out the rampant growers, and replacing them with choicer, small plants; they are so much more delightful.

Which flowers are best to plant in a small rock garden? Such things as the drabas, *Aubrieta deltoides, Gypsophila repens, Myosotis alpestris, Nierembergia rivularis, N. caerulea, Primula vulgaris, Armeria caespitosa, Veronica teucrium rupestris, Androsace sarmentosa, A. villosa,* and *Rosa rouletti.* Avoid the use of coarse creeping plants; they will overrun the garden.

Can you suggest some plants for a very steep rock garden? *Thymus serpyllum* and its varieties, *Cerastium tomentosum, Sedum spurium, S. hybridum, Phlox subulata,* sempervivums, *Lotus corniculatus, Ceratostigma plumbaginoides, Antirrhinum asarina, Muehlenbeckia axillaris,* and *Campanula carpatica.*

Which perennial plants can I use for a very exposed location in a rock garden? *Arabis albida, Anemone pulsatilla, Phlox subulata* varieties, *Veronica teucrium rupestris, Cerastium tomentosum, Dianthus deltoides, D. plumarius, Lamium maculatum, Aquilegia canadensis, A. vulgaris, Campanula carpatica,* and *Dicentra eximia.*

Can you suggest a few small, decorative plants to fill small crevices in rocks and tiny pockets? My garden is in full sun. *Draba aizodes, Globularia repens* (*G. nana*), *Sedum dasyphllum, Sedum acre minus, Sedum anglicum minus,* and sempervivums (the tiny kinds).

Which are some good plants for shady corners in my rock garden, for spring flower? *Anemone nemorosa* (several kinds), *Brunnera macrophylla, Chrysogonum virginianum, Epimedium niveum, Iris cristata, Phlox divaricata laphami, Phlox stolonifera, Pulmonaria succharata,* and *Saxifraga umbrosa.*

Which perennials, not over 10 ins. in height, bloom between June 15 and September 15, and are suitable for a rock garden in shade? *Chrysogonum virginianum, Corydalis lutea, Mitchella repens, Myosotis scorpioides, Sedum ternatum, S. Nevi, Allium Moly, Saxifraga cortusaefolia, Arenaria montana, Gentiana asclepiadea, Cymbalaria muralis, Scilla sinensis,* and *Dicentra formosa alba.*

Which are some small summer-blooming plants for the shady rock garden? *Chrysogonum virginianum, Cotula squalida, Mitchella repens, Sedum ternatum,* and *S. Nevi.*

Which are the most hardy rock-garden plants that will grow in semi-shade? *Primula polyanthus, P. veris, P. vulgaris,* epimediums, aubretias, aquilegias, *Iris verna, Phlox divaricata laphami, Chrysogonum virginianum, Viola odorata, V. priceana, Vinca minor, Lysimachia nummularia, Sedum ternatum, Ceratostigma plumbaginoides, Asperula odorata,* trilliums, erythroniums, and dodecatheons.

Will you name rock plants that will grow and bloom in the shade of a large oak tree? *Phlox divaricata laphami, Dicentra eximia, Chrysogonum virginianum, Asperula odorata,* erythroniums, trilliums, *Gaultheria procumbens, Mitchella repens, Iris verna, Vinca minor, Lysimachia nummularia,* and *Primula veris.*

Can you name several plants which will grow between rocks of a patio in very sandy soil; preferably fast growers? *Arenaria verna caespitosa, Thymus serpyllum* and its varieties, *Sedum acre, Dianthus deltoides, Muehlenbeckia axillaris, Mazus reptans,* and *Ajuga reptans.* Keep the soil reasonably moist.

Which rock plants require acid soil? Rhododendrons, azaleas, Mountain Laurel, pieris, shinleaf, partridge-berry, *Cypripedium acaule,* erythroniums, galax, and shortia.

Will you name a dozen or so of the choicest and most unusual plants that I may hope to grow in my rock garden? *Androsace lanuginosa, Androsace sarmentosa, Armeria juniperifolia, Campanula cochlearifolia alba, Dianthus callizonus, D. neglectus, Saxifraga burseriana, S. irvingi,* and encrusted saxifragas.

Will all kinds of rock-garden plants grow successfully in a garden without rocks? Yes, although many of them look better against or between rocks.

ALPINES

What is the best site for alpines? A gentle slope facing northeast or northwest.

What soil is best for alpines? One that is not too rich. A neutral, porous soil, well drained, and with grit and cinders to lighten it, will be satisfactory for most alpine plants.

Need I know a lot about alpines to have a good rock garden? No. You may use, more or less exclusively, plants from high, intermediate, or low altitudes. A good rock garden need not be filled with "high-brow" plants. It should afford a happy glimpse of Nature's play with rocks and plants—be it in a mountain scree or on a roadside ledge.

Would you advise me, a beginner, to try an alpine garden? No. Most of the best rock gardens one sees are not alpine gardens, but bits of small-scale, intimate mountain or hillside scenery, with occasional patches of true alpine flora.

Why are alpine plants so difficult to grow? Because the conditions prevailing in lowland rock gardens are so utterly different from those at or above timber line: the heavy winter pack of snow, the short summer, pure, crisp air, and chilly baths of mountain mist. One must learn gradually to devise acceptable equivalents or approximations to these conditions.

Can you name a few alpine plants not too difficult for an amateur

to grow? The following high-mountain plants (not all strictly alpines) are suggested: *Armeria juniperifolia, Androsace lanuginosa, A. sarmentosa, Campanula cochlearifolia, Dianthus alpinus, D. callizonus, Douglasia vitaliana, Gentiana acaulis,* and saxifragas (encrusted and kabschia kinds).

What are the best alpine campanulas for the rock garden? Campanulas *allioni, alpina, cochlearifolia, elatines, fragilis, lasiocarpa, portenschlagiana, poscharskyana, pulla, raineri,* and *tomasiniana.*

What winter care should be given alpines? Cover lightly with evergreen boughs or salt hay after the ground is frozen—usually in December.

BULBS FOR ROCK GARDEN

How should chionodoxa (glory-of-the-snow) be used in the rock garden? Scatter the bulbs in groups of 2 dozen or more in various places among low ground covers. They may also be used effectively beneath shrubs that may form a background to the garden.

Will you give a list of crocuses suitable for the rock garden? Spring-flowering: crocuses *aureus, biflorus, chrysanthus* and its varieties, *imperati, susianus, tomasinianus.* For autumn: *cancellatus albus, longiflorus, pulchellus, speciosus* and its varieties, *zonatus.*

Can you suggest some good narcissi for the rock garden? The best kinds are the small ones, such as *Narcissus minimus, cyclamineus triandrus, t. albus* (angel's tears), *concolor, bulbocodium* (hooppetticoat daffodil), and *B. citrinus.* The sweet jonquils and campernelles can also be used, such as *Narcissus jonquilla, j. flore-pleno,* and *odorus.*

Can you tell me kinds of tulips to plant in a rock garden and what conditions they need? The best are the species tulips, also called "botanical" tulips. These need well-drained soil and sunshine. Plant them about 6 or 7 ins. deep. The following are among the best: *kaufmanniana, acuminata, clusiana* (Lady Tulip), *dasystemon, greigi, praecox, praestans, fosteriana* varieties, *sylvestris,* and *turkestanica.*

Which spring-flowering bulbs are suitable for the rock garden? Squills, glory-of-the-snow, snowdrops, spring-snowflakes, crocuses, grapehyacinths, miniature daffodils. And also dogtooth violets, fritillaries, calochortuses, brodiaeas, and *Iris reticulata.*

Which bulbs are suitable for a rock garden at the side and front of the house? *Crocus* species (for fall and spring), *Galanthus nivalis* (snowdrops), *Leucojum vernum* (snowflake), *Chionodoxa luciliae* (glory-of-the-snow), muscari (grapehyacinths), scillas (squills), narcissi species, colchicums, Tulips *kaufmanniana* and its hybrids, and *dasystemon.*

When are small spring-flowering bulbs planted in the rock garden?

In late August plant snowdrops, winter-aconites, autumn-flowering crocuses, and colchicums. Plant the small daffodils and crocuses in September and others, mentioned in previous replies, in October.

I wish to plant a number of small bulbs in my rock garden. Should I dig up the other plants before planting the bulbs? How deep must I plant the bulbs?   Unless the soil needs improving it is not necessary to remove the plants. Use a bulb trowel (a tool with a narrow concave blade), push it into the soil through the mat of plants, pull the handle toward you, and then push the bulb into the soil and smooth the plants back again. Plant these small bulbs in groups and closely together. The depth at which they are set should be, roughly, 3 times the depth of the bulb.

EVERGREENS

Can you tell me some evergreens for a rock garden which will withstand severe winter exposure?   *Taxus cuspidata, Juniperus communis, J. horizontalis, J. sabina tamariscifolia, Pinus mughus, Pieris floribunda,* and *Ilex glabra.*

Which are some small evergreens that may be used effectively in a rock garden?   *Juniperus procumbens nana* (for a low, flat spread), *Juniperus squamata prostrata* (to drape over a rock), *Juniperus horizontalis* "Bar Harbor"; the dwarfest and most compact of Japanese yews and of hemlocks.

What soil does Daphne cneorum require?   This is a much-debated question. Its success seems to depend mostly upon climate. It does better in the cold parts of New England (with a winter covering), than in warmer climates. Plant in a well-drained soil, away from the fiercest sun.

SHRUBS

Will you suggest some shrubs to use in a rock garden near the front of my house?   Rhododendrons and azaleas are suitable. Mountain-laurel, *Daphne mezereum,* and *D. genkwa* would also look well against a taller evergreen background.

Will you name a few small shrubs that may look well in a small rock garden?   *Spiraea decumbens, S. bullata, Cotoneaster microphylla, Berberis verruculosa, Ilex crenata helleri.* In part shade and an acid, humusy soil, *Rhododendron obtusum* and its varieties, and *R. racemosum* should be satisfactory.

Which shrubby plants would make a good background for our rock garden along the side of the garage?   In east to northeast exposures: rhododendrons, azaleas, laurel, pieris, Japanese holly, and *Mahonia aquifolium.* In sunnier exposures: *Berberis koreana, B. vernae, Symphoricarpos chenaulti,* and perhaps an upright yew.

I have a natural spot for a rock garden about 25 ft. long by 5 ft. wide, on a slope exposed to north and west winds. Are there any shrubs sufficiently hardy to winter in such a location? *Rhododendron mucronulatum, Daphne mezereum, Enkianthus campanulatus, Forsythia ovata, and Cercis chenensis* should do well.

SPECIFIC ROCK GARDEN PLANTS

What is the proper treatment of ALYSSUM SAXATILE which has grown "leggy"? It is best to raise new plants from seed. This plant does not usually last much longer than 3 years. It is inclined to rot away during winter. If it survives, wait until new shoots appear near the base of the plant, then cut the leggy, long ones away.

Does AUBRIETA remain in bloom for a long period? No. Its blooming season is short. However, it flowers in very early spring and is worthy of a place in the garden.

Are the plants called CINQUEFOILS suitable for the rock garden? Can you suggest a few? Many cinquefoils (potentilla) are excellent, others are worthless weeds. *Potentilla nepalensis, tridentata,* and *verna* are worth trying. Give them full sun and well-drained, gritty soil.

How best to grow pinks in the rock garden? Dianthuses do best in a well-drained, sunny position. Do not make the soil very rich and do not overwater them. They are good on gentle slopes, planted so that they can spread over the top of a rock, or in flat, well-drained pockets. Start with young, pot-grown plants if possible, and plant them out at about 9 ins. apart. Some kinds die after a time, so it is best to keep raising a few fresh plants each year.

What kinds of DIANTHUS do you suggest for a rock garden? *Dianthus deltoides* (Maiden-pink), *plumarius* (Grass-pink), *gratianopolitanus* (Cheddar-pink), and *neglectus* (Glacier-pink).

What can I do to make GENTIANA ANDREWSI grow? It appreciates a moist, semi-shaded situation, preferably on the edge of a pond, and a deep, humusy soil. Top-dress in spring with peatmoss mixed with a little cow manure.

Which IRISES are suitable for the rock garden? Irises *reticulata, gracilipes, arenaria, pumila* (in many varieties), *dichotoma, minuta, cristata, cristata alba, lacustris, tectorum,* and its variety *album.*

What conditions do PRIMULAS need in the rock garden? A rich, moist soil and a shady or semi-shady situation. Some, like *Primula pulverulenta,* grow best in almost boggy conditions along the sides of streams. Practically all need plenty of moisture. If very moist conditions cannot be given, grow them in shade.

Will you suggest some primulas for the rock garden? Primulas:

polyantha, veris (the cowslip), *farinosa, bulleyana, rosea, denticulata, frondosa,* and *japonica.*

What care should be given LEONTOPODIUMS that were raised from seeds? The edelweiss likes a well-drained, limy soil, full sun in spring, semi-shade in summer, and light protection in winter. Either evergreen boughs or salt hay should be used, as leaves pack too hard and keep the plant waterlogged, which may result in rotting. From seed they should bloom well the second year. Carry the plants over in a cold frame, in pots, the first year.

Will you name a few PENSTEMONS that would grow in my rock garden? Are they difficult to grow? *Penstemon glaber, heterophyllus, rupicola* and *unilateralis.* These are not difficult. They require gritty soil and do not like a position that becomes sodden in winter. They are not long-lived plants and in order to maintain them it is necessary to raise a few each year.

What soil is suitable for PHLOX subulata? Any light, well-drained garden soil.

Where does Phlox subulata grow wild? In the Eastern, Western, and Southern parts of the United States, on dry banks and in fields.

Do most of the Western species of phlox require scree conditions in the Eastern states? Yes, they seem to do better under either scree or moraine conditions in the East.

What are some good kinds of phlox for a rock garden, not tall ones? Some of the most suitable besides the various varieties of *Phlox subulata* are *Phlox amoena, divaricata* (and its variety *laphami*), *douglasi,* and *stolonifera.*

What is the best place in the rock garden for SAXIFRAGAS? What kind of soil? A partially shady situation facing east or west. Soil should be gritty, open, and well drained. Mix garden soil, leaf-mold, and stone chips, or screened cinders, in about equal proportion, and have a foot depth of this in which to plant. Limestone chips are beneficial for the encrusted saxifragas.

Which saxifragas are not too difficult to grow? Saxifragas: *aizoon, apiculata, cochlearis, decipiens* (a mossy type, requiring partial shade), *hosti, macnabiana, and moschata.*

How many species and varieties of rock-garden SEDUMS are there? Approximately 200. Perhaps not more than 50 distinct and useful kinds are available in nurseries.

Which are the best sedums? Sedums: *Album, anglicum, brevifolium, caeruleum* (annual), *dasyphyllum, ewersi, kamtschaticum, lydium, middendorffianum, nevi, oreganum, populifolium, pilosum, reflexum, rupestre, sempervivoides, sexangulare, sieboldi, spurium ternatum, stoloniferum, hybridum,* and the self-sowing biennial *nuttallianum.*

Can I get information regarding the culture of sedums? Most are easily propagated from cuttings taken in the fall or spring. They root best in sand, either in flats or in cold frames. When well rooted, transfer them into small pots or put them directly into their permanent places in the garden. The location should ordinarily be sunny, the soil sandy and well drained. Western-America sedums prefer a semi-shaded position.

Are the SUNROSES (helianthemums) hardy? Do they require much care? They are not very hardy; they thrive fairly well in the vicinity of New York but farther North they are doubtful subjects. They need no more care than ordinary rock-garden plants. Give them a well-drained soil in a sunny location. Protect them in winter with salt hay or evergreen boughs, and cut them back to within a few inches of their crowns in spring, to encourage fresh growth.

Do helianthemums survive the winter without protection? That all depends upon the winter, and upon where they are growing. In a sheltered spot they would probably come through. In an exposed position, cover them with evergreen boughs. They are not overhardy in lower New York State.

MORAINE GARDEN

Can you explain what a moraine garden is? How is it made? A moraine is constructed for the purpose of growing certain alpine plants from high altitudes. The garden contains little or no soil, the growing medium being mostly stone chips and shale. The important factor is water. The most complete moraines have cool water circulating below the growing medium so that the roots of the plants are in a cool, moist medium much as are alpines in their native haunts. A moraine can be built in a water tight basin 2 ft. deep and of any length and breadth. A foot-thick layer of stones is laid in the bottom. The remaining space is filled with a mixture of 5 parts crushed stone (½ in.), 1 part sand, and 1 part leafmold. Water is supplied during the growing season through a pipe at the upper end and the surplus is drawn off by one at the other end 12 ins. below the surface. Sub-irrigation is sometimes dispensed with and the garden is then known as a "scree."

Will you give me a list of plants suitable for a moraine garden? Aethionema, androsace, *Arenaria montana, Dianthus sylvestris, Campanula speciosa, Silene acaulis,* and saxifragas (the encrusted kinds).

PATHS

What are the most suitable kinds of paths for the rock garden and how are they constructed? See Paths, this section.

PAVEMENT PLANTING

How are plants grown between the flags in a pavement? For the plants to succeed, the flags should be laid on sand overlying several inches of soil. Watering during hot, dry weather is very helpful.

How are plants arranged in a pavement planting?   Do not overdo the planting or it will look untidy. Use for the most part flat types of plants, with an occasional taller plant to relieve the monotony.

How are plants planted between flagstones?   Planting is first done as the flat stones are laid. When the spot for a plant is selected, the plant is set so that when the surface is leveled for the next flagstone, the top of the plant is resting at the correct level. The stone may have to be chipped to avoid crushing the plant.

Which plants are suitable for planting in a flagged walk?   Those that will withstand much walking are: *Festuca ovina glauca, Sagina subulata,* and *Tunica saxifraga.* Others to use are *Thymus serpyllum* varieties, *Mentha requieni* (both fragrant), *Alyssum montanum, Erinus alpinus, Veronica repens,* and *Lysimachia nummularia.*

POOLS

How do you construct a small pool for the rock garden?   See Pool Construction, this section.

I have a hillside rock garden with an uneven 6-ft.-diameter pool. Will you give me advice as to plants for inside the pool and for outside to hold up the dirt which seems to wash away with each rain?   Plant *Nymphoides peltatum* inside the pool. *Caltha palustris* (marsh-marigold) along the edge, also *Primula rosea, Trollius europaeus,* and 2 or 3 *Lobelia cardinalis.* In between plant solid with *Myosotis scorpioides,* which will hold the soil.

A small informal pool not only adds interest to the landscaping but can provide congenial conditions for moisture-loving plants.

STEPS—PLANTING

I have some rough flagstone steps and wish to set some plants in

them. How should I arrange them? What kind should I use? The width of the steps will have to be considered in the arrangement. The primary purpose of steps is to link certain areas. Plants, if used, are for decoration. Don't overplant and avoid regularity. Low plants should be used mostly with an occasional bushy one interspersed. The sides can be more thickly planted than the centers. (For kinds, see Pavement Plantings.)

WALL GARDENS

What exposure for a wall garden? Eastern, except for shade-loving plants such as ramondia, haberlea, *Saxifraga sarmentosa,* English ivies, and certain ferns. For these a northern exposure.

What is the best type of rock for a wall garden? For an informal effect, any natural, porous rock with a good facing surface; squarish pieces, such as one might use for an ordinary dry wall, are best. A good wall garden can be made of bricks.

How does one make a wall garden? Much like a dry retaining wall, but the joints are packed with prepared soil and the stones are tilted backward to keep the soil from washing out and to direct the rain water toward the plant roots. To prevent squashing of roots, chink the horizontal joints with small pieces of stone. Place plants in position as the laying up proceeds, and firm the soil well at the back of the wall.

What special upkeep does a wall garden need? Upkeep is reduced by using suitably compact, small, rock-hugging plants. Remove all old flower stalks. Pull out weeds and excess seedlings. Prune and thin so as to maintain a balanced distribution of planting effect. On top of the wall, provide a watering trench or trough, and use it freely to prevent drying out in summer.

Wide terrace with planted dry wall.

How are plants planted in a wall? In a wall garden, building and planting are done at the same time. If the plants are located at the joints, the soil is packed in, the plant set, a little extra soil added, and then the stones are placed. Chips placed between the stones near the plants prevent them from sinking and squeezing the plants. If planting has to be done after building, the job is more difficult. The roots must somehow be spread out in a narrow space, and the soil rammed in with a piece of stick. Don't plant fast-growing plants near slow-growing ones or the latter will be smothered.

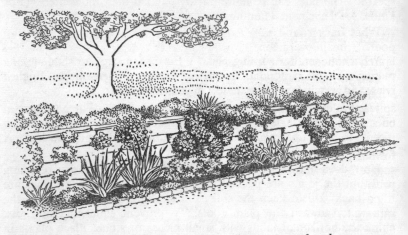

In planting a wall care must be taken to spot the plants with a natural-looking irregularity that avoids any studied pattern or design.

What summer upkeep is necessary for a rock wall?   Keep plants well watered and weeded. Spray if necessary.

Can you tell me what spring care should be given a rockery made in an old stone wall?   Trim dead pieces off plants; fill washed-out cracks with new soil. Push heaved-out plants into soil or take them out altogether and replant.

What winter cover for a wall garden?   Stick a row of pine boughs into the ground thickly enough to provide shade from the brightest sun of winter. Or place a row of two-by-fours, slanting against the wall, and over them stretch a burlap cover. The pine boughs will be better looking.

What winter care is necessary for a rock wall?   Cover with evergreen boughs when the ground is frozen. Take off during early April.

Which plants are particularly suitable for use in a rock wall?   All the sempervivums, Sedums: *hybridum, coccineum, nevi,* and *sieboldi, Nepeta hederacea,* Campanulas *carpatica: cochlearifolia,* and *rotundifolia, Silene caroliniana,* Linarias: *pallida* and *aequitriloba, Phlox stolonifera, Achillea ageratifolia,* and *Mazus reptans.*

Are wall gardens easy to maintain?   They are at their best in moist climates (England) where there are not long drought periods. If left unwatered in long summer droughts many of the plants will die. They require more attention than other types of gardens, especially care in watering.

WATER GARDENS

(*See also Pool Construction*)

PLANTING

What background materials should I use for my small informal pool? Small evergreens, yew, arborvitae, cedar, hemlock, azalea, laurel, rhododendron, leucothoe, euonymus, cotoneaster, daphne.

Can you tell me some flowering shrubs I can put around my pool? Viburnum, forsythia, abelia, mockorange, lilac, deutzia, kolkwitzia, spirea, azalea, rhododendron, laurel, lonicera. Shrub roses would also be a good choice here.

I want a formal-looking clipped hedge around the sides of my formal pool, which is at the rear of my garden. What would you suggest? Yew, hemlock, barberry, box (for sheltered positions), privet.

Can I have a successful fish pond in a plot about 9 × 15 ft.? How could anything so small be landscaped? Why not pave the area with flagstones, leaving wide cracks between stones? These could be planted with rock plants. The pool would be the central feature.

Have you any planting suggestions for rim of a pool? Astilbe, cardinalflower, Japanese iris, loosestrife, marshmarigold, rosemallow, Siberian iris and moneywort.

I have a rocky ledge by my pool. What evergreen might be grown over it? Depending on size of ledge and pool, low growing bearberry (arctostaphylos), or one of the creeping junipers might be used. For larger pools, there is nothing quite as graceful as a dwarf weeping Canada hemlock planted with its branches hanging down over the rocks.

Which flowering plants can be grown in a pool other than waterlilies? Floatingheart (*Nymphoides peltatum*); true forget-me-not; waterhyacinth (*Eichornia*); waterpoppy (*Hydrocleis*); water-snowflake (*Nymphoides indicum*). The last 3 are not winter hardy.

What can be used to break the monotonous flatness of a lily pool? Tall-growing water plants, such as American and Hindu Lotus; calla;* cattails (if pool is large); flowering rush; yellow and blue flags; taro;* water plantain.

With what flowers shall I border informal pool 6 × 10 ft.? *Spiraea venusta* and *S. filipendula*, *Iris ochroleuca*, *Trollius ledebouri*, *Lythrum salicaria*, hemerocallis, *Liatris pycnostachya*, *Myosotis palustris semperflorens*.

*Not winter hardy

SPECIFIC WATER PLANTS

HINDU LOTUS

Which is the best way to keep sacred lotus through winter? If growing in a pond that is drained during the winter, cover the roots with a sufficient depth of leaves to prevent the frost penetrating to the tubers. When this plant is grown in water 2 or 3 ft. deep, usually no winter protection is necessary.

WATERHYACINTH

How can I grow waterhyacinth? Float in 6 ins. water above a box or tub containing 6 ins. or more of soil. Keep from drifting by confining within an anchored wooden hoop. Bring plants indoors before frost.

How do you winter waterhyacinths that have been in an outside pool? Bring them indoors before the leaves are injured by cold. Float them in a container of water which has 3 or 4 ins. of soil in the bottom. Keep in a sunny window in a temperature of 55° to 60° F.

WATERLILIES

What is proper soil for waterlilies? Heavy loam, composted for a year before use with cow manure in the proportion of 2 to 1. If this is out of the question, use rich soil from vegetable garden.

What shall I use to make waterlilies bloom better? Possibly your plants are starved. Divide and replant in the soil recommended above, adding a 5-in. potful of bone meal to each bushel of soil.

How can I make waterlilies blossom in a small artificial pond? See answer to preceding question. Perhaps, however, the failure of your plants is due to insufficient sunshine. Waterlilies need full sun all day for best results.

How large should containers be for waterlilies? Depends on the variety. Small-growing kinds can be grown in boxes 15 × 15 × 10 ins., while the tropical varieties can be grown to advantage in sizes up to 4 × 4 × 1 ft.

In a small concrete pool is it better to cover the bottom with soil or use separate boxes for waterlilies? The lilies are better off if the bottom is covered with soil, but it is easier to avoid muddying the water in the pool if the soil is confined in wooden boxes or similar containers.

How deep should the water be over waterlilies? Six ins. to 3 ft. Preferably 1 ft. for tropical varieties, 1 to 2 ft. for hardy varieties, provided this is enough to prevent roots from freezing in winter.

What is the most practical way of caring for a waterlily pool in the

winter? If the pool is small enough to be bridged by boards, do so and then cover with a sufficient thickness of straw or leaves to prevent the water from freezing. If the pool is drained and the lilies are growing in tubs, move the tubs together and cover around and over them with leaves held in place with wire netting or something similar.

Supposing the mud is not sufficiently deep to support the growth of waterlilies? Plant the lilies in rich soil in a shallow wicker or chip basket, or fruit crate with openings sufficiently wide to allow roots to emerge, then gently slide the planted container into the pond.

How often should waterlilies be divided? Whenever the container becomes so crowded that growth is poor—usually after 3 or 4 years.

Would colored pond lilies grow where wild white ones grow in a lake with muddy bottom? Yes.

Which waterlily can be grown in a pool fed from an underground stream? Water is cold the year around and is in dense shade. Waterlilies will not grow in such a location.

How can I plant HARDY WATERLILIES in a natural pond? If the pond has a rich mud bottom, merely tie a heavy sod or half brick to the tuber or rhizome and drop it in the pond where water is between 1 and 3 ft. deep.

When is the best time to plant hardy waterlilies? When ice has left the pond in the spring, but they may be planted successfully up until mid-June.

Should hardy waterlilies be left outside in the pool through the winter? (New York.) Yes, if they are growing in water so deep that there is no danger of the roots freezing—18 ins. should be enough in your locality.

How early can TROPICAL WATERLILIES be set out? (New York.) Not until all danger of frost is past and the water has become warm—about the second week in June in the vicinity of New York.

How are tropical waterlilies planted? Pot-grown plants are commonly used. A hole is scooped in the soil of the container deep enough to receive the ball of earth about the roots, then the roots are covered with soil, taking care not to bury the crown of the plant.

Can tropical waterlilies be kept through the winter as other bulbs are? It is difficult to carry over tropical waterlilies unless one has a sunny greenhouse. When it is possible to find small tubers around the crown of the old plant, these may be gathered in the fall, stored in sand, protected from mice, and started in an aquarium in a sunny window in April.

Can I carry my Dauben Nymphaea over the winter? Lilies of this type produce young plantlets on the leafstalks. If a greenhouse or sunny window is available, the plantlets can be gathered in the fall, planted in a watertight vessel about 12 ins. in diameter, filled to within

3 ins. of its rim with soil, the remainder of the container being filled with water.

Can tropical waterlilies be carried over the winter in this climate? (New York.) Not out of doors. See answer to 2 preceding questions. Usually it is better to obtain new plants from dealers each spring.

During the past 2 summers some sort of leaf miner has eaten the leaves (making marks like Chinese ideographs) of my waterlilies. Consequently the leaves soon die. What are they and how may I get rid of them without injuring the fish in the pond? The larvae of a midge— *Chironomus modestus.* Waterlily foliage is sensitive to insecticidal sprays, so it is best, whenever possible, to use mechanical means to get rid of pests; therefore pick off infested leaves as fast as they appear, and destroy by burning, which will ultimately eliminate the miner.

We have an old pond on our place but now it is almost one solid growth of waterlilies. How can these be eradicated? By spraying the waterlily foliage with a mixture of half 2,4-D and half 2,4,5-T in early August, applied at the rate of one gallon of concentrate (containing 2 lbs. of acid equivalent of 2,4-D and 2 lbs. of acid equivalent of 2,4,5-T) in 2 gallons of water. Or sodium arsenite has proved effective as a spray—15 lbs. of sodium arsenite in 100 gallons of water.

WILDFLOWER GARDENS

SOIL

What soil and fertilizer should be used for wildflower planting? Generally speaking, the soil should approximate that in which the plants grow naturally. Woodland plants thrive in rich leafmold. Many prefer slightly acid soil. No artificial fertilizer should be used; well-rotted compost is next best to natural leafmold.

What fertilizers are recommended for woodland wildflowers? None. Leafmold is enough.

Should the soil around wildflowers be cultivated? The weeds should be kept out, but the soil does not need cultivating.

PLANNING

What is the best location for a wildflower garden? This depends on the type of flowers to be grown. Some wildflowers grow naturally in woodlands, and others in a sunny meadow. Try to make the condition in your garden most like the one which the particular plants came from.

Should a wildflower garden be attemped in an ordinary backyard garden? If so, what type? No, not in general. However, an informal sort of garden may be made, using the more common types of either woodland flowers or meadow flowers.

What plants go well with mertensia, bloodroot, and Dutchman's-breeches to fill in when their foliage dies down in late spring? Use Christmasfern or evergreen woodfern with mertensia and bloodroot; use spleenworts and grapeferns among the Dutchman's-breeches. These ferns do not have crowding habits and are almost evergreen. Their colors are good with the flowers mentioned.

Which wildflowers and trees can be established in dry, sandy, stony soil? Trees for dry, stony soil in your location are the Redcedar (*Juniperus virginiana*) and the locust (*Robina pseudoacacia*). Many shrubs will grow, such as bayberry, barberry, scrub oak, raspberries and blackberries, sumacs, blueberries. The blackhaw may assume the stature of a tree. Flowers include many of the flowers of the open field—daisies, asters, blackeyedsusans, everlasting.

PROPAGATION

Is it best to grow wildflowers from seed, or to buy the plants? Choice plants may be started from seed. Plants of most varieties may be purchased.

Which wild native plants may be started from seed and how is this done? Practically all of the field flowers, such as asters, milkweeds, goldenrods. Also columbine, pale corydalis, climbing fumitory (vine), celandine poppy, bloodroot, early saxifrage, bishop's cap, foamflower, and painted cup. With more patience, try arbutus and fringed gentian. The seeds are best started in flats in a protected cold frame. Sow in early winter or spring, using a light, sandy, leafmoldy soil mixture.

What is a good all-around soil mixture in which to sow wildflower seeds? One half ordinary garden soil, ¼ leafmold, and ¼ coarse fresh-water sand, thoroughly mixed and worked through a ⅛-in. mesh sifter to remove all stones and lumps.

How long can wildflower seeds be kept before planting them? Much depends on what kind they are. Some, such as trillium, bloodroot, and others that are produced in a more or less pulpy berry or pod, should be sown immediately before they dry at all; many other harder and thinner kinds can be kept for 5 or 6 months. A good general rule is to sow as soon as the seed is ripe, regardless of the time of the year.

Which kinds of wildflower seeds can be sown in a cold frame late in the fall? Practically all of the perennial kinds, especially those which flower in midsummer or later. Keep the sash on the frame to protect from winter rains, and shade with slats or cheesecloth to prevent undue heating before spring.

I want to have thousands of beautiful kinds of wildflowers all over my meadow. Can't I get them by strewing handfuls of seed in all directions—a "wildflower mixture," you know, like I see advertised in the catalogues? Sorry—but you can't. Only the toughest and commonest, such as daisies and goldenrod, will catch hold and grow, so all you'll really have in a couple of years will be a bumper crop of weeds. Rather raise the kinds you want from seed sown in a place where they won't be overrun, and set the plants out in the meadow when they're big enough to hold their own.

What wildflowers self-sow so quickly as to become pests if planted in the garden? Goldenrod, cattails, wild carrot, jewelweed, ironweed, blackeyedsusan, sunflower, asters, golden ragwort, mullein, daisy, and many others.

I am not a botanist but like to identify wildflowers. Can you give me one or two references to well-illustrated books that would help me identify wildflowers from illustrations? Wild Flowers—Homer D. House; Macmillan Co. 1934. The Macmillan Wild Flower Book, C. J. Hylander & E. F. Johnston, Macmillan 1954.

COLLECTING

How can wildflowers be identified? By a study of botany or by reference to a reliable illustrated book on the wildflowers growing in your locality.

Which wildflowers cannot be collected from the wild without breaking the conservation laws? Nearly every state has its own list of native plants under conservation, so a complete list of all protected species is impossible. Some of the more important kinds are trilliums, trailing arbutus, Mountain Laurel, all native orchids, anemone, lilies, dodecatheon, Fringed Gentian, cardinalflower, Birdsfoot Violet, bluebells, wild pink.

Where can wildflowers be obtained? There are special dealers in wildflowers throughout the country who carry all types of these plants.

How do you start a wildflower preserve? Start a wildflower preserve by acquiring a spot that already has enough trees and flowers and beauty to suggest preserving. Gradually bring in groups of plants which you wish to include and see that they are planted in situations such as they seek in nature. This involves a good working knowledge of the soil and other conditions which the plants prefer and matching these conditions in the places you plant them.

May a flower preserve be joined with an arboretum? It should be a splendid addition to an arboretum.

BOG

What conditions are necessary for a bog garden? Is it different from water gardening? Generally a swampy piece of ground, not under water, but where at all times there is plenty of moisture and usually too soft to walk upon. In water gardens the plants are immersed or floating. In bog gardens, the plants grow free above the soil.

Which plants grow in wet marshland? Swamp milkweed, marsh-marigold, Joepyeweed, yellowflag, blueflag, cardinalflower, loosestrife, forget-me-not, sedges, marshmallow, water plantain, Yellow- and White-fringed Orchises, and many more.

Are tall-growing wildflowers, such as hibiscus, cardinalflower, and lobelia, suitable for the wild garden? Yes. They are best grown in the bog garden or in a moist border.

Which wildflowers are suitable for planting near a naturalistic pool in sun and shade? *Iris pseudacorus, Iris prismatica, Aruncus sylvestris, Vernonia noveboracensis, Anemone canadensis, Asclepias incarnata, Calla palustris, Caltha palustris, Chelone glabra, Gentiana andrewsi, Hypoxis hirsuta, Lilium superbum, Parnassia caroliniana.*

Which wildflowers do you suggest for the edge of a slow-moving, shaded stream? Cardinalflower, boneset, turtlehead, Great Lobelia, Fringed and Bottle Gentians, forget-me-not, monkeyflower, mertensia, blueflag (iris), marshmarigold, American globeflower. A little distance from the stream, but where they profit by some of the moisture, you can grow Yellow ladyslipper, trilliums, Yellow Adders-tongue, Fringed Polygala, Solomonseal, false Solomonseal, foamflower, Jack-in-the-pulpit, White Violet, windflower (anemonella).

MEADOW

Can you give me some pointers on planning and setting out a meadow wild garden? The meadow where wildflowers are to be grown should be open, sunny, and preferably fenced with either a rustic fence or rock wall. The soil for common meadow flowers should be dry, porous, and preferably a little sandy. Most meadow flowers are easily grown from seed and then transplanted. Weeds should be kept away from the plants so that they are not choked out. Room should be allowed for them to reseed themselves and form natural-looking patches.

What are the general cultural requirements for growing meadow wildflowers in the garden? The conditions should be as much like those of a meadow as possible: full sun, plenty of room for the plants, and undisturbed conditions. The soil should be porous and loamy except for moist meadow plants.

What sun-loving wildflowers are suitable for rural garden planting to give color and succession of bloom? *Phlox amoena,* April to May; *Iris cristata,* May; *Corydalis glauca,* May to June; *Epilobium angustifolium,* June to July; *Gillenia trifoliata,* June to August; *Campanula rotundifolia,* June to October; *Cassia marilandica,* July to August; *Asclepias tuberosa,* July to August; *Aster linariifolius,* September; *Aster ericoides,* September to October.

Which wild plants will grow well in a sunny meadow? Daisies, blackeyedsusans, the goldenrods, butterflyweed, phlox, Joepyeweed, hawkweed (devil's-paint-brush), yarrow, thistles, ironweed, lupine, Pearly and Sweet Everlastings, American Artichoke, tansy, chicory; New England, Smooth, and New York Asters, trumpet creeper and Bush Honeysuckle, Queen Anne's lace, wild sweetpea.

WOODLAND

How can a woodland wild garden be planned and arranged? A woodland garden made for wild plants should simulate natural wild conditions. There should be shade and semi-shade formed by such trees as grow in the woods. The soil for wood plants should be rich and leafmoldy and slightly damp. The plants are best placed in natural-looking clumps around the base of the trees. A few rocks may be used as focal points, and plants placed around them.

How does one go about starting a wildflower garden beginning with a piece of wild woodland in Vermont? It's just a small patch about ¼ acre. How do you get cardinalflowers started to grow in such a garden? Start your wild garden by gradually replacing and replanting under and around trees, along paths, etc. You will have greatest success with the plants that grow naturally in Vermont woods. Cardinalflower (*Lobelia cardinalis*) likes the stream sides, will grow in partial shade almost in the water, although it sometimes thrives when transplanted to garden soil with less moisture.

Will bloodroot, trillium, and columbine grow under pine trees? If not, what will grow there? The plants mentioned grow well under oak trees. They will grow under pine trees if the shade is not too great and the soil is loamy. Why not try partridge-berry for ground cover, also the club mosses? Plant Christmasfern and Shieldfern. Pipsissewa and shinleaf (*Pyrola elliptica*) will be dainty but difficult additions, as well as wintergreen (*Gaultheria procumbens*) and bunchberry (*Cornus canadensis*).

What are the best methods of growing wild plants under shady conditions? Try to create the conditions in which the plants grow naturally. The amount of shade, moisture, and kind of soil are all important. If under oak trees, you may plant most of the early spring flowers, such as bloodroots, Dutchman's-breeches, partridge-berry, hepatica, bishop's cap, violets, shinleaf, woodbetony, and many ferns and club mosses, such as Shieldfern, polypody, Christmasfern, spleenworts. The club mosses include ground cedar, runningpine, and staghorn. The last, however, are very difficult to transplant.

What are the general cultural requirements for wildflowers? Such as grow in the woods? A leafmoldy soil, semi-shade, and undisturbed conditions.

What mulching materials are suitable for woodland wild plants? Fallen leaves and evergreen boughs.

Do woodland wildflowers require a mulch? A mulch of leaves is helpful.

When woodland wildflowers have been transplanted from their natural habitat, should they be protected over winter? Yes, especially the first year to prevent heaving.

Do woodland wildflowers require any special care in planting? They need the same careful planting as all flowers. Put them in well-dug soil with enough room for the roots and do not crowd them. Tamp the soil firmly around them.

My property is a Gray Birch grove. Which wildflowers can I plant in among the birches? Under your Gray Birches you may grow speedwell (*Veronica officinalis*), violets, wild strawberries, Pearly Everlasting, pipsissewa, shinleaf, *Phlox divaricata,* Rue and Wood Anemones, mertensia. Ferns: Christmasfern, spleenwort, and polypody; the lycopodiums (club mosses.)

Can you suggest a group of native American wildflowers for planting in a wooded lot on home grounds? *Aralia nudicaule, Aralia racemosa,* trilliums, *Dicentra eximia, Gillenia trifoliata, Shortia galacifolia, Tiarella cordifolia, Actaea alba* and *A. rubra.*

Which wildflowers will grow in a beech grove? Springbeauty (claytonia), wild columbine, harebells, hepatica, violets, mertensia, *Phlox divaricata, Trillium grandiflorum,* Jack-in-the-pulpit, Red Baneberry, the anemones, Yellow Ladyslipper (if moist), Solomonseal, false Solomonseal, bloodroot. Ferns: Walking and the woods ferns.

Which wildflowers will grow in a woodland where there are hemlocks and oaks? A few are Pink Ladyslipper, Painted Trillium, Wood Lily (*L. philadelphicum*), arbutus, bellwort, *Iris verna,* wintergreen, Purple-fringed Orchis, Wood Anemone, partridge-berry, Wood Aster. Shrubs: rhododendron, wild azalea (Pinkster bloom), and laurel.

SPECIFIC WILDFLOWERS

ANEMONES

I have tried several times to transplant Rue Anemones (Anemonella thalictroides) from the woods, without success. What could be wrong? They should be dug with a large ball of soil right after flowering, before the leaves die down. Take enough of the soil in which they are found to establish them in their new location. Plant in light shade. They require light, moist soil and are indifferent to acidity. The Wood Anemone (*A. quinquefolia*) requires moderate acidity.

What are the soil conditions required by the Wood Anemone (A. quinquefolia)? Moist, open woodland. Likes the borders of streams.

Must have moderately acid soil. Dig with a large ball of soil just after flowering.

ARBUTUS

What is the correct name for trailing arbutus or mayflower? *Epigaea repens.*

How can I grow trailing arbutus? Best to get pot-grown plants from a nursery, since they more easily adapt themselves to changed soil conditions. Where arbutus grows in abundance in nature there is usually a sandy base to the soil, often ancient sandy river beds, or along the shore as on Long Island or the pine barrens of New Jersey. Soil should be light, strongly acid, and rich in organic matter, with good drainage.

BLUETS

I should like to have a large patch of bluets (or quakerlady or innocence, as they are called). How can this be done? They are best in a rather moist, acid soil, in full sun. If you get them from the wild, put them in a place as much like the one they were in as possible. They should reseed themselves and form a patch.

What kinds of bluets are there besides the common quakerlady? Only one, if you are thinking of kinds that are worth planting. This one is the Creeping Bluet (*Houstonia serpyllifolia*), from the southern Appalachians. It is a mat-forming, rather short-lived perennial that flowers profusely for about 3 weeks in May. It will usually self-sow freely.

Dogtooth Violet (left) and Bloodroot, two of our most charming native spring flowers.

BLOODROOT

How is bloodroot transplanted? Take care to get the whole root. Set it carefully in a well-dug soil in light shade, in August. Indifferent to soil acidity.

How may one germinate bloodroot seed?   Collect the seed capsules just before they burst open. When seeds have ripened, they may be planted immediately in a prepared spot in the garden where they are to stay.

BUTTERFLYWEED

Is butterflyweed difficult to transplant from the field to the garden? *Asclepias tuberosa* is, as its scientific name implies, tuberous-rooted. In moving a mature specimen, a very large, thick ball of earth must be dug with it in order not to break the tubers. It can be transplanted in fall. Is one of the last things to appear above ground in spring.

Can I grow butterflyweed from seed?   Yes. Sow in fall or spring— preferably the latter. Transplant seedlings to place where they are to grow when about 6 ins. tall, being careful not to break the very long taproots. Give full sun and well-drained soil.

CARDINALFLOWER (LOBELIA CARDINALIS)

Is cardinalflower suitable for wild plantings?   Yes, if you have a moist, partly shaded situation. It is ideal for the edge of a stream or naturalistic pool.

How can cardinalflower be propagated?   By late-fall or early-spring sowing of fresh seed; by dividing large plants; and by pinning down a strong stalk on wet sand in August and half covering it with more sand until young plants start where the leaves join the main stem.

COLUMBINE

I have heard that wild columbine (Aquilegia canadensis) grows much taller and fuller in good garden soil than in the wild. Is this true?   Yes, but the improvement is limited to the stems and foliage; the flowers remain the same size. The result is a plant devoid of most of the grace and charm which make it so attractive in the wild. We recommend retaining its natural characteristics by giving it a rather poor, dryish soil.

What causes wild columbine to rot off at the crown when other things flourish around it?   Columbine is used to thin, poor, neutral soil. Perhaps your soil is too moist, or the roots may be burned by too much fertilizer. Or it may have been attacked by columbine borer.

CREEPING JENNY (LYSIMACHIA NUMMULARIA)

Where can I plant creeping Jenny?   In a low, damp, pasture-like location in the sun.

DUTCHMAN'S-BREECHES

What is the Latin name for Dutchman's-breeches? In what climate do they thrive?   *Dicentra cucullaria*. The plant grows in thin woods and on rocky slopes, from New England south to North Carolina and west to South Dakota and Missouri. Prefers neutral soil.

FERNS

Which wild ferns can I plant in my woodland wildflower garden? Those which grow in your locality in wooded sections. Give them conditions as nearly as possible like those in which you find them. Among the best possibilities are Evergreen Woodfern, Christmasfern or Swordfern, Sensitivefern, Ostrichfern, Interruptedfern, Royalfern. (The last 3 need very moist situations.)

Why can't I grow Walkingfern successfully in my rocky woodland? I give it just the kind of place it likes, but the leaves turn yellowish and just barely stay alive. Sounds as if the soil is acid, as is likely to be the case in a region where the rock ledges and outcrops are granite. Walkingfern appears to be a lime-lover, so we suggest having your soil tested for acidity.

In what section of the United States does the Climbingfern, Lygodium palmatum, grow as native? The Climbingfern, *Lygodium palmatum,* strangely enough is a native of fields in which shrubs are abundant, often in old river beds. It is found sporadically along the East coast and abundantly in the pine barrens of New Jersey.

GENTIANS

Is there any way to start or plant blue gentians? Fringed Gentians need a very moist situation in sun. Turn the soil, sow absolutely fresh seed on the surface in autumn, press it in, and cover with tow cloth to prevent washing. Remove tow cloth in spring as soon as frost is out of ground. Or, if you prefer, buy pot-grown seedlings.

Is Bottle Gentian a biennial? And is it hard to grow? Bottle or Closed Gentian (*Gentiana andrewsi*) is definitely a hardy perennial. It is easy to grow in rather heavy, dampish soil that is kept cool in summer by the shade of other plants.

HEPATICAS

What sort of soil is preferred by hepaticas? Can they be placed in a wildflower garden? There are 2 native hepaticas: *H. acutiloba,* with pointed 3-lobed leaves, and *H. americana,* with rounded 3-lobed leaves. Common near Atlantic seaboard. Either can be planted in the home garden in shaded locations, near rocks, if soil is suitable. A neutral soil is preferred, though the last-named is considered more tolerant of acid.

IRIS

Which wild irises can be used in the garden? *Iris cristata,* which needs a protected, moist situation and is indifferent to soil acidity.

I. verna, wooded hills, very acid soil. *I. versicolor,* marshes, wet meadows, thickets; needs some sun. *I. prismatica,* marshes, swamps; full sun.

JACK-IN-THE-PULPIT

Can Jack-in-the-pulpits be grown in the wild garden? Yes. Give them a deeply prepared soil. If they are transplanted from the woods, take care to get all of the roots and tubers.

LYCOPODIUMS (CLUB MOSSES)

When is the best time to transplant such things as princesspine? Transplant runningpine and other lycopodiums early in the spring before new growth starts. All club mosses are difficult to establish if conditions are not very close to their native habitats. May be moved any time if the place is damp enough.

MARSHMARIGOLD

Is it difficult to transplant marshmarigolds? No, very easy. Dig or pull the plants gently from their position in marsh or stream. Do not let roots dry out. Replant promptly in similar situation in edge of stream or naturalistic pool.

How can I propagate marshmarigolds? The simplest way is to divide the clumps in spring, right after flowering. Merely wash the mud away from around the roots so you can see what you're doing, and separate the numerous small crowns (with their roots and leaves) with your fingers. Replant at once in bog garden or in edge of slow-moving stream or near outlet of naturalistic pool.

MERTENSIA

Is mertensia easy to grow in the garden? Yes. Though *Mertensia virginica* is found in very moist situations—chiefly along the edges of slow-moving streams—it is adaptable to partly shaded positions in the average garden.

How can I keep rabbits from eating up my mertensia plants? The only way we know of is to get rid of the rabbits, by fair means or foul. Mertensia seems to be a special favorite of theirs in some localities.

ORCHIDS

How can I get wild orchids without breaking the conservation laws? Purchase them from a wildflower specialist.

How many native American cypripediums (ladyslippers) are there? Which of these are suitable for use in the garden? There are about 10 native cypripediums, of which the following are the best for naturalistic gardening (none are suitable for gardens in the ordinary sense

—they need special soil and care): *Cypripedium acaule* (pink); *C. montanum* (white); *C. parviflorum* (yellow); *C. pubescens* (yellow); *C. reginae,* (white and rose); *C. candidum* (white).

Can ladyslippers be transplanted to a semi-wild garden successfully? When should transplanting be done? Yellow ladyslippers, both *Cypripedium parviflorum* and the larger *C. pubescens* and the Showy Ladyslipper, *C. reginae,* are transplanted with less risk than most other types. Best done in late summer or fall, but may be accomplished in spring if a firm root-ball is taken to prevent injury or disturbance to the roots.

Which of our native cypripediums are perennial? How deep should roots be set? All are perennial. Roots should be set so that the growing bud, formed in fall, is just under the surface. Use rich woods soil, the surface kept from drying out with a thin layer of oak leaves. Whenever you transplant these cypripediums, take as much as possible of the soil in which they have been growing.

Can you tell me what to do with a moccasin plant after it is through blooming? If by moccasin plant you mean our native Pink Ladyslipper, *Cypripedium acaule,* and if it is planted in a suitable place, you need do nothing after it blooms. An oak-leaf mulch in fall is desirable.

Does Showy Ladyslipper (Cypripedium reginae) require a neutral soil? (Minnesota.) It generally is found in the wild where the soil is boggy and acid but is said to tolerate neutral soil.

ORCHIS

Where will I find the Showy Orchis? The Showy Orchis (*Orchis spectabilis*) and the Pink Ladyslipper (*Cypripedium acaule*) inhabit rich, moist woods from Maine to Georgia, especially oak woods and hemlock groves. The Showy Orchis, however, is said to be tolerant of nearly neutral soil if rich enough.

Where will the Purple-fringed Orchis grow? In woods, swamps, and meadows, or locations in the garden which simulate such conditions.

Where can I plant the White-fringed Orchis in my wild garden? If you have a bog garden, plant it there. Native to swamps and bogs.

Can I grow the Yellow-fringed Orchis in my garden? Perhaps, if you have a strongly acid, continuously moist wild garden.

PARTRIDGE-BERRY

Can partridge-berry be grown in the wild garden? Yes, especially if it is damp. It requires an acid, rich woods soil.

PHLOX DIVARICATA

How can I get Phlox divaricata and what are its uses? It can be purchased from many nurseries, especially those which deal in wild plants. Its uses are innumerable. Plant in open shade of deciduous trees. It blends well with mertensia, trilliums, and other plants of the open woodland. Self-sows.

PITCHERPLANT

Can pitcherplant (Sarracenia purpurea) be grown in the wild garden? Yes. This is a good bog-garden subject.

SHOOTINGSTAR

Is shootingstar a good wild-garden subject? Yes. *Dodecatheon meadia* is a showy wildflower suitable for woodland planting in slightly acid or neutral soil.

SPRINGBEAUTY (CLAYTONIA)

What are the cultural requirements of springbeauty (Claytonia)? Damp, leafmoldy soil and full shade in summer.

TRILLIUM

Which trilliums are best for the wild garden? *Trillium grandiflorum* (Large-Flowering White Trillium); *T. nivale* (small white, earliest); *T. luteum* (yellow); *T. stylosum* (rose); *T. californicum* (sessile type in white or red).

Can trilliums be purchased? Yes, specialists in wild plants and some other nurseries list them.

How can trilliums best be propagated from seed? The best way to propagate trilliums is by division of old, large clumps. Absolutely fresh seed, sown before it has a chance to dry, may germinate the following spring, but growth is very slow and all conditions have to be just right.

VIOLETS

Are violets dug up from the woods suitable for planting in the wild garden? Yes. They are easily transplanted.

What sort of conditions does Birdsfoot Violet need? Give a dryish, well-drained, sandy, very acid soil in full sun.

WINTERGREENS

Will you please name and describe some native wintergreens? Spotted Wintergreen (*Chimaphila maculata*) with white-veined lanceolate evergreen leaves; showy white flowers. Pipsissewa (*Chimaphila umbellata*), rather like the above but with wedge-shaped unmarked evergreen leaves and smaller flowers, sometimes blush pink. Shinleaf (*Pyrola elliptica*), oval basal leaves, persistent but not evergreen; white flowers on 5- to 10-in. stalks, in racemes. Round-leaved American Wintergreen (*Pyrola americana*), leaves basal, rounded; showy blush-white flowers on tall stalks. Creeping Wintergreen (*Gaultheria procumbens*), evergreen, blunt, aromatic leaves; creeping subterranean stems; blush flowers in leaf axils; edible red berries; 2 to 6 ins. tall. Flowering Wintergreen or Fringed Polygala (*P. paucifolia*), evergreen leaves; rose-purple, fringed flowers, or, sometimes, white; lowgrowing, and spreading.

How is pipsissewa (Chimaphila umbellata) propagated? By cuttings of new growth taken the first half of July and rooted in sand in a seed flat.

GARDENS OF OTHER TYPES

CHILDREN'S GARDEN

How much space would you suggest giving a child in which to make his own garden? This depends on the size of the child and on how much space is available. A little tot should have a tiny space—4 or 5 ft. square. The area may be increased as he grows older.

What would be a good location to give a child for a garden? A spot that has full sun all day, where the ground is in good condition and easily workable. Children are easily discouraged if their garden does not produce, so do not select any unfit "leftover" area.

Which plants would be suitable for a child to grow in his own garden? Bright, easily grown annuals, which can be raised from seed: zinnias, marigolds, alyssum, scabiosa, and portulaca. These will give him an opportunity to learn how seeds are planted and what the plants look like as they come up. A few easy perennials might be given him to plant too. If a fence encloses his garden, morningglories can be used to cover it.

Will you list some easy vegetables that a child might grow from seed? Carrots, beets, leaf lettuce, beans, radishes, and New Zealand spinach.

I am very much interested in planning a garden that will interest my children. Just what arrangement would you suggest? I have in mind something to go along with their own yard and playhouse. Any garden for children should be scaled down to their size. They like intricate patterns and odd plants. Paths should be narrow, and all plants relatively small. Choose varieties that will stand the maximum amount of abuse. Leave plenty of play space.

CITY GARDENS

Will you give some hints on making a city garden? The keynote of the city garden is simplicity. Remember that you cannot grow all the flowering plants that thrive in the country. If you have shade, plant interesting shrubs that will tolerate shady conditions, and some ground covers, such as pachysandra and ivy. Get a few pieces of suitable furniture and arrange them attractively. Pots of bright flowers, or window boxes, may be set about in sunny places. Vines are good for most city gardens, as they afford protection as well as greenery. (See also City Conditions, Section III.)

ENGLISH GARDEN

How does one begin to plan an English country garden? Is there any set plan or style to follow? This subject is too large to cover in a few words. Better consult such books as *Gardens for Small Country Houses,* by Gertrude Jekyll and Lawrence Weaver; *English Flower Garden,* by W. Robinson.

FRAGRANT GARDENS

I would like some fragrant annuals in my garden. What do you suggest? Nicotiana, nasturtium, sweet alyssum, petunia, marigold, stock, heliotrope (tender shrub), mignonette, sweetpea.

Will you name some bulbs for a fragrant garden? *Crocus versicolor* and *C. biflorus; Scilla italica* and *S. campanulata; Fritillaria imperialis;* hyacinths; narcissi (jonquils and hybrids; poetaz; poeticus; tazetta); tulips: Ambrosia, Arethusa, Dido, De Wet, Leda, Early Yellow Rose; lily-of-the-valley; scented irises (rhizomes, not bulbs); Liliums: *auratum, candidum, longiflorum, regale, speciosum;* tuberose.

What are some fragrant hardy flowers? *Dianthus caesius* and varieties; *Dianthus caryophyllus* and varieties; scented bearded iris; lily-of-the-valley; *Viola odorata* and varieties; *Lavandula officinalis;* hemerocallis; buddleia; primula; clematis; sweetwilliam; monarda; phlox; peony; roses; Arabis Snowcap; salvia.

Which herbs shall I plant in a fragrant garden? See Herbs.

Which flowers shall I plant for night fragrance? Nicotiana; moonvine; petunia; *Pelargonium triste;* nightblooming waterlilies.

Will you tell me which geraniums to buy for fragrance? *Pelargonium tomentosum* (mint); *P. graveolens* (rose); *P. limoneum* (lemon); *P. odoratissimum* (nutmeg.)

What will give fragrance in the late garden? Chrysanthemums, clematis, wallflowers.

Which shrubs shall I plant for fragrance? Pink (winterbloom) and Swamp Azalea; *Jasminum nudiflorum* and *J. primulinum;* benzoin; magnolia; Flowering Almond; lilac; honeysuckle; daphne; roses; mockorange; strawberry-shrub; English Hawthorn; wisteria; witchhazel. Tender: lemonverbena; rosemary; heliotrope.

KNOT GARDENS

What is a knot garden? A garden of low-growing plants or hedges planted in a formal, intricate design. Common to medieval landscape design, when colored sand was often used to form the paths or sections which outlined the beds. Now used in parks, herb gardens, and formal gardens.

A "knot" design herb garden. The herbs used are: 1. Thyme or Roman Wormwood; 2. Sweet Violet or Santolina viridis; 3. Lavender cotton or dwarf Lavender; 4. Germander or Rosemary.

What plant materials can be used for a knot garden? Boxwood, artemisia, santolina, iresine; low-bedding flowers; herbs.

OUTDOOR LIVING ROOM

What is an "outdoor living room"? An area with comfortable tables and chairs set aside for lounging and loafing. It should be secluded, at least partially walled in by evergreens, shrubs, or other plant material. It is desirable to have the outdoor living room away from the house, but easily accessible. The ideal "room" gives a view of the garden through an arch in the hedge or by leaving one side unscreened. It is often placed in the shade of a large tree. Some people like to include equipment for barbecues and picnics in this area.

Invitation to leisure: at least one corner of the garden, no matter how small, should be arranged for outdoor living.

We are planning a simple rose garden in an outdoor living room

surrounded by poplar trees. **Will you help us with the layout?** The typical rose garden is formal in design. Square or circular areas divided into small beds by narrow paths, and provided with a central feature such as a sundial, make an effective arrangement. (See also Roses and previous question.)

ROOF GARDENS

What soil mixture should be used to fill the boxes on a roof garden? A good, friable loam is ideal. Avoid heavy clay or very sandy soil.

What kind of fertilizer should I use for the plants on my roof garden? Liquid manure, or a complete commercial fertilizer.

Should one use a mulch on the soil in roof-garden boxes? Yes; a mulch will help prevent sudden drying out of the soil from wind and sun on the roof. Peatmoss, rotted manure, or leafmold could be used.

Can one grow vegetables successfully on a roof? Yes, with full sun and good soil, a few can be grown. In boxes about 8 ins. deep grow lettuce, parsley, radishes, bush beans, endive, onions (from sets), New Zealand spinach, Swiss chard. Try stump-rooted carrots and beets. Tomatoes planted in deeper boxes, staked and sheltered so that they will not blow over, will probably thrive.

I would like to grow some herbs on my roof garden. Do you think they would be successful? Yes, they probably would. Herbs are a good choice for the shallow boxes usually used on a roof. Try thyme, chives, parsley, mint, sage, and basil. (See Herbs for soil and culture.)

Will you give a list of annual flowers for growing on a roof? Marigolds, zinnias, ageratum, petunias, calendulas, alyssum, lobelia, portulaca, celosia, iberis, forget-me-nots, salvia, corcopsis, aster, scabiosa.

I am planning to make the boxes for plants on my roof garden. Can you give me some suggestions? Your boxes should be made deep enough to hold 8 to 12 ins. of soil. They can be as wide as you like. Use cypress wood that will withstand water. Provide drainage holes in the bottom of each box so that the soil will not become sour. The inside of the boxes can be painted with asphaltum to protect the wood, and the outside with several coats of durable outdoor paint.

I want to grow some vines on my roof. How could I effectively support them? Make an arbor over part of the roof. This would not only be a good support for your vines, but would also supply shade and some shelter on the terrace. Otherwise, use a trellis against the side of the building, or put vine supports along the side of the building, on which to tie the vines.

What kind of furniture can I use for my roof garden? Any comfortable, well-designed furniture that will withstand the weather. Avoid types that must be taken in each time it rains. Metal chairs and tables are good, if kept well painted, and are heavy enough not to blow over; or stout wooden ones. If you care to be different, make your own furniture out of boxes and barrels, and paint with bright colors.

I want to make a roof garden that is good-looking but will not be expensive. Will you make some suggestions? Edge the railing or wall with window boxes painted dark green or any color which fits your scheme. Grow such plants as petunias, ageratum, geraniums, alyssum, marigolds, and calendulas. Some potted plants can be arranged about the roof. If you can get some large boxes or barrels, try a few shrubs, such as privet or forsythia, or trees, such as cedars or yews, for a background. Train vines against the wall or building. Ivy, honeysuckle, or morningglories would do well. Comfortable chairs and tables will be needed.

What can be done on a flat roof, approximately 10 × 10 ft., on the west side of an apartment? Can dirt be put on the roof to sufficient depth to raise anything successfully? Six to 8 ins. of soil will successfully grow many flowers or even a few vegetables. Check with engineer before putting this considerable weight on roof. Otherwise confine efforts to a few soil-filled boxes.

I have some large roof-garden boxes. How can I tell if the soil is sour? How can I fertilize the earth before we plant? If in doubt, have a soil test made. For most plants add lime every 2 years. Bone meal and dried cow manure are excellent fertilizers; or use any complete commercial fertilizer. Do not mix lime and fertilizer at one time. Add lime in fall or very early spring, and fertilizer at planting time.

SUNKEN GARDENS

I have a natural spot for making a sunken garden. How can I plan this? The sunken garden is viewed from above and the basic layout is very important because of this. An informal or untidy effect would spoil it. A formal garden, with a path running through the center, and a center of interest at the end, would probably work out well. If your garden is well drained, you might plan a formal rose garden; or an herb garden with thyme-planted steps and borders of fragrant plants around the four sides of the area in front of the walls. Leave the center in turf.

There is an old foundation on our property, where a house burned down. Would this make a good place for a sunken garden? Yes, it should be excellent. You may have to provide drainage, if water collects in the foundation. Build steps down into the garden of the same kind of stones as the foundation. Perennials of doubtful hardiness and shrubs, which need much protection from cold winds, can be incorporated in your planting plan.

WINDOW BOX GARDENS

What special problems are involved in window-box gardening? First provide appropriate boxes with holes in bottom for drainage. Put in 2 or 3 ins. of cinders or broken brick, and fill with rich, porous soil. Plant with appropriate material in spring. Regular attention to watering is of prime importance. Fertilize as often as necessary.

Can you give some pointers on making window boxes? Make box to fit window space, but if the length is in excess of 3 ft. make in two sections. For good results the box should be not less than 8 ins. deep and 10 ins. wide. Use cypress or white pine at least 1 in. thick. Bore ½-in. holes, 6 ins. apart, in bottom for drainage.

What is the best soil for window boxes? One that is rich, with plenty of humus to retain moisture. Use 2 parts loam, 1 part rotted manure or leafmold, with a 5-in. pot of bone meal mixed with each bushel.

Are wooden window boxes better than those made of concrete? They are inexpensive and less weighty to handle if they have to be moved occasionally. On the other hand, they are less permanent.

Are the metal "self-watering" boxes satisfactory? Yes; but don't place too much reliance on the "self-watering" feature.

Can an old hot-water tank (cylindrical) be used as a porch box? Yes. Have a tinsmith cut out a strip equal to ⅓ to ½ of the circumference for the entire length. Punch holes in the opposite side to drain off surplus water.

Is there any flowering plant suitable for window boxes which will hold up all summer and be colorful? Lantana. Get potted plants in May; usually then in flower, they will bloom until frost. They stand heat, drought, and city conditions, but are at their best when well watered and pruned occasionally to restrain lanky growth. Stand partial shade, but prefer full sun. Balcony petunias are also good.

The garden club in our town wants to promote a window box project in the hope of winning more plant growing enthusiasts. Can you refer me to a publication which covers this subject completely so our committee can be well informed? Yes, "Window-box Gardening" by Henry Teuscher, published by Macmillan, 1956, covers the subject thoroughly.

Which flowers grow in window boxes? Among the most satisfactory are begonias, geraniums, fuchsias, ageratum, petunias, dwarf marigolds, torenias, pansies, sweet alyssum, morningglory, vinca, sedum, balsam, portulaca, and lobelia.

Is there a blooming plant that will grow in window boxes under

awning? (West Virginia.) None that you can be sure of. Try *Begonia semperflorens* varieties, petunias, and *Lobelia erinus* varieties.

What would you suggest for flowers (not tuberous begonias) for window boxes that are very shaded? Would like plenty of color. You will probably have difficulty with any flowering plant if the shade is heavy and continuous. Fuchsias, *Begonia semperflorens*, torenias, and lobelias will stand as much shade as any.

What shall I plant in a window box, outdoors, on north side? (Washington.) Flowering plants: tuberous begonias, fuchsias, lobelias, torenias. Foliage plants: aucuba, boxwood, Japanese Holly, Dwarf Yew, arborvitae, privet, English Ivy, vinca, Kenilworth Ivy.

What could we plant in outdoor front-stoop window boxes which will survive New York City winter climate, such as evergreen, yew, dwarf pine, etc.? Among the most satisfactory plants are small yew, arborvitae, Japanese Holly, privet, and English Ivy. All suffer, however, when the soil is frozen solid. Make sure soil is well soaked in fall. *Sedum acre* and *S. spectabile* will survive year in, year out.

What can be put in a window box (southern exposure) during the winter months? (Virginia.) Small evergreens, boxwood, arborvitae, junipers, spruces, with English Ivy and trailing myrtle to droop over edge. This material cannot be expected to thrive permanently, however, because of poor environment.

Is it necessary to put ivy and myrtle grown in window boxes into the ground for the winter? If the soil about their roots freezes solid, they cannot take up water to replace that lost by leaves, and the plants die. Place boxes on ground, pack manure or straw well about them, and cover with burlap or light layer of straw.

How early can pansies be planted in outdoor window boxes? (North Carolina.) Pansies are much hardier than most people realize. The established plants can be put in the outdoor window box as soon as the severe portion of winter is passed. Plants grown indoors should be hardened off by gradually exposing them to cooler temperatures before setting them in the outdoor boxes. March 15, or even earlier, in your locality, might be about right.

Are hanging baskets practical? Yes, provided they are made right with plenty of moss on the outside of the soil and are never allowed to dry out.

MISCELLANEOUS

CACTI FOR OUTDOORS

What are the hardiest kinds of cacti? *Opuntia compressa* (*vulgaris*), *O. fragilis, Echinocereus viridiflorus,* and *Pediocactus simpsoni.*

Are there any varieties of cactus, other than opuntia, that can be left outside all winter in south Jersey? You might try *Echinocereus viridiflorus* and *Pediocactus simpsoni.*

Will cactus from the Arizona desert thrive in Oklahoma? Those native from north of Phoenix will possibly grow if given a thoroughly well-drained and sheltered position.

Can spineless cacti of the type that Luther Burbank developed be grown in a climate which is hot and dry in the summer and cold and wet in the winter? No. The spineless opuntias do not thrive where wet winters are experienced.

What are names of some cacti that will live out of doors in south central North Carolina? *Opuntia compressa* (*vulgaris*), *O. fragilis, O. rhodantha,* (*O. xanthostemma*), *O. polyacantha, O. imbricata, O. basilaris, O. ursina, Echinocereus viridiflorus, E. reichenbachi, E. baileyi,* and *Pediocactus simpsoni.*

GOURDS

WHAT TO GROW

Will you tell me which gourds to grow for curing—gourds to be used for winter decoration? White pear, bicolor pear, goose egg, ringed pear, spoon, miniatures, ladle, warty hardhead, snake, *lagenaria* in variety.

Which kinds of gourds are suitable for bird houses? The ordinary dipper gourds as well as others of the *lagenaria* genus.

How can I produce dipper-type gourds? Have heard it is necessary to tape the neck of the gourd. Dipper gourds are known to seedsmen under that name and culture is the same as for other gourds. Shaping of necks is not ordinarily necessary for dipper gourds, but if you want to modify their shape this could be done.

CULTURE

Is there any fertilizer that will cause gourd plants to grow more rapidly? The same provisions that are made for cucumbers and melons will work well with gourds. Use a 5–10–5 fertilizer or a combination of manure and a smaller amount of fertilizer, or stable manure and superphosphate. Stable manure alone is also satisfactory.

How do you raise gourds? Gourds are not particularly difficult to grow. They can be allowed to run on the ground but are better planted along a wire fence or provided with a trellis. General requirements are about the same as for cucumbers and melons—a moderately rich, well-fertilized soil with reasonable moisture supply. They thrive under a wide range of conditions, and most varieties of small gourds will mature in the Northern part of the country. Seed is sowed about 1 in. deep and plants are thinned to 2 or 3 ft. apart, according to varieties. Dusting may be necessary to control the striped cucumber beetle. In Northern climates plants may be started under glass as are cucumbers and muskmelons. Shallow cultivation should be practiced to control weeds.

What is the earliest date gourds can be planted? Gourds are planted at about the same time as cucumbers, 2 or 3 weeks after average date of last killing frost in the spring or at about the time tomatoes are set out. Gourds will not stand frost.

How do you start gourds from seed? Ornamental gourds are usually raised in pots from seed sown in April or May and transplanted out in June. Some find it advisable to sow gourd seeds directly in pots (in the greenhouse) made of pressed peat and dried manure. When set out in the ground these quickly disintegrate but save the roots from being disturbed in the transplanting operation. Seed may also be sown outdoors when danger of frost is past.

How can one take care of gourds after they are picked so that they will not decay? Gourds should be thoroughly matured on the vines before they are picked. They will not stand freezing if they are still succulent. If by necessity they are taken at the immature state, they should be handled with the utmost care and allowed to dry and cure indoors, but mold is likely to attack them. Some recommend washing gourds, but wiping with a soft cloth is probably better. Disinfectant solutions may be of some service, but not too much. To keep gourds in their natural state, waxing is one of the best methods, using ordinary floor wax and polishing lightly. Some use shellac, but this changes the color and appearance. Some also like to decorate and paint them in simple or fanciful fashion. Stems should be left on the gourds, removing them from vines by cutting. Maturity may be judged by feeling them, but it is not wise to test with the fingernail. They should be dry and the stem should be withered.

What is a good spray to combat the stem borer of gourds? It is best to grow the gourds on ground where curcubits have not been grown the previous year or where their refuse remains. Early summer squash may be used as a trap crop. When the borer is already at work in the vines, surgery is resorted to, cutting lengthwise of the vine with a thin knife to destroy the larvae, then the cut portion is covered with earth and little harm is done to the plant. Rotenone spray or dust applied 3 or 4 times may be effective in destroying the borers just after they are hatched.

Is there a gourd society in this country? Yes. The Gourd Society of America, Inc., Horticultural Hall, Boston, Massachusetts.

WEEDS

GENERAL

Can you keep weeds down; and how? By constantly attacking them while they are yet young, and above all by preventing them from seeding. On cultivated ground, use the cultivator and hoe, plus hand weeding; on lawns, hand weeding and good culture to encourage desirable grasses; on drives and paths, weed killers.

I have 6 acres, not worked for about 20 years, full of weeds. What is the best way to get rid of them? Is it best to plow in fall or spring? Maintain a bare fallow through one season. Plow in spring and harrow or plow shallowly at frequent intervals throughout summer, so the surface is never permitted to show any signs of green growth.

We intend fencing our lot (natural pickets) in spring. Adjoining are open fields. How can I keep down weeds at base of fence on the outside? If you are not planting too close to inside of fence, use regular weed killer. If the right one is selected, most of the broad-leaved weeds will be killed and one can easily keep the grass mowed to prevent tall weeds from becoming established.

Would it be advisable to burn all dried-up flowers and weeds in our flower garden in early spring? (Due to illness, garden was not tended in fall.) Under the circumstances the burning treatment would be satisfactory. The seeds produced by the weeds are already dispersed, however, so burning will not materially reduce the season's weed crop.

Is there any method other than burning trash or dry brush on a seedbed, to kill weed seeds? Burning is not very satisfactory, for weed seeds will stand considerable heat. A good method is to keep the bed moist to encourage germination and then to hoe 2 or 3 times (allowing 10 days between each hoeing) to destroy seedlings. Sterilization with chloropicrin (which see) is also effective, but special equipment is needed.

How can I get rid of weeds before and during growth of parsley, besides weeding when small? Hand weeding in the rows and frequent hoeing between the rows are the best methods for annual weeds. If the ground is infested with perennial weeds, these should be dug out to the last root before the parsley is sown.

Is it possible to spray carrots to control the weeds? Yes, several so-called selective sprays are now being used by the vegetable growers for this very purpose. For latest information on these in your area, consult your Agricultural Extension Service.

In August I put turf-builder around a privet hedge. Six weeks later a broadleaf weed came in thick around hedges. Could it be the turf-

builder? Turf-builder is a proprietary plant food that certainly does not contain weed seeds. It probably stimulated the growth of weeds present in the soil, thus proving its efficiency as a fertilizer.

Is there anything that will kill weeds, yet not destroy flowers or vegetables? While certain selective sprays have limited uses in the control of weeds in grainfields and in lawns, no substance has been (or probably ever will be) found to meet the requirements you state. This is because many weeds are closely related botanically to favorite flowers and vegetables.

I have heard that "Sovosol", a dry cleaning fluid, is a weed killer. How can it be applied? This is sprayed lightly at full strength on the young weeds in the garden. Care should be taken to hold the nozzle of the spray gun close to the weeds, so that the wind will not blow the spray to valued plants. This spray is particularly effective in controlling small seedlings of purslane in early summer.

What can be done to keep a cinder drive free from weeds? Procure a commercial weed killer from a dealer in horticultural supplies, and use according to directions. Crankcase drainings, diluted with kerosene so that they can be sprayed over the drive, are alternatives.

What is the name of a compound to put in paths between flower beds to eliminate weeds? Any good commercial weed killer will do this. Be careful not to let any of it get onto the flower beds, lawns, or other places where you desire vegetation to grow.

What is best to use in killing weeds in a brick drain? Providing the drain does not carry water into a pond or stream used by fish or animals, any commercial weed killer should prove effective.

Is 2, 4–D dangerous to use? No, providing normal caution is taken in pouring the material and in *thoroughly cleaning the sprayer* afterward. However, extreme precaution should be taken in applying it on a windy day since the wind may blow the material, which is highly volatile, to quite a distance where it can kill other vegetation.

How can I tell different kinds of weeds and grasses? *Weeds,* by Walter Conrad Muenscher (Macmillan, 1955) and *Weeds of Lawn and Garden,* by John M. Fogg (Univ. of Penna. Press, 1945) are two excellent books on this subject.

SPECIFIC WEEDS

Am planting a garden over an old asparagus bed and have tried many ways to kill the asparagus, even to digging up the crowns, but the stuff persists. How may I rid myself of this nuisance? Keep digging. Every time an asparagus stem appears dig out the root from which it arises.

How can one get rid of bindweed on lawn without killing roses,

trees, and shrubs by using poison? You probably cannot, especially if the weed is intertwined with the shrubbery. Digging out would be the only solution here.

How can I exterminate an extremely hardy vine resembling a morningglory, having white flowers and seemingly endless roots? Doubtless a bindweed, a pernicious weed with fleshy roots which descend several feet, every fragment of which will grow. Where it exists, either don't plant anything and constantly hoe, so that no leaves can build up a food store in the roots, or plant only low-growing crops which can be hoed frequently so that no vines can get started. Also it has been determined that the proper application of 2, 4–D while the weed is actively growing can kill it nearly 100%.

How can I get rid of Bermuda Grass? Where ground freezes, plow or fork shallowly in fall so roots are exposed to air through winter. Farther South rely upon forking out and frequent cultivation; or smother with crop of fall-sown rye, followed by crop of cowpeas or velvet beans. Chemical methods of eradication have not proved too successful.

What can I do for Bermuda Grass in flower borders? (Tennessee.) In your section, Bermuda Grass doubtless is a troublesome weed, but it is used to make lawns in the South. In the borders it must be kept down by frequent hoeing.

How can I clear land of blackberry vines? Spray vines twice during season, when foliage is present, with ammonium sulfamate; strength, 1 lb. to 5 gals. of water. The solution reaches the roots through the vines and kills them. Also, 2, 4, 5–T can be used as a spray since this has proved very effective in eliminating blackberries which are not killed by 2, 4–D alone. The best time to apply the first spray is when the leaves are almost fully developed.

Narrowleaf Plantain, a deep-rooted pest in lawns; watch for and dig up seedling plants. (Right) The Broadleaved Plantain.

Can you name a formula to kill buckthorn or plantain? At what time of year should it be used? Dig out by hand or mow down and burn before seeding stage is reached. Also spraying with 2, 4–D weed killers early in the summer affords good control.

Which is more effective in killing weeds 2, 4–D or a material under the trade designation of 2, 4, 5–T. The latter has proved more effective especially on difficult-to-kill plants like poison-ivy, sumac and blackberries.

We have some patches of Canada Thistle in our garden. Is digging them up the best remedy? Yes, if the work is well done. Any pieces of root left in the soil will grow, however, and digging should be followed by repeated hoeings.

We have a large hay field next to us with a few bad patches of Canada thistle. The seeds blow over into our garden. Can these patches be eliminated by spraying? Yes. Use sodium chlorate as a summer spray (1 lb. per gal.) and again in early September when regrowth has occurred. Sometimes 2, 4–D has also proved effective.

What is the best way to clean cattails and rushes from lake edge? The only practicable method is to dig them out completely. If surface of lake could be lowered for a considerable period, they may die out from lack of moisture.

What is the best method of fighting crab grass? Pull every seedling as soon as big enough to recognize, thus preventing seeding (crab grass is an annual). Fertilize lawn generously to stimulate desired grasses. (See also Lawn and Turf Areas.)

Crab grass: bane of the lawn maker.
For control see Lawn and Turf Areas
(page 638).

How can creeping Jenny be eradicated? Creeping Jenny is a name applied to a golden-flowered lysimachia as well as to the white-flowered wild morningglory. The former is controlled by hand forking and frequent surface cultivation. (For control of wild morningglory, see other answers.)

How can I fight the curse of a neighbor's dandelion seed blowing into my yard? Three procedures are possible: eliminate dandelions on neighbor's property; dig out young dandelions as fast as they appear in your yard; learn to tolerate dandelions. Probably best and easiest means of eradication is to spray both your neighbor's dandelions and yours with 2, 4–D or some specific chemical weed killer. Effective control is easily maintained this way.

What is the best method for controlling dandelions? Digging them out. Alternate methods are: cut the plants off well below surface and drip a few drops of sulphuric acid onto the cut root; spray with an iron sulfate solution (1 lb. to 1½ gals. water) every 10 days; or spray with 2, 4–D.

Dandelion: to control, cut tap root well below ground with an asparagus knife and prevent stray plants from seeding.

How can one effectively destroy dock weeds? Specimens of small size can be pulled out when soil is very wet. With larger plants, cut tops off an inch below ground surface, pierce root with a skewer, and pour a few drops of sulphuric acid (or a large teacupful of salt) on cut surface.

What can be done to get rid of "dodder," also called lovevine, gold-thread, strangleweed, Desire's-hair, and hellbind? Dodder is a parasitic annual. Cut down and burn all infected plants before the dodder has a chance to seed.

What method of controlling chickweed do you recommend to the home gardener? In flower and vegetable garden, surface cultivation; remove *at once* every plant, with its spreading root system, as it appears, *and destroy*. In lawns, fertilize to encourage growth of grasses. Use lime if soil is at all too acid. Another method is to dust lightly with sulfate of ammonia on a dewy morning, and water well the same evening. More than one application may be necessary. Also a mixture of TCA and 2, 4–D to which a wetting agent has been added has proved successful as a spray control.

Chickweed: one of the worst pests in gardens. Remove plants—getting all the roots—in early spring, and burn.

In absence of sulfate of ammonia, what would be a good substitute for control of chickweed? Spraying with 2, 4–D gives fairly good control. Dimet and Sodar are new and effective.

Will you suggest a remedy for much-branched, green, leafy weed

with tiny daisy flowers each having 5 white petals? I think it is called galinsoga. This is an introduction from tropical America. It is very sensitive to frost, but is an annual and so over-winters as seed. Hand pulling large plants *before seeds form* and cultivation to kill young ones are most practical remedies.

Is it possible to remove Johnsongrass or quackgrass from a vegetable garden so that it will not be back the next season? These are two distinct species. Both may be eliminated by forking out as much as possible by hand, taking pains to get every root, and then by repeatedly cultivating the surface throughout summer. Johnsongrass is particularly resistant, and vigorous methods must be used. Advances have been made recently in the use of 2,2 dichloroproprionic acid at proper strengths in the control of Johnsongrass. We suggest contacting one of the large weed-chemical manufacturing companies now for a trade name product of this material and its proper use.

Lambsquarters is common in my garden. How do you keep it down? This weed usually favors rich soils. It is controlled by cultivating and is easily hand pulled. When the plants are young, lambsquarters makes excellent greens.

We have a shrub called Mexican bamboo which is becoming a nuisance. How can it be eradicated? This is *Polygonum cuspidatum*. If you want other plants to grow in same place, dig it out as thoroughly as possible, then cut every shoot off that appears when not more than an inch high. Otherwise use commercial weed killers. Some of the chemical weed killers have given partial control of this pernicious pest but it must be sprayed several times at proper intervals before it can be killed out altogether.

I have a weed which grows very tall and multiplies rapidly, roots are red and run under the ground and sprout. What is the proper name and how can I kill it? Probably *Polygonum cuspidatum*. Only relief other than poisoning ground with weed killer is to dig out all roots (which go very deep) and keep surface hoed afterward to kill any sprouts that appear.

What will kill moonvine or wild morningglory? Dig out as much as possible, then keep the ground surface cultivated at frequent intervals so that no new shoot ever attains a height of more than 2 ins. before being cut off. Spraying with 2, 4–D and 2, 4, 5–T also gives good control if spray is applied to plants when they are actively growing.

How can a fairly large patch of nettle in a field be eliminated? By repeatedly mowing so that the plants are never permitted to get more than a few inches high. Also, by spraying the plants when young with a commercial weed killer.

Nutgrass is a troublesome weed in my garden. Can you suggest a

means of eliminating it? This is not really a grass but a sedge which is partial to wet places. Drainage, followed by a year's clean cultivation, is the only real remedy.

What can be done to destroy petunia seedlings? I would like to plant something else in the former petunia bed, but the petunias come up by the hundreds each year. Hand weeding and scuffle hoeing after the seedlings are up are the only practicable means. The hoeing will not only destroy the petunias but will also encourage the growth of whatever else you may plant in the bed.

Can you suggest any means of getting rid of plantain (both narrow-and broad-leaved) in quantity? Digging, even with a special tool, is slow and laborious. Plantains on lawns can be killed by using a pinch of salt in the center of each plant on a hot day. Two or 3 drops of sulphuric acid will also serve. There are compounds sold that will kill broad-leaved weeds in lawns when dusted on. (See Lawns.) Spraying with 2, 4–D also proves effective.

How can I get rid of poisonivy without spending a fortune? Syringe or spray the plants while green with fuel oil or crankcase oil thinned down with kerosene. Spray in late spring with sodium sulfamate or a mixture of 2, 4–D and 2, 4, 5–T, and again when new young leaves are formed in late summer. A final spray or two the following year should eradicate the bed, but it should be remembered that getting rid of poisonivy is no one-shot proposition.

How can I eliminate poisonivy? By the use, according to the maker's directions, of the Du Pont spray, ammonium sulfamate. By digging out the roots.

How may I get rid of poisonivy growing in a bed of lily-of-the-valley? Get someone immune to poisonivy to carefully dig up the bed. Transplant lily-of-the-valley to another location for 2 or 3 years. Meantime eliminate any ivy that appears on old site.

What is the poison-oak plant and how can it be destroyed? Poison-oak (*Toxicodendron quercifolium*) is similar to poisonivy (*T. radicans*), but has more oaklike leaves. Spray with ammonium sulfamate according to maker's directions.

Every summer my garden is invaded by purslane. What can I do? This is an annual that develops rapidly in warm weather and rich soil. Attack vigorously with hoe and cultivator while weeds are yet tiny. If plants get large, rake them up and burn or compost, otherwise they will root and grow again. To keep areas of very small seedlings under control without hoeing, one can spray with one of the dry cleaning fluids, one of which is termed "Sovosol".

Which is the most effective way of ridding ground of quackgrass? It grows in soil around shrubbery and cannot be exposed to anything that would harm these plants. In the spring work the whole area over with a spading fork and carefully remove all underground stems of the grass. Follow this throughout the summer by forking out every piece of the grass that appears before the leaves are an inch high.

How can I eradicate redroot (pigweed)?   Practice clean cultivation. Mow plants down before they reach the seeding stage.

How do you get rid of sandburs?   Practice clean cultivation. The plant is an annual and cannot reproduce if all plants are hoed or pulled out before they seed.

How can I destroy sheepssorrel and at the same time use the ground for vegetables and flowers?   Sheepssorrel is a sure sign of poor, infertile, and, usually, acid soil. Apply fertilizer generously and test for lime needs. Nitrogenous fertilizers are especially helpful.

How can I eradicate sumac?   The most satisfactory remedy is to grub out the roots. It has also been killed out by three consecutive cuttings, the first when the plant is actively growing in late spring, and the other two following shortly thereafter when regrowth has again started.

Is there any method of destroying sumac other than digging it out?   Spraying young foliage with a mixture of 2, 4–D and 2, 4, 5–T when half mature in spring and a second time when regrowth is at about the same stage, has given good control.

I have an old trumpetvine root in the ground and want to plant a fruit tree instead. How can I kill the heavy root so it won't take the strength from the fruit tree?   The only satisfactory procedure is to dig out the trumpetvine root and turn over and fertilize the soil before planting the fruit tree. Other than digging out root, the best way of killing the old root is to paint the stump with a concentrated solution of sodium sulfamate, or chip down the bark around the stump and insert small crystals of sodium sulfamate.

How can I get rid of white clover in my garden?   White clover in lawns may be discouraged by maintaining the soil on the acid side. Liming encourages its growth. If troublesome in flower and vegetable garden, hoeing and hand weeding are recommended.

What is best method of getting rid of white snakeroot?   Grub out the roots.

How is the best way to get rid of wild carrot?   The plant is biennial and does not reproduce itself if it is cut down before it reaches the seeding stage.

Wild garlic is becoming troublesome. How shall I eliminate it?   A most pernicious weed, once established. If area is not too large, hand digging, followed by destruction of every bulb, is best. Cultivate surface frequently. Spraying with 2, 4–D or a combination of 2, 4,

5–T has proved successful but best results are obtained when leaves are actually growing. Poor results occur when bulblets are dormant.

How can wild grapevines and poisonivy be killed out? These seem to cover every rock and bit of space on our farm. Goldenrod and milk-weed mingle with these weeds. Both poison ivy and wild grapes are effectively killed when sprayed two or three times while still actively growing with a mixture (half and half) of 2, 4–D and 2, 4, 5–T. If this is delayed until late summer, a very poor killing results.

Can wild morningglory be exterminated around the trunk of fruit trees without killing or damaging the trees? Maintain a circle of bare ground around the tree and keep this clean of all growth by scuffle hoeing every few days throughout 2 successive growing seasons. As an alternative, cover infested area with heavy roofing paper for 2 seasons.

Poison Ivy (left); (right) Virginia-creeper, often mistaken for it.

How can I get rid of wiregrass? This name is applied to several distinct species of grasses, and also to a kind of rush. Several of these indicate soils low in fertility. Some are annuals, some perennials. Frequent cultivation and prevention of seeding are recommended treatments.

How can I kill a large and vigorously growing poplar tree on our property. I do not want to go to the expense of cutting it down at this time? Cut the bark from the trunk in strips about 6″ long in a circle around tree, place some crystals of sodium sulfamate between them and the trunk, tying the strips back in place and let nature take its course from there on.

I have a poplar tree, recently cut down but the roots keep sending up suckers. How can I kill this two and a half foot stump once and for all without having to dig it out? Make a groove or hollow in the stump and place a half cup-full of crystals of sodium sulfamate there which will gradually dissolve in rain water and be absorbed by wood.

Can I spray brush while it is dormant in the winter and still expect

a good kill? Yes, using a mixture of 2, 4–D and 2, 4, 5–T in kerosene and directed to the base of the plants so that the stems are thoroughly wet on all sides.

In reading a trade magazine I saw an advertisement of a power company spraying brush along the power lines to kill the growth. Can I use this same material on my property? Certainly, it is usually a mixture of 2, 4–D and 2, 4, 5–T mixed with water for use when plants are in leaf, and mixed with kerosene when plants are dormant. It is easily applied and very effective on many plants.

We have an old pasture covered in spots with hawthorns as much as 6" in diameter. How can I best eliminate these plants without having to pull each one out with a tractor? Try spraying the lower base of the trees with a concentrated solution of 2, 4–D and 2, 4, 5–T in the winter while trees are dormant.

ODDS & ENDS

Will you explain the meanings of floriculture and horticulture? Horticulture covers the cultivation of all plants that may be grown in a garden. Floriculture is that branch of horticulture that deals with the growing of flowers—often used to denote the commercial culture of flowers outside and under glass.

What is meant by "deciduous" trees and shrubs? Those which shed their foliage in the autumn. Some, which retain their dry leaves, all or partly, through the winter, like beech and some oaks, are commonly included in "deciduous" trees.

Is it possible that a chain or a peg fastened to a tree at a certain distance from the ground will ever be further from the ground, no matter how old the tree? No, there will be no elevation of anything driven into a tree at a given point.

How much sunshine and air circulation do most blooming plants need? Some flowering plants are happiest in all the sunshine possible. Others appreciate shade during the hottest part of the day, and some are tolerant of a good deal of shade. All appreciate good air circulation but dislike drafts.

Will you tell me how to change the color of flowers? For instance, what would the procedure be if I wanted to raise a blue marigold? Colors in flowers result from inheritance. You cannot get a blue marigold. In some instances (hydrangea) chemicals like aluminum added to the soil change the color from pink to blue.

What is the usual procedure in the treatment of seed by X ray for the origination of new varieties? Both time of exposure and intensity of the rays seem to affect the results. Sometimes dormant seeds are irradiated and sometimes young flowers. Write to Research Laboratory, General Electric Co., Schenectady, New York.

We hear so much about "activated" phosphorous and its use in fertilizers, as well as the use of some of the by-products in the manufacture of atomic energy. Where can I write specific questions concerning how these materials can be used in growing plants?   Address all questions to the Brookhaven National Laboratories of the Atomic Energy Commission, Brookhaven, Long Island, New York.

What use are radio-active fertilizers in growing plants?   Chiefly of value as tracers, since their uptake and transfer from one part of the plant to another can be traced either on photographic film or by Geiger counters.

Will you state what effect, if any, the moon has on planting gardens? The moon has no effect on planting gardens.

What is the truth about planting in the signs of the zodiac?   There is no scientific basis for these superstitions.

SECTION III

Ornamental Plants and Their Culture

INTRODUCTION

BY MONTAGUE FREE

MOST OF our leading garden plants have their origin in wildflowers. A few have been cultivated for so long that the original species is unknown or uncertain. They have been greatly changed by domestication, so that they are quite different from the wild prototypes. Hybridizing and selection have improved the form, size, color, and garden value.

Taken as a whole, the number of different kinds and varieties of garden flowers available to the home gardener is staggering. He can easily become bewildered by the great array of different types from which to choose. No one should attempt to grow all the varieties of the more important plants in the average home garden. It is wisest to select a few that are known to be especially adapted to the region.

Many flower lovers prefer to specialize in one or a few groups and become experts in growing roses, irises, dahlias, or chrysanthemums. There is much to recommend the practice, because the gardener comes to know his particular plants thoroughly. Those who are familiar with the interesting habits of their plants get the most fun from gardening. It is usually better to learn to grow one kind well, and to be thoroughly acquainted with its many varieties, than to dabble with all sorts of plants and know little about any of them. Most of the leading horticulturists of the country have been specialists to a certain degree, and have then in turn mastered the culture of many groups.

PLANTS AS GARDEN MATERIAL

The real gardener is interested not only in the plants themselves, but also in the garden pictures he can create with them. Floriculture is a combination of both science and art. Each complements the other. To be able to grow good flowers without the skill to use them artistically in and about the home furnishes only part of the enjoyment from them that is possible. Merely using plants and flowers for decorative purposes, without understanding their culture, is an empty form of art.

Joining a garden club or special flower society is to be recommended. Such organizations are dedicated to the improvement of horticulture or to promoting the culture and development of a particular flower. Besides furnishing helpful information through their meetings and publications, they give an opportunity to become acquainted with other gardening hobbyists. The friendships and sociability encouraged by horticultural organizations are by no means a minor factor in making the world a better place in which to live.

The gardener who knows something of plant structure, plant physiology (which deals with the functions of the various plant parts), and ecology (the relation of plants to their environment) finds such knowledge helpful in dealing with problems of plant culture. Furthermore, a smattering of general botany adds greatly to the pleasures and interest which come from gardening.

Structure of the Plant. All of us know that the function of the *roots* is to anchor the plant in place and to absorb water containing dissolved nutrients from the soil. The botanists can tell us, in addition, that roots of most plants, in order to remain healthy, require air. When we know this we appreciate more the importance of cultivation which, among other things, admits the air to the soil. We can also understand why some plants fail to thrive when set in poorly drained soil from which the air is driven by waterlogging. Knowing the need of roots for air we can see the importance of adequate underdrainage for plants growing in pots and the need to avoid overwatering which drives out air from the spaces between the particles of soil.

The information that water, with its dissolved minerals, is absorbed mainly near the root tips indicates to us that fertilizers should be applied to that area where the roots are actively growing, and not in close proximity to the stem or trunk, where there are few if any actively "feeding" roots.

Plant stems, in addition to supporting the leaves and flowers, provide a connecting link which distributes water (with the dissolved nutrients absorbed by the roots and the food materials manufactured in the leaves) between the roots and other parts of the plant. The internal structure of the stem has an important part to play in some aspects of plant culture. For example, in those plants which have two or more seed leaves the stem contains a layer of actively growing cells between the bark and wood: this is the *cambium layer*. It is essential for the gardener engaged in grafting or budding to be aware of this because the cambium layer of the understock must be brought into close contact with that of scion or bud to be grafted on it; otherwise union cannot take place.

The leaves are the factories of the plant where water, containing dissolved minerals absorbed from the soil, and carbon dioxide, taken in by the leaves, are combined to form complex food substances which are then transferred by the sap to other parts of the plant where they are needed. When we realize the importance of the work carried on by the leaves we can readily understand the necessity of keeping them healthy and why we should never remove too many of them. If the work of leaves were more widely understood, there would be fewer beginners expecting a harvest of edible roots from young beets from which all the leaves have been cut for use as "greens." The function of leaves is recognized in the oft-repeated advice to leave plenty of foliage when cutting such flowers as gladioli, peonies, or tulips, and thus avoid weakening the underground parts.

The flowers produce seeds and thus provide a means of reproduction. Commonly they are "perfect": that is, the male and the female elements are contained in a single flower—as in a rose, or a sweetpea. But sometimes they are "monoecious"—that is, with stamens and pistils in separate flowers on the same plant; for example, corn, squash, and oak. In some cases the male and female flowers are "dioecious" and are produced on separate plants, as in holly and willow. While, contrary to a widespread impression, it is never necessary to have plants of both sexes growing in proximity for flowers to be produced, fruits are possible on dioecious plants only when both sexes are growing fairly close together. Also many varieties of fruits, such as apple, pear, plum, and cherry, although their flowers are "perfect," require another variety of the same kind growing near by to provide cross-pollination, because their own pollen is incapable of securing a good "set" of fruit.

Environment Is Important

Often it is helpful to the gardener to know the kind of surroundings in which the plants thrive in the wild state. The study of such environment is known as plant ecology. Some plants are found always growing in the shade; others revel in hot, dry situations. They must, in most cases, be accorded similar conditions when we grow them in our gardens. Again, some plants are more perfectly at home in heavy clay soils, while some thrive in sand. There are those which have to be grown in water, and others which languish if their feet are too wet. Some plants demand a soil with an acid reaction; some prefer a soil which is abundantly supplied with lime; and others—many of them— seem almost indifferent to the chemical reaction of the soil. It is obvious that the right kind of soil and its proper preparation are among the most important factors in plant culture.

Some knowledge of the natural environment of plants is of great help to the gardener. Species that thrive in sheltered positions, for instance, cannot be expected to do well if fully exposed to storms and winds.

Other things also have to be considered, such as shelter and exposure to wind. Climate, of course, has a very important bearing. In some regions the extreme cold of winter prohibits us from growing some plants outdoors throughout the year, and to others the heat of summer may be inimical. Many plants are adapted to dry air; and in this group we find a large proportion which are successful as house plants. The polluted air of large cities is fatal to many plants, but there are some which can endure it; these, of course, are of special interest to those whose gardening has to be conducted in urban surroundings.

Competition for food, light, and air among themselves, and from other plants, is another environmental factor which affects growth. In order to secure room for adequate development it is necessary for us either to thin or transplant the seedlings which we raise; and it is also necessary to insure that they are not starved, smothered, or crowded by weeds.

Information bearing on these environmental factors can be obtained from observation, from books, and from the experience of friends. But sometimes if the gardener's special bent is the cultivation of rare and unusual plants, he may have to experiment for himself before he is able to discover a location and conditions in which his plants will thrive. A knowledge of the natural environment is always helpful, but there are isolated cases where plants seem to thrive better under garden conditions when their usual environment is changed. An example is our native cardinal flower, which grows naturally in wet places, usually in shade, but which, in our garden, we find does better in the rich soil of the perennial border where it gets sun for most of the day. The wise gardener first selects plants which are adapted to the environment of his garden. If he is ambitious to grow other kinds, he must change the environment to suit them if that is possible.

Propagation of Plants

Starting new plants is an absorbing garden operation which never loses its thrill. Even an old-timer like myself, who has been an active gardener for more than forty years, can still get a kick out of watching seeds germinate (though I no longer dig them up the day after planting to see if they have started to grow!), and from inserting cuttings with the expectation of getting roots on them.

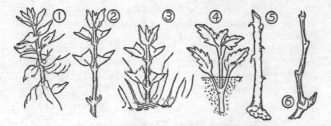

PROPAGATING PLANTS BY CUTTINGS

Many plants are readily propagated by means of cuttings —a trick which the amateur can readily master. Most commonly used for house plants, perennials, tender annuals, and some shrubs, are softwood cuttings. In (1) above such a cutting is being made; (2) shows it trimmed up, ready for (3) inserting in sand or sand and peat-moss, to root. (4) Cutting properly inserted in rooting medium. (5) Hardwood cutting of rose, showing callus formed at bottom. (6) "Mallet cutting" of grape.

Nature increases plants by means of seeds, spores, bulbils, tubers, rhizomes, runners, offsets, suckers, and stolons. The gardener uses all these methods and in addition makes cuttings of stems, leaves, and roots. He also increases his plants by division, by layering, and by budding and grafting.

During the past ten years or so several new methods, or variations of old ones, have come to the fore. Among them are: the use of constant mist, (see p. 246) and a plastic film, Polythene, sold under various trade names, as an aid in rooting cuttings and in propagation by means of air-layering. New rooting media have also come into the picture. These include: powdered glass, shredded styrofoam, perlite and mixtures of these.

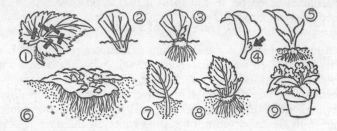

LEAF CUTTINGS

Some species of plants are readily propagated by leaf cuttings. (1) and (6) show begonia leaf cut across main ribs and laid flat on moist sand, with new plants starting from cuts; (2) and (3) show triangular leaf cutting of begonia; (4) and (5) leaf cutting with bud; and (7), (8), and (9) leaf cutting of African-violet, and young plant developed from it.

Keeping Plants Well and Happy

The Art of Transplanting. The gardener's job is not finished when he has started or purchased his young plants. They must be properly cared for in order to get best results from them. The seeds may be sown where they are to mature (after proper preparation of the soil, of course); and then they have to be thinned, the soil cultivated, and weeds kept down. Sometimes seeds are started either in seed pots indoors or in seedbeds out of doors. Then the seedlings have to be transplanted once or oftener before the plants are installed in their permanent location. Cuttings usually are started in a propagating frame, and their subsequent treatment involves transplanting. Transplanting is usually done to temporary nursery rows, or to pots, preliminary to their final shift to the garden. In some cases, however, the rooted cuttings can be transferred directly to the garden.

Transplanting is an important operation. It must be done at the right season for best results, and care must be taken to avoid undue injury to the root system. Usually trees and shrubs are transplanted when they are more or less dormant, provided the ground is unfrozen. Most of them can be moved either in spring or fall, but for best results some require spring transplanting. Frequent transplanting (every year or two), when the trees are young, produces roots that make possible transplanting, even when they are of large size, with little injury. Each transplanting inevitably shortens the wide-spreading roots, and this causes the remaining roots to branch freely. Thus the plant produces a compact mass of fibrous roots which enables it to be transplanted easily. For this reason plants obtained from a nursery (where regular transplanting is practiced) can be moved with much less loss than those which are dug from the wild.

Seedlings, and young plants in general, can be transplanted when they are actively growing because it is possible to move them with the root system almost intact. There are some exceptions among those plants which produce a deep taproot. Carrots and annual poppies, for example, cannot be transplanted with good results. Occasionally transplanting is done to promote fruitfulness, as with dwarf fruit trees, growing in rich ground, which are making excessive branch and leaf growth at the expense of flowers. The loss of roots brought about by transplanting often results in checking such vegetative growth and promoting the formation of flower buds.

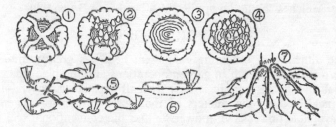

PROPAGATING BULBS, ROOTS, AND RHIZOMES

Hyacinth bulb (1) cut across bottom to induce formation of bulblets (2). Hyacinth bulb (3) scooped out at bottom, to produce bulblets (4). Old iris rhizome (5) cut into sections or divisions, and divisions planted (6). Dahlia root cut into sections, each containing an eye (7).

Benefits of Cultivation and Mulching. Cultivation is the term applied to the loosening of the surface soil. It aids in the aeration of the soil, enables rain to penetrate more easily, and, perhaps most important, it helps keep down weeds.

Cultivation is accomplished in many ways, and a variety of tools is involved. In pots or flats a pointed stick or an old dinner fork may be used. For cultivating soil in crowded areas there are various types of hand cultivators. In flower borders the scuffle hoe is the most useful tool, while in the vegetable garden either the scuffle hoe, draw hoe, or wheel hoe may be brought into action. In large areas, where the crops are grown in rows, either motor-driven or horse-drawn cultivators are used.

Cultivation after rains is usually recommended to prevent the formation of a surface crust and to kill weed seedlings; but cultivation must not be done until the moisture has had a chance to penetrate and the surface is beginning to get dry. Frequent cultivation is essential to cope adequately with weeds. It is much easier to kill them while they are still in the seedling stage. Furthermore, this prevents them from stealing the food and moisture which properly belong to the cultivated crops.

A mulch is sometimes applied in order to lessen or obviate the necessity for cultivation. Paper treated to make it somewhat waterproof has in some cases been successfully used. Some plants, however, do not respond to a paper mulch and under garden conditions there are several objections to it, such as its appearance, the difficulties of anchoring it to the ground, and of working among the plants without disturbing it.

Ordinarily mulches of organic materials, most of which can be incorporated with the soil at the end of the growing season to decay and form humus, are the most practical, and serve the purpose better. Mulches should be applied in a layer 2 or 3 ins. thick.

LABOR SAVING

The difficulty of obtaining competent help has greatly influenced modern gardening, both in garden operations and the plant materials.

Even though his garden is only a small one the gardener has not been neglected by the makers of motorized equipment. There are now available power lawn mowers, either the conventional reel kinds or the rotary types with all sorts of attachments ranging from snow removal to tillers.

Other labor-saving devices include metal strips which can be pushed into the ground to make a barrier between the lawn and flower border. This, to a large extent, eliminates the tedious job of trimming the whiskery grass by handshears. If even this short chore is hateful an electric trimmer can be bought which will enable him to do the job without that backbreaking effort that gets a man down.

Mulching the surface as a means of controlling weeds is another labor-saver. Among the organic materials that can be used for mulching are: buckwheat hulls, peatmoss, ground corn cobs, shredded sugar cane (bagasse) sold as chicken litter, salt-meadow hay, grass clippings, sawdust, wood chips, excelsior and pulped newspaper. Most of these serve a triple purpose—that of making it easier to control weeds; conserving soil moisture by checking evaporation; and adding organic matter. Naturally there are some drawbacks to the wide use of mulches. Among them are the possibility of an increase in the slug population and the temporary depletion of available nitrogen in the soil. Fortunately these drawbacks can be counteracted by putting out slug bait containing metaldehyde, and by keeping a close watch on the plants and applying quick-acting nitrogen in the form of nitrate of soda or sulfate of ammonia at the first sign of yellowing foliage.

As part of the endeavor to cut down on labor there is a diminution of interest in bedding plants which have to be started fresh every year; and a trend toward permanent plants, especially trees and shrubs, which once they are planted take care of themselves, to some extent at least. Among the newcomers in woody plants are Moraine locust, a form of Honey locust (*Gleditsia triacanthos,* var. *inermis*); a spineless variety; and a form of this, the Sunburst locust, in which the new leaves are yellow. Another new tree is a form of Schwedler maple, sold as Crimson King. This, although it does not quite live up to the colored pictures in the advertisements, is an advance over the dull summer color of Schwedleri. Among the comparatively new shrubs are the contorted hazel (*Corylus avellana contorta*), *Chaenomeles* (*Cydonia*) Spitfire, a columnar form; and a hybrid *Viburnum carlcephalum* (*V. Carlesi* x *V. Macrocephalum*).

Watering. Plant physiologists tell us that the plant nutrients in the soil can be absorbed by the roots only when they are in solution. The necessity for abundant moisture is therefore obvious. Cultivation and mulching both have a bearing on the conservation of moisture already in the soil. In recent years the value of cultivation has been questioned by some investigators regarding the moisture-holding value of a dust mulch, but most practical gardeners still accept it.

In addition to conserving the moisture already in the soil it is sometimes necessary to *supplement* the rainfall. This is accomplished by irrigation, or by watering with the aid of a hose or watering pot.

Simple method of applying water in a fine spray without wasting time "hose-holding."

The important thing to remember about watering is that light sprinklings, which penetrate the soil only an inch or so, are not desirable, because they encourage roots to come to the surface where they are exposed to too much heat from the sun and where they may be killed by cultivation, or by drought if for any reason the daily sprinkling is neglected. When watering is done, *it should be thorough,* so that the soil is wet, if possible, to a depth of 6 to 8 ins. Do not water again until the soil begins to get dry.

The same principle should be followed when watering potted plants. Sometimes it may be desirable to let the soil become so dry that the plant is almost wilting. The soil shrinks when drying, and this opens up pore spaces, permitting the entrance of air which, as we have already seen, is a necessity for the roots of most plants.

Pruning. In a reaction against the plant butchering which went under the name of pruning many gardeners have come to look on all cutting back of plants as a practice to be avoided. Actually, however, pruning is not altogether bad. By pruning it is possible to aid the

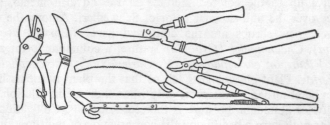

Types of pruning equipment. The pruning shears and pruning knife (left) are the most useful in the small garden.

rejuvenation of sickly plants and assist in the control of insect pests and fungous diseases. Pruning can be used to correct faulty habits of growth, to promote interesting branch formations, and to bring about earlier blossoming. In certain cases it is possible to develop larger flowers on longer stems by pruning to reduce the number of flowering shoots. The complete removal of dead and dying branches is an operation that can be safely performed at any time.

There are several principles which are helpful to the would-be pruner:

(1) Severe pruning *when the plant is dormant* stimulates the production of strong, leafy shoots; contrariwise, pruning *when the plant is actively growing* tends to check exuberant growth and helps bring about the formation of blossom buds.

(2) Trees and shrubs which *blossom early,* in the spring, ordinarily should be pruned immediately after they flower; while those which bloom in summer or autumn, on shoots of the current season's growth, can be pruned in the spring.

(3) In general, the aim of the pruner should be to maintain the natural habit of growth of the tree or shrub. Sometimes, however,

when plants of definite outline are required (as, for instance, privet hedges, or shrubs or small evergreens used as accent points in a formal garden), "shearing" or light surface pruning is practiced. This alters and controls the plant's habit of growth.

(4) Pruning, limited to *pinching out the tips* of the growing shoots, (called "pinching back") stimulates branching and develops a plant of compact habit. Chrysanthemums are commonly thus treated. The same principle is sometimes followed with woody plants, with the same purpose in view.

(5) In pruning, *no stubs should be left* which will die and decay. The cuts should be made close to the supporting branch or trunk, or just above a bud—preferably one which is pointed in the direction it is wished to have the bush or tree develop.

(6) Wounds more than an inch or so in diameter should always be painted with a protective covering to keep out moisture and spores of disease organisms.

In pruning shrubs with a natural, loose-growing or drooping habit—such as forsythias, deutzias, and weigelas—old stems are cut out clear to the ground if thinning seems necessary.

Pruning is a complex subject full of interest and worthy of the thoughtful study of all gardeners.

Winter Protection. Gardeners everywhere commonly grow plants which are not able to survive the winter without help. In some cases this requires that the plants should be dug up and stored in a frost-free place, such as a greenhouse, cellar, or cold frame. Often sufficient protection is afforded merely by placing a mulch of insulating material on the soil over the roots. Sometimes the tops have to be covered to protect them from the effects of drying winds and winter sunshine.

Plant Supports. Some of the most useful decorative plants have twining or climbing habits. To be effectively displayed, such plants usually have to be provided with supports. These may be walls, fences, pergolas, arches, trellises, or poles stuck in the ground.

There are other plants which are not climbers but which, under garden conditions, have weak stems likely to be toppled over as a result of heavy rains or strong winds. These can be held upright by staking and tying, or by pushing twigs in between and around the clump before the plants have attained their full height.

Plant Enemies. In addition to all these operations, plants have to be protected from the various insect pests and plant diseases to which they are subject. In keeping the garden free from pests, sanitation must be practiced, plus close observation to note any departure from the normal so that remedial measures (fully discussed in Section VIII) can be put into effect before much damage has been done.

There has been tremendous increase in growing plants in the home. This interest has been sparked by the furor attendant on the amazing success of the culture of Saintpaulia (African-violet). In part this is due to the discovery that many kinds of plants can be grown without any daylight at all, merely by the use of fluorescent lights combined with a sufficient number of the ordinary tungsten light bulbs to provide from 300 to 600 ft. candles. The result of this has been that many plants which formerly were believed to be unsuited for culture in the home can be grown without too much difficulty.

ENVIRONMENT

CITY CONDITIONS

PLANT MATERIAL

I have a small yard in the heart of the city. Will you suggest flowers for cutting that I can grow from May until October? Columbine, pinks, thalictrum, iris, zinnia, marigold, cosmos, petunia, nasturtium, eupatorium, phlox, calendula.

What are the best varieties of ANNUAL FLOWERS for a small, sunny city back-yard garden? Alyssum, China-aster, balsam, calliopsis, candytuft, celosia, cynoglossum, dianthus, four-o'clock, lobelia, dwarf marigold, annual phlox, portulaca, salvia, verbena, dwarf and medium zinnia.

Which annuals would you advise for a very small half-shaded city garden? Balsam, begonia, calliopsis, campanula, celosia, cleome, lobelia, nicotiana, petunia, torenia, vinca, viola.

Which annuals and potted plants stand shade in a city garden? Very few. Lobelia, nicotiana, and torenia thrive in partial shade. Begonia, fuchsia, and lantana are good. Potted plants include begonia, caladium, calla, fuchsia, Zanzibar Balsam.

How can I grow sweetpeas? (New York City.) As a rule, they do not succeed in or around New York. Sweetpeas should be planted either in late fall or *very* early spring (mid-March if possible) in full sun. They need cool weather to come to perfection. Soil is prepared 18 ins. deep, rotted manure being mixed in. Seeds are planted 2 ins. deep in a 4-in. trench. As plants grow, trench is filled in and supports are provided for vines to climb on—twiggy branches, chicken wire, or stakes.

Which are the best varieties of PERENNIAL flowers for a small city back-yard garden? Ajuga, *Alyssum saxatile, Anchusa myosotidiflora,* aquilegia, Artemisia Silver King, astilbe, hardy aster, campanula, chrysanthemum (hardy), coreopsis, daylily, *Dianthus barbatus,* bleedingheart (both tall and dwarf,) *Eupatorium coelestinum,* gaillardia, heuchera, hosta (plantainlily), tall bearded iris, lily-of-the-valley, mertensia, *Phlox divaricata,* platycodon, plumbago, sedum and sempervivum in variety, tradescantia, viola.

Are there any other BULBS which furnish bloom in a city garden besides narcissi and other early spring ones? Calla, caladium (colored leaves), tuberose for very late bloom, most lilies that are listed as easy of culture and tolerant of partial shade, gladiolus for sunny, well-drained situations, small-flowered dahlia.

How can we grow EVERGREEN trees successfully in New York City? Select only ones that are known to be smoke- and gas-resistant. Give them good soil, occasional fertilizer, plenty of water, and protect them from dogs. The trick is to select resistant species such as: Austrian pine, *Pinus nigra;* Japanese black pine, *P. Thunbergi;* and American holly. But don't be too disappointed if they fail. None will survive in closed-in shaded places, except, possibly, Japanese Yew.

Which evergreens are suitable for a shady city garden? *Broadleaf evergreens*—andromeda, azalea, *Ilex crenata,* kalmia, leucothoe, mahonia, rhododendron, wintercreeper, abelia, pyracantha (the last two semi-evergreen), and varieties of yew.

How shall I care for evergreens in the city? Soil should be prepared to a depth of 18 to 24 ins., incorporating well-rotted manure and leafmold. Transplant only in early fall or spring. Never allow roots to dry out, and wash foliage frequently with fine but strong spray from hose. Broadleaf evergreens require acid soil.

We don't want a paved area in our city garden, and it is too shady for a lawn. What GROUND COVERS are best (perennial preferred)? English Ivy, suitable for formal as well as informal gardens; and vinca (common periwinkle) which has blue flowers in the spring. A pleasing effect is achieved with ajuga, either green or bronze-leaved, which has blue flowers in spring, good foliage all season, and is very hardy.

How can I have a good LAWN in the city? Difficult unless garden gets at least 6 hours of direct sunshine. Soil should be rich and deep (at least 8 ins.) with good drainage. Prepare soil and sow a good grade of lawn seed (without bent grasses) in early September.

What can I plant in a shady CITY ROCK GARDEN? If you furnish proper soil, rich in leafmold, you can have an attractive planting of ferns, small-leaved ivies, and native woodland wildflowers, with small bulbs—such as chionodoxa, snowdrop, Siberian squill and crocus—for spring bloom.

Can ROSES be successfully grown in a city garden? Yes, providing there is abundant sunshine, deep, rich soil, and the garden is outside of congested metropolitan areas.

Can you suggest roses which succeed best in a city garden? Area is open and sunny. Excelsa, New Dawn, and Paul's Scarlet Climber are good climbers; Mme. Jules Bouche, President Macia, Radiance, Soeur Therese, and Talisman are good hybrid teas. Gruss an Teplitz is excellent, but needs much room.

What deciduous SHRUBS tolerate shade in a city garden? Aralia; calycanthus (sweetshrub); deutzia; *Euonymus alatus;* rose-of-Sharon; hydrangea; kerria; privet, clethra (sweetpepper bush); rhodotypos (jetbead); stephanandra; viburnum in variety.

Can you recommend any distinctive shrubs for a city garden? We don't want only privet and forsythia! If your soil is good, the following will succeed: *Abelia grandiflora; Acanthopanax sieboldianus; Berberis julianae; Euonymus alatus,* brilliant red foliage in fall; *Pyracantha coccinea lalandi* (firethorn)—transplant only when young, preferably potted; stephanandra; tamarix.

Which small ornamental and FLOWERING TREES can you recommend for a city garden? *Aralia spinosa* (devils-walking-stick); flowering crab, peach, plum, Japanese cherry; Flowering dogwood (only for more open situations and good, deep soil); hawthorn; honey locust; *Magnolia soulangeana;* Russian olive; umbrella catalpa; weeping mulberry.

Would a pink hawthorn or a mountain-ash grow in a city garden? Hawthorns do very well, but mountain-ash is completely intolerant of urban conditions.

What good-sized trees stand city life? We don't want ailanthus. Catalpa, ginkgo, London Plane, *Magnolia soulangeana,* Norway Maple, Paper Mulberry, Pin Oak, willow.

We cannot build new fences for our city garden and would like VINES which would cover the old ones within a year or so. What can you recommend? Fastest-growing and most tolerant perennial vines are fleeceflower (*Polygonum auberti*); Hall's Honeysuckle; kudzu-bean (dies to the ground in winter but grows rapidly every summer); Virginiacreeper for shade particularly. Hyacinth bean, or morning-glories, if annuals are preferred.

Which is the fastest-growing vine to cover an old brick wall in city? Either Virginiacreeper or Boston Ivy.

PROBLEMS

It is difficult to maintain humus supply in our city garden because

everything has to be carried through the house. Could I grow "green" manure? Yes. Plant winter rye seed in late September in bare places, and dig under in spring.

What locations and conditions in an average city home are suitable for starting seeds in flats? South or southeast window, with sunshine available for the major part of the day; fresh air without direct drafts or chilling; even temperature not exceeding 65° F. during daytime, 10° lower at night; humidity, provided by syringing, pans of water, or humidifiers; freedom from cooking or heating gas fumes.

How can we keep dogs away from plants? If the dogs belong to you, fence off a small exercise yard for them; it is an aid in training the dogs. If they do not, low wire fencing or special curved wire guards may be placed around shrubs or borders. Spraying individual plants with a solution of 40 per cent nicotine sulfate, 2 teaspoons to 1 gal. of water, is sometimes effective; as are proprietary preparations sold by garden supply dealers. Spraying must be renewed at intervals.

FOUNDATION MATERIAL (GENERAL)

What are some good, low-priced materials for foundation planting under adverse conditions? Coralberry, Five-leaved Aralia, Gray Dogwood, jetbead, physocarpus, privet.

Will you give suggestions as to medium-height foundation planting, without using evergreens? Bridalwreath, *Cotoneaster apiculata,* Five-leaved Aralia, Flowering Quince, Japanese Witchhazel, lilac, Persian Lilac, *Rosa rugosa, Deutzia gracilis, Viburnum dilatatum,* and *V. wrighti.*

Will you name several hardy foundation plantings which will not take up much width in the bed and will not look too dilapidated in winter? Low shrubs, in general, tend to spread horizontally. The following are narrow or compact. *Deciduous shrubs:* Anthony Waterer Spirea, *Berberis thunbergi erecta,* dwarf privet, *Physocarpus monogynus. Evergreens:* Redcedar varieties, Chinese Column Juniper (both narrow, tall-growing), Hatfield and Brown's Yews, Spiny Greek Juniper.

What is a good evergreen or deciduous shrub to use for foundation concealment—one that will not grow more than 2 or 3 ft. high and will not be too bushy? Most dwarf shrubs tend to be broader than tall. The following are slow-growing and can easily be kept at 3 ft. by careful pruning: *Berberis thunbergi erecta, Picea glauca conica; Taxus canadensis stricta,* and *Taxus media hatfieldi* (yews); *Thuja occidentalis rosenthali.*

What would be a good thing to plant between two windows to fill blank wall on south side of house in full sun? There is only 4 ft. from house to lot line and ground is sandy, from excavating cellar. Most plants die from heat. The house is Cape Cod style. *Juniperus chinensis columnaris,* or *Juniperus virginiana cannaerti.* Remove the poor soil, and replace with good, light, loamy soil enriched with about ⅕ part of leafmold.

Which shrubs and flowers would be best to plant along a house that has a high foundation? These shrubs average around 4 or 5 ft. in height: coralberry, *Cotoneaster apiculata,* Fragrant Sumac, Maple-leaf Viburnum, *Physocarpus intermedius,* hydrangea, Sweetpepper Bush; Vanhoutte Spirea. Some tall perennials are boltonia, delphinium, Michaelmas daisy (*Aster novibelgi*), rosemallow, *Helenium autumnale.*

What is a suitable planting on west side of house along foundation, space about 6 ft. from house to driveway? Deciduous materials: *Cotoneaster apiculata,* Flowering Quince, *Physocarpus monogynus,* rose-of-Sharon, Rugosa Rose, Slender Deutzia. Evergreen kinds: dwarf hemlock varieties, Spiny Greek Juniper, *Juniperus virginiana; Taxus cuspidata nana* (if kept pruned), also *Taxus media browni, hatfieldi,* or *hicksi* (yews).

Which is best evergreen for a corner? Want a tall one that is graceful and smooth and not too spreading, for yard is small. (D.C.) Arborvitae, Chinese Column Juniper, redcedar varieties.

What would be suitable foundation plantings for an old (1792) farmhouse in southern New Hampshire? The shrubs that grow naturally in the fields and woods of your area and which are in harmony with the general surroundings. Arborvitae; arrowwood; Canada Yew; chokeberry (*Aronia melanocarpa*); *Rosa humilis;* Flowering Raspberry; hemlock; highbush blueberry; Maple-leaf Viburnum; Mountain Laurel; pinkster-flower (wild azalea); Prostrate Juniper (*Juniperus communis depressa*); winterberry. Of exotic shrubs, lilacs would not be out of place, nor would *Chaenomeles lagenaria,* Japanese Quince or *C. japonica* (Dwarf Japanese Quince).

What can be done with 3 feet of space under eaves which does not get any natural moisture in summer? This space is always barren, and nothing seems to grow even though watered with the hose. Such a spot should be watered with unfailing regularity. Occasional neglect may be ruinous. Improve soil by working in leafmold or peatmoss. If this is done, try *Symphoricarpos chenaulti, Berberis thunbergi erecta* (Truehedge Columnberry), Spirea Anthony Waterer. These will grow about 3 to 4 ft. high.

How may one grow shrubbery about the house that has eaves projecting 3 feet, without excessive watering? A 6-in. layer of peatmoss at the base of roots and a generous amount of it mixed in planting soil would limit artificial watering.

Does close foundation planting (3 ft. away) affect walls of house in any way—possibly causing dampness on inside walls? Probably not. While the planting keeps sun and air from the walls, it also sheds rain and the roots absorb much water.

FOUNDATION MATERIAL FOR SHADE

FLOWERING

Which plants bloom in a location next to a garage wall where very little sun reaches the ground except in late afternoon? Balloonflower, bugbane, columbine, coralbells, meadowrue, monkshood, plantainlily, Showy Sedum (*Sedum spectabile*).

What would give me profusion of color, or at least greens, on a narrow strip (about 10 ins. wide) on driveway and against the house? Strip is on the north side and therefore sunless. Ferns, goutweed (*Aegopodium podagraria variegatum*), Japanese Spurge (*Pachysandra*), lily-of-the-valley, plantainlilies.

What are good perennials for the shady north side of the house? It is at the front, and there is a space approximately 3 × 14 ft. between the house and the walk around the house. Astilbe in variety, balloonflower, columbine, coralbells, daylily, *Eupatorium coelestinum*, plantainlily, *Anemone japonica*.

EVERGREENS

What can I plant in shade of building under oaks, on a sandy ridge? Nothing worth trying, unless you prepare the ground thoroughly, mixing in abundant humus, leafmold, and some very old manure. Having prepared an acid mixture of this sort, try rhododendrons and Mountain Laurel.

Can azaleas and rhododendrons be used in a foundation planting about the house? Yes, but special precautions must frequently be taken to keep the soil acid. The stucco or brick foundations contain cement, which is alkaline. Rain falling against this washes a certain amount of lime into the soil close to the house, frequently resulting in its gradually becoming alkaline.

Can I safely put in a foundation planting of evergreen trees where the outer branches of the street maples reach? Probably only the native yew would thrive; and at the point farthest from the maples, perhaps a hemlock or two. The Japanese Yew might survive, but would not thrive. Both the shade overhead and the roots below would trouble evergreen trees.

The planting north of my house looks spindly. Which evergreens can I use to replace it? In soil well prepared with leafmold and old manure try *Taxus canadensis* and its variety *stricta*. In the somewhat more sunny ends, hemlock, especially its dwarf varieties, and Japanese Yew. In an acid, humusy soil try *Rhododendron maximum*. At the more sunny ends: *Rhododendron carolinianum*, Mountain Laurel, and *Pieris floribunda*. All of these are evergreen shrubs.

Which plants for foundation plantings are best suited for northern New England? Especially for shady north side of house?   Evergreens would be best, especially the broad-leaved types, such as Mountain Laurel and Mountain Andromeda. Because of shade only a small amount of flowers could be expected from any plants. Yews would be useful.

SHRUBS

Can you advise if there is any flowering shrub which will grow in a totally shady place in the front of the house—north side? (New York.) Few, if any, shrubs will bloom satisfactorily in complete shade. *Rhododendron maximum*, Mountain Laurel, and jetbead (*Rhodotypos scandens*) are worth trying. One of the best shrubs for north exposures, totally shaded by the house (not over-hung by trees), is *Euonymus patens*.

What can be planted, to grow successfully, on the north side of the house? The ground is covered with fine green moss.   Prepare the ground deeply, mixing in a liberal supply of leafmold and old manure. Then you may safely try *Euonymus patens*, *Symphoricarpos orbiculatus*, *S. albus laevigatus*, honeysuckle (lonicera) various kinds. If you will prepare an acid soil, such a situation may do well for rhododendrons, Mountain Laurel, azalea, pieris.

Which shrubbery is best for foundation planting in a very shaded spot facing west?   Deciduous shrubs: *Symphoricarpos chenaulti*, *Rhodotypos scandens*, *Physocarpus monogynus*, *Lonicera morrowi*. Evergreen shrubs (for acid soil): *Rhododendron maximum*, *R. catawbiense*, *Pieris floribunda*, *P. japonica*, Mountain Laurel.

Which shrubs would best grow on north side of porch facing east, with a joining hallway next to it? Prefer something not to grow over 5 to 6 ft. high that would flower with some fragrance, as it will appear on front of house.   Chokeberry, mockorange, sweetpepper bush (*Clethra alnifolia*), *Viburnum carlesi*, Winter Honeysuckle.

Which inexpensive ground and foundation plants can be used to fill in north-side foundation?   Low to medium-height shrubs: *Viburnum patens*, *Mahonia aquifolium*, *Symphoricarpos orbiculatus*. Taller shrubs: *Lonicera tatarica*, *L. morrowi*, Regel Privet. Ground covers: *Pachysandra terminalis*, *Vinca minor*.

Which shrub can be used beside a house for sort of a hedge, to grow 5 ft. high? Not much sun hits spot, and not too good a soil.

I don't want barberries. Amur River Privet, Five-leaved Aralia, Gray Dogwood, Siberian Peatree.

GROUND COVERS

Is it harmful for ground ivy to grow over ground where flowers (perennials and annuals) grow? If the other plants are small, the ground ivy (*Nepeta hederacea*) may smother them.

What ground cover flowering plants are suitable for a steep bank with northeast exposure? *Ajuga reptans,* Japanese Honeysuckle, moneywort (*Lysimachia nummularia*), *Vinca minor.*

What can I use for ground cover between sidewalk and curb, on a 2-ft. bank, 3½ ft. wide, with some shade? *Vinca minor,* Bowles variety.

We have a small, steep terrace shaded by trees. It is next to impossible to grow grass on it. Last year I planted ivy (Hedera helix gracilis), which seemed to grow only fairly well. Was our selection wise? *Hedera helix gracilis* is a well-recommended plant for dry banks and will probably do much better when it has become established. Try giving it a mulch of leafmold or well-rotted cow manure this winter.

What is the best coverage to plant where there is full sun, on a hill? Grass and weeds make it hard to cut. Honeysuckles are good, so are trailing roses. Ask your local nurseryman to supply you with suitable kinds.

What is the most beautiful flowering ground cover for Regal Lilies in a perennial border? *Myosotis sylvatica* (forget-me-not) should please you.

Which evergreen euonymus vine would grow well as a ground cover? Purple-leaf Euonymus (*E. coloratus*).

What is a good ground cover to plant along house wall between two houses, space about 4 ft. wide running north and south, with steppingstone path in center? Strip gets rain but not dew. Would like something deep-rooted, short, and not viny. *Arenaria montana* (Mountain Sandwort), *Arenaria verna caespitosa* (Moss Sandwort). Both of these are very low, tufted-growing grass substitutes; they are the best plants available for planting between flagstones in a walk.

Which ground cover do you suggest to border a stream? Moneywort (*Lysimachia nummularia*) which is also known as Creeping Jenny or Creeping Charlie—(take your choice!), is an excellent semi-evergreen ground cover which might be used near the stream.

FOR BULB BEDS

What is a good ground cover for my tulips? Pansies may be used to advantage to flower with the tulips, also forget-me-nots, especially to underplant yellow tulips. To follow these, petunias would give a good display until frost.

Will it be harmful to bulbs left in the ground if they are over-planted with annuals for summer bloom? Not if the bulbs are planted at the proper depth and the soil is enriched annually. Any kind may be used—from alyssum to zinnia—that will conform to the situation.

Is it practical to plant seeds of annuals over spring bulbs, in the fall? Not if desirable mulch of manure is placed over beds. Wait until mulch has been removed in early spring.

What is the best way to start annuals for planting in a bulb bed? Those kinds which give best results from an early start, such as ageratum, petunia, snapdragon, torenia, and verbena, may be started under glass in March and set out between the bulbs in late May. Marigold and zinnia may be transplanted at this time; or they may be sown where they are to flower, especially if a late display is most desirable. These kinds are best sown in place: sweet alyssum, California Poppy, candytuft, coreopsis, *Gilia capitata,* nigella, portulaca.

I have a triangular bed of tulips in the front lawn. What fairly low-growing plants can I place between the tulips after the foliage dies down? The bed is partially shaded in the morning. For color and profusion of bloom nothing will outdo petunia for the purpose, particularly those of the bedding type. Other good dwarfs are ageratum, sweet alyssum, portulaca, verbena.

FOR SHADE

What can I do to get grass to grow under oak trees? If trees are low-headed and dense, remove lower branches and thin top to admit more light and air. Better, perhaps, use a shade-enduring ground cover, such as pachysandra, ivy, ajuga, or gill-over-the-ground.

Grass will not grow on a terrace which is quite shady. What is the best ground cover for such a location? The terrace is about a 45° slope. Japanese Pachysandra, English Ivy, Hall's Honeysuckle, *Ajuga reptans.*

We have just planted a flowering cherry tree in our back lawn. Will you tell us what to grow around the tree? Something that blooms early spring to late fall and spreads around to cover the earth under tree. Only annuals would give you flowers from summer into autumn; petunias, for instance. For a permanent ground cover, try the evergreen periwinkle or Japanese Spurge. The former has blue flowers in the spring; the latter no appreciable flower at all.

Which ground cover might be used under large elm trees? *Ajuga reptans,* Canada Yew, English Ivy, *Euonymus fortunei,* ferns, yellowroot, (*Xanthorhiza apiifolia*). Best of all, *Pachysandra terminalis,* the Japanese Spurge.

What would be a good ground cover under large plantings of 3-year-old lilacs? *Veronica rupestris, Plumbago larpentiae, Phlox divaricata,* and *P. stolonifera, Ajuga reptans;* but these or any others will likely pass out of the picture as the lilacs get older.

What will really grow under maple trees as a substitute for grass? *Pachysandra terminalis* is the court of last resort, especially under Norway Maples. If this will not grow, nothing will; you might as well save time and money and stop further experimentation. Maples cast dense shade and their roots are very near the surface.

Which ground cover shall I plant (other than sedums) in shade under maples? Most things I try grow leggy and floppy. See preceding answer. Manure and dig soil and try Japanese Spurge, moneywort, periwinkle, English Ivy, or *Ajuga reptans.*

Is there a low-growing or creeping plant that would form a carpet for a shady pine grove in southern Vermont? The pines are young and do not shed enough needles to cover the ground. Partridgeberry (propagated by seed), Mother of Thyme (easily propagated by division); blueberries—especially the smooth-leaf low-bush blueberry (propagated by seed); yellowroot (easily propagated by root division). As the pines increase in size they may be expected to kill everything beneath them.

How can I plant English Ivy from cuttings for low cover under tree? Suggest rooting the cuttings first in propagating frame, then prepare soil well with leafmold or rotted manure. Plant rooted cuttings 6 to 8 ins. apart in early spring and keep watered until established.

Is Japanese Spurge (pachysandra better than creeping myrtle for a ground cover in the shade? Yes.

What fertilizer or special care is needed to maintain healthy pachysandra plants? Pachysandra prefers partial shade. Dig soil 8 ins. to 1 ft. and incorporate manure before planting. If foliage of established plantation is not deep green, spread a ¼-in. layer of dehydrated cattle manure on the surface of the soil in the fall.

Does pachysandra grow better in acid or alkaline soil? It is reasonably tolerant. If the soil is quite acid, plant pachysandra; if alkaline, use English Ivy.

SANDY SOIL

Which annuals grow best in very light, sandy soil? Sweet Alyssum, *Lobularia maritima,* arctotis, calendula, California Poppy, castor bean, geranium, lantana (a tender shrub treated as annual), marigold, nasturtium, petunia, *Phlox drummondi,* portulaca, *Cleome spinosa,* statice, verbena, zinnia.

Which hardy flowers grow best in sandy loam soil?   *Penstemon barbatus,* butterflyweed (*Asclepias tuberosa*); *Nepeta mussini,* false-indigo, *Anthemis tinctoria, Phlox subulata, Achillea ptarmica,* The Pearl.

Which perennials grow best in very light, sandy soil?   Achillea; *Anchusa italica; Arabis albida; Arenaria montana;* armeria in var.; *Artemisia abrotanum* (old-man); *A. stelleriana* (old-woman); *Cerastium tomentosum; Dianthus deltoides;* globe-thistle; lupin; *Nepeta mussini;* Oriental Poppy; balloonflower; *Salvia azurea; Santolina incana;* sedums; yucca.

Which shrubs and trees are suitable for a sandy soil in a sunny location?   With proper, ordinary care in planting and after care until established, the following commend themselves: Medium to tall shrubs—*Elaeagnus umbellata;* hydrangea (various); hypericum; *Hippophae rhamnoides* (seabuckthorn); *Lespedeza thunbergi;* bayberry; *Rosa rugosa; R. setigera; Robinia hispida* (rose-acacia); *Vitex agnuscastus;* tamarix. Tall-growing—Siberian Peatree; Russian Olive; Goldenrain Tree.

Which edging plants, preferably flowering kinds, will do well in dry, sandy soil?   Several kinds of statice (armeria); *Sedum hybridum, S. ellacombianum,* and *S. spurium*; Silver Mound Artemisia (A. *schmidtiana nana*).

SEASHORE

Which ANNUALS are suitable for planting near the ocean?   Sweet alyssum (*Lobularia maritima*); California Poppy; geranium; lantana (tender shrub treated as annual); petunia; *Phlox drummondi;* portulaca; nasturtium; *Cleome spinosa;* verbena. If sufficient depth of topsoil (6 to 8 ins.) is provided, and sufficient water in dry periods, practically all annuals that grow successfully inland, provided the low-growing types are selected.

Which PERENNIALS endure salt spray and high winds?   Tall-growing kinds will require staking in windy places. Among perennials able to withstand salt spray and shore conditions are Carpathian Bellflower (*Campanula carpatica*); *Allium schoenoprasum;* daylily; echinops (several kinds); *Erigeron speciosus;* eryngium (several kinds); gaillardia; Bearded Iris; coralbells; statice; perennial flax; lythrum; New York and New England Asters; pinks; rudbeckia; sedums; *Silene maritima;* statice (armeria)—several kinds; veronica; *Yucca filamentosa.*

Are there any SHRUBS which will grow near the shore exposed

to salt-laden air? Yes, but immature leaves are damaged by salt-laden fogs in spring and late spring. This applies to native shrubs also. The following are good: arrowwood, bayberry, beach plum, chokeberry, coralberry, groundselbush, highbush Blueberry, inkberry (*Ilex glabra*), Japanese Barberry, *Rosa rugosa* and *R. humilis,* and *R. lucida,* Russian Olive, seabuckthorn, shadbush, sumac, winterberry, and tamarisk in several varieties.

Which TREES are most suitable for seashore planting? Birch; Black Jack Oak (*Quercus marilandica*), but does not transplant well; Chinese Elm does fairly well; hawthorn; pepperidge (*Nyssa sylvatica*), but does not transplant well; Red Maple; sassafras; White Poplar, White Willow; mulberry.

Which evergreen trees resist salt air? American Holly, best broad-leaved evergreen; Austrian Pine; Japanese Black Pine—best; Redcedar especially good.

Which evergreens will grow best near salt water with danger of water occasionally reaching roots? (Massachusetts.) No evergreen tree hardy in Massachusetts will *thrive* where salt water reaches the roots occasionally. Redcedar is best bet.

Will you suggest protective planting for sloping shore bank, about 18 ft., which is inclined to wash, due to wind, rain, high water? Chesapeake Bay area. Toe of slope *must* first be stabilized with retaining wall of timber, boulders, or concrete. Abutting properties, if similarly subject to attack, should also receive attention. Study the vegetation of similar situations and plant that material closely on your own bank. Beachgrass, bearberry, elaeagnus, goldenrod, povertygrass, Sand Blackberry, sumac, Virginiacreeper, wild grape (Fox or Frost Grape), and wild roses are good, especially *Rosa rugosa.*

Which fertilizers are best for sandy seashore gardens? Seashore soils usually are benefited by heavy applications of humus (rotted leaves, grass, or other vegetation) and old, well-rotted barnyard manure. This is largely to improve their physical condition. Moderate applications of commercial fertilizer will help build up the nutrient content of the soil. Applications should be small but frequent.

SLOPES; BANKS

I have a steep bank at the end of my lawn to the street. Can you advise the best plants to keep the soil from washing away? Cover it with plants that make a dense mat, or tangle of growth: Japanese Barberry, Japanese Honeysuckle (especially in shade), *Juniperus horizontalis,* matrimonyvine, *Rosa wichuraiana,* yellowroot (especially in shade). If low-growing plants are desired, Japanese Spurge, or trailing myrtle.

What would you suggest to plant on a bank, across the front of our yard, about 4 ft. high off the highway and about 375 ft. long? Akebia, English Ivy, Japanese Honeysuckle, Japanese Spurge (if shaded), Memorial Rose (*R. wichuraiana*), *Vinca minor.*

What can I plant on a sunny south slope now covered with tufted grass? Coralberry, Five-leaved Aralia, Fragrant Sumac, Gray Dogwood, jetbead, Rose Acacia, Scotch Broom.

What can I plant on a dry, sunny slope (southern exposure, formal surroundings) on which it is impossible to grow any grass? Japanese Barberry, Box Barberry, Chenault Coralberry, Tibet Honeysuckle.

What can best be planted on a sandy slope that will cover well, look nice, and keep sand from blowing? *Arenaria montana, Cerastium tomentosum, Dianthus deltoides* and *D. plumarius* (Cottage Pink). Mix equal parts of seed of Domestic Rye Grass and Chewings's Fescue Grass, and add 1 part of the seed to 10 parts of soil by bulk, and broadcast this. If your home is near the seashore, dig up roots of wild perennials, mostly weeds and grasses, that are growing above high-water mark, divide them, and plant them on your property; surround the plants with a little soil when setting them.

What are good shrubs for south slope of a gravel hill, soil loose and sandy? Try barberry, Beach Plum, Scotch Broom.

What can be used for fast coverage of a steep bank, heavy clay soil? We now have barberries, but after 2 years they are not covering very quickly, and deep gorges are being cut in the bank. Suggest keeping barberries in but also plant clumps of Hall's Honeysuckle, or bittersweet. Fill gullies with brush to catch and hold soil. Mulch slope with manure, to check washing.

Which flowering plants can be planted on a sandy, rocky bank? *Phlox subulata, Gypsophila repens,* and columbines are suitable perennials; use a good half pailful of soil in each planting hole. Buy seed of single mixed portulaca, mix it with screened soil (1 part of seed to 10 parts of soil); broadcast the mixture, and look forward to a fine display in summer.

SHADE

WHAT TO PLANT

In a shaded location, which flowers will bloom in each month of the season? The month of bloom may vary with the degree of shade and the geographical location, but one can depend upon the following plants to flower in the broader seasonal divisions of spring, summer, and fall. *Spring:* barrenwort (epimedium); bleedingheart, *Ajuga reptans, Pulmonaria saccharata,* spring bulbs (chionodoxa, muscari, scilla, etc.), *Mertensia virginica. Summer:* daylily, foxglove, Fringed Bleedingheart (*Dicentra eximia*), monkshood, plantainlily. *Fall: Aconitum autumnale, Eupatorium coelestinum,* and *E. urticaefolium, Anemone japonica.*

Which low-growing flowering plants thrive best in shade? Epimedium in variety, *Ajuga genevensis* and *A. reptans, Dicentra eximia, Iris cristata,* lily-of-the-valley, *Pulmonaria saccharata, Lysimachia nummularia, Vinca minor,* plantainlily.

Which flowering plants will grow well in an area that receives only about 2 or 3 hours of strong sun daily? Iris, phlox, anemone, digitalis, coreopsis, *Primula japonica,* veronica, bleedingheart, primrose.

Due to many trees adjacent to the entire length of south side of yard, my garden stretch is damp and shady all day. What type of planting would you suggest? Arrowwood, *Monarda didyma,* Fiveleaf Aralia, Cornelian Cherry (*Cornus mas*)*;* Mountain Laurel, plantainlily, spicebush (*Lindera benzoin*).

What can I grow to cover a small space under a cluster of oak trees, on the type of rock-garden material? Unless utterly shaded: barrenwort (epimedium), Fringed Bleedingheart. If only lightly shaded: *Iris cristata* and *I. gracilipes.* Or little evergreen shrubs, in not-too-heavy shade, in acid, humus soil: *Rhododendron indicum balsaminaeflorum, R. carolinianum.*

Have had no success with shade-loving plants, put near trees. Have enriched the soil but trees take all moisture. Would a mulch be of use? I can use blue grass clippings, old flax straw, rotted or regular grain straw, but peat is not available. Nor is a garden hose available. If your trees are maples or elms, your problem is a diffi cult one. Try *Pachysandra terminalis,* Japanese Spurge, planting it in the spring while the ground is moist—after first spading and raking the ground—then apply a mulch as well. This plant will often succeed where nothing else will.

Which flowers grow the best in tubs on a terrace that is shaded very heavily from a tree that is in the center? You will have to bring into bloom elsewhere, and use for temporary effects on the shaded terrace, any flowering plant that lends itself to pot culture; such as hydrangea varieties, lantana, geraniums, calla, caladiums (for colored foliage).

I have a row of Lombardy Poplar trees. Can I plant flowers in front or back, or in between spaces? Yes, particularly on the sunny side: *Aquilegia canadensis, Iberis sempervirens, Digitalis purpurea,* Rose Paul's Scarlet Climber, *Anemone japonica.*

What could one plant in shade of a mulberry tree? If a mere ground cover is wanted, prepare the area, working in leafmold and some old manure, and plant either Japanese Spurge or periwinkle; the former 6 to 9 ins. apart each way, the latter 8 to 12 ins., depending upon size of plants. If shade is not very dense, the following shrubs may, with proper preparation, be used: symphoricarpos (any), *Clethra alnifolia,* Morrow Honeysuckle (about 7 ft. tall). In an acid, humus soil: *Azalea rosea* and *A. calendulaceum.*

ANNUALS AND PERENNIALS

Which annuals can I grow in a section that is in complete shade after the trees are in full leaf? Practically none. Try cornflower, flowering tobacco, and nasturtium.

Which annuals grow best in a shady location? In general annuals must have sunlight to grow satisfactorily. There are a few, however, which get along fairly well in the shade: *Begonia semperflorens, Torenia fournieri,* cornflower, flowering tobacco (nicotiana), *Myosotis arvensis, Impatiens balsamina, Lobelia erinus, Vinca rosea,* monkeyflower, nasturtium, pansy, Tuberous-rooted Begonias (which see).

West garden border of my house is shaded half the day; would you name 6 annuals that would bloom in it? *Begonia semperflorens, Torenia fournieri,* monkeyflower, calliopsis, cornflower, petunia.

Which are best annuals for partial shade and all-summer flowers? Balsam, flowering tobacco, lobelia, *Vinca rosea,* nasturtium, petunia.

Will begonias grow and bloom outdoors in a spot that is shaded all day, but not densely so? And how should soil be prepared for them? They get along very well in partial shade. Soil must be moist but well drained. Work into it generous quantities of leafmold, old rotted manure, or other humus material; also dressing of bone meal. (See also Tuberous-rooted Begonias.)

I have a semi-shady spot in my perennial border in which I have been able to grow only wild violets. Can you give me some suggestions? The ground in this spot is inclined to remain damp. Astilbe in variety, beebalm, bugbane, bugle (*Ajuga reptans*), buttercup, cardinalflower, ferns, Great Blue Lobelia, plantainlily in variety.

Which perennials can be grown in a dry, shady place? Bugle, *Aquilegia canadensis,* moneywort, Red Baneberry, White Snakeroot, *Aster ericoides.*

Which perennials should I plant on terraces in the shade of immense forest trees high up the hill? Balloonflower, bleedingheart, coralbells, daylily in variety, ferns, foxglove, *Anemone japonica.*

What can I plant in a damp place in the shade of a neighbor's garage? Hardy primulas are good for spring, along with lily-of-the-valley. Pachysandra and English Ivy are good ground covers. Foxglove, funkia, forget-me-not, ground ivy, and periwinkle. Tuberous-rooted begonias may be planted every spring if soil is well drained.

SHRUBS

Which shrubs will grow in a shaded place? Andromeda (*Pieris floribunda*);* arrowwood (*Viburnum dentatum*); Cornelian-cherry; Five-leaf Aralia; hemlock;* jetbead; Mountain Laurel;* *Rhododendron maximum;* spicebush (*Lindera benzoin*); Sweetpepper-bush (*Clethra alnifolia*); yellowroot (*Xanthorhiza simplicissima*); American Yew.

Which shrubs can be planted near front of house shaded by tall maple trees? If the soil is full of tree roots, very few plants will get along well; try Five-leaf Aralia.

What kind of shrubs will grow the best along the west side of the house in almost constant shade of large oak trees? If you will prepare a deep, humusy, acid soil, this would seem fine for rhododendrons, azaleas, Mountain Laurel, leucothoe, and picris.

Will shrubs do well near evergreen trees? Near—yes; not *under* them. On the north and northeast sides, in properly prepared acid soil, even rhododendrons, laurels, and such might do well.

SUN

Which shrubs will thrive along the south side of a brick house in full sun? In deeply prepared, enriched, well-drained soil, kept sufficiently moist in summer, your choice is almost unlimited. Within the limits of permissible ultimate height and width, select from catalogues any good shrubs which require no special conditions or shade. Avoid rhododendron, azalea and, generally, evergreen shrubs.

Which shrub would suit an open, sunny, enclosed corner atop a retaining wall? Whatever you plant, prepare the soil 18 ins. deep with leafmold, old manure, and some peatmoss. See that the place does not dry out in summer. Usually, for a place like this, a shrub is best which will drape its branches somewhat over the wall. You might plant any of these: *Cotoneaster racemiflora*, *Lespedeza thunbergi*, *Rosa hugonis*, *Spreaea arguta* or *S. thunbergi*, *Forsythia suspensa* varieties.

What would you suggest as a fairly low, long-blooming flower for about 2-ft. space between brick house and sidewalk on south side of house? Harmony Marigolds would be excellent. Or dwarf zinnia, or the little blue *Torenia fournieri* (wishboneflower).

Can you suggest an edging for a 24-in.-wide border between house and driveway. South side of house. Germander, *Teucrium chamaedrys*. This may need some pruning which may be done in the spring by thrusting a spade in the soil alongside the row to check its lateral growth, using shears to trim the top growth.

*Evergreen

WET GROUND

Are there any flowers or flowering shrubs that like wet ground throughout the year? Perennials: cardinalflower, loosestrife (*Lythrum salicaria*), rosemallow. Shrubs: *Viburnum den tatum, Cephalanthus occidentalis, Aronia arbutifolia,* Swamp Azalea (*A. viscosum*).

The boundary line of my property is quite low and wet. I have put up a 5-ft. fence. Which vines would grow in such soil (clay)? Which shrubs or hedges could I plant there as a screen? *Vines:* porcelain-vine (*Ampelopsis brevipedunculata*); Dutchmanspipe, bittersweet, Japanese Honeysuckle. *Screen:* *Clethra alnifolia, Viburnum cassinoides, Ilex verticillata, Lindera benzoin.*

Our lot is about 1 ft. lower than the lot next door. Consequently, after a rain water stands in this spot for some time. The space is 3 × 6 ft. I would like the names of low-growing shrubs that would not interfere with the grass. The spot receives sun all day long. Do you have any other suggestion as to what to plant on the spot? *Aronia arbutifolia,* Dwarf Willow (*Salix purpurea nana*), *Ilex glabra,* snowberry (*Symphoricarpos*), *Itea virginica.* Pruning may be necessary to keep them low.

What shall we plant on a space which is liable to be flooded during bad storms? Rosemallow, Japanese Iris, *Lythrum salicaria.*

How should sides of a stream be treated or built up to prevent caving in? The stream, which meanders for 210 ft., is about 1 ft. deep and 18 ins. wide; it is completely dried out in the dry season. Set some large rocks in the bank, at 10 to 15 ft. apart. Plants mentioned in preceding question should hold the bank once they are established.

Which annuals grow best in wet soil, in the shade? Jewelweed and monkeyflower.

Which perennials will thrive in wet soil? Beebalm, boneset; cardinalflower, *Iris pseudacorus;* Japanese Iris; Joepyeweed, *Lythrum salicaria,* marshmarigold, rosemallow, starwort (*Boltonia asteroides*).

What herbaceous planting is suitable for the sides of a small stream which becomes a full storm sewer after a rainfall? *Myosotis palustris semperflorens, Lysimachia nummularia, Iris pseudacorus, Lythrum salicaria.*

Which shrubs will thrive in wet soil? Buttonbush (*Cephalanthus occidentalis*), *Aronia arbutifolia* and *A. melanocarpa,* Highbush Blueberry, *Lindera benzoin,* Siberian Dogwood, *Clethra alnifolia,* sweetshrub (*Calycanthus floridus*), Swamp Azalea (*A. viscosa*), winterberry (*Ilex verticillata*).

Which trees will thrive in wet soil? American Elm, Pin Oak, Red Maple, Swamp White Oak, sycamore, Sour Gum (*Nyssa sylvatica*); Weeping Willow.

What kind of trees and shrubs shall we plant around a swimming pool? *Trees:* Red Maple; Sour Gum (*Nyssa sylvatica*); Sweetgum (*Liquidambar styraciflua*); sycamore; Weeping Willow. *Shrubs: Cephalanthus occidentalis, Lindera benzoin, Clethra alnifolia.* Leaves and fruits falling in the water might be objectionable, if planting is too close to pool.

Which flowering plants will grow in a boglike spot? Japanese Iris, Siberian Iris, astilbe, flowering rush, marshmarigold, cardinalflower, *Primula japonica* and *P. pulverulenta,* trollius, *Myosotis palustris,* loosestrife.

ORNAMENTAL PLANTS AND THEIR CULTURE

(For soils and fertilizers in general, see also Section I; for individual plants, see under Specific Plants, this section. For plant material for special decorative effects, see also Landscaping, Section II.)

GENERAL CULTURE

CULTIVATION

What are the reasons for cultivating the surface soil? To kill weeds and maintain a loose surface that is readily penetrated by rain. It helps also in soil aeration in those cases where a crust forms on surface.

In cultivation, should the soil be left level or mounded around plants? Generally level cultivation is best, because it exposes less surface from which soil moisture can evaporate. When it is desirable to get rid of excess soil moisture, hilling or ridging is sometimes practiced. Corn and similar crops are mounded with soil to help them stay erect; potatoes to prevent "greening" of the tubers.

How soon after a rain should one hoe the soil? When it has dried to such an extent that it no longer sticks to the hoe in sufficient amount to impede the work.

Is it desirable to cultivate the surface every week? No. Cultivate according to circumstances rather than by the calendar. Hoe after rains to prevent the formation of a crust, and to kill weeds when the surface has dried somewhat. If no more rain falls, hoe only to kill weeds.

How deep should surface soil be cultivated? This depends on character of soil, time of year, and the root formation of the plants cultivated. Sometimes it may be desirable, in some soils, to cultivate deeply—3 to 4 ins.—early in season to dry the surface. Later shallow cultivation, 1 in. deep, is preferable to avoid injury to crop roots. Modern tendency is toward shallow cultivation.

My soil forms a crust after every rain. What shall I do? Cultivate with hoe or cultivating tool to break crust; or use a mulch of organic matter. (See Mulches.) Improve soil by adding bulky organic material—strawy manure, partly decayed leaves, sedge peat, peatmoss—annually until condition is cured.

Does a dust mulch really conserve soil water? Probably not in most soils, if the soil is stirred to a depth of more than 1 or 2 ins. Moisture in the loosened soil is quickly lost by evaporation and the dust mulch is likely to absorb all the water from light showers before it has a chance to reach the soil occupied by roots.

MULCHING

See also Winter Protection under Perennials, Evergreens, etc.

What is meant by mulching? The application of various materials —usually organic—to the soil surface to hold moisture in soil, to prevent weed growth, and, in some cases, to help keep the ground cool.

Essential small tools for the gardener—shovel, hoe, iron rake, trowel, and spading fork.

Should mulches be applied early in spring? Better wait until soil has warmed up. The chief reason for mulching is to conserve moisture in the soil during hot, dry weather.

Once a mulch has been put on, is it necessary to do anything further about it? Not much; just keep it loose. Peatmoss must be watched because it is likely to pack down after a heavy rain, forming a felted surface when dry which sheds water like a roof.

Mulches are put on to conserve water in the soil. Don't they also work in the opposite direction by absorbing rain which otherwise would reach crop roots? Yes, to some extent. Some mulch material, however—buckwheat hulls and cranberry tops, for example—allows easy penetration of water and does not absorb a great deal. Examination of soil after rain will show whether or not mulch is too thick.

What can I use to mulch my perennial border? I want something

not unsightly. Peatmoss, leafmold, buckwheat hulls, shredded sugar cane, pine needles, coconut-fiber refuse. Peatmoss and pine needles might make the soil too acid in some gardens, unless lime or extra nitrogen is used with them.

Of what value, if any, are grass cuttings for garden beds, and how should they be used? They are of use as a water-conserving mulch, and if incorporated with the soil after they are partly decayed they add to its humus content. They should be spread in a layer of 1 to 2 ins. thick.

Is a paper mulch practicable in a small garden? Scarcely. It is objectionable on the score of appearance, and because it is difficult to anchor it. Not all plants do well under a paper mulch.

What are the advantages in using mulch paper in the garden? It keeps moisture in soil; it eliminates cultivation; it keeps down weeds, but is difficult to keep in place, and will tear readily.

Is Polythene plastic film good material to use as a mulch? It can be used, but it is difficult to apply. One has to anchor it to prevent it from blowing away; and it is also essential to make provision for the ingress of water by punching holes in it. Except that it does not tear easily it has the same defects as mulching paper.

Can Polythene be used to mulch newly planted shrubs? Yes. In this case it can be used to advantage. Cut off a square of three or four feet, slit to a little beyond the center, put it in place and anchor it by covering each corner with soil. It is desirable to punch a few holes in the plastic film so that water can get in over the entire space.

My cottage is on a salt-water beach; is it beneficial or injurious to mulch with seaweed washed up in abundance on shores? Or could the presence of salt kill plants? Seaweed makes an excellent mulch. The amount of salt present should do no damage unless the seaweed is used in excess.

Since peatmoss is getting so high in price, would shredded sugar-cane fiber answer the purpose of peatmoss for mulching, especially around acid-loving plants such as azalea and rhododendron? Yes. It works very well.

What is your opinion of the use of coffee grounds? We can get a bushel a week, and we have a heavy clay soil. Coffee grounds make an excellent mulch, but should not be used too thickly, or air will be excluded. ½ in. deep is sufficient.

What plants would be benefited by mulching with pine needles? Pine needles are especially good for cone-bearing evergreens and acid-soil plants such as rhododendrons.

How about the use of well-rotted sawdust around plants, and on lawns, as a mulch? Sawdust makes a satisfactory mulch during the summer. Do not apply deeper than 1 in. unless it is mixed with sulfate of ammonia at the rate of 1 pound to 100 sq. feet.

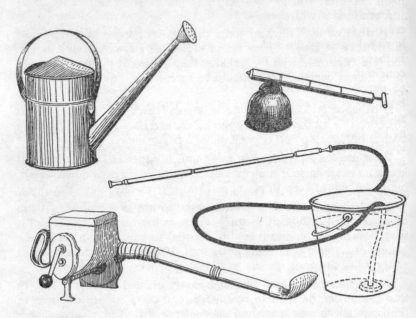

Types of sprayers and dusters for applying insecticides and liquid fertilizers. Watering can; small hand sprayer; crank duster for small garden; and "trombone" sprayer.

WATERING

How should one water flowers?   Water in at planting time if the soil is dry. When growth is active, and soil is really dry, water before the plants suffer. Mere surface sprinkling does no good. Give enough to wet the soil 6 ins. down. Cultivate the surface as soon as dry enough to work freely.

Are there any objections to spraying or watering plants in the evening?   Some authorities believe that if the foliage is wet when the temperature is falling, the plants are more susceptible to attacks by disease organisms. Under outdoor conditions this is probably not important, but in greenhouse or hotbed it is wise to spray or water early in the day.

Is it harmful to water plants when sun is shining on them?   Generally speaking, no. But, theoretically, it is better to water in early morning or in evening, so that water has a chance to penetrate the soil before much is lost by evaporation.

When watering newly set annuals, should water be applied to the

soil, or over all by sprinkling?   If water is in limited supply, leave depression around each stem and fill with water. If ample, sprinkle whole bed, making sure water penetrates several inches.

I mulched my kitchen garden with wood chips and sawdust. The crops did not grow at all well. The foliage looked peaked and yellowish. I presume this was caused by acid soil as a result of the mulch. Is there anything I can do to counteract this?   It is doubtful if this condition is caused by acid soil. More likely it is due to the depletion of nitrogen by the need for nitrates of the microorganisms which bring about the breakdown of the organic matter in the mulch. Apply sulfate of ammonia—1 pound to 100 square feet; or nitrate of soda at 1½ pounds. You should test the soil and, if it shows a reaction of less than pH 5.5, pulverised limestone should be applied—the amount is contingent upon the degree of acidity plus the character of the soil (more will be needed if it is a heavy clay). Your county agricultural agent should be consulted on this matter.

I have read somewhere that when undecayed organic materials are put in or on the soil that it is necessary to add chemical fertilizer to supply food for bacteria that cause its decay. How much and what kind?   Chemical fertilizer is not absolutely necessary but it is usually more convenient to obtain. Nitrogen is the element that is most likely to be lacking; this can be provided by sulfate of ammonia at one pound to 100 square feet, or 1½ pounds of nitrate of soda. Phosphorus can be added by superphosphate at 5 pounds to the same area. Organic fertilizers such as poultry manure can be used at 5 pounds to 100 square feet, or sheep manure at the rate of about 10 pounds. It is important to watch the behavior of the plants and if they become yellow indicating nitrogen deficiency, use quick acting nitrogen such as nitrate of soda or sulfate of ammonia, either in liquid, or dry and watered in.

PRUNING

See also under Trees, Shrubs, Evergreens, etc.

Please give us otherwise "green-fingered" amateur gardeners the real low-down on what, to me, has always been mystifying and most vexing—the art of pruning. There simply must be some fundamentals that apply. Are there not some simple rules to follow?   Read the section on pruning in the introduction to this division and the answers to the pruning questions. Then, if you are still in doubt about pruning, follow the advice which Mr. Punch gave to those about to marry— "Don't."

What is the difference between shearing and pruning?   Shearing is a form of pruning in which all young shoots extending beyond a definite line are cut off. Pruning proper involves cutting individual shoots or branches with a view to improving the tree or shrub.

When is the best time to trim trees? If the purpose is to check growth, it is better to prune trees when they are actively growing. Ordinarily, however, trees are pruned when they are dormant, in the fall or late winter. This stimulates strong shoot growth.

What is meant by "dormant"? Plants are said to be dormant when they are not actively growing. In deciduous trees and shrubs it is a period between leaf fall and starting into growth the following year.

Is it all right to trim trees in the winter? Yes, provided the temperature is not too low. From the standpoint of comfort for the operator and the danger of breaking surrounding branches when they are brittle from frost, it is desirable not to prune when it is very cold. However, it is preferable to wait until late winter.

How can I avoid tearing the bark on the trunk when cutting off large limbs? Make the first cut from underneath the branch, cutting upward until the saw binds. Then cut from above, which results in the removal of the branch. The stub may now be cut off with safety by sustaining it with one hand while the few last cuts with the saw are being made.

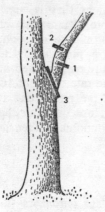

*Proper way to cut off a large limb.
(1) – make an "under cut" near trunk;
(2) – saw off limb, leaving stub; (3) –
saw off stub as close to trunk as possible.*

Is there any special rule to follow when making the cuts in pruning? Yes; branches should always be cut off close to, and parallel with, the branch from which they spring. When shoots are shortened, the cut should be made just above a growth bud, pointing in the direction you wish to have the tree develop.

Should a single or double leader be developed? Generally speaking, a single leader is preferable, especially for those trees which naturally grow with a single trunk. Some trees, and all shrubs, have a diffuse habit and cannot well be restricted to a single leader.

Does pruning help make a tree bushy? Yes, if it is limited to cutting off the tips of the leading shoots. It can be done during the growing season if the tree is too vigorous.

Is it better to use hedge shears or pruning shears when trimming trees into globes, squares, etc.? If the leaves are large, as in linden, cherrylaurel, etc., it is better to use pruning shears, because the use of hedge shears results in obviously marred leaves. In the case of small-leaved trees, hedge shears can be used.

What is used to paint over wounds made in pruning? Several coatings of shellac, renewed when necessary, are excellent. Or you could use tree-wound paint, obtainable from horticultural supply houses, asphaltum paint, or white lead and linseed oil in which a little lampblack has been mixed to make it less conspicuous.

Is pruning of any help in the case of trees infested with scale insects? Yes. Branches dying as a result of attack by scale insects should be cut off. This will tend to strengthen the rest of the tree. The cut-off branches should be destroyed by burning and measures taken to kill the insects remaining. (See Scale—Section VIII.)

Is pruning sometimes used as an aid in controlling plant disease? Yes; for example, canker on roses, and fire blight on trees and shrubs of the apple family. The affected limbs must be cut off well below the point of injury, and the tool used should be disinfected after every cut.

We have a young tree with the center broken off; will it grow into a tree or should we dispose of it? If there is a strong side shoot near the break, it could be trained to take the place of the broken leader. Tie a stout stake securely below the break, and let it project two or three ft. above it; then tie the side shoot to this.

How can I keep tree wounds from bleeding? Maples and birches, if pruned in spring, will bleed, but this is temporary. Another form of bleeding is caused by "slime flux," and this is often very difficult to control and may cause the bark to decay if it persists for a considerable time. Sometimes a short length of pipe is inserted to carry off the flux, or in the case of large wounds the wood is scared with a blowtorch. These practices, however, are not always effective.

What tools are necessary for pruning? For close work on trees, a narrow-bladed pruning saw is desirable. In some cases it is helpful to have one attached to a long pole to get at branches which otherwise would be difficult to reach. To cut branches ½ in. in diameter, or less, sharp pruning shears should be used, or a pruning knife. In pruning old, overgrown shrubs, long-handled "lopping" shears are useful.

DISBUDDING AND PINCHING

What is meant by disbudding? The removal of some flower buds while they are still small, so that those remaining will develop into flowers of larger size. Plants on which disbudding is commonly practiced include carnation, chrysanthemum, dahlia, peony, rose.

When are plants disbudded? As soon as the buds to be removed are large enough to handle, usually about the size of a pea or bean.

How often should plants be pinched to force blooms? Should they be kept pinched as long as they bloom? Pinching a plant delays blooming instead of forcing it, but results in a bigger, more stocky plant. Some plants, such as snapdragon, give good, bushy plants with only 1 pinching. Others, such as chrysanthemum, may be pinched 3 or 4 times until late July. A plant such as geranium, after the first pinching (soon after rooting), may be pinched just beyond each flower bud as it appears.

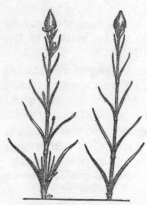

Disbudding—pinching out most of the buds in order to secure fewer but larger blooms—is often practiced with some plants, such as carnations, dahlias, chrysanthemums, and roses.

What plants should I pinch; and when? These are a few examples: coleus, carnation, chrysanthemum, dahlia, fuchsia, heliotrope, iresine, salvia, and the garden geranium. One pinching, when the plants are a few inches high, may be sufficient, but in the case of coleus and chrysanthemum, pinching may be repeated more than once if extra-large plants are desired. Some woody plants are pinched back during the growing season to make them more compact.

What is meant by "terminal bud"? The topmost bud on a shoot.

ROOT-PRUNING

What are the reasons for root-pruning? To promote formation of fibrous roots, to induce blossoming, and to check excessive shoot and leaf growth.

How many roots should be cut off when root-pruning a tree or shrub to check growth or induce flowering? Impossible to say definitely, for each specimen is a problem in itself. Sometimes cutting the taproot is all that is necessary, and sometimes one or more horizontally spreading roots also must be cut. Root-pruning is a hazardous practice not to be attempted by the beginning gardener.

What is the technique of root-pruning? If the tree or shrub is a large one, dig a trench halfway around the tree (distance from trunk depends on size of tree) and sever all thonglike roots encountered. Do the other half the following year—if necessary. Sometimes one must undermine the tree to cut the taproot.

Can I, by root-pruning ahead of time, make it possible to move some shrubs with greater safety? Yes. In the spring thrust a sharp spade into the ground to its full depth all around the shrub a few inches inside the digging circle. This will induce the formation of fibrous roots which will enable it to be easily moved the following fall or spring.

Is there any simple method of dwarfing plants? It is helpful to start off with naturally dwarf varieties. Restrict the roots by growing the plants in comparatively small containers, or by root-pruning if in the open ground. Prune the top at frequent intervals during the growing season by shortening new growth. In the case of fruit trees (which see) the use of a dwarfing understock is indicated.

SUPPORTS

What is the best method of staking perennials and annuals? The type of support varies with the subject. Those with only comparatively few slender stems (delphinium, for example), should have individual slender stakes to which the stems are loosely tied. Low, bushy plants can be supported by twigs stuck in the ground around them before they have completed their growth. For others, such as peonies, wood or metal hoops, on 3 or 4 legs placed over the plants, afford the best solution.

Many flowers require support, and many devices have been developed for this purpose. Detail drawing (upper right) shows proper method of securing plant stem to stake: string is first tied tight around stake; then ends are tied in a loose loop around stem.

Any pointers on staking plants? Always maintain the natural habit of growth. Don't tie stems in a bundle and fasten to a broomstick. (See answer to preceding question.)

How can one obtain twiggy shoots for staking perennials? Save all suitable material from shrub pruning. Keep one or more privet bushes solely for this purpose—cutting off the twigs early in the fall so that they will dry up and not grow when stuck in ground. Gray birch twigs are ideal, if available.

I want to use espaliered trees to enclose a small flower garden. How can I support them? If in a continuous row, use galvanized wire stretched tightly on posts; or a wood fence with horizontal members. Isolated specimens are best supported on wooden trellises.

How are "espaliered" trees or shrubs supported on walls? Sometimes by fastening directly to the wall, but this is considered undesirable where exposed to full sun in regions having hot summers. They can be fastened to wires strung on brackets 6 ins. or more from wall, or on wood trellises, thus allowing circulation of air between plant and wall.

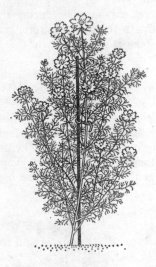

Staking an annual (cosmos). Tie is first made fast around stake and then looped loosely around stem of plant.

How can I attach trained shrubs directly to a wall? Use broad tape; or use cloth or leather (old gloves) cut into strips ½ in. wide, 3 to 6 ins. long, passed around branches and fastened to wall with stubby nails. Also special wall nails are obtainable from firms dealing in horticultural supplies.

I want to use vines for "accent points" in my flower garden. What is best for holding them up? Use redcedar posts, sunk 2 to 3 ft. in the ground, or a "tepee" support (see page 762).

What are the best supports for roses, vegetables (such as tomatoes, peas, pole beans, etc.), fruit trees in bearing, etc.? See Index for specific plants to be supported.

PLANT PROPAGATION

See also Cold Frames, Hotbeds, Greenhouse, and Propagation under Plant Groups.

What are the various methods of plant propagation? Seeds, spores, bulbils, cormels, tubers, rhizomes, runners, offsets, suckers, stolons, layers, division, cuttings, grafting.

SEEDS

What are the main factors in seed germination? Quality and freshness in seed. Correct temperature, even moisture supply, and sufficient air. Some seeds must never be allowed to become really dry (usually these are stratified in a moist medium); some must be sown as soon as they are ripe; some wait a year or more before germinating; and some require an "after-ripening" period at low temperatures.

How can germination be hastened in hard-shell seeds? Soak in warm water overnight, or longer, to soften shell; or nick hard shell of large seeds with a sharp knife. Sometimes seeds are treated with acids, but this is not recommended for beginners.

What is meant by "stratification" of seeds? It is the term applied to the practice of storing seeds over winter, or longer, in moist material such as sand or peatmoss. Seeds which lose their vitality if allowed to become dry (oak, chestnut, etc.), and "2-year seeds" (hawthorn, dogwood) are commonly so treated.

Should seeds be treated with a disinfectant before planting? Yes, if trouble has been experienced in the past with seed-borne diseases. (See Section VIII.)

BULBS; CORMS; TUBERS

What is the usual method of propagating bulbs? By digging them up when dormant and taking off small bulbs formed around the mother bulb. They should be planted separately, and grown on to flowering size.

Is there any way of inducing bulbs to form offsets for propagating purposes? Planting shallower than normal is supposed to be helpful. Commercial growers, in the case of hyacinths, either scoop out the base of the bulb, or cut into it in several directions to induce the formation of bulbils. Special after-treatment is necessary.

What are offsets? Shoots with short stems with a miniature plant at the end—sometimes applied to the small bulbs produced around the mother bulb. Typical offsets are produced by houseleeks. They may be taken off and used to start new plants.

How are plants propagated by tubers? By separating or cutting, and planting. Sometimes, as in the potato, the tuber may be cut into several pieces, each having an "eye," or growth bud.

Can the little gladiolus bulbs that form on the old ones be used? Yes. These are known as cormels (the large bulb is really a corm) and may be planted 1 in. deep in rows in the spring in much the same way that one would sow peas.

CUTTINGS—GENERAL

What is meant by softwood cuttings? These are made from shoots that are still actively growing, and are taken from hardy shrubs during May and early June. Nurserymen sometimes place suitable plants in greenhouses to force young growth for cuttings.

What is meant by half-ripe wood cuttings? Cuttings of half-ripe wood are taken when the shoots have finished growth but are not yet mature. July and August are suitable months.

What are hardwood cuttings? Hardwood cuttings are made from fully matured shoots, generally of the current year's growth. These are taken after there have been a few frosts, packed in moist sand or peatmoss, stored in a temperature of 35° to 40° F., and planted out the following spring.

How does one propagate softwood and hardwood plants? This depends entirely upon the plant under consideration. In most cases softwood plants may be increased by stem cuttings, and many of the hardwood plants may be increased in the same way; but there are innumerable exceptions in both groups.

What is the best and surest way to root cuttings for the average amateur? I have a cold room in cellar, no heat, facing east, with two small windows. Also have a dark closet behind the furnace where it is always warm. The dark closet behind the furnace is most unsuitable. Probably you could root most of the commoner shrubs and house plants in the cellar room if the cuttings were placed near the window. However, you would be more likely to succeed with a small cold frame or propagating box in a shady place in the garden.

How best can one propagate plants from cuttings without greenhouse or hotbed? Many shrubs, some trees, most of the plants used for summer bedding, herbaceous perennials, many rock garden plants, and several house plants can be propagated during the summer almost as readily in a cold frame as in a greenhouse or hotbed.

What is Polythene? Polythene or Polyethylene is the name given to a plastic film which has the properties of permitting the passage of gases and retaining water vapor.

How is Polythene used in plant propagation? It is used in the same way as glass. Among the advantages as compared with glass are: its light weight; it usually eliminates any need for additional watering. It is also used to enclose the moist sphagnum moss when air-layering is practiced.

How can I make a propagating frame? An ordinary cold frame is satisfactory; or you can use a box 10 to 12 ins. deep, covered tightly with a pane of glass. Make ½-in. drainage holes in bottom; cover with 1 in. of peat moss, and put in 4 ins. of some rooting medium (such as sand or sand and peatmoss) packed down firmly.

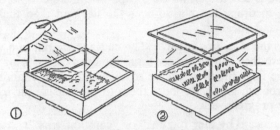

A miniature greenhouse for indoor use. Panes of glass, set around sides of a deep flat, are held in place by sand or compost in which cuttings are to be placed or seeds sown. A fifth pane of glass forms the "roof." By this simple arrangement moisture for the plants can be controlled.

A bulb pan or a flower pot, covered with an inverted glass jar, makes an excellent miniature propagating frame for the amateur gardener. In it cuttings can readily be rooted.

What are the essentials in using Polythene in rooting cuttings? Thoroughly soaking the rooting medium; and completely enclosing the cuttings. When only a few cuttings are to be rooted they are put in a flower pot which is then put in a Polythene bag and the open end is tightly closed. Or, on a slightly larger scale a shallow box (flat) can be used. In this case some kind of support is needed to keep the film from contact with the cuttings. It can be wire coat hangers or willow twigs. After the cuttings are inserted and have been thoroughly watered the whole is wrapped in plastic, taking care that no opening is left to permit the escape of moisture. The best way to do this is to drape the plastic over the flat and then tuck the sides and ends underneath it.

What is the after-treatment? The cuttings are put in a well-lighted place where they can be shaded from the direct sun during the hottest part of the day. In six weeks or so they should be examined, and if they are rooted, gradually inure them to the outside air by loosening the cover progressively.

What is meant by the "fog box" or "constant mist" system of propagation? This is a method whereby cuttings are rooted by keeping their leaves constantly moist by subjecting them to a fine mist-like spray.

I am interested in the possibilities, on a small scale, of rooting cuttings by constant mist. How does one go about it? You will need a nozzle that will deliver about 1½ gallons of water per hour, and water pressure of 30 to 50 pounds. This should be sufficient to cover an area of about one square yard. The site should be in the open in full sun; if in a windy location a windbreak may be necessary which may be of plastic fastened to a wooden frame (about 4 by 3 feet). There must be free drainage, therefore the rooting medium should be coarse sand, and the pots or flats should be placed on a platform of galvanized hardware cloth raised an inch or two above the ground.

Is it necessary to keep the spray going all the time? No, it is not—although no great harm will accrue if it is left on night and day. It is considered desirable however to have an intermittent mist. This may be accomplished by the installation of an electronic leaf which automatically shuts off the water when it is wet and turns it on when it is dry.

What are the advantages and the drawbacks of this method of rooting cuttings by constant mist? *Pro.* It enables us to root larger cuttings than is possible by conventional means; and cuttings usually considered difficult often may be rooted with ease.

Con. on the other hand, while you may have a hundred percent rooting, there may be great mortality when they are transplanted. The operation was successful but the patient died! Doubtless means will be devised to overcome these defects.

Will you please tell me something about air-layering by using plastic film?   This is a method that can be used successfully outdoors on a large number of different trees and shrubs. Here is the way of it. With a sharp knife cut a slit in a stem at the point where it is desired to have roots form. (Other ways of wounding the stem are to cut a small notch in the stem or to remove a cylinder of bark, about an inch long.) The wound is wrapped with a wad of moist sphagnum moss, which is tied in place with twine, preparatory to covering it with the plastic film which should be between 2 and 4 thousandths of an inch thick.

When is the best time to make the layer?   This has not yet been definitely determined. Probably early spring.

Is it a foolproof method?   It is not. Care must be taken to avoid getting the medium too wet. This involves squeezing out as much of the water as possible prior to applying the moss; also in putting on the wrap it is essential to ensure that no water gets in. Thus be careful to have the overlap on the underside; and see that the ties, both top and bottom, are made watertight by taping them spirally so that rain cannot seep in.

How does one know when to remove the layer?   When roots are visible through the plastic. The removal of the layer is probably the most critical period. The layers, when they are rooted, should be treated for a time as though they were unrooted cuttings, by potting them, keeping them in a closed and shaded cold frame, and gradually hardening them off. (See page 261 for details.)

What is the best material in which to root cuttings?   Sand is most commonly used, but recently a half-and-half mixture of peat and sand has become popular for almost all kinds of cuttings. Sifted coal ashes, sphagnum moss, decayed spruce or pine needles vermiculite and perlite are other materials used for special purposes.

Is there any special trick in inserting cuttings?   Make individual holes with a pointed stick; or make a narrow trench by drawing a blunt knife or label through the rooting medium. It is important to be sure that the bases of the cuttings touch the rooting medium and that it is well firmed about them.

Is there any reason for cutting back leaves when inserting cuttings in wet sand?   The reason for cutting back leaves is to prevent undue loss of moisture from the plant tissues by transpiration. Its value has been questioned by some propagators in recent years, and it is probably only necessary in the case of cuttings with very large leaves.

Why do professional growers use a powder when planting cutting in wet sand? Is this powder a talc, or some special powder?   A root stimulant is used for the purpose of obtaining a higher percentage of rooting, to shorten the time required for the production of roots, and, in many instances, to obtain a bigger root system. Talc is sometimes the carrier with which small amounts of active chemical substances are mixed.

Which chemicals are used as stimulants for cuttings? Many chemicals have been tried—indoleacetic acid, naphthaleneacetic acid, etc. —and others are under trial. Indolebutyric acid seems to be most generally used at present.

Why are acids used, and what kinds are used, to promote good cuttings? Most cuttings root better in an acid than in a neutral or alkaline medium. Old-time propagators frequently added vinegar to water applied to cutting beds. (See answer to preceding question.)

Are chemical stimulants poured on sand used to root cuttings? Or are the cuttings kept in water? The use of stimulants applied to the sand has not proved very satisfactory, and it is now customary to apply it to the base of the cuttings before they are inserted in the sand. The cuttings are not kept in water to form roots, but some of the substances used to induce rooting are made up in solution in which the base of the cuttings is allowed to stand for a given number of hours.

Can anyone use root-inducing chemicals? As prepared for general use these can be very readily applied by anyone. The most popular are in powder form. The bases of the cuttings are merely dipped into this before being inserted in the rooting medium.

Is the use of commercial rooting preparations safer than the older methods? Provided that the instructions of the manufacturer are strictly followed, the use of such preparations is quite as safe as the older methods, and in many cases a better root system is produced in a shorter time.

How do you treat cuttings started with the aid of chemical stimulants? The treatment of cuttings after the application of the root-inducing stimulant is the same as for untreated cuttings.

What about the use of Vitamin B_1 and hormones in rooting plants? Vitamin B_1 is probably present in sufficient quantities in any soil reasonably well supplied with humus, so that the addition of this substance is unnecessary (see also Section I), but in soils deficient in humus it may be of service. If by hormones you mean the substances now on the market for facilitating the rooting of cuttings, there is little room for doubt that they are a definite aid to propagation.

What is the general treatment of cuttings after they have been placed in a propagating frame? Keep rooting medium moist and frame closed until roots have formed, then gradually increase ventilation to harden cuttings. Frame must be in a shady location, or shaded by a double thickness of cheesecloth on sash.

How can one know when a cutting has developed roots, and is

ready to be transplanted?   When it is judged that sufficient time has elapsed for roots to have developed, gently pull on 1 or 2 cuttings, and if they offer resistance it is a good indication that they have rooted. Most of the plants commonly rooted in summer produce a good root system in from 6 to 10 weeks. Many conifers, however, require as many months.

How are cuttings treated after rooting?   Those rooting early (July, August) are potted up, and the pots plunged in sand, peatmoss, or ashes in a cold frame, to be planted out the following spring. Late rooters may be left in the rooting medium. Both kinds should be protected by scattering salt hay, or similar litter, among them after first severe frost.

ROOT AND LEAF CUTTINGS

Can root cuttings be put in ordinary soil, or must sand be used? A sandy soil is desirable, as there is less probability of the root cuttings decaying, and a better root system is produced.

Rooted leaf cutting of sansevieria or snake-plant, with roots sufficiently developed for transplanting.

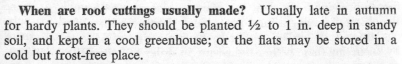

When are root cuttings usually made?   Usually late in autumn for hardy plants. They should be planted ½ to 1 in. deep in sandy soil, and kept in a cool greenhouse; or the flats may be stored in a cold but frost-free place.

Does it make any difference which end of a root cutting is inserted in soil?   Yes. In order to be certain that the right end will be uppermost, it is customary to make a straight cut across the upper end of the cutting and a sloping cut at the basal end. However, with thin cuttings (such as phlox), both ends are cut straight across and the cuttings are laid flat.

How many kinds of root cuttings are usually made? When true roots, as distinguished from underground stems, are being dealt with, there is only one type of root cutting. Such cuttings are usually from 1 to 3 ins. long, depending upon their thickness.

How are cuttings of fine, stringy roots made? Cut them into lengths of an inch or a little more and lay them flat in the container in which they are to grow.

Are root cuttings more sure than stem cuttings? This depends entirely upon the plant to be propagated. The roots of all plants do not produce buds, and in these cases it is useless to attempt to reproduce them by root cuttings. In those instances where past experience has shown that a plant will produce buds on severed root pieces, this method is generally a little less trouble than stem cuttings.

What type of plant is mostly propagated by root cuttings? Many plants can be raised from root cuttings. These include apple, pear, cherry, rose, blackberry, horse-radish, phlox, trumpetcreeper, daphne, locust, bouvardia, and many others. It must be understood, however, that if root cuttings are made of grafted or budded plants, it will be the understock that is propagated.

Are any indoor plants propagated by root cuttings? Not many of the more familiar house plants are propagated from root cuttings, but dracaena and bouvardia are sometimes increased in this way.

Will leaves make new plants if treated in the same way as stem cuttings? In some cases, yes. Among the plants commonly propagated in this way are African-violet, gloxinia, Rex Begonia, pick-a-back plant, and many succulents, such as the sedums.

Can all plants be propagated by leaf cuttings? No. Some will root—croton, for example—but never form a growth shoot. If, however, the leaf cuttings are taken with a growth bud and a sliver of the parent branch attached, they are successful in the case of most of the plants commonly increased by stem cuttings.

LAYERING

What is meant by layering? As generally understood, layering means bringing a shoot of the plant into contact with the earth with the object of having it form roots. Such shoots are slit with an upward cut, twisted, or girdled, either by having a ring of bark removed, or by encircling them with a tight wire, in order to induce the formation of roots at the injured part. This injured part must be covered with soil and kept moist.

How long before layers are ready to transplant? Many herbaceous plants will form roots in a few weeks. Shrubs layered in the spring will usually have a satisfactory root system by the end of the growing season. Some shrubs, such as rhododendrons and others that form roots slowly, require 2 years. After new roots form, the layers may be severed from the parent plant to become new plants on their own roots.

How many kinds of layering are there? Layering may be broadly divided into two classes: (a) layering in the ground, and (b) air layering. Class (a) may be divided into simple layering, serpentine layering, continuous layering, and mound layering. In all these ways it is necessary to bring the branches to ground level. Air layering

Some plants, such as the Strawberry-begonia or Strawberry-geranium (Saxifraga sarmentosa) multiply themselves by runners, which are easily rooted in pots while still attached to the parent plant.

(b) refers to rooting stems at points above the ground, by means of "layering pots" filled with soil; or by wrapping moist moss around the stem.

When is layering done? Spring is the best time, as in most cases a good root system will then be developed before winter. It may be done at any time, however, but in the colder parts of the country

New plants produced by layering. English Ivy (1) rooting at each joint or leaf node. (2) "Serpentine" layering, with stem covered at intervals, to induce rooting.

the roots may be torn off the layers due to winter heaving if plants are layered at a later period.

What is the best kind of wood for layering? If shrubs are to be layered, stout, 1-year-old shoots are preferred, as they form a root system much more readily than older wood.

How large should the layers be?   Not so large as implied by the over-optimistic advertisements of dealers! If the layer is made in the spring it should, in general, be put at the base of the shoots made the preceding year; if it is a summer job shoots of the current season are preferred.

Is there a limit to the size of branch used in layering?   For practical purposes, yes. The younger they are the more readily they may be expected to root. However, layering frequently takes place when large branches, many years old, come in contact with the ground, but it may take many years before they form a root system sufficiently large to support them independently.

SUCKERS; STOLONS; RUNNERS

How are plants propagated by SUCKERS?   If the plant is not grafted and is a type that produces suckers (lilac, for instance), rooted suckers can be dug up, cut back, and planted to produce new plants.

What is a STOLON?   A branch which grows downward and roots at the tip, where it comes into contact with the soil. When rooted, it may be detached from the parent, dug up, and planted, to lead an independent existence. Forsythia and matrimonyvine commonly produce stolons.

How are plants propagated by RUNNERS?   Merely by digging up the runners when rooted. In special cases, to avoid root disturbance, small flower pots may be filled with earth and the developing runner fastened to the soil with a hairpin.

GRAFTING

What is meant by a "graft"?   A graft is the union of parts of 2 plants in such a manner that they will grow together to form 1 plant. It consists of 2 parts: the *understock* and the *scion*. The union of these 2, by grafting, results in a new plant having the roots of one plant and the branches, leaves, flowers, and fruit of the plant from which the scion was taken.

What is double grafting?   This refers to the practice of first grafting onto the understock a scion that will unite readily with it, and later grafting onto the first scion a second one of a kind that will unite with it but will not unite satisfactorily with the understock when grafted directly upon it.

Can any plant be grafted on any other plant?   Only those plants that are closely related can be grafted.

What is a scion?   A scion is one of the 2 parts necessary when making a graft, and consists of a short portion of stem of the plant that is to be duplicated. It usually contains 2 or more buds, and the base is cut in such manner that the cambium, a layer of actively growing tissue between bark and wood, or a part of it, will come in direct contact with the corresponding layer of the understock, which is cut to fit the scion.

What is meant by understock? The understock is the part that constitutes the root system of a grafted or budded plant. Seedlings, or pieces of root, or rooted cuttings, are generally used as understocks. It is the part to which the scion or bud is attached that is to become the new plant.

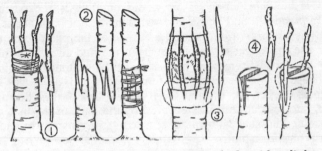

Grafting is an interesting operation which, with a little practice, the amateur can accomplish. Above are shown (1) bark grafting; (2) whip or tongue grafting; (3) bridge grafting; (4) cleft grafting. In each case the detail sketch shows how the scion (or bud wood) is cut.

When is grafting done? Grafting is usually practiced in spring, either in the open or in greenhouses, just as the understocks are beginning to break dormancy. The understocks should be beginning growth while the scions must still be dormant. For this reason the scions are buried in the ground or kept on ice until required for grafting. Summer grafting of some ornamental trees and shrubs is also practiced.

Why are plants grafted? To propagate horticultural varieties which do not "come true" from seed; to increase plants which are difficult to propagate by other vegetative means, such as cuttings or divisions; to modify growth of scion by use of dwarfing understocks, etc.; to hasten flowering; and to produce plants of special form as when "weeping" trees (mulberry, elm, etc.) are "worked" on a tall understock.

TYPES OF GRAFTING

How are ornamental trees grafted? In several ways, depending upon the plant being grafted. Splice, whip, veneer, and side graft are probably more commonly used than others, but saddle grafting and grafting by approach are other forms frequently employed.

What sort of roots are ornamental trees grafted on? Can any root be used? The kind or root that an ornamental tree is grafted on must be very closely related to it. Oaks cannot be grafted on elms, for example, nor beech on ash. Even in a group as large as the oaks, not all oaks can be grafted on just one kind of oak.

What is meant by BUDDING? Budding is a form of grafting by means of which a single bud and a portion of its surrounding bark are brought in contact with the cambium layer of a suitable understock.

How is budding done? T or shield budding is the commonest form. In practice a bud and a narrow, thin strip of bark about ¾ in. in length is cut from a bud stick (a branch of the plant to be propagated). The thin sliver of wood, cut from the bud stick with the bud, may or may not be removed, according to the custom of the budder. A T-shaped cut is made on the understock, and the edges of the bark on the leg of the T lifted. The bud is then pushed down, from the top, into the cut until it is covered by the bark of the understock. It is then tied in place with raffia, soft string, a rubber strip, or a narrow strip of plastic film.

What is a bud stick? A bud stick is a shoot, usually of the current year's growth, from which buds are cut for budding.

Why is budding practiced in preference to grafting? Because only 1 bud is required to produce a new plant, consequently a given amount of scion wood will furnish more buds than scions for grafting, as each scion would require about 4 buds. In the case of stone fruits, budding insures a better union than grafting. Also, since less time is consumed in budding than in grafting, it is preferred where suitable.

When is budding done? Budding is usually a summer operation, as it can be done only when the sap is running and the bark lifts easily from the wood. June, July, and August are the usual months.

How does grafting differ from budding? The principal differences are in the time of year when each is performed, and the amount of scion or budwood required. A graft consists of an understock and a scion; i.e., a short length of shoot containing 2 or more buds. In budding, an understock is also required, but in place of a scion a single bud is inserted on the understock.

Has the plant on which the bud is placed (understock) any influence on the budded portion? Very definitely in many cases. Weak-growing garden roses are much more vigorous when budded on a suitable understock than when on their own roots. Recently dwarf apple trees have attracted much attention. Such trees are dwarf because they have been budded or grafted on understocks that cause dwarfing.

What is BARK GRAFTING?   The tree is prepared as for cleft grafting (which see) but the branches are not split. Instead, a slit is made in the bark, about 1½ ins. long, from the stub down. The scions are prepared by making a sloping cut at their bases, but a shoulder is cut at the top of the slope so that the lower part of the scion, which is to be pushed under the bark, is quite thin. Several scions may be placed on one stub, depending upon its size. On large stubs the scions may be secured with brads; on smaller ones they are tied in. All must be covered with grafting wax.

What is the purpose of BRIDGE GRAFTING?   This form of grafting is confined to the repair of tree trunks (particularly fruit trees) which have been entirely or largely girdled by rodents. Its purpose is to maintain a connection between top and roots. Unless the girdled portion is bridged in this way the tree will shortly die.

How is bridge grafting done?   Trim away ragged bark. Make longitudinal slits above and below wound and loosen bark. Cut scions (from the tree being operated on) of 1-year-old wood about 3 ins. longer than the wound. Bevel each end with cuts ½ to 1 in. long; bend scion in middle; insert under slit bark; fasten with small brads. Cover points of insertion with grafting wax. Scions should be placed every 2 ins. around the trunk.

What is CLEFT GRAFTING?   Cleft grafting is one of the simpler forms, and involves the insertion of scions cut to a long wedge shape in a cleft of the understock. It is chiefly used in "making over" fruit trees and in grafting certain herbaceous plants.

What is the purpose of cleft grafting?   The particular value of this form of grafting is in the conversion of unsuitable kinds of apples, pears, and sometimes such stone fruits as cherries and plums, to the production of fruit of better quality, or greater productiveness.

How is cleft grafting done?   Cut back all branches to be grafted to leave a shapely tree; smooth over the cut faces; split each cut end with a grafting chisel. Cut scions with a wedge-shaped base about 1½ ins. long. Open cleft with end of chisel and insert scions, 2 in each cleft. See that the inner edges of bark on scions and stock are in contact. Tie in the scions on small branches; on the thicker ones this will be unnecessary. Cover scions and all parts of the cleft with grafting wax. If both scions unite, the weaker one may be cut off level with stump the following spring. At least one branch should be left to be grafted the second year, otherwise there will be an enormous growth of water sprouts.

When is cleft grafting carried out?   In spring, as soon as the buds show the first indication of swelling. The scions must be completely dormant.

What is WHIP GRAFTING?   The base of the scion is cut across with a downward, long, sloping cut, about 1¼ ins. long, then an upward cut ½ in. long is made on this face, commencing about ½ in. from the lower end of the first cut. The understock is cut in a similar way. Press the tongue of the scion into the cut in the understock until the one face covers the other. Tie together with raffia or soft string, and cover the union with grafting wax; or pack in moist material and treat the same as hardwood cuttings.

What is the procedure in whip grafting if the understock is much thicker than the scion? The first cut should be straight across. Then on one side of the understock, and near the top, cut off a strip of the same length and width as the cut face of the scion. Cut a tongue in it as previously described; tie; wax. Where scion and understock are not exactly of the same width it is most important that the inner edges of the bark of scion and understock *come in contact on one side* of the joint; otherwise they will not unite.

GLASS

COLD FRAMES

Should every garden have a cold frame? Not necessarily. Some gardens are too small for a standard-size frame. However, cold frames are a handy addition to the smallest gardens, even if there is space for only a 2 × 4 ft. frame.

How can I make a simple cold frame? Use a 12-in. plank for back, a 6-in. one for front. Make ends of one 6-in. plank and half a 6-in. plank cut diagonally lengthwise (to allow for slope from back to front) cleated together. Standard sash is 6 × 3 ft., so width of frame should be 6 ft. and the length made up of units of 3 ft. plus about 1¼ in. allowance between each sash to accommodate cross ties, usually 1 in. thick. Above specifications do not allow much headroom—a height of 9 to 12 ins. front and 15 to 18 ins. in back is preferable.

Can I make a cold frame in December? I have a large, dry cellar where I can thaw out the ground. It is possible to construct a cold frame of wood in December, and get the soil in place ready for spring planting.

I have been informed that plants will not do so well in a cold frame constructed with concrete walls instead of wood. Is this true? No, it is not true. In fact, concrete frames can be kept more sanitary.

How deep should the layer of cinders or coarse gravel be when preparing the soil in a cold frame? What should be the composition of the soil that is placed over the cinders; and how deep should it be? Cinders should be deep enough to allow for good drainage—usually 3 ins. or so. This would differ in various soils. In light, well-drained soil no gravel or cinders are used. Over this use about 6 ins. of a mixture of equal parts humus, garden soil, and sand.

How do you make a seedbed in a cold frame? If soil in frame is a sandy loam, spread a 2-in. layer of sifted leafmold and mix with the upper 6 ins. If soil is clayey, remove 6 to 8 ins. and replace with a screened mixture of sand, loam, and leafmold.

What should be added to the cold frame each year, and at which season should this addition be made? Well-rotted manure or leafmold shortly before plants are to be set.

CARE OF PLANTS

How do I go about starting plants in a cold frame? In March and April seeds of annuals and vegetables that can be transplanted may be sown, either in flats or directly in a bed of good, friable soil. Seeds of perennials may also be sown at this time. In June greenwood cuttings of some shrubs may be rooted in a few weeks if kept under rather close conditions and shaded from bright sun. In August seeds of pansy, forget-me-not, and English Daisy can be sown for early-spring bloom outdoors.

What is the best way to use cold frames (of which I have quite a few) to obtain maximum year-round efficiency? Seeds of perennials and biennials can be sown in cold frames in summer, and the seedlings transplanted and wintered over in same. A cold frame is also a convenient place in which to root greenwood cuttings of certain shrubs, inserting in sandy soil in June and July and keeping closed for a few weeks until rooted. A frame provides good conditions for seed flats of certain woody plants (as dogwood) over winter; also to winter stock plants of chrysanthemums and other perennials not reliably hardy. With the approach of spring sow certain annual flowers and vegetables for early planting outdoors. In April and May a frame is useful to harden off greenhouse-grown plants for a short time before planting out. Any vacant space in summer could be utilized for the growing of tomatoes, melons, and cucumbers.

Is it possible to get early blooms from bulbs and other spring plants in a cold frame? Pansies and forget-me-nots from August-sown seeds flower well in a cold frame in early spring. Good divisions of polyanthus primrose planted at the same time would also reward with nice flowers. The chaste flowers of Christmasrose open to perfection under cold-frame protection. Potted bulbs of narcissus, tulip, scilla, and snowdrop can be plunged in the frame in October to be brought out early in the year for flowering indoors if need be, or planted directly in the frame to flower in place. Leave the sash off until freezing weather threatens, and ventilate on all warm days during winter. In very severe weather it would help to have the frames banked outside with leaves, and the sash covered with mats or similar material.

Can violets be grown in cold frames for flowering in spring? Yes. Plant strong, field-grown plants in early September. Cover with sash for a few days to help them recover, keep moist but admit some air, and shade lightly from bright sun. When established, give all light possible and plenty of air until hard freezing weather. Put mats or some other covering over the sash on very cold nights, and ventilate on every warm day in winter.

Will you tell me how to operate cold frame with plants in pots and flats? Provide a bed of sifted ashes 4 to 6 ins. deep on which to stand plants during early spring. If to be kept in frame throughout the year, pots should be buried to their rims to conserve moisture in summer and help to prevent breakage from frost in winter. (See answers to preceding questions for general management.)

Why do I have such a hard time growing plants from seeds in cold frames, even though care and thought have been used? Plants grown in frames require more careful attention than when grown in the open. Correct soil, temperature, watering, *and especially* ventilation, all are of utmost importance. Attention to these should produce satisfactory results.

I have a cold frame. When the soil freezes do I fill it in with salt hay and close it for the winter; or do I have to give it ventilation on warm days? A light covering of salt hay put on plants when the soil freezes will give added protection. Ventilate on warm days. If the frame is vacant, a covering of hay or leaves will keep out some frost but is hardly necessary.

How would you manage a small cold frame containing little perennial seedlings and some very choice perennial slips for rooting during winter? See that the soil is moist before hard freezing. After this, lightly cover the plants with clean litter, such as salt hay or pine needles. Provide ventilation on warm days.

When plants are stored in a cold frame over winter, what protection should be provided? Cover with a mulch and then use a mat over the glass. Put a mulch around the outside of the frame.

Is commercial fertilizer good to put in a cold frame to give added heat? Commercial fertilizers are of no value in this respect. (See Hotbeds.)

HOTBEDS

What is the difference between a hotbed and a cold frame? A cold frame has no other heat than that provided by the sun. A hotbed is heated by fermenting material, electricity, steam, or hot water.

How can I make a medium-size, manure-heated hotbed to start early tomato plants? Assuming you have the frame complete, a pit should be made 2½ ft. below ground level and the same size as the frame. Then mix 2 parts fresh stable (horse) manure with 1 part unrotted leaves. Turn 2 or 3 times at about 4-day intervals, and moisten if dry. When well heated, place mixture in the pit in 6-in. layers, each one well packed, until there is a solid 2-ft. bed, or a little more. Finish off to ground level with 4 to 6 ins. of good, fine soil in which to grow the plants.

Is it necessary to line a hotbed pit? If soil holds together, and if only a temporary hotbed is required, no. Permanent hotbed pits are usually lined with concrete or boards.

I am planning to raise flower and vegetable plants for sale to gardeners. Which is the best way of heating my beds each 6 × 17 ft.? If this is a more or less permanent proposition, the installation of electric heating cable or of electric bulbs, arranged in series, would be the best if possible. A mixture of 2 parts fresh stable manure and 1 part leaves of the previous fall would be the best fermenting material. You can, however, raise good flower and vegetable plants for amateurs' gardens in just sun-heated frames.

I expect to start a hotbed March 1. Manure is available February 15 and March 15. How can I store the February manure so I can make use of it later? The manure you gather in February can be left piled, either indoors or out, for hotbed use in March.

When is the best time to start a hotbed in northern Vermont? Late March is soon enough. Put the sash on the frames before snowfall, so they do not have to be emptied of snow.

Does the depth of manure in a hotbed depend on climate? Yes, to some extent. Around New York City 2 ft. is the usual depth. Farther North 2 ft., 6 ins., is desirable; in the South 18 ins. or less is enough.

How much soil should be put over the manure in an outdoor hotbed? If seeds are to be sown directly in the bed, about 6 ins. of good, friable soil is sufficient. If to be sown in flats, then 1 in. or so of soil over the manure will do.

How does one know when a manure-heated hotbed is ready for sowing seeds? Stick a hotbed thermometer in the manure and close the frame. When the temperature *recedes* to 90° F. (it will go higher at first), it is safe to sow seeds.

Does the manure in a manure-heated hotbed have to be changed every year? Yes, it will not heat up a second time. Clear it out after the plants are removed and use it in the compost heap.

What can be used for hotbeds in place of horse manure besides electricity? Under certain conditions, such as where the frames are close to a greenhouse, it is possible to heat them with steam or hot water piped from the greenhouse system. Or a pipe may be run from the house heater if the frame adjoins the house.

Is there anything besides leaves suitable to mix with manure in the making of a hotbed? If obtainable, tanbark and spent hops give good results in prolonging the period of heat in a hotbed. Chopped cornstalks can also be used.

How, or in what way, are cornstalks used for a hot bed to take the place of manure for heating in the hotbed? Cut stalks into 1- or 2-in. lengths, wet thoroughly, pack in 2-in. layers to a total depth of 6 ins. in excess of depth when manure is used. Sprinkle each layer of 18 sq. ft. (area of standard hotbed sash) with ½ lb. cottonseed meal, ½ lb. ground limestone, and 3 oz. superphosphate. This increases heat and improves fertilizing value of cornstalks when rotted.

Can one raise hotbed plants without manure? In recent years electric heating cable or ordinary light bulbs, arranged in series, with thermostatic control, have often been used in place of manure for heating hotbeds. The installation is good for some years, and the disagreeable features of the old-time hotbed procedure have been eliminated. (See preceding queries and answers.)

When and how may a hotbed be prepared to supply a small garden in town? If obtainable, special electric heating cable is more convenient for city gardeners than fresh stable manure for providing heat in a hotbed. Where spring is slow in arrival, last half of March would be soon enough to start. If neither method is practical for you, sun heat alone would do for an early start in the frame, as compared to outdoor sowing.

Can glass substitutes be used successfully on hotbeds? Good plants have been grown beneath glass substitutes, but the sash must be in first-class condition, and may not be good for more than 1 or 2 seasons.

Is it necessary to ventilate hotbeds? Yes; every day except in severe weather. Tilt the sash on the side or end opposite to the direction from which the wind is blowing.

Are any special precautions necessary when watering seedlings in hotbed? Yes; because of humid air seedlings are specially vulnerable to attack by "damping-off" fungi. Water in morning, so that leaves dry more readily. Water only when soil begins to get dry.

Do hotbeds need any special protection during cold snaps? If started when freezing weather is still to be expected, the frames are usually banked with manure or coal ashes. When specially cold nights are anticipated, the sashes are covered with mats or boards as an additional protection.

How is it best to make a hotbed for seeds to be left outdoors all the year around if the seedlings should have to stay 2 or more years? In this case a cold frame will serve the purpose better than a hotbed. Depending on kinds, the seeds could be sown in the fall or spring, and the seedlings transplanted in the bed of the frame until ready to plant outside.

GREENHOUSE

HARDENING OFF

What is meant by "hardening off"? The process whereby plants are gradually inured to change in environment.

Is it necessary to "harden off" plants before they are moved from greenhouse or hotbed to open ground? Yes. A sudden change to more intense sunlight, lower humidity, and exposure to wind, is injurious to them.

How does one harden off plants which have to be moved from a greenhouse into the open? By transferring them first to a cold frame, where they are gradually exposed to outdoor conditions by progressively increasing the amount of ventilation until, at the expiration of 10 days or so, the sash is entirely removed.

Potted plants which I place on my sunny terrace during summer have their leaves scorched when they're transferred from the greenhouse. Is there any way of overcoming this? Ventilate greenhouse as freely as possible for a week before they are moved. Keep them in a partially shaded location outdoors for a week or so before putting them on the terrace.

EQUIPMENT

What essential equipment is needed in the small greenhouse? Soil, leafmold, or peatmoss; sand; fertilizer; pots; flats; watering can; trowel; sprays and sprayer; labels; water.

WHAT TO GROW

I am building a small greenhouse. Will you give me information on early planting of vegetables and flowers to transplant for summer production? Start about mid-February. Follow instructions given under annuals, vegetables, and propagation for details of planting. If house is to be heated, even though no higher than 45° F., chrysanthemums, azaleas, etc., and forced spring bulbs, could be used for fall and winter display.

I am building a 10 × 12 ft. home greenhouse. Can you give a few pointers as to what I can grow? Assuming the minimum temperature is 55° F., the following could be raised from seeds: begonia, calceolaria, cineraria, cyclamen, primula. Obtain plants or bulbs from dealers of the following: acacia, azalea, camellia, Easter Lily, erica, gardenia, genista, gloxinia. Books on this subject include *The New Greenhouse Gardening* and *How to Grow Rare Greenhouse Plants,* both by Ernest Chabot, published by Barrows, and *Beneath the Greenhouse Roof,* by C. H. Potter, published by Criterion Books.

Which plants, besides geraniums, can be grown in a small home greenhouse maintained at 55° to 65° F., and also planted in borders during summer? Fuchsia, begonia, lantana, abutilon, acalypha, and heliotrope.

Which flowers are suitable for an amateur to grow in a small greenhouse for winter bloom? Among the easiest are calendula, stock, snapdragon, forget-me-not, daffodil, tulip, freesia, chrysanthemum, and buddleia. All of these grow in a night temperature of 45° to 50° F.

I have a glass-covered frame over the well which is outside of our home (east side); normally it is used to give light and air in basement. Will you advise which plants or vines might do well? Also what type of soil would produce best results? English Ivy; chrysanthemums could be dug up and potted when budded; also such annuals as carnation, petunia, and marigold not completely flowered out could be dug from garden to finish out the season. Begonia of the bedding type lifted and cut back would flower well in spring. Bulbs: daffodil, tulip, freesia, and amaryllis should do well. For summer, coleus. A good soil mixture would be 2 parts good loam, 1 part leafmold, ½ part sand; 5-in. potful bone meal to each bushel.

How can I start a small greenhouse, and which flowers are the most popular to sell? As this is a commercial venture you had better consult a book, such as *Commercial Floriculture,* by Fritz Bahr. Public taste varies in different locations. Your local florists are best fitted to inform you concerning most popular flowers.

Which plants, other than the little English Daisy and blue forget-me-not, would be suitable to raise in a small greenhouse for small corsages? What other flowers would you suggest? Ageratum, alyssum, babysbreath, candytuft, cornflower, lily-of-the-valley, linaria, lobelia, French Marigold, annual phlox, primrose, Sweetheart Roses, and verbena.

Which plants will grow most successfully in my small lean-to greenhouse (southwest exposure)? (There is no heat except what comes from cellar; it is cold nights, but warm during the day.) Chrysanthemums, Jerusalem-cherry, decorative peppers, hardy bulbs, herbs.

What can I grow in a practically unheated lean-to greenhouse? Strong specimens of various early-flowering hardy perennials could be dug in fall and potted or planted to flower well in advance of their season. Hardy bulbs; St. Brigid Anemone, Kurume Azalea, snapdragon, calendula, stock, larkspur, clarkia, nigella, *Phlox drummondi*, and annual chrysanthemum should all do well. Early vegetables and choice rock-garden plants could also be grown.

Am unable to heat my greenhouse. What practical use can be made of it, if any? If span-roofed and fully exposed, perhaps best to wait until March, and then sow seeds of flowers and vegetables that can be transplanted for early start outdoors. If there are benches of soil, such plants as radish, beet, lettuce, and carrot could be sown and grown inside until big enough to use. During summer, chrysanthemums could be grown to finish before winter really started. Hardy, early-flowering plants dug and planted in fall would give earlier blooms than those left outdoors.

TEMPERATURES

What temperature should be maintained in a small greenhouse? Depends on what is grown. A minimum night temperature of 50° to 55° F. will suit a large variety of plants commonly grown.

At what temperature should a small greenhouse be kept to germinate various seeds, and at same time keep seedlings at right temperature? For usual run of annuals and vegetables, night temperature of 50° to 55° F. with rise of 5 to 10° in daytime is about right. Seed pots or flats may be stood in propagating case, having slightly higher temperature until they germinate; or placed near heating pipes until seeds *start* to sprout.

Will you advise as to minimum night temperature acceptable for small greenhouse for winter growing of sweetpea, stock, snapdragon, calendula, and begonia? Fifty degrees. The sweetpea, stock, and calendula would do better at 45° F., the begonia at 55°F.

Is temperature of 65° to 70° F., maintained by hot-water heat, correct in a flower conservatory? Depends upon what is to be grown. For general-purpose house a night temperature of 50° to 55° F. (with a 5 to 10° rise in daytime) would be right.

We are keeping a coal furnace going in our one-wing greenhouse. How low can the temperature drop at night without harm to plants? Depends on what is being grown. Azalea, calceolaria, camellia, cineraria, cyclamen, erica, genista, hydrangea, primula, violet, and many others can endure 45° without injury.

I have a greenhouse built alongside of my house at the basement windows. I use it for starting vegetable and flower seeds, and heat it with warm air from the basement through the windows. What temperature should I have in it? A night temperature of at least 45°, and better close to 55°, would be suitable. The day temperature would vary according to sun heat, but ventilation should be increased if it rises above 65°.

Is bottom heat more important than the temperature around the plants? It is under certain conditions of plant propagation, and for the growing of some plants under glass. For general culture it will not take the place of air temperature.

GENERAL CARE

What is proper soil mixture for flower seed sown in small greenhouse built off basement window? Want to avoid damping off. One part each loam and leafmold and 2 parts sand. A formaldehyde dust (used according to directions on container) may be mixed with the soil before sowing; or pots could be prepared and drenched with boiling water a day or two previous to sowing seed, to check damping off.

How is it possible to tell when soil in pots is dry? By sight, touch, and hearing. If soil looks dry, feels dry, and the pot "rings" when tapped with knuckle or stick, watering is necessary, provided the plant is in active growth.

How often should pot plants be watered? The correct answer is "when needed." The need varies with the kind of plant, its condition, and environment. When plants are in active growth, water when the soil appears to be getting dry; give enough to *wet the soil all through*.

What is the procedure in watering newly potted plants? Be sure the ball of soil is thoroughly moist at potting time. Water well immediately after potting, then wait until the soil is dry on surface. It is very easy to overwater newly potted plants. If they tend to wilt, syringing the foliage once or twice a day will be beneficial.

Is the amount of watering and damping down influenced by weather? Yes. On cloudy, moist days little is needed, especially if temperature is low. When it is sunny and dry, especially in winter when artificial heat is used, much more water must be applied to keep the air moist and plants from wilting.

Is there any way of cutting down on the need for frequently watering pot plants? Bury pots to their rims. Outdoors: in earth, ashes, sand, or peatmoss. Indoors: in cinders, pebbles, peatmoss, or sphagnum. If this is done, great care must be taken to avoid overwatering in damp, cloudy weather, and when plants are not actively growing.

How often should greenhouse plants be sprayed with water; and when? Tropical foliage plants can be sprayed every sunny day. This is an excellent prophylactic measure against insect pests. Generally plants in bloom should not be sprayed because of the danger of marring flowers. Spraying should be done in the morning, after plants have been watered.

How can humidity be controlled in a greenhouse? By careful attention to heating, ventilating, and wetting down of the paths and other interior surfaces, and the balancing of these factors to produce the desired result. A wet-bulb thermometer is useful to indicate the relative humidity.

Is it necessary to sprinkle frequently to keep air humid in greenhouse? Depends on what is grown. Cacti and succulents get along

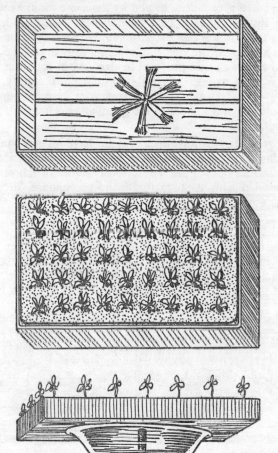

The "wick method" of keeping soil moist for seedlings or cuttings—especially useful where plants must be left to themselves for several days. Wick (made for this purpose) inserted through hole in bottom of flat is spread out in several directions; flat is then planted and placed over pan or pail, filled with water, which is drawn up by wick as soil needs it.

in dry air. Most cool-house plants—primroses, cyclamens, stocks, house plants, etc.—with moderate humidity, provided by sprinkling walks once or twice on dry, sunny days. Tropical plants from moist climates may require the sprinkling of walls, floors, and benches 3 or 4 times a day.

I have a small greenhouse heated by kerosene room heater, supplemented by thermostatically controlled electric heater. A large bucket of water is kept on top of heater to supply plenty of humidity. Temperature is kept at 55° to 60° F. Geranium growth is good, but leaves brown and fall off. Some progress in size, but in time the same thing happens. What is wrong? Probably insufficient humidity. Wet down floors once or twice a day. Fumes from your kerosene stove may be escaping into the atmosphere of the greenhouse. Have you a flue from stove to outdoors?

What direct effect, if any, does coal gas have on greenhouse plants? Am thinking of a small greenhouse heated by a small stove. Even minute quantities of coal gas will seriously injure or kill plants. If you have in mind placing a stove *inside* the greenhouse, drop this idea at once.

REPOTTING

When is the best time for repotting? For plants that are rapidly increasing in size, whenever the roots get crowded in the pots. For plants which have "settled down" and slowly increase in size, at the end of the resting season—usually midwinter or late winter.

A well-lighted bench corner assists materially in carrying on the various greenhouse operations.

When do plants need repotting? When pot is crowded with roots and available plant nutrients are exhausted. Also when, because of poor drainage, overwatering, or unsuitable soil, the roots are unhealthy.

How does one repot a plant? Prepare new pot by cleaning it and putting broken pots, small clinkers, or something similar in the bottom for drainage—from ½ in. to 2 ins., depending on size of pot, and the plant's need for quick drainage. Cover with ½ in. moss or fibrous loam. Remove plant from old pot by turning it upside down and tapping rim of pot on bench or table. Place in new pot at correct depth; fill around with new soil; tamp soil firmly with a potting stick—a small piece of lath will do. Surface soil should be a sufficient distance below rim for convenience in watering.

Would good soil brought from country and stored in boxes make good potting soil? Should box be kept inside or out of doors? Yes; but such soil may need modifying by addition of leafmold, sand, fertilizer, etc., according to needs of plants. Store inside only for convenience in use. Outside storage will do no harm.

REPOTTING A PLANT

Removing plant from pot. Rim of pot (1) is rapped sharply on edge of bench or table to remove rootball; (2) root-ball is loosened up to remove some of old earth; (3) crock (drainage material) and more earth removed from bottom of root-ball. Plant is now ready for repotting.

Plant is placed in larger pot, partly filled with fresh soil, and (4) more soil filled in around it. Cross section of pot (5) with crock over drainage hole. Soil is tamped in firmly (6) around old root-ball.

VENTILATION

What about ventilation in a small greenhouse? Open ventilator daily, even if it is only a mere crack, for a short time. Avoid drafts by opening on the side opposite to that from which wind is blowing.

When air outside is warm and still, ventilate freely except when plants requiring high humidity are grown, when it is necessary to exercise discretion to maintain air moisture.

REST

How are plants "rested"? By lowering the temperature and reducing the supply of water to their roots. Northern plants become more or less dormant in winter; some (certain bulbs) in summer, as a means of tiding over summer drought. Certain tropical plants almost completely suspend activities during the dry season.

How can I tell when my greenhouse plants need rest? By close observation, and by reading up on the culture of specific plants. When a plant has grown actively for 6 to 9 months it may indicate its need for rest by yellowing and dropping leaves; example, the poinsettia.

For how long should plants be rested? Varies with the subject; amaryllis, October to February; poinsettia, January to May; tulips, May to November. These are approximate resting periods of some commonly grown examples.

INSECTS

I am growing vegetables under glass and have trouble with whitefly. What kind of fumigant is best to use? Have tried nicotine fumes. Surest control is hydrocyanic gas (a most deadly poison) generated by use of cyanogas. Use strictly in accordance with manufacturer's directions.

What is the best way to fumigate a small home greenhouse (8 × 12 ft.) with ground benches? Green aphids seem to have taken over. Fumigate with tobacco dust according to manufacturer's instructions. Be certain that fumes have no access to dwelling house.

SPECIFIC GREENHOUSE PLANTS

Are ABUTILONS easy to grow in a small greenhouse? Yes. Take cuttings from outdoor plants in September, or from greenhouse plants in February. Pot in ordinary soil. Pinch tips of shoots occasionally to induce bushiness. They like sunshine and temperature, about 50° F. at night. Can also be raised from seeds.

Can small plants of yellow-flowered "mimosa" (ACACIA) be grown in pots? Several kinds are well adapted for growing in pots in cool greenhouse (night temperature, 40° to 45° F.). Try *A. armata, A. pubescens, A. drummondi,* and *A. longifolia.*

What is the correct treatment for an acacia plant grown in a tub

in a greenhouse? Cut old flowering branches back to length of 6 ins. Retub or top-dress as necessary, using light, porous, peaty soil. Spray tops to encourage new growth. After danger of frost has passed place outdoors, with tub buried nearly to rim. Bring inside before freezing weather in fall. Keep cool. At all times give plenty of sun. Beware of dryness at root. Feed established plants during summer.

What is the proper way to winter an ALLSPICE tree? The allspice tree (*Pimenta officinalis*) is not suited to outdoor growing where freezing temperatures occur. If the plant is in a tub, it could be wintered in a cool greenhouse or other suitable light place under cover, where the temperature range is between 40° and 50° F. Water only enough to keep the soil from getting bone dry.

How shall I plant and care for bulbs of AMARYLLIS (hippeastrum) in greenhouse? Pot bulbs firmly in porous loam enriched with dried cow manure and bone meal, using pots 4 ins. to 6 ins., according to size of bulbs. Leave top half of bulb out of soil. Keep nearly dry until roots form, then gradually increase water supply. Spray foliage with clear water on bright days. Temperature 60° to 65° F. at night, 70° to 75° F. by day. Give full sunlight until flowers appear, then light shade. (See also under Tender Bulbs.)

I would like to grow ANEMONES from seed for blooming in my greenhouse. How is it done? Sow in April or May. Transplant individually to 2½-in. pots. Grow in summer in cool, shaded cold frame or greenhouse (pots buried to rims in sand or ashes). Repot into 4-in. pots, or plant 6 ins. apart in benches, in September. Grow in cool temperature.

Will ANTHURIUMS thrive in a greenhouse where Cattleya Orchids grow well? Indeed they will. Both need humid atmosphere and a 60° F. temperature at night. Pot the anthuriums in a mixture of orchid peat, sphagnum, and charcoal. Keep moist at all times.

What greenhouse conditions best suit ANTIRRHINUMS (snapdragons)? Night temperature 45° to 50° F.; full sunshine; free air circulation; light but rich soil; 9 ins. to 1 ft. between plants in benches; or 4-in. to 6-in. pots; judicious feeding when in vigorous growth. Avoid wetting leaves. Pinch plants in early stages to encourage branching. Propagate by seeds or cuttings.

When should snapdragon seed be sown for fall flowering? For early-spring flowering (in greenhouse)? From middle to end of May for fall. Late August or early September for spring.

I saw the interesting and beautiful flowering vine, ARISTOLOCHIA ELEGANS growing at the Brooklyn Botanic Garden. I would like to grow it in my own greenhouse. Can you tell me how? Very easily. Sow seeds in light soil in spring and grow seedlings in sunny greenhouse where night temperature is 55° F. Prune plants back each spring, and top-dress or repot as necessary. Unlike some aristolochias this one is not evil-smelling.

Can you give me instructions for forcing spireas (ASTILBE) for Easter blooming in a greenhouse? Plant strong clumps in fall in pots just large enough to hold them; plunge in cold frame; bring indoors January or later; give plenty of water and grow in light position. They need from 10 to 14 weeks, in temperature 55° to 60° F., to bring them into bloom.

What treatment should be accorded greenhouse AZALEAS that are kept from year to year? After flowering, trim plants back lightly, repot if necessary (using an acid, peaty soil), and grow in temperature of about 60° F.; spray frequently to encourage new growth. Plunge outdoors, in sunny or partially shaded place, from June to September, then bring into cool house in light position. Never let plants suffer from lack of moisture in the soil.

I am greatly interested in BEGONIAS and, having acquired a small lean-to greenhouse, would like to grow a collection. What temperature, etc., should I maintain? Night, 55° F., rising 5 or 10° in daytime. Shade lightly during March, April, and September; more heavily from May to August. Ventilate to keep atmosphere buoyant rather than stagnant; damp down sufficiently to keep air fairly humid. Be sure to keep house clean at all times. (See also Begonia—Section VII.)

How can I grow BOUVARDIA? Propagate by stem or root cuttings in spring. Grow in sweet (slightly alkaline) soil that is well supplied with humus yet is porous. Give plenty of water during active growing periods. Plenty of sunlight is needed, and a greenhouse temperature of about 55° F. Keep plants pinched freely during early growth to make them bushy.

What soil does a BOUGAINVILLEA (grown under glass) require? If in a pot, a rich but porous soil is needed. If planted in a ground bed, a less rich soil is preferable. Good drainage is essential, and the soil should be coarse (not sifted) and loamy.

The florists' winter-blooming BUDDLEIA—how can I grow it in the greenhouse? There are 2 types—*asiatica* (white) and *farquhari* (light pink). Root cuttings in spring; pinch out tips of young growing plants to encourage bushiness; plunge pots outdoors in summer; use good, rich soil; feed when pot-bound. Bring into greenhouse before hard freeze, and keep cool; give plenty of sun and air. Never let them suffer from dryness.

I would like to have a succession of BULBS for my greenhouse. Which bulbs shall I buy, and how plant them? Paper-white Narcissi can be planted at 2-week intervals, from October 1 to January 1. Roman Hyacinths, at 3-week intervals, from September to December

1. Callalilies are constant bloomers. Plant amaryllis in November. Lachenalia planted in September will bloom for Christmas. Try velheimia also. Plant tulips in November. (See also Tender Bulbs.)

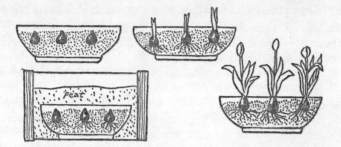

Tulips for indoor bloom: bulbs are planted with tips level with soil surface; stored in a cold frame, pit, or cool cellar for several weeks to form roots; brought indoors to cool temperature to start top growth; and then given higher temperature and abundant water to develop flowers.

Will you give instructions on raising CALCEOLARIA from seeds? Sow in shallow pans, well drained, using sand, leafmold, peat, and loam in equal parts, sifted through ¼-in. sieve. Firm soil, make level, sow seeds, and gently press them in with tamper. Moisten by standing pan in vessel of water for half-hour. Cover with pane of glass; shade with newspaper. When seeds germinate, tilt glass; remove entirely after few days. Keep cool.

What conditions are needed to grow calceolarias in the greenhouse? A well-drained soil that contains a liberal amount of humus, together with some cow manure and bone meal. Give free circulation of air; shade from strong sunshine; provide a cool, moist ash bed beneath the pots, uniform moisture, and a night temperature of 50° F.

How is it possible to force calceolarias into bloom early? I used to see them in full bloom at the Spring Flower Show in New York. By using electric light to provide supplemental illumination for about 5 hours each evening from November on.

I would like to grow some CALENDULAS for winter flowering in my greenhouse. Can you tell me how? Sow seed of good greenhouse strain in early August. Prick off seedlings into small pots, and later set out in benches (14 or 15 ins. apart), or pot into 5-in. pots. Use rich soil. Grow in full sun with night temperature of 45° to 50° F. Good air circulation is necessary.

Is it possible for me to grow CARNATIONS for winter bloom, along with other greenhouse plants? Yes, if the other kinds are chosen so that their needs are similar; however, carnations are usually at their best when grown in a house by themselves. They need full sunlight, free ventilation, and night temperature of 45° to 50° F. Soil must be sweet, fertile, and porous. It is usually advisable for the amateur to buy young plants rather than attempt to propagate his own.

When should carnation cuttings be made? Late November or December or January. Select strong growths from near the base of flowering shoots and remove with a slight side twist. Insert in sand bench in greenhouse where night temperature is 50° F. Shade with cheesecloth or newspaper for a week or two.

What causes carnations to split? Splitting is caused by overfeeding, and especially by a too-high temperature, which induces rapid development. Carnations are cool-temperature plants, so growth must be gradual and the temperature at night kept evenly at about 52° to 55° F.

What are important points for an amateur grower (with a small greenhouse) to bear in mind when growing indoor CHRYSANTHE-MUMS in pots? Secure healthy stock. Keep plants repotted as they grow (without permitting them to become potbound) until they are in their flowering pots. Feed after flower buds have set. Keep greenhouse cool (night temperature of 40° to 45° F.). Full sunshine is necessary.

What kind of soil is best for growing chrysanthemums in pots? A rich mixture containing plenty of mellow, fibrous loam, about a sixth part by bulk rotted cow manure, a good sprinkling of bone meal, a generous dash of wood ashes, and sufficient sharp sand to keep the whole porous. A sandier mixture, without manure or fertilizer, is preferred for the first potting of cuttings.

Can greenhouse chrysanthemums be planted in the vegetable garden in the summer and then be dug up in fall and transplanted to soil beds in greenhouse? Yes. Plant in fertile soil. Dig up carefully before severe frost (keeping as much soil on roots as possible), replant, and then water thoroughly. Shade from bright sunshine for a few days and lightly sprinkle foliage with water to prevent wilting.

Can large chrysanthemums be grown in a greenhouse, and at what temperature? List some names of large varieties. Cool (40° to 50° F.) greenhouse culture is best for large-flowered chrysanthemums. (See previous questions for culture.) Barbara Phillips, yellow; Henry Woolman, crimson; Louisa Pockett, white; Nagirroc, bronze; Vermont, pink, are good exhibition varieties.

How does one propagate greenhouse chrysanthemums? After blooming, old plants are cut back close to ground and stored in a light place (just above freezing). In January or February they are placed in temperature of about 45°, and young shoots, that soon appear, are made into cuttings when about 2 ins. long. These are inserted in sand propagating bench.

What culture is required for CINERARIAS? Sow seed June to September. Transplant to flats, later to small pots. Keep potted on as plants grow, using rich, porous soil containing fair amount of humus. Grow in full sunshine during winter weather, and stand pots on cool, moist bed of ashes. Keep moist; spray with water on sunny days. Grow cool (night temperature of 40° to 45° F.).

Do cinerarias need much feeding? They are heavy feeders; therefore provide rich soil, but do not use liquid fertilizers until they are well rooted in their flowering pots; then feed once or twice a week until flowers are open. Cease feeding when flowers open.

How is the fragrant, yellow-flowered genista handled in the greenhouse? Correctly named **CYTISUS** racemosus. After blooming, shear plants and repot, using sandy, peaty, fertile soil. Spray with clear water to encourage new growth, and grow in cool, sunny greenhouse. Plunge pots outdoors in sunny place through summer, and bring in again in fall. Night temperature of 40° to 45° F. Propagate by cuttings in spring.

Can bleedinghearts (DICENTRA spectabilis) be forced into bloom early in the small greenhouse? Yes. Plant strong roots in fall or winter in pots just large enough to hold them. Bury pots to rim in cold frame; about February bring into light greenhouse (temperature of 45° to 50° F.). Keep soil moist.

What soil and culture are required for EUCHARIS grandiflora (Amazon- or Eucharis-lily)? It needs tropical greenhouse conditions. Soil rich, medium, well drained. Must be partially dried off for a month or 6 weeks twice a year, to induce blooming. Feed generously with organic fertilizer when growing.

How can I grow the tender Maidenhair FERN in my little greenhouse? Adiantums are easily grown in a temperature of 60° to 65° F., if the atmosphere is kept humid. Pot in a sand-peat soil. Avoid wetting foliage, but keep soil evenly moist (except that plants may be rested by partially drying off for a couple of months in winter). Propagate by division in early spring.

Can I grow ferns in a conservatory? What is the best temperature? Ferns do well in a conservatory. Keep the temperature above 55° F., and the house shaded in summer. Adiantum, pteris, davallia, nephrolepis (in variety) are good kinds to start with.

When should I sow FORGET-ME-NOTS (myosotis) for blooming in greenhouse? Also hints on culture? Sow in May or June. Select variety recommended by seedsman for greenhouse culture. Transplant seedlings 3 ins. apart in flats. Later pot, or plant in benches. Grow in cool, airy conditions. Shade from strong sunshine. Keep soil always moist.

What causes GERANIUMS (pelargoniums) suddenly to turn yellow and then die? Gas in the air; poor drainage; overwatering; underwatering; or disease might cause this.

What is the best way to propagate geraniums that damp off or rot before rooting? Expose cuttings to sun for one day before setting in rooting medium. Water after planting, then keep on the dry side until roots are formed.

I have GERBERIAS that were raised from seed in my greenhouse; the potted plants are now nearly a year old, but have never bloomed. Why? Gerberias need rich, well-drained soil. Crowns should be just above soil level. Feed with liquid manure as blooming period approaches. Should be grown in cool house (night temperature of 50° F.).

Can you give me advice on how to raise and grow HYDRANGEA for blooming in greenhouse? Propagate by cuttings from February to May. Grow in light, well-drained loam in temperature of 50° and full sun. Pinch once or twice before June. Keep in cold frame, water freely, and spray foliage with water during summer. From September on keep drier, and just above freezing. Start into growth in temperature of 45° in January or February.

How is the LEOPARD-PLANT (Farfugium) grown? The correct name is *Ligularia kaempferi.* Ordinary greenhouse culture, or conditions that suit ferns or saintpaulia (temperature around 60° F.), shade, and high humidity; but avoid wetting the leaves much.

What is Russian Statice? Can I grow it in my little greenhouse? This is *LIMONIUM suworowi.* Sow seeds in September in sandy soil. Prick off seedlings into well-drained flats, and later pot singly into 4-in. pots. Grow in full sun, in temperature of 50° to 55° F. Be careful with watering and watch out for aphids.

I have a breadfruit plant, so called. Will you tell me more about this plant, and how to care for it? Probably it is *MEXICAN BREADFRUIT* (not related to real breadfruit) or ceriman— MONSTERA *deliciosa;* often sold as philodendron. Its fruits are edible. Prefers a warm, moist atmosphere, but will grow almost anywhere provided the temperature does not fall below 50°. When planted in good soil, it is a vigorous grower, climbing high on tree trunks by means of its stem roots. It succeeds well as a pot plant.

What treatment do Calanthe ORCHIDS require? Pot in spring in a mixture of fibrous loam, sand, and old cow manure, being sure drainage is perfect. Water with extreme care at first; more generously as roots take possession of soil. Shade spring and summer. Grow in warm temperature. Reduce water supply when foliage begins to die away in fall. After blooming, keep dormant pseudobulbs in warm, dry place until spring.

What kind of soil should I use for potting a Cattleya Orchid?
Soil (in the ordinary sense) is not used for epiphytic orchids such as cattleyas. Instead they are potted in osmunda fiber (the wiry-roots of osmunda fern). With a potting stick pack the fiber firmly between and around the roots. Recently, because of the difficulty of obtaining osmunda fiber, different materials have been tried as substitutes. Among the most promising are bark fragments or wood chips; the bark of fir and birch chips have proved to be satisfactory. One advantage of using bark or chips is that they make it much easier for the beginner to pot orchids.

Would an amateur be likely to have any chance of success in raising Dendrobium nobile from seed?   No. The raising of orchids from seed calls for specialized skill and closely controlled environment.

I have some PALM tree seeds. Can you tell me how to plant these?
Plant in sandy, well-drained soil in 4-in. flowerpots (in flats, if quantity is large). Space seeds about 1 in. apart, and cover about ½ in. deep. Keep moist in temperature of about 70° F.

How are PANSIES grown for flowering during the winter in the greenhouse?   Seeds are sown in July, and resulting plants are grown in cold frame until October, when they are planted in benches, or in pans of sweet, light, fertile soil. They are grown in a light, cool greenhouse, and flowers are picked promptly to prevent seed forming.

Which PRIMULA would you recommend for growing in a small home greenhouse (temperature of 45° to 50° minimum)?   *Primula malacoides* (white, lavender, pink, red); *P. sinensis* (same color range); *P. stellata* (same color range); *P. kewensis, P. verticillata,* and *P. floribunda* (all yellow). It may be well to avoid *P. obconica* because it causes dermatitis in some people.

Will you give some pointers on growing greenhouse primulas?
Soil, medium loam with plenty of humus; grow in cool temperature; keep pots standing on layer of moist ashes; shade in summer-time; keep soil moist at all times, but not waterlogged; feed dilute manure water when final pots are filled with roots.

Can you tell me how to grow greenhouse RANUNCULUS from seeds?   Treat exactly as greenhouse anemones (which see) from seed. Both like a porous soil that is well supplied with humus.

Can I force Crimson Rambler and other climbing ROSES into bloom early in my greenhouse?   Obtain strong plants in November and set in pots just big enough to contain roots easily. Use medium-heavy, fertile soil. Bury pots to rim in deep cold frame. Bring inside, in January, to temperature at first 45°, later 55°. Spray with clear water to encourage growth. Water freely. No pruning necessary.

How should roses be pruned when they are potted, in fall, for spring forcing in the greenhouse?   Tall-growing ramblers and climbers not at all, other than removal of any dead or broken growths. Dwarf polyanthas, hybrid teas, hybrid perpetuals, etc., cut back to within 9 or 10 ins. of base. Leave strong shoots longer than weak shoots.

Which varieties of roses are best for blooming in tiny greenhouse during early spring? Polyanthas, such as Ellen Poulsen, Gloria Mundi, Edith Cavell, and Orange Triumph; and miniature roses, such as Oakington Ruby, Pixie, Rouletti, and Tom Thumb.

Would it be practical for me to grow roses for cut flowers in a very small greenhouse in which I want to grow a good many other kinds of plants? Hardly. To grow cut-flower roses with even moderate success demands fair space and rather exacting conditions. Why not try a few plants in pots?

What makes the leaves turn yellow and fall off my miniature rose plant? Poor drainage in the pot; not enough light; too much water; too rich a soil; too high a temperature; red spider infestation, and black-spot disease—one or more of these may be responsible.

I would like to grow SALPIGLOSSIS in pots for spring blooming in the greenhouse. Is this possible? Quite practicable. Sow seeds in sandy soil in August; transplant seedlings; and later pot them individually. Beware of burying plants too low in soil. Water with care. Afford full sunlight and grow in temperature of 50° F. Fumigate with tobacco if aphids appear.

Would it be possible to grow a Bird-of-Paradise-flower (STRELITZIA) in a greenhouse built against my house? It should be. Healthy specimens need a large pot or tub, good drainage, medium-heavy soil, plenty of water, and feeding when pot-bound. They like abundant light and a night temperature of 50° to 55° F.

Can you tell me how to grow in winter the feathery STEVIA that is used for mixing with cut flowers? Propagate by cuttings taken from January to March. Keep plants potted on as one does chrysanthemums. Plunge pots outdoors from May to September, then bring into cool greenhouse (temperature of 45° to 50° F.). Water well at all times. Feed when pot-bound.

Are STOCKS good flowering plants for the home greenhouse? Yes. They can be grown either in pots or in benches. Sow seeds August to January, using rich, sweet soil. Finish in 4- to 6-in. pots. If planted in benches, set branching types 8 × 6 ins. apart; non-branching types closer. Grow in full sun and night temperature of 40° to 45° F.

Can you give instructions for growing SWEETPEAS in a greenhouse that has scarcely any artificial heat? Sow in October in sweet, moderately fertile soil, preferably in a ground bed. Rows should be 3 ft. apart. Thin plants to 6 ins. apart. Ventilate freely, and avoid encouraging too much growth until February. Provide strings or other means of support. Feed when flower buds form. They need full sunshine. They can also be grown in 10-in. pots (though not so well), using brushwood for support.

Trees and Shrubs

DECIDUOUS TREES AND THEIR CULTURE

WHAT TO GROW

How can I start an arboretum?   Professor Sargent, first director of the world-famous Arnold Arboretum, used to say that in order to start an arboretum one should have a thousand acres of land and a million dollars' endowment. The best advice would be to consult some recognized arboretum authority to ascertain what can best be grown in the proposed locality, how much it will cost to plant and care for it, what future purpose will be best fulfilled by the arboretum, and how this can be accomplished most economically.

Which trees are undesirable on the home grounds because of their spreading, greedy roots?   Maple, elm, and poplar.

Which food plants (shrubs or trees) can be used on a lawn of less than 1 acre, without detracting from the ornamental aspects?   For beautiful blossom, any of the fruit trees. For added beauty of fruit, any of the showy-fruited apples and crabapples. If acid soil, blueberries for autumn color. For early-spring blossom and good jelly fruit, the flowering quinces. Hickories and black walnuts are very acceptable as ornamental trees.

Which tree would be a good companion for a magnolia in front of the house?   If it is a Star Magnolia, the Arnold Crabapple might do well. If it is a Saucer Magnolia, a fringetree could be used.

Which trees can you plant close to the house to be sure their roots will not get into the drains?   The kinds will depend upon soil and the amount of space you can sacrifice for shade. Avoid the following: elms, maples, willows, and poplars.

We live in the country. Our driveway is on the north side of the house and unprotected. Driveway is east and west. On which side of the drive should trees and shrubs be planted to avoid snowdrifts?   On the side away from the house, providing the winds causing those drifts come from a northerly direction.

How near the house is it safe to permit an oak or elm to grow?   An elm could grow nearer than an oak (say 10 ft.), for the elm has high, wide-spreading branches and would eventually top the house. The oak, on the other hand, would have wide-spreading branches nearer the ground and might have to be twice the distance from the house so that its branches would not interfere with the building.

Will maidenhair (ginkgo), and laburnum grow in the northeast? Yes.

DISTINCTIVE FOLIAGE

What tree can I get whose leaves have a silvery effect? Silky White Willow, 30 to 80 ft.; White Poplar, 30 to 70 ft.

We are going to buy a few more trees with handsome foliage. We already have a Hedge Maple and an American Beech. What else? English Oak, Black Oak, corktree, Fernleaf Beech, Honey Locust, especially the Moraine and/or the Sunburst varieties.

We do not like dense-leaved, heavy-looking trees, such as Norway maples. Prefer airy, delicate foliage. What do you suggest? Birch, poplar, Honey Locust, willow.

Are there any trees with distinctively tinted spring foliage? Not many. Here are a few: Katsura Tree (*Cercidiphyllum japonicum*); flowering cherries (*Prunus serrulata*); sourwood (*Oxydendrum arboreum*); some Japanese Maple varieties; Schwedler Maple, Purple Smoke-tree (*Cotinus coggygria var. purpureus*).

I should like to plant a few small trees with good autumn foliage. Will you name a few? *Cornus florida*, dogwood, and its varieties; *Cercidiphyllum japonicum*, Katsura Tree; *Crataegus phaenopyrum*, Washington Thorn; *Oxydendrum arboreum*, sourwood.

FAST GROWING

We would like to plant a good shade tree that would grow rapidly. Which of the following grows more rapidly: mountain-ash, Chinese Elm, Silver Maple, or Rock Maple? Chinese or Siberian Elm is the fastest, with the Silver Maple a close second.

Can you give me some idea of a fast-growing shade tree for about a 61 × 50 ft. back yard? The Siberian Elm, *Ulmus pumila*. However, it grows so fast that proper steps should be taken to prune it regularly and vigorously each year to keep it at the height you prefer.

Will you name some fast-growing trees for southern New England? Elms, especially the Siberian Elm, Red Maple, Silver Maple, pine, Red Oak, oriental cherries, and American ash.

Which tree of rapid growth is best to plant for shade about a new home? Goldenrain tree, Flowering Dogwood, Washington Thorn, apple if the house is small. Elms, Red Oak, and Sugar Maple.

What kind of shade tree should I plant that has a rapid growth, is well shaped, is comparatively clean during the summer, will not re-

quire spraying, and whose lower limbs, when mature, will not be less than 15 ft. from the ground? Tuliptree (*Liriodendron tulipifera*) and Sweetgum (*Liquidambar styraciflua*) are favorites. Other good ones: sycamore, Scarlet Oak, and Pin Oak.

FLOWERING

Which small ornamental flowering trees would you recommend besides fruit trees and dogwoods? Laburnum, silverbell, redbud, magnolia, goldenrain-tree, crabapple, flowering cherries.

What is a good tree to use on a small place: one which will not have too wide root spread? Crabapple, magnolia, flowering cherry.

What type trees should be planted, on front of lot, for decorative purposes, where large trees are not desired because of their effect on the lawn? Are dogwoods, flowering cherries, etc., suitable? Dogwoods and crabapples are both superior to flowering cherries for this purpose.

What kinds of trees can be planted in a pasture used by hogs (that they will not root out or eat)? Hawthorn.

FRUITING—FOR BIRDS

Can you name a few small trees with decorative fruit? *Cornus florida* (dogwood); *Crataegus phaenopyrum* (Washington Thorn), and *C. mollis* (Downy Hawthorn); *Sorbus aucuparia* (European Mountain-ash).

Which trees provide food for birds? Cherries, mulberry, mountain-ash, hawthorn, small-fruited flowering crabapple, flowering dogwood, hollies, fringetree, buttonwood.

LAWN TREES

Which are the best deciduous trees for specimen lawn planting? Flowering cherry, weeping willow, Norway Maple, dogwood, American Elm, beech, and Moraine Locust. Among the fruits, apple is best, although crabapple is often used.

Will you name some lawn trees good for the windy southern New England coast? Red Maple, Red Oak, poplar (especially White Poplar and Quaking Aspen), sassafras, White Willow, sourgum.

FOR SHADE

Can you suggest a shade tree nice for a back yard? Canoe Birch; yellowwood.

What are the best deciduous trees to plant for shade on landscaped grounds? Elm, maple, apple, red oak, European Birch, buttonball are good.

How does one identify the sex in shade trees? The only certain way is to study the flower, when open. Those with flowers having both stamens and pistils are bisexual. Most trees, especially fruits, are of this type. Then there are trees like the hollies, willows, and mulberries which have only pistillate or fruiting flowers on one tree—these are the female or fruit-bearing trees. Staminate (male) flowers are produced on a separate tree. These latter are the male or nonfruiting trees.

CULTURE

SOIL

How should I prepare the ground for planting trees? Over a well-drained subsoil there should be, throughout the area, a foot of good topsoil. Beyond this, prepare individual planting holes for trees to a depth somewhat in excess of the depth of root balls or root systems. Remove any excavated soil of poor quality and improve the remainder with leafmold and some old manure.

Most trees and shrubs seem to grow poorly in my soil, which is very sandy. What can I do? Select kinds especially suited for light, very sandy soil. For any others work in, around their root spread, a liberal quantity of peatmoss, leafmold or humus and some old manure.

My soil, though well drained, is heavy, clayish. It bakes and cracks in summer. Will it do, generally, for trees and shrubs? You should lighten it by mixing into all planting areas, about a foot deep, a liberal quantity of fine cinders (not fine ashes). At the same time work in some humus matter (leafmold, peatmoss, rotted manure). In addition you might try a synthetic soil conditioner such as Krilium.

Few trees and shrubs succeed on my place, which adjoins a swampy tract. What can I do about this? The only cure for lack of drainage is to provide it. Either raise the level of your ground considerably, or limit your selection to those trees or shrubs which will accept the condition. Among these are aronia, *Azalea vaseyi,* blackalder, buttonbush, gordonia, Pussy Willow, tupelo, Weeping Willow.

My soil is shallow, with hardpan beneath. Any special precautions when planting trees and shrubs? Before investing heavily in planting, break up the hardpan so that it will let water through. For the run of ordinary shrubs there should be a depth of about a foot of good soil; for trees, about 2 ft. Neglect of these things may greatly limit your success.

What will I plant in front of an apartment house, where the soil is "sour," of yellow clay, and the spot shady? Have tried several types of evergreens. An unpromising condition. In amply prepared pockets, try untrimmed privet, bush honeysuckle, or *Euonymus patens.* Or, in an elaborately prepared, acid, humusy bed, rhododendron and Mountain Laurel. If tree roots intrude, the prospects of success are poor.

What do I use to make soil acid? See Acidity—Section I. Three to 6-in. layer of oak leafmold, rotted pine needles, or acid peatmoss is one way of acidifying soil. Aluminum sulfate applied at varying rate (4 oz. to 12 oz. per sq. yd., depending upon the alkalinity of the soil and the degree of acidity required) is another, but generally less satisfactory, method. Flowers of sulfur can also be used making the initial application at the rate of 6 ounces per square yard.

Our soil is rich but moist and acid. What tree do you advise— something with good autumn color? Sweetgum (Liquidambar) would be a tree for you. The fall color is crimson. Red (Swamp) Maple, tupelo, pepperidge, or sour-gum (*Nyssa sylvatica*) are also appropriate.

TRANSPLANTING

Is fall preferable to spring for the planting of trees? Yes; with certain exceptions. Birch, redbud, magnolia, certain hawthorns, and all doubtfully hardy or notoriously finicky kinds are best set out in spring. Plant bare-rooted trees when the leaves drop. They will then continue to produce new root growth well into the winter, even under the frozen surface.

What is your opinion of winter planting? By this you probably mean moving in the depth of winter with a frozen ball of earth about the roots. This method is often used successfully by professional tree movers. For the average gardener, it should be avoided, because specialized equipment is needed to do the job successfully, except with very small specimens.

What is the advantage to be gained from a mass of fibrous roots? Ease of transplanting. Good nurserymen transplant their trees and shrubs regularly, thus inducing fibrous root growth. Or they root-prune their stock by dragging a U-shaped blade beneath the soil of the rows, thus severing wide-spreading and deep-penetrating roots.

Can all deciduous trees be moved with bare roots? Probably yes, if sufficient care is taken; but experience shows that some kinds— birch, dogwood, magnolia, oak, for example—are best transplanted with a ball of earth.

How large a tree can be transplanted? It depends upon the kind of tree. Fibrous-rooted, easily transplanted kinds, with trunk up to 1 ft. in diameter if proper machinery and equipment are available.

I have a shade tree 10 ft. high that I want to transplant. How do I dig it up? Dig a trench around it 18 ins. deep. If many thick roots are encountered, keep farther away from trunk. With a digging fork carefully pick away the soil from roots, moving it into trench. Sway top back and forth to loosen remaining roots, and transplant before they dry out.

When planting trees is it best to mound the dirt around them, or leave a pocket to hold moisture to soak down to the roots? Do not mound the soil. Have it flush with the grade when planting is completed. It will then probably settle a couple of inches below grade, which is proper. A slight, saucerlike depression is sometimes advisable to facilitate watering.

Is it necessary to cut back trees when they are transplanted? If so, how much? Not if they are balled and burlapped. If the roots are scant in relation to the top, reduce the lateral growths in the crown, leaving the leader unpruned. If roots and tops are balanced, pruning may not be necessary.

Is it desirable to wrap the stems of newly planted trees with burlap? How long does one keep the wrappings on the tree? It is excellent practice. The bare stem is the most vulnerable part of the transplanted tree. Keep the wrappings on as long as they can be tolerated. They will prevent sun cracks on the bark. Spraying with a liquid solution (Wiltpruf, Protex) is sometimes employed instead of wrapping.

Is it necessary to support the stem of a newly planted young tree? In wind-swept places, and where school children pass—yes. Before setting the tree, drive a stout stake into the center of the hole and snuggle the tree up to it. Fasten it by means of non-abrasive tape, crossed between stake and tree. Large trees are usually held firm by securing them with wires to 3 or 4 pegs driven in ground around tree several feet from it.

What should be done in the spring for fall-translanted shade trees? Do what necessary pruning may have been deferred in the fall planting. Check over fastenings, and prevent chafing of the bark. Replenish the mulch if necessary.

How can I help my newly transplanted trees (large) to form a new and strong root system? If planted in proper soil, do not overfeed your trees, nor overwater. Keep a mulch at the base. Keep bandages on the stems. Prevent drying out of the soil.

When transplanting trees why do they shoot from the ground instead of the branches? When suckers appear at the base, and no growth develops in the top, there is trouble. It is probably due to root injury and failure to prune top.

Is it correct, in pruning newly fall-set shade trees of 5 to 8 ft. in height, to cut back the whip or leader ⅓ or more as most garden books recommend? Do not cut the leader back. When necessary, reduce competing growths so as to prevent the development of future crotches.

When planting trees in the fall of the year, when is the best time

to prune them? Practice varies. If roots and tops are well balanced, pruning (if any is needed) may be deferred till spring. If roots are scant and tops large, the top should be reduced; leave the leader untrimmed, but reduce side branches.

Should fall-planted trees be pruned? Not necessarily. If a tree has properly balanced roots and top, pruning, if any, may be deferred till spring. If the roots are scant or poor, tops should be reduced, retaining the leader and pruning laterals.

What is meant by "heeling in"? The *temporary* planting of trees or plants, close together, in a trench—with at least the roots covered, and properly watered. It serves to tide plants over an interval between their receipt and permanent planting. If so kept over winter, they should be laid in a little deeper (usually at an angle of 45°) and covered, over all, with a thick layer of straw, leaves, or other mulch.

We heeled in 150 tree seedlings in November, and the weather prevented us from planting them. Will they be ruined, or can they be planted in spring? It depends upon the kinds of trees and on the severity of the winter. It would have been much safer to have buried them, if deciduous, in a trench covered with a mulch of straw.

CARE

When shall tree food be given to shade trees? November and April are perhaps the best times to apply fertilizer, whichever month is most convenient to do the work.

How can I stimulate the growth of newly planted flowering trees? If the planting hole was well prepared no special stimulant should be needed until the trees are well established. However, it is good practice to put a mulch of manure on the soil over the roots in the fall.

How shall I feed an old tree which seems to be weakening? An old tree responds well to loosening the soil beneath and just beyond the spread of the branches. Do this in the fall, and put on a layer of 2 to 3 ins. of rotted manure. In spring incorporate this with the topsoil, in readiness for reseeding if need be. If this method is not possible, then make holes with a crowbar 2 ft. apart and 18 ins. deep. Distribute a complete fertilizer (such as a 10–6–4) in the holes and fill with fine soil. A fair application is 1 lb. for each inch of circumference of the trunk. Take measurement above ground-line bulge.

Three years ago I started a grove of various shade trees on a plot 100 × 250 ft. There are approximately 100 trees. I am keeping the place very clean of any weeds with a small power cultivator, thereby also loosening the soil for better penetration of rain. The trees seem to do well. But am I right in keeping the plot scrupulously clean? The longer you keep the plot cultivated the more vigorously you may expect the trees to grow, but as it is an ornamental plantation and the trees are now well established and growing to your satisfaction, you can sow it down to grass. This would slow down the rate of growth a little but otherwise would not be injurious.

What is the procedure to follow when watering trees? Give thorough soaking so that soil is moist to a depth of 2 ft. If necessary, loosen topsoil with spading fork to facilitate penetration of water. Or use a tool (obtainable from horticultural supply houses) designed to deliver water below surface by means of a hollow, pointed rod.

Why is it that after a spring and summer of heavy rainfall, the trees, including the oaks, this fall shed their leaves earlier than usual? This is one of the things about plants not always of easy explanation. Rainfall is not the only determining factor; temperature may be equally important, and a period of cold weather toward the end of the summer undoubtedly hastens leaf fall.

The grade has to be changed around my house, necessitating a "fill" averaging 2 ft. around a large oak tree. Will this harm the tree? It will probably kill it. (See following question.)

Can anything be done to help trees survive when grade over their roots has to be raised? Build a "well" of rocks around trunk, keeping it at least a foot away. Spread a 6-in. layer of coarse gravel on soil. Lay agricultural tiles in rows, radiating from well to outer spread of roots. Bring these to surface of the fill by means of tiles, set vertically, at end of each line. The purpose of all this is to admit air to soil in which roots are growing. Unless soil is exceptionally well drained it might be wise to install drain tiles, 2 ft. below original grade, to prevent roots from suffering from too much water.

How deep is it safe to raise the grade over roots of trees? Depends on the kind of tree and soil in which it is growing. Six inches probably would not harm surface rooters, such as elms and maples, especially if the soil and fill is porous. Willows and ash can endure even more fill than this. The statement has been made that trees can survive a fill of 8 to 10 ft. if protected by a dry well.

What can we do to stop a tree from bleeding? This depends upon the kind of tree and the cause of the bleeding. If it is merely bleeding due to pruning in spring such trees (for example, maples and birches) as should be pruned in summer, the bleeding soon stops. If it is due to "slime flux," it may be exceedingly difficult to control. (See Section VIII.)

What is used to treat a decayed hole in a tree? Is common cement used to fill hole after it has been cleaned out and treated? For sterilizing the cavity use copper sulfate, 1 lb. dissolved in 3 gallons of water; or bichloride of mercury, 1 oz. to 7½ gals. of water. (Both these substances are poisonous to animals and human beings.) Cement mortar or concrete is one of the materials used for filling.

Will the roots of trees affect a garden?   The roots of some trees are very objectionable. For instance, maples root right up to the surface of the ground, and elms are nearly as bad. Oaks and hickories are deep rooting and cause less interference with other plants. But the most serious objection to trees is to the amount of moisture they take out of the soil; and with it any soluble plant food in the vicinity.

How do you tell when a tree is bark bound?   Newer branches outgrow older portions. Bark seems tight and lifeless. To remedy the condition, scrape off the dead outer bark and scrub the trunk with soapy water. Some authorities suggest making a longitudinal slit through the bark with a sharp knife.

Does smoke from a smelter damage trees?   Yes. Trees growing near a smelter may be seriously injured or killed, particularly if growing in such a position that the smoke is constantly carried to them by the prevailing wind.

For what reason are the lower parts of trees whitewashed? Also when is proper time, spring or fall?   To prevent growth of moss and lichens, and to destroy insect eggs. But with the development of improved insecticides—which are much more efficient—it is little practiced nowadays. Early spring is probably the best time to apply it.

What is used to whitewash yard trees?   Lime and water. But why whitewash them? Its only value is for the destruction of lichens, as its use as an insecticide is now recognized as negligible.

How can I prevent seed formation on trees and shrubs?   By cutting off the dead flowers.

KILLING ROOTS

How can you kill tree roots growing in the sewers?   Dissolve 1 lb. or more copper sulfate crystals (poisonous) in hot water, and pour down a drain. If pipe is badly matted it must be cleared by plumber with roto-rooter machine. The copper-sulfate treatment will tend to prevent the return of tree roots; but the only sure remedy is to eliminate offending trees or install root-proof pipes.

Can you tell me a sure way of killing a large buttonball tree and stopping the roots from growing farther without cutting the tree down? I have girdled the tree, and filled holes bored into it with copper sulfate.   It should be unnecessary to do anything more to the tree; but to prevent shoots coming up from the stump, uncover the larger roots for some distance and peel the bark off them.

Is there any way to prevent elm tree feeder roots from spreading all over the lawn? I have heard that the United States Government recommends trenching the grass plot 12 × 36 ins. deep, and lining both sides and bottom of trench with tar paper. Will that work?   This will work for a time. It would be better to sink a concrete trench into the ground. The deeper it is, the less the opportunity for the roots to grow underneath it and up to the surface on the other side. It may be necessary to dig down beside such a barrier every 4 or 5 years and cut all the roots growing around it.

How can I prevent roots from shrubs in a neighbor's yard from taking over in a seeding bed of mine? They have become a very thick mat, stopping growth and preventing even digging tubers like dahlias. Dig a trench 2 ft. deep along boundary and install a barrier below soil surface. This may be a narrow concrete wall, sheet metal, or the asphalt-impregnated roofing material which comes in rolls.

How can one combat shrub roots where shrubs and flowers are in the same bed? Chop off roots annually in the spring with a spade or a lawn edger; or install barrier as described in previous question.

What season is best for ridding property of wild cherry trees and elderberry bushes; and what is the best method? If possible, grub them out by roots with mattock; or pull up with tractor in early fall and burn when snow is on the ground. If cutting down is the only practicable method for you, do so in summer and chop off sprouts as soon as they appear. This will starve roots.

How can I remove a wild cherry tree and not have some shoots appear later? This tree is on a lawn. Cut down tree, grub out stump and largest roots. Any suckers that appear will be cut off when lawn is mowed. The remaining roots will soon die if no foliage is allowed to grow to nourish them.

What can I use to kill out a large lilac bush; also a tree? Can be done by application of salt or commercial weed killers to soil; but as the tops and stumps will have to be removed in any case, to avoid unsightliness, it is best to cut them down and grub out largest roots.

I cut a hickory tree down to about 20 ft. from the ground. The tree is a foot in diameter. I would like to put a large birdhouse on the part that remains. What can I use to prevent the tree from sprouting from what remains and still have a strong pole for the birdhouse? Cut off a ring of bark at the base of the tree, or better still take all the bark off; the stump will then last longer.

What can you do when a neighbor to the south plants poplar trees and shuts off all sunlight along the entire lot line? Dig 3-ft. deep trench along lot line, cut off all roots encountered, install barrier of asphalt roofing material, and plant shade-loving material. Cut off branches projecting over your boundary.

How best can I kill a sycamore tree which is growing so fast that it shades our perennial garden? It is about 8 or 9 years old. Is there any chemical that can be used? If so, how? The safest way to kill the tree would be by cutting off a ring of bark about 6 ins. wide all the way around the trunk. Any chemical you might use on the roots would also kill any other plants near it. Why not take it out?

What is the best method to get rid of alder and alder roots so that we may greatly enlarge our vegetable garden?   If there is much ground to clear, pulling them out with a tractor would be the cheapest. If there are only a few, then grub them out. Subsequent plowing would cut up the smaller roots.

How can old roots of large trees be removed from the ground when other trees are growing?   If you attempt to take out the old roots there is sure to be some injury to the roots of the growing trees. The extent of the injury will depend upon how greatly the roots are intermixed. If the old roots must come out, dig them out with a grubbing ax. But it will do no harm to the growing trees if the old roots are left to decay.

Is there anything you can put on tree stumps to make them rot quicker?   Drill holes in the stump with an auger, fill with saltpeter, or with sulfuric or nitric acid, then place stoppers in the hole. *Use with care*, as the acid will burn clothes or flesh when it comes in contact with them.

TREE AND SHRUB PROPAGATION

CUTTINGS AND SEEDS

How should I store oak and maple seeds over the winter?   It is better to sow as soon as ripe. This is particularly necessary with some of the white oaks. Maple and some oak seeds may be kept until spring by mixing them with sand in a box (stratification) and covering them with 6 ins. of soil outdoors.

Can trees be started from cuttings?   The percentage of rooting of many kinds is so small as to make this method impractical. (See Propagation, Cuttings, this section.)

What general procedure is followed in making cuttings of shrubs? Softwood cuttings are usually from 3 to 5 ins. long, whereas hardwood cuttings may be from 5 to 8 ins. long. Softwood cuttings must be rooted in a close, humid atmosphere such as that provided by a cold frame. Hardwood cuttings are taken in the late fall, after there have been a few frosts, stored in sand in a cool cellar (or buried in the earth) until early spring, when they are set in the open ground. (See also page 246, mist propagation.)

When making cuttings of shrubs and trees is the time of year, or the condition of the wood, the determining factor?   Probably the condition of the wood is the more important, but as the most desirable condition occurs only at a particular time of year there is a rather narrow range during which the best results may be obtained.

SPECIFIC TREES

AILANTHUS

Of what special value is the ailanthus tree? It is useful in city back yards, where it grows rapidly and endures almost any soil conditions, smoke, and dust.

Why do some ailanthus trees give off a disagreeable odor when in flower? These are the male, or staminate, trees. The female, or pistillate, plants are inoffensive.

What is the ultimate height of the tree-of-heaven (ailanthus)? Sixty feet.

BIRCH

What is the difference between the Paper Birch and the Gray Birch? Paper Birch bark peels off in shreds; Gray Birch does not. Paper Birch has horizontal black marks on its bark; Gray Birch has triangular black patches. Gray Birch has softer wood, subject to fungous disease, and is comparatively short-lived (20 to 30 years), while Paper Birch survives more than twice that long.

Which species of birch has white bark and several stems that come from the ground? Gray Birch (*Betula populifolia*).

I bought some White Birch trees and when they came the bark was gray instead of white. Did they send the wrong trees? Probably not. When very young the bark is gray; turns white later.

Would a Weeping Birch make a good tree to plant in front of a house? No. This is a variety of the European Birch, all of which are susceptible to the pernicious bronze birch borer. The best birch is the Canoe or Paper Birch, native all over New England, and a splendid ornamental, very resistant to the bronze birch borer.

Are birch and sycamore trees suitable for shade on a small property? Birch trees would be better because they are considerably smaller. The sycamore takes a great deal of room. (See "What to Grow," this section.)

At what time of the year should Weeping White Birch trees be planted? (Missouri.) In the spring, if bare-rooted. In the case of large specimens, balled, burlapped, and platformed, autumn or winter should be safe in your climate.

When is proper time for transplanting birches? (New York.) In the spring, before growth starts. In the milder parts of the state, balled and burlapped trees may be moved almost throughout the winter.

Is it practical to plant White Birch in this locality (25 miles east of Pittsburgh, Pennsylvania)? Please give directions for type of soil, and any special care necessary to keep it healthy. Yes, it can be planted. All it needs is a good, well-drained soil, preferably on the sandy side. Susceptible to serious infestations of leaf miners which can be kept in check by spraying. (See Section VIII.)

Last spring we planted a 14-ft. Paper Birch tree (it was balled in burlap). It did not fully leaf out and was attacked by aphids for which we sprayed. The tree did not seem to do well. Is there anything we can do for it this spring to make it healthier? Birch trees do not transplant too readily, but if yours was properly balled it should survive. Try placing a mulch of old manure, peat, or leafmold over the surface of the soil occupied by the roots. Put this on in May, after the soil has had time to absorb some warmth.

What is the life span of birch trees? Can they be planted near fruit trees? Yes, the birch tree—especially the Paper or Canoe Birch (*Betula papyrifera*)—will live to be 50 to 75 years old or more. These trees do not send up suckers, nor do they harm fruit trees in any way.

Vandals have removed a cylinder of bark 6 or 8 ins. wide from my Canoe Birch. Will it harm the tree? Yes, if the inner bark has been removed. The leaves may start into growth because the sap passes up through the wood to the branches, but the roots will ultimately die of starvation because the food which nourishes them passes downward through the bark. If the injury is discovered early enough, it can sometimes be repaired by bridge grafting—which see.

If a young White Birch tree is pruned, do the branches need to be treated where pruned? It is unnecessary to paint wounds when they are less than ½ to 1 in. in diameter. Large wounds should be covered with tree paint or something similar to keep out moisture and spores of disease organisms.

Can White Birch be raised from cuttings? It is next to impossible to root White Birch from cuttings.

BLACKGUM

See Sourgum.

BUCKEYE

See Horsechestnut.

BUTTONBALL

See Sycamore.

CATALPA

What is the origin of the so-called umbrella tree? This is a dwarf form of catalpa (*C. bignonioides nana*), usually grafted or budded, at a height of 6 ft. or so, on straight, single-stemmed plants of *Catalpa bignonioides*.

I have 2 catalpa trees; bark is becoming loose and the part of one

top looks rather dead. Can I save these trees? Your description suggests root trouble, possibly due to poor drainage; or frost injury. Cut out all dead branches, and note whether the wood below the loose bark is also dead, for if it is you may have difficulty saving the trees. If the grade has been changed, this may have produced conditions unfavorable to the trees.

How do you prune an umbrella (catalpa) tree? It is the practice to cut it back annually if a formal effect is desired. Prune during the growing season; or in spring just before growth starts. It may, however, be left unpruned; then the head will present a more natural appearance and increase considerably in size over pruned specimens.

Should all the branches of the so-called umbrella tree be cut away in the fall? It is the usual practice to cut them in the fall, but this leaves an ugly stubby knob. If pruning has to be done, delay it until just before growth starts in the spring. (See preceding question.)

Is there any special way of trimming a catalpa tree if it has branched out too close to the ground? Mine is about 2 ft. from ground and the leaves are so heavy they smother the grass underneath. The lower branches may be cut off to raise the head of the tree. It should be done gradually, taking not more than 1 or 2 in any one year.

CHINESE ELM

How far apart and how close to the house should Chinese Elms be planted? How close to septic tank and drainage bed? Keep them some 25 ft. away from drains. If you have in mind a row of them, plant no closer than 25 ft. apart, and at least 20 ft. from the house. A single tree might be set closer to the house if for some reason that should seem desirable.

What is wrong when a Chinese Elm does not thrive? It is impossible to give a definite answer without more information. The soil may be at fault, but more probably you have not had it long enough for it to become established.

When and how should I prune a Chinese Elm, now about 10 ft. high, and very bushy, with lowest branch about 3 ft. from ground? Growing V-shape on top. If a high-headed tree is required, prune by removing 1 or 2 of the lowermost branches every year. This can be done in early spring before growth starts. It might be desirable to eliminate the "V," because of the danger of splitting, by removing the weaker of the 2 branches forming it.

How should I trim Chinese Elm trees for effective shade? Cutting back the tips of the main shoots will stimulate branching and thus make the head more compact to provide denser shade.

Will you give suggestions for pruning (not trimming) Chinese Elms

to globe shape and square shape?   When trees are trimmed to formal shape by shearing them, usually no further pruning is necessary.

I planted 2 Chinese Elms which have grown along entirely different lines. One grew very rapidly, with spreading, upright branches and sparse foliage. The other grew slower, with dense foliage, and has a tendency to droop, very similar to a weeping maple. Since I prefer the second, could you tell me whether there are 2 varieties, and the name of the second?   There are many variations in the Chinese (also called Siberian) Elms, unnamed as yet. Ask some nurseryman to propagate the one you like from cuttings.

CORKTREE (PHELLODENDRON)

What does a Chinese Corktree (phellodendron) look like?   It is a round-headed, wide-spreading tree. The leaves are compound, with 7 to 13 leaflets, aromatic and handsome.

ELM

What is the best time to put out American Elms?   Either in early spring or in autumn, after the leaves drop.

At what season should elm trees be trimmed?   During the growing season, if it is desired to check growth. Otherwise pruning may be done in the fall or late winter.

EUONYMUS

Can you tell me why euonymus does not have berries in the fall? It has white blossoms in the spring, and was supposed to have berries in the fall.   Euonymus species frequently perform in this fashion. They are probably alternate-bearing, like our fruit trees. It may also have been that weather conditions were such that when the pollen was ripe it was not distributed properly by wind or insects. Fertilize with a complete fertilizer containing ample amounts of available phosphorus and potash. This could be done in the very early spring.

GINKGO

For what special uses is the ginkgo suitable?   The ginkgo, or maidenhair, is quick growing, resistant to smoke and fumes, and therefore useful as a city tree. It is picturesque and erratic in its habit of growth and is remarkably insect and disease resistant. Autumn color is clear yellow.

Will you tell me something of the history of the ginkgo tree? How long has it been grown in this country?   The ginkgo, since ancient times, has grown about temples in China. It is sole survivor of a large group of plants with a long geological ancestry, perhaps unchanged for a million years. Is probably more ancient than any other tree except the Dawn Redwood, *Metasequoia glyptostroboides*. Introduced in this country in the early nineteenth century.

When and how shall I transplant 2 5-foot ginkgo trees, standing 4 ins. apart, with roots intertwined? In the spring, before growth starts. Try to untangle the roots. If you can do no better, save the roots of one intact and cut those of the other if necessary. Set as deeply as they stood. Water them well. Mulch the base, and prevent soil drying.

HONEY LOCUST

Is the Honey Locust good for the small place? I have recently seen one without thorns. The Thornless Honey Locust (*Gleditsia triacanthos inermis*) is a very desirable, lacy-leaved tree. It may, however, grow too tall for a small property. It is more slender than the common Honey Locust, which is undesirable under certain conditions because of the vicious thorns on trunk and branches and its habit of suckering freely.

HORNBEAM

What is the difference between the American and the European Hornbeam? The native tree reaches a height of about 30 ft. while the European one grows to 50 ft. and is more vigorous when young. The European is more treelike; the American tree is hardier North.

HORSECHESTNUT (BUCKEYE)

What is the difference (if any) between horsechestnut and a buckeye? Generally speaking, the horsechestnut has 5 to 7 leaflets in a cluster, while the buckeye has only 5. Also the horsechestnut attains greater height, and the fruits, flowers, and leaves are larger. We commonly think of *Aesculus hippocastanum* as "the" horsechestnut. This is a native of Europe. The members of the Aesculus genus native in America we commonly consider buckeyes.

Is the horsechestnut a good lawn tree? Yes, though rather untidy and, unless pruned to a high head, it is difficult to get grass to grow beneath it.

How long will it take for a 35-ft. horsechestnut tree to re-establish after transplanting? It is about 10 ins. in diameter at base. If successfully moved into a suitably moist, well-drained soil, it will probably take 2 years for the tree to resume approximately normal growth.

LARCH

We have a tree which looks like a pyramidal evergreen but loses its foliage in winter. What is it? A larch; probably the European Larch (*Larix decidua*).

Is the larch a desirable lawn tree? Yes. The European Larch is best for lawns, while the American Larch (commonly known as tamarack and hackmatack) is best in low, moist places.

Would a larch tree make a good growth in rather heavy clay soil? (Ohio.) Yes, it might grow well in a heavy clay soil, but it prefers a cool, rather moist atmosphere such as that of the lower mountainous regions of the northern and northeastern United States.

How and when should a larch be transplanted? (New Jersey.) In fall or spring, with a ball of earth.

LIQUIDAMBAR (SWEETGUM)

In the late fall I purchased from an Ohio nursery a sweetgum or liquidambar tree 10 ft. high. It was then covered with bright red leaves, beautiful fall coloring. Here it has not shown any fall coloring, only a drab yellow; why? (Pennsylvania.) It should have a western exposure and plenty of available nitrogen to make vigorous growth. Often it takes several years after transplanting to really "reach its stride." Soil conditions often affect coloring.

MAPLE

I would like to have a maple tree but haven't much room. What shall I select? The Hedge Maple is comparatively small, its leaves are handsome, but it casts a rather heavy shade.

What kind of hard maple has reddish or purplish leaves all summer? The Schwedler Maple has a reddish tinge to the foliage throughout the season. Crimson King is a new variety said to be an improvement on Schwedler.

What kind of maple is Acer negundo? Commonly called Box Elder or Ash-leaved Maple; this is a large, rapid-growing tree which withstands cold, dryness, and strong winds.

Will you please tell me the common names of the following maples: Acer circinatum, A. macrophyllum, A. floridanum, and A. grandidentatum? 1. Vine maple; 2. Bigleaf Maple; 3. Florida Maple; 4. Bigtooth Maple.

In what kind of soil and location do HARD MAPLES thrive? In any not utterly sandy soil of fair quality; not too acid and well drained.

I have a maple tree facing northwest, which gets a lot of wind. The branches are very short and high up. Can you advise how to get a fuller and shadier tree? It is probable that on the windy side the branches will always be shortest, as it is so exposed. You might try feeding it with a good tree food, or mulching the ground under the branches with manure.

What is best time to transplant maple trees about 12 to 15 ft. high?

In the spring, before growth has started; or in the autumn, after leaves have dropped.

My maple grows very thick and casts too dense a shade. How can I overcome this? Thin out superfluous branches during the summer months. Do this in such a way that the tree has a pleasing branch pattern. In some instances you may find it necessary to cut branches up to 10 ft. long. Always make the cuts close to the parent branch.

How can the top 6 ins. of soil be kept clear of roots of a 30-year-old hard maple? This is a surface-rooting tree, and there is no means of preventing the roots coming to the surface without injuring the tree in the attempt.

How hardy is JAPANESE Red Maple? What sub-zero temperatures can it endure? Probably cannot live through consistently sub-zero winters.

What location and what kind of soil should the Japanese Maple have (the cut-leaved variety)? A well-drained, open situation and a light loam of fair quality, but not necessarily rich. Mulch the soil around newly planted trees.

Would you recommend covering with burlap my Japanese Red Maple tree? (New York.) If you do not mind the appearance, this is a good idea. Japanese maples are subject to winter injury. They may stand uninjured for a number of years, and then some abnormal winter condition will cause one side of the tree to die.

My Japanese Maple has unsightly, withered leaf edges. I am told that the soil isn't right. Is that so? Condition is probably caused by sunscorch during the period of soft spring growth, at which time the leaves are extremely sensitive. All you can do is provide some slight protection from the brightest sun in the spring.

How can one root cuttings of dwarf Japanese Maple? Take cuttings in June and place them in a shaded cold frame or glass-covered box. Unless you have had some experience with the propagation of plants you may not be very successful. Usually propagated by grafting.

What is the NORWAY Maple like? A large, massive, quick-growing tree with big, dark-green foliage. It creates a shade so dense, and its roots are so greedy, that practically nothing can be made to grow under it.

When is the best time to plant Norway Maple? As soon as the ground has dried off and warmed up so as to be thoroughly workable; *before* the trees start into growth.

When is the best time to cut large lower limbs on Norway Maples? Should cuts be painted? If so, with what? As soon as the leaves have fallen; or in summer. When the wound has dried, paint with shellac, tree-wound paint, or white lead and linseed oil.

Why does a RED MAPLE tree turn green in the summer? This is quite normal for some varieties.

When is the proper time of year to prune an ornamental Red Maple tree? In the spring. If it is a matter of promoting bushiness and checking growth, shoots may be shortened during the growing season.

I have a SILVER MAPLE tree on which the leaves dry up before fall. One other Silver Maple tree on the same place is all green. What may be the reason? Probably a difference in soil or moisture conditions. However, it may be due to a leaf blight.

I should like to transplant some SOFT MAPLES. How much should they be pruned? It would depend upon the relative proportions of roots and tops. If roots are scant and coarse, reduce the length of side branches, leaving the leader intact.

What causes the bark on a large soft maple tree to split and hang in tatters? Apparently the tree is otherwise healthy. It is natural for the bark on old soft maples to peel off; this need cause no alarm, provided the bark immediately below that which is peeling is in good condition.

When and how does one plant and care for SUGAR MAPLE trees? Where can they be bought? Sugar Maples may be purchased (by that name) from many nurseries. Plant in the spring, before growth has started; or in autumn after the leaves have dropped. They require no special care or coddling and will thrive in any well-drained soil of fair quality.

MOUNTAIN-ASH

What can be done to make mountain-ash produce more berries? Does it need a special soil? Mountain-ash or rowan-tree (*Sorbus aucuparia*) will grow well in any reasonably good garden soil. However, if your trees have reached the age where they may be expected to fruit heavily, and fail to do so, they may be in need of fertilizer.

Would the mountain-ash be hardy here where dogwood trees are not? (Northern Maine.) Yes.

How close to house can I plant a mountain-ash tree? I want its shade to fall on roof of sun parlor. As close as is consistent with comfort and convenience. As close, if you wish, as 5 or 10 ft. It would develop more perfectly if set at least 15 ft. away.

Is a mountain-ash 6 ft. high easily transplanted in the fall? (New Jersey.) In New Jersey—yes.

I have a 3-year-old mountain-ash. Would moving harm the tree; and could you advise as to the best time? Move it in the spring. Dig the entire root system. Have the hole large enough to accommodate it in a natural position. Water well, and place a mulch about the base.

Why doesn't my mountain-ash, age 5 years, bloom?   If your tree is healthy, it should bloom within the next year or two. When the growth is very vigorous, blooming is sometimes delayed; but it is too early to worry about that on a 5-year-old tree.

What treatment will encourage bloom on young mountain-ash trees? As they get older they should flower more freely, but there is no treatment that will insure equally free flowering every year. Whatever the age of the tree, in some years it will flower more profusely than in others. Make sure the supplies of phosphates and potash in the soil are adequate.

Why does my mountain-ash have a tree full of blossoms but only about 10 clusters of red berries in the fall? The tree is 6 years old. Weather conditions at flowering time may have been too cold or too wet, so that only partial pollination took place.

My mountain-ash is weak. I fed it last spring with Treewiz. Bloomed with heavy crop of seeds, then became thin. When may I prune? Some branches are weak and broken. It is in an open northeast location.   The production of a heavy crop of seeds is a severe drain upon the resources of a tree and may account for the appearance of thinness. Feed it at least after every heavy fruiting. Cut out the broken branches immediately. Any other pruning should be done in spring before growth starts. Have you looked for borers in the trunk? (See Section VIII.)

I planted a small mountain-ash tree this summer. The branches are long and growing more perpendicular than I like. Would pruning help? If so, when should it be done?   Shorten the young shoots about ½ in late winter. During the growing season, if any shoots show excessive vigor, pinch out their tips.

I know that the berries of mountain-ash are bright orange, but what are the blooms like?   Broad clusters of creamy white flowers in May.

OAK

Which are the fastest-growing oaks?   Red Oak and Pin Oak.

How can I identify the different oaks?   Black (*Quercus velutina*), bark very dark brown; inner bark orange; leaves to 10 ins. long, 7 to 9 ins. broad, toothed lobes, shining dark green above. White (*Q. alba*), very light bark; leaves to 9 ins. long; 5 to 9 rounded lobes. Red (*Q. rubra*), leaves to 9 ins. long; 7 to 11 pointed lobes, indented halfway to middle; pale beneath. Scarlet (*Q. coccinea*), leaves to 6 ins. long; 7 to 9 very deep, pointed lobes; bright green. Pin (*Q. palustris*), pyramidal form; lower branches drooping; leaves to 5 ins. long; 5 to 7 oblong, pointed lobes; bright green.

When is the best time to transplant oak trees?   In the spring, before growth starts.

Why must a Pin Oak be transplanted in the spring only?   Practice indicates that bare-rooted Pin Oaks are better planted in the spring only. Balled, burlapped, and platformed trees are often moved successfully in the fall or winter.

When and how should a small oak, grown from seed, be transplanted?   In the spring, before growth commences. Dig out the whole root system. Have the hole wide enough to accommodate it; water the soil thoroughly; place a mulch at the base and see that the roots do not lack moisture at any time.

When is the proper time to transplant 5-year-old oaks; and how?   In the spring, before growth starts. (See preceding question.)

In transplanting Red Oak trees is it wise to cut the tap root?   When transplanting oak trees not previously transplanted, it is inevitable. Young trees may survive it, but old trees will resent it and are, therefore poor planting risks.

How should I feed a Pin Oak?   Put a 3-in. mulch of manure over the root area, in fall or spring.

What does my soil need to make White Oak leaves turn red in the fall instead of just drying up? Also, my Pin Oak leaves turned brown with very little of the normal red.   White Oak leaves seldom turn red—usually purplish—in the fall. Pin Oak leaves should turn a brilliant red some seasons when climatic conditions are just right. If your tree has a full western exposure, has plenty of nitrogenous fertilizer, and the weather is just right, it should turn the desired red. But the reasons vary considerably from year to year, some years resulting in "good" color and other years being decidedly "poor."

PEPPERIDGE

See Sourgum.

PLANE

See Sycamore.

POPLAR

During heavy, wet, unseasonable snow, when leaves were on trees, several Bolleana Poplars with trunks over 4 ins. in diameter broke off and had to be trimmed 'way down. What trimming shall I do on upright branches from low side branches?   Paint wounds; leave upright branches to develop.

What time of year should Lombardy Poplars be topped?   Ordinarily Lombardy Poplars are not planted in situations where it is necessary to cut off their tops. If it has to be done, they may be cut back at any time without injury. Cutting back during the growing season checks growth; during the dormant season it promotes strong, leafy shoots.

How can I choose new leaders for some Lombardy Poplars which lost their tops due to a severe wind and rain storm? Select the strongest shoot near to the top and center of the tree, to make new leader. Cut off the splintered stub just above the shoot. Make a slanting cut which will shed rain, and paint the wound.

SASSAFRAS

Is it easy to transplant sassafras trees from the wild? This interesting tree, with large, various-shaped leaves which turn brilliant yellow, rose, and scarlet, is not easily transplanted. Choose trees not more than 10 or 12 ft. high.

My yard has numerous sassafras trees growing. Do they have any ill effect on the soil? No. They are desirable trees, especially when they reach maturity. Picturesque in winter because of its gnarled branches; very wind resistant.

SOPHORA

What is the sophora tree like? What is its common name? *Sophora japonica* is called Japanese Pagoda-tree or Chinese Scholartree. It has a rounded top with leafage which suggests the locust and casts a light shade. In summer it has small, yellowish-white, pealike flowers in large panicles. Hardy as far north as Massachusetts. Though it may attain a height of 60 ft., it remains small for many years.

SOURGUM (NYSSA SYLVATICA)

I am told that a Sourgum, (also known as Blackgum, Tupelo, and Pepperidge) would be appropriate for a place with poor drainage. What is this tree like? In silhouette when young a little like Pin Oak. Slow-growing, moisture-loving, attaining a great height; very hardy; distinguished tree; noted for scarlet, crimson, and copper foliage in autumn; difficult to transplant.

SYCAMORE (PLANE, BUTTONBALL)

Sycamore, planetree, or buttonball tree—which is the correct name? All three common names are used for sycamore.

What is the best plane tree for city streets? London Plane (*Platanus acerifolia*).

What is the difference in appearance between the bark of the American Plane and that of the London Plane? When the bark is shed the trunk of the American is white; the London Plane is yellowish.

Are the plane trees, buttonballs and sycamores the same? Yes. Sycamore is primarily the term used in forestry.

What is the rate of growth of a plane tree? When young, averages about 2 or 3 ft. of growth in height each good growing season.

Does London Plane prefer spring or fall planting? What are best soil conditions? Plant in early spring or in the fall. It will grow well in any good soil.

Does the plane tree shed its bark untidily? Yes; but the white inner bark thus disclosed is definitely decorative.

Can a sycamore root about 3 in. in diameter growing out of slope be removed without harming tree? If the tree is well provided with roots on the side away from the slope, cutting off the root should not hurt the tree. As soon as the cut surface is dry, cover it with tar or hot asphalt.

When is the best time to cut large lower limbs on sycamore? This may be done in late winter or early spring before growth begins. It is not advisable to cut off more than 1 or 2 limbs at one time because of the danger of promoting excessive sappy growth.

TULIPTREE (LIRIODENDRON TULIPIFERA)

Which tree is it that grows tall and stately and has cream, green, and orange tulip-shaped flowers in June? In autumn the coloring is yellow. Tuliptree (*Liriodendron tulipifera*). It does not flower, however, until it has attained good size—probably 10 years or more after planting.

Is it possible to grow tuliptrees in northern New York State? Near Rochester and Buffalo—yes. In the upper Adirondacks—no.

How shall I prune a tuliptree that was transplanted this spring, having 3 or 4 new shoots at the base? The original tree died. Before growth starts in the spring remove all shoots but the strongest. Avoid leaving any stubs which might decay.

TUPELO

See Sourgum.

WILLOW

What is a good willow (not weeping)? White Willow (*Salix alba*).

When is the best time to move a willow tree? In the spring, before growth starts.

Can a 4-year-old WEEPING WILLOW be moved from one side of lawn to the other side without injuring the roots? It can be moved safely, but not without cutting some of the roots. This will not be serious. Willows move easily in moist soils.

How far should a Weeping Willow tree be planted from a sewer? Are their roots a particular menace to sewer pipes? At least 25 ft. or 30 ft. away. Their roots are very likely to be troublesome.

Will the roots of willow trees damage concrete pits, septic tanks, or drilled wells? I am anxious to plant a pair near these things and have

been told that the roots damage underground constructions. The roots of willows will enter the tiniest crevices where they may obtain moisture, and unless all joints are screw joints or are filled with lead you may have considerable trouble in a few years.

Is a Weeping Willow tree self-pruning? I notice all the small limbs have dropped off; or is this caused by a disease? Many willows shed some of their twigs annually by the development of what the botanist calls "abscission layers." Probably this is what your tree has been doing. Not a disease.

SPECIFIC DECORATIVE FLOWERING TREES

CHERRY

Are there flowering cherry trees whose leaves unfold brown and then turn green? Yes. Among these are Sargent Cherry with single pink blossoms, and Kwanzan (*Prunus serrulata lannesiana*) with double pink ones.

Which flowering cherry trees have white and pale pink flowers? Try 2 beauties, Naden with semi-double fragrant blossoms in pink and white, and Shirotae with double white flowers.

I once saw a cherry tree blooming in autumn. What was it? It must have been Autumn Cherry (*Prunus subhirtella autumnalis*), pink, which blooms in spring and again sparingly in the fall.

What is the best way to propagate Nanking Cherry (Prunus tomentosa)? Either from seeds, which should be stored cool, 40° to 50° F., in moist sand over winter; or from cuttings taken in July and placed under a bell jar; or in a cold frame kept closed until roots are formed.

CRAB, FLOWERING

Can you recommend a few decorative crabapple trees? Arnold Crab (*Malus floribunda arnoldiana*), pink and white blossoms, yellow fruits; Carmine Crab (*M. atrosanguinea*), blossoms red-purple-pink, red fruits; Toringo Crab (*M. sieboldi*), pink to blush flowers, fruits orange-yellow; Sargent Crab (*M. sargenti*), white blossoms, dark red fruit.

I have a sunny space alongside my house about 10 ft. wide. Will you recommend a flowering tree that will not spread too much and will not grow over 20 ft. tall? Any one of 20 different kinds of crabapples.

Would you advise spring planting of flowering crab? Yes.

What is the best way to move flowering crabapple trees 3 ins. in diameter, about 8 ft. high? Balled, burlapped, and platformed—

preferably in the spring; but safe enough in the autumn, after the leaves have dropped.

Where should a BECHTEL CRAB TREE be planted? What kind of soil and drainage? How to prune, if at all? Plant in good soil with good drainage and plenty of sunlight. Needs little (if any) pruning —only the removal of diseased or broken limbs.

What is the care of Bechtel Crab trees? Need no special care except the application of a dormant oil spray every few years if scale is bad in your area, and elimination of cedar trees if cedar-apple rust is prevalent.

Why doesn't my Bechtel Flowering Crab bloom? It is 10 ft. tall and a nice tree. It will bloom—all crabapples do eventually. It is simply that in some soils it takes longer than others. Try applying super-phosphate, 6 oz. per sq. yd., and forking it into the soil under the tree in the fall or early spring.

I have planted a Bechtel's Crabapple, 3 ft. high. Does one prune it much the first year? Assuming that it was pruned at the time it was transplanted (by cutting it back about ⅓), further pruning is not likely to be necessary except for the removal of dead branches.

What care does the DOLGO CRAB tree need in winter? No more care is needed than would be given an apple tree. A mulch of manure spread around in the fall would be helpful.

Is there any way of preventing a flowering crabapple from increasing in size too rapidly, without loss of the flower display? Yes. Shorten young shoots each season, about ½ when they are ⅔ grown.

DOGWOODS

Does the Flowering Dogwood tree come in any color except white? Yes, there is pink or rose form listed as *Cornus florida rubra*.

What is the Japanese Flowering Dogwood like? Similar to our native flowering dogwood, but the flowers (bracts) are pointed instead of blunt. The Japanese species ·(*Cornus kousa*)blooms a few weeks later. The berries grow together in a head and seem, from afar, to resemble cherries.

Should soil for dogwood be acid or alkaline? It grows well in both, if not extreme. Slightly acid preferred.

What is the best fertilizer for dogwoods? How applied and when? Flowering Dogwood (*Cornus florida*) is usually planted in spring. In such cases mix a 10–6–4 with a good compost at the rate of 4-in. potful to a wheelbarrow of soil, and use this to fill about the ball of soil. Thereafter, if necessary, fall applications of 10–6–4. A 4-in. tree (diameter of trunk) will need 10 lbs. applied over the area covered by spread of branches and a little beyond.

I have been told that white Flowering Dogwood (Cornus florida)

would not bloom if planted in an unprotected place, but only if in a wooded place. Is this true? (Michigan.)   This may be true in the colder parts of Michigan, where the wooded areas give it winter protection and prevent its buds from winter killing from too severe cold. Farther south the dogwood will do well either in the open or in wooded areas.

When is the best time to move dogwood from the woods to a garden?   In the spring only—before growth starts.

Should the pink dogwoods be planted at a different time from the white kind? (Kentucky.)   Both white and pink dogwoods can be planted at the same time. Transplant with a ball of earth—not bare root, unless plants are very young.

Are dogwood trees, 3 to 4 ft., hardy in northern New York?   In Rochester and Buffalo—yes; but in the Adirondacks these trees are frequently subjected to such low temperatures that winter killing results.

How soon after transplanting wild dogwood do they bloom?   From 1 to 5 years, depending on the size and age of the plant and the growing conditions.

What would cause a white dogwood to show only 2 bracts to a flower, every flower, every season?   Winter injury—the outside bracts being killed or stunted by severe weather. Also there may be individuals in which this is characteristic. Such specimens should be replaced with normal plants.

What makes all the buds fall from my white dogwood in the spring? They set perfectly in the fall, but just drop off.   They are frequently killed by severe winters. This is especially true in New England.

Can dogwood be grown in this section? Our soil is alkaline. My tree had about 6 leaves on all summer. (Utah.)   Give it the best garden soil you have available. Mix acid leafmold with it. The chances are the summers are too hot and the winters too cold for Flowering Dogwood (*Cornus florida*) to amount to very much in many sections of Utah.

I have a white dogwood tree 5 or 6 years old. Appears to be very healthy, but does not blossom. What should be done?   Merely have patience; and try working superphosphate into the soil about the roots.

My pink dogwood has faded to a dirty white. Is there anything I can fertilize with and bring back to original lovely pink?   Possibly a heavy application of a nitrogenous fertilizer would help. It might be that the pink-flowering part has died and you now have the white-flowering understock left in its place, since pink dogwoods are usually grafted plants. If this is the case, and the understock only remains, it will never have pink flowers.

What is the treatment to insure blooming of red dogwood? Every well-established Flowering Dogwood should bloom if the soil is normal. If it does not, a 3-ft. ditch 18 ins. deep could be dug around the tree several feet from the base. Superphosphate should be mixed with the soil as it is returned to the ditch. This treatment frequently results in aiding the flowering of dogwoods, and of wisterias.

A transplanted twin (2-stemmed) wild dogwood bloomed for the first time this year. When is the proper time to cut the shoot or twin which does not bloom? Any time, preferably just after flowering. However, both branches will bloom eventually.

When is the best time to prune and transplant a dogwood tree? Ours has small flowers, and is getting too large. The branches have fallen over the ground and rooted themselves. Can I use these in any way? Dogwoods can be pruned either in the spring or fall, but are most easily moved in the early spring. The branches that have rooted can be cut off and transplanted, and in this way should make separate plants.

When can native dogwood trees be trimmed? Any time; preferably just after they are through blooming.

What winter protection should be provided for very young dogwood trees? Mulching the roots with peatmoss or rotted manure would help the first year or two.

Is it true that there are 2 kinds of dogwood trees—male and female? No; dogwood flowers are "perfect," having both stamens and pistil in the same flower. They are borne in clusters and form the center of what commonly is considered the dogwood "flower." The large "petals" are really bracts or modified leaves surrounding the clusters of the tiny *true* flowers.

Is it difficult to grow dogwoods from seed? (North Carolina.) No. Sow 1 in. deep in late fall; protect carefully from mice; and leave outdoors all winter to freeze. Germination will begin in spring, and may continue for a year. Transplant when 4 ins. high.

Will pink dogwood tree seedlings bloom true? Probably not. They should be propagated either by grafts or budding to insure the young plants having the identical characteristics of the parents. These are termed asexual methods of propagation. Propagation by seed is the sexual method.

Can I propagate pink or red Flowering Dogwood from seeds? The seedlings are not likely to be red-flowered. The usual method is to graft scions of a colored form on seedling understocks of the common flowering dogwood. Layering is practicable if it is possible to bend the branches down to earth to root them. (See Propagation.)

RUSSIAN OLIVE (ELAEAGNUS)

See Shrubs.

FRINGETREE (CHIONANTHUS)

Is the Fringetree native? What is it like? Yes. This tree or large shrub bears loose, shredlike tassels of fragrant green-white flowers, in May or June, and has glossy tapering leaves. Male plant has larger flower trusses, but female has plumlike fruits in September.

GOLDRAINTREE (KOELREUTERIA)

Is there any tree I can get that has yellow flowers? Goldraintree and laburnum, which see.

I want to try an uncommon flowering tree. What do you advise? Please describe same. The Goldraintree (*Koelreuteria paniculata*) is a small, decorative tree with rounded top. Large panicles of small yellow flowers bloom in July or August. In September it has papery pods, and the foliage turns bright yellow.

Would a Goldraintree be appropriate on a small informal place? We like yellow blossoms. (Mid-New England.) Excellent, if given a sheltered location; otherwise branches may be killed back during severe winters. It likes full sun.

GORDONIA

What is the Franklinia alatamaha, also known as Gordonia alatamaha? A beautiful shrub or small tree originally from Georgia. Introduced to cultivation in 1790 by John Bartram, who discovered it on one of his plant-collecting trips to the South; it has since never been found in the wild. It has handsome, glossy, bright green leaves about 5 ins. long. In autumn its foliage turns orange-red and it bears cup-shaped, fragrant white flowers to 3 ins. across, with handsome golden anthers. A large specimen in Bartram's Garden near Philadelphia was long supposed to be the only living specimen. All other specimens in cultivation are believed to have been propagated from the Bartram tree, which is now dead.

Does the "lost tree" (gordonia) have any special requirements? Mine does not grow well. It prefers a moist but well-drained soil. Not reliably hardy inland far north of New York City.

Does the Franklin-tree (gordonia) require an acid or alkaline soil? There is a conflict of opinion on this point. Usually it is considered that an acid soil is preferred, but some have found that it responds to an application of lime.

Is Loblolly Bay (Gordonia lasianthus) hardy in Pennsylvania? Probably not. Native from Virginia to Florida. *Gordonia alatamaha* (see previous questions), if sheltered, may be hardy to Massachusetts.

HAWTHORN

What color are the flowers and berries of the hawthorns? To choose a few popular kinds—Washington Thorn and Cockspur Thorn have white flowers; English Hawthorn has several varieties, single and double, varying in color from white to scarlet. These all have red berries, the Washington Thorn bearing the most decorative ones.

What is a May Day Tree? Perhaps you mean the May-tree of England, which is a hawthorn, either *Crataegus oxyacantha* or *Crataegus monogyna.*

Do you need 2 trees to make hawthorn bloom? No.

I transplanted a hawthorn tree in November. Is it natural that the leaves should die in a few days? I cut back all the tips of the branches at the time of transplanting. If planted with bare roots (which would be hardly advisable), then any leaves left on the tree would promptly wither. But this would not be harmful so late in the season.

What is the reason why a very flourishing pink hawthorn tree starts to shed its leaves in early August and has new leaves and even blossoms in September? Can this condition be corrected? The fact that the hawthorn sheds its leaves in August suggests that the tree has been attacked by spider mites, or by a leaf blight. For the spider mites use diluted miscible oil as a dormant spray; for the blight, use Bordeaux mixture. See also Section VIII.

When should red hawthorn trained on a wall be pruned? It should be pruned, after flowering, by shortening new shoots as they are produced during the summer. The following spring, before growth begins, thin out some of the weakest shoots if they appear to be crowded.

How shall I prune my Paul's Double-Scarlet Hawthorn? If it is growing vigorously, and you wish to keep it within bounds, shorten the leading shoots in July. If growth is weak, cut out branches in late winter, having in mind the desirability of maintaining its interesting branch pattern.

LABURNUM

I saw in June a small tree that had flowers like wisteria, only yellow in color. What was it? Goldenchain Laburnum (*L. anagyroides*).

How hardy is the Laburnum vossi? This is now called *Laburnum waterei;* probably the hardiest of the laburnums. However, it is not reliably hardy much farther north than New York City.

Will you describe necessary soil, exposure, and give any other suggestions for culture of "Golden Tree," which I understand is a variety of laburnum? (Massachusetts.) These trees prefer a sandy soil, not too acid, which must be well drained. Protection from cold winds is also necessary.

Will you give some advice on the culture of Laburnum vossi? I have had difficulty growing this tree. This should not present any difficulties provided it is growing in a well-drained position. (See previous question.) Do aphids attack it? If so, spray with nicotine whenever they are present; otherwise they may completely ruin the new growth.

MAGNOLIA

How can I learn about every species of magnolia? Would suggest *Magnolias,* by A. G. Millais, published in 1927 by Longmans, Green & Co., New York.

Are Magnolias fraseri, macrophylla, kobus, and soulangeana lennei hardy in Pennsylvania? Yes. All these should be hardy in Pennsylvania except in the coldest areas.

Are the following varieties of magnolias good for southern New York: M. glauca (Sweet Bay), M. acuminata (Cucumbertree), and M. hypoleucea (Silver Magnolia)? Yes.

Would any magnolia trees be hardy north of New York City? Would their leaves be evergreen? Leaves would not be evergreen. The Cucumbertree, the Saucer Magnolia, and the Sweet Bay (or Swamp Magnolia) are hardy in Boston.

Will a magnolia tree grow around Woodridge, New York? Certainly. The Star Magnolia, the Cucumbertree (*Magnolia acuminata*), or any one of several varieties of the beautiful Saucer Magnolia should all do well.

Sweet or acid soil for magnolias? Slightly acid, pH 6.5

When is the best time to transplant magnolias? In the spring, even during, or immediately after, the flowering period. Move with as good a ball of fibrous roots as it is possible to obtain.

Should a small potted magnolia tree be kept growing in the house in sunny window for the winter, to be planted outdoors in the spring? Do not attempt to keep the magnolia growing through the winter, as it requires a rest at that time. Keep it in a cool cellar or garage, but do not allow the soil to become entirely dry. It may be planted in the garden in the spring.

When may I move magnolia trees from woods to garden, and what treatment should be given? In the spring. The Cucumbertree (*Magnolia acuminata*) is not easily transplanted from the wild. Get as many of the fibrous root ends as possible. Have the hole wide enough to accommodate them. Mulch the soil over the roots. Wrap the trunk with burlap, and spray tops with Wilt-pruf *before digging*.

What are the "rules" for growing magnolias? Magnolias require rich soil, therefore the addition of cow manure is advisable. While they require a moist soil for best results, it is equally important that it be well drained. For most, a position with full exposure to the sun is desirable.

Will you give the year-around treatment which would be best for the growth of Magnolia soulangeana in my locality? Particularly the establishment of young trees. (Pennsylvania.) Once the plants begin to grow satisfactorily after they are planted in the garden they require little in the way of extra attention. A mulch over the roots, particularly a mulch of cow manure, will feed them and keep the roots cool in summer.

How can I get results with a magnolia in this district? (Pennsylvania.) The Star Magnolia is the easiest to grow and is also the hardiest. If it is given a good soil and a dormant oil spray applied in case scale appears, it should do well. The many varieties of the Saucer Magnolia (*Magnolia soulangeana*) can also be grown with no particular attention other than the supplying of good soil.

Our Magnolia soulangeana, planted in October, had scant bloom and very few leaves the following spring and summer. Will it survive? We mulched with cow manure in fall. What else can be done? Magnolias frequently make very little growth during the year after they are transplanted. Mulching is beneficial. For the first winter at least, protect from sun and wind with a screen of burlap, evergreen branches, or boards. It should make good growth after the first year.

What can I do to make a magnolia bloom? I have had the tree for 5 years and it is 7 ft. high and grows well, but has never bloomed. Our soil is sandy. It is possible that you have a seedling of one of the tree magnolias, in which case it may be 3 or 4 or more years before the tree blooms. As the growth is satisfactory, do not worry.

I have a Magnolia soulangeana which was in bloom when I bought it from the nursery; it bloomed the next season but hasn't bloomed for two seasons. What should be done? Magnolias resent moving and sometimes take a few years to become established after transplanting. If it is planted in good soil in a well-drained position it will soon resume its flowering. If you have any doubt about the quality of the soil, top-dress it with cow manure.

How do you cut back a Magnolia glauca (6 to 7 ft. tall) when transplanting? If it was moved with a good ball of fibrous roots you need not cut it back; if moved bare-rooted with a good root system, and it must be pruned, reduce the main stems to about ⅔. If it appears to be making good growth, do not cut it.

My young magnolia produced many sucker shoots this summer. Should they be cut or left on? If the shoots originate from below the ground line, they probably come from the understock on which the magnolia is grafted, and should be cut off. If, however, they come from *above* the ground line, they may be left, provided they are not too crowded.

How should I protect magnolias, planted in spring, during the

first winter? (Michigan.)   Sometimes it is advisable to wrap the trunks in burlap, especially for the first winter. If the plants are small, you might build a burlap screen about them for the winter and even partly fill it with leaves, which would aid in protecting the roots from too-severe winter cold.

Do young magnolia plants (4 to 5 years) need winter protection? The magnolias commonly grown should not need protection at that age unless your garden is so situated as to be exposed to northwest winds. If that is the case, erect a screen on that side of the plants.

Can you start a new magnolia from cuttings from an old tree? If so, how can it be done?   Some of the magnolias may be rooted, but they are very difficult. Sideshoots, about 5 ins. long, are generally the most successful. Cut very close to the branch, so that a little of the old wood is taken also. They must be kept in close, humid conditions until rooted. A cold frame or glass-covered box in a place out of the sun would be required. Magnolia stellata (and possibly others) can be easily rooted by the "mist" method. See page 246.

A branch was broken from my young magnolia bush. It has one bud on it. I placed it in a bottle of water and it started blooming. How can I grow roots on it?   You can't! (See answer to preceding question.)

Where and how should magnolia seeds be planted?   Soak in water until fleshy covering can be removed. Plant seeds ½ in. deep in soil of cold frame, or in cool place over winter. They will germinate the following spring.

PEACH, FLOWERING

When is the best time to transplant a flowering peach? (New Jersey.) In early fall or in spring.

PLUM

How and when shall I prune Purpleleaf Plum (Prunus pissardi)? Severe pruning of trees related to plums and the stone fruits generally is to be avoided. Unless there is some urgent reason to the contrary, pruning of *Prunus pissardi* should be restricted to shortening "wild" (too energetic) shoots during the growing season.

REDBUD (CERCIS)

Which other native tree would make a good companion to the white-flowered dogwood? The redbud; it flowers simultaneously and likes a similar environment.

What does redbud look like?   In open places it has wide crown and grows 15 or more ft. high. In shaded and crowded quarters it will grow taller and slimmer. It has deep pink, pea-shaped flowers which grow in clusters along the stems. The leaves which follow are large and roundish.

Can redbud be successfully moved in fall?   Redbud is not one of the easiest shrubs to move, and spring is much safer than fall for the operation. Move it with a ball of earth, held by burlap, attached to the roots and, unless the soil-ball is very firm, do not attempt to remove the burlap when the plant is in its new position.

This is the second year for a redbud tree. Will it bloom this spring if I move it quite early?   Do not expect redbuds to flower much the first spring after transplanting. Do not transplant them unless necessary. They are not very good-natured about being moved.

Why does my redbud tree not bloom freely? Has grown nicely, but has very few blossoms.   Redbuds, dogwoods, and some other flowering trees often fail to produce flowers during periods of vigorous growth. Do not feed your tree with nitrogenous fertilizers.

SHADBLOW (AMELANCHIER)

What is a good small flowering tree for light woodland?   Serviceberry (*Amelanchier canadensis*); also called shadblow or shadbush. It has delicate white flowers in spring.

Does the serviceberry grow well near the salt water's edge?   Yes. Thicket serviceberry, *Amelanchier oblongifolia*, endures salt-laden winds.

SILVERBELL (HALESIA)

Is the silverbell a desirable small tree?   Yes. Its main attraction is in spring, when the dainty white flowers are produced.

Where would the silverbell be attractive?   On the edge of woodland in company with a ground cover of Mertensia, violets, and other woodland flowers.

SMOKETREE (COTINUS)

What gives the smoketree its name?   When the seed pods form in June they produce whorls of gray-lavender hairs. As they become full blown the bush seems enveloped in a whorl of smoke.

What would be the reason for my young smoketree not growing taller? I have had it 6 years and it is only the same height as when I bought it.   Either it is being recurrently killed by cold winters, or the soil is not to its liking. Would suggest fertilizing with well-rotted manure in the fall, *after* digging it up and examining the roots and transplanting it to some new situation which you know has fertile soil.

Why does my smoketree blossom but not set any seeds? The blossom stems wither and drop off. It is more than 20 years old.   The sexes are sometimes on separate individuals and this particular plant is probably the male or staminate type which never bears fruits.

I have a smoketree 6 years old and more than 10 ft. high. Why doesn't it bloom? It gets leaves, but no flower buds. You may have the native smoketree, which is sparing of its smoke! The European (*Cotinus coggygria*) is more floriferous.

My smoketree has leaves with beautiful autumn coloring, but no "smoke." The seed panicles do not produce the "smoke" effect until the shrub is fairly mature.

How should a smoketree be trimmed to tree form, instead of a bush? No attempt should be made to change common smoketree (*Cotinus coggygria*) to tree form—it naturally forms a bush. American Smoketree is occasionally seen as a tree. This form can be encouraged by the gradual removal of the lower branches, starting when the tree is young.

YELLOWWOOD (CLADRASTIS)

What tree is it that has white flowers resembling wisteria? It has a sweet perfume. I saw it at night and it was beautiful. It was probably yellowwood, *Cladrastis lutea.*

Will yellowwood resist high winds? No. The wood is inclined to be brittle.

DECIDUOUS SHRUBS AND THEIR CULTURE

WHAT TO GROW

Can you give me a list of uncommon, but worth-while, hardy shrubs? *Berberis mentorensis; Buddleia alternifolia; Cotoneaster divaricata; Euonymus alatus* and *E. europaeus; Jamesia americana; Kerria japonica; Rubus deliciosus* (thimbleberry); *Shepherdia argentea* (buffaloberry); *Symphoricarpus vulgaris* (snowberry); *Viburnum burkwoodi; V. carlcephalum.*

We cannot afford evergreen foundation planting for our little place. Could you suggest good shrubs, and a few with interesting winter habit? Flowers not essential. Regel Privet, Fiveleaf Aralia, shrub dogwoods with colored branches, Cork Bark or Winged Euonymus, European and Japanese Barberry.

What deciduous shrubs should we plant under our windows to harmonize with the evergreen shrubs which are already there? Azaleas in variety, Flowering Quince, *Abelia grandiflora*, cotoneaster, (various low-growing varieties) *Viburnum carlesi.*

Will you name a few pretty shrubs, beside lilacs and forsythia, that grow rather heavy and would make a "wall" for an out-of-door

room? Beautybush (*Kolkwitzia amabilis*); chokeberry (*Aronia melanocarpa elata*); Gray Dogwood (*Cornus paniculata*); honeysuckle (*Lonicera korolkowi*); *Viburnum dilatatum*.

Which shrubs will give us bloom in the garden from spring to fall? We have a narrow strip on one side of our house. *April*—forsythia; *May*—*Spiraea prunifolia* and Vanhoutte spirea, lilac; *June*—mock-orange, beautybush (*Kolkwitzia*), lilac (continued); *July*—vitex, Snowhill Hydrangea, roses, buddleia; *August*—Peegee Hydrangea, roses, rose-of-Sharon; *September*—rose-of-Sharon and roses (continued), clematis.

Will you list some dwarf shrubs? *Juniperus horizontalis; Juniperus horizontalis plumosa; Mahonia (Berberis) repens; Euonymus radicans; Euonymus Fortunei minimus (kewensis); Daphne cneorum; Cotoneaster horizontalis* and *C. adpressa; Prunus nana*, Rose Max Graf.

Can you name some shrubs which can be used for training on walls? *Cotoneaster horizontalis;* English Hawthorn (*Crataegus oxyacantha*); firethorn (*Pyracantha coccinea*); Flowering Almond; *Forsythia suspensa;* goldenchain (*Laburnum anagyroides*); *Jasminum nudiflorum;* matrimonyvine (*Lycium halimifolium*); peach (*Prunus persica*).

Which bush can be planted near a window, as a screen which will stand much trimming? If by trimming you mean close shearing, privet will take it. As an irregular bush that will tolerate removal of some growths and still flower, try forsythia; but prune out old growths right after blooming.

BERRIES

In order to have a continuous succession of colorful berries along a driveway, which shrubs should be planted? The driveway has very little sun during the summer. To provide fruits throughout late summer and winter use the following: barberries, Cornelian Cherry, Red-stemmed Dogwood, Gray-stemmed Dogwood, Siebold's Viburnum, American Highbush Cranberry, and Linden-leaved Viburnum.

Can you name a few shrubs with outstandingly bright fruit? *Aronia arbutifolia brilliantissima; Berberis amurensis japonica, B. koreana, B. vernae,* and *B. vulgaris atropurpurea;* callicarpa species; *Cotoneaster zabeli miniata, C. dielsiana,* and *C. francheti; Euonymus europaeus; Ilex laevigata,* and *I. verticillata; Rosa rugosa; Symplocos paniculata; Viburnum dilatatum,* and *V. setigerum.*

Are there any shrubs with decorative fruit, other than the usual bright reds? Beautybush (bright lilac); Yellowberry Flowering Dogwood (yellow); Gray Dogwood (white, on red stalks); privet, several kinds (black); Sapphireberry (*Symplocos paniculata*) (clear blue);

Chenault Coralberry (*Symphoricarpos chenaulti*) (pinkish); *Viburnum cassinoides* (at first white then pinkish, later black).

What are some of the names of berried shrubs and their culture? Barberry, viburnum, shrubby dogwood, and cotoneaster. For culture see Specific Plants.

BIRDS

Which shrubs, easily grown in part shade, will attract birds? Buckthorn (*Rhamnus cathartica*); Fragrant Thimbleberry (*Rubus odoratus*) red (*R. strigosus*) and blackcap (*R. orientalis*) raspberries; Red-berried Elder (*Sambucus pubens*); viburnum species; shadblow (*Amelanchier canadensis*); chokeberry (*Aronia arbutifolia*); *Cornus alba, C. mas,* and *C. racemosa; Ilex glabra; Lonicera morrowi;* chokeberry (*Aronia arbutifolia*).

What shrubs should I plant to call birds to my garden? (Vermont.) Bush honeysuckle, chokeberry, cotoneaster, honeysuckle, shadbush, spicebush, wild roses, and most other berry-bearing shrubs.

BLOOM

We would like succession of bloom in our shrub border. Our place is informal and we like native plants. Can you help us? February and March—Vernal Witchhazel; April—spicebush, Cornelian Cherry, shadblow, redbud; May—Pinkshell Azalea, dogwood, rose-acacia, Red Chokeberry, rhododendron, viburnum—various; June—Silky Dogwood and Gray Dogwood, Mountain Laurel, Snow Azalea, rhododendron, Prairie Rose, Flowering Raspberry; July—Jersey Tea (*Ceanothus americanus*), Showy Cinquefoil, summersweet (*Clethra alnifolia*); August, September, and October—colored foliage and pods and berries; witchhazel (*Hamamelis virginiana*).

What shrubs can be planted to bloom from early spring until late fall? To obtain a succession of bloom, one must plant several plants which bloom in sequence. *Hamamelis mollis* (earliest); *Abelia grandiflora,* 12 to 15 weeks; *Potentilla fruticosa,* 10 to 12 weeks; *Spiraea bumalda* Anthony Waterer, 8 to 10 weeks; forsythia in variety, 3 to 4 weeks; vitex, 8 to 10 weeks; *Hibiscus syriacus,* 8 to 10 weeks; azaleas; lilacs; rhododendrons; roses; hydrangeas; rose-of-Sharon; common witchhazel (latest). (See preceding question.)

Can you name some shrubs with fragrant flowers? Honeysuckle (*Lonicera fragrantissima*); mockorange (*Philadelphus coronarius* and *P. virginalis*); *Viburnum carlesi;* clethra; common lilac; *Daphne cneorum;* sweetshrub.

We are planting a little old-fashioned summer cottage with old-time shrubs. Can you remind us of a few blooming from June to September? June—rose-acacia, mockorange, sweet azalea, shrub roses, *Spiraea bumalda,* lilacs, hydrangea; July—sweetshrub, smoke-bush, hydrangea; August—summersweet, rose-of-Sharon.

Will you name 5 deciduous shrubs desirable for flowers, berries, and foliage color? *Aronia arbutifolia, Berberis koreana, Viburnum prunifolium, Vaccinium corymbosum, Chaenomeles lagenaria* (Japanese Quince).

FOLIAGE

Which shrubs have distinctive autumn color, other than the brilliant reds and orange shades? Here are a few: *Abelia grandiflora* (reddish-bronze); *Cotoneaster divaricata* (purplish); *Mahonia aquifolium* (chestnut and bronze tints); *Viburnum carlesi* (purplish-red); *V. tomentosum* (purplish).

Can you name some shrubs with outstandingly bright autumn foliage? *Berberis koreana, B. vernae, B. thunbergi pluriflora,* and *B. dictyophylla; Cotoneaster adpressa; Euonymus alatus* and *E. alatus compactus;* fothergilla; *Gordonia alatamaha; Itea virginica; Rhodo dendron arborescens, R. schlippenbachi,* and *R. obtusum kaempferi; Rhus aromatica; Stephanandra incisa; Vaccinium corymbosum; Xanthorhiza simplicissima.*

I am partial to shrubs with foliage of a fine, lacy quality. Can you mention a few? *Acer palmatum dissectum* varieties; *Abelia grandiflora; Berberis vernae; Cotoneaster dielsiana; Neillia sinensis; Rosa hugonis* and *R. eglanteria; Spiraea arguta, S. thunbergi; Symphoricarpos chenaulti;* tamarisk; *Rosa hugonis.*

Will you name a few shrubs with aromatic foliage? *Calycanthus floridus, Comptonia asplenifolia, Cotinus* species, *Elsholtzia stauntoni, Benzoin aestivale, Rhus aromatica, Rosa eglanteria, Rhododendron micranthum* and *R. racemosum.*

CULTURE—GENERAL

SOIL; FERTILIZER

How should I prepare the ground for planting shrubs? The subsoil must be well drained. Plow or disk in a layer of leafmold and old manure, thus providing a 1-ft. depth of good topsoil. Prepare planting holes to required depths. Remove the excavated soil that may be of very poor quality; improve the better part with leafmold or humus and old manure, for refilling holes. (See also Soil Preparation—Trees, this section.)

What is the best fertilizer to use to stimulate the growth of shrubs? In the planting of shrubs, use leafmold, peatmoss and old manure mixed into the soil. For established shrubs, a mulch of the same. In default of these ingredients, top-dress with a balanced commercial fertilizer.

What is the best commercial fertilizer to use around shrubs? A 10–6–4 if making weak, short growth; or a 0–12–4 if blooms are scant.

Are commercial pulverized manure and peatmoss as beneficial for shrubs as raw cow or horse manure for mulching? Just about, provided the soil is not made too acid thereby.

Which of these shrubs like a soil with lime? Barberry, Japanese Quince, mockorange, Irish Juniper, crapemyrtle, nandina, and roses? Any of them will grow in an alkaline soil. Roses seem to do best in a slightly acid soil, however.

PLANTING, TRANSPLANTING CARE

I want to plant a double row of mixed flowering shrubs between lawn and garden, using tall and medium varieties. How far apart should they be planted in order to avoid either a sparse or a crowded appearance? As you do not give the names of the shrubs you intend to use for your border, exact directions cannot be given. As a general rule 4 to 5 ft. should be sufficient distance between plants in the front row; about 6 to 8 ft. between those in the back row.

When is the best time to transplant flowering shrubs? Spring and fall are the most suitable seasons, but the transplanting of all shrubs which are recognized as difficult to move and all tender shrubs should be undertaken only in spring. In spring, transplant before the shrubs begin to leaf. In fall, as soon as the greater part of the leaves have fallen; but at this season planting must cease before the ground freezes.

In setting out roses, shrubs, and large perennial plants, the soil (unless wet) is made firm about the roots with the feet or a tamping stick.

PLANTING DETAIL

Can most flowering shrubs and berry bushes be set out in the fall and winter, instead of waiting until spring? Shrubs (with some exceptions) and berry bushes may be safely set out in the fall; but the work should be undertaken as early as possible, while there is still sufficient warmth in the soil, to develop new root growth. It is impossible to plant satisfactorily when the soil is largely composed of frozen lumps.

Could I transplant between December 15 and end of March the following: common lilac, French pussy willow, forsythia, deutzia,

syringa, snowball, hydrangea, and bridalwreath?   Do the transplanting in late March rather than in December.

Is the fall the best time of year to plant trees and shrubs in a climate as cold as that of central Vermont?   No; early spring is better.

How does one go about digging up shrubs for transplanting?   If they are small, thrust a spade to its full depth in a continuous circle, at a sufficient distance from center to avoid undue root injury, and pry out. Roots are likely to extend at least as far as the spread of the branches.

Is it necessary to cut back shrubs when they are transplanted? If so, how much?   Balled and burlapped specimens need not be pruned after planting. Vigorous young shrubs of quick-growing kinds are best pruned to about half the length of main stems. Older, bare-rooted shrubs, with poorish root systems and large tops, are best pruned back to from ⅔ to ½ their length.

What is the reason for cutting back shrubs when they are transplanted?   It reduces the plant to a size more easily supported by a disturbed root system; it reduces the area exposed to the drying effect of wind and sun, and divides the vigor of the new growth over a smaller number of growing points. (See "Pruning.")

How low should fall-planted barberry, Spiraea Vanhouttei, and althea be pruned?   With the barberry and spirea cut out, at about ground level, half of the strongest stems; reduce the remainder about half their length. If the althea is on a single stem, it must not be cut to the ground. Cut out some of the branches at a point where they fork, and shorten the remaining ones to ½ or ⅓ their length.

Why do shrubs bloom well some years and others very poorly? Last spring my forsythia and flowering crab had only a few blooms.   For two reasons. Some winters are cold enough to kill the flower buds of plants such as forsythia. Then, too, many flowering and fruiting ornamentals, such as crabapples, bear alternately—that is, they have profuse flowers and fruits one year and but few the next year. There is little the homeowner can do to change this sequence.

PRUNING SHRUBS

See also General Pruning, this section.

Do all shrubs get pruned? How does one know which to prune? It is not necessary to prune all shrubs. Some are benefited by pruning —such as most varieties of roses and certain flowering shrubs whose branches become crowded and cluttered with worn-out wood which does not bloom freely. Generally speaking, if a shrub does not give satisfaction it is worth while to try the effect of pruning. Prune, in the main, *only* where necessary to keep materials within their allotted space, and to keep them at the highest pitch of effectiveness.

Is it better to prune flowering shrubs in spring or fall?   Few, if any, should be pruned in the fall in Northern climates. Generally, shrubs which blossom on old wood (forsythia, for example) should be pruned in spring immediately *after* flowering. Those whose blossoms are produced on shoots of the current season may be pruned in the spring before growth starts.

Which shrubs should be pruned in the fall? (South Carolina.) Where severe winters are experienced it is desirable to defer pruning until the worst of the winter has passed. In your section fall pruning might be permissible for those shrubs which produce their blooms on young shoots of the current season. Examples are H.T. roses, P.G. hydrangea, rose-of-Sharon, and late-blooming tamarisks.

When is the best time to prune a hedge? Hedges are best pruned when their young shoots are nearing the completion of their growth. With many hedges, one trimming at this time is sufficient; with others a second trimming may be necessary in late summer. In order to keep a fast-growing privet hedge in shipshape condition, trimming has to be done several times in a season. (See Hedges.)

What is the reason back of the recommendation to avoid, during the dormant season, the pruning of shrubs which blossom on the old wood? Because such pruning results in loss of branches which would produce flowers the following spring. Sometimes exceptional circumstances make it desirable to sacrifice flowering wood to attain a definite purpose; as, for example, when old, scraggly lilacs are cut back to rejuvenate them, reduce their height, and make a more compact bush.

Why are some shrubs pruned back every spring to mere stubs? This is done in the case of some shrubs which, though pruned back short, will flower on the new growth made after pruning. It affords a method of keeping them within limited proportions, without sacrifice of blossom. It is often done with Hills of Snow Hydrangea, vitex, abelia, and Spirea Anthony Waterer.

Should you remove dead flowers from shrubs? Yes—if you want to increase the bloom of plants such as lilacs the next year. No—if you wish these plants to produce fruits.

Should shrubs, such as mockorange, Hills of Snow Hydrangea, rose-of-Sharon, weigela, roses, and beautybush, be pruned the first fall after spring planting? Shrubs usually require little if any pruning the first year after planting—certainly not in the fall. In the spring Hills of Snow Hydrangea and rose-of-Sharon may have the growth of the preceding year cut back ⅔.

When is the proper time for, and what is the correct method of, thinning out shrubs and bushes that have not been cared for properly for years? Should they be cut to the ground and allowed to grow up again? Indiscriminate cutting to the ground may upset the balance between root and top. Thinning out crowded branches can be done during the winter. Those shrubs which normally are pruned by shortening the shoots of the preceding year in the spring should be so treated. Any large, overgrown specimens may be cut back ⅓ to ½.

How many branches should be left when shrubs are espaliered against wall? Average is about 1 ft. apart, but this is determined by the character of the shrub. Enough should be left so that the wall is well covered when the branches are clothed with leaves and shoots during the growing season.

WINTER PROTECTION

Are leaves good for mulching shrubs in the fall? Yes, where a mulch is desirable. Oak leaves are especially valuable around rhododendrons, and should be left in place finally to rot down.

I have read that maple leaves are not the right kind to use for a winter covering. Is this true? It all depends on what is being covered. They could be safely used as a mulch among shrubs. They are not so good as a cover for many perennials, as they tend to make a sodden mass with a smothering effect.

What is "salt" hay? It is hay from salt marshes cut and dried the same as ordinary hay. It is used for covering plants in winter as protection. May be obtained from dealers in horticultural supplies or nurserymen in your vicinity.

Do shrubs have to be covered for the winter with peatmoss or salt hay after their first winter? No.

When is the proper time to remove mulching around shrubs? For the sake of appearance, when the spring cleanup is under way. If manure was used, leave all possible for the benefit of the shrubs. In the case of rhododendrons and related plants, a perpetual mulch is desirable.

PROPAGATION

Generally speaking, when should I take slips from hardy shrubs? The majority root most readily during July and early August. Lilac and beautybush are two notable exceptions. The latter part of May, while the shoots are still growing, is the best time for lilac and mid-June for beautybush.

How are slips from hardy shrubs rooted? By placing them under preserving jars, bell jars, or in a cold frame, in a shady place. Sand, or a sandy soil, forms the best rooting medium.

What procedure should be followed after slips taken from hardy shrubs have rooted? (Wisconsin.) They may be potted up singly, or be planted in boxes. In the Northern states it is exceedingly risky to plant them in the open ground late in the fall. The pots or boxes should be stored in a cool place, such as a garage or cold cellar, where they will not be subjected to hard freezing. In the spring they may be planted in the open ground. (See also Propagation, Cuttings, this section.)

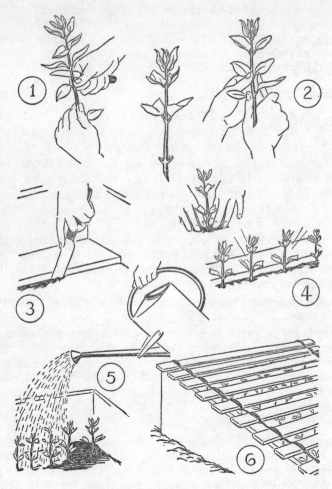

SUMMER PROPAGATION WITH SOFTWOOD CUTTINGS

(1 and 2) Making the cutting or slip, and trimming it up, ready for planting. (3 and 4) Marking line with knife in rooting medium (sand), inserting cutting, and firming sand along row of cuttings. (5) Watering in the cuttings. (6) Shading frame from sunshine, with lath screen. Sometimes it is necessary to cover with glass sash also.

Are there any shrubs which can be increased by division? Yes. Some types of boxwood, hydrangea, rose, spirea, etc.

SPECIFIC SHRUBS

ABELIA

How would abelias harmonize with broad-leaved evergreens? Very well. They like peaty soil as the evergreens do, but not too much shade.

Are Abelia grandiflora and the crapemyrtle hardy in the Pittsburgh, Pennsylvania, area? *Abelia grandiflora* is hardy in Pittsburgh, but the crapemyrtle may not prove completely hardy. Certainly it should be tried only in the most protected areas.

How long is the blooming season of Abelia grandiflora? From June or July to late October, or even November.

ARALIA, FIVE-LEAF (ACANTHOPANAX)

A nurseryman recommends acanthopanax for planting in shade. Is it any good? Flowers and fruits negligible; beautiful 5-parted, lacy leaves; fast-growing, well shaped; will grow under trees or in any shaded place, or in full sun; drought resistant. Height about 5 ft.

ALMOND (PRUNUS TRILOBA)

How do you prune a Flowering Almond (Prunus triloba)? The flowers are produced on the shoots made the preceding year, therefore, as soon as the flowers fade, cut back flowering shoots to within 2 ins of the point of origin.

Can I root cuttings of an almond? Yes. The cuttings must be taken in July and placed in a cold frame, or glass-covered box, in order to have the requisite moist, humid conditions to induce rooting.

AMORPHA

What is the Indigobush? Is it hardy in northern Ohio? Indigo-bush (*Amorpha fruticosa*) is somewhat weedy, with purplish flowers, in spikes, during June and July. Will grow in poor soil, and should be hardy in northern Ohio.

AZALEA

See Ericaceous Shrubs.

BARBERRY

What is Korean Barberry? A very decorative shrub growing 6 to 7 ft. high, erect when young and then spreading and arching. Thick, broad, wedge-shaped leaves turning orange-red in autumn. Small yellow flowers in spring, followed by scarlet berries in fall.

Is there a barberry suitable for a very low hedge? Yes. Box Barberry (*Berberis thunbergi minor*), very like a miniature of the well-known Japanese Barberry. There is also a variety called Truehedge Columnberry. It grows narrower and more erect. Good for its fine autumn color.

When shall I transplant barberry bush 3 years old? How far apart? When to prune? Barberry bushes of the kinds that lose their leaves every fall may be transplanted in spring or fall, while they are leafless. Evergreen kinds are better transplanted in spring. If they are to be planted in a shrub border where every plant is to be allowed enough room for normal development, the smaller kinds may be allowed 4 to 5 ft. and the taller ones 6 to 7 ft. at least. Pruning should be done immediately after transplanting.

When shall I prune barberry? Barberry ordinarily requires little if any pruning, except in those cases when a special shape is desired, as in hedges, or in a formal garden. Then the practice is to shear it when the new shoots have almost completed their growth in late spring.

I want to drastically prune my barberry. Should it be done in spring or fall? If it has to be cut back, do it in the spring. It may suffer from winter injury if done in the fall.

If Japanese Barberry bush is trimmed to the ground in December, is it possible to transplant same in the spring to another spot in garden? If any small part of the stems were left above ground, you may safely move it in the spring. If cut clear to the ground, then wait until new growth starts.

How can the Truehedge Columnberry Barberry be raised from seed? This plant is what botanists term a "clon." It will not reproduce itself from seed.

How can I best propagate Japanese Barberry? The simplest method is from seeds, which should be stored in a cool place in moist sand over winter, and sown very early in spring. Or they may be rooted from cuttings taken in July and kept in a closed cold frame until rooted.

BAYBERRY (MYRICA)

When is proper time to transplant bayberry bushes? (New Jersey.) Spring; or, in New Jersey, early autumn.

Wild bayberries were planted on the north side of house. Will these grow? Not a good situation. They prefer open situations, and will take only very light, partial shade.

What is proper cultivation of bayberry? Where may it be obtained?

It is by nature a shrub of open, sunny, sandy coastal tracts. Therefore, in cultivation, it should be kept out of shade. It is a poor-soil shrub. Plant it, balled and burlapped, in the spring, in non-alkaline soil. Few nurseries grow it. One may have to obtain it from dealers in native plants.

BEARBERRY (ARCTOSTAPHYLOS)

Is Bearberry (Arctostaphylos uva-ursi) a good ground cover to plant just back of a dry retaining wall? Yes, one of the best if there's plenty of sun and the soil is well drained and sandy. Be sure to get only pot-grown plants from a reliable nursery; wild plants are *very* difficult to transplant.

What conditions are necessary for growth of Bearberry? Full sun or light shade, well drained and aerated, very sandy soil, slightly acid.

BEAUTYBUSH (KOLKWITZIA)

I've heard about kolkwitzia. What is it like? Beautybush is top ranking. It suggests weigela, but is finer by far. Flowers are smaller, more abundant, and a pale pink with yellow throat, in early June. Slow-growing. Ultimate height to 9 ft.

Last year I planted a Beautybush. It has not bloomed and has thrown out only one new shoot. It gets morning sun and careful attention. Should it not have flowered? Next spring prune back the one shoot. It will probably branch out and begin to form a solid shrub. It might flower the following spring. The Beautybush often doesn't flower at an early age.

What kind of fertilizer should be used on a Beautybush to get it to bloom? No need for special fertilizer. This shrub often does not flower at an early age. Wait. It is worth waiting for.

Should a Beautybush (Kolkwitzia amabilis) be pruned? If so, when? If the bush is crowded, cut away the oldest flowering branches to the ground immediately the flowers have faded. Otherwise, little or no pruning required.

How can I start new plants from my Beautybush? Either from seeds, which take several years to reach flowering stage; or from cuttings. Cuttings must be of soft wood, i.e., taken from the tips of the shoots while they are still growing actively. If taken at a later stage, they will form a large callus but generally fail to form roots. Softwood cuttings can only be rooted in a shaded cold frame or glass-covered box.

BENZOIN

At approximately what age does Lindera benzoin (Spicebush) flower? Does it make a good screening shrub? How far apart should

it be planted for that effect? Is it thoroughly winter hardy in Connecticut? It begins to flower when 5 to 8 years old. In New England it grows to about 8 to 10 ft. tall. Makes a fair screen, with plants set 5 to 6 ft. apart. It is relatively pest free and requires no special attention, but is not completely hardy in the most severe winter.

BLUEBERRY

I want to grow blueberries for their ornamental foliage. Any special soil requirements? Make soil acid by mixing with it rotted oak leaves (which see), rotted pine needles, or peatmoss. Maintaining a 3-in. layer of oak leaves or peatmoss on soil over roots is a good plan to help keep soil moist.

BROOM (CYTISUS)

What is the scientific name of the shrub called "Scotch Broom"? It has yellow flowers similar to sweetpeas, with the seed borne in a pod like peas. Has it commercial possibilities? *Cytisus scoparius.* Probably no commercial possibilities except as an ornamental. Is used in a limited way for making brooms, in basketry, for thatching, etc.

What soil is best for Scotch Broom? It succeeds well in many places in poor, almost barren sand dunes, roadsides, and embankments. It prefers a light, sandy soil, non-alkaline. The admixture of a little peat will be helpful. Plant in well-drained, open places. Start with small plants—pot-grown, if you can get them.

BUTTERFLYBUSH (BUDDLEIA)

Which kinds of buddleia bloom in late summer? There are several, but the varieties of *Buddleia davidi,* with flowers ranging from mauve to deep purple, are the best.

Which buddleia is the most reliably hardy? *Buddleia alternifolia,* which has short, dense clusters of fragrant blue flowers in June.

Where would be the best place to plant buddleia? In a sunny place or shady place? Makes its best growth in full sun.

How should buddleias be planted? Buddleia, dug from a nursery, should be planted in spring. Probably the roots will have been roughly pruned when the plant is received, but before planting they should have any ragged ends cut clean. Plant an inch or two deeper than previously, and pack the soil carefully between the roots. Cut the stems back to 2 ins. from the point where growth started the previous spring. Give full sun.

Is it too late to cut branches from Buddleia in April? I understand they should be cut late in November. Spring is the correct time to prune buddleias. They should not be cut back in the fall because of the danger that a severe winter will injure them and necessitate still more pruning in the spring.

Is it advisable to debud the first spikes of buddleias?   No particular advantage to be gained from this practice.

Should butterflybush be cut down every year in Pennsylvania? In your section the effects of winter are almost certain to make pruning necessary. Wait until the buds begin to grow in the spring, then cut the top down to vigorous shoots.

Is Buddleia alternifolia pruned in the same way as the butterfly-bush buddleias?   No. Its flowers are produced on old wood; therefore pruning should be done immediately *after* flowering, merely thinning out crowded shoots and shaping up bush.

What care should be given buddleia (butterflybush or summer-lilac) for winter protection?   A mulch of littery material around the base is all that may be needed. It is advisable not to cut the tops back until spring.

Can butterflybushes be grown from slips? If so, how is it done? When are cuttings made?   Yes. The cuttings, 4 to 5 ins. long, are made in July or August, from side shoots. Cut off the bottom pair of leaves, and make a clean cut through the stem, just below the joint from which the leaves were cut. Insert ⅓ of their length in sand, in a propagating case.

CARYOPTERIS

What is caryopteris like?   The one commonly grown (*Caryopteris incana*) is a shrub bearing bluish flowers. It is not fully hardy in the North, where it is treated as a perennial herb.

How should one prune caryopteris, and when?   Wait until the buds swell in spring and then cut back each branch to a strong-growing bud. If winter killed to ground, remove dead stalks in early spring.

CHASTETREE (VITEX)

Is chastetree really a tree? Mine is more like a shrub.   It may develop into a small tree in a favorable climate. In the North its young branches often are killed by low temperatures, which make it assume a shrubby habit.

Does chastetree (Vitex macrophylla) require acid soil?   It appears to reach its best development in a sandy peat. This would indicate a preference for a non-alkaline but not highly acid soil. It grows readily enough in average, light garden soils.

How and when is proper time to prune chastetree (Vitex macrophylla)?   This blossoms on shoots of the current season and should be cut back in spring. Wait until growth begins (it is a late starter) and cut back the branches to strong-growing buds.

COTONEASTER

What are some of the best cotoneasters for border planting?
C. hupehensis, 6 ft. high; *C. salicifolia floccosa,* 10 ft.; *C. zabeli-miniata,* 6 to 8 ft.

We are looking for a cotoneaster which is lower growing than C. horizontalis. What do you suggest? *C. adpressa* grows only 9 to 12 ins. high; has glossy berries in fall like *C. horizontalis,* but it is hardier.

How can I grow the cotoneasters successfully? Give them a sunny position, in well-drained soil. *Protect young plants from rabbits* in rural districts.

CRAPEMYRTLE (LAGERSTROEMIA)

What kind of soil does crapemyrtle need? It has no special requirements, and will thrive in any ordinary garden soil.

What is the proper care of crapemyrtle as to fertilizer, trimming, watering, and winter protection, if needed? (Maryland.) Crapemyrtle has no special soil preferences. Fertilize by mulching with rotted manure in the fall, which will also help protect the roots against winter injury. If in an exposed location, cover the top with cornstalks. Shorten shoots of the preceding year ½ to ⅔ in the spring. Cut back flowering shoots when the blossoms have faded. Water only during droughty periods.

Why did my 8-year-old crapemyrtle fail to bloom the past summer? Two of them have always bloomed beautifully until last season. (Kentucky.) The chances are that they were injured by the very severe winter.

Can you advise why my crapemyrtle shrubs do not bloom? (Brooklyn, New York.) I have had these shrubs for 4 years and protect them each winter. They bloomed only the first year after planting. Winter injury and not enough heat during the growing season. They bloom freely about once in 10 years as far North as this. Grow in the warmest, sunniest situation; cut back in the spring to strong-growing shoots.

The crapemyrtle, an old bush, very tall and about 10 ft. from an oak, is thrifty as to foliage but no blooms. We have a stratum of clay soil but have put in many tons of topsoil and plenty of fertilizer. What is wrong? The proximity of the oak may be a factor in the failure of the crapemyrtle to bloom. Omit nitrogenous fertilizers and try the effect of an application of superphosphate to the soil over the roots, at the rate of 6 oz. per sq. yd. Maybe the soil is too acid.

Can a crapemyrtle be protected sufficiently to winter safely out of doors in a climate where the temperature falls to 10 to 15° below zero? No.

How shall I care for crapemyrtle, and do they need pruning? (California.) Not satisfactory in southern California. Pruning consists of cutting back the shoots, immedately after flowering, to encourage new growth and further flowering.

CYDONIA

See Quince.

DAPHNE

What is the name of the daphne which blooms very early? February Daphne (*D. mezereum*). It is valued for its early blooming, and lilac-purple fragrant flowers. Height may reach 3 ft.; stiff, erect; deciduous.

Why do the leaves of a Daphne mezereum turn yellow and drop off during the months of August and September? It is characteristic of this species to shed its leaves during drought in late summer.

DEUTZIA

Are there any low-growing deutzias? If so, when do they bloom? *Deutzia gracilis,* with white flowers in May; *Deutzia rosea* has pinkish flowers, otherwise resembles the preceding.

What are the advantages of the tall deutzias? Are they interesting in winter? Their flowers are showy; otherwise their foliage and their branch pattern are uninteresting.

When should I transplant deutzias? In spring or early fall.

When is the proper time to trim deutzias? They should be pruned by cutting out worn-out and crowded flowering shoots immediately the blossoms have faded.

DOGWOOD (CORNUS)

See also under Decorative Flowering Trees.

Which dogwood shrubs have colored twigs in winter? *Cornus alba* (Tartarian D.), bright red twigs; *Cornus stolonifera* (Red Osier D.), deep red; *Cornus stolonifera flaviramea* (Goldentwig B.), yellow; *Cornus paniculata* (Gray D.), gray; *Cornus sanguinea* (Bloodtwig D.), dark blood-red; *Cornus sanguinea viridissima* (Greentwig D.), green.

What color are the berries of the dogwood shrubs? Tartarian Dogwood, whitish; Silky Dogwood, pale blue; Bloodtwig Dogwood, black; Pagoda Dogwood, dark blue; Red Osier Dogwood, white or bluish; Gray Dogwood, white.

How are the shrubby dogwoods used to best advantage? In masses as woodland border, or as an informal hedgerow planting of mixed shrubs.

I have had a Cornus mas (Cornelian Cherry) for 3 years, but it has not grown. Can you prescribe? Takes a few years to become established. If you have given it good soil, fertilized it occasionally with well-rotted manure or a complete commercial fertilizer, and given it plenty of water, you have done the best you can for it.

ENKIANTHUS

What is Enkianthus campanulatus like? A graceful, upright shrub with an ultimate height of 12 to 15 ft., but slow-growing. In May and June it bears drooping clusters of yellowish bell-shaped flowers. Its chief value is in its foliage, glossy turning brilliant orange and scarlet.

What deciduous shrub with good autumn color can we put in among the evergreens at the east and west side of our house? *Enkianthus perulatus,* growing to 6 ft., would be a good choice because, like the broad-leaved evergreens, it prefers acid soil. Use *E. campanulatus* if a taller shrub is required.

EUONYMUS

I have seen a shrub which has curious corky flanged bark on its branches. Its leaves turn deep rose in the autumn. What is it? Winged Euonymus (*E. alatus*).

FORSYTHIA

What different kinds of forsythia are there? About 5 species; several varieties. Among the best are, urnlike in form *F. intermedia spectabilis;* and fountainlike (or drooping), *F. suspensa.*

There is such a difference in the number of flowers on forsythias that I wonder if it is due to soil or location; or if there is more than one kind of plant. (Arkansas.) There are several kinds of forsythia. *Forsythia intermedia spectabilis* is a very showy one.

What is the hardiest forsythia? A species called *F. ovata,* earliest to bloom; flowers, however, are less effective and more amber in color.

When is the best time to transplant forsythia? Does it require cultivation? This shrub may be safely transplanted in spring or fall, any time that it is leafless. Cultivation around newly transplanted shrubs for a period of 1 or 2 years is decidedly beneficial.

Our forsythia had a late fall bloom this year. Will that impair the spring bloom? Yes, for the flower buds are formed in the fall, and if some open then the bloom the following spring will be just so much reduced.

Why do forsythias bloom around the bottom of bushes only? Because in cold areas the flower buds—present all winter long—are killed by low temperatures except where they are protected by a blanket of snow.

I have forsythia on southwest corner of our house, about 6 years old; used to bloom in spring; now blooms in October and November. Why? The chances are the autumns have been unusually mild in this particular location.

Why doesn't my forsythia bloom? The buds seem to dry up. They have been killed by winter cold. Try *Forsythia ovata*. This is the most hardy of all the forsythias.

How and when should forsythia be pruned? Cut out some of the oldest branches annually, making the cut not far from the base of the bush. This can be done in February, and the cut branches brought indoors and placed in water to force them into bloom; or wait until the bush has flowered, and prune it immediately the flowers have faded.

How do you prune forsythia when grown too high? Cut it back to the required height immediately after flowering.

How can I keep forsythia bushes from getting so awfully straggling? Make them more compact by pinching out the tips of strong-growing shoots during late spring and early summer. Comparatively compact varieties, such as *F. viridissima* and *F. ovata,* are preferable if there is an objection to a straggling habit.

Can forsythia or goldenbells be pruned in fall as well as in spring? Usually the shrub gets very awkward after spring pruning. Forsythia produces its flowers on preceding year's growth, and any cutting back during the time it is dormant results in a diminution of the floral display in the spring. Try pinching out the tips of strong-growing shoots during the growing season.

When is proper time to trim Weeping Forsythia? The beauty of this variety is in its long, trailing growth. It should not be trimmed in the usual sense of cutting back the tips. Thinning out crowded branches is permissible in the spring immediately the flowers have faded.

HAZELNUT

Are there any garden forms of the European hazel nut that are grown for their beauty rather than the production of nuts? There are two outstanding ones. One is a variety of the filbert (*Corylus maxima purpurea*). The other is the European hazel (*Corylus avellana* var. *contorta*), which is interesting rather than beautiful. The leaves of *purpurea* are dark purple, especially in early spring; and in *contorta* the stems are twisted and curled in a way that makes it an excellent conversation piece.

HONEYSUCKLE (LONICERA)

Do the honeysuckles have berries?   Yes. Amur, Morrow, and Tatarian Honeysuckles have red berries. There are also yellow-fruited varieties of the two last named. Mistletoe Honeysuckle has white fruit.

Can you mention a few desirable honeysuckle bushes?   Fragrant Bush Honeysuckle—April, white; Morrow Bush Honeysuckle—May, cream-yellow; Blueleaf Bush Honeysuckle—May, pink; Amur Bush Honeysuckle—May, white; and Tatarian Bush Honeysuckle—May, rose and white.

How can I best propagate bush honeysuckle?   In order to have plants of uniform kind, it is best to root the plants from cuttings. Many of them root quite readily from hardwood cuttings, and this is the simplest way. Or they may be raised from cuttings taken in July and kept in a closed cold frame until rooted.

HYDRANGEA

Varieties

Will you tell me what is the real name of the hydrangea with pink or blue flowers?   Bigleaf Hydrangea (*Hydrangea macrophylla*). There are many varieties of this species, both with blue flowers and with pink flowers. Rosea is a popular variety with pink flowers.

What are some hydrangeas other than the usual Peegee and Snow Hill?   Try Panicle Hydrangea, the parent of Peegee, with flowers more opened out, not so "top-heavy"; Climbing Hydrangea (*H. petiolaris*), as vine or shrub; Oakleaf Hydrangea, with interesting foliage.

Culture

What exposure to sun should hydrangeas have?   The common species do best in full sun, although they will stand slight shade.

Do Oakleaf Hydrangeas need a shady or sunny location?   Shady.

What plant foods do hydrangeas need and when?   They require no special fertilizer treatment. The use of well-rotted manure or a mixed commercial fertilizer in the spring is satisfactory.

Can a hydrangea tree be transplanted in my state in the month of October or November? (New York.)   Yes.

Would transplanting a large hydrangea into another section of the garden cause injury to the plant?   No, not permanently, if properly done. Transplant in early spring.

When is the best time to move hydrangeas?   Either fall or early spring for very hardy types; spring in the case of "French" hydrangeas.

Should a potted hydrangea with a large beautiful blue flower which came from a hothouse be transplanted to the outdoors? (Kansas.) No, not in Kansas. It would not live over winter.

My mother gave us a 4-year-old hydrangea to transplant in our yard. Could you tell me what to do to make it bloom next year? Protect canes from winter injury by covering them in the fall with cornstalks or something similar. Do not cut back the canes in the spring any more than is necessary to remove injured tips.

Does Peegee Hydrangea require any special care? I don't seem to be able to grow them. One of easiest shrubs to grow. Needs no special care.

Why do the leaves on my pink hydrangeas appear yellow and mottled? The soil is too sweet or alkaline. Have it tested and add aluminum sulfate to reduce the pH value to 6.8 or lower.

What would cause a hydrangea to stop flowering after having bloomed beautifully for 3 seasons? Too much shade, poor soil, over-fertilization, improper pruning, and winter injury are some of the more important factors that affect the flowering of hydrangeas.

Why do my French hydrangeas bloom some years and not others? (New York.) Cold injury to the flower buds is the most common reason for failure to flower. The flower buds are formed in the fall, and if the winter is severe they may be killed even though the plant is not seriously injured.

Why has my hydrangea plant (French type) not bloomed for 15 years, even though it grows well and is kept pruned? (Massachusetts.) Undoubtedly the flower buds which form in the fall are killed during the winter. Give more winter protection by covering with leaves, held in place by chicken wire, etc. Pruning at the wrong time of year (each spring or fall) will prevent flowering by removing the flower buds. Prune immediately *after* blooming (late July).

After blooming should the old flowers be cut from hydrangeas? Not necessarily, unless they are unsightly.

Do hydrangeas bloom on old or new wood? Some common species, such as *Hydrangea paniculata grandiflora* and the Hills of Snow type, bloom on new wood, and may be pruned in the early spring. On a few other types, particularly the common greenhouse or French (*Hydrangea macrophylla,* formerly called *H. opuloides*) varieties, the buds originate near the tips of the canes formed the preceding year, and should be pruned *after* flowering, or not at all.

How near to the ground do you prune hydrangeas? This depends on the species. *Hydrangea arborescens* can be cut off at the ground each year. (See preceding answer.)

When is the proper time to cut back a blue hydrangea? This species (often called French hydrangea) should be pruned immediately after flowering. Pruning in the fall or in the early spring will reduce the number of flowers or prevent flowering.

What is the best way to prune a standard hydrangea?   Since round, uniform tops are desired, all branches should be cut back so that only 2 or 3 buds are left at the base of each old stem. Pruning should be done on this type (*Hydrangea paniculata grandiflora*) in the early spring.

How should Peegee Hydrangeas be pruned?   This is the strong-growing shrubby type which sometimes almost attains the dimensions of a small tree. It blossoms on shoots of the current season, and if large heads of bloom are desired, the shoots of the preceding year should be cut back to one bud in the spring.

When should the Oakleaf Hydrangea be pruned?   Immediately after flowering. This is another species, like the French type, in which the flower buds form in the fall. Since the buds are likely to be injured during severe winters, the plants should be protected.

I never get any blooms on my French hydrangeas. Is this because I cut them to the ground every spring?   Yes. Many varieties of French hydrangea fail to bloom if severely pruned in spring. Merely cut back the tips of canes injured by winter.

Why do my hydrangeas have so many leaves and so few flowers?   Too much nitrogenous fertilizer and improper pruning may encourage the growth of foliage instead of flowers. In warm climates the common French hydrangeas may not set flower buds in the fall because of high temperatures.

Why do not the pink and blue hydrangeas flower for me outdoors? (Connecticut.)   Some bear flowers only on last summer's branches. These will not flower outdoors in your climate. Some flower on the current summer's growth; these should flower in your garden. The 2 types are not clearly distinguished in books and catalogues. Search out plants which bloom outdoors in your locality, in gardens or nurseries, and obtain stock of these.

What care should be given blue hydrangeas for the winter? (Eastern exposure.)   Wrap in burlap or straw, and mulch soil heavily with leaves.

Should hydrangeas be covered during winter in this section? (New York.)   The blue- and pink-flowering hydrangeas only need be protected in winter in this locality.

Can blue hydrangeas be propagated?   Yes, by cuttings. However, the flowers may appear as pink when grown under different soil conditions.

Color (How to Change)

What causes pink hydrangeas to turn blue?   Experiments have conclusively demonstrated that the presence of aluminum in the tissue of hydrangea flowers causes the blue coloration.

Can all kinds of hydrangeas be made to produce blue flowers? No. Only the pink varieties of the common greenhouse or French hydrangea (*Hydrangea macrophylla*) will turn blue.

Could the Oakleaf Hydrangeas and Climbing Hydrangeas be made to have pink or blue flowers?   No.

Will my hydrangeas be blue if I plant them in an acid soil?   Pink varieties of the common greenhouse or French hydrangea produce blue flowers when grown in acid soil (pH 5.5 or below). Soil acidity is an indirect factor in the production of blue flowers because of its relationship to the solubility of aluminum in the soil. The aluminum is soluble and can be absorbed by the plants when the soil is acid (pH 5.5 or below). In neutral or slightly alkaline soil the aluminum is insoluble.

What chemical will change the color of hydrangea flowers to blue? Aluminum sulfate is the most effective chemical, but common alum (potassium alum) will also bring about the blue color.

Can dry aluminum sulfate be mixed with the soil to produce blue flowers?   Dry aluminum sulfate may be used in the spring at the rate of 1 lb. for each square yard of ground area. It may be necessary to repeat the treatment for several years. Aluminum sulfate may also be mixed with the soil when it is prepared. The soil should be tested to determine its reaction (pH). If the soil is neutral, mix in thoroughly ½ lb. for each bushel.

How does one make hydrangeas growing in pots have blue flowers? Water 5 to 8 times, at weekly intervals, with a 2½ per cent solution of aluminum sulfate (1 lb. to 5 gals. water). Use 1 gal. to each plant.

If rusty nails are put in the soil will a hydrangea produce blue flowers?   Rusty nails or any other form of metallic iron has no effect upon flower color. Potassium alum (common alum), however, will induce blue coloration.

How can I make a blue-flowering hydrangea produce pink flowers? The soil should be made neutral or very slightly alkaline (pH 6.7 to 7.2) by the addition of lime. Too much lime will cause mottling of the leaves, as the result of a lack of iron. The required amount of lime should be deeply and thoroughly mixed with the soil. It is best to lift the plants in the fall, shake off as much soil as possible, and replant it in the especially prepared lime soil.

How can one prevent discoloring of hydrangea flowers?   Flowers of intermediate hues between pink and blue are produced when the soil reaction is between pH 6 and 6.5. If pure blue flowers are desired, add aluminum sulfate to make the soil more acid (pH 5.5). For pink flowers, add lime to bring the soil reaction to pH 6.8 to 7.0.

KERRIA

What is Kerria japonica? This shrub grows 4 to 8 ft. high and produces bright yellow flowers. Variety pleniflora is double and more vigorous. Both have green stems. It is a shrub of easy culture, and does well in part shade.

I have an old kerria shrub, but only 1 or 2 branches bloom. How can I treat or prune it? Winter injury or crowded branches may be responsible for its failure to bloom. Cut out weak shoots in spring and remove flowering branches as soon as the flowers have faded.

How can I best propagate Kerria japonica pleniflora? Either by means of cuttings in July, which must be kept in close, humid, shady conditions until rooted; or by hardwood cuttings, taken in late fall, buried in the soil over winter, and set in the garden in early spring.

LILAC (SYRINGA)

Types and Varieties

What are the best lilacs (French hybrids) in each color? A *few* of the "best" lilacs are: white—Edith Cavell (double) and Marie Finon; violet—Cavour and Marechal Lannes (double); blue—President Lincoln, Olivier de Serres (double); lilac—Marengo, President Fallieres (double); pink—Lucie Baltet, Macrostachya; magenta—Congo, Marceau; purple—Ludwig Spaeth, Mrs. W. E. Marshall.

Are there ever-blooming lilac bushes? No.

What are so-called "own-root" lilacs? Those lilacs so propagated that the roots and tops are from one continuous piece of plant, i.e., not grafted with two pieces grown together as one. Hence, they are not susceptible to the serious graft-blight disease. "Own-root" lilacs are the best kind to buy.

Would you consider a Syringa japonica (Japanese lilac) a good lawn specimen tree? How tall does it grow? Yes. It may grow 40 ft. high and more but usually is under 20 ft.

What is the difference between species lilacs and the other, or common, lilacs? Lilac species are the wild lilacs of the world found growing in uninhabited places. The "common lilacs" are usually considered either natural hybrids, which have appeared in gardens, or (more frequently) as the direct result of hybridizing efforts.

Why are French hybrid lilacs so called? Because hybridizers in France have had much to do with their production.

Culture

What kind of soil and nourishment are best for lilacs? Any fair, not too heavy, well-drained, alkaline garden soil. If needed, every other year apply a 3-in. mulch of cow manure, alternated with a dose of lime. Do not feed them unless the need is indicated, lest they grow too tall and must be cut back.

Please advise when to plant a lilac bush; spring or fall?   Either. Lilacs are among the easiest of plants to transplant and will grow under almost any conditions.

I planted lilac the last of November. Was it too late?   Probably; but if ground didn't freeze until late December this date for planting should have been satisfactory.

Can a large lilac bush be moved and continue blooming—that is, without waiting several more years?   Yes, if moved with a large ball of soil about the roots, and if the branches are pruned back ⅓ in the operation.

How long do lilacs have to be planted before blooming?   This depends on many things, such as soil, skill of transplanting in the soil, etc. Some plants, grown properly, will bloom profusely when only 4 ft. tall. Others may take years before they will start to bloom.

I transplanted a lilac bush. Should the leaves be stripped at the bottom in the spring or left alone?   Always prune off some of the branches when transplanting; approximately ⅓ of the total branches is a good average. Stripping off the leaves is not a good practice in this case.

What is the ultimate height of the French lilacs?   Depends on the variety; 10 to 25 ft.

Which lilacs, if any, will thrive with only forenoon sunshine?   All lilacs need sunshine. The less sunshine they have the fewer the flowers.

Will you give me information pertaining to the culture, pruning, and general care of own-root, French hybrid lilacs, for specimen bloom? I have a collection of young plants comprising 12 varieties.   The general care of these lilacs is no different from that of any others. For specimen blooms, cutting out a few of the weakest flowering shoots in winter is helpful. Read other questions and answers.

Why do the leaves on new lilac bushes turn brown?   Transplanting injury, lack of sufficient water, or too much fertilizer.

We have lilacs of different species, some more than 10 years old. The foliage always looks clean, but the plants never have any buds or flowers. Neighbors have flowers on their lilacs. Why not ours?   When lilacs fail to bloom, 4 things can be tried, since every lilac should bloom if grown properly: 1. Thin out some of the branches at the base of the plant. 2. Root-prune by digging a 2-ft. ditch around the plants. 3. When the soil is removed from the ditch mix with it a generous amount of superphosphate (about 8 oz. to every 3 ft. of ditch) and return the soil to the ditch. 4. Apply lime if soil is acid. One of these methods, or a combination of all, should force the plant to bloom. Some lilacs, like many other plants, are alternate-blooming, flowering profusely one year and sparsely or not at all the next. This, unfortunately, is to be expected.

Why do lilacs fail to bloom even though flower buds are formed? This may be due to severe drought in the late summer after the buds have been formed.

We have old-fashioned lilacs, large clumps 8 or 10 years old, that have only 5 or 6 blossoms each year. Can you suggest what is cause for not blooming freely? Probably too many young suckers at the base. Cut out most of these and you probably will be repaid with good blooms.

I have some Persian Lilacs, also French Lilacs, none of which seem to do well. What kind of soil and conditions do they require? They need a good alkaline soil with sufficient moisture throughout the summer. Try applying lime in spring and a 3-in. mulch of manure in fall to see if they help.

Pruning

How does one prune lilacs to keep them a decent height and still have blooms? Do not give all the pruning in one year, but over a period of several years. Do not allow them to become too dense, for this forces them to grow high. Allow each branch room to grow, and "top" it at the 6-ft. height.

Should lilacs be pruned? Yes, prune out most of the young suckers and all of the dead or diseased wood. Some of the older branches could be cut out also, to allow more light to reach the branches in the center of the plant. Prune just *after* blooming.

How much pruning should lilacs have? When is the time to to it? Just enough pruning to keep the center open, to cut out dead and diseased wood, keep down the suckers, and to remove the dead flower stalks. This may best be done immediately *after* they are through blooming.

My lilacs are 10 ft. tall. How can I bring them down to eye-level height? In 2 ways: 1. Cut them down to within 2 or 3 feet of the ground and so start entirely new plants. 2. If this is too drastic, do the same thing, but over a period of 3 years, hence thinning out only ⅓ of the branches each year and allowing for continuous bloom.

Will severe pruning force old-fashioned lilacs to give more bloom? Yes, it may; but do not expect flowers for a year or two.

What is the best way to cut back very old, tall, uncared-for lilac bushes? Cut them down nearly to the ground.

What is the best way to start growth again on lilac bushes—all the growth seems to be at the top, leaving the lower part very unsightly. Can it be done? Yes; cut back to within a foot of the ground, and start all over again.

What can be done, if anything, to prevent lilacs from suckering?
There is no preventive measure, but once started this suckering habit
should be stopped immediately merely by cutting out a majority of the
young suckers.

Should any suckers be allowed on French Hybrid Lilacs?   Yes, if
they have been propagated on their own roots. However, if they have
been grafted, the suckers from the understock may prove to be either
California Privet or some very different lilac. Therefore *all* should be
cut out of grafted plants.

**My French Hybrid Lilacs were propagated by cuttings and are grow-
ing on their "own roots." Can I allow suckers to grow?**   Yes—to
some extent. A few of these can be allowed to grow to replace the
older branches which are cut out or to allow the bush to increase in
size. Do not allow all to grow, however, as the bush will become too
dense, and flower formation will be decreased.

**Is it necessary, or better, for the bushes, to cut off dead flowers
from lilacs before they bloom again?**   Yes. Cut them off as soon as
they are finished blooming. This prevents seed formation and allows
more nourishment to go to the flower buds for the next year.

**What is the proper time and method of root-pruning lilacs to bring
them into bloom?**   Dig a 2-ft. trench in spring slightly within the outside limit of the branches, in this way cutting all roots encountered.

How can you stop lilacs from spreading into your neighbor's yard?
Sink a concrete barrier down in the soil, or continually dig and cut
roots on that side of the plant.

Propagation

How do you start new bushes from an old lilac bush?   The best
method is to raise a new stock from cuttings; or, if it is not a grafted
plant, rooted suckers may be dug up, tops cut back ½, and planted.

**I have a lilac bush "President Grevy"; one branch has flowers of a
different color, pale pink with a yellow center. How can I propagate
this sport? It is not from the rootstock, as it appears on a bush 10 ft.
high.**   Either by cuttings, or by grafting or budding it on California
Privet. This privet is not recommended as an understock, but in order
to work up a stock of the "sport" that has occurred on your lilac,
you would be justified in using it until you could obtain enough plants
on their own roots, i.e., from cuttings.

When should lilac cuttings be made?   While the shoots are still
growing, usually about the middle of May. Make cuttings 5 to 6 ins.
long; remove bottom leaves; make a clean cut through stem ¼ in.
below place where leaves were attached. However, lilacs are sometimes raised from hardwood cuttings (taken in early winter) which are
planted in boxes of sand and kept in cool but frostproof sheds until
spring, when rooting takes place.

How is lilac best rooted from cuttings? Outdoors, cold frame, or greenhouse? Either in propagating cases in a greenhouse, or in a shaded cold frame. The cuttings are placed in sand and kept in a close, humid atmosphere until rooted. (See preceding question.)

How is Persian Lilac propagated? Either from seeds sown in spring, or from cuttings in May. Also from suckers.

Will lilacs root from the buds on the stems if placed in sand? It is possible that this method of propagation might be successful if cut off with a sliver of old wood, with leaf still attached.

Pests and Diseases

The leaves of my lilacs are a gray-green instead of true shade. What is the remedy? The chances are they have mildew. This happens especially in the late summer or during a moist season. It is not serious and can be ignored. Dusting with powdered sulfur as soon as mildew appears is the remedy.

What is lilac "graft blight"? This is a disease occurring on plants which have been grafted on California Privet understock. A plant which has this disease will look sickly, have yellowish leaves, and may die even in good growing weather. The only remedy is to dig up and destroy such a plant.

How can one eliminate chlorosis in lilacs? This is not well understood. Chlorosis occurs even on healthy plants growing in normal soil during dry seasons. During the following year the same chlorotic plants may appear healthy. About all one can do is to see that they have some fertilizer and lime, and water thoroughly during dry spells.

MIMOSA

Will a mimosa tree survive a Michigan winter? The hardiest mimosa—*Albizzia julibrissin rosea*—might be tried in southern Michigan. This proves fairly hardy in Boston, Massachusetts. The mimosa of the South will not be hardy.

Are you supposed to prune mimosa trees? Yes, when they require it to make them shapely. Where they grow rapidly, they incline to be too flexible and "weak-backed" unless pruned.

MOCKORANGE (PHILADELPHUS)

Which are some of the best mockoranges? *Philadelphus coronarius* (the old-fashioned syringa); also certain Lemoine hybrids as, for instance, Avalanche and Mont Blanc, with single flowers; Virginale, semi-double; Girandole and Boule d'Argent (double); and certain *cymosus* hybrids like Voie Lactee, Conquete, Banniere, Norma, and Rosace.

Will you give me a statement on the comparative merits (ease of

growth, hardiness, floriferousness, fragrance, shape, and height) of the following hybrid mockoranges: **Banniere, nivalis, Norma, Pavillon Blanc, Pyramidale, and Voie Lactee?** These are all of approximately equal hardiness—not reliably hardy north of Philadelphia—but they are being grown as far North as Boston. They are all about 5 to 7 ft. tall; equally easy to grow; but vary in beauty and amount of flowers and fragrance. Using another hybrid, "Avalanche," as a basis for good flower and the old-fashioned fragrant *P. coronarius* as best for fragrance, and rating these both at 10 points, the varieties could be rated as follows: Banniere—flower, 5; fragrance, 4; *nivalis*—flower, 3; fragrance, 6; Norma—flower, 6; fragrance, 4; Pavillon Blanc— flower, 2; fragrance, 0; Pyramidale—flower, 3; fragrance, 0; Voie Lactee—flower, 2; fragrance, 2.

I once saw some mockoranges with large double flowers. What might they have been? Virginal, or perhaps Argentine; beautiful but less hardy than some.

Why don't my mockoranges, planted last spring, bloom? They have so much brush in them. They need a year or two in order to recuperate from the shock of transplanting. Thin out a few of the branches if they are too crowded.

Although pruned, why does Mockorange Virginal not bush out, but grow only lanky shoots at the top? This variety is naturally gawky. It can be made a little more compact by pinching out the tips of lanky shoots when they are actively growing.

How should I trim an overgrown mockorange bush? Thin it out during winter by cutting the oldest branches as near the ground line as possible. Shorten those remaining about ⅓, if it seems necessary. This drastic treatment will result in few, if any, flowers the following spring.

When and how is the best way to prune a mockorange shrub? Immediately after flowering by cutting out the oldest and weakest shoots, making the cuts as near the ground line as possible.

PRIVET

See also Hedges, this section.

If a privet is not pruned, what kind of flowers does it have? And berries? Cream-white flowers in small panicles somewhat like lilacs, but with a distressing odor in midsummer. Berries are black.

What is the name of a privet which forms a broad bush? Regel Privet—*Ligustrum obtusifolium regelianum.*

What is the best time to prune Amur River Privet? When grown as a bush, needs no pruning. As a hedge it should be sheared when the new growth is 6 to 8 ins. long. Repeat shearing in August.

QUINCE, FLOWERING (CHAENOMELES (CYDONIA) JAPONICA)

What colors are to be had in flowering quinces? When do they bloom? The following are some varieties of *Chaenomeles lagenaria:* Nivalis—white; Double Scarlet; Corallina—salmon-pink; Baltzi— rosy pink; Columbia—deep rose; Marcocarpa—red; Rubra Grandiflora—deep crimson. One known as Spitfire, a newcomer, is noteworthy because of its narrow form and upright growth. It can be used for accent or for hedges. Its flowers are deep crimson.

What kinds of flowering quince bushes are there? Are some varieties taller than others? The tall shrub *Chaenomeles* (also called *Cydonia lagenaria*) grows to about 6 ft. high. The dwarf species (*C. japonica*) is a broad, low shrub, growing to 3 ft. high. A still lower variety (*C. j. alpina*) spreads into a low patch seldom over 1½ ft. high.

I have a flowering quince (red) that does not bloom, although the plant is 6 years old. The sprout was taken from a beautiful bush which blooms each year. This plant has never bloomed and it's planted beside 2 other quinces that bloom each year. Why? It may well be that the original plant was a grafted plant and the understock was the common quince, which blooms only after reaching some size. Would suggest that you check the 2 in foliage. If they differ, discard yours. If they do not differ, check them again when the parent is in flower next spring.

The blossoms of my flowering quince are produced toward the center of the bush and are not well displayed. Can this be avoided? Yes. Prune the bush by shortening the new shoots as they are produced throughout the summer. This will cause the formation of flower spurs near the tips of the branches.

I have a shrub in my garden that I have been told is a variety of flowering quince. It has never bloomed and I was wondering what could be done to force it to bloom. Would pruning help? Summer pruning will help, as described in the preceding answer. The incorporation of superphosphate in the soil over the roots, at the rate of 6 oz. per sq. yd., may be helpful. Root-pruning (which see) should be resorted to if these measures fail.

How can I slip my flowering quince? The flowering quince may be treated in the same manner as flowering almond (which see).

Is the fruit of the so-called "burning bush," or Chaenomeles japonica, edible? It is very sour, but can be used in making jellies. Incidentally "burning bush" is a misnomer as an English name for this shrub. It is more correctly applied to the wahoo, or strawberry bush, *Euonymus americanus,* which see.

ROSE-ACACIA (ROBINIA)

What is a rose-acacia?   A hardy shrub native to the Allegheny Mountains. Grows to 12 ft. with dark, rich green foliage and racemes of rose-colored, pealike blossoms in late spring.

Where shall I plant a rose-acacia shrub?   In a spot protected from heavy winds, in light soil. Good for dry banks and as a screen. It suckers freely and, if neglectd, forms a dense thicket.

Do rose-acacia shrubs have to be grafted stock to bloom, or can they be taken from old plants?   No. If the old plants spread from year to year by suckers then it is a simple matter to dig up and re-plant some of the suckers, and so form new plants. However, rose-acacia is sometimes grafted high to form "standards," in which case any growth taken from the base would merely increase the under-stock, probably black locust.

ROSE-OF-SHARON (HIBISCUS SYRIACUS)

What colors does the rose-of-Sharon come in?   Double—white, pink; single—purple, red, blue, and white.

The most beautiful rose-of-Sharon I have seen has single lavender-blue flowers with carmine eye. What is its name?   Coelestis.

What is shrub-althea?   Same as rose-of-Sharon, *Hibiscus syriacus.*

What kind of soil does rose-of-Sharon thrive in? Mine was doing poorly. I put lime around it and it died.   It needs a deep soil which has plenty of water—even a tendency to be very moist occasionally. A complete fertilizer and water would possibly have saved your plant.

Can rose-of-Sharon shrubs or trees be transplanted in the fall?   May be safely transplanted in fall except in places subjected to high, cold winds during the winter.

What is the correct care of rose-of-Sharon? (Maine.)   There are many places in Maine where the rose-of-Sharon simply will not grow because of winter cold. Where it will survive, cut back the last year's shoots to about 4 buds early in the spring. This heavy pruning usually results in heavy flower production—providing, of course, it has good soil.

What is the cause of my rose-of-Sharon buds falling off before they open?   Partly a varietal characteristic. Other factors might be insufficient phosphorus or potash in the soil; too little or too much soil moisture; or attack by aphids.

When and how should rose-of-Sharon (Hibiscus syriacus) be pruned?   Blossoms are produced on shoots of the current season, so the shoots of the preceding year can be cut back to within 1 bud of their point of origin in spring, with no loss of blooms. However, this heavy pruning makes an ungainly bush, and many good gardeners prefer to prune them lightly or let them go unpruned.

What are the best conditions for rose-of-Sharon? Can it be budded or grafted? Rose-of-Sharon (*Hibiscus syriacus*) will grow quite well in any reasonably good garden soil. It may be budded or grafted, but this trouble hardly seems justified, as most of the varieties root very readily from cuttings taken in the summer.

RUSSIAN OLIVE (ELAEAGNUS)

What shrub would give a distinct silvery effect? Russian Olive (*Elaeagnus angustifolia*), with narrow leaves, silvery on reverse side, a shrub to 20 ft. high; Silverberry (*E. commutata*)—bushy, to 12 ft., leaves silver on both sides, fast-growing; Cherry Elaeagnus (*E. multiflora*), leaves silvery beneath, grows 4 to 9 ft.

Does Elaeagnus have flowers or fruits? Flowers inconspicuous but strongly fragrant in *E. angustifolia,* Silverberry, and *E. umbellata.* Small, yellow-silvery berries on Silverberry; brown-red berries on *E. umbellata.*

In what manner and how severely should Russian Olive (Elaeagnus angustifolia) be pruned if 3 years old and about 15 ft. high? Usually needs no pruning when growing in poor, dry soil and a sunny location to which it is adapted. Yours evidently is in rich ground and should be pruned by shortening lanky growths about midsummer.

SNOWBERRY (SYMPHORICARPOS)

How and when should the snowberry bush, Symphoricarpos, be trimmed? If it is behaving itself by producing plenty of fruits on a shapely bush, leave it alone. If not, cut it down to the ground in late winter.

SPIREA (SPIRAEA)

I would like to know if I should snip the tips of bridalwreaths? If so, when? Do not snip off the tips, as this spoils the grace of the bush. Instead, cut out some of the shoots as soon as the blossoms have faded.

Is it possible to trim and drastically reduce bridalwreath (Spiraea prunifolia) in size? Yes; cut back all flowering shoots immediately the flowers have faded. Shorten those remaining, if necessary, to reduce to the height required.

How should Spirea Anthony Waterer be pruned? This is a late bloomer, producing its flowers on shoots of the current season; therefore, it may be cut back about ½ in the spring, just as growth begins.

We have a number of spirea plants on an old lot which are much too large and tall for our present building lot. How drastically can these shrubs be pruned? Spireas in general can withstand severe pruning. It may be done in late winter, but this results (in the case of early-blooming varieties) in no blooms the following season.

STEPHANANDRA

What is stephanandra? A shrub with panicles of white or greenish flowers. *S. incisa* is drooping, with deeply lobed leaves; *S. tanakae* has larger leaves, shallowly lobed. These are hardy in the North with some winter protection.

How do you make cuttings of stephanandra? Most descriptions make it difficult to understand. Cuttings of half-ripe wood root readily in July. From shoots of normal thickness cut off the terminal 4 to 5 ins. Remove 1 or 2 of the lowest leaves on the cutting so formed, and make a clean cut through the stem, just below the joint from which the lowest leaf was cut. The cutting is then ready for placing in moist sand in a shaded cold frame. Or make hardwood cuttings, 6 ins. long, in November, pack in moist sand in a cool place (or bury outdoors over winter), and plant in early spring.

SUMAC

Can Fragrant Sumac be closely trimmed, down to say 4 ins.? When? Yes; in the spring before growth starts. But better leave it a little longer than 4 ins.

SWEETSHRUB (CALYCANTHUS)

What color are the flowers of sweetshrub (Calycanthus)? When does it bloom? Reddish or purplish brown. Blooms in June and July.

Is calycanthus a difficult shrub? We planted one, pruned it, and gave it plenty of water, but it slowly died after having come out in full leaf. Calycanthus should not present any great difficulty, though it is sometimes slow to start into vigorous growth after moving. The treatment you gave your plant appears to be correct. If you make another attempt, cut out at least half of the older stems at ground level, and reduce the remainder about half their length. Be careful not to give too much water.

A sweetshrub bush which formerly produced very fragrant flowers now continues to have lovely blooms which, however, have no scent. Is there anything that can be done? No, unless you wish to try fertilizing it heavily with well-rotted manure or some complete commercial fertilizer. Sometimes increased vigor produced in this manner will make the flowers more fragrant.

STRAWBERRY-BUSH (EUONYMUS AMERICANUS)

Does the Strawberry-bush require pruning? Strawberry-bush or Brook Euonymus (*Euonymus americanus*) ordinarily does not need pruning. Any "wild" shoots (those which in growth greatly outstrip the majority) may be shortened in late winter or during the growing season.

I have a Strawberry-bush I wish to move. Can I do it more successfully in the late fall or in the early spring? Early spring is preferred; but as you are moving it from one position to another in your own garden it should be quite safe to move it in the fall as soon as it has lost the greater part of its leaves.

TAMARISK

What does a tamarisk (tamarix) look like? Handsome, picturesque shrub with a plumy effect. Leaves resemble heather. Flowers pink to white. Some of the hardiest (to southern New England) are *T. parviflora, T. pentandra,* and *T. odessana.*

I have been told that the tamarisks can stand ocean spray and wind. Is that true? (Massachusetts.) Yes. It is one of the finest of all shrubs for shore planting, and thrives in sandy soil.

When and how is a tamarisk pruned? We have one which has 6 or 7 long branches which begin at the ground level and sprawl. Pruning depends on the group to which it belongs. Some bloom early on old wood, while others flower on wood of the current season. The first type should be cut back severely after flowering; the latter in the spring. In both cases the (approximately) 1-year-old shoots should be cut back ½ to ⅔.

VIBURNUM

Which viburnums do you recommend for autumn coloring and fruiting? Linden viburnum (*V. dilatatum*); witherod (*V. cassinoids*); Wright, or Oriental (*V. wrighti*); Mapleleaf (*V. acerifolium*); Blackhaw (*V. prunifolium*).

Which viburnums have the most effective flowers? Double-file Viburnum (*V. tomentosum*); Japanese Snowball (*V. tomentosum sterile*). The former has flat flower heads which seem to lie along the horizontal branches.

Which viburnum would lend itself best to foundation planting? The sweet-scented and early blooming *V. carlesi;* or, *V. carcephalum* which has larger heads of bloom.

Which viburnum will stand the most shade for woodland planting? Mapleleaf Viburnum, also called Dockmackie (*V. acerifolium*).

Is there a low, compact viburnum? Yes; Dwarf Cranberry Bush (*V. opulus nanum*), to 2½ ft. high.

Does Viburnum carlesi prefer a neutral soil? It will grow well enough in any approximately neutral garden soil of good quality, and not likely to become parched.

Why is Viburnum carlesi so difficult to grow on its own roots, and Viburnum burkwoodi so easy when the plants are practically identical? This is one of Nature's many as-yet-unanswered questions. In fact,

V. carlesi is one of the parents of *V. burkwoodi*—which only makes the answer more difficult.

When and how should I prune Viburnum carlesi? Usually does not require any pruning. If the center of the bush becomes crowded, superfluous shoots may be thinned out immediately after flowering.

Why did my Viburnum dilatatum fail to produce berries? It may have been that a cool rainy spell predominated just when the pollen was ripe. This would have prevented insect activity and wind from disseminating the pollen at the proper time.

Can you suggest reasons why three Japanese Snowballs (Viburnum tomentosum sterile) I planted died? The European Snowball (V. opulus roseum) American Cranberrybush (V. trilobum) lived. Possibly killed by winter. The Japanese Snowball is not so hardy as the European.

When and how can I prune my snowball bush (viburnum) which has grown too high and too shaggy? You might take a chance on cutting it back immediately after flowering; or in early spring if you are prepared to sacrifice the season's crop of bloom; but often snowball bushes do not respond well to severe pruning.

I have a snowball bush 5 or 6 years old that has never bloomed. What is wrong with it? The flower buds have probably been killed by winter cold. May be lack of nutrients in soil.

WEIGELA

Is there a weigela with very showy blooms? Yes, variety Bristol Ruby, with red blossoms; or Eva Rathke or Vanicek both of which have a tendency to recurrent bloom from June to August.

What is the best way to treat a weigela bush that is very old and produces very few flowers? Thin out the bush by removing some of the oldest branches during the winter. Cut them as near as possible to the ground line. Annual pruning should consist of the removal of worn-out flowering branches as soon as the blossoms have faded.

WILLOW, PUSSY

Will a Pussy Willow do well in dry soil? Pussy Willow (*Salix discolor*) adapts itself to a dry soil but prefers a moist. In dry soil it may become quite susceptible to diseases, and it will grow more slowly and remain smaller.

Why does my Pussy Willow burst forth in December and not in spring? (Massachusetts.) Mild winter days frequently force pussy willows into premature growth, especially if the tree is growing in a protected spot.

When is best time to prune Pussy Willows? If it is desired to have the "pussies" develop on long, wandlike shoots, the tree should be pruned severely before growth starts by cutting back all of the shoots made the preceding year to 1 or 2 buds. Otherwise no pruning is necessary.

Is it best to let a Pussy Willow grow in a bush or tree form? How tall should it grow?   It is best to keep it in bush form by pruning out any central leader that may appear. The height depends upon conditions, varying from 10 to 20 ft.

How can I start Pussy Willows in ground? What time of year? As soon as the frost is out of the ground in spring make cuttings 8 to 10 ins. long. Place ¾ of the cutting in the ground.

WINTERBERRY (ILEX VERTICILLATA)

I have seen a shrub in the wild which in fall has shining scarlet berries close to the stem after the leaves are gone. What is it?   Probably winterberry (*Ilex verticillata*).

Two good plants for autumn and winter color— American Holly and its relative, the native Winterberry. The latter is much hardier, but is not evergreen.

How can winterberry or blackalder be used?   In a shrub border, preferably in moist soil. It grows somewhat lank, so plant it in back of lower shrubs as, for instance, inkberry, an evergreen relative.

Does blackalder (winterberry) require wet feet or does it grow in spite of the water?   Winterberry is a shrub often found in the wild state in swampy ground. However, it grows quite successfully in any good garden soil, provided it is not too dry.

Will you tell me the best way to move, transplant, and grow the blackalder or winterberry holly?   Dig it carefully in the very early spring, with or without a ball of earth about the roots. Place in a good garden loam, slightly on the moist side if possible. Prune back ⅓. Water well.

WITCHHAZEL (HAMAMELIS)

Where would you plant a witchhazel?   In the woodland, or in the rear of a shrub border, or near a window of the house so the blossoms may be enjoyed from indoors at close range. They are not showy, but valued for their time of bloom.

What is the ultimate height of the witchhazel?   The tallest witchhazel your answer man has seen was an old specimen of the native *H. virginiana,* some 40 ft. high. That is exceptional. Another native species, *H. vernalis,* usually remains less than 8 ft. high.

When do the witchhazels bloom?   October or November—native witchhazel; February or March—Japanese, Chinese, and Vernal.

Will witchhazel grow in half shade? Is it worth growing?   Witchhazels are eminently suited for planting as undershrubs in wooded places. Their unseasonal flowers are more interesting than spectacular. Showiest in flower is the Chinese (*H. mollis*). Where open woodland situations are to be planted, the witchhazels are well worth while.

EVERGREEN TREES AND THEIR CULTURE

WHAT TO GROW

What does coniferous mean?   It means cone-bearing. Among the cone-bearing trees are firs, spruce, pines, Douglasfir, and hemlocks.

What are retinosporas?   This is a term applied to juvenile or immature forms of false-cypress (*Chamaecyparis*) and arborvitae (*Thuja*).

What are the best evergreen trees for specimen lawn planting? (Northern New England.)   Douglasfir, White Fir, hemlock, White and Red Pine; arborvitae, yew, and Hinoki Cypress if small trees are preferred.

I want to put some evergreens back of my White Birch trees. What would harmonize?   Hemlock or Red Pine.

Would like a few dignified evergreen trees. What do you suggest that would in time become very large?   Hemlock, White Pine, Red Pine, firs, and most spruces where climates are not too hot.

Will you recommend some medium-size, erect-growing evergreen trees?   Arborvitae (*Thuja occidentalis*); Redcedar (*Juniperus virginiana*); Chinese Juniper (*J. chinensis*); Upright Yew (*Taxus cuspidata* and *T. media* varieties).

Can you suggest some drooping evergreen trees to plant beside our garden pool?   Weeping Hemlock, Weeping Norway Spruce, Weeping Douglasfir.

We are planting a wildflower sanctuary in our woodland. Which evergreens would be the best to introduce there?   Hemlock, rhododendrons, Canada Yew.

What is the fastest-growing evergreen?   In the northern United States this is probably the hemlock, although the White Pine might run first when grown in good soil.

Are there any evergreen trees with berries?   Redcedars have blue-gray berries, and the yews sometimes have red berries, but they usually drop quickly.

What are some evergreens that can be grown for Christmas decorations?   Hollies, all kinds, both deciduous and evergreen; pine, spruce, fir, hemlock, arborvitae, juniper, yew, Mountain Andromeda, Japanese Andromeda, Mountain Laurel, rhododendron, etc. Spruce and hemlock quickly drop their needles when cut unless stood in water.

I wish to set out 50 or 75 evergreens for use later as cut Christmas trees. What kind of trees would you recommend for western Pennsylvania?   Douglasfir (*Pseudotsuga taxifolia*). Balsam Fir is best if it will grow in your section.

LOW-GROWING

What evergreens, 4 to 6 ft. high, are spreading in habit?   Common and Pfitzer Juniper, Japanese Yew, Sargent Weeping Hemlock.

Two types of small evergreens; the prostrate or spreading varieties are desirable for banks or terraces.

Which low evergreens could be used to edge our terrace in a sunny, dry location?   Pfitzer Juniper, plumy; Globe Redcedar, compact.

Which formal evergreen would be suitable for each side of our sunny front door?   *Picea glauca conica,* the Dwarf Alberta Spruce.

Is there a dwarf evergreen with red berries in winter?   Yes, dwarf forms of Japanese Yew.

Are there any evergreens which will remain low—not more than 2 ft.?   Mugho Pine; Spreading English Yew; Compact Japanese Yew; many dwarf junipers, such as Bar Harbor and tamarix; Maxwell Spruce, and other dwarf varieties. After several years it may be necessary to slow down rate of growth by summer pruning.

Are there low-growing conifers suitable for a rock garden?
Spreading English Yew, Dwarf Japanese Yew, Dwarf Hinoki Cypress,
Andorra Juniper, Bar Harbor Juniper; dwarf forms of Mugho Pine.

*For picturesque effects in the rock garden, or
in more or less formal plantings, such evergreens as Mugho Pine and the Oriental or
Chinese Arborvitae are selected.*

**Which evergreens would make suitable foundation planting for the
four sides of a large farmhouse? Are fruit-bearing bushes practical
for such use?** Evergreens would be selected from the rhododendrons
(for shady areas), yews, arborvitaes, and junipers. Yes, fruit-bearing
shrubs, such as the blueberry, viburnum, and cotoneaster, would be
assets in such a planting.

*For foundation plantings low-growing evergreens
that stay low (such as Pfitzer Juniper and Dwarf
Alberta Spruce) are a wise choice.*

CULTURE

SOIL

What kind of soil is best for evergreens? A soil suitable for most
kinds is a good loam, well drained, but somewhat retentive of
moisture. On such a soil, additional nourishment may be supplied for

yews, which like a rather rich diet. Junipers, pines, and Douglasfir should not require it. Most broad-leaved evergreens need an acid soil.

Can good results be expected from evergreen trees planted on land stripped of its topsoil? Such land is not suited for the intensive cultivation of evergreen trees, but pockets may be prepared for occasional trees. In a clayish subsoil, prepare these pockets by mixing in cinders and humus matter; in sandy soil, work in plenty of humus.

Our soil is dry. Would pines and junipers be advisable? Yes, most pines and junipers tolerate dry soil.

FEEDING

What is the best fertilizer for dwarf evergreens? Some, including dwarf junipers and pines, will require none, unless the soil is very poor. Arborvitae, yews, and chamaecyparis like some fertilizer. The best way to apply nourishment to established plants is by applying a top-dressing of leafmold or peatmoss mixed with old manure before snow falls.

Do evergreens need a leaf-and-manure fertilizer? In planting—depending upon the quality of the soil—mix more or less leafmold and old manure with the planting soil. For established evergreens in good soil, nothing more than a top-dressing of the same. Yews like a top-dressing of old manure.

Can evergreens be fed in the winter? A rich mulch (2- to 3-in. layer of manure or leafmold) applied before snow falls, or during open weather in winter, is beneficial.

How often should bone meal be placed around evergreens? Do not use bone meal. Use, rather, somewhat acid artificial fertilizers; or, still better, top-dressings of leafmold or peatmoss with some old manure. (See previous question.)

TRANSPLANTING

How are evergreens transplanted? Very small specimens are moved with a ball of earth, held in place by burlap, attached to their roots. Large specimens should be moved with a platform beneath them, installed by someone with experience.

When is it best to transplant small evergreens in southern New York State; and how? Either early September or early spring. Dig a hole twice as wide and twice as deep as the root system of the plant; have plenty of good soil available; be certain there is drainage at the bottom of the hole. Set in plant carefully—no deeper in soil than it formerly grew—untie burlap and remove it (if possible without the root ball collapsing, otherwise tuck it in between the side of the hole and the root ball) fill in soil, make firm, and water thoroughly. Leave a slight depression in soil about plant so that it will receive plenty of water until it becomes well established.

I would like to change several little evergreens to another location. When and how do I go about it?   If plants are small, dig them in the spring with the best possible root-ball. Plant in a friable soil mixed with leafmold or old manure. Water thoroughly; mulch the base to prevent drying out. If larger trees, transplant either in spring or early autumn.

When is the best time of the year to plant little evergreens (seed-lings)?   In the spring, when the ground has dried and warmed so that it is friable; and before the evergreens have started growth.

When is the best time to transplant evergreens?   For well-grown nursery grades, spring, before growth has started; or early autumn, from August 1 on. For plants that have not been transplanted recently, spring is best. Large trees, properly balled and platformed, may be moved in the spring, or as late into the autumn as the ground can be dug.

Evergreens planted with the burlap on do not grow for me, although I have raised beautiful evergreens. Should I remove burlap instead of slitting it?   Unless it might break a weak root-ball, remove the burlap; at least open the knots, spread it out in the bottom of the hole, or cut it off close to the base of the ball.

How early in the spring can evergreens be transplanted?   Wait till all frost is out of the ground and the soil has dried off and warmed up, so that it is thoroughly workable. Transplant evergreens before they have started into growth.

When does the fall planting season for evergreens begin?   Generally, as soon as the early summer growth has become hardened. In the case of pines, spruces, and firs, this means as soon as the annual growth has been completed and has hardened and the terminal buds firmly "set." In dry seasons, one usually waits for a favorable moist spell of weather.

In New York, what are the best months for planting evergreens? And what months in spring and fall are the deadlines for planting?   Plant preferably in early September (first choice); or March to April (second choice).

Which evergreens could be planted in December?   In lower New York State large specimens of the hardy kinds, if properly balled and platformed. While December is late for smaller evergreens, one might take a chance on them, if they had solid, fibrous root-balls, and were handled carefully.

Is it O.K. to move evergreens in midwinter, so long as the ground is not frozen, but may freeze up any time after the planting?   Safe enough for large trees, dug with solid fibrous root-balls, carefully planted, well watered, and mulched. Not advisable for small evergreens; unsafe for trees that have not been previously transplanted.

Why do I lose so many evergreens, purchased with solid-looking balls and tightly burlapped? Possibly because these good-looking trees had been dug and kept out of the ground for some time prior to your purchase. Freshly dug trees, promptly planted, stand a far better chance of succeeding than "pre-dug" stock.

I often find roots of dead evergreens packed hard in a dry ball, despite repeated soakings. How come? Root-balls dug in clayish soil, or puddled in clay, when planted in a lighter soil may easily become caked hard, so that water cannot penetrate them. Loosen the surface of hard-looking balls before planting.

Why do so many evergreen trees die after transplanting? There are many possible causes. Trees may not have had fibrous root systems; they may have been dug with inadequate root-balls, or planted at the wrong season; they may have perished from drought; or they may have been tender kinds.

Will oak sawdust, if it is put in the ground while transplanting evergreens, help them or do harm? On a soil deficient in humus, if no other humus-forming material is available, a little rotted hardwood sawdust may be helpful. But when possible use leafmold, woods earth, peatmoss, or old manure.

CARE

Our water supply comes from a deep well and is quite hard. We have planted many seedling evergreens. Will it be harmful to use well water on them; and will it injure the foliage should any get on it? Alkaline water is definitely harmful to all broad-leaved evergreens, and might injure some narrow-leaved ones, such as pines, hemlocks, spruce, fir, cypress. Foliage will be injured through damage done to the whole plant by introducing alkali into soil, not by contact of water with leaves.

Should one cultivate around evergreens? Cultivation at the base of established evergreens may disturb surface roots and do more harm than good. Keep the soil from caking, rather, by means of a mulch of leafmold or peatmoss, with perhaps a little old manure.

Should one at all times keep a mulch about the base of evergreen trees? Mulch all newly planted evergreens. While a mulch will be helpful to many established evergreens, not all kinds require it if planted in a suitable soil.

What is the reason that evergreens, such as Pyramidal Arborvitae or Scotch Pines, turn a rusty brown and lose their needles? This may represent only a normal shedding of old foliage. Drought and soil exhaustion may cause premature shedding. Virorous growth and proper sanitation tend to reduce it.

My arborvitae has a lot of brown leaves. I have dusted it with

sulfur. Can you give any advice? Prevent caking of the soil, and see that the roots do not lack water. Just before ground freezes, give a very thorough soaking. Keep a mulch of leafmold or peatmoss about base.

I have poor luck with Mugho Pine and Koster Blue Spruce. I lost two Mughos, and the spruce doesn't look well. What is wrong? Both kinds, unless transplanted frequently in the nursery, makes coarse roots, which mean great risk in transplanting. Most losses are due to this. Secure transplanted, fibrous-rooted plants. These will usually grow right along in any fair soil, if planted where they get sun.

Would the exhaust from autos, blowing into the evergreens, cause their death? Repeated and protracted exposure to these gases may cause the death of evergreens, especially hot exhaust gas on a cold winter day.

Should healthy evergreen trees turn yellowish? Color is not a natural condition. No. A yellowish discoloring may indicate any of several causes of trouble: poor drainage, overwatering, or a poor quality of soil.

In the planting about our house one corner plant died 6 months after planting. A reset did the same. The soil was examined, and no lime pocket was found, nor sign of insect trouble. All other plants are doing well. What may have been the trouble? Corner plants often suffer from a strong draft of air. This may be fatal to newly planted trees. A windscreen might prevent the trouble.

I have cedars and Pfitzer Junipers, planted about 2 years ago. They are not growing and look dry, although I have tried to treat them right. I hoe around them and water thoroughly. They are on west side of open porch (not very close to porch) and pretty far apart. What do they need? Examine them for spider mites. It these are found, spray promptly and repeatedly with malathion. The ground may be hard and poor. Cultivate and apply a mulch.

Do evergreen trees need shade or sun? Nearly all prefer an open situation. The native yew prefers shade. Balsam fir and hemlock prefer a situation open overhead, but some partial protection from the brightest winter sun from near-by tall trees.

When is the best time to apply a dormant oil spray to evergreens (in central Pennsylvania)? What should the temperature be? Early spring; but this kind of spray should always be used on evergreens most carefully, for if too strong, it will quickly burn the foliage and possibly kill the plant. It will remove "bloom" from types such as Blue Spruce. Temperature should be under 65° F.

How can I straighten spruce and other evergreens bent from snow-storms? Pull them back into position. Light trees may be held in place by stakes; larger ones by guy wires or ropes fastened to pegs in the ground, or to overhead points. After a snowstorm, go over your evergreens and shake off snow with a broom or the back of a rake.

PRUNING

When and how should an evergreen be trimmed to make it bushy instead of a tall tree?   Different kinds may be trimmed at different times, but the season which will suit all is in late June or July period of soft spring growth. In upright growing kinds, trim both top and side branches so as to avoid a chopped-off effect.

What can one do to train evergreens to be bushy instead of tall and straggly?   Trim them annually, from the start. And see that those which like a rich soil, such as yews and chamaecyparis, are kept supplied with a nourishing top-dressing.

Can evergreen trees, which have been allowed to grow too tall near the house, be trimmed back?   It can be done with the kinds which will "break" readily from the old wood; but not with pines, firs, spruce, or Douglasfir. Trimming back, however, may leave large evergreens in an unsightly condition.

Can evergreen trees be kept low by cutting the tops?   Yes; but a radical "topping" will spoil the appearance and natural beauty of most—especially pines, spruces, and firs, which will not "break" from the old wood, and will remain stunted.

Is it advisable to heavily prune small evergreens to control shape?   With the exception of erect-growing pines, spruces, firs, and Douglasfir (which are best left with a minimum of pruning), most young evergreens will be benefited by pruning uneven shoots that they will eventually make more solid and compact plants.

Does it harm a spruce or pine to cut branches from it for indoor purposes?   It may not threaten the life of a large tree, but may easily spoil its appearance.

Can evergreens be trimmed in winter?   Never prune them during freezing weather. Do not trim in winter any of those evergreens which make one annual shoot terminated by a prominent bud, like pine, spruce, fir, and Douglasfir. These should be trimmed in early summer. Young shoots of pine may be shortened before the needles develop.

WINTER PROTECTION

Will you outline winter care of untransplanted seedling evergreens, and of once- or twice-transplanted ones?   For the seedlings and once-transplanted, a covering with dry leaves in late autumn; for the twice-transplanted, a mulch over the ground and light branches (not necessarily evergreen) laid over the rows or beds. Water the plants thoroughly just before winter hard freezing and previous to applying mulch.

How should pines and junipers be cared for during the winter?
If well established, no special winter protection is needed. In the case
of newly set plants a mulch of leaves or other littery material, applied
as the ground is about to freeze, might be helpful and would certainly
do no harm.

**How should I care for Douglasfir, Picea omorika, Austrian Pine,
and Mugho Pine in the winter? (New York.)** The evergreens mentioned are quite hardy in New York and need no special winter
protection.

**Is it true that I shouldn't mulch with oak leaves around my small
firs?** There is nothing harmful to firs in oak leaves; but in a planting
near the house, for instance, the leaves may be too loose to be the
best mulching material.

**What is proper procedure for protecting low evergreen shrubs and
trees in the winter (located at the seashore with only the house to
protect them)?** If the soil is dry, give a good watering before the
ground freezes, then put on a mulch of leaves or litter several inches
deep. Protection from wind is probably important, and this may be
afforded by sticking evergreen boughs in the ground around them. In
some cases it may be advisable to erect a temporary windbreak made
of boards or burlap.

**Will it be worth while to cover bases of evergreens with partly
decayed leaves now (January) after the ground has been covered with
snow for some time? The trees were planted in October.** If the
snow is likely to remain all winter, there is no need for a mulch at
this time; but if a midwinter thaw occurs, then it would be advisable
to spread leaves to curtail bad effect of alternate freezing and thawing.

Is there any way to prevent windburn on evergreen trees? The
injury referred to is probably the scorched appearance of foliage
sometimes noted in the spring, especially on firs. This is caused by
the sun in winter and can be prevented largely by placing trees so
that they will have some slight protection from the brightest sun in
winter.

**How shall I take care of evergreens in winter, when they can-
not be watered?** There is not much to be done in this case. In some
cases, such as small specimens in a foundation planting, or in a very
exposed position, evergreen boughs could be stuck in the ground
around them to give some protection from winter sun and wind. A
liquid latex preparation has been sprayed on with good results.

PROPAGATION: SEED AND CUTTINGS

Is it possible for an amateur to raise evergreens from seeds? Yes,
providing one has reasonable patience and is prepared to give careful
attention to the seeds and seedlings. (See following questions.)

How can I grow evergreens from seed? Sow fall-collected seed in spring in shallow boxes filled with light, well-drained soil. Cover, to about diameter of seed, with sifted soil. Place flats in cool, shaded cold frame and keep evenly moist. When watering, avoid disturbing surface soil. Transplant when large enough to handle.

How do you keep seeds of evergreens until planting time? Store in tins, jars, or tight paper bags that are nearly airtight, in a cool, dry place.

When should evergreen tree seed be planted; and how old should the seed be? Seed collected in fall should be sown in spring. Older seed, kept under proper conditions, will germinate, but vitality becomes progressively less with each passing year.

Can evergreens be propagated by using the clippings for cuttings? (Wisconsin.) Most of the yews, junipers, cypresses (chamaecyparis), arborvitaes, and some of the spruces may be propagated by means of clippings. These may be taken in late August, but as a rule many of them do not form roots before winter, therefore a greenhouse is desirable, particularly in your climate. If you have a greenhouse (night temperature 50° to 55° F.) you could also take cuttings in November and December.

What is best temperature to root pines and spruces from slips in hothouse beds? The percentage of pine cuttings that can be rooted is so small as to make this method almost valueless. Some of the spruces may be rooted, and for these a greenhouse with a night temperature of 50° to 55° F. is required.

Will you describe the simplest way to start cuttings of arborvitaes and junipers? Take the cuttings in the latter part of August, and set them out, about 1½ ins. apart, in boxes of sand. The boxes should not be more than 4 ins. deep, but any convenient size; the sand must be made firm before the cuttings are put in. Keep them in a cold frame until there is the possibility of the sand freezing, then place them in a cool, frostproof storage for the winter.

Should boxes filled with sharp sand and leafmold, containing cuttings of yew and boxwood, be placed in deep shade, or in semi-shade, for best results? The important thing is that the cuttings must not be directly exposed to the sun, except possibly very early in the morning or late in the evening. Beyond this give all the light possible.

SPECIFIC EVERGREENS

ARBORVITAE

See also Hedges.

Which arborvitae would be best in our Northern climate, to serve

as a boundary-line screen? Pyramidal Arborvitae, *Thuja occidentalis fastigiata.*

Would an arborvitae stand city conditions? Not very well but it will grow in the city if conditions are not too severe. Needs good moist soil and sunshine for at least half of the day.

Will Golden Arborvitae do as well in shade as in sun? No. All "colored" evergreens require full sun to bring out their peculiar coloring.

When is the best time to plant arborvitae? What soil? Plant in spring, before growth starts, or early fall, up to October 1; baby trees, only in the spring. Dig them, in spring or fall, with solid root-ball. Set as deeply as they formerly stood. Fill around the ball with friable soil enriched with humus, and water this down well. When settled, add more soil, flush with the grade. Mulch the base, and in dry weather administer occasional soakings.

How shall I care for an arborvitae foundation planting? Do not set plants in shaded areas; see that they do not lack for water; just before winter, give a thorough soaking; spray promptly and repeatedly in case of spider mites; keep the soil from caking. In a poorish soil, a mulch of leafmold or peatmoss, with a little old manure, will be helpful.

Why are arborvitaes so hard to grow? They are by nature lovers of open situations and moist soils. Their use in foundation plantings, therefore, is highly artificial and unnatural. (See previous questions.)

Can an arborvitae be pruned if the tree becomes too tall and thin? When is the proper pruning time? This can be done effectively in the case of quite young plants. Pruning and topping will do little good to old plants. Pruning should be done during the period of soft spring growth. To improve the denseness of old plants, apply a nutritious top-dressing of leafmold and old manure.

When and how is the best time to trim arborvitae? During the period of soft spring growth shear the outer surface slightly, trimming the extremities of the soft growths. Close shearing results in a dense, formal appearance; light shearing in a less formal appearance.

CEDAR

Could I grow a Cedar-of-Lebanon here? What is its botanical name? (Southern Pennsylvania.) *Cedrus libani* would probably grow for you, but it is not hardy much farther North, though a strain of the cedar-of-Lebanon, said to be fairly hardy, has been introduced by the Arnold Arboretum near Boston.

CRYPTOMERIA

What is the cryptomeria like? The Japanese Temple-cedar is a rapid-growing tree with tufted branches. It attains 125 ft. in Japan. It is not hardy much above Zone VI. In this country is handsome when young, but soon becomes scrawny.

CYPRESS

I have a tiny dwarf tree which has frondlike foliage and seems very tolerant and hardy, and looks very well in the rock garden. What is it? It is probably Dwarf Hinoki Cypress (*Chamaecyparis obtusa nana*).

FIR

What does the Nikko Fir look like? Large, broadly pyramidal tree with spreading upturned branches, and glossy dark-green leaves. Needles spread upward forming a V over the twig. Identify it by its grooved branchlets.

What is a good fir as a specimen tree? (New Hampshire.) White Fir (*Abies concolor*).

Which of the evergreens is very dark in color, of pyramidal form, tall, and with pendulous branches? This is probably the Douglasfir (*Pseudotsuga taxifolia*), one of the best.

Will you suggest some good fir trees? Douglasfir, White Fir, Nikko Fir, Nordmann Fir, Veitch Fir.

Can we grow fir trees in a dry, rather hot part of the East? Probably not; they require a cool, somewhat humid climate; but if you must try one, the White Fir would probably do best.

Can one grow a Balsam Fir in New Jersey? Perhaps; but it does best north of Connecticut; or in mountains south of Virginia.

Do fir trees grow well in a fairly sandy soil? How early in spring can they be planted? Yes, in a somewhat sandy soil, enriched with leafmold or other humus matter. Plant not too early in the spring. Wait till the ground has dried and warmed.

How can I grow Christmas trees in Massachusetts? In New England the "Christmas tree" is usually the Balsam Fir (*Abies balsamea*), which requires the cool, moist climate of the mountains. It has a difficult time in the warmer areas about Boston, and on Cape Cod. If the climate is right, young trees 6 to 18 ins. high can be set out in any field and be expected to begin to yield suitable Christmas trees in from 7 to 10 years. However, because of the time element involved, only marginal land should be used for this purpose.

Is it wise to buy a tubbed fir Christmas tree and then, on a mild day, after the holidays, plant it outdoors (the hole having been previously dug and filled with leaves)? From a viewpoint of gardening economy better buy proper kinds and grades of trees for ornamental use, in the proper seasons, and buy your Christmas trees cheaply, without balls. However, many living Christmas trees are successfully set out after the holidays.

How does one plant trees used indoors as Christmas trees? Prepare the planting hole in advance. Fill and heap it over with leaves. Have planting soil ready indoors. Keep the tree moist; remove it promptly, after use, to a cool place. Plant on a frost-free day, and water thoroughly. Apply a thick mulch, and place a burlap screen around it.

How can I prune a fir tree which is growing too tall and narrow? Does it need fertilizing? The soil is very poor. Many fir trees grow naturally tall and narrow. It is not practicable to prune back a fir tree after it has reached any great size. In poor soil, apply a nutritious mulch of leafmold and some old manure at the base.

Would four Douglasfir trees take all the nourishment from 4 lots 25 × 100 ft.? No, not at all. The shade, however, might make it difficult to grow most other plants.

HEMLOCK

We have an extremely shady garden. Would any evergreens do well for us? Hemlocks and yew only.

Which evergreen trees obtained in ordinary woods would be best to put around a home? I wish to stunt their growth. How is this done? Hemlocks would be best of all, for they can be kept at any height merely by trimming or clipping their new growth, once or twice a year, in the early summer and late summer or early fall.

What type of soil is best for young hemlocks? Do they require much water? A light loam, rich in humus. In an ordinary garden soil, up to 25 per cent of leafmold or other humus may be worked in; in a light, sandy soil twice this amount. Hemlocks should not be permitted to suffer for lack of water; but do not keep the soil drenched.

When is the best time to transplant hemlocks? (New York.) Either very early in the spring, before growth has started, or in early autumn, during favorable, moist weather, up to about October 15.

What conditions and methods are advocated for most successful transplanting of hemlocks from woods in same locality? The safest method is to root-prune the tree a year in advance of moving. When actually transplanting, the roots should all be carefully dug and *not allowed to dry out* while the plant is being moved from one place to the other.

Can a 25-ft. hemlock, once transplanted, regain new needles on branches now bare, due to moving of tree to different spot in garden? If the bare branches do not develop new leaves during the spring following transplanting, they never will. In that case, remove the dead branches.

What is the proper care of hemlock trees?   They prefer a situation sheltered from strong winds and a soil very rich in humus. They revel in leafmold. Use lots of it when planting, and apply a leaf mulch about the base. Do not let them get dry, and, in dry autumns, soak the soil thoroughly just before winter. If set in a sun-scorched place, partial shade will be helpful in establishing seedling trees.

Why do hemlocks die back soon after planting?   They should not. The trouble may be due to one or more of several causes: lack of a good, solid, fibrous root-ball when transplanted; improper planting; lack of humus in the soil; lack of water; or windy exposure.

How would you propagate hemlock from cuttings? Do they need heat?   In July make cuttings 3 to 4 ins. long. Insert in a mixture of sand and peat, in boxes, in shaded cold frame. They root slowly, and if it is possible to carry over to the following year any not rooted in the fall, the percentage of rooting would be greater. For this a warm (50° to 55° F.) greenhouse is desirable.

JUNIPER

Which juniper would grow tall, compact, and narrow?   Canaert Redcedar. Or one of the Chinese junipers, such as *J. chinensis columnaris,* would be good.

Are Irish Junipers of same family as Redcedar trees? Can they be safely planted near apple trees?   Yes, they both belong to the genus *Juniperus.* They serve as alternate hosts for the cedar-apple rust, and should not be grown within several hundred yards of apple trees.

Will Irish Juniper do well in an east foundation planting? Mine don't look very good. Red spider might be the trouble, as they were not sprayed this year.   A northeast exposure would be better. This juniper is subject to winter burn on the sunny side. Spider mites are often injurious; but the effect would spread over the entire tree, not merely on the sunny side.

How can I keep my Irish Juniper from turning brown each spring?   Keep the brightest sun in winter from the foliage, either by locating the junipers in a northeast exposure, or by means of a burlap screen or other protection.

Are cedar and Redcedar the same thing?   No. The word "cedar," when correctly used, applies to the genus *Cedrus*—a group of trees native in North Africa, and southwest Asia. These are quite different from our native "Redcedar" (*Juniperus virginiana*) of the eastern United States.

What is the best time of year to transplant Redcedar from a field?   Cedars over 7 ft. high should be root-pruned in September and moved a year later, or in the spring thereafter. This will ensure a fibrous root system, so necessary to successful transplanting.

What can be done to improve the appearance of Redcedar trees planted in front of a house? Examine them for the presence of spider mites. If these are present, spray promptly and repeatedly. Cultivate the surface lightly, without disturbing roots. Mulch with leafmold or peatmoss and a little old manure. See that there is no lack of moisture.

What time of year should I plant Spreading Juniper? Spring, after the ground has become thoroughly workable, before growth has started; or early autumn. In lower New York State, up to about November 1. In dry autumns, take advantage of such wet spells as may come along.

What fertilizer do Spreading Junipers need? Established, thriving plants, in soil of fair quality, need none. In poor soil, apply a top-dressing of leafmold or peatmoss mixed with some old manure. Avoid alkaline fertilizers.

What winter and summer care does an erect cedar or juniper, 2 to 3 ft. high, require? Is it possible to prevent dead branches at the base? Is this due to dogs? Examine branches for spider mites. If found, spray promptly. See that the soil does not cake. Apply a mulch. Dogs may well be responsible for injury to lower branches.

When are junipers pruned; and how? The principal annual pruning is done during the period of soft spring growth. If a formal appearance is desired, a second, lighter pruning may be given, about September 1, to upright-growing kinds like the Redcedar.

Can I cut about 27 ins. off the top of a Meyer Juniper without damaging the tree for summer growth? Our tree is too tall. Yes, you may reduce the height by cutting back. It will produce new growth below the cut, which will eventually cover the stubbed effect.

Please tell me the right way to trim Savin Junipers. Can the long branches be trimmed back? For proper development, Savin Junipers should be pruned rather heavily in their young stages. This will make them bushy. When old branches are pruned back, they may be slow in producing new growth and the effect may be unsightly.

After the top is broken off a Silver Juniper, Juniperus virginiana var. argentea will it ever be a nicely shaped tree? It will readily develop a new leader of acceptable appearance within 2 or 3 years. The process may be helped by staking up the new leader and pruning back competing growths.

How long does it take for juniper berries to get ripe; and when is the time to pick them? Some junipers will never have berries. Only the female (pistillate-flowering) trees bear fruit. The Rocky Mountain Redcedar (*Juniperus scopulorum*) and several other junipers take 2 years to mature their fruits. These could be picked in the late summer or early fall of the second year.

How do nurserymen increase junipers? I have done it by slicing a

branch and burying it until it roots, but there must be a quicker way. Either by cuttings or grafting. Cuttings are placed in the greenhouse in summer or early winter. Cuttings of some junipers will remain alive and in good condition for more than 2 years without rooting. Grafting is done early in the year.

Can I start Pfitzer's Juniper from cuttings? It is possible but this juniper does not root too readily. Make cuttings, about 5 ins. long, in latter half of August. (See Propagation, this section.)

PINE

Which is the more satisfactory, Red Pine or Austrian Pine? They are similar, but the former is less susceptible to insect pests than the latter.

We like pine trees, but our soil is moist. Would any of them do well? White Pine (*Pinus strobus*) and Pitch Pine (*P. rigida*) are occasionally found growing wild in swamps in New Jersey. In the South, Longleaf Pine (*P. palustris*) could be planted.

We were advised to buy pine trees for our garden near the windy seashore. Is Scotch Pine a good choice? Yes. Japanese Black Pine is most resistant however.

I would like to plant a pine tree which is not coarse in texture. What do you suggest? Use either White Pine or Japanese Red Pine.

How can I tell the principal pine trees apart? Many of them by the length of their "needles," and the number of each cluster (fascicle). White Pine—5 in a cluster, 5 ins. long (soft bluish); Austrian Pine—2 in a cluster, 6½ ins. long (stiff); Scotch Pine—2 in a cluster, 3 ins. long (twisted); Red Pine—2 in a cluster, 6 ins. long (glossy); Japanese Black Pine—2 in a cluster, 4½ ins. long (sharp-pointed).

What is the best fertilizer to keep a pine tree healthy and growing? Is bone meal O.K.? Bone meal when transplanting, but it is not a complete fertilizer, which may be applied later on. However, if the ground is of good quality and the tree healthy, no feeding will be required. At the slightest sign of soil exhaustion, apply a top-dressing of leafmold or peatmoss mixed with old manure.

Can pine trees be planted all year 'round? No. Not during the period of soft growth, from May to August.

I have some fine 4-year-old White Pine and Norway Pine. When is the best time to transplant them, and should they be in full sun or partial shade? (Wisconsin.) Transplant in spring, before growth starts. Mulch the surface. An open situation is best, but some temporary shading would be desirable.

When is the best time to transplant pine trees? (New York.) In the latitude of New York City fibrous-rooted trees may be transplanted either in the spring, or in the autumn, between August 1 and November 1. Pines not previously transplanted had better be planted in the spring only, with as good a ball as possible.

How should pine trees be transplanted?   Untransplanted trees over 6 ft. high should be root-pruned (which see) in September and moved a year later. Transplanted trees with fibrous root systems may be dug with a ball of roots, burlapped, in the spring or in early autumn. Water down the filling soil. Fill the hole flush with the grade. Mulch soil over roots.

Is it too late to transplant pine trees that were set out as seedlings, and are now about 10 ft. tall?   No. Root-prune (which see) them in September; move them a year later, or in the spring of the second year. They should then have developed sufficient fibrous roots to facilitate successful transplanting.

How old may pine trees be transplanted safely?   There's no age limit. The only limits are those set by available machinery for moving, and by obstructions in the path of travel.

Should grass be kept away from the ground around young pines? Yes.

When and how does one prune Mugho Pines?   When the candle-like spring growths have about reached their full length, but before the leaves have spread out, cut these "candles" back partly. When they are reduced to ¼ or ⅓ their length each year, a Mugho Pine will form a dense, cushionlike plant.

I have a matched pair of Mugho Pines. One is getting larger than the other. Is it possible to trim them back?   Yes. In the annual pruning of the candlelike spring growths, cut those on the larger plant a little farther back than those on the smaller plant. This ought, in a year or two, tend to even the two plants up. Do not prune into the old wood.

What can be done to save young pine trees badly browned by the heat from burning brush?   If the scorched branches produce new leaves in the spring following injury, no harm will have been done. If not, nothing can restore the damage; cut off the burned parts.

Will you please tell me what makes our pines so thin looking, and with brown edges?   Probably unsuitable environment, such as inadequate underdrainage, or too much shade.

Are pine trees started by seed or cuttings?   Pine trees are started from seeds sown in spring. Some varieties are grafted. Most species and varieties are exceedingly difficult to raise from cuttings.

Can pine trees be grown from seed?   Yes. Seed ripens September to November, the cones that produce the seed being 2 or 3 years old. Collect cones before seed has shed and place in shallow boxes in warm, dry place. (See answers to other inquiries.)

Is there any disease that pine trees catch from fruit trees? No, but the white-pine blister rust lives for part of its life on gooseberry and currant bushes. This is a very serious disease.

REDCEDAR

(See Juniper.)

SPRUCE

Which are some of the outstanding spruce trees? Oriental Spruce (*Picea orientalis*); Siberian Spruce (*P. omorika*); Colorado Spruce (*P. pungens*) (some varieties of this are bluish in tone).

What is the best fertilizer for Blue Spruce? An occasional top-dressing of leafmold or peatmoss with old manure mixed into it. When planting, mix leafmold and some old manure with the planting soil.

I have planted spruce trees in oyster shell. I was advised to use sulfate of ammonia and pine needles to make the soil acid. Was it wrong? Oyster shell is not suitable for evergreens. Add a large quantity of acid humus material, such as peatmoss, hemlock or pine-needle leafmold.

What type of soil is suitable for spruce trees? A good loam, enriched with humus. Untransplanted trees over 6 ft. high should be root-pruned in September and moved a year later. Trees previously transplanted should be dug with a good ball, either in spring or in early autumn. Water the soil after planting. Fill flush with the grade. Mulch.

Should ground be frozen to remove spruce and pine from woods to lawns? Not necessarily. The main thing is to secure an adequate, solid ball of fibrous roots and earth. Large trees are sometimes most conveniently moved with frozen balls.

How much space should be available in front of a home to plant a Blue Spruce? It should have an area 20 ft. or more in diameter in which to grow.

In a Blue Spruce, successfully transplanted last year, the old foliage has lost its bright color. Will it return? This happens often when in transplanting or transit a Blue Spruce is tied in tightly or crowded. The blue, waxy coat of the foliage rubs off and does not renew itself. Subsequent new growth will eventually cover up the dull inner foliage. The color rubs off most readily on the soft new growth.

I have had little success with Blue Spruces. Will you give information on their culture? Be sure to procure transplanted, fibrous-rooted plants. Plant in a well-drained, sunny place in any fair, loamy soil. Plant in the spring before growth starts, or shortly after August 1, during suitable damp weather. Water plentifully; mulch the base.

Keep the roots moist, but not too wet, and in dry autumns soak thoroughly just before winter.

What is the proper care for Norway Spruce and Blue Spruce seedlings, now 1½ ins. high? Assuming that they were planted in well-prepared planting beds, merely keep under lath shades, and maintain soil moisture with a light, fine surface mulch.

Can you prune and shape a Blue Spruce? If so, when is the proper time? Yes. Prune only during the period of soft spring growth. The shaping process may sometimes be aided by tying in misdirected branches and staking a crooked leader.

How shall I trim sides of Colorado Blue Spruce too wide for parking space? If this involves cutting into old wood, it will not be found practicable. Better move the whole tree back from the drive.

I have a Blue Spruce which is growing lopsided. How shall I trim it? If the leader is crooked, stake it. If any branches can be tied into place, do this before you use the pruning knife. If it is a matter of one or more protruding branches in an otherwise well-balanced plant, then reduce these branches as necessary.

How does one prune Blue Spruces to prevent them from growing too large? They are by nature tall-growing trees. They may be kept down artificially by means of annual prunings or shearings, during the period of soft growth in spring. This involves the snipping off of the extremities of the shoots.

Can spruce trees be kept trimmed to a small size? Yes, by means of annual prunings during the period of soft growth. This will result in plants of compact, formal appearance. Once so treated, plants will never again develop into normal, natural-looking specimens.

In 2 spruce trees that serve as windbreaks the lower branches are dying. How can I improve their appearance and discourage any great increase in height? Once the lower branches have died, nothing will bring them back to life, and no new growth will replace them. To prevent further loss of lower branches, remove all crowding near-by growths which may shut out light. Keep a mulch about the base; eventually cut off top shoots if necessary.

Can I get information about propagating Blue Spruce? Can they be increased by cuttings? They can be rooted from cuttings, but not very readily. Use shoots of one year's growth with a very small "heel" of old wood, inserted in January in a propagating case in a warm greenhouse.

How can Moerheim Blue Spruce be propagated? Usually propagated by grafting; cuttings taken in January may be rooted, but not readily, in a warm greenhouse.

How, when, and where should one plant seeds of Norway Spruce and Colorado Blue Spruce? Sow ¼ in. deep in a bed of fine soil, shaded by lath screens, until seeds have germinated; or in flats in cold frame in spring.

Will handling spruce and cedar Christmas trees, after they have been in the house, cause a bad case of poison on the hands and face? Such a difficulty is not common. Some individuals might be allergic to the resins in these trees, but cases of poisoning are rare.

YEW

Which yews grow in tree form? English Yew and the single-stem Japanese Yew; but they rarely attain great height in this country except in the Pacific Northwest.

Which yews make upright growth? Hatfield, Hicks, and Irish Yew (where winters are not severe); also Japanese Upright Yew.

Hemlock will not survive here but we have had best success with Japanese Yew. What else shall we plant? There are several varieties of yew, available from nurserymen, which differ in shape and height. These could be used.

Do dwarf yews prefer an acid soil? No, they will grow well in either acid or alkaline soils.

When is the best time to move yews? Either in spring, before growth starts, or in early September.

Should Dwarf Japanese Yew be fed? If so, what and when? Not necessarily. If their color is good, leave them alone. Dwarf Japanese Yews always grow slowly. Well-rotted manure makes a good fertilizer, when needed.

I have 2 Japanese Yews. One has retained its dark green, but the other has a slight yellow cast. Why? Frequently Japanese Yews are grown from seed. Then there are wide differences in the resulting plants. Height, shape, and color of foliage are all variables in such instances.

My Japanese Yew is dying. I have given it plenty of water and fertilizer, sprayed the foliage, all to no avail. What is the trouble with it; and how can I correct it? The roots of this plant are probably being attacked by the grubs of the strawberry root weevil. This is frequently controlled by the use of poison baits for the beetles, and pyrethrum sprays (soaked into the ground above the roots) to kill the grubs which are actually doing the damage by feeding on the roots.

I planted 2 yews 4 years ago. One seems to be dying. It has been this way for 2 seasons. Foliage is green but very thin. There are no grubs around roots. This is a condition frequently related with finding aphis on the roots. If this is not the case, the explanation could be in some peculiar soil condition. Would suggest digging the plant up, removing the soil about the roots, and transplanting in some other situation.

When is the best time to trim Japanese Yew? Just after growth has been completed, in late June or early July.

Should yew trees be trimmed in August, or are they prettier left untrimmed? Usually they are prettier untrimmed when grown as specimens, but some years a small amount of trimming (which really can be done any time) is necessary to keep certain branches from growing too much out of proportion to the rest of the plant.

Should low-spreading yews, in foundation plantings, be pruned? Not if they stay low and do not grow out of proportion to the other plants.

Should the branches of Taxus cuspidata capitata be tied for winter protection or supported in some way? The branches break easily. This might be done if they are growing in situations where snow and ice will accumulate on them, as under the eaves of the house.

How can I best propagate Japanese Yew for a hedge? Seedling yews would be the best for this purpose, as they grow upright. The seeds require stratification for a year before being sown, and grow slowly during their first few years. Probably better to buy small plants.

Is there any method for the home gardener to raise Japanese Yew? I have a yew hedge, but some have died and I need more to fill in. If you have a hotbed (either manure or electric), take cuttings in the early summer; insert in pure sand in the hotbed. Keep temperature of sand 80° to 90° F. Shade, keep moist, but not wet, and rooting should take place in 4 to 6 weeks. Then plant rooted cuttings in carefully prepared soil and mulch well over the first winter.

Can you advise how to grow the Taxus or Japanese Yew from seeds? Clean the fleshy pulp from the seed; stratify by placing alternate layers of moist peatmoss and seeds in a box; keep at a temperature of 30° to 40° F., and sow in the early spring. Some seeds may not germinate for a full year, so don't be discouraged if they all do not come up the first year.

How can I raise seedlings from berries on a Hicks Yew? This can be done (see preceding question), but Hicks Yew is a hybrid and seedlings of it will not all have the characteristic upright shape of the Hicks Yew. A better method would be to propagate by cuttings taken in early summer.

BROAD-LEAVED EVERGREENS

(See also Ericaceous Shrubs)

Which broad-leaved evergreens will grow best in New York City? *Ilex crenata* (Japanese Holly); *I. opaca,* (American Holly); Rhododendron hybrids; *Rhododendron obtusum amoenum.*

Which is a good informal evergreen, besides rhododendron and laurel. Either inkberry (*Ilex glabra*), or leucothoe.

Which broad-leaved evergreens can be planted beneath a bay window? Mountain Andromeda, evergreen azaleas, leucothoe. A few dwarfish rhododendrons, such as the Carolina Rhododendron.

Can you suggest a very low, dainty evergreen, suitable for planting near a front door? *Daphne cneorum* is low and spreading, with narrow little leaves, producing pink flowers in April, and often again in September.

What kinds of native shrubs, besides azaleas, need acid soil? Rhododendrons and all other broad-leaved evergreens; blueberries, huckleberries, and bayberries. As a general rule, provide acid soil conditions for all kinds that grow naturally in oak or evergreen woods.

SPECIFIC BROAD-LEAVED EVERGREENS

BOXWOOD

I have heard about Korean Box; what is it like? It does not grow more than 3 ft. high, resembles dwarf box, and is the hardiest of all the boxwoods.

Will box grow in woods soil, or should we use lime? Boxwood should grow well in woods soil, if not too acid. A reaction of pH 6 to 8 is considered best.

In making an English Box garden in a space 50 × 75 ft., what should spacing be? This depends on the height at which the box bushes will be kept. If a height of 3 to 4 ft. is desired, then plants could be spaced 18 ins. apart, for a hedge. Single specimens, if allowed to grow unclipped should be allowed a space at least 5 ft. in diameter.

What fertilizer should I use on boxwood? Well-rotted manure is best. Commercially prepared chemical fertilizers should be used with discretion, for fear of burning the foliage.

What is the best time of year to move large boxwoods? Commercial tree movers transplant them at any time of year. The amateur might best do it in early spring, or very early fall.

Would small boxwood plants, of which we have a number to be transplanted, do well along a cemented parkway about the building? How far apart should these be planted? When? These would grow satisfactorily if given good soil and sufficient room. They should be set 10 ins. apart if this is the dwarf variety, *Buxus sempervirens suffruticosa*. Transplant in early spring.

Should boxwood be covered for a time after transplanting? If the weather is very hot, shading with a burlap screen will help cut down the water loss. Also syringing the foliage during the evenings of hot days will aid young boxwoods in pulling through. Covering such young plants the first winter is a good practice.

What winter and summer care do boxwoods require? A thick mulch of leaves or straw on soil for the winter; plenty of water during hot, dry summer weather.

Many of the leaves of my boxwood drop off in midsummer, and the plants become unsightly. What causes this? Probably the box-wood leaf miner (which see), the most serious of boxwood pests. The tiny maggots tunnel within the leaves, causing irregular swellings or blisters in the leaf.

What material should I use to spray my boxwoods for boxwood leaf miner? Timing is most important. Keep a close watch on the under-sides of the leaves during late April and early May and when the pupae are beginning to get active it is necessary to spray right away with DDT. A better way to determine the timing is to open some of the blisters and if the pupae have black heads it is time to spray. When the infestation is heavy one spraying is not sufficient; so, spray with lindane early in summer. Follow directions on the containers and observe all precautions.

When is the best time to trim boxwood? Late June.

Can boxwood be trimmed close to the ground in order to thicken the growth at the base of the plant, where many of the limbs are very lanky? In the case of old plants with very thick trunks and branches it is practically impossible to coax new growth from the base. In young plants, this may be feasible, but cutting heavy branches back severely should be avoided.

How shall I protect old, very large, and dense boxwood during winter? Prune out any dead or diseased branches. Thoroughly water, if ground is dry. This is frequently necessary, for winter injury may result if they enter winter with dry roots. Cover with burlap supported on wood frames if injured by winter in previous years.

What makes some box turn reddish brown in winter? Is there any remedy? Either too-low temperatures, or too much bright, warm sun while the ground is still frozen. The remedy is to protect the box-wood with a screen of wood, burlap, or pine boughs.

What makes boxwood winter kill? Many complex physiological factors. The chief cause for winter killing is bright, warm sunshine in early spring, while the ground remains frozen. Another cause is low temperature.

Is the Truedwarf Box hardy in Boston? It will survive with pro-tection, but is not reliably hardy there.

How can I root cuttings of boxwood? Put them in boxes of sharp sand in July or August, and keep in a cold frame until there is danger of sand freezing. Then remove them to a frost-proof building. Keep the sand moist, but not wet, during the winter months.

Can you tell me how to root the slow-growing boxwood? (Georgia.)

Boxwood roots readily in a cool greenhouse if the cuttings are taken in November. However, in Georgia they could be rooted in a cold frame and kept there over winter if precautions are taken to prevent frost heaving the cuttings out of the sand.

DAPHNE

I have tried out Daphne cneorum five times and had no luck. I tried full sun; half shade; shade in sandy soil enriched with fertilizer; wet soil; dry soil; and also clay soil. Can you advise?   There is a controversy as to whether this plant does best in alkaline or acid soil. As a matter of fact, it grows in *both* types of soil. What is more important is that the soil should be a sandy loam and well drained. Shade has little to do with it. Such successive failures as indicated above would point to the possibility that the acidity or alkalinity of the soil might be at fault, and the soil should be made nearer the neutral point.

Is it possible to transplant a daphne which has been in one place for 5 years? (Michigan.)   If the daphne is growing satisfactorily in its present position it would be better not to attempt to move it. If it must be moved, transplant in spring, with a ball of earth attached to the roots.

What is the proper method of pruning Daphne cneorum? My plants sprawl all over the place.   It is the nature of this species to be wide-spreading. Pinching out the tips of the growing shoots will help keep it more compact.

Can Daphne odora be pruned?   Daphnes are inclined to resent severe pruning. You can keep them compact by pinching out the tips of the growing shoots.

Should a daphne plant receive special protection during the winter?   Generally it seems desirable to protect *Daphne cneorum* from winter sun and wind, though some plants come through perfectly without, even when exposed to morning sun. A loosely arranged overcoat of pine branches is sufficient.

How can an amateur best propagate the dwarf daphne?   The Rose Daphne can be rooted from cuttings, but with difficulty, by usual means. Under constant mist 100 percent rooting may be expected. Shoots may be layered in the usual way. Another method (mound layering) is to place sandy soil in among the shoots in the form of a mound, leaving only a few inches of the ends of the shoots protruding. At the end of the season the earth is drawn away and the rooted shoots are potted singly. The great objection to the latter method is that the resulting plants are rather spindly.

EUONYMUS

Which evergreen euonymus does not climb but remains a shrub?

E. japonicus, not reliably hardy north of Washington, D.C., and varieties of *E. radicans* (now called *E. fortunei*). One is the variety *carrierei.* Another is *E. r. vegetus,* but this will climb if near a wall.

HOLLY (ILEX)

What is the difference between Osmanthus aquifolium and holly? Osmanthus is often mistaken for holly because of the similarity of the foliage, but they are easily distinguished by the opposite leaves of osmanthus and the alternate leaves of holly. There is no close botanical relationship between the two.

What is the hardiest kind of holly? We have a "Christmas garden" and would like to add this to it. (Massachusetts.) The American Holly (*Ilex opaca*) might grow near the coast, or if protected; English Holly probably would not. *Ilex pedunculosa* and the native inkberry, *I. glabra,* are the hardiest, but they do not look like the Christmas holly.

Does the American Holly grow low or high? Both the American and English hollies are trees, growing eventually to 50 ft. or more in height.

What kind of soil does the American Holly prefer? A light, sandy soil, containing some decaying leafmold. Heavy clay soils should be avoided in planting hollies.

What fertilizer shall I use for American Holly? If it is growing well, do not apply any fertilizer. Well-rotted leafmold, worked well into the soil, is about the best material which can be applied. In the South, rotted manure can be applied in the late fall as a mulch, but is best used only sparingly on American Hollies in the North. Hollies prefer a light, sandy soil.

When is the best time to plant a holly tree? In early September; or early April, just as the new leaf buds begin to open.

When and how is it best to transplant holly, especially in a hedge? In areas where the climate is moist, either spring or very early fall. In the eastern United States very early spring is usually best. The plants should be dug carefully with a ball of earth about the roots. If planted as a hedge, space 2 ft. apart.

How can I most successfully transplant hollies? The safest way is to move them with a ball of earth about the roots. If they are to be dug up in the woods, sizable trees should be root-pruned (which see) a year in advance of transplanting.

Are there any real hollies that can be grown in Ohio? Of the evergreen hollies, the English cannot be grown satisfactorily in Ohio, but our native American Holly (*Ilex opaca*) is worthy of a trial in the warmer parts.

Is it possible to raise holly that is used for Christmas decorations

in Maine, or is that too far North? Maine is too far North. The northernmost limit for American Holly is Cape Cod. English Holly can be grown very little in the northeast except on Long Island and further south near the coast.

Can I get holly to grow in my garden? (Michigan.) It is doubtful if either the American or the English Holly will grow in Michigan except in extremely well-protected situations.

Is it true that in Ohio holly should be planted where the winter sun will not hit it? It is not the winter sun so much as the high, dry winds of late winter which injure holly trees. If these are prevalent, it will pay to protect the holly trees from such winds.

Where is the beautiful English Holly grown commercially? In the moist region of Oregon and Washington.

Have set out native American Hollies, using leafmold and dirt from the woods as a fill around the roots. How should I fertilize and care for them from now on? You have done the best possible. Keep the soil moist, sprinkle the tops in the evening of hot days throughout the first summer. If you have good soil, do not fertilize until one year after transplanting.

How shall I care for small holly trees? Water well, especially through the first summer after transplanting. Apply a mulch of well-rotted leafmold in the fall, and place a protective screening of burlap or pine boughs about them the first few winters.

Why do some English Holly trees have no berries? The male or pollen-bearing trees never have berries. Only the trees with the female or pistillate flowers will fruit.

I have a thriving grafted English Holly which sets good berry crop each year. When the berries are half formed, they all drop. Have tried less water, more water, and fertilizer—with no results. Why? This sounds very much as if the female flowers had not been properly fertilized with pollen. A male tree should be near by to make certain pollination occurs.

We have a female English Holly which flowers, but no berries set. Tried grafting male cuttings, but none took. Would you suggest trying budding instead? If so, what type of bud and when and where on the limbs should I do the budding? English Hollies can easily be budded. Use the shield bud, commonly used in propagating peaches. Insert buds in August or very early September. Be certain that only the pointed leaf buds found on the more vigorous shoots are used. Insert buds only on the current year's growth. (See Propagation.)

What is the matter with a holly tree that has stopped producing berries, even though male trees are present? Such incidents are difficult to explain. Some trees are alternate in their bearing habit, having a large crop of fruits one year and very few fruits the next.

Sometimes a cold, rainy season, just when the pollen is ripe, prevents its distribution by wind and insects.

A holly tree purchased 3 years ago, which then had berries, has failed to produce them since. The pH of the soil is 5.4, and there is a male tree within 70 ft. Why does it fail to bear? It may be recuperating from the shock of transplanting. Fertilize and water well. Berries will soon be formed if the near-by tree really is a male.

When and to what extent should holly trees be pruned? Pruning, especially of fruiting plants, might be done just before Christmas, by cutting short branches for decoration. Other pruning should be limited to taking out dead or diseased wood and crossed branches. Slight trimming, to make the tree dense and compact in habit, can be done during early spring, before growth starts.

How can one tell sex of a lone holly plant? I want to buy more but don't know sex needed. Observe the flowers, which are very small and inconspicuous, and appear in June. The pistillate or fruiting flowers have a well-developed pistil in the center, and undeveloped stamens. In the male flowers the pistil is small and undeveloped, and the stamens bear pollen.

Should you plant more than one Burford Holly for it to bear berries? No, the Chinese Holly (*Ilex cornuta*) (of which the Burford Holly is a variety) is unique among the hollies in this respect. The fruiting plants will bear fruits even though their flowers do not receive pollen from male plants.

How is English Holly propagated from cuttings? In a greenhouse, either in sand or a mixture of sand and peat. Use cuttings 4 to 5 ins. long taken in August or September. Shade with cheesecloth.

How is American Holly propagated from cuttings? Usually in a greenhouse, though it may be done in a cold frame. Cuttings should be 4 to 5 ins. long, of the current year's wood, taken in August or September.

INKBERRY

Does inkberry have attractive flowers? If not, why is it popular? While the inconspicuous flowers are small, it has attractive black berries and glossy leaves, somewhat like box. It is hardy and shade enduring.

MAGNOLIA

See also Flowering Trees.

Is Magnolia grandiflora hardy North? There is a large specimen growing in a sheltered spot in Brooklyn, New York, but it is not usually hardy north of Washington, D.C.

MAHONIA

Is Oregon Grapeholly the low-growing shrub with leaflets something like holly? This is *Mahonia aquifolium* (Oregongrape). The leaves vary in color from deep green to rich purple-red. If its environment is suitable and not too exposed, it has yellow flowers followed by little grapelike bunches of black berries. It prefers half shade.

Which is the hardiest kind of mahonia for use as a ground cover? *M. repens.*

What exposure suits the mahonia? A northeast exposure, where it gets enough winter sun to bring out the bronzy colors in the foliage, but not enough sun and wind to scorch the leaves.

Is mahonia (Oregongrape) hardy at sub-zero temperature? Yes, it will withstand temperatures of 5 to 10° below zero. Persistent temperatures any lower than this will probably cause injury.

How and when shall I trim mahonia, planted on north side of the house? Some of it grows upright, but part lies almost on ground. I thought there was only 1 kind of mahonia, but I seem to have 2 different kinds. There are several kinds, 2 of which are commonly grown in the East, one upright and shrubby—*Mahonia aquifolium,* and another which is really a ground cover—*Mahonia repens.* They can best be pruned in early spring before growth starts. *M. Bealei* and the closely related *M. japonica,* which are dubiously hardy on Long Island, N.Y., are excellent in the southern states.

PYRACANTHA

Are any of the pyracanthas hardy? Yes. *P. coccinea,* or firethorn, is fairly hardy in the middle states. Sometimes winter kills in the vicinity of New York City.

Would like to plant 2 pyracanthas, one either side of large living-room window, to grow against house. However, there are 3 small oak trees, about 9 to 12 ft. distant, on front lawn. Would their shade cause the pyracantha not to fruit, or to lack color? Planting where you suggest would not be advisable. For an abundance of berries full light is needed. Though the oaks may not be very big at present, it is probable that in a few years they would cast a shade too dense for the pyracanthas to fruit satisfactorily.

When is the best time to transplant Pyracantha coccinea lalandi? A difficult plant to move successfully, particularly if it has attained any size. Spring is the most suitable season, and it must be moved with a ball of earth. Do not attempt to remove the burlap when replanting. A more certain method is to enclose the ball of earth in a box when transplanting.

What can one do to make pyracantha bushes have more berries?
Keep in good health and growing vigorously. They frequently bear
good crops only in alternate years. A fertilizer rich in superphosphate,
combined with root-pruning if bush is growing vigorously, might
aid in increasing fruit production. Full sunshine, or at least uninter-
rupted light, is a requisite.

*Firethorn—most colorful of ber-
ried shrubs for winter.*

How should pyracanthas be treated when dead branches appear?
Pyracanthas are susceptible to fire blight, a serious disease of apples
and pears, their close relatives. When this appears, cut out the
branches immediately and burn them. The cut should be made
considerably below the injured part. (See Section VIII.)

**Last year my pyracantha was full of berries. This year it had none.
Why? How can I keep it from growing so tall?** Most berried shrubs
are alternate in their bearing, producing heavy crops one year and
light crops the next. Pyracantha can be restrained at any height by
pruning—preferably in summer.

How are pyracantha cuttings rooted? Take the cuttings in July
and place them in 3 to 4 ins. of sand in a fairly deep box. Cover the
box with a sheet of glass, and keep it in a position out of the sun but
with good light; or root them in a cold frame.

VIBURNUM, EVERGREEN

Is there a good evergreen viburnum? Yes, Leatherleaf Viburnum
(*V. rhytidophyllum*), with long, oval, leathery wrinkled leaves. Protect from too much winter sun. Not reliably hardy north of Philadelphia, Pennsylvania.

ERICACEOUS SHRUBS

What does "ericaceous" mean? This term is applied to the plant
family Ericaceae, consisting mainly of shrubs and small trees which
in general require a sandy, peaty acid soil. Among the Ericaceae are
the following: andromeda, arbutus, heather, enkianthus, wintergreen,
blueberry, Mountain Laurel, sandmyrtle, leucothoe, pieris, rhododendron (including azalea).

CULTURE

What fertilizer ingredients, in what formula, would you suggest for feeding ericaceous plants, and at the same time maintain acidity in the soil? Tankage or cottonseed meal applied at the rate of 5 lbs. per 100 sq. ft. is satisfactory for small plants. For large plants use 6–10–6 fertilizer in which cottonseed or soybean meal is used to supply ¼ to ½ of the nitrogen. Apply at the rate of 2 to 3 lbs. per 100 sq. ft. of bed area. If the soil is sufficiently acid, 7½ lbs. nitrate of soda, 10 lbs. superphosphate, 2½ lbs. sulfate of potash could be used to approximate the above formula. (See also Azalea and Rhododendron.)

What soil is best for Mountain Laurel? Moist, acid, bountifully supplied with humus. Grows well in rhododendron soils.

Do rhododendrons, Mountain Laurel, etc., require special soil? Yes. A well-drained subsoil beneath, 12 to 18 ins. of topsoil containing up to 50 per cent acid humus matter. A totally uncongenial soil should be removed bodily, and replaced with a suitable compost. For acid humus, use pine, spruce, hemlock, or oak leafmold; or peatmoss. Peatmoss, mixed with a little very old manure, makes a good soil for plants of this type.

Can I condition my alkaline soil for rhododendrons with aluminum sulfate? If your soil is rich in humus matter—yes, but flowers of sulfur is safer. Periodic applications may be required to maintain a properly acid condition. Do not expect success with aluminum sulfate in uncongenial soils poor in humus. Acidity is only one factor in preparing a soil suitable for plants of the heath family.

My soil is very acid, but rhododendrons do not grow well; why? The soil may be too acid, and poorly drained. Bring it up to pH 5.5 by adding pulverized dolomitic limestone. Dig out bed to a depth of 18 ins., put in 6 ins. cinders and return soil.

SPECIFIC ERICACEOUS SHRUBS

AZALEA

What to Grow

What types of azaleas would be hardy for this section of the country? The temperature often goes to 20° below, but not for any great length of time. (New York.) Many azaleas can be grown in northern New York and New England. Some are *calendulacea, nudiflora, rosea, vaseyi, arborescens, viscosa, schlippenbachi,* and *obtusa kaempferi.* Many of the Ghent hybrids are also worth a trial, and will grow and bloom even when temperatures drop as low as 20° below zero.

What are the best varieties of azaleas to plant in southern New York State? Practically any of the azaleas except the Kurume and the India varieties. Many of the colorful Ghent hybrids are hardy even as far North as central Maine.

How can I lengthen the period of bloom in azaleas? By selecting types which bloom successively. The following should insure 2 months of continuous flowers from early July to late August: *Azalea mucronulata, A. vaseyi, A. nudiflora, A. calendulacea, A. arborescens,* and *A. viscosa.*

Are there any azaleas which will grow in swampy places? *Azalea viscosa* grows naturally in swampy ground. *A. vaseyi* is also satisfactory.

What can you combine with azaleas for summer and fall bloom? Soil is part clay. Have put oak-leaf mulch around azaleas, but nothing else seems to thrive. For a midsummer shrub, try *Clethra alnifolia.* For autumn flower, the low, matting, blue-flowered Ceratostigma. For both of these the clay soil should be lightened with sand and peat.

Soil and Fertilizer

What conditions are necessary for growth of Ghent azaleas? These deciduous azaleas need a fairly open situation and deep, well-drained acid soil, with ⅓ humus-forming materials—leafmold from oaks or evergreens, rotted hardwood sawdust, or peatmoss.

Where and in what soil should I plant Pinkshell Azalea? Light shade such as that given by thin woodland. Deep, moist soil, with plenty of humus.

How can I be certain a soil is acid? Send samples to your county agricultural agent or to State Agricultural Experiment Station for testing; or buy one of several soil testing kits available for just this purpose. (See Acidity—Section I.)

Our soil is definitely alkaline, but I want to grow azaleas and rhododendrons. What should I do? The best way is to excavate the soil in the area for planting to an approximate depth of 2½ ft. Place in the excavation only acid soil rich in humus.

With a soil only slightly alkaline, how does one make it acid with a minimum amount of trouble? The *second* best way of acquiring an acid soil is to apply aluminum sulfate to the soil in question, at rates depending on the alkalinity, or pH. Following figures indicate reaction of soil at start, and amount of aluminum sulfate per sq. yd.: pH 5.5 to 6.0, ¼ lb.; pH 6.5 to 7.0, ½ lb.; pH 7.0 to 8.0, ¾ lb. This should be well watered in, and the soil again tested at the end of 2 weeks. If the soil has not reached the desired acidity, to a depth of 6 to 12 ins., apply sulfur at ⅙ of the rate given above.

How acid should soil be for azaleas and rhododendrons? For most of them, pH 5 to 6.

Should a soil in which azaleas and rhododendrons are growing be tested more than once a year? Only if the plants fail to grow well.

Do deciduous azaleas and evergreen azaleas need the same amount of soil acidity? Yes.

Will coffee and tea grounds sprinkled around azaleas help to acidify the soil? Would this practice be harmful? No, it would not acidify soil to any marked degree; but it would not be harmful.

What is the best time of year to feed azaleas? They can be fed either in early spring or fall.

We use cottonseed meal for fertilizer a great deal down here. Can this be used on azaleas? (South Carolina.) Yes. A mixture of 2 lbs. of cottonseed meal and 1 lb. of ammonium sulfate, used at the rate of 1 to 2 lbs. per 100 sq. ft., makes a very good acid fertilizer. (See also under Rhododendron.)

What type of soil does wild azalea (Azalea nudiflora) require? A normally moist, acid soil.

Transplanting

When is the best time to put out azaleas? (Georgia.) In your region, late summer and fall planting only are preferable. Most varieties of azaleas, however, can be transplated in full bloom, if they are carefully dug, balled, and burlapped.

At what season of the year should wild azalea (wild honeysuckle) be transplanted? It can be transplanted either in the fall after its leaves have dropped or in the early spring, before new growth starts. Spring is the preferred season. Should be carefully dug to preserve all roots, with soil adhering to them. The roots should not be allowed to dry out while plant is being moved.

Why do I have trouble growing azaleas dug in the woods when those purchased from nurserymen do very well indeed? Most plants growing in the woods have considerably longer but fewer roots than if they were grown in the nursery, where they are periodically root-pruned. In digging azaleas in the woods usually much of the root system is cut off.

Culture

What summer and winter care do azaleas need? Water thoroughly during drought in summer. Mulch with oak leaves, pine needles, or peatmoss to maintain acidity and to protect roots in winter. Tender varieties should have evergreen boughs or burlap placed about them.

Is it possible to grow rhododendron and azalea successfully in Ohio? What are the soil requirements? Yes. Azaleas are easier to grow than the evergreen rhododendrons, but both can be grown from Maine to Florida, and west to the Mississippi River, *providing* they have acid soil, plenty of moisture, and not too severe winter temperatures.

What is the proper treatment for azaleas the year 'round? Our bushes are not blooming. (Minnesota.) Many azaleas, especially in the colder parts of the United States, have their flower buds killed by very low temperatures. Plant only the hardiest kinds in cold areas, such as the Pinkshell Azalea, Flame Azalea, Pinxterflower, and some of the Ghent hybrids.

How can I grow azaleas (which come from West Virginia) between lakes Ontario and Seneca, in soil that is not naturally acid? First make the soil acid. Practically anything which is hardy in the mountains of West Virginia will prove hardy in central New York.

I have 2 plants of Azalea rosea and 2 of Azalea nudiflora. They have been in for 3 years and both of the former have bloomed each year, but the latter never have. Why? What degree of temperature is the minimum under which the Azalea nudiflora will bloom? Both these azalea species need acid soil, and if grown in identical conditions the one should bloom if the other does. *Azalea nudiflora* will bloom even though temperatures fall considerably below zero.

Have a wild azalea. How can it be made to bloom? If collected in Massachusetts this is probably *Azalea nudiflora*. If given acid soil, plenty of water, and a mulch of pine needles, oak leaves, or peatmoss, it will undoubtedly bloom well in 2 years' time.

How do you pinch back azaleas? Merely pinch off end of growing twigs. This will force several side buds to grow, and will result in a bushier shrub.

How should azaleas be pruned? Cut out diseased or dying branches from the base of the plant. Often it is advisable to cut off a few twigs here and there to force out thick growth. Otherwise they need little pruning.

Should seed pods be pruned from azaleas? Cut off dead flowers before seed pods form, then more strength will go into flower-bud formation for the next year.

When should azaleas be sprayed? How often? Lace bug and red spider are the most serious pests of azaleas. (See Section VIII.)

Winter Protection

Do azaleas need winter protection in vicinity of New York? How is this best provided? Only the more tender evergreen sorts need the kind of protection provided by a burlap screen or pine boughs, so placed about the plant as to protect it from high winds and sun. All azaleas will do better if provided with a mulch of some acid material (oak leaves, pine needles, or peatmoss) about their roots in winter.

Should azaleas be covered completely for the winter? If by this is meant the complete covering of leaves, the answer is, No! But if a mere shading of the plant is meant, this proves very helpful when tender varieties are being grown.

Should young azaleas be covered for the winter if they are not sheltered by shrubs?   The evergreen varieties might well be covered, since these are the least hardy. Covering material should be light, allowing air circulation.

How can potted azaleas purchased at the florist and full of buds and flowers, be taken care of so as to bloom again?   Most of the florists' potted azaleas are Kurume azaleas, and are not hardy north of Philadelphia, Pennsylvania. They will grow out of doors the first summer but will be killed by winter cold. In the South, such plants can be planted out of doors in acid soil, protected the first winter, and usually come through in fine shape.

Should azaleas be kept in hothouses or a lath house during the winter months? (California.)   This really depends on the section of California and the kind of azalea. The more tender sorts should not be exposed to more than a few degrees of frost.

Should azaleas have a mulch about their roots? Why?   Yes. Because their roots grow best when the soil is cool and moist. In the winter a mulch protects the roots against extremely low temperatures.

Is it good to cover azaleas and rhododendrons with manure?   Not if it is fresh. Well-rotted manure can be used in moderation without injury to the plants.

When should a mulch be applied to azaleas?   It is well to put a mulch over the roots just before winter weather sets in. This, if not more than a few inches deep, may be left on until time to place new mulching material for the next winter.

What makes a good mulching material for azaleas and rhododendrons?   Oak leaves, pine needles, and acid peatmoss. Upon decomposition all these are beneficial to the growth of this type of plant.

I have no oak leaves but plenty of maple leaves. Could I use these as a mulch?   It would be better to use peatmoss instead. Maple leaves tend to pack closely when wet, thus keeping air from the plant roots. When very tightly packed they frequently "cake" and have been known to kill azaleas for this reason. Also, maple leaves are alkaline when decomposed.

Propagation

Are azaleas propagated by seed?   Azaleas are propagated from cuttings, by grafting, and also from seeds, depending upon the kind and the purpose for which they are needed. Any of the wild forms, native or exotic, may be raised from seeds, as the seedlings will reproduce the characters of the parent. Hybrid forms and "sports" cannot be reproduced from seeds.

How can I start azalea from seed? Collect seed pods in late fall when they are ready to open. Keep dry, and in February shake seeds out on milled or ground sphagnum moss 1 inch deep on top of acid soil well firmed in pots. Keep moss moist, preferably by using a fine mist spray from time to time. In several months seedlings should be of right size to prick off and transplant.

Can azaleas be propagated by cuttings? It is exceedingly difficult to root cuttings of the native azaleas, but some of the more familiar garden forms, such as Snow, Hinodegiri, Torch, and Amoena, can be rooted with good success in July. The cuttings should be about 3 ins. long, taken (just after new growth is completed) from the tips of the shoots and placed in a rooting mixture of sand and peat in a cold frame.

Are azaleas propagated by grafting? The grafting of azaleas is almost entirely confined to some of the tender kinds, normally grown in greenhouses. Propagating cases in a warm greenhouse are needed, and the grafting has to be done very skillfully to be successful.

EVERGREEN

How can I grow the evergreen azaleas? They need much the same conditions as rhododendron, with which they are now included by botanists.

A group of Azalea Hinodegiri have become too large. Can they be clipped rather severely, after next bloom, without injury or serious loss of future bloom? Yes, they withstand heavy pruning.

Will you discuss winter protection for azaleas in this region? Mine fail to blossom in the spring; most of the leaves are brown and new growth is slow to start. During the summer they grow well. (Northern New York.) The evergreen types are not completely hardy in northern New York. If you build a screen of burlap or pine boughs, this may help to bring them through in better condition; but if the flower buds are killed, even with this protection, then the thing to do is to plant a hardier variety. *Azalea calendulacea, A. nudiflora,* and *A. viscosa* are among the hardiest of the deciduous azaleas.

Last June and July I made over 200 evergreen azalea cuttings of the current season's growth, 3 to 5 ins. long. I dipped half in Rootone and the other half in No. 1 Hormodin powder, placed them in a mixture of sand and peat, in a shady open cold frame, and kept bed moist, with temperature around 70° F. After 4 or 5 weeks the leaves would fall, leaving a dried, withered stem, minus roots. Where was my mistake? If by the term "open cold frame" you mean that you did not put the sash on the frame, then that was the mistake. Except for removing condensed moisture from the glass, the frame should be kept closed for 6 weeks, after which a *little* ventilation is desirable. Some of the tender greenhouse azaleas do not root readily from cuttings and, consequently, are grafted.

What evergreen azaleas are hardy in New Jersey? Amoena Azalea, magenta; Hinodegiri Azalea, strong rose color; and Rose Azalea, white.

HEATHER (CALLUNA)

I want to plant a little "sheet" of Scotch Heather. What kind of soil? Choose a well-drained situation. Prepare a cushion, fully a foot deep, made up of about ⅓ garden loam, ⅓ sand, and ⅓ highly acid leafmold. If the latter is not available, use peatmoss instead, and add a little very old manure.

Can heather be satisfactorily grown out of doors in the vicinity of New York? Scotch Heather grows quite well, in peat soil, along the Eastern seacoast. The plants usually kill back in about 3 years, and new plants should be used for replacement.

Should Scotch Heather be pruned? Early-blooming varieties should be cut back to the base of the flowering shoots as soon as the blossoms have faded. In sections where heather suffers from winter injury it should be cut back in spring just as growth is beginning.

MOUNTAIN LAUREL (KALMIA LATIFOLIA)

When does Mountain Laurel bloom, and what color are the blossoms? Will it stand shade? Deep pink buds and pink-white flower clusters, in June. Sun or shade.

Must Mountain Laurel have shade? Will grow in full sun if soil conditions are right, but seems to do best in partial shade. For soil and culture see rhododendron.

What are some uses for Mountain Laurel? Foundation planting; mass planting, in woodland: among azalea, rhododendron, leucothoe, ferns, hemlock.

When is the proper time to transplant the wild Mountain Laurel? In the early spring, before the buds have started growth.

Is Mountain Laurel hardy in Cleveland, Ohio, without any protective covering? Yes; but be certain the soil in which it is planted is acid.

In transplanting laurel from woods have been generally unsuccessful, even with utmost care exercised on basis of rules governing growth of this plant. Any specific reasons? Sounds like soil trouble. Perhaps by bringing in considerable leafmold and soil from woods you could succeed in growing it.

Will you give proper culture for Kalmia latifolia? Mine is 7 or 8 years old and has never bloomed, though it seems to be healthy.

If the plant is healthy, this shows it to be growing in good soil. You might try the effect of superphosphate (15 to 20 per cent) applied beneath the mulch, at the rate of 4 oz. per sq. yd. Perhaps the shade is too dense.

LEUCOTHOE

What is Leucothoe catesbaei? How is it used? An evergreen with arching stems clothed with handsome long racemes of white flowers and long, oval leathery leaves. Acid soil and partial shade. Good for woodland plantings, with rhododendron, laurel, and hemlock.

How can I grow leucothoe? Needs well-drained, acid soil containing ⅓ or more organic matter—acid leafmold or peatmoss. Partial shade preferable.

PIERIS

When do the "andromedas" bloom? What are the blossoms like? Mountain Andromeda (*Pieris floribunda*) has erect panicles of tiny cream-colored waxy bells in May. Japanese Andromeda (*Pieris japonica*), drooping panicles slightly longer than on the Mountain Andromeda, in April to May.

Would Japanese Andromeda be hardy in northern New England? No; but our native Mountain Andromeda probably would be.

What is the difference between our native Mountain Andromeda and the Japanese species? The native (*Pieris floribunda*), though hardier, is not so easily content nor is it as handsome of leaf and flower as *P. japonica*. The latter is better suited to formal plantings and the former to woodlands.

Which andromeda has leaves that turn reddish bronze in winter and new spring leaves with a rose-colored cast? Japanese Andromeda.

What soil is required by the andromedas? Moist, peaty or sandy soil. Part shade desirable.

Would Pieris japonica stand through the winter on Long Island, if planted on a north or west exposure, with a peatmoss mulch? Yes, if the winter winds are not too high. *P. floribunda* is more hardy, while *P. japonica* is easier to grow.

RHODODENDRON

What to Grow

Which types of rhododendron are the hardiest and the most satisfactory for growth in southern New England (as mass planting, not as specimen plants)? The Giant Rosebay (*Rhododendron maxi-*

mum) is the hardiest of all the rhododendrons. It is not so colorful as some of the hybrids, but it can be used for massing.

What are some of the best and hardiest rhododendron hybrids? Red—Atrosanguineum, H. W. Sargent; pink—Abraham Lincoln, Roseum Elegans; purple—Purpureum Elegans, Purpureum Grandiflorum; white—Album Elegans, Album Grandiflorum.

What color are the flowers of different native rhododendrons? Carolina Rhododendron, pink; Catawba Rhododendron, rosy-purple; Rosebay (*R. maximum*), pale pink.

How tall does the Carolina Rhododendron grow? Six ft. maximum height; usually less under cultivation.

Soil and Fertilizer

I would like to grow rhododendrons here. How can I make soil acid? (Illinois.) See under Azaleas for method of making soil acid. In Illinois, especially the northwestern part, the summers are very hot and dry and the winters very cold, which is extremely hard on rhododendrons. Precautions should be taken to give foliage and roots plenty of moisture in the summer; also to give winter protection, especially in exposed situations.

My soil is very dry, and some of my rhododendrons have died. What should I do? Mix decomposed vegetable matter (rotted manure, rotted oak or pine leaves and peatmoss) with the soil. Then apply a mulch of rotting oak leaves, pine needles, or peatmoss about the base of the plants. All these help to conserve moisture.

What is a good fertilizer for rhododendrons and azaleas? Mr. C. O. Dexter of Sandwich, Massachusetts, has recommended the following mixture, and it has worked very well indeed: 7 lbs. of Chilean nitrate of soda, 3 lbs. muriate of potash, 20 lbs. superphosphate; use 2 to 3 lbs. per 100 sq. ft.

What is the best formula for fertilizers for rhododendrons and azaleas, to help their color but not too much of a growth stimulant? The fertilizer mixture mentioned above is excellent for this purpose, for although it carries some nitrate, it contains high percentages of phosphates and potash, and these aid primarily in flower production.

What fertilizer should one give rhododendrons growing in a poor, sandy soil? Add decaying vegetable material, such as rotted manure, decaying oak leaves, pine needles, and peatmoss. Chemical fertilizers alone added to a poor, sandy soil would not be sufficient.

Is flowers of sulfur a desirable fertilizer for azaleas and rhododendrons? It acts as a fertilizer, for in making the soil more acid it releases certain materials which were not formerly available to the plant.

Planting and Culture

Will rhododendrons grow in full sun?   Yes; but partial shade is preferable.

Are there any particular requirements, as to sun or shade, for rhododendrons?   Rhododendrons bloom most profusely in the full sun; but if grown in partial shade they will bloom sufficiently well to be attractive. In deep shade most varieties bloom very little.

Do rhododendrons and azaleas need the same general growing conditions?   Yes, except that rhododendrons will grow better in shaded situations.

When should rhododendrons be planted?   Preferably in the early spring.

Where should rhododendrons be planted?   Where they get some shade and some direct sunlight. Also, they should be protected from high winter winds. Their roots should not be allowed to dry out at any time.

My place is exposed to wind from ocean. Will rhododendrons thrive?   No. In any case they need shelter from strong wind especially in winter.

How old must rhododendrons be to bloom? Mine are 5 years old, growing well in prepared acid soil and partial shade, but do not bloom. Many rhododendrons bloom when they are about 5 years old. This particular plant may be growing too fast vegetatively. Root-pruning might be practiced by pushing a spade into the soil around the base of the plant, not too near the stem. Or you might try superphosphate (15 to 20 per cent), applied beneath the mulch, at the rate of 4 oz. per sq. yd.

Can you tell me why my rhododendron did not bloom although it has healthy foliage and growing conditions (acid) are favorable?   It may have been that the flower buds were killed by an unusually cold winter. Also, rhododendrons are like many other ornamentals in that they bloom profusely one year and very little the next. There is little that the amateur can do about this "alternate-bearing" habit.

How is Rhododendron maximum made to bloom better?   This species does best only in the shade. Ornamentally it is not so good as the earlier-flowering hybrids, because the flowers appear *after* the new growth has started, and this frequently hides the flowers. Plenty of moisture, acid soil, and an acid mulch are helpful aids.

Winter Protection

Would it be helpful or harmful to tie burlap sacks around the branches of my rhododendrons and to cover the buds, in winter?   It would be harmful. Air must circulate about these plants in the winter, and wrapping stems and branches would not permit this. It is far better to build a *screen* of burlap about them, slightly open at the base to permit free air circulation at all times, but also giving a screening and shading protection.

What is the best protection for rhododendrons exposed to strong winds?   Burlap screens, or screens of evergreen boughs, so designed and placed as to give protection from winds, and some shade during winter months—especially February and March.

When should leafmold mulch be applied to rhododendrons?   In fall.

Propagation

How are rhododendrons propagated? Can they be propagated by hardwood cuttings?   The large-flowered garden kinds are usually grafted, but Carolina, Rosebay, and Catawba Rhododendrons are raised from seeds. Some of the hybrid kinds can be raised from cuttings taken in August, but with most of them the percentage of rooting is not very large.

Can I root leaf cuttings of Rhododendron?   Dr. Henry T. Skinner has had good success in rooting leaf-bud cuttings. These were made in late July by cutting leaves with a sliver of wood together with a growth bud attached. These were treated with a root-inducing growth regulator and inserted in a mixture of 3 parts by bulk of quartz sand and 2 parts peatmoss. They were kept in a propagating frame in a greenhouse until they were rooted.

Can rhododendron cuttings be rooted by the constant mist method?   Yes, it is well worth a trial.

What is the proper time for grafting rhododendrons?   Rhododendrons are generally grafted, in heated greenhouse, during January and February. (See also Grafting, this section).

Can rhododendron grafting be done outdoors?   While this is not altogether impossible, it is not a method to be recommended, as there would be too many failures for every union obtained.

What is the type of graft used on rhododendron?   The veneer graft is most commonly used. The understock is not cut back at the time of grafting. A downward, slanting cut is made on the stem of the understock, about 1½ ins. long and about ⅓ of the way through the stem. A second cut into the stem (at the base of the first) removes the piece of bark and attached wood. The base of the scion is cut to correspond to the cuts on the understock.

Can any kind of root be used as an understock for grafting rhododendrons?   No. It must be another rhododendron. The one most commonly used for understocks is *Rhododendron ponticum*. The tenderness of this species, however, makes it anything but satisfactory for the purpose in this country.

How should rhododendrons be separated? Rhododendrons as a rule should not be "separated" in the same sense that one thinks of separating perennials. They grow as individual plants, often in clumps. Any attempt to divide these clumps would probably prove disastrous.

Insects and Diseases

See Section VIII.

Is there any insect that destroys the leaves of rhododendrons? The lace bug is the most serious pest of rhododendron foliage. This is a small insect with lacelike wings appearing on the undersurface of the leaves. It appears in May and June, to be followed by a second infestation later in the summer.

When should rhododendrons be sprayed to control the lace bug? What material should be used? Spray as soon as the insects appear, usually in June. Several materials are available for control. Use nicotine-soap solution; or lindane, 1 tablespoonful of 25 percent to 1 gallon; or malathion emulsion at 1 teaspoonful per gallon. Spray forcibly on the *under* surfaces of the foliage, on a cloudy day when the temperature does not exceed 80° F. Spraying in full, hot sunshine will burn the foliage. (See Section VIII.)

SPECIFIC TENDER SHRUBS

ACACIA

Can we grow the yellow-blossom acacia trees one sees in California? (Connecticut.) No, they will not endure temperatures much below 20° F.

Where can I get plants of the acacia with small yellow blossoms? Can it be grown in the garden? (Missouri.) Many California nurseries can supply acacias. They are perennials (either trees or shrubs). They are not hardy where winter temperatures drop below 20° above zero.

BAY TREE (LAURUS)

How hardy is bay tree and when is the best time to trim to formal shape? It is not really hardy north of Philadelphia, Pennsylvania. Trim when the new shoots have almost completed their growth. A second trimming may be necessary if the first stimulates the production of new shoots.

CAMELLIA

See also Regional Section.

In a Southern garden I saw a shrub or plant that I became very much interested in. The owner called it Camellia japonica. It had a

double flower like a rose and as large. Please tell me where I can buy this shrub? (Pennsylvania.) Camellias in many beautiful forms and colors can be obtained from Southern nurseries. *C. sasanqua* will be hardy with you in Pennsylvania.

Soil, Fertilizer, and Planting

At what pH do camellias grow best? Will they do better at 5.7 to 6.2 or from 6 to 7? Camellias are less particular in this regard than gardenias and some other plants. They should thrive in either of the soils mentioned providing it is physically in good condition and is fertile.

What soil preparation is necessary for camellias? (California). Make the soil rich and friable to a depth of at least a foot, or, better still, 2 ft. Mix with it very generous amounts of leafmold, or peatmoss and very old rotted manure. Good compost may also be used.

What is the best fertilizer for camellias? When should it be applied? Old cow manure (or dehydrated manure or cottonseed meal, plus compost) applied as a mulch at the beginning of the growing season, followed, a few weeks later, by a light dressing of any complete fertilizer.

Are chemical plant foods good for camellia bushes? They respond best to organic fertilizers of a comparatively mild character. Old rotted manure, cottonseed meal, and bone meal are all excellent.

What is the best way to start and grow camellias? For outdoor culture, prepare ground so that it is rich and well drained but retentive of moisture. Select lightly shaded position. Obtain good plants from nursery of repute. If possible, visit gardens and nurseries where camellias are grown and familiarize yourself with their needs.

When is best time to move Camellia japonica? During the dormant season, in winter or in early spring.

Culture

Can camellias be forced to bloom earlier? If so, how? They can be encouraged to bloom early by planting them in sheltered locations; a more certain method is to grow them in pots, tubs, or planted out in ground beds in a cool, airy greenhouse.

What causes few blossoms rather than many on a well-fertilized camellia bush? Possibly the plant is in too dense shade. Some protection from strong sunlight is helpful, but lack of sufficient light is harmful. Also overfertilization may result in too vigorous growth at expense of flower production.

What is it that eats holes in camellia leaves? Have never found anything on them, and no spray that I have used seems to do any good. Probably the Asiatic beetle or the black vine weevil. Before specific advice can be given, a surer diagnosis is desirable. Send specimens to your State Agricultural Experiment Station. Spraying with lead arsenate probably best control.

What causes my camellia leaves to fall off? Damage to roots due to careless transplanting; waterlogged soil; lack of sufficient water, particularly during growing season; or spray damage.

What causes the leaves of an apparently healthy camellia plant to turn brown just before coming into blossom? This may be due to very cold weather, disease, or extreme drought. Spray injury could also be responsible.

My camellia has rusty coat on buds, and they do not open in the spring. What should I do? (Texas.) You seemingly have a variety unsuited to outdoor conditions. There are some kinds that are satisfactory in greenhouses, but not outdoors. Replace plant with variety recommended by local nurseryman.

Will frequent sprinkling of camellias while in bud cause the buds to rot and drop off? I understand they should be sprinkled during hot weather. Spraying of the foliage during hot weather is beneficial. Make sure, however, that the ground also is kept moist to a good depth. Do not be deceived by merely wetting the surface.

Why do many full buds fall off my red camellias late in the season? They are planted on the east side of the house, with just the morning sun. Should they be moved? The commonest reason for bud-dropping is lack of sufficient moisture at the roots of the plant. This is particularly true of secondary buds that develop if a late frost has killed early growth. Certain diseases also cause bud-dropping.

Propagation

Can I increase my favorite camellia by layering? Yes. See Propagation. In June or July, nick a low branch with a knife, bend to the ground, hollow out a little trench, and lay the branch in this. Cover with sandy soil and use a brick or other heavy object to prevent motion. Be sure that the layer is kept constantly moist.

How and when can we start camellias from cuttings? July. Select firm, young growths, 3 or 4 ins. long; cut away lower leaves and cut stem horizontally below joint with sharp knife. Plant firmly in sand or sand and peatmoss. Keep lightly shaded, moist, and in humid atmosphere. Slight bottom heat helps rooting.

Diseases and Pests

See Section VIII.

What makes the buds on my Soeur Therese Camellia turn brown on edges of petals? This may be due to flower-blight disease. Send specimens to your Agricultural Experiment Station for examination.

What spray can I use to destroy the Asiatic beetle which is destroying my camellia plants? Spread lead arsenate (1 lb. to 100 sq. ft.) over surface of ground and wash it well into soil. Spray foliage with 5 lbs. lead arsenate and 4 lbs. wheat flour to 100 gals. of water. (See Section VIII.)

What is the scurfy white substance on the under side of my camellia leaves? This is tea scale, and must be controlled by carefully spraying with an oil-emulsion spray during late summer and fall. (See Section VIII.)

The leaves on one of my camellias have large, dark spots, and drop off the tree. What causes this? Possibly the black mold disease, which is often associated with another infection called spot disease. Spray with Bordeaux mixture, or dust with dusting sulfur.

GARDENIA

See also House Plants.

In growing gardenias, we are advised if the leaves turn yellow to use aluminum sulfate around them. How much shall I use and how often? Use at the rate of from 4 to 12 oz. to each 10 sq. ft., and frequently enough to keep the pH of the soil at 4.5. A soil test is necessary to determine this.

I know Capejasmine (gardenia) requires acid soil. I have fed copperas and aluminum sulfate, but still the leaves are yellow and smutty-looking, and no blooms. Can anything be done? Use more natural methods of acidifying the soil. Mix oak leafmold, rotted pine needles, or granulated peatmoss with the soil, 1 to 3. The smutty appearance is indicative of the presence of scale insects. Spray with a good contact spray to get rid of them. (See Section VIII.)

When is the best time to transplant a gardenia, crowded in its present location? At the very beginning of the growing season, when new shoots and leaves are observed to be starting.

May gardenia plants remain outside in garden all year 'round? (New York.) Even with protection gardenias are not hardy in New York. Virginia is about as far North as *Gardenia florida* can be successfully grown outdoors.

How can I make gardenias bloom in my yard? The Capejasmine or *Gardenia florida* needs a sheltered, sunny position, a moist (not waterlogged) acid soil, and protection from frost.

Is it necessary to protect small gardenia plants by building frame around them, and wrapping with sacks? They need protection of this kind if there is danger that they will encounter frost.

JASMINE

Which jasmines are hardy North? None reliably hardy though

Jasminum nudiflorum (a good wall shrub), blooming very early before leaves appear, can be grown in the vicinity of New York City if given a southern exposure with the protection of a sheltering wall. *J. humile,* an erect evergreen to 20 ft. with yellow flowers, and *J. officinale,* climbing, with white flowers, are grown near the seaboard in the Middle Atlantic states.

Can jasmine (the flowers of which are used for tea) be grown as far North as Cleveland, Ohio? Not very well. In a protected spot it might live through the winter; normally one would expect it not to be hardy.

OLEANDER

How can I succeed with oleanders in my garden? (California.) They are easily grown out of doors in the South. Watch for scale. (See Section VIII.)

Will you tell me how to start slips of oleanders? Cuttings taken in July and August root readily in sand if kept in close, humid surroundings such as a cold frame or glass-covered box. Or shoots may be kept in water until rooted, and then potted in soil.

POMEGRANATE

What soil is best for pomegranate? A heavy, deep loam. Suited only to tropical and subtropical climates, or for the greenhouse.

When should a pomegranate (flowering) be pruned? Shorten strong-growing shoots about ⅓ when they have almost attained their full length.

HEDGES AND WINDBREAKS

WHAT TO GROW

What would be the best kind of hedge to set out on the north side of a lot? This depends on the height. For under 6 ft. a yew hedge would be good, but expensive. For over 6 ft. a hemlock or White Pine hedge. These are evergreens and so would give protection 365 days a year. Evergreen hedges cost more, but they are worth it for their winter protection.

Which flowering hedge would look well around a vegetable garden? It should be low so that it will not shade the vegetables. Spirea Anthony Waterer, with its flat-topped, deep red-rose flowers would give color to the area. Prune back after it has bloomed and more blossoms should follow.

Which flowering shrubs would make good hedge plants, even if unpruned? Barberry, especially upright-growing types; *Abelia grandi-*

flora; Peatree or Peashrub (*Caragana*); Japanese Quince, especially the variety "Spitfire"; deutzia; hydrangea, bush honeysuckle, spirea, common lilac, many of the viburnums. Unpruned privet makes a good tall hedge or screen.

What are the beautiful hedges made of that one sees in England? Can they be grown here? (Maryland.) Many different species are used. Perhaps you have reference to the English Hawthorn and English Holly combination. This could be done here by substituting American Holly for the less-hardy English species.

What would be a good low deciduous hedge, not above 2 ft. high, to put around a sunken garden? One of the dwarf barberries (*Berberis thunbergi minor*); Slender Deutzia; the dwarf Cranberrybush Viburnum (*Viburnum opulus nanum*).

What would be good as a fairly high deciduous hedge for screening? Acanthopanax, Corkbark or Winged Euonymus, rose-of-Sharon, privet, buckthorn, Vanhoutte's Spirea, various lilacs.

Could you suggest some good deciduous trees which would screen our garage driveway from our out-of-door sitting room—something natural-looking for an informal place where there is plenty of room? (Massachusetts.) European Beech. It can be sheared.

What is the name of a hedge plant that would grow at least 6 ft. tall? I do not want privet or barberry. The one I have in mind has dark berries on it. The American Cranberrybush with red berries (*Viburnum trilobum*); or the Glossy Buckthorn with red and black berries (*Rhamnus frangula*).

What is the difference between buckthorn (Rhamnus cathartica) and Alder Buckthorn (R. frangula)? Which is better for a hedge? (Maine.) The former, because it is hardier than Alder Buckthorn. The latter, however, has pointed glossy leaves, while the former has dull rounded ones.

What is the best fast-growing hedge for screening (not privet)? (North Carolina.) Myrtle (*Myrtus communis*); Laurelcherry (*Prunus laurocerasus*); Portuguese Laurelcherry, (*Prunus lusitanica*).

Is a flower border or a shrub border better to screen a vegetable garden from view? Either kind of border would be proper; shrubs would be the more permanent. Why not plant a yew hedge, which would not take up more than 2½ to 3 ft. of width; or a single, informal row of *Spiraea Vanhouttei;* or bush fruits, such as blueberries or gooseberries?

What hedges are recommended for the lazy gardener who prefers not to have the work of clipping every week? Truehedge Columnberry; the Upright Privet (*Ligustrum lucidum erectum*); Truedwarf Box, Dwarf Winged Euonymus, the Dwarf Hedge Yew, and other similar plants are ideal for the lazy man's hedge. They need practically no clipping. At most this need be done but once a year.

What hedge would be best for city property—one that would need least attention?   One of the best would be the Five-leaved Aralia (*Acanthopanax sieboldianus*). Japanese Barberry hedges are also good under adverse conditions; and privet, of course—but this needs attention.

Can you suggest a neat, small, broad-leaved evergreen shrub to use at the edge of a terrace? (We want to have the plants untrimmed, but not more than a few feet high.)   English Ivy trained on a frame; Boxleaf Holly (*Ilex crenata nummularia*); Dwarf Box; *Euonymus vegetus*. Warty Barberry (Berberis verruculosa).

What is the rate of growth of a Canadian Hemlock hedge? Which low shrubs would go well in front of it?   A well-established young hemlock hedge in good soil will average at least 18 ins. a year. Such a hedge in itself is very beautiful, but if shrubs have to be placed in front of it, some low-growing types—coralberry (*Symphoricarpos*), Slender Deutzia, roses, Oriental quinces, and the like—might be used.

What kind of evergreen can I grow for a hedge, not more than 6 ft. high, that will keep a neat shape without shearing?   Hicks Yew will do this, although it will take quite a few years for it to grow 6 ft. high if small plants are purchased. Farther South the Irish Yew would be ideal.

What could be used for a low evergreen hedge (not box) for between vegetable garden and lawn?   A yew called *Taxus canadensis stricta*, or *Ilex crenata convexa* (commonly called the Convex-leaved Japanese Holly), would answer.

Would spruce trees make good hedges? (New Hampshire.)   Yes. Norway Spruce (*Picea excelsa*) either trimmed or untrimmed; also various forms of White Spruce (*P. glauca*).

Are there any evergreen barberries for hedge purposes?   Yes; Juliana Barberry, with black berries, grows to about 5 ft. *Berberis verruculosa*, with tiny holly-like leaves, growing about half as tall, is also suitable.

What hedge material would give a soft, blue-gray tone?   Pfitzer Juniper.

Can you give us advice on which evergreens to grow across the front of our place to form a hedge that people can neither see over nor through?   Either *Ilex crenata*, Redcedar, or American Arborvitae (all are evergreen).

Could we have an evergreen hedge, unclipped, which would have berries?   Yes, firethorn (pyracantha).

Which evergreen would make a handsome hedge that, without trimming, need never exceed 6 ft.—preferably less?   Dwarf Hinoki Cypress (*Chamaecyparis obtusa compacta*). Also, other dwarf forms of this evergreen.

Which trees, other than native hemlock, make a good hedge?   Northern exposure, semi-clay soil. The hedge is wanted for beauty as well as to serve as a windbreaker. White Pine, Red Pine, redcedar, Serbian Spruce.

Which tall evergreen—not too expensive—would you suggest for use as a fence along boundary line? Hemlock or White Pine.

FERTILIZERS AND PLANTING

What is a good fertilizer for hedges? Any complete commercial fertilizer, or well-rotted manure. For instance, 5–10–5 might be applied at the rate of 5 to 10 lbs. per 100 ft. of hedge, depending on the size of the plants.

How shall I plan a hedge? Decide whether you want it low or high, thorny or flowering, evergreen or deciduous. Just why you want it. Then select the best plant material to fit the need.

How does one plant a hedge? Dig a trench 2 ft. wide, 1 to 2 ft. deep, close to property lines, but at a safe distance away from sidewalk or street, so hedge will have plenty of space to expand up to the size at which it is to be permanently maintained. Put well-rotted manure on bottom of trench, then some good soil, and tramp firm. Space plants 1 to 3 ft. apart (depending on size), filling in soil about their roots. Make firm, and water in well. Cut back severely if a deciduous shrub is being used.

How far apart (approximately) should 6- to 8-ft. shrubs be planted for screening purposes? It depends upon the kinds used and on how quickly you want a solid screen. For instance, rose-of-Sharon might be set 6 to 7 ft. apart and the Morrow Honeysuckle 8 to 10 ft.

When is the best time to move a hedge of flowering shrubs? Should they be cut back? We want to keep them as large as possible for a screen. They can be moved after leaves have fallen in the autumn; or in the early spring. In transplanting their tops should be cut back about ⅓ for best results.

TRIMMING AND TRAINING

What is the best way to prune hedges? Different sorts of plants used as hedges demand different treatments. Large plants like White Pine and spruce should be allowed to retain approximately their outline. Hemlock hedges should always be much wider at the bottom than at the top. Large privet hedges should also be somewhat wider at the bottom, although smaller ones may be trimmed with the sides vertical. Regels Privet and other shrubs of that sort should be allowed to grow as naturally as possible. Hedges of dwarf yew should be broader than they are high. Dwarf boxwood and other edging plants can be trimmed to a rectangular shape.

How should one prune a deciduous hedge the first year? Cut back to within 6 to 12 ins. of the ground at planting time. Lightly shear whenever new shoots reach a height of 10 to 12 ins. if a close, compact hedge is needed.

Should hedges be trimmed to any special shape? Wider at bottom, preferably with a rounded top.

Do all hedge plants have to be trimmed several times in the season? No. Most evergreens can be kept tidy with one shearing. The same is true of such deciduous shrubs as althea, barberry, buckthorn, and spirea.

Should hedges be trimmed during the winter? This can be done with no injury to deciduous hedges, if hardy.

How shall I cut a hedge to make it grow? Cutting or pruning never makes a hedge "grow." It is good soil, fertilizer, and plenty of water offered the roots which really make the hedge grow.

I have heard that constant trimming devitalizes a hedge. Is this true? Yes, to some extent. Privet, for example, sheared every 3 weeks is more likely to succumb to the effect of a severe winter than one sheared only 2 or 3 times during the growing season.

Are electric hedge shears satisfactory? Yes; a good type will do the work in about ¼ the time required with hand shears.

Is it necessary to cultivate the soil along a hedge? Yes. Primarily to keep out weeds, which might grow and choke lower branches of hedge.

SPECIFIC HEDGE PLANTS

How shall I plant an ARBORVITAE hedge? (Topsoil is rather poor and only 9 ins. deep.) Dig a trench 2 ft. wide and 1½ ft. deep. Put topsoil on one side. Either remove 9 ins. of subsoil and replace with good soil; or take out 3 ins. and fork in 4 to 5 ins. of rotted manure or leaves and make firm by tramping. Return topsoil, and proceed with planting. The young trees should be set from 18 ins. to 3 ft. apart, according to their size.

When and how should an arborvitae hedge, about 18 ins. high, be trimmed? Top it evenly, during the period of spring growth, to about 1 ft. high. Thereafter, if you want a solid hedge, permit it to gain each year not more than 6 ins., until the desired height has been reached. From then on keep it closely sheared.

What is the best treatment to produce a thriving BARBERRY hedge? Give it good soil to grow in from the start. Fertilize with manure or commercial fertilizers once a year if needed. Keep watered during very dry spells. In trimming, keep the hedge slightly wider at the base than at the top.

When, and in what manner, should barberry and privet hedges be

trimmed? Always trim hedges so that they are wider at the base than the top, thus giving the lower branches plenty of exposure. Trimming might best be done when the young shoots are half grown, or nearly full grown, in late spring. However, trimming can be done without injury at practically any time.

What time of year is best for planting a BOXWOOD hedge? Either early spring or early fall.

To make CHINESE ELMS form a thick hedge, what procedure should be followed? Cut them back hard. Any plants up to 3 ins. in diameter at the base (and possibly larger) could be cut back to within 6 ins. of the ground. Then a trimming before active growth has stopped, and another a month later, will aid in forcing bushy growth.

I planted a hedge of TRUEHEDGE COLUMNBERRY, 18 to 24 ins. tall, last spring, cutting back half the growth, and trimming the new growth occasionally throughout the summer. Although no plants were lost they did not bush out enough from the base. What procedure shall I follow? How far should they be cut back next spring? These plants never will bush out at the base, for this is a columnar or upright-growing variety. If the shoots at the base have their ends pinched off occasionally, this may help somewhat. It is only necessary to trim the tops once a year. If the plants are still too far apart to make a hedge, move them closer together.

What is the cause of scant foliage on lower part of a MONTEREY CYPRESS hedge? (California.) Not sufficient room at the base. Hedges should be *wider* at the base than the top; this gives the lower branches plenty of sunlight and exposure. When hedges are clipped perpendicularly, or narrower at the base than at the top, the lower branches can be expected to become sickly and die.

What is the best way to grow a thick EVERGREEN hedge and yet not stop its upward growth too much? Allow it to elongate upward a full year untrimmed, then merely trim off the terminal buds of the branches several times during the next season. If it thickens up well in that year, allow it to grow with little trimming the next, and so on.

Will a HEMLOCK hedge thrive in a northwestern exposure without protection from sweeping winds? Depends on the area. If in the middle states, or in the South, yes. If in the extreme northern parts of Minnesota, Illinois, Wisconsin, where winds are high and extremely cold, some "burning" might result in winter. If in Midwest, where winds are very hot and very dry in summer, the answer is, No!

In planting 18-in. hemlock bushes for a hedge, should spacing be 2 ft. or less? Best spacing would be 18 ins. apart.

When do you shear a hemlock hedge? Shorten new growth about the end of June.

When is best time to prune a LAUREL hedge? This can be pruned any time; the best time (i.e., when one trimming would do the most good) is when the new shoots have nearly completed their growth for the current year. To avoid cutting leaves, use knife or pruning shears rather than hedge shears.

How about purple LILAC for a hedge? It makes a splendid tall hedge, but you must remember that the more it is clipped the more flower buds are removed. Also, in many places it must be sprayed annually for bad infestations of lilac scale.

At what season should a PEASHRUB (caragana) hedge be trimmed for the first time? At the time it is planted; not again until the very early spring of the next year.

How does one trim WHITE PINE into a compact hedge, solid from the ground up? Trim during the period of soft growth, reducing the new, candlelike growth, but not pruning into old wood. Permit only a slight annual gain in height. Shape the hedge so that it tapers up from a wide base to a narrower, rounded top. Keep the base free from weeds.

PRIVET

How do I go about planting a privet hedge? If soil is fairly good, no special preparation is necessary beyond removal of weeds and trash. An overrich soil may cause privet to grow embarrassingly fast. Stretch a line as a guide in planting. Starting at one end, dig a hole deep enough to set the plant 3 ins. deeper than it formerly grew. Dig hole for the next plant and use soil for covering roots of first plant; and so on to end of hedge, when the soil removed in making the first hole can be used for filling in around the last plant.

I want to plant a Waxleaf Privet hedge. Please tell me how tall this privet grows? How far apart to set plants? And if they need lime. (New Jersey.) This privet, untrimmed, may grow to 30 ft. in height. For a hedge, space 18 to 36 ins. apart, and keep trimmed to height desired. Privets grow well in either acid or alkaline soil, but this species would be hardy only from southern New Jersey southward.

In the first warm spell can I broadcast some bone meal around my California Privet hedge so that it may get a quick start in spring? I planted the hedge last May. You can, but the "early start" would be doubtful for bone meal is very slow in taking effect. You might better use a commercial fertilizer, or well-rotted manure.

How low should a privet hedge be cut when planted? Shorten all branches at least ⅔.

What is the procedure in trimming a newly planted privet hedge, to make it bushy? Shear it whenever the new shoots attain a length of about 1 ft., cutting them back ½.

What is the best thing to do with an old overgrown privet hedge?
Cut it off 6 ins. above the ground, and in this way force it to start
anew.

How often is it necessary to shear a privet hedge? About 3 times
during the growing season, giving the last clipping early in September.
It is better to shear every few weeks if a very trim hedge is required.

**How and when should Ibolium Privet be trimmed to make thickest
hedge, about 15 to 18 ins. high?** Cut off to a few inches above the
ground when it is planted, and then shear at the required height
several times a year.

**I was unable to trim and shape privet hedge last fall. Now it is
unsightly. When is the earliest time to trim?** A privet hedge can be
trimmed any time of year except late summer, when a trimming might
force new growth which would not mature by winter.

What makes privet hedge die from the roots? The common privet
(*Ligustrum vulgare*) is subject to a serious blight which kills the plants
and for which there is no known cure. Better use some other kind;
they all do well in normal soils.

How can I start a hedge from cuttings without a cold frame? See
Propagation. Privet can be raised from cuttings set in sandy soil in
early spring. One or 2 years after the cuttings are set they may be
transplanted to form the hedge. When planting the hedge set the plants
about 3 ins. deeper than before, and as soon as the planting is finished
cut all the shoots back to a few ins. above the soil to insure a dense
base to the hedge.

**When is the time to make cuttings of privet hedges? How do you
go about doing it?** Late spring or early summer is best. Take 6-in.
cuttings of the new wood, and place them in sand in a hotbed, with
some bottom heat if possible. Keep moist but not wet, shade, and they
should be rooted in 4 weeks or less.

At what time of the year should a SPIREA hedge be trimmed?
Just after it has flowered, then one gets the full benefit of the flowers.

**How can you get a hedge of spireas 2½ ft. apart, to grow together
at the bottom?** Best plan would be to cut it down to the ground and
thus force it to make bushy new growth. If it doesn't grow together
then, reset the plants 18 ins. apart—as they should have been set in
the first place.

**I planted a hedge of 6- to 8-ft. NORWAY SPRUCES 3 ft. apart.
How should I trim them so that they will stay thick and rich at their
base?** Top in the spring to 5½ or 6 ft. Thereafter, in the annual
shearing, allow only little gain in height. Trim sides no more than
necessary for an even appearance. Shape the hedge so that it tapers
from a wide base to a narrow, rounded top.

Can TAMARISK be used for a hedge? It makes an excellent

informal hedge. If late-blooming species, cut back in spring. If a May or June flowering species, cut back when flowers have faded.

Can you tell me whether a GOLDEN WILLOW hedge would be suitable for a boundary around a farm building? (Iowa.) If a tall, quick-growing hedge is required, the willow would be quite suitable.

What distance apart should JAPANESE YEW (2 to 3 ft.) be planted for a straight border-line hedge? Eighteen inches is best, but if this costs too much 24 to 30 ins. would do. It would take the hedge a longer time to grow together in the second instance.

When is the best time to trim a yew hedge? It can be trimmed almost any time. Trim "wild" shoots in spring; give main shearing at end of June.

Do you approve the use of ROSA MULTIFLORA as a hedge plant? No! It grows much too large for use on small properties. A 3-year-old can be 8 ft. high and 12 ft. across.

WINDBREAKS

For how great a distance does a windbreak exert its influence? About twenty times its height.

Which trees are suitable for use as windbreaks? If soil is sandy, Red Pine and the Riga variety of Scotch Pine. For sandy loam, White Pine, Douglasfir, spruce. For heavy soil, arborvitae, Balsam Fir, White Spruce.

We need a windbreak on the west line of our property. The spot is quite shaded. Would Scotch or Jack Pine thrive there? No, not in shade. Use hemlock if height is needed; or Japanese Yew, upright form.

Which evergreens are best to use for windbreak? We get heavy windstorms from the southwest, and the garden is on a hill sloping to the south. Red Pine.

What can I plant for a hedge and windbreak—something that will grow fast? There is a strong north wind all summer; space is ample. The Siberian Elm is one of the fastest-growing trees we have. Plant it thickly, about 5 ft. apart, if the hedge is to be over 20 ft. high; about 3 ft. apart if hedge is to be nearer 10 ft. high. It is one of our best trees for dry climatic conditions.

I haven't much room on my property but would like a windbreak on the north and west sides. Any suggestions? Plant arborvitae; redcedar; upright form of Japanese Yew; or White Pine. Keep in bounds by annual pruning.

What would make a good windbreak for a garden that is exposed on all sides? Closely set evergreens, such as cedar, hemlock, or arborvitae, are good. A 6-ft. paling fence or a storm fence might also help.

VINES AND THEIR CULTURE

How do different vines climb? By clinging rootlets, such as English Ivy, trumpetcreeper, euonymus; by adhesive disks, such as Boston Ivy; by coiling tendrils, as balloonvine, *Cobaea scandens*, sweetpea; by stems which twine, such as wisteria, bittersweet.

Is any special preparation needed before planting vines to grow on a house? Make sure there is sufficient depth (1½ ft.), and width (2 ft.) of good soil. All too often the planting area next to a foundation is filled with builder's rubbish.

WHAT TO GROW

See also Landscaping.

I have a partially shaded back yard in the city. Which flowering vines could be grown on the fence? Cinnamonvine (*Dioscorea batatas*); silverlace-vine (*Polygonum auberti*); wisteria. The last will bloom only if it can climb to where there is sun. All these vines need a trellis, or to be supported in some way.

Which flowering vines would look well growing over a stone wall? We would like to enjoy seeing the flowers from our porch, 100 ft. away. Perennial pea, wisteria, clematis, hyacinth bean, trumpetvine, rambler roses.

Which flowering vines will cling, without support, to the wall of our garage? Trumpetcreeper; Climbing Hydrangea; Boston Ivy.

Which vines shall I grow on our clapboard house, which will need painting occasionally? Do *not* use climbing vines, such as the ivies, Climbing Hydrangea, or trumpetcreeper; nor wisteria, which will thrust strong stems between the clapboards, sometimes destroying them. Honeysuckle, silverlace-vine, clematis, akebia, should do well. A trellis hinged at bottom will be advisable so you can lay it (with the vine) down at painting time.

Which hardy flowering vines will stand the winter in southwest corner of Massachusetts? Elevation 1800 ft. Bittersweet, trumpetcreeper, sweet-autumn clematis.

Which vines would you suggest for growing on stone walls, chimneys, and house walls? *Euonymus fortunei* (*radicans*); *ivy* (*Hedera*), small-leaved varieties; *Cotoneaster horizontalis*. The latter is not a vine but can be trained as such.

Which vines will grow and climb in oak shade? Virginiacreeper, wild grape, bittersweet.

Which are the best climbing vines for this area (S. E. New York)?

Clematis, bittersweet, Hall's Honeysuckle, silverlace or fleece-vine, and wisteria.

Which vines will thrive in water?   None, in the northern United States.

Is it in good taste to plant climbing roses and climbing honeysuckle to grow up the four wide pillars along stucco porch of a stucco bunga-low? I plan to plant a few low evergreens and shrubs for foundation planting around the whole house.   Yes; but from the standpoint of good growth of the plants, it would be better to plant either roses or honeysuckle, not both.

What kind of a flowering vine or climber will grow every year to a height of 15 or 20 ft. on the north side of a house, where it would get the early morning and late-afternoon sun?   Sweet-autumn Clematis, silverlace- or fleece-vine. Also *Cobaea scandens,* an annual.

Which vine can be planted on top of a ledge where soil is very shallow and dry in ordinary years? Foliage is desired to keep dust from house.   Very few vines would do well under such circumstances, but bittersweet and Sweet-autumn Clematis might be tried. Virginiacreeper is another possibility.

Which flowering vines are satisfactory for use on the north side of a house, in shade during most of the day?   It is improbable that any flowering vine will thrive very well, but you might try trumpet honeysuckle, climbing hydrangea, or silverlace-vine. *Cobaea scandens,* annual, and mountainfringe (adlumia), a biennial, might do well.

What are some of the easiest-grown and most beautiful flowering perennial vines?   Wisteria, honeysuckles, trumpetcreepers, silverlace-vine, Sweet-autumn Clematis.

I have a terrace 13 × 14 ft.; no roof over it; sunny most of the day. I want to "grow a roof." What would you suggest? Something that will grow fast and give protection in summer, and at the same time something that will be decorative and useful as a more perma-nent screen. How about a grapevine? How long would it take to provide a screen, and how many should I plant? The soil is sandy.   Grape-vines would serve well. Plant 4 on each of two opposite sides. It will take at least 3 to 4 years to cover this area. The kudzuvine might cover the areas in a shorter time—but it has no grapes!

Which perennial vines are good for screening purposes?   Kudzu-vine, the fastest-growing vine; Dutchmanspipe, also fast-growing, with large, rounded leaves; turquoiseberry (*Ampelopsis brevipeduncu-lata*); easy to grow, and with profuse foliage and berries. The first named however, behaves as a herbaceous perennial in the north.

Which vine gives quickest growth for trellis at window for shade?   Kudzuvine grows the fastest (and the most!) of any of our "perennial" vines. Where it is not hardy, bittersweet, the Fiveleaf Akebia, or the Bower Actinidia, might be used. All these are rapid-growing vines and have smaller and more interesting leaves than the large, coarse-leaved gloryvine (*Vitis coignetiae*) which is about the fastest-growing of the grapes.

Which flowering vine would be pretty to cover top of cave, the end and sides of which will be planted as a rock garden? Sweet-autumn Clematis, or rambler roses.

Is there an evergreen vine which will cling to a wall in shade? English Ivy (*Hedera helix*); Wintercreeper (*Euonymus fortunei radicans*).

Which evergreen vine do you recommend to hang down from the top of a driveway wall? Wintercreeper (*Euonymus*), or English Ivy, where hardy.

What is the best creeping vine for walls of stucco? *Euonymus fortunei* or one of its varieties is very good. Boston Ivy usually adheres well also.

Which ivy can I plant by the doorway that will hang down from the top in a place that is shaded most of the time? Either Boston Ivy or English Ivy; the last being evergreen. Give both good soil in which to grow; keep moist during dry weather.

Is there some small-leaved vine which will cling to rocks? Would like something besides ivy and euonymus. (Delaware.) Creeping Fig (*Ficus pumila*). Its small leaves lie flat. Not reliably hardy north of Baltimore, though it has been known to survive 80 miles north of New York City.

ANNUAL VINES

We have rented a summer cottage and would like to grow some annual vines to cover lattice. What would be appropriate, easy to grow, and have attractive flowers? Morningglory, moonflower, scarlet runner bean, hyacinth bean (dolichos), *Cobaea scandens*.

Which vine can be grown over a poultry fence to provide shade, and for concealment? Have tried Heavenly Blue Morningglory, but chickens eat it. Is there any annual vine distasteful to poultry? Try canarybird-vine, climbing nasturtiums, hyacinth bean, wild cucumber, Japanese hop (humulus), scarlet runner bean, and cardinal-climber. Mix seeds together, sow quite thickly along the bottom of your fence, on outside. Chickens may take some and leave enough of others to give you a show. If necessary, thin to stand about 1 ft. apart.

Can you suggest vines—annuals—which will grow in a place which has shade ¾ of the day? Try cup-and-saucer-vine (*Cobaea scandens*), hyacinth bean, morningglory, and cardinal-climber.

Will you give the correct information of how to grow adlumia or

Alleghenyvine from seed? I have not been at all successful. Reproduce the conditions natural to this native plant of the northeast United States. Give it a cool, damp situation, as it would be in woodland, protected from sun and wind, with shrubs to climb on. It is a biennial.

What does the Scarlet Runner Bean look like? It resembles in leaf and habit the pole beans we grow in our vegetable gardens, but the blossoms are larger and scarlet in color. The pods and green beans are edible.

I saw a beautiful vine twining on strings to cover a cellar window wall. It had purple sweetpea-like flowers in late summer, and then broad, flat, red-purple beans. What was it? Hyacinth bean (dolichos) of easy culture.

Is the Cup-and-saucer-vine (Cobaea scandens) a satisfactory annual? Yes, if started indoors 6 weeks before ground warms up. Plant individual seeds in pots or plant bands. Set out at tomato-planting time. Grows to the top of a 3-story house in one season. Lovely foliage, tendrils; showy buds, flowers, and seed pods late summer and autumn. Foliage colors red-purple in light frosts. Grows on until hard freeze.

Is MOONFLOWER a good annual vine? Yes. Large leaves, beautiful, fragrant, night-blooming flowers late summer and autumn. Give it something to climb high on. Start indoors. (See Cup-and-saucer-vine.)

What is the proper procedure in propagating moonflowers? Sow seeds. Proceed as suggested for morningglories below or start seeds in individual pots indoors in early April.

Is there a variety of moonflower which climbs and has colored flowers? Moonflower is a twining night-bloomer with white flowers. There are also pink varieties. Twining day-bloomers are morningglories.

Which large-flowered MORNINGGLORIES are best? Heavenly Blue, Scarlett O'Hara—crimson; Pearly Gates—a white sport of Heavenly Blue. Start indoors in pots for early bloom in the North.

I would like some morningglories for a window box; not the large-flowered varieties. You want the Japanese type, which are to be had in white, crimson, purple, blue, and other colors. They grow 2 to 8 ft. high, while Heavenly Blue grows 10 to 20 ft. The dwarf morningglories grow only about a foot high.

Should I plant morningglories in the same place a second time? Theoretically it is wrong; but practically there is little objection. Dig the soil deeply, and work in decayed manure; if, after a few seasons, morningglories seem to be doing less well, sow instead hyacinth bean, *Cobaea scandens,* or tall nasturtiums.

Will you tell me how to make Heavenly Blue Morningglories grow?
Dig soil 1 ft. deep, mixing bone meal with it, ¼ lb. per sq. yd. Sow
seeds about ½ in. deep and 2 ins. apart, after soaking in water overnight. Thin out to 6 ins. from plant to plant. Make your sowings at
the base of a fence, trellis, or some similar support.

Do morningglories require a rich soil?   Soil of average quality is
good enough. If it is too high in nitrogen, you may have large plants
with small flowers; if you work in a balanced fertilizer, however, they
should have large flowers and remain in bloom for a longer period
each day.

**Had some Heavenly Blue Morningglories and watched for seed,
with no success. How are they propagated?**   They grow readily from
seeds which you purchase. It is possible that fertile seeds cannot be
collected in your part of the country. Seeds are produced in large
quantities for the trade in southern California.

**Is there any known way to keep morningglories open longer in the
morning?** No.

**When picking morningglories, how do you keep them open in the
house in a container?**   Cut buds at sunset, selecting those ready to
open. Keep in water up to their necks in a cool cellar overnight. Clip
stems and place in position in morning. Moonflowers cut in late
afternoon will open in containers indoors.

How tall will climbing NASTURTIUMS grow? How do they cling?
To 6 ft. They climb by means of coiling leaf stalks.

SWEETPEA

See Annual Flowers.

PERENNIAL VINES

AKEBIA

**What do you recommend to mask an ugly leader pipe near our
front entrance?**   *Akebia quinata* deserves such a place where one
views it closely. It has dainty oval leaves, five to a group, and a
decorative manner of growth. It will festoon itself around any upright
support. At intervals along a leader pipe the vine will have to be
tied up. Sun or shade suits akebia.

**Is there any vine, except English Ivy, that remains green during the
winter, and that is suitable for covering the side of a frame building?**
The Fiveleaf Akebia (*Akebia quinata*) is worthy of a trial. It climbs
by twining and would have to be supplied with wire for support. It
is not completely evergreen, but leaves remain on the vine long into
the winter. Another evergreen vine, *Euonymus radicans,* would satisfy

these requirements but it is susceptible to serious infestations of scale, and so must be used with caution.

Does akebia have flowers?   Small rose-purple waxy flowers neither conspicuous nor numerous, but very interesting at close range.

AMPELOPSIS AND PARTHENOCISSUS

I have cement blocks about 4 ft. high on the 3 sides of my porch and would like to know what will grow up and cling to these blocks so they will not be conspicuous. It is on the north side, therefore not much sun.   Wintercreeper or St. Paul Virginiacreeper (*Parthenocissus quinquefolia hirsuta*).

What plant will cover a stone wall where the location is hot, dry southern exposure?   The ordinary ivy which flourishes on the north wall does not thrive here. Boston Ivy or St. Paul Virginiacreeper.

Which deciduous ivy is the best to cover a stone wall? What kind of soil? Should it be covered by a mulch for the winter?   The Boston Ivy, St. Paul Virginiacreeper, or even the Virginiacreeper could be used to cover a stone wall. These do not need any special soil, simply a good garden loam. No winter mulch is required.

How shall I order an "ivy" which has deeply cut leaves and berries which turn lilac to bright blue?   This is porcelainvine (*Ampelopsis brevipedunculata maximowiczi*).

Which deciduous ivy has the best autumn coloring?   Virginiacreeper (not a true ivy) has the most brilliant crimson foliage in autumn.

Where would Virginiacreeper grow?   In the woods, on the ground, up a tree, in the sun or shade, along a wall, on the sand dunes. Very hardy and very adaptable.

What kinds of deciduous clinging vines are there?   Among them are Virginiacreeper and its several smaller-leaved varieties. Then there is Boston Ivy and its small-leaved varieties, and trumpetcreeper.

BITTERSWEET

I have heard that the Oriental species of bittersweet is better than our native kind. Is that so?   It is more vigorous and has better foliage, but the fruits are about the same.

How would bittersweet look growing on a trellis by the front door? As it is rather rampant, we doubt if you would like it there. Its chief charm is in its dark bare stems with their clinging berries in fall and winter.

If bittersweet seeds are planted, how long will it take before the vine produces berries? Does bittersweet prefer acid soil?   About 3 years. They grow well in either acid or alkaline soil.

At what time of year can bittersweet be planted?   Spring or fall.

Will bittersweet climb on a stone chimney? Not unless you provide a wire around which it can twine. It is a *twining* vine not a *clinging* one.

How can I make my small patch of bittersweet larger? Allow some of the shoots to touch the ground, cover portions of them with soil, and they will soon take root, especially if you cut part way through the vine on the under side of the portion to be covered with soil.

What causes blossoms to fall from stems at base of a bittersweet vine? Probably the male flower blossoms, which never have any fruits and fall off the plant after the pollen has been dispersed.

I have several bittersweet vines on trellises. The clusters which I gather in fall are usually small and imperfect. Is there anything I can do so that these vines will produce clusters such as I see in the florist shops in the fall? Be certain that 1 or 2 strong male or pollen-bearing plants are close by, preferably growing in with the fruiting vines. Another method is to note when they bloom in June, obtain cut branches of male flowers from some distant plant, put in bottle of water, and tie up in your fruiting vine. Leave there for 2 weeks and the pollen distributed by insects and winds will fertilize the pistillate or fruit-bearing flowers, insuring a good crop of fruits.

Should bittersweet be pruned while growing? Mine grows 4 or 5 ft. high and then starts long runners 7 or 8 ft. long and of course there is no trellis for them. Yes, it can be pruned while growing.

I have a bittersweet vine. When should the berries be picked for winter bouquets? Any time after heavy frosts.

I have read that only the female plants of bittersweet have berries. How can you sort the seedlings to discard male plants? They can't be sorted as seedlings. It is necessary to wait until they are old enough to bloom.

CLEMATIS

I am interested in clematis. Which species or variety is best in bloom, and easy to care for? *Clematis paniculata,* the Sweet-autumn Clematis, is one of the easiest of all to grow. The Jackman Clematis can be grown fairly easily if the soil is alkaline.

Which clematis is it that one sees in our woodland? Rock Clematis, *Clematis verticillaris,* blooming in May or June; or virginsbower, *C. virginiana,* with white flowers in August to September. Must climb into sunlight to bloom well.

Could you tell us the name of a clematis with rosy-pink flowers about 2 in. across? There are 4 petals and yellow stamens. Bloom in May. Pink Anemone Clematis (*C. montana rubens*).

Is there any clematis with red flowers that is easier to grow than the big-flowered hybrids? Scarlet Clematis (*C. texensis*) is a native of Texas. Grows to about 6 ft., with flowers about 1 in. long; blooms July to September.

Can you tell me a yellow clematis that would grow in Maine? I saw a beautiful small variety (on the ground) in Canada but could not find its name. *Clematis tangutica,* the Golden Clematis, is certainly worthy of a trial. It is the best of the yellow-flowered species, a native of China. Will need winter protection.

Culture

What is the best exposure for Jackman Clematis? (Illinois.) In Illinois as protected a situation as possible, but not complete shade. All clematis bloom better where the vines reach full sun, but they like shade at their bases.

What fertilizer does clematis need? Should one cultivate around it, or are the roots near the surface of the ground? Most clematis varieties require lime and a cool, moist soil, best supplied by a mulch of leafmold. Roots are very near the surface.

Is it always necessary to shade the roots and lower stem portions of clematis? This is necessary on most of the many large-flowered hybrids, but it is not necessary on our native clematis types nor on the Sweet-autumn Clematis.

What type of trellis is best for clematis? Chicken-wire netting supported in rigidly upright position on a light frame.

Will different varieties of clematis, planted very close, "cross," thus spoiling the species? No, this will not change the plants or flowers a particle. Seeds from the flowers might yield seedlings of mixed parentage.

How can I grow large-flowered clematis? They do well for 6 months or a year, and then die. Unfortunately many large-flowered clematis are susceptible to a rather serious disease which kills them during the summer months. No manure should be applied, nor should water be allowed to stand at the base of the plants. If the disease occurs, spray with wettable sulfur at once, and again in a week or ten days.

Pruning

How and when should one prune clematis? Those which bloom on old wood (such as *C. florida, montana,* and *patens*) need little or no pruning beyond the removal of dead or diseased wood. The *lanuginosa, jackmani,* and *viticella* types bloom on wood of the current season, and may be cut back in spring before growth begins.

A white clematis planted in the fall grew about 10 or 12 ft. the following summer, but did not flower. Should I have pinched it back

after it was 3 or 4 ft. high? No. Let it grow and gain nourishment; it will bloom the second or third year.

When and how should Clematis paniculata be pruned? In many places in New England this clematis will be killed to the ground by winter cold. In such places it should be pruned back, in early spring, to just above where the buds break. In situations where it does not kill to the ground, merely cutting out some of the older wood is all that is necessary.

Should clematis be pruned in fall or summer? I notice some cut them down to ground, but I have never cut mine and have lovely vines. What is the best preventive for aphis? If you have lovely vines, continue the same treatment. Cutting them down does not help. (See preceding questions.) Aphis can be controlled by spraying with nicotine sulfate.

Should a Clematis jackmani be trimmed or pruned in springtime? Yes; but only if the vine is cluttered up with a mass of unproductive shoots.

Propagation

Can you start clematis from cuttings? Clematis are rather difficult to propagate. This can be done either by cuttings or seeds. For the amateur, sowing the seed in the fall is the easier method. Many of our large-flowered hybrids must be propagated by cuttings, or by grafting.

Can clematis be grown from slips? Many varieties may be rooted from slips in the latter part of July. Cut young shoots into 6- to 8-in. lengths, making the basal cut between joints. Place them in a glass-covered box or cold frame, and keep out of direct sunlight until rooted. Most of the large-flowered named varieties are grafted.

DUTCHMANSPIPE

Which vine would make a good solid screen to hide the compost pile? Please describe Dutchmanspipe. Dutchmanspipe would be fine if grown on a series of vertical cords or slats. The big roundish leaves, 10 ins. in diameter, overlap each other. Flowers, nondescript in color, resemble a Dutchmanspipe.

EUONYMUS FORTUNEI; WINTERCREEPER, EVERGREEN BITTERSWEET

Which one of the wintercreeper vines has berries like bittersweet? The best of the berried varieties is the Bigleaf Wintercreeper (*E. fortunei vegetus*).

Our wintercreeper is especially noticed because of its leaves, which are variegated sometimes with white or pinkish tones. What variety could it be? Silver-edge Wintercreeper (*E. fortunei gracilis*).

Which euonymus vine has very tiny leaves?   Baby Wintercreeper (*Euonymus fortunei minimus*).

Which is the hardiest of all evergreen vines that will cling to a stone wall?   Wintercreeper (*Euonymus fortunei*) and its varieties.

Is Euonymus fortunei the new name for what we used to call Euonymus radicans?   Yes. It is now *Euonymus fortunei radicans*. (Until the botanists decide to change it again!)

I have a euonymus which I thought would climb on a wall, but it remains a bush. What is the trouble?   It must be the variety called Glossy Wintercreeper (*E. fortunei carrierei*) which is shrubby, non-climbing. There is another shrubby variety which remains so unless planted near a wall (*E. fortunei vegetus*), the Bigleaf Wintercreeper.

GRAPE

See Fruits—Section VI.

HONEYSUCKLE

Which honeysuckle has flowers that are yellowish on the inside and rose-purple outside?   Everblooming Honeysuckle (*Lonicera heckrotti*).

Please describe the Scarlet Trumpet Honeysuckle (Lonicera sempervirens). I believe it used to grow in gardens long ago.   Yes, it is long in cultivation. Orange-scarlet flowers with long tubes, yellow inside, produced from May to August.

What low-growing variety of honeysuckle would you recommend for a northern exposure, with semi-shade?   Hall's Honeysuckle—but watch out; it is a pernicious weed if it gets out of bounds.

What low vine may one plant under the shade of a large maple tree, but unprotected from the wind; one which will grow with myrtle, where grass will not?   You might try Hall's Honeysuckle, but it is very difficult to coax anything to grow under most maples.

Our honeysuckle vine (2 years old this past spring) had only one spray of bloom. Why? The foliage is beautiful and healthy-looking.   It needs time to become well established before it will bloom properly.

My honeysuckle lost all leaves in midsummer, then bore leaves and blooms and seeds at one time. What should be done this year?   Give it more water. This was probably due to unusually dry weather.

Does Japanese Honeysuckle eventually work its way into water drains? Should it be planted near them?   Like the roots of most plants it probably will, but usually the roots won't do much damage in this respect.

How does one trim out honeysuckle which is very thick, and about 12 ft. high?   If there is too much wood, it may be necessary to cut it off at the base and start all over again.

Will you tell me whether honeysuckle vine can be pruned, and at what time of the year? Prune it in the early spring when the buds are breaking. Unless the vine is to be restrained within a limited area, it is necessary to prune out only dead or diseased wood.

What is the proper way to prune a honeysuckle for profuse blooming? Mine is a cutting about 3 years old, with very few flowers. Is a trellis necessary? Don't prune; allow it to grow profusely on some support, and if good soil, plenty of water, and sunshine are available, it will soon bloom well.

HYDRANGEA

How tall does the Climbing Hydrangea grow? How does it climb? *Hydrangea petiolaris* can grow 50 ft. or more in time, but it is slow. It clings to a wall without support, sends out branches at right angles to the wall, and blooms in June.

What kind of flowers does the Climbing Hydrangea have? Flowers are white, in round, flat, open clusters, resembling some of the viburnum flowers.

IVY

How can one tell whether an ivy is a variety that will be hardy if placed outdoors? We want to plant some on a new cottage chimney. Try several. The hardiest evergreen variety is the Baltic Ivy (*Hedera helix baltica*). If this winter kills, no English Ivy will grow there.

What does Baltic Ivy look like? Its leaves are slightly smaller than those of the typical English Ivy, and the white veins are often more prominent.

Which evergreen vine can I plant on north side of brick house? English Ivy, if a tall-growing kind is required; otherwise, use wintercreeper, which is hardier.

Which vine is suitable for planting on west slope, to cover up ground and stay green all the year 'round—one that won't spread too much? Baltic Ivy.

SECTION III-B

Bulbs, Tubers, and Corms

INTRODUCTION

BY F. F. ROCKWELL

THE VARIOUS bulbs and other bulb-like plants—those which form tubers and corms instead of true bulbs—have more rapidly gained in popularity during the last decade or so than any other group of decorative plants. The reasons for this growing popularity are not far to seek, for many bulbs are much more rewarding for the time and room required for their culture, than are most other flowers. Moreover, a considerable number of them flower very early in spring and add brilliant color to the garden scene by the time most perennials and shrubs have begun to don their summer garments of green.

There are still many gardens, however, where one looks in vain for any sight of spring bulbs other than a few long out-dated daffodils and perhaps a planting of that ubiquitous, sensational tulip Red Emperor. The owners of such gardens are overlooking a wide range of easily grown plants which could provide them with beautiful and interesting flowers, very literally, from one end of the year to the other, for there are a number of bulbs and corms that may readily be flowered indoors. The most easily obtained and grown of these are commented on in the following pages. You can add to your store of garden pleasures by becoming acquainted with them.

HARDY BULBS, CORMS, TUBERS, ETC.

WHAT TO GROW

Which hardy bulbs may be used in permanent plantings? Among the most satisfactory are narcissi, grapehyacinths, squills, chionodoxas, snowdrops, crocuses, the hardier lilies, alliums, colchicums, and camassias. Tulips may give several years' bloom without being taken up, especially if planted deep (to ten inches).

Which bulbs can be left in the ground the year round? Alliums, brodieas, calochortus, camassias, chionodoxas, colchicums, crocuses, erythroniums, fritillarias, grapehyacinths, hyacinths, tulips, narcissi, irises, leucojum, ornithogalum, lilies, puschkinia, squills, shootingstars, snowdrops, snowflakes, sternbergia, and zephyranthes.

We have spring-flowering bulbs. Which hardy bulbs shall I plant for summer bloom? Hardy kinds: summer-hyacinth, hardy begonia (*B. evansiana*), lycoris, garden lilies, sternbergia, colchicum, fall-flowering crocuses, *Scilla chinensis,* zephyranthes and some of the flowering onions or alliums.

SOIL AND FERTILIZER

What kind of soil should I use for spring-flowering bulbs? A rather light, but fertile and well-drained, slightly acid soil is best. Avoid the use of fresh manure. Very old manure and bone meal are good fertilizers.

Bulbs do not multiply readily in the soil in my garden. Tulips do not last over 3 years. What element in the soil is lacking? Possibly your soil is not suitable, but this is not unusual for tulips. Heavy, clayey soils are not conducive to increase. Most bulbs prefer a loose, fertile soil that has been well worked to a depth of 10 or 12 ins.

Does well-rotted manure above, but not touching, the bulbs rot them? No. But it is much better to spade the manure under before planting, so that it is well below the bulbs, but not in direct contact with them.

PLANTING AND TRANSPLANTING

How deep should bulbs be planted? Is the general rule 4, 5, or 6 times the thickness of the bulb? No general rule can be applied to all bulbs. Some lilies should be planted 8 or 9 ins. deep, others 2 ins. deep; so the depth varies. If possible, obtain specific information for each kind before planting. If this is not available, a rough rule that can be followed in the case of the hardy spring-flowering bulbs is to cover them with soil equal in depth to 2 or 3 times the diameter of the bulb.

How late in the fall may bulbs be planted? Bulbs planted in December will grow and thrive, and instances are known of January-planted bulbs succeeding. But earlier planting is recommended.

Early-flowering bulbs arrived after sub-zero weather and snow. How can I take care of them over winter and when can I plant them? They are winter aconites, scillas, tulips, etc. Keep in cool, dry place and plant any time when ground thaws, up to January. An alternative would be to plant bulbs in pots or flats of soil and cover with 6-in. layer of sand or cinders outdoors. They cannot be kept over winter out of the soil.

Can spring-flowering bulbs (tulips, narcissi, etc.) be put in the

ground in January in Maryland with any success? Yes, if the bulbs have kept well in storage until this time; but it is much better to plant them earlier.

Can you plant bulbs in spring that call for planting in fall? Certain hardy, summer-flowering bulbs can be held in cold storage and planted in spring as, for instance, lilies; but fall planting is better. Spring-flowering bulbs must be planted in fall.

Bulbs held temporarily, awaiting planting, should be stored in a cool, dark place, away from artificial heat, and safe from rodents.

Can a person plant bulbs of all kinds in spring? Only summer- and fall-blooming kinds can be planted at that time.

Will bulbs planted in September bloom in the spring if they sprouted, and in some cases bloomed, in October and November? Surely bulbs that bloomed in October and November are fall bloomers rather than spring bloomers. They will retain this characteristic from year to year, and will not bloom in spring. Spring-blooming kinds that sprouted before planting will probably bloom in spring.

Will daffodils, scillas, and similar bulbs bloom after the first season, and multiply, if planted the first week of December? Yes. It would be better, however, to plant them somewhat earlier.

Can you take up crocus and jonquil bulbs, separate, and replant them as soon as the leaves die down? Or must you wait until fall? Yes. It is always best to transplant narcissi before mid-July.

Should bulbs be watered after planting? This is usually not necessary. Very little moisture is needed for their early root growth, but in case of a long, dry spell with no rain within a month after planting, a thorough watering is beneficial.

What is the best way to handle the small bulbs one finds growing on older bulbs? Plant them separately in specially prepared nursery beds where the soil is loose and fertile. Grow them on in these beds until they reach blooming size.

CULTURE

What can be done with spring-blooming bulbs which come through the ground in December, due to a warm spell? Probably planted too shallowly. Cover them carefully with a layer of sifted earth, sand, or cinders; mulch with leaves or other covering.

If true bulbs have their flower bud within them, do they need full sunshine in order to bloom?   Yes, they need sunshine and moisture to bring the blooms to maturity.

Does it weaken the bulbs to cut flowers of hyacinths, tulips, and narcissi, being careful not to remove more than one third of the leaves?   Any removal of foliage has a weakening effect.

Does it inhibit next year's bloom to pick flowers of the bulbous plants—daffodils, narcissi, etc.?   No; not if most of the foliage is left. This is needed to manufacture food that feeds the bulb and produces the next year's bloom.

What can I do with the unsightly foliage of my spring-flowering bulbs after bloom is over?   Removal of foliage before it has matured (turned yellow and wilted) is sure to prevent normal bloom the following year, as the maturing foliage provides nutrients for the flowers to come. Water in dry spells to keep foliage growing as long as possible. Overplant maturing bulb foliage with shallow-rooted annuals, such as petunias, which spread and cover the unsightly dying leaves.

Do spring-flowering bulbs need fertilizer after planting?   An application of a complete plant food should be applied and gently raked into the surface each spring just after the first weeding. In light, sandy soil a second application in late spring after bloom is over is also advisable.

Do you advise the use of a summer mulch on bulb beds?   Yes, by all means. A mulch of peatmoss, sawdust, pine needles, buckwheat hulls, shredded sugar cane or other similar material may be applied early in spring after weeding and fertilizing. If bed is later overplanted with annuals, the mulch remaining on the bed will help to control weeds and retain moisture through the summer heat.

What causes bulbs to disappear in the soil? Such hardy bulbs as jonquils, tulips, lilies, and irises are examples.   Unsuitable soil or location; cutting the flowers without leaving sufficient foliage to make food to fatten up the bulbs; cutting of leaves before they wither naturally; and disease or the depredations of rodents.

How short a rest period should bulbs have after being taken up from the soil?   This varies with the kind of bulb. Colchicums and lilies, for example, should be replanted with least possible delay, as also should narcissi. Tulips are stored out of ground for 3 months or more without harm.

PROTECTION

Should tulips, narcissi, and jonquils have mulch (leaves) over them

in fall? When should they be uncovered? Not necessary except in extremely cold sections (Zones 2 and 3, see map) unless you are in an area subject to frequent alternate freezing and thawing. Damage is then from "heaving" of roots and bulbs from soil. Under these conditions cover *after* the ground has frozen hard, with leaves, peatmoss, or salt hay. This keeps ground uniformly cool and prevents damage to roots by heaving. Uncover gradually when growth appears.

RODENTS

Have had much trouble losing lily and tulip bulbs in winter. Some rodent makes burrows 3 ins. below surface of ground. Have used wire baskets in planting, but to no avail. Also poison and traps. What can I do? You may have to encircle the whole bed with fine mesh wire netting, 12 inches wide, buried vertically, and extending 2 to 3 inches above ground surface. Do not *mulch* bed until ground is well frozen.

SPECIFIC HARDY BULBS

ALLIUM

Do flowering alliums possess that unpleasant onion odor? Ordinarily not, unless the stems or leaves are crushed or bruised. *Allium tuberosum* (sometimes sold as *A. odorum*) has violet-scented flowers.

Are there any flowering onions that are suitable for outdoor gardens? Many species of allium are excellent for planting in borders. Among the best are *tuberosum* (white), *moly* (yellow), *stellatum* (pink), *caeruleum* (blue), *flavum* (yellow), *senescens glaucum* (lavender), *pulchellum* (pink-lavender), and *schoenoprasum* (rose-purple).

What soil and treatment do Allium flavum and other summer-blooming onions require? A rather light, well-drained loam is best, although they will thrive in most soils, providing drainage is good. Full sunshine is preferred by most species. Divide and transplant whenever crowded: either fall or early spring. Most are very easy to grow.

ANEMONE

Will anemone tubers survive winter in New York (Long Island) if planted in fall? Will they bloom if planted in spring? If so, when should they be planted in the vicinity of New York? Rock-garden tuberous-rooted kinds (such as *apennina, blanda, ranunculoides, quinquefolia,* and *nemorosa*), are hardy and should be planted in fall. The florists' tuberous-rooted kinds are not hardy. You might try storing them in a cool place (40°) over winter, and planting them in the spring.

How should one plant tuberous anemones, such as nemorosa, ranunculoides, etc.? Plant in early fall in porous soil containing generous proportion of humus. Set tubers 2 or 3 ins. apart, and cover about 2 ins. deep. Light woodland shade is needed.

ARUM

I have a lily plant which produces a flower, dark purplish in color, almost black, on a stem 8 ins. tall, with leaves 5 × 3 ins. It seems to prefer the cold, for it survives our occasional frosts. It becomes dormant in summer. Could you please identify? Probably Black Calla (*Arum palaestinum*).

BELAMCANDA

Can you tell me something about a plant called Blackberry Lily? *Belamcanda chinensis,* a hardy iris relative from the Orient, is now naturalized in many parts of this country. Easily grown in sun or light shade, and propagated by seeds or division. Orange flowers, spotted with purple-brown, are followed by blackberry-like fruits. Blooms in the summer.

BRODIAEAS

What treatment do brodiaeas, such as grandiflora, capitata, and ixioides, need in the garden? Plant in fall in gritty soil in full sun. Set bulbs about 2 ins. apart and cover 3 or 4 ins. deep. Protect with light winter covering of salt hay or similar material.

Are brodiaeas good bulbs for Eastern gardens? Many are excellent, and they should be used more extensively. Among the most satisfactory are *bridgesi* (violet), *capitata* (lavender), *coccinea* (red and green), *douglasi* (lavender), *grandiflora* (purple), *ixioides* (yellow), *lactea* (white), and *laxa* (purple-blue).

Can you tell me the name of the floral firecracker plant? *Brodiaea coccinea,* one of the many fine species of this genus native to western America. The flowers bear a close resemblance to a gaily-colored bunch of firecrackers.

CALOCHORTUS

Can calochortus (or Mariposa Tulips) be successfully grown in the Middle Atlantic states? Yes, but they are not very easy to keep from year to year. Plant at twice their own depth, late in fall, in bed of specially prepared, very gritty soil. Protect lightly through winter. Water freely when growing, but keep bed as dry as possible in late summer and fall. They need sunshine.

CAMASSIA

Will you tell me something of camassias and their care? They thrive in any good garden soil that is not too dry; prefer full sun or light shade; bloom in May (flowers blue or white), then die down. Plant in early fall, so that bulbs are 4 ins. below surface and 7 or 8 ins. apart. Do not transplant as long as they bloom well.

Are camassias good garden flowers? Very good indeed, and worthy of being more widely planted. Most of them are native Americans and are of easy culture. Apart from their garden value, their spires of starry flowers are excellent for cutting purposes.

CHIONODOXA

Does the bulb glory-of-the-snow (chionodoxa) need any special care? One of the easiest and loveliest of hardy spring-flowering bulbs. Plant in the fall in any fairly good soil, 3 ins. deep, 2 or 3 ins. apart. Do not disturb for many years after planting. Top-dress every 2 or 3 years with fertilized soil. They will increase and improve with passing of years. Excellent for planting in low-growing ground covers such as vinca or bearberry.

COLCHICUM

How deep should colchicum be planted; and how often divided? Cover the tops of the bulbs with not more than 3 ins. of soil. Divide every third or fourth year.

What soil and situation are best for colchicums and when should they be planted? Soil should be rich and reasonably moist (but not wet). Light shade. Plant in early August.

Is it difficult to raise colchicum (C. autumnale) from seed? Not difficult, but it requires patience. Sow when ripe in pans of humusy soil and plunge in shaded cold frame. Keep uniformly moist.

CONVALLARIA (LILY-OF-THE-VALLEY)

Can lilies-of-the-valley be grown in an absolutely shady place? Yes. They will grow in dense shade if the soil is fairly good, but will probably not bloom so freely as when in partial shade.

When should the ground be made acid for lily-of-the-valley? This may be done at planting time, by incorporating generous amounts of leafmold or peatmoss with soil. Each year the bed may be top-dressed with sifted leafmold.

Should lilies-of-the-valley be fertilized to have more blossoms? If so, when and with what? They appreciate a top-dressing of well-rotted cow manure in fall. Do not allow them to become overcrowded.

How can I grow lily-of-the-valley? What kind of soil? I have no success. A moist, but not wet, soil that contains generous amounts of humus. Improve soil by spading in rotted manure, leafmold, peatmoss, etc., and by adding bone meal. Lily-of-the-valley prefers light shade. Plant in spring.

The bed in which I have very fine clumps of giant lilies-of-the-valley has been okayed as to soil, sunshine, and shade; they have splendid foliage. Why is it they do not multiply, and produce only a few stems of bloom? The soil is basically clay, though it has been enriched. If the soil is very rich, the foliage will be good, but flowers scarce. Let the plants become firmly established, then they will flower when the excess nutrients are used up.

Is there any difference in size of lilies-of-the-valley, or can you make them grow to be a good size? How?   The largest-flowered variety is named *fortunei*. Old, worn-out plantings usually produce few small flowers. Lift, separate, and replant in newly fertilized soil every 3 or 4 years.

Why don't my lilies-of-the-valley bloom? They look thrifty.   Probably in too-dense shade; or the plants are too thick, and need dividing and replanting.

How do you grow clumps of lily-of-the-valley for forcing for cut blossoms?   Plant clumps in very rich, sandy loam. When pips are ¼ to ⅜ in. thick and ⅞ to 1 in. long, cut away from clumps with as much root as possible. Wrap in bundles and place in cold storage, 28° to 32° F., for at least 3 months. Best results however are obtained from specially prepared pips.

Are the roots of the lily-of-the-valley poisonous?   Yes. The druggists' convallaria, which is used as a heart tonic, is made from lily-of-the-valley roots.

CROCUS

When shall I plant crocuses, and how?   Spring-flowering kinds in September and October. Plant in light, fertile soil, in sunny place. If among grass, only where grass can remain uncut until leaves have died away in late spring. Plant 2 or 3 ins. apart and about 3 ins. deep. Fall-blooming kinds should be planted in July or August; or transplanted in June or early July.

Should crocuses be planted in beds, or with grass, to look natural? They appear best when planted among grass or some low ground cover, such as creeping thyme, mazus, or *Veronica repens*. A good method is to throw handfuls of the corms over the ground surface so that they fall in natural drifts, and then plant each corm where it falls.

DAFFODILS (NARCISSI)

Many of the early spring-blooming plants would not be worth a second glance if it were not for the fact that they are harbingers of spring. Daffodils, on the other hand, would be important even if they bloomed in June or August.

The daffodils belong to the genus *Narcissus,* and while all daffodils are narcissi, it is not quite correct to say that all narcissi are daffodils. In a general way the term is the common name for the genus, but certain species, like *Narcissus jonquilla* have a special common name, and in this case it is jonquil. Some 10,000 varieties have been introduced. The color range of the group is limited largely to yellow, orange and white, but apricot tones and a few clear pinks have recently been created. Perhaps other colors will sometime be available.

Daffodils have much to recommend them. While a given species may not succeed in all parts of the country, there are types that do well in warm climates, and others that thrive where the winters are severe. They are highly prized in rock gardens, borders, and in small intimate gardens, and they may be naturalized in woodlands and meadows. They are also of value as cut flowers.

Daffodils border a woodland walk. Ideal for the purpose because they take care of themselves.

Soils; Fertilizers

What type of soil is needed to grow narcissi?   Any garden soil is suitable providing it is deep, well drained, and fertile. Avoid planting in hot, barren soils, or where the soil remains wet for long periods.

Will narcissi thrive in wet soils?   No. The water table (level below which all spaces in soil are filled with water) should not stand nearer the surface than 18 ins. for any appreciable length of time.

What is correct preparation of soil for planting narcissi?   Spade to a depth of 12 ins. and place rotted manure in bottom of bed. Cover so that at least 2 ins. of soil separates the manure from bases of bulbs. Incorporate 4 to 5 lbs. of 5–10–5 fertilizer per 100 sq. ft.

Can you tell me how to prepare a bed in which to grow daffodils for exhibition?   The classic recommendation is to excavate a trench 18 ins. deep, dig into the bottom an 8-in. layer of well-rotted manure, and on this spread a generous sprinkling of bone meal. Cover with

6 ins. of good topsoil (without manure), set bulbs on this, and cover with any fairly good soil.

How should one fertilize narcissi that do not need lifting and replanting?   Top-dress in early fall with bone meal and in early spring with a complete fertilizer and compost or old, well-rotted manure.

Is superphosphate a safe fertilizer to use on narcissi beds?   Yes. It may be forked in at planting time, or applied as a top-dressing just as the foliage breaks ground in spring.

With what can I feed my daffodils to increase size of blooms for exhibition?   Dilute liquid cow manure judiciously applied at intervals in spring, from the time flower scapes appear, helps immensely. Keep beds well watered. If reduction in size and quantity of bloom is caused by overcrowding of bulbs, fertilizer does not help. When foliage becomes crowded and bloom falls off (4 to 6 years after planting), dig after foliage matures, separate bulbs and replant.

Planting

What type of situation is best adapted for daffodils?   A lightly shaded slope, sheltered from drying winds, with deep and well-drained soil.

Can daffodils be naturalized among trees?   Light woodland affords an ideal location for daffodils which, under such conditions, thrive and increase abundantly.

*A good way to use daffodils: informal or natural-
ized planting under tree.*

When is the best time to plant daffodils?   August, September, or early October, with preference for the earlier dates.

Daffodil bulbs ordered from seedsman usually do not arrive until fall, yet I am told to transplant those that are in my garden in July. Why?   Bulbs in storage remain dormant for some considerable time after those in the garden have developed new roots. Bulbs are harmed by moving after root growth is far advanced. Early planting is always advisable.

I transplanted narcissi bulbs in October. They all died. Why?
If transplanted later than October 1, the root system, then in active growth, is severely disturbed; serious injury may result.

Can daffodil bulbs be planted as late as December? Yes; dormant bulbs can be planted any time before the ground freezes solid. Well-stored bulbs have been planted with success as late as February. Earlier planting, however, is much to be preferred.

Is it possible to plant narcissi in spring right after frost is out of ground? The immediate results may be quite unsatisfactory. If sound bulbs are available at that time, plant them, as they may improve the following year.

Is it true that if you transplant narcissi in spring, they will not bloom? If so, why? It is scarcely possible for them to bloom satisfactorily if removed from the soil. By spring the bulbs have a fully developed root system and the disturbance of transplanting causes a serious setback. If taken up in clumps of soil, with roots intact, they may bloom fairly well.

About what distance should be left between full-sized daffodil bulbs when planting? It depends upon the effect desired, and also upon the variety, because bulb sizes vary considerably. A minimum distance of from 3 to 6 ins. should be allowed. For colonizing, the bulbs should be set in a pleasingly informal pattern rather than evenly spaced.

How deep are daffodils planted? In light soils large bulbs are set with their bases 6 to 8 ins. deep; in heavier soils, 5 to 7 ins. deep. Small bulbs should be planted shallower than those of larger size.

Does deep planting encourage daffodils to multiply? No. On the contrary, it checks rapid division. Shallow planting induces rapid multiplication. Deep planting tends to build up strong-flowering bulbs.

Can daffodils be interplanted with tulips to produce early flowers and thus extend the blooming season of the planting? Yes. This is an entirely satisfactory combination.

Culture

How are daffodils cared for? Plant in good deep soil. Water during dry weather, especially after flowering, to keep foliage green as long as possible. Remove faded flowers. Fertilize yearly. Lift and separate every third or fourth year.

What are the moisture requirements of narcissi grown outdoors? They need ample supplies during the growing season, particularly in spring, when the flower scapes are developing.

When should daffodils be lifted for storage through the summer? Or is it better to leave them in the ground all year? Summer storage is not recommended for daffodils. If they must be dug, July is the best time. Store in dry place, as cool as possible down to 50°.

What time of the year should daffodils be separated? July; by then the foliage has fully matured and the bulbs are quite dormant. After separation, replanting should be done at once.

Do narcissus bulbs naturalized among trees have to be dug and replanted at intervals? Yes, do this whenever they become so crowded that the quantity and quality of the blooms have deteriorated. This may be as often as every third year, or as infrequently as every 5 or 6 years.

Daffodils left in one place too long (right) produce grassy foliage and poor flowers. Dividing old clumps and replanting will produce blooms like those at left.

Will daffodils bloom the spring after they have been divided and reset? Yes, if of blooming size: 1½ to 2 ins. diameter for trumpet varieties, 1 to 1½ ins. for smaller varieties; and ⅝ to 1 in. for the *triandrus, cyclamineus,* and *jonquilla* types.

What should be done with clumps of narcissi and daffodils that won't bloom? After the foliage has died down, dig them up, separate the bulbs, fertilize the soil, and replant.

How can I get miniature daffodils to bloom every spring? Plant in a sheltered place in moist, but not waterlogged, soil. Water freely during dry periods whenever foliage is present. Dig up, separate, and replant every 3 years.

Can daffodil bulbs which have bloomed indoors in pots be stored after blooming, to be used next year? Not for forcing again. If kept well-watered until ground is in satisfactory condition, they may be planted outdoors and will bloom in future years.

Do narcissi bloom the second year? Under favorable conditions yes, and for many successive years. Bulbs that are forced into bloom early indoors cannot be forced satisfactorily a second year.

I have heard that it is harmful to cut the foliage off narcissi when they have finished blooming. Is this so? Yes; the leaves are needed to produce food to plump up the bulbs in readiness for next season's flowering. Never remove foliage until it has died down, or at least turned yellow.

Daffodils planted the end of September are now (late October) through the ground. Will they survive? They probably will. Throw an additional 2 ins. of soil over them. They were undoubtedly planted too shallowly.

Can you tell me why double jonquils do not mature their blooms? Hundreds of stems come up with empty cases at the tops. They are overcrowded and are robbing each other of nutrients and moisture. Dig up the bulbs, separate them, enrich the bed, and replant. Water thoroughly during dry weather in the spring.

Propagation

What is the simplest way for an amateur to increase a limited stock of a choice narcissus? Plant bulbs shallowly (about 4 ins. deep) in a well-prepared bed—preferably in a cold frame. Give good cultural care and lift, divide, and replant every second year.

Is there any rapid method of vegetatively propagating daffodils? In summer large bulbs can be sliced vertically into many sections (each containing a small portion of the basal plate). The sections are then planted in peatmoss and sand. Mild bottom heat stimulates production of new bulblets.

How are narcissi raised from seeds? Sow in late August in rows 6 ins. apart in a well-prepared seedbed in a cold frame. Cover seeds ¾ in. deep. Shade the bed, keep uniformly moist, weeded, and covered with salt hay or other protection during winter. Allow seedlings two summers' growth, then lift and replant with wider spacing.

Why can't I get daffodil seeds to come up? It is possible that the seeds are not fertile, or perhaps your cultural care is incorrect. Hand pollination of the flowers should result in fertile seed. See previous question.

Pests and Diseases

Are daffodils subject to pests and diseases? Several diseases and some insect pests may be troublesome, but these usually do not appear in garden plantings. If trouble is suspected, remove affected bulbs and send samples to your State Agricultural Experiment Station for diagnosis and advice.

Is the hot-water treatment of narcissus bulbs effective? Yes, as a control for eelworms, bulb flies, and mites. The treatment consists of soaking for 4 hours in water maintained at 110 to 111.5° F. One pint of formalin to each 25 gals. of water is added if basal rot is present. Bulbs must not be treated too early or too late in the season. There are now many new chemical miticides on the market.

Varieties

What is the difference between a daffodil and a narcissus? These names are interchangeable, although "daffodil" is applied particularly, but not exclusively, to those kinds which have large, well-developed trumpets. The Latin name for the entire group is *Narcissus*.

What is a jonquil? A jonquil hybrid? The true jonquil is *Narcissus jonquilla*, a species that has slender, rushlike foliage and sweet-scented flowers in clusters. Jonquil hybrids are horticultural developments of this species, usually with larger flowers. The large-trumpet narcissi, or daffodils, are sometimes miscalled jonquils.

What are the names of some white and bicolor trumpet daffodils? White: Beersheba, High Sierra, Mount Hood, President Carnot, Roxane, Ada Finch. Bicolor: Jefta, Sylvanite, Spring Glory, Queen of Bicolors.

Can you tell me some good varieties of large-cup daffodils? Francisca Drake, Dick Wellband, Scarlet Leader, white perianths, orange cups; John Evelyn, E. H. Wilson, South Pacific, white perianth, yellow cup; Scarlet Elegance, Krakatoa, Fortune's Bowl, yellow perianth, orange cups.

What are some of the best small-cup narcissi? Alcida, white and yellow, Lady Kestevan, Firetail and Limerick, white and red; Sunrise, white with golden rays in pale cup; Nette O'Melveny, white with lemon cup edged orange; Hera, white with pale lemon cup.

Are there any small-flowered white narcissi for a rock garden? The following are *triandrus* hybrids: white or cream, Moonshine, Shot Silk and Thalia, with starry perianths, bell-like small trumpets; Agnes Harvey, white; *triandrus albus* (Angel's Tears), 6 ins. white, 2 to 3 flowers to a stem.

What are the names of some of the Jonquil Hybrids? Trevithian, fragrant, golden, starry, 2 to 3 flowers per stem; Golden Sceptre and Golden Perfection, golden yellow; Tullus Hostilius, yellow; *campernelli odorus,* single, golden, very small.

Please give me names and descriptions of some late-blooming daffodils. Azalea, pink cup; Bridegroom, white, yellow crown; Cover Girl, pink cup; Daphne, double fragrant white; Geranium, red-crowned cluster-flowered, fragrant; Gremlin, white, starry with lemon cup; Moonshine, white with bell-shaped trumpets.

Please name some mid-season daffodil varieties. Gertie Millar, white with flaring primrose cup; L'Innocence, white poetaz; Moonglow, sulphur yellow trumpet; Mount Hood, white trumpet; Trevithian, fragrant yellow jonquil hybrid.

What is the double white narcissus that looks like a gardenia, smells sweet but does not bloom very freely? *N. alba plena odorata* is a notoriously shy bloomer. It prefers a moist situation. Try instead, Daphne, Cheerfulness and the even newer Swansdown, all white doubles.

Can you suggest some very early daffodils? February Gold, small yellow trumpet, a *cyclamineus* hybrid; Ada Finch and High Sierra, white trumpets; Grapefruit, lemon trumpet; Hallowe'en, yellow trumpet; Riootous, two-toned double; South Pacific, white and yellow; Twink, primrose and orange double.

ERANTHIS (WINTERACONITE)

I have not had success with winteraconites, although I planted them in a favorable situation early in October. Can you suggest cause of failure? Too late planting. They should have been planted at least 2 months earlier. They quickly deteriorate when kept out of ground.

What conditions do winteraconites (eranthis) need? A woodsy, non-acid soil in light shade. They often do well on gentle slopes, and once planted should be left undisturbed. Set tubers 3 ins. deep and about same distance apart.

EREMURUS

Are Foxtail-lilies hardy? These stately (5 to 12 foot) members of the lily family produce from star-shaped, fibrous rootstocks, rosettes of narrow leaves which send up blooming stalks bearing heavy racemes of bell-shaped white, pink, yellow or orange flowers in late spring. They are hardy to Zone 4 if heavily mulched after ground freezes hard. Do not remove mulch until late spring frosts are past as early spring growth may be frost-nipped. For this reason a northern exposure is desirable.

ERYTHRONIUM

What are the habits and culture of dogtooth-violets? *Erythronium dens-canis* is a woodland plant which likes a constantly moist position in partial shade.

What is the proper depth for planting dogtooth-violet bulbs, and how late may they be planted for spring blooming? Plant with top of bulb 3 ins. below surface. September is latest month for planting. They quickly deteriorate if kept out of soil long.

Are the troutlilies or dogtooth-violets easily grown in gardens? They are among the most lovely of plants for lightly shaded places where soil is deep and humusy, and possibly moist. Unfortunately many of them gradually deteriorate when planted in Eastern gardens, but they are well worth replanting from time to time.

FRITILLARIA

What is the guinea hen flower? *Fritillaria meleagris*. The speckled, pendant blooms are curious rather than beautiful. A good rock garden subject.

What is the culture for crown imperial?   *Fritillaria imperialis*, like many others of its genus, is capricious, sometimes doing well, and then again, for no apparent reason, failing to thrive. Plant in July in deep, limy soil, in light shade. Leave undisturbed as long as it continues to thrive.

GALANTHUS (SNOWDROP)

I am very fond of snowdrops. Where and how shall I plant them? Plant in early fall, setting bulbs 3 to 4 ins. deep and about 3 ins. apart. If possible, choose a porous soil that contains fair amount of humus, and a lightly shaded position. They multiply fairly rapidly if congenially located.

How often should snowdrops (Galanthus nivalis) be lifted and transplanted?   Do not disturb them unless absolutely necessary; they thrive best when left alone. If transplanting becomes imperative, do it after foliage dies down. Do not keep bulbs out of ground longer than necessary.

HYACINTH

Can hyacinth bulbs be planted outside in November for spring flowers?   Yes, but a month earlier is preferable.

Can I plant hyacinth bulbs in the spring? If so, will they bloom the first summer?   Only the so-called summer-hyacinth (*Galtonia candicans*) can be planted at this time. It blooms the first summer. The spring-flowering Dutch hyacinths are planted in fall.

Will hyacinths be injured if moved after the leaves show? Yes, they will suffer somewhat. If absolutely necessary it can be done, providing every care is taken to keep a large ball of soil intact about the roots.

Will Hyacinthus amethystinus grow in light shade? When does it bloom?   Yes. It blooms end of May and early June in vicinity of New York. A fine species for the home garden. It looks like a grape hyacinth. Plant bulbs in fall, 3 to 4 ins. deep.

LEUCOCRINUM

Are starlilies annuals or perennials? I have had them in the house summer and winter so far, but they increase so fast, I won't have room for them all another winter. Will they stand the winter in the flower bed?   Starlilies or sandlilies (leucocrinum) are hardy perennials. They are native from Nebraska to the Pacific coast.

LEUCOJUM

A friend gave me a clump of leucojum which I greatly admired in

her garden 2 years ago. **They have never bloomed in mine. Why?**
This plant dislikes root disturbance and the transplanting may have
caused it to skip blooming for a couple of years. Leucojums enjoy a
soil rich in leafmold and a sunny or very lightly shaded position.

**I bought bulbs of Leucojum vernum, which books say grows 6 ins.
tall. Mine grew 2½ ft. Was the soil too rich?** The plant often sold
as *Leucojum vernum* (Spring Snowflake) is the later-blooming and
much taller *L. aestivum* (Summer Snowflake). The former has but
2 flowers on each stem; the latter usually 4 to 6.

LILIES

Lilies have been called both the most fascinating and the most
exasperating of all garden flowers: fascinating because of their beauty
of form and coloring; exasperating because of frequent failures and
disappointments. However, few ornamental plants have as great decorative value or are better adapted to garden planting design. Because they are closely linked with art and religion, they are interesting
for sentimental reasons.

In nature different species are found under the most diverse conditions: some grow at high altitudes, others at low; some inhabit the
desert, while others are found in damp meadows. They come from
both dry and humid climates, and from cold and warm regions. Is
it any wonder that as a group they used to appear capricious when
included in a garden planting?

While lilies have been cultivated in gardens for a long time, it is
only within the past decade or so that they have really been domesti-
cated. For centuries efforts to hybridize the wild species had proved
almost futile. Once a few hybrids were obtained, however, these
intercrossed readily. The result has been new races or groups of man-
made lilies which are infinitely easier to grow in gardens than were
their progenitors. Today lilies have become flowers for every garden.
They are invaluable for cutting as well as for the landscape effects.

Soils; Fertilizers

How should soil be treated before planting lilies? Well-drained
garden soil that is in good condition requires no special treatment.
Spade it well, allow it to settle, and plant the bulbs. It is desirable,
but not necessary, to mix some peatmoss with the soil for the eastern
American lilies, and for *Lilium hansoni*.

Do lilies require sweet or acid soil? In most cases the acidity of
the soil is not important. The foliage of a few kinds, however, becomes chlorotic or yellowish in alkaline soil. *Hansoni, speciosum, canadense,* and *superbum* are some of these. Where this occurs the lilies
benefit if a layer, several inches thick, of peatmoss is spaded into
the soil.

What kind of fertilizer is best for lilies? A good garden fertilizer, or almost any complete fertilizer that is relatively high in potash. One good formula is 5–10–10. Manure should not be used, as it may encourage losses from basal rot.

Can bone meal and cottonseed meal be used in ground where lily bulbs are to be planted? Yes, these are excellent.

When is the best time to fertilize lilies? Early spring.

Planting

How and when should hardy lily bulbs be planted? The ground should be dug and leafmold or peatmoss added. Plant stem-rooting kinds, such as *L. regale,* with the tops of the bulbs about 6 ins. under ground; bottom-rooting kinds, 2 or 3 ins. Sand placed below and above the bulbs helps drainage. Most lilies are best planted in autumn.

How deep should Easter Lily bulbs be planted? With a 4- to 6-in. cover of soil over the tops of the bulbs. They are hardy, of course, only in mild climates.

When is the best time to plant Regal Lilies? Early fall. They may be planted in spring providing the bulbs have been carefully stored.

When is the best time to plant Madonna Lilies? And how deep? Late August or early September. Somewhat later planting will do if the bulbs are not available earlier. Set them in a sunny site and do not cover the top of the bulb more than 2 ins.

When is the best time to divide and transplant various kinds of lilies? When the tops begin to die. Somewhat earlier or somewhat later lifting will not materially affect the performance of the plants the following year.

I find it necessary to move Madonna Lilies to another place in my garden. When should this be done? Shortly after the flowers have withered.

How often should Regal Lilies be divided and reset? Only when the number of stems indicates that the plants are becoming crowded.

Can you tell me how to take up Regal Lilies? The leaves often stay green until cold weather. Also, how about the roots? I was always afraid to cut off roots, so I just took the plants up and set them in a new place, although I wanted to ship them. If necessary to replant, do so in fall about a month before ground freezes hard. Ship with roots intact.

Should lilies be moved in spring? How deep should they be planted? They may be moved if taken up with considerable soil about their roots. Plant at the same depth in the new site as they were before being moved.

Problems

What should a beginner look for when purchasing lily bulbs?
Try to get mosaic-free bulbs of reliable species, and avoid kinds known to be difficult. A well-grown Maxwill or *henryi* is much handsomer than a diseased *auratum* or *japonicum*.

Just what is a "stem-rooting" lily?   Most garden lilies are stemrooting; that is, they produce most of their roots from the stem that grows upward from the bulb. For this reason most lilies are planted deeply so that they will have a long portion of their stem underground.

Why do lilies become spindly after a season or two? If this is caused by lack of food, what is it best to do?   The Sunset Lily increases rapidly and becomes so crowded after 2 or 3 years that it is necessary to dig, separate, and replant the bulbs, otherwise only weak, non-flowering stems are produced. Many other lilies eventually become crowded and need separating.

I have a lily which does not bloom every year. One year it blooms with 7 or 8 blossoms, the next it fails to flower, and grows only about 1 ft. tall. Can you give me any information regarding this?   Some lilies fail to bloom because they become crowded; others because of disease or because of frost injury to the growing point.

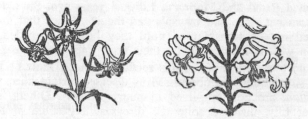

Meadow Lily (Lilium canadense) *and Regal Lily* (L. regale), *two of the most satisfactory for garden use.*

Does Lilium speciosum rubrum bloom in August; and can it be planted in spring?   It blooms in late August or September. It may be planted in spring.

I cannot grow Auratum Lilies. What do they need?   They usually fail because they become infected with mosaic disease. Try again with mosaic-free bulbs, planted away from other lilies, in ground that has not grown lilies recently.

I have planted 12 Formosa Lilies and not a one to show for it. I've tried to do just as nurserymen say, but no luck. Is something wrong with soil?   Probably not. *L. formosanum* is susceptible to mosaic disease and also to basal rot, which is caused by a soil fungus. Try some of the new disease-resistant hybrids.

If different kinds of lily bulbs are planted in the same bed, will the different species mix?   They will not mix if by mixing is meant that the pollen of one kind will influence adjoining plants so that their characteristics change. Varieties with wandering, underground stems may invade the territory of other near-by species.

Should Easter Lily bulbs be taken up and dried before replanting? (Texas.)   No. If it is necessary to move them, take them up late in the season and replant promptly.

Two other good lilies for amateurs—Hanson and Shuksan.

I planted Regal and Madonna Lilies 4 years ago. Should I have taken them out since and transplanted them?   Lilies that are doing well need not be transplanted until they become crowded, which condition will be manifested by their numerous short, weak stems.

Why do lilies "run out" in this section? (Pennsylvania.)   Because of their susceptibility to obscure virus diseases certain lilies, such as *L. auratum,* are not long-lived in many sections. Others, such as the Tiger Lily, thrive despite the diseases. Try some of the new horticultural types, such as the Mid-century Hybrids and Centifolium Hybrids.

Culture

How shall I plant and care for lilies of various kinds?   Plant Madonna Lilies in late August or September; all others when bulbs are received. Madonna Lilies are covered 2 ins. deep to top of bulb; most others 6 ins., more or less, depending upon the vigor of the plant. Mulch for winter with straw or marsh hay. After ground freezes mulch during the growing season with peatmoss or lawn clippings. Keep down weeds, fertilize with a complete fertilizer, and water if season is dry.

Will you give me some information about growing Madonna Lilies? Mine have always failed.   Deep planting is a common cause of failure. The top of the bulb should not be more than 2 ins. from surface of the ground. Any good garden soil, well drained, and a sunny site are suitable. Use organic fertilizer but no manure or peatmoss near the bulbs. Spray, if necessary, against botrytis blight, which see.

The Regal Lily is considered easy to grow, but mine are small. Do they like lime or an acid soil? Dry soil, or a fair amount of water? Failure may be due to plants being infected with mosaic disease, from which they will not recover. Soil conditions may be unfavorable. The Regal Lily prefers a fertile soil, well supplied with organic matter. Watering during dry weather and mulching to conserve moisture are beneficial. The presence or absence of lime is not important.

What are the cultural requirements of Lilium speciosum rubrum? What ground cover shall I use over them? Any good, well-drained garden soil in full sun or light shade. Low-growing, shallow-rooted plants such as pansies, violas, Scotch pinks, canterburybells and low-growing ferns are the best ground covers for lilies.

Would you please give me information on culture of the Mount Hood Lily? This is a form of *Lilium washingtonianum* which is rather difficult in gardens. Plant 10 ins. deep in well-drained soil that is supplied with an abundance of organic matter; provide a surface mulch to conserve moisture.

May ground where lilies are growing be hoed? Yes, but with extreme care. Many lilies appear late in spring and careless hoeing may result in chopping the shoots off below ground. Lily roots are near the surface and are damaged by deep hoeing. A summer mulch of leafmold, lawn mowings, peatmoss, or bagasse will eliminate the necessity for much cultivation.

What sort of mulch should be used around Madonna Lilies? Lawn clippings, leafmold, or peatmoss.

Does it harm lily bulbs to cut the flowers? Unfortunately, yes. One can scarcely avoid removing a considerable proportion of the foliage together with the blooms, and these leaves are needed to manufacture food to build up the bulbs for the next season's growth. Some kinds can be cut every second year without serious damage.

How do you get long stems on Regal Lilies? Long stems are produced on well-grown plants that are free from disease. Cultural requirements are a fertile soil well supplied with organic matter, mulching to conserve moisture, and the annual application of a complete commercial fertilizer. Old plants with numerous stems should be divided, and the bulbs replaced in enriched soil.

Should lily blooms be left on plants, or should they be picked off before seeding? Remove flowers as they fade. This favors the development of larger plants the following year.

Should lily stems, after they have dried up and died, be left, or

should they be cut off or pulled off? They should be removed. They may be pulled up gently if it is desired to save the bulblets which are found at the bases of the stems of certain species; otherwise they may be cut off.

At what time of year should lily bulbs be dug? Do not dig unless it is necessary to move them to another location or divide them. Take them up when the tops begin to die.

Should Regal Lilies be lifted every spring? Absolutely not. Lilies should never be dug unless they are overcrowded or unless it is desired to move them to another location.

Do we cover Madonna, Regal, and philippinense lilies because they are not quite hardy, or to prevent freezing and thawing? Lilies are mulched to prevent damage to the bulbs from low temperatures and to prevent injury to the roots from alternate freezing and thawing.

At what temperature should lily bulbs (Regal) be kept during winter? They are hardy and should be left in the ground over winter. In cold regions protect with a 6- or 8-in. straw mulch. (See next question.)

My lily bulbs arrived too late to plant outside. I have buried them in sand in a cold fruit cellar. Will they be all right? Yes, if temperature is kept just above freezing. It would have been better, however, to have potted them before storing in the cellar.

Propagation

Can lilies be grown from seed? Seeds of such lilies as *regale, tenuifolium, amabile, concolor, formosanum, henryi,* and *willmottiae* germinate promptly. Plant in early spring in flats of good soil, and leave in a cold frame, under lath shades, for 2 seasons. Water and weed regularly, and mulch or cover the flats with boards during winter. At the end of the second summer plant the seedlings out in nursery beds for another year or two, mulching the beds for winter. Plant seeds of *auratum, speciosum, martagon,* and native American lilies in spring. They will not send up leaves until the following spring. If the flats are stacked during the first summer no weeding, and only occasional watering, will be necessary. At end of the third season the plants should be large enough for the nursery bed.

What is the most successful way to propagate Regal Lilies, and how long before blossoms may be expected from seed? By seed. The larger seedlings should bloom during their third season.

Our Madonna Lily set seed after it bloomed. Could I plant the seed this winter in a box in the house? Madonna Lily seeds may be started in flats in the house any time during the winter.

I have some Lilium formosanum started from seeds sown last March. The bulbs are still pinhead size. How can I make them grow

faster? Water them every 2 weeks with water in which commercial fertilizer has been dissolved at the rate of 1 tablespoonful to 1 gal. of water.

When and how should lily bulblets be planted? Remove bulblets borne at bases of the stems when stems are cut down in fall. Plant them in a nursery row for a year or two until they are large enough to transplant to the border. Bulbils borne in the axils of leaves of some varieties may be planted about 1 in. deep as soon as they begin to drop from the plants.

How can I propagate the Gold-banded Lily (Lilium auratum)? Remove the bulblets from the bases of the stems in the fall and plant them out in a nursery for a year or two until they are large enough for the border.

I have three Madonna Lily bulbs grown from scales I took from large bulbs last August. What should I do with them until next August? I have them potted in the house now. Keep them growing in the pots until next August, when they may be planted in the garden.

Can small bulbs of Regal Lilies, that appear almost on top of the ground, be separated from the main plant and be planted deeper to increase the stock? Yes.

My Lilium umbellatum formed new bulbs on top of the ground. I covered them with 4 ins. of soil and mulched them with leaves. Will they come through the winter? Yes. To prevent crowding, bulblets which form near the surface of the ground on the bases of the stems, should be removed every year or two, and planted elsewhere.

How do you separate lily bulbs when you wish to start new plants? Dig, and break up the clumps in fall. The small bulbs on the bases of the stems may also be saved. Lilies which do not increase by bulb division nor by stem bulblets may be propagated by removing a few of the scales from the bulbs as soon as the flowers fade and planting these an inch deep in a light soil.

How do you propagate Regal Lilies from the flower stems? As soon as the last flowers fade, jerk the stems from the bulbs and "heel them in" (plant them) so that their lower quarters are covered with soil. In fall, when the stems are dead, remove the small bulbs from the bases and plant them 2 ins. deep.

Pests and Diseases

What is the best way to avoid mosaic disease in lilies? Plant only bulbs known, or guaranteed, to be free from mosaic. Or grow the bulbs from seed away from all lilies and other bulbous plants. When you see any sign of disease, dig up the plant and burn it at once.

What is the treatment for basal rot in Madonna Lilies? It is caused by a fungus. If detected before the bulbs have rotted much, remove decayed tissue, dip bulb for 20 mins. in 1 part formaldehyde to 50 parts water, and replant in a new location.

What is the recommended treatment for botrytis blight of lilies? Spray at weekly intervals with Bordeaux mixture. This disease is most serious in wet seasons.

How can I prevent field mice or moles from destroying Regal, Madonna, and other lily bulbs? Plant the bulbs in cages of wire netting of a large enough mesh to let the stems grow through.

Is it true that L. philippinense and Tiger Lilies are disease carriers and should be removed from the garden? They may or may not have mosaic disease. *L. philippinense* is usually raised from seeds and is therefore mosaic-free, but it may acquire the disease later. The Tiger Lily in the trade often, but not always, has mosaic. The health of these lilies is determined only by an examination of the leaves in the spring or early summer.

Varieties

Please tell me what new hybrid lilies to choose for my garden for bloom from June to September. I am not a specialist. Aurelian Hybrids; Bellingham Hybrids; Fiesta Hybrids; Golden Chalice Hybrids; Mid-century Hybrids; Olympic Hybrids, Rainbow Hybrids.

What lilies are long-lived? Healthy bulbs give long life. Buy only from a reliable dealer. Some of those most likely to live long in your garden are *hansoni, regale,* Maxwill, *superbum, henryi, speciosum, candidum* and *tigrinum*. Try also some of the new hybrids.

Which are the best lilies for dry soils? *Pumilum* (*tenuifolium*), *regale,* Maxwill, *formosanum, candidum, umbellatum* varieties, *tigrinum* and *princeps*. It is helpful, in conserving moisture in dry situations, to mulch the soil with peatmoss, lawn clippings, or some similar material.

What is the botanical name of the commonly used Easter Lily? *Lilium longiflorum*. Several varieties of this lily are grown by florists, among them *giganteum, harrisi, formosum,* Erabu, and Creole.

LYCORIS SQUAMIGERA

Which lily is it that shows its leaves in the spring, then dies, and in August sends up stalks which have a pink-lavender bloom? *Lycoris squamigera,* sometimes sold as *Amaryllis halli*.

How shall I care for Lycoris squamigera? Plant in September in light, loose soil, either in full sun or light woodland shade. Set bulbs so that their tops are 5 ins. deep and spaced 5 or 6 ins. apart. Leave undisturbed for many years.

Why did Lycoris squamigera fail to bloom since transplanting 2 years ago? It is in sunny, well-drained location. Bulbs multiplied, but

sent up no flower stems. It often happens that transplanted bulbs of this species refuse to bloom for 2 or 3 years after transplanting.

I have 2 Amaryllis halli, now 4 years old. They came up in the spring, and the leaves are healthy and long; they die down in July but never bloom. Can you help me? Maybe you planted small bulbs. If in a suitable soil (deep, light, well drained) and location (full sun or light shade) they should grow and eventually flower.

When do you dig Amaryllis halli? Some seed houses say after the foliage dies and before they bloom; others, after they bloom. Correct name of this plant is *Lycoris squamigera*. Best time for transplanting is immediately after they have bloomed.

MUSCARI (GRAPEHYACINTH)

How late can grapehyacinth (muscari) bulbs be planted? They may be planted any time before the ground freezes hard; but it is better to plant them in early fall.

Do grapehyacinths multiply? If so, when can one transplant them? Yes; they multiply freely. Self-sown seedlings come up in great numbers. Lift bulbs as soon as foliage has died down and transplant immediately; or store in cool, dry place until fall.

Can I keep grapehyacinth bulbs, without planting, till next spring? No. If you cannot plant them in open ground, plant them closely together in shallow boxes of soil. Stand outdoors and cover with leaves or hay during winter.

When should grapehyacinths, which have been undisturbed for years, be reset? To what depth? They may be lifted and replanted when the foliage has died and become completely brown. Plant 2 ins. apart, and cover tops of bulbs with 3 ins. of soil.

I have 2 varieties of muscari; one sends up top growth in fall. Which variety is it? How do I care for them over winter? The nomenclature of the species and varieties of muscari is very confused. Several of them produce foliage in the fall. They are quite hardy and require no special winter attention.

ORNITHOGALUM

Can you give me some information about ornithogalums? (Texas.) More than 100 kinds exist. They are natives of Europe, Asia, and particularly Africa, belonging to the lily family. Many kinds should be hardy in Texas. They need a fertile, sandy soil. See article in Bailey's Standard Cyclopedia of Horticulture, available in most libraries.

Is the very fragrant Ornithogalum arabicum hardy in the vicinity of New York City? Not generally so, although it will winter and bloom if given a very sheltered position, porous soil, and winter protection.

OXALIS

Will oxalis survive the winter months? *Oxalis violacea* and *O. acetosella* are hardy, and are sometimes grown as rock-garden plants.

PUSCHKINIA

Will you give me directions for growing a scilla-like bulbous plant called puschkinia? Plant in early fall about 3 ins. deep and same distance apart, in light, well-drained, fertile soil, either in full sun or very light shade. Do not replant more often than necessary. Need for this is indicated by reduction in number of blooms produced.

SCILLA

What is the best way to plant and care for the blue scilla? Plant S. sibirica in fall in deep, loose soil that is fairly fertile. It thrives for years without disturbance. Do not remove foliage until it has completely died down. The scillas, with large, potatolike bulbs (S. hispanica and S. nonscripta), are set 5 ins. deep. Other kinds about 3 ins. deep.

In the rock garden at a botanical garden I saw a pink scilla (squill) blooming in late August. What could this be? *Scilla chinensis* (sometimes known as *Scilla japonica*), an easily grown kind that self-sows freely. It thrives in ordinary garden soil in sun or light shade.

Which scillas are best adapted for planting in a shaded situation, in soil containing lots of leafmold? The Spanish Bluebell (*Scilla hispanica*) and the English Bluebell (*Scilla nonscripta*). Both may be had in blue-, pink-, and white-flowered forms.

STERNBERGIA

What is the name of the rich golden-yellow flower that looks like a crocus (but more substantial) and blooms in September? *Sternbergia lutea*. Plant bulbs 4 or 5 ins. deep in August, in quite porous soil and sheltered situation. Cover lightly during winter. This species resents root disturbance.

TULIPS

The May garden would indeed be dull without tulips. They are one of the "musts" of the mixed perennial border because they are unsurpassed in their wide array of harmonious colors and in their reliability. The range of hues covers the entire spectrum and all its tints and shades except pure blue. What artist would not revel in tubes of tulip colors as a medium for painting garden pictures?

For generations tulips grew in the fields and gardens near Constantinople before they found their way to Holland in 1571. Few plants have been molded to such an extent into the economic and social life of a nation. Even though grown in all the temperate regions they are still thought of as Dutch.

In the course of history, tulips have had their ups and downs. Soon after their introduction into Holland they reached a peak of popularity never before or since achieved by any plant. Men speculated and gambled with them as is done today in cotton, corn, and oil. The prices of new varieties soared to staggering heights. A single bulb of the variety Semper Augustus once sold for 13,000 florins, the equivalent of $6,500. Then came the crash; and the economic and financial structure of the entire nation was threatened. The popularity of tulips vanished, and for years they were hidden in the small home gardens of the poorer people of Holland only to rise again and become a leading industry.

Tulips are valuable in many kinds of garden plantings. Their best use is in the border, where they combine beautifully with all other plants. They may be planted in formal beds, where they take on an appropriate quality of stiffness and constraint. In small, intimate groups about the garden, they offer friendliness and charm. Because they are so easy to grow, they force well in the window garden. For flower arrangements, their form is distinctive and their coloring delightful.

Soil and Fertilizer

What kind of soil suits tulips best?   A fertile, well-drained, light loam, at least 12 ins. deep. They will grow satisfactorily, however, in a wide variety of soils.

Will tulips grow well in a bed that is located in a wet spot in my garden?   No. Good subsurface drainage is of the utmost importance in growing tulips. The bulbs will quickly rot in waterlogged soil.

Is it necessary to change the soil yearly in beds where tulips are planted?   Desirable, but not essential unless disease is present. Changing the soil every 3 years should control fire blight, basal rot, etc.

What can I add to my garden soil to make my tulip bulbs grow larger?   Coarse bone meal and commercial fertilizer, mixed with the soil at planting time, and well-rotted manure, set 2 ins. under the bulb with a soil separation layer between the bases of the bulbs and the manure, will aid.

How should soil be prepared for a tulip bed?   Dig to depth of 10 or 12 ins. Place 2 ins. of well-rotted manure in the bottom. A dressing of bone meal or commercial fertilizer, worked into the bed, is also beneficial.

What common fertilizers are good for tulips?   Bone meal, superphosphate, dried and shredded cattle manure, sheep manure, and commercial fertilizers, such as a 4–8–4 or 5–10–5.

Is it worth while to put commercial fertilizer on a tulip bed in late fall? Yes, but better in spring. Apply and water it in immediately.

What is the best fertilizer for tulips? Bone meal is probably best, because of its slow-acting properties. Complete commercial fertilizers, of low-nitrogen content, and superphosphate are also satisfactory. Avoid all fresh manures. Liquid manures should be used only in weak dilutions.

Is it well to put manure on my tulip bed? Manure is practically wasted when put on the surface. It should be used only in the bottom of the bed. Best winter covers for tulip beds are salt hay, clean straw, peatmoss, and rough compost.

Planting

When is the best time to plant tulips? October 15 to November 1, except where a short growing season makes earlier planting necessary. A good general rule is to plant 2 to 4 weeks before the ground freezes.

How late can one plant tulips and still hope for fair results? (Ohio.) December 15 in your section. However, if bulbs are sound they may be planted later.

How can I save tulip bulbs which are not in the ground at the time of the first hard freeze? Build a fire over the frozen ground and thaw it out, or else chop through the crust and plant. Tulips cannot be held a full year out of the ground.

Could tulip bulbs be planted in January or February if the weather permits? Yes, if sound and well preserved. By February the flower buds contained in the bulbs are usually dead. However, this procedure may result in saving the bulbs so that they will flower the following year.

What happens if tulips are planted in early spring? They grow very short, and usually do not flower the first year.

On December 2 I planted tulip bulbs in a prepared bed. Is this too late for them to make root growth? How will their spring growth be affected? They should grow and bloom. Their stems will be shorter, and their blooms not so large as those of earlier-planted bulbs.

My tulip bulbs are very soft. Would it be advisable to plant them? Soft tulips result from too early digging or hot, dry storage. They can be planted, and should recover by the second growing season.

How does one obtain even results from tulip plantings? Flowers all the same height, and all of one kind blooming together with flowers of the same size? By planting good-quality, even-sized bulbs at the correct season and setting them all at the same depth. Professional gardeners accomplish this by removing soil from the bed, placing the bulbs, and then refilling with soil. For the very best results new bulbs of the same variety or the same type should be planted each fall.

Will tulip bulbs just thrown in any way grow?   They may grow but will not be satisfactory. They should be set properly on their bases, and at a suitable depth.

Is it true that tulip bulbs do better when planted 10 or 12 ins. deep as stated by some bulb growers?   Deep planting prevents tulips splitting up and saves the task of digging and separating them every 2 to 3 years. Large bulbs may do well planted with their bases at this depth but shallower planting is usually more advisable if bulbs are small. Deep planting retards breaking up of each bulb into several smaller ones and therefore makes it possible to leave the planting undisturbed for several years.

Do you agree that if tulips are planted 9 ins. deep they'll never have to be moved?   No; but they will need replanting less frequently than shallowly planted bulbs. They will eventually have to be transplanted.

Do you favor very deep planting for tulips; 10, 12 or 14 inches to the bottom of the bulb?   Only if the bulbs are unusually large. Top-size bulbs should be planted 6 to 10 ins. Oversize Jumbo bulbs (13 to 14 centimeter or larger) may be placed deeper.

Will tulips planted less then 6 ins. deep bloom next spring?   They should, providing they are not subjected to too much frost.

What happens if you plant tulip bulbs too deeply or too shallowly?   If planted too deeply, small bulbs will waste their strength pushing through to the ground level. If too shallowly, they may heave out of the ground, or freeze completely.

How shall I plant Darwin tulips to get the best results in this climate? (Pennsylvania.)   Obtain top-size bulbs. Plant in October in fertile, well-drained soil, covering the bulbs 6 or 8 ins. deep. After the ground freezes hard, mulch lightly with leaves, salt hay, or evergreen branches. Remove this covering gradually in spring. Feed with diluted liquid fertilizer and water freely during dry spells.

In planting 1,000 tulips in beds 36 ins. wide should I dig the dirt out to a depth of 6 or 8 ins. and replace after setting the bulbs? I want to plant annuals without lifting tulips.   Your method is quite satisfactory, but it is quicker to prepare the bed and then plunge the bulbs into the ground, using a long-shanked trowel. Annuals can be planted over bulbs planted 6 ins. deep or deeper.

How soon will it be safe to plant tulips in the same bed again after they are lifted? They occupied the bed for 3 years.   Unless the soil is changed, or unless bed has been sterilized, allow a 3-year period between tulip plantings.

What causes the "dropping" of tulip bulbs? (By this I mean that

**the bulbs grow lower than the parent bulbs.) Will the bulbs growing
up on the stem produce true to variety?** Tulip bulbs "drop" when
planted too shallowly. Bulblets on the stems can be used for propagation and will come true to the variety.

Culture

**Is it true that American-grown tulips are very poor and that only
about 40 per cent will grow?** Definitely false. Good-quality, American-grown tulips bloom 100 per cent, and usually are earlier blooming. They are preferred by commercial growers for early forcing.

How can I grow tulips successfully? (Tennessee.) Plant bulbs, in
your section, from October 20 to November 5, in beds that have been
dug to a depth of 12 ins. and are enriched with bone meal and humus.
Cover the bulbs to a depth of 6 ins. If a drought occurs in spring,
water frequently and thoroughly.

**How can I get larger tulip blooms? I plant only top-size bulbs ob-
tained from a reputable dealer.** Fertilize each September with 5 lbs.
of a 4–8–4 fertilizer to each 100 sq. ft. of bed. Water freely during
dry periods in spring. Do not remove leaves when cutting flowers.
Remove faded flower heads to prevent seed production. Never remove
leaves, or dig bulbs, until tops have dried completely.

**What extra steps can I take to keep my Darwin tulips in fine con-
dition, now that tulip bulbs are so expensive that I can't replace the
present supply?** Top-dress beds with compost and bone meal. Feed
in spring with commercial fertilizer. Water frequently during growing
season. Cut flowers high up on stem as soon as they begin to fade. Dig
up and separate every 2 or 3 years, and replant in enriched soil.

*Success with tulips (and other spring-flower-
ing bulbs) depends largely on thorough preparation of the soil before planting.*

**Will tulips bloom as well the second year after planting as they do
the first?** If the soil is well prepared, moisture is provided during
the growing season, and the flowers are removed immediately after
blooming (but the foliage left intact), there will be very little difference between the quality of the first and second year's blooms.

**Could tulips be satisfactorily grown in a porch box 5 ft. long, 15 ins.
wide, and a foot deep; northwest exposure?** Not unless the box was
packed around, bottom, sides, and top, with straw, salt hay, or other

material to prevent the soil from freezing solid. It would be better to plant the bulbs in shallow pots or bulb pans and set them out in window boxes filled with damp peatmoss.

Can bulbs which have been forced be made to produce flowers outside? If so, how? They can be planted outside if the soil is well fertilized, but the number of flowers as well as their size is usually disappointingly small. If you intend to try this, be sure to keep the forced plants watered and growing so that they retain their foliage as long as possible.

Is it good policy to leave tulip bulbs in the ground all summer? It is quite practical. Tulips can remain 2 to 3 years without disturbing. Do not remove foliage until it has died down.

Can tulips be left in year after year? I have some that have been in for some years and they look very good. As long as the bulbs continue producing satisfactory blooms, keeping them in the ground is a good time-saving practice. It is usually better, however, to dig them and separate them every 3 years.

What is the best treatment for a planting of tulips which are to be left in the ground? Cut flowers off as soon as they fade. Keep watering the bed in dry weather until the foliage has completely died down. Fertilize in spring.

I had beautiful beds of Darwin tulips. I left one bed in the ground and covered it with manure. Will the tulips ever bloom again? If so, when? They should bloom again, in normal fashion, next spring.

Will tulip bulbs bloom again if flowers are cut? They should bloom the following year providing most of the foliage is left to die down naturally.

If all that comes up from a tulip bulb is one large leaf and no bloom stalk, will that bulb, or the increase from it, ever bloom? This indicates the need for digging and separation. First-year bulblets produce only one big leaf. Both the bulb and its increase may eventually bloom if planted in enriched soil. This "growing on," however, may prove tiresome, and for practical purposes it is often better to discard such weakened bulbs and start afresh with new stock.

Last year I lost about 1,000 tulips. Do they run out? One bed was replanted after bulbs were lifted and separated, but many died. Would lack of snow affect them thus? (Minnesota.) No. Losses may be caused by disease, rodents, or lack of fertility. In your section, shallowly planted bulbs need the protection of a winter mulch.

What is the best method of producing tulips from bulbs which have bloomed 2 years and now show nothing but leaves? Dig up the bulbs in July or early August. Replant only those having a diameter of 1 in. or more. Set small bulbs in rows, in vegetable garden or elsewhere, to grow on.

Is it advisable to prevent small tulip bulbs from blooming the first year, thus to obtain larger bulbs for the next year? Yes; but do not remove buds until they show color.

Can tulips be lifted and packed in dirt until the tops are dry so as to save the bulbs; or should they be planted deeper so that I can plant "glads" above them? Tulips can be lifted and carefully "heeled in" in a shallow trench until their tops are fully dried. They may then be separated and stored, and be replanted in the fall.

Should tulip bulbs be taken up each year and separated? Should they be covered with leaves in the fall? No. Dig them up and separate them every 2 to 3 years unless the ground is wanted for other purposes. (See answer above.) A winter mulch is desirable where temperatures go much below zero.

Is it wise to dig up tulip bulbs in May or June, and store them away to replant in fall? (Missouri.) This is too early. In your section July 1 would be better. When the bulbs are thoroughly dried, give them a good dusting with sulfur and store in a cool, dry place.

How often should tulip bulbs be removed from the soil and replanted? In light soils, every 2 years; in heavy soils, every 3 years. Bulbs planted 6 to 10 ins. deep require separation less frequently than those planted 4 ins. deep.

Is it all right to dig tulips in the fall for transplanting? Tulips can be dug and transplanted as late as October 1. An earlier date is better, however, as vigorous new root growth begins in October and continues until hard freeze.

How should tulip bulbs be handled after digging in fall? Tulips should not be dug in fall unless absolutely necessary. If they are, they should be immediately replanted.

Can tulips be moved in spring before blooming? No, it is impractical and will prevent the bulbs from blooming. It is also dangerous to the future welfare of the bulbs.

Do tulips need to be cured in the sun after digging? They should not be exposed to the sun, even a 30-minute exposure to full sunshine may crack the coats on the bulbs. Cure them by storing in a cool, dry place protected from sunlight.

What is the best way to store tulip bulbs through summer? Dry them thoroughly, dust well with sulfur, and hang them in ventilated bags from the rafters of a cool, dry cellar, shed, or garage.

I expect to move this winter and have taken my tulips out of the ground and have them stored in my basement. I covered them with soil. Would it be better to keep them dry and in a bag? Store them dry. Dust the bulbs with sulfur and keep them in open boxes or ventilated bags.

How can I keep tulips over winter, to plant in spring? This is not a good practice. If it must be done, store at 34° to 40° F. Tulips cannot be kept over safely for periods longer than 6 to 8 months.

When do you reset tulip bulbs that have been lifted and stored through the summer? No sooner than September 15. October 15 is better, if the bulbs are storing well.

What should be done with small tulip bulbs taken up in spring but not planted the following fall? Will they grow in size if planted next spring—not for bloom but for bulb growth? They are hardly worth bothering with. Small bulbs will have wasted most of their substance by being stored so long.

Winter mulch is applied after the ground freezes.

Is it important to cover the ground after planting tulip bulbs when the weather is freezing? (Long Island.) In sections as cold as Long Island it is wise to cover tulip plantings with salt hay or a similar protection. Apply this after the ground is frozen. Do *not* use manure for mulching tulips.

When should strawy manure be placed on tulips? Any manure may be a dangerous covering for tulips, as it sometimes harbors botrytis blight. Use only clean straw and apply it after a hard freeze.

Propagation

How is the crossing of tulips accomplished by the amateur? By the same methods used for most other flowers. Ripe pollen is transferred, with a camel's-hair brush, from the stamens of the male parent to the receptive stigma of the seed-bearing parent. All stamens are removed from the female parent before they ripen and shed pollen, and the flower is covered with a paper or plastic bag, to prevent accidental pollination.

Is it true that it takes 7 years to grow tulips from seeds? During this time is there any top growth? No. Tulips often produce blooms in 3 years from seed. Top growth appears on the young seedlings.

Is it worth while for the amateur to attempt growing tulips from seeds? No. The chances of getting desirable flowers are very small. The growing of seedlings for breeding work is a tedious job, best left to the specialist.

Could you give detailed directions for growing tulips from seeds? Seeds should be planted in light, well-drained soil in a cold frame in summer. Dig the bulblets the following year when the foliage has died down, and plant them 3 or 4 ins. deep in nursery beds in fall. The soil should be enriched for the young bulbs. It is a tedious process that appeals only to the most interested amateurs and to breeders of new varieties.

How do tulip bulbs multiply? By offsets (young bulbs), which grow from the base of the mother bulb. These are separated and are grown on to flowering size in specially prepared nursery beds.

How can the little tulip bulbs be taken care of so that they can produce full-size bulbs that will flower? When tulip bulbs are dug up, there are so many little ones. Immediately replant the small bulbs 3 to 4 ins. deep in good soil, or they may be stored in a cool place in a mixture of *slightly* moist peatmoss and sand to be replanted in fall. Allow flower buds (if any) to develop until they show color, then nip them off. Allow foliage to ripen, then dig bulbs and store until following fall. Have soil well enriched at all times.

Why, after large clusters of tulip bulbs are dug, do the small bulbs completely wither after a short period in storage? Small bulbs are often immature when dug. They have high water content and little stored food. Loss of water causes withering. See previous question.

Diseases and Pests

Are tulips subject to disease? Tulip diseases include fire blight, gray bulb rot, shanking, root rot, and mosaic. For all of the above, destruction of infected stock and a change of soil or sterilization of the infected soil are the only effective remedies.

Last year some of my tulips had small greenish spots on the leaves; the spots grew larger and many of the leaves turned yellow. Some buds failed to open. What was the trouble; and what can I do? Botrytis or "fire" blight. Remove and burn infected leaves; dig bulbs each year, and burn all showing infection. Replant in a new location, where no tulips have been grown for several years.

What causes new colors and varieties to appear in tulip beds after a few years? Do the bulbils or offshoots produce other varieties? Are the new forms seedlings? Change of color is usually due to disease mosaic. Infected plants should be removed or the virus will spread through the entire planting. It is unlikely there would be any self-sown seedlings.

I have a number of named tulips that have bloomed every year, and now some of them are striped. I move them every 3 years. Is this a disease? Striping and splotching of tulips are the results of a virus disease. There is no cure. See question above.

Do moles eat tulip bulbs during winter or early spring? This is a moot question. Many gardeners believe moles do eat bulbs. Others contend mice and other pests follow the mole runs and destroy the bulbs.

What can I do to keep pocket gophers from eating tulip bulbs? (Idaho.)   Use commercial rodent repellents, poisons, or cyanogas, in the form of dust forced through a special air pump made for the purpose.

How do you prevent mice and squirrels from eating tulip bulbs? There are many good commercial rodent repellents and poison baits. Avoid applying winter mulch until *after* ground has frozen. In extreme cases surround and cover plantings with fine wire netting spread beneath ground.

Varieties

What tulip types are generally available? What are their characteristics?   Species or botanical and their hybrids: most of them low-growing and very early; a few, like Red Emperor, very large. Single Earlies, blooming just after Species: many fine yellows and oranges in this group and many are fragrant—10 to 16 inches in height. Double Earlies: double form of Single Earlies, long lasting, especially when cut. Triumphs and Mendels bloom next: they are crosses between Single Earlies and Darwins, 20 to 24 inches. Peony-flowered are double Triumphs, resembling peonies; long lasting. Cottage: tulips with tall, flexible stems, yellows and oranges but no purples, lavenders or bronzes. Darwins: the largest and most important group with large, globular flowers on very tall stems; colors range from white, yellow and orange through pinks, salmons and reds to lavenders and deep purples. Breeders bloom after Darwins and produce large, stiff-stemmed cup shaped flowers in golds, bronzes, browns, purples. Parrots are late flowering tulips with lacinated and twisted petals, excellent for arrangements. Lily-flowered; blooming late, with graceful, goblet-shaped blooms with pointed, recurved petals.

Which tulips make a good garden, but are not too expensive? Glacier, white; Mrs. John T. Scheepers, gold; Insurpassable, lilac; Lafayette, deep violet; City of Haarlem, red; Crimson Giant; Pride of Zwanenburg, rose; Clara Butt, pink.

How shall I select varieties of tulips for May flowering?   From the catalogue of a reputable dealer select kinds which appeal and which are within your price limit (the highest-priced varieties are not necessarily the best). Make your selection from the Darwin, cottage, and breeder sections. If possible, visit tulip plantings in May and make your selections then.

Are the single, early-single, and early-double types of tulips satisfactory for spring bedding?   Yes. They are lower-growing and earlier-flowering than the Darwins, breeders, and cottage tulips, but their flowers usually do not last so long in good condition. Many of the Single Earlies are delightfully fragrant.

What is a parrot tulip?   One of a group with petals curiously twisted, frilled, and colored so that they are thought to resemble the plumage of a parrot. Fantasy is one of the best-known varieties.

Is there a black tulip?   This name is applied to a very dark, maroon-black variety called La Tulipe Noire.

Is there a yellow Darwin tulip?   Yes. Niphetos Sunkist, Mrs. John T. Scheepers and Yellow Giant. The cottage tulip Inglescome Yellow is often known as the yellow Darwin. It is a fine, inexpensive variety.

Which of the "botanical" tulips are most satisfactory for an ordinary garden?   *Kaufmanniana* (the Waterlily tulip); *clusiana* (the Lady Tulip); *sylvestris* (the Florentine Tulip), *Fosteriana*, red, large; *praestans*, red.

Please name some desirable Species Hybrid Tulips.   *Fosteriana* Cantate, Princeps and Red Emperor, all red; *Kaufmanniana* Caesar Frank, Elliot, Gaiety, The First and Vivaldi, all white or cream with red or rose exterior stripes; Scarlet Elegance, multiflowered; *praestans* Fusilier, red, multiflowered.

TENDER BULBS, CORMS, TUBERS

GENERAL

How often should bulbs be watered when being forced in a dark, cool room?   Until growth starts, just enough to keep soil moist. All forced bulbs, while in active growth, require constant supplies of moisture, and should never be allowed to dry out.

Do the following need to be placed in dark to form roots: freesias, St. Brigid Anemone, ranunculus?   Freesias, no. Anemone and ranunculus preferably, but not necessarily. All should be started in cool temperatures.

How long a rest period must bulbs that have been forced in pots have before being replanted?   Hardy bulbs, such as narcissi, tulips, hyacinths, etc., should be discarded or planted out of doors after forcing. Tender subjects, such as hippeastrums, haemanthus, oxalis, lachenalias, etc., should be rested from the time the leaves have died away naturally and completely, until they show evidence of starting into growth again.

Can I store bulbs in an old-fashioned cellar which is damp?   If too damp, many bulbs will rot. Suggest you make provision for better ventilation, which should result in drier conditions.

Can bulbs which are nearly, but not quite, hardy in Northern states be successfully wintered by mulching heavily before the ground

freezes? Many of them can. Plant them in a border on south side of a building when frost occurs. Before severe weather sets in, surround border with boxlike frame 12 ins. deep, fill with leaves, and cover with tar paper to shed rain.

SPECIFIC TENDER BULBS

(See also under House Plants.)

ACHIMENES

How are achimenes grown? Pot rhizomes about 1 in. apart and ½ in. deep in pans of sandy, humusy soil early in spring. Water carefully at first, more freely as growth develops. Temperature 60° to 65° F.; atmosphere moist. Keep air dry and cooler when flowers appear; shade from strong sun; feed when actively growing. Gradually dry off at end of growing season, and store when dormant.

Achimenes died after blooming. How long do bulbs remain dormant, and where shall I keep them during this period? From late summer until March or April plants remain dormant. Keep rhizomes mixed with dry sand, stored in temperature of 45° to 50° F. during this period.

ACIDANTHERA

Can acidantheras be grown outdoors, like gladioli? Yes, where the growing season is long; but in most parts of the country it is better to plant several bulbs together in good soil in large pots or tubs; or plant outdoors in a lightly shaded garden bed rich in humus after all danger of frost is past. Dig, dry and store when frost threatens. Grow outside during summer and bring into cool situation indoors before frost. After blooming, dry off and rest.

AGAPANTHUS

Is the blue Africanlily hardy, or must it be protected (in New Jersey)? Agapanthus is not hardy where more than very light frosts are experienced. In New Jersey it should be wintered in a light, cool, frostproof cellar, or some similar situation.

ALSTROEMERIA

Are alstroemerias hardy in New York? How are they grown? *A. aurantiaca* survives on Long Island when established; however, most kinds need protection of a cold frame, or may be grown by planting out in spring and lifting and storing in cool cellar through winter. They need an abundance of moisture (without stagnation) during growing season.

AMARYLLIS

What is an amaryllis? *Amaryllis belladonna* of South Africa is the only plant to which this name truly belongs. It is tender north of Washington, D.C. Requires deep planting and full sun. The name is commonly applied to hippeastrums, which hail from South America, as well as to sprekelia (Mexico), lycoris (Asia), sometimes to vallota (South Africa), and occasionally to crinum and other genera.

AMARYLLIS (HIPPEASTRUM)

Will red and white amaryllis bulbs bloom in summer garden? The florists' amaryllis, or, as it is more correctly named, hippeastrum, cannot be successfully grown as a garden plant except in warm sections, such as Florida and California.

Is there a way to have amaryllis (hippeastrum) bloom at a more desirable time? They are winter and spring bloomers. The exact time of flowering can be controlled to some extent by varying the temperature in which they are grown, and also by the methods employed to ripen them off in the fall.

Do amaryllis (hippeastrum) bulbs absolutely need to rest? Yes. However, some individual bulbs exhibit much less of a tendency to go completely dormant, and lose all of their foliage during the rest period, than others.

During the past summer my older amaryllis (hippeastrum) bulbs have grown some new bulbs. I will soon have to rest the large bulbs. How can I save the small ones? Would it be safe to separate them? Rest young bulbs with mother bulb, and separate at potting time. Plant young bulbs individually in small pots of sandy soil, and give same treatment as older specimen.

Is there a blue amaryllis? The "Blue Amaryllis" is *Hippeastrum procera* from Brazil, a plant rare in the United States. In recent years it has bloomed in the New York Botanical Garden, in Florida, California, and perhaps elsewhere. The flowers are lavender-blue or violet-blue, and very handsome.

BABIANA

I have a bulb called babiana. Will you please tell me how to care for it? Exactly same treatment as freesia, which see.

BEGONIA (TUBEROUS-ROOTED)

Are tuber-rooted begonias annuals? They are tender perennials. They bloom the first season if seed is sown early indoors.

Do tuberous-rooted begonias need any special attention except shade? The stems on mine seemed so brittle, the flowers fell off almost before they were open, and the tubers diminished considerably in size.

They need a loose, woodsy soil containing plenty of humus, even moisture, good drainage, and shelter from strong winds. They like well-rotted cow manure.

Where can I plant, and how can I start and care for, tuberous-rooted begonias? Purchase tubers in early spring. Plant in pots of light soil indoors for 6 or 8 weeks before plants are to be set outside. Set plants in open ground when all danger of cold weather has passed. Sheltered, shaded position necessary and soil enriched liberally with humus. Keep moist throughout summer.

What is proper soil mixture for tuberous begonias, for boxes placed on ground outside? One part good garden soil, one part sand, one and one half parts flaky leafmold, one half part old, rotted manure. Add bone meal, 1 pint to a bushel of compost. You may vary this mixture somewhat, but result should be a rich, but porous, humusy soil.

Will growing plants of tuberous-rooted begonias, set out in May or June, do as well as the tubers? Well-established plants set out from pots after the weather has become warm and settled should do as well as, and will produce earlier flowers than, tubers set in the open ground.

Should tuberous begonias be lifted before or after first hard frost? Before the first killing frost. A light frost that just touches the foliage will not harm them.

What should be done to tuberous begonias in the fall? (Outdoor grown.) Dig them up before severe frost, and spread out in flats (leaving soil adhering to roots). Put in sunny, airy place, and allow to ripen off. When stems and leaves have died, clean off and store the tubers in dry sand, soil, or peatmoss, in a temperature of 40° to 50° F.

My tuberous-rooted begonias "run out." Is there a way to grow them so they will bloom year after year? Too heavy a soil, strong competition from the roots of other plants, lack of fertility, or any other factor that discourages growth may account for this. If grown under favorable conditions, they will last for many years.

How can I grow tuberous-rooted begonias indoors? Start tubers in flats of leafmold or peatmoss in temperature of 60° F. in spring. When growth is 2 or 3 ins. high, pot into 4-in. pots, using loose, rich soil. Later pot into larger pots as needed, but *avoid overpotting*. Keep moist at all times; feed established plants; shade from bright sunshine; keep atmosphere moist; protect from wind.

Can tuberous begonias be used in house when taken from garden? No, at least not the same year. After a season's growth in the garden they need a winter's rest. They may be started into growth again the following spring.

Do tuberous begonias grown as house plants need a rest period?

Yes indeed. They must be dried off and completely rested during the winter. At end of summer, plants begin dying back naturally.

How can one propagate tuberous begonias? From seed. By rooting cuttings made from the young growths, or by carefully cutting the tuber into pieces. This last operation is done in spring just after growth has started. Be sure that each piece of tuber retains a growing sprout. Dust cut surfaces with fine sulfur before potting up.

Will a cutting from a tuberous-rooted begonia grow a bulb or tuberous root, and will it bloom? Cuttings taken in early spring (they are made from the very young shoots) will bloom well the first season and will form tubers that may be stored in the usual way through the winter.

Can you tell me if there is any way to increase tuberous begonias? By leaf or other cuttings? They can readily be propagated from cuttings made from the young growths, which are taken (when a couple of inches long) from the parent tuber and inserted in a moist, warm sand propagating bed.

CALADIUM

I bought a beautiful potted plant of fancy-leaved caladium, but it began to die in fall. What did I do wrong? It is natural for this plant to die down in fall, remain dormant, through the winter, then start into growth again in spring.

Would it be practicable to plant the beautiful colored-leaved caladiums out of doors in summer and dig them up in fall and store them in cellar through winter? Entirely so. Select a partially shaded location. Prepare soil well and incorporate humus with it. Plant tubers after ground has warmed up. Water freely in dry weather.

How can I care for bulbs of colored-leaved caladiums that have been dormant through winter in pots of dirt in which they grew last season? To start into new growth, remove tubers from old soil and place in shallow boxes of moss, leafmold, or peat, just covering tubers. Keep moist and in temperature of 70° to 80° F. When growth has started, pot up again, using a light, rich, humusy soil.

CANNA

Will you please let me know how to cut cannas to plant in spring? Use a sharp knife and cut so that each division consists of one good eye on a substantial piece of rootstock.

How early should cannas be started? They can be started indoors as early as February 1, and then potted into 4-ins. pots. For roots that are to be planted outdoors, without potting, start 4 to 6 weeks before planting (after danger of frost).

What is the proper method of starting cannas in the house? Plant divisions separately, in 4-in. pots. Water sparingly until growth has started, and then heavily. Use bottom heat to start.

What is the best soil for cannas, and how deep should they be planted? Any ordinary soil. Plant so that the "eye" is less than 2 ins. below the surface.

How shall I care for canna roots during winter? Dry thoroughly after digging. Dust lightly with sulfur and cover with clean sand or peatmoss kept slightly moist. Store in cool, dark cellar, and inspect often to see if drying occurs. If too dry, sprinkle sand or soil with water occasionally.

How can I keep canna roots over the winter? We have no basement. Dig a pit 3 ft. deep. Line bottom with 6 ins. of ashes, put roots in, and cover with 6 ins. of sand. Pack down litter, such as leaves, straw, etc., and cover pit with burlap bags, or an old rug.

How should canna roots be divided before storing for the winter? Do not divide in fall. Store whole, and cut in spring.

Cannas planted last year grew large and healthy, but very few developed flowers; they were small and poor. Why? Poor, runout planting stock is most likely responsible. Too much nitrogen could also be the cause. Cannas need fertilizer containing high phosphoric content. Lack of sunshine may also be responisble.

Is it a good plan to dig cannas and store the roots over the winter? (Georgia.) No. In the lower South it is a good practice to allow cannas to grow without moving until the clumps become very matted. Every 3 or 4 years dig the clumps, sometime during the winter, separate the roots, and set the divisions in new beds of well-enriched soil.

CLIVIA

Will you please tell how to grow clivias in pots? Pot in rich, well-drained soil. Do not repot oftener than absolutely necessary. Water to keep soil always moist; shade from sun; feed when growing actively. Give winter temperature of 50° to 60° F. In summer keep outdoors in shade.

COLOCASIA (ELEPHANTSEAR)

Is the elephantsear a kind of caladium? How do you grow it? Often sold as *Caladium esculentum,* but correct name is colocasia. Plant tubers in pots indoors in spring. After all danger of frost has passed, set outdoors in moist, rich soil. After first frost, dig up, dry off, and store in a cellar or similar place.

CRINUM

Is the Milk-and-wine-lily (Crinum fimbriatulum) hardy? (Pennsyl-

vania.) It is not generally hardy in Pennsylvania. If planted in light, well-drained soil against the south side of a building, and well covered, it may survive.

Can you recommend some good varieties of crinum for growing in North Carolina? A grower in that state reports best success with the following kinds: *kirki, kunthianum, erubescens, fimbriatulum, longifolium, moorei,* Powelli, and Cecil Houdyshel.

DAHLIAS

Few flowers have attained such wide popularity as the dahlia. Yielding readily to the handiwork of plant breeders, it has produced innumerable forms and colors. In the early days the breeding work was aimed at increasing the size of bloom. When flowers were obtained as large as dinner plates, the gardening public began to feel they were coarse, and too big to be artistic. The hybridizers were not disheartened, but proceeded to develop miniature types. Today the size of different varieties varies from ½ to 15 ins. in diameter, and the plants are from 18 ins. to 7 ft. in height!

The colors, clear and rich, include all the hues except clear blue. The petals have a crystalline texture which gives a luminous or translucent quality to the color. In addition to the pure spectrum hues they embrace the rich, warm tones of the sunrise and the soft, full tints of the sunset. There are flower forms to suit any fancy. Some varieties are dense, full, and formal; others are loose, shaggy, and carefree. There are ball-shaped types, singles, and some even mimic the forms of other flowers, such as the peony, orchid, and anemone.

The dahlia hails from Mexico, where it may be found growing at altitudes from 4,000 to 8,000 ft., among the broken rocks of lava beds, and where the temperature is moderate and rains are frequent. As with other plants, its native habitat suggests many clues to successful culture: good drainage, plenty of moisture, cool temperatures.

In garden plantings dahlias are not combined with other plants to the extent they might well be. Many gardeners feel that they are difficult to use except by themselves in mass plantings. Yet when skillfully placed in the perennial border, or in front of shrub plantings, they give a magnificent effect. Dahlias should be more generously used in the flower gardens of America to give added color in the late summer and fall.

Soil and Fertilizer

What type of soil do dahlias need? They will grow in a wide variety. Important points are porosity and free drainage, reasonable humus content, and sufficient retentiveness, so that the plants do not suffer from lack of moisture. Any good vegetable garden soil is satisfactory.

l for dahlias? A week or 10
surface rough. Then broadcast
lia hills, 5 lbs. raw bone meal
of potash. Leave until day of
fertilizer, breaking all lumps

good to add to soil for dahlias.
of heavy soils are appreciably
l cinders. They have no value
light soils, nor to excess on

place every year? What is best
a.) Yes. After roots are dug,
s acid, broadcast ground lime-
ter rye and turned under just
nsylvania about the first week

m for dahlias? At planting
with 1 lb. muriate of potash
10 hills. About July 10 give
ertilizer (4–10–10). Finally,
x 3 lbs. raw bone meal, 4 lbs.
otash together and rake this
y closer than 6 ins., nor more

or Agrico as a fertilizer for
al is rather slow-acting.

place. Should I use them on
a valuable source of potash.
either dig the ashes into the
to 15 lbs. per 100 sq. ft., or
ptember.

Excellent. A diluted solution
ken manure, and applied at
re developing, increases both

hey need free circulation of
urs each day, freedom from
ense shrubbery, and a fertile,

rt shade? Full sun.
rtially shaded place? They

require direct sunlight at least 6 or 7 hours each day. More is desirable.

In planting dahlias, should they be kept a certain distance from other flowers?   Not more than is necessary to permit both the dahlias and the other flowers to grow and develop satisfactorily. Dahlias should not be crowded.

What distance apart should dahlias be planted?   From 3 to 4 ft. for the taller kinds; somewhat less for the miniatures and pompons.

How soon can dahlias be planted in pots indoors before they are transplanted outdoors?   For May planting outdoors, pot during April.

What is the proper planting time for dahlias?   After all danger of frost has passed, usually about May 15 in the vicinity of New York City.

Can the tubers that develop on dahlia plants be replanted with success?   Yes. This is the most common method of perpetuating dahlias.

Can the tubers formed by the dahlia that one buys in pots and sets out in late spring be held over and used the following year?   Yes. They are entirely satisfactory.

Which is better, to leave dahlias in bunches or to plant the tubers separately? I have mine put away in bunches for the winter.   Always divide the clumps before planting.

If the necks of dahlia tubers are injured, will the plants bloom?   Dahlia tubers with broken necks will not grow.

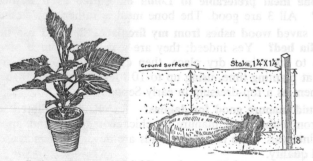

Left—pot-grown dahlia plant. Right—correct method of planting: one root, with strong eye, cut from clump.

Can dwarf or "bedding" dahlias be started in 3- or 4-in. pots and be planted out after tulips are dug?   Start seed, sowing in flats or bulb pans, indoors in March. Grow on, transplanting into pots of suitable size, and set out in open garden beds when all danger of frost is over and ground has warmed up.

Dahlia catalogues list plants as well as roots of certain varieties. I would like to try plants next season. How do you handle them? When received, remove from carton but leave in pots. Soak in shallow water to freshen. Set out in late afternoon or on a cloudy day. Dig holes 6 ins. deep; remove plants from pots; set so that root-balls are just covered with soil, and leave finished surface around plants 3 ins. below grade. If following day is sunny, shade. Plants will take hold in a few days. Gradually fill holes with soil as plants grow.

How are dahlia tubers planted, after clumps have been divided? First set stout stakes in place; at base of each stake, dig a wide hole 6 ins. deep; loosen up bottom. Lay tuber horizontally, with neck near stake and with eye pointing upward. Cover with soil so that tuber is just hidden. As eye grows, keep filling in soil so that it is kept just covered until surface grade is reached.

Culture

I am afraid my method of tying up dahlias is not very successful. They are always damaged in storms. What do you suggest? Plant in a position not too exposed to wind. Sisal binder twine is good for tying. Make 2 tight half hitches around stake; twist ends of twine twice around each other in front of stake; loop around stem tightly enough to afford support but not to cut, and tie with a square knot. Tie each stem separately and securely; do not bunch together like sheaf of wheat.

Is it necessary to hoe or cultivate around dahlias? Early in the season frequent surface cultivation is very beneficial, but it should be dispensed with about 10 weeks after planting, at which time beds should be mulched with peatmoss, bagasse, buckwheat hulls or other similar products which may be locally available. Do not cultivate when plants are in bud or bloom.

How do you prune dahlias in summer in order to get fall blooms? Allow only one main stalk to grow. When plants reach about 10 ins. in height, pinch out their centers just above the second pair of leaves. Side branches which develop should be pinched also. Remove any flower buds that appear before August 1.

How much water do dahlias require? Unless weather is very dry, they need none until they commence to bloom. Then water thoroughly, soaking the ground every week or 10 days whenever rainfall is insufficient.

Is mulching dahlias a worth-while practice? Yes. Early in the season maintain a "dust mulch" by frequent cultivation. At beginning of August cover surface of ground with a 2- or 3-in. layer of litter, salt hay, grass clippings, peatmoss, or similar material.

How are dahlias disbudded so that they have large blooms? When the buds appear (usually in clusters of three), pinch out all except the central one of each group. New lateral shoots will appear. All of these below the remaining bud, except the 2 nearest to the main stalk, should be pinched out. This will not only produce large blooms, but will keep plants low and bushy and will encourage the development of long stems.

What is the proper method to produce strong-stemmed dahlias that will support large blooms when cut? Remove all but 1 stalk from each plant. After 3 sets of leaves develop on this, pinch out its tip. Laterals will soon grow and eventually become main branches. All laterals and sublaterals other than the 4 main branches should be pinched out, except for the 2 sublaterals that develop near the base of each flowering stem.

How are exhibition dahlias grown? By planting healthy stock of suitable varieties, and by intelligent attention to cultivation, watering, spraying, disbranching, disbudding, and fertilization.

How many days should one allow from planting time for blooms of giant dahlias to develop for show? From 80 to 120 days, depending on the variety. A hot, dry season may cause blooms to mature from 10 to 15 days later than normal.

When and how do you cut dahlia flowers for exhibition? After sunset on the evening before the show. Cut with long stems, trim off any leaves not needed, and immediately stand the stems in water. Carry indoors and then trim the base of each stem by cutting it slantwise under water. Keep in a cool, dark place until they are packed for transportation.

Storage

How soon after digging should dahlia bulbs be divided and stored? After clumps are dug allow them to dry in the sun for 4 to 5 hours before storing. Do not divide until some months later (March or April).

At what temperature should dahlia roots be kept over winter? I always lose half my roots each year. From 40° to 55° F.

What care do you suggest if part of the dahlia bulb is injured in lifting? Remove injured tubers with a sharp knife or pruning shears. Sprinkle the cut surface with sulfur.

I planted dahlia tubers (pompons and giants) and now have 12 plants each with a cluster of from 5 to 7 tubers. How shall I store them? In a cool (45 to 55°) cellar, or in barrels or boxes lined with newspaper and placed where the temperature is not more than 55° nor less than 40°. Examine periodically to see that they are not becoming mildewed, nor drying up.

Should dahlia roots be wrapped in paper or packed in earth for

winter storage? Either. Allow soil to cling to clumps to prevent excessive drying. Peatmoss makes a good material in which to store them.

Will you tell me how to store dahlia roots in a modern basement? After digging, turn upside down and dry in sun for 4 to 5 hours; pack in barrel or box lined with newspaper. Allow soil to cling to clumps to guard necks from breaking and to prevent excessive drying. Keep as far as possible away from furnace.

What is your opinion of the practice of washing dahlia tubers as opposed to leaving on dirt? Either may be satisfactory. If soil is left, it tends to prevent excessive drying and reduces danger of necks of roots being broken. If tubers are washed, make sure that they are well dried before storing. Pack in peatmoss.

May dahlias be stored out of doors if buried below the frost line? Yes, if well below the frost line.

What makes dahlia roots rot after they are dug up? We put ours in the garage, and in about 3 weeks they had all rotted. Probably the temperature went down below freezing. There are also several rot organisms which affect stored dahlia roots.

A short time after digging my dahlias the roots shriveled and became soft. What was the reason? They were dug after the first frost. You probably kept them in a warm place and thus dried them out too fast.

Why do my dahlia tubers sprout after storing? They were put away in peatmoss in the cellar. Storage place is too warm. Take care they are not near a heater. Temperature during storage should not be above 55° F.

My dahlia bulbs in storage are beginning to sprout. I have them packed in sand. Will this harm them? Not if it happens in spring when planting time is approaching. Sprouting in winter weakens roots and should be prevented by storage at 40° to 55°.

My dahlia bulbs were not dug this fall. Will they die? Snow is on ground now, and lowest temperature has been 5° above zero. They will not survive if the tubers are frozen.

Problems

What causes large dahlias to wilt as soon as cut? Large-flowered dahlias always wilt if cut during the day. Cut in late evening, well after the sun is down, or *very* early in the morning. Dipping ends of the stems in boiling water for 1 or 2 minutes has a tendency to keep the flowers fresh.

We have dahlias which never bloom. Does their age have anything to do with it? Not if they are healthy. Dahlia "stunt," a virus disease, and tarnished plant bug often prevent flowering.

Why do dahlias with large flowers have very thin stems? The excess buds were pinched out. Some varieties naturally have weak stems. Excess nitrogen and too little potash also cause this condition.

My dahlia garden is between two buildings. I get very good plants, but the frost kills the buds before they bloom. Is there any way to speed the blooming of dahlias? Your plants may not receive sufficient sun. Plants in shade tend to become soft and to bloom late. Possibly you have late-flowering varieties. These should be planted early.

Why do my dahlias have so many leaves and so few flowers? Probably because of too much shade, or too much fertilizer. Attention to pruning and disbudding may help.

Can Coltness Gem Dahlias be carried over from year to year? I want particular colors; otherwise the ease with which they are propagated from seeds would make winter storage foolish. Yes, treat the roots exactly as you do other dahlias.

Why do some dahlias, of varieties supposed to be tall, stay low? Very possibly because they are infected with mosaic disease or "stunt." Check with a skilled grower or with your State Agricultural Experiment Station. Destroy diseased plants.

One of my choice dahlias had no tubers this fall. Why? This may be because it received improper fertilization. There are some dahlias, particularly choice varieties, that are very poor root producers. If the plant was grown from a cutting made *between* the joints, it would bloom, but would not form tubers.

My dahlias make good growth and lots of flowers but never form tubers. What can I do to encourage the plants to grow large, plump bulbs that will keep over winter? Probably you use an unbalanced fertilizer. Excess nitrogen will cause the condition you describe. Try more potash and phosphate. (See preceding question.)

I planted dahlias, took great pains with them, and although they were very thrifty they did not flower. They bloomed last year. What is the cause? Lack of blooms may be caused by not enough sunshine, surface cultivation continued late in the season, too much nitrogenous fertilizer, insects or disease.

Some years my dahlias bloom; other years they don't. What is wrong? Weather conditions have some effect on the blooming of dahlias. If water is not supplied artificially, a dry season may cause poor blooming. See other questions.

How can I stop my dahlias from growing 9 ft. tall, with very little bloom? Probably too much shade, or fertilizer containing too much nitrogen. Allow only one main stalk to grow from each plant, disbranch, and disbud as described in other answers.

Why do my dahlias refuse to bloom? They have plenty of water

and fertilizer and are planted in good garden soil. They have southern exposure. The plants grow strongly but have few, poor blooms. Is the air circulation good? Dahlias should not be planted along the side of a house or close to a hedge. They may be infected with insects such as thrips, leaf hoppers, borers, or tarnished plant bug; or with mosaic or "stunt." Try a change of stock. Dahlias planted in same soil year after year sometimes deteriorate.

I have a dahlia that grows about 8 ft. tall and has lots of buds, but they never open up. Why? It grows lots of nice tubers. These symptoms are suggestive of tarnished plant bug injury.

What causes imperfect dahlia blooms? Diseases, as stunt; pests, as leaf hoppers, tarnished plant bug and thrips; unfavorable weather conditions.

Has anyone discovered the cause of the variation in color in some bicolored dahlias? The exact cause is not definitely known. Bicolored varieties seem to be particularly unstable and tend to run back to solid colors.

What dahlia has the record of growing to the greatest height? Complete records are probably not in existence. The tallest reported by a well-informed source is a plant of One Grand, 13 ft. in height.

Do the tubers of the Coltness Hybrid dahlias store successfully, and, if so, are the flowers as good? They do; and will bear good blooms when planted the following year.

For what particular purposes are dwarf dahlias suited? For decorative garden beds or borders, for providing cut flowers, and for exhibiting at flower shows.

I have heard that dahlia bulbs were used as a food. Is there any reason why they should not be so used; are they habit-forming or harmful in any way? According to the authoritative Sturtevant's *Notes on Edible Plants,* "it was first cultivated for its tubers, but these were found to be uneatable." It is reported that sugar can be made from them.

Propagation

How are dahlias propagated? By division of the clumps of roots; by cuttings; by seeds; and, much more rarely, by grafting.

How are dahlias increased by cuttings? Undivided clumps are planted in a cool greenhouse in January or February. Cuttings, each with sliver of tuber attached at the base, are prepared when shoots are 3 ins. or so long, and are inserted in a propagating bench (bottom heat 65°; atmosphere, 5° lower), or in a flat. Shade and a "close" atmosphere are supplied. When roots are an inch long, cuttings are potted up individually. Ordinary stem cuttings may also be used, but the basal cut should be made just below a node.

Can I increase my dahlias in the house by cuttings?   It is scarcely practicable. They need rather special conditions, and for best results should be made early in the year when it is difficult to provide a correct environment in the average home.

What types of dahlias bloom the first year from seed?   All types. The Coltness Hybrids and others that are grown chiefly for mass-color effects in the garden, rather than for perfection of their individual blooms, are the kinds most commonly raised from seeds.

Dahlia root placed in moist peatmoss or sand to start sprouts. When cut, the sprouts root readily to produce individual pot plants.

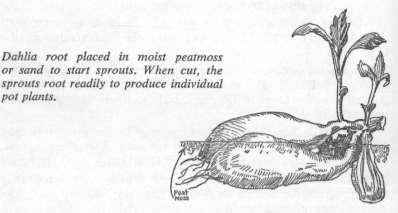

How can I save seeds from my dahlias?   After petals have fallen, allow the flower head to dry on the plant (wax paper or plastic is sometimes wrapped around heads so that they dry quicker). Gather heads before killing frost and place them in a dry cellar until they have fully dried out.

Do dahlias grown here (Mount Vernon, New York) have a long enough growing season to make good seeds?   As a rule seeds saved from dahlias grown in the vicinity of New York are not fertile. The best seeds are produced in California, where the growing season is much longer.

How should dahlia seeds be started?   Sow in pots or flats of light, sandy soil, February to March, in temperature of 60°. Transplant seedlings (when second pairs of leaves have developed) individually into small pots. Grow on in a sunny location, with temperature of 55°. When roots crowd small pots, replant into 4-in. pots.

Is it necessary to remove the tubers from seedling dahlias, and when?   No; the small tubers are left on, and set out with the seedling plants.

How can I hybridize dahlias?   Some large dahlia growers maintain beehives in their gardens, and the bees carry the pollen from plant to plant. Others employ hand pollination, which involves using a camel's-hair brush to transfer the pollen of one variety to the pistil of another.

How are new varieties of dahlias developed? They are selected from seedlings. Some responsible dahlia growers make a specialty of raising and selling dahlia seed saved from the leading exhibition varieties.

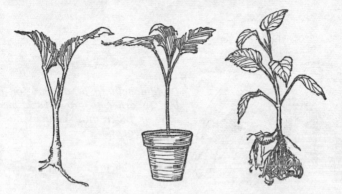

Left   dahlia cutting rooted, ready to pot up; right —dahlia seedling, ready for transplanting. (Note small tuber already beginning to form.)

How were the giant dahlias developed from smaller ones? By systematic breeding, based on hand cross-pollination, and by carefully selecting the most promising seedlings. This work has been carried on over a long period of years.

Can dahlias be divided immediately after they are dug in fall, or must they wait until spring when they are sprouted? Is any special instrument used for this purpose? It is better to wait until spring, when eyes are visible. Use any good, sharp knife with a stout, fairly long blade.

How should dahlia clumps be divided? By using a sharp knife and pruning shears. Each division of a clump should include a portion of the old stem attached to the neck of a tuber; on each should be a visible eye capable of developing into a sprout.

Is there any danger of dividing dahlias too much? Yes; unless you are experienced there is a danger of cutting into undeveloped eyes.

How can I divide dahlia bulbs when absolutely no eyes are visible? *Do not* divide until eyes appear. If clumps have a tendency to be slow in "eying up," put them in a flat with damp peatmoss and place near the furnace. This will cause eyes to develop in a few days. If eyes fail to appear, the stock is "blind" and will not produce plants.

Should each clump of dahlia roots be separated so as to plant only 1 root in a place?   Yes. Be sure each division has an eye (bud) from which a shoot will develop.

Are dahlia bulbs which shrivel up after division any good?   They will probably produce weak plants. After dahlia roots are divided, they should be kept in slightly damp peatmoss until planting time.

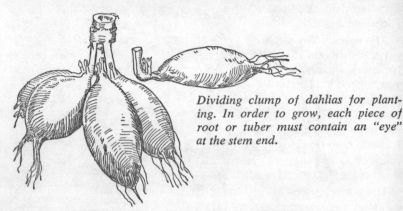

Dividing clump of dahlias for planting. In order to grow, each piece of root or tuber must contain an "eye" at the stem end.

How can I know a live dahlia tuber from one that will not grow, when dividing for spring planting?   Roots that will grow possess eyes (buds) which usually appear on part of the stalk or old stem of the clump. Many clumps produce "blind" roots. These should not be planted.

Diseases and Pests

My dahlias are not growing well. I suspect mosaic disease. What are the symptoms?   The plants are usually dwarfed; the leaves are smaller than normal and show a yellowish mosaic, or spotting. Pale-green bands are often developed along the midribs and larger secondary veins.

Is there any cure for mosaic disease of dahlias?   No. Ruthlessly dig out and destroy affected plants. Under no circumstances propagate from them. Spray to control aphids, as they transmit the disease from plant to plant.

What is the cause of dahlia "stunt"?   A temporary dwarfing, not carried over from year to year, may result from attacks of such insects as tarnished plant bugs, leaf hoppers, thrips, and aphids. Virus diseases may cause real stunting, which is not curable. Virus-infected plants should be promptly destroyed.

What is the recommended treatment for dahlia wilt disease?   Two wilts attack dahlias—one caused by a fungus, the other by a bacterium. Destroy all affected plants. Use only healthy tubers for propagation. Move dahlias to new ground, or sterilize the soil with formaldehyde or chloropicrin.

How can I recognize and control red spider on dahlias? It is commonest in hot, dry weather. The leaves become yellowish or pale brown. With a hand lens the insects, usually covered with a fine web, can be seen crawling on the under sides of the leaves. Forcible spraying with clear water is helpful. Spray also with wettable sulfur. (See Red Spider.)

My dahlias are attacked by small bugs that jump off the leaves when disturbed. The leaves are turning yellow and becoming brittle. No holes appear in the leaves. What is insect, and what remedy do you suggest? This is leaf hopper. Spray at weekly intervals with a pyrethrum, DDT, or all-purpose spray. Keep all weeds cut down in vicinity.

I have had a lot of trouble with corn borers in dahlias. How can I check their ravages? Spray or dust twice a week with DDT or rotenone from August to October inclusive. Pick off infested blooms. Burn old stalks at end of season. (See Corn Borer.)

Does more than one kind of borer attack dahlias? Yes. The common stalk borer hatches out in May, eats a hole in the stem, and usually remains until August. Watch for holes in stems and probe with fine wire to kill borers. Destroy all coarse weeds in the vicinity.

I have found large shell-less snails eating dahlia flowers. Can I do anything other than hand-pick? Clean up all rubbish and debris. Slugs hide under stones, bricks, boards, etc., during the day. Spread poison bait around. (See Slugs.)

Varieties

What are the names of some of the leading varieties of large-flowering dahlias? New Look, Director Carl G. Dahl, Jane Cowl, Lois Walcher, Mrs. Geo. Le Boutillier, Murphy's Masterpiece, Sunrays, Volcano, and Yellow Glory.

Can you recommend some good exhibition dahlias? Jane Cowl, Jack of Hearts, Fanny Levy, Florence M., Murphy's Masterpiece, Sunrays, Maffie, Crowning Glory, Alabaster and The Real Glory.

What are some good varieties of miniature dahlias? Easter Greeting, Elsie, Gertrude, Kate, Marie, Park Yellow, Tacita, Red Head, Sunburst, Coltness Hybrids and Unwin Dwarfs.

Can you name a dozen good pompon dahlias? Atom, Betty Ann, Betty Malone, Dot, Ebony, Little Edith, Little Herman, Little Red Wing, Little Snow White, Morning Mist, Sherry.

What are 2 or 3 of the best dahlias for cut flowers? Jersey Beauty, Bishop of Llandaff, Newport Wonder, Dr. J. Beyer, Venita.

Is there a definite trend toward small-flowering varieties of dahlias?
Yes; largely because they require less space and less attention in regard to disbranching, disbudding, and staking. In many ways they are more useful than the large-flowering types both in the garden and as cut flowers. They are listed in catalogues as "miniature" dahlias.

EUCHARIS (AMAZONLILY)

Will you give me the recommended method of growing the Amazonlily? *Eucharis grandiflora* bulbs should be planted, several together, in large pots containing rich, well-drained, fibrous soil. Avoid repotting unless necessary. Give temperature of 65° to 75° F., plenty of moisture when growing, and shade from bright sun. Foliage is evergreen, so plants should never be dried off completely.

FREESIA

What conditions are necessary for growing freesias successfully?
Well-drained but fertile soil; strict care in matter of watering; cool (45° to 55° F.), airy, growing conditions; and fullest possible exposure to sunshine. Sound, healthy bulbs of fair size are a prerequisite.

What is the secret of watering freesias? When first potted, give thorough soaking; place in cool situation; and cover with several inches of moss or leaves. When growth starts, remove moss, and water to keep soil only just moist. Gradually increase supply of water as leaves develop, and water generously when well rooted and in full growth. After blooming, water freely until foliage begins to fade, then gradually reduce, and finally withhold water entirely.

Do freesias need a high temperature? Quite the contrary. They thrive best where the night temperature does not exceed 45° or 50°, with a daytime rise of 5° to 10° permitted.

How shall I fertilize freesias grown in pots in winter? Mix bone meal with potting soil. When flower buds begin to show, feed at weekly intervals with dilute liquid cow manure. Vary this occasionally by using a good complete fertilizer.

My freesias grew at first, but before they were very high they died, and green scum grew on top of soil. What was the cause? Poor drainage, overwatering, or both. Freesias abhor too much water during their early stages of growth.

GLADIOLI

The gladiolus species, from which the modern garden varieties have been developed, grow wild along the shores of the Mediterranean Sea and in South Africa. The true species are of little significance as garden plants. The flowers are small, the colors often harsh, and the forms uninspiring. It is a far cry from the unattractive wild-lings to the glorious flower we know today as the gladiolus.

Always popular as a specialist's flower, particularly with men, the gladiolus now takes its place beside the rose, the camellia and the iris in that an All America Gladiolus Selections Committee has come into being (1956) to test and study new varieties and to grant each year awards to those considered most outstanding. The first variety so honored was Royal Stewart in 1956.

The ease with which gladioli can be grown anywhere in the United States undoubtedly contributes to their popularity. They are not particular in their soil requirements. They do well in warm exposures. While they tolerate neglect better than many other plants, they also respond to good treatment. Of upright growth, they require little room, so that large quantities of flowers can be produced in a limited area. They are therefore ideal for small gardens.

Usually they are grown in beds or in rows in the cutting garden. However, if combined with other plants in the mixed border they will add much color interest. Gladioli are more important as cut flowers than as decorative garden plants. They keep exceptionally well, and the form of the spike is especially well adapted for use in various types of arrangements.

Soil and Fertilizer

Do gladioli take the strength out of the soil? I have 20 acres on which gladioli have been planted for the last 2 years, but the soil has been fertilized each time they were planted. Gladioli do not exhaust the soil, particularly if fertilizer is used, but repeated growing of "glads" in the same soil may result in an increase in prevalence of disease, and this may make bulbs unsalable.

I am interested in raising gladiolus bulbs. Does the soil have to be very fertile for best results? Fertile, but not excessively rich.

What is your suggestion for the best fertilizer to be used for gladioli? A 4–10–5 mixture. Avoid animal manures, as they are apt to cause disease in the corms.

Which fertilizer shall I use when I plant gladioli in my flower border? Providing the soil is in good condition, almost any complete fertilizer will be satisfactory. Bone meal and unleached wood ashes mixed together are excellent. Avoid fresh manure; leafmold and of course commercial fertilizers are satisfactory.

What type soil should "glads" have to be most successful? A well-drained, sandy loam in which gladioli have not been grown for the past 3 years.

Will "glads" grow in sandy soil? Fine specimens can be grown in sandy soil if enough moisture is supplied.

Planting

How am I to pick out the right kind of gladiolus bulbs to plant?
Best for planting are clean No. 1 bulbs, or corms 1½ ins. or more
in diameter, with small scars, which proves they were grown from
small corms. Very large, flat corms are less desirable than moderate-
sized ones with greater depth.

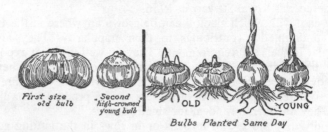

*Gladioli corms: small, "high-crowned" young
corms are preferable to larger-sized, old flat ones.*

Do gladioli prefer sun all day, or partial shade?   Full sun, although they can be grown in partial shade.

How early can "glads" be set out?   As soon as frost is out of the
ground. Little is gained by extra-early planting, and sometimes later
plantings bloom first.

When is best time to plant gladioli; and how deep?   Make first
planting about May 1, and follow with successional plantings up to
early July. Set corms 4 to 6 ins. deep.

*Trench method of planting gladioli: corms are set
in deep furrow (with fertilizer mixed with soil in
bottom) and the trench is gradually filled in—
thus smothering small weeds—as the plants grow.*

**When should I plant "glads" to bloom in September and mid-
October?**   Between June 15 and July 1.

**Will the flowers of late "glads" be as large as if the bulbs were
planted early?**   Late flowers should be larger than early ones of the
same variety, because cool nights produce larger flowers and better
color in gladioli.

How deep do you advise planting gladioli; and how far apart in rows? Four ins. deep in heavy soil and 5 to 6 ins. in light, sandy soil. Three ins. apart is close enough in the rows for good spikes. Space rows 18 to 30 ins. apart.

What is the best method for planting gladioli? In rows, like vegetables. They can then be given better care and will produce better spikes.

Can gladiolus bulbs be planted too closely to each other? The old rule is to plant the diameter of the corms apart, but small sizes, at least, should be given more room.

Is it advisable to cut large gladiolus corms in two when planting? How deep should the cormels be planted? They can be cut in two providing each piece has part of the root base and an eye; little can be gained by so doing, however. Cormels should be planted about 2 ins. deep.

The gladiolus bulbs which I planted along the borders of my shrubbery failed to grow well. What is wrong? Gladioli are not able to compete successfully with the roots of strong-growing trees and shrubs. Try planting in well-prepared soil away from the influence of roots.

Can gladiolus corms be used after not having been planted one year? Gladiolus corms are of little use the second year; but bulblets are still good the second year, and those of hard-to-sprout varieties grow better then.

Culture

What is the best way of supporting "glads" so they do not fall over? Tie to individual slender stakes, or place stakes at intervals along both sides of the rows and stretch strings from stake to stake. Hilling up soil around the bases of the stems is also helpful.

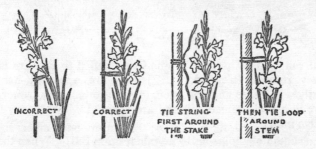

Method of staking gladiolus spike to prevent injury by wind.

Do "glads" need much watering? The soil must be well drained, but they need an abundance of moisture, and if the season is at all dry they should be watered liberally, particularly after the sixth or seventh leaf begins to develop.

How are gladiolus bulbs grown to such mammoth sizes as 4 to 5 ins. in diameter? Some varieties under good conditions make 4- and 5-in. corms, but a good, thick 1½-in. corm is more satisfactory.

Do gladiolus bulbs need to be taken up every year? They are killed by freezing, and so should be dug and stored in a cool, dry cellar over winter.

How can I keep my late "glads" from sprouting? To keep your corms from sprouting store them in a cool, dry, dark place, in slatted or screen-bottom trays. The temperature should be evenly maintained, at as near 40° as possible.

Taking up gladioli for winter storage. Plants are loosened in the soil, pulled up gently to save the cormels, and placed in flats to dry before cleaning. Tops may be cut off just above corms to save space.

What can I do with "glad" bulbs that I failed to take up last fall? Are they ruined? (Kentucky.) Gladioli are only half-hardy and ordinarily will freeze and rot if left in the ground over winter, unless they are in a well-drained soil and are covered with a heavy layer of protective mulch.

When should gladiolus bulbs be taken up in fall? When the leaves start to turn brown. A good new corm is formed 6 weeks after blooming.

When is it best to take up gladioli, and what is the proper way to keep them—in a basement; in sand, or in earth? Lift with a fork after the first frost, taking care not to damage the corms, and store not over 2 or 3 corms deep in trays in the basement. Do not cover with sand or earth.

Should gladiolus corms be trimmed close before storing? The tops should be cut off close to the corm at digging time. The husk should never be removed while in storage, as it helps the corm to retain its moisture.

How can I store gladiolus bulbs to keep them from shrinking and drying out in winter? If stored in a cool cellar, they will not shrink or dry out.

What about temperature for "glads" in winter? The ideal temperature is 40°. Never allow them to freeze.

Problems

Will a light frost on gladiolus bulbs ruin them; and how can I tell if they are still all right? A light frost will not harm the corms. If they are badly frosted, they will dry out and become very light in weight.

How does one develop larger gladiolus bulbs for larger blooms instead of having the bulbs multiply? Where 1 bulb is planted, 2 or 3 grow from it, all about the same small size. To prevent gladiolus corms from splitting all the eyes but one may be cut out before planting. However this is a practice seldom resorted to.

Why do gladiolus bulbs produce large blooms one year and none or very poor ones the next? Possibly your bulbs were dug too soon after blooming, or perhaps you cut the stems too low when picking flowers. Corm diseases or thrip may be factors.

Why do glad bulbs keep getting smaller from year to year? Too-early digging; taking too much foliage when flowers are cut; or poor growing conditions.

Why do my gladiolus bulbs exhaust themselves within 2 or 3 years and produce inferior blooms? Varieties vary greatly in this respect; some will produce good spikes for a number of years, others for only a single season. Gladiolus scab is often responsible.

What makes my gladiolus flower stems develop crooked necks? Not all varieties of gladioli "crook," but those which do should be planted so that they bloom in the cool weather of fall.

How can I prevent my gladiolus bulbs from becoming flat, rather than high-crowned? A high crown was at one time considered a mark of perfection, but Picardy and its children are never high-crowned, and there are few good "glads" today not related to Picardy.

. **Will small "glad" bulbs, such as No. 6 size, bloom the first season if planted early enough?** No. 6 size corms of most varieties will bloom, although the spikes will be short and the flowers few.

I have 200 gladiolus seeds planted and they have grown 8 ins. tall and have fallen over. They look healthy. Will they be all right? Gladioli, the first year from seed, look like grass. They should form small, mature corms in about 12 weeks.

Why don't gladioli bloom all at one time? Blooming time varies according to the size of the corms and the variety. A large bulb of Maid of Orleans will bloom in 60 days, and a small bulb of Bagdad, a late variety, will take 150 days.

Are gladioli true to color? They normally come true to color, although color sports often appear among the smoky shades.

Why did my assorted-color gladioli all turn yellow after the first year? Gladioli do not normally change color. Your yellow-flowered kind must be a robust variety and the only one to survive.

What makes gladioli of different colors gradually change to one color after a few years? Many people think that gladioli change color. What actually happens is that the more robust-growing varieties in a mixture outlive and out-multiply the weaker-growing ones.

My gladiolus bulbs end up with a growth on the bottom. Is this natural, or is it a disease? If so, what is the treatment? Gladioli in growing form new corms on the tops of the old ones; the old corms remain attached to the bases of the new ones; they are easily removed 3 or 4 weeks after digging. Often a cluster of tiny cormels grow from the base of the new corm.

Propagation

What is the best way to increase gladioli? By saving and planting the small bulblets that form around the large corms.

CORMELS   LARGE CORM CUT
                       FOR PLANTING

The cormels, planted early in spring, like peas, produce by autumn small corms, some of which usually flower the following year. Right—large old corms, with more than one sprout, can be cut before planting, to increase stock of a favorite variety.

How are gladiolus bulbs raised from many small bulbs that develop on each large one? The small corms are stored through the winter, and are planted in rows in well-prepared soil much as are larger corms (except that they are not set so deeply). They are then grown on to flowering size.

What is the best way to get gladiolus bulblets to sprout quickly and evenly? Soak them in tepid water for 2 or 3 days, before planting. Also plant them as closely together as 20 to the foot as they seem to like company.

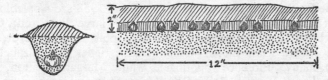

FROM SMALL BULBS

Small gladioli corms are planted out in nursery rows, to grow on into flowering-sized bulbs for another year.

In the propagation of "glads," what is the procedure of handling the bulblets or cormlets gathered from old bulbs, until the next planting season? Treat them with flake napthalene, and store in a cool, dry place in an open crate.

How are new varieties of gladioli developed? They are raised from seeds. Most improvements are obtained from seeds collected from hand-pollinated flowers.

How can "glads" be raised from seeds? Plant them in a light, friable soil in an outdoor bed early in spring, while the ground is still cool. Sow the seeds rather thinly in shallow drills, spaced so a cultivator can be used between them. Cover about ¼ in. deep. Corms the size of a pea or smaller should develop the first year, and most of these will bloom the second year.

Pests and Diseases

Should gladiolus bulbs be treated before planting? Certain fungous and bacterial diseases are sometimes carried on the corms. If these are suspected, disinfect by soaking for 20 minutes, just before planting, in a solution of 1 part mercuric chloride in 1,000 parts of water, by weight. Rinse thoroughly in clear water immediately before planting.

What should be done to stop wireworms from damaging gladiolus bulbs? Wireworms are usually bad only in newly made gardens, or where trash is allowed to accumulate. (For control, see Section VIII.)

How can I check the ravages of cutworms among my gladioli? Clean the ground of all weeds and other unwanted growth in fall. Use a poison bait. (See Cutworms, Section VIII.)

What is the most satisfactory method of combating gladiolus thrips?
In fall after corms are dug, dust with 5% DDT or with malathion
dust. In spring when plants are 6 inches high, spray or dust every
10 days with the same.

Varieties

**Will you please give me a list of some of the best gladiolus
varieties?** A.A.G.S. Selections for 1957 and 1958 are Appleblossom,
white flushed pink; Royal Stewart, very large light red; Carib-
bean, blue-violet, Maytime, ruffled deep pink and Emperor, rose-
purple with a white blotch. Other good varieties are Elizabeth the
Queen, mauve; Florence Nightingale, white; Margaret Beaton, white,
scarlet throat; Picardy, flesh; Red Wings; Spic and Span, deep pink;
Vagabond Prince, mahogany and bronze; and Voodoo, smoky.

What are the uses of Miniature Glads? Please name a few varieties.
Miniatures are generally useful in mixed border plantings and espe-
cially as cut flowers. They are more informal than the standard
varieties and the spikes are more graceful for use in arrangements.
BoPeep, salmon-pink Loveliness, shrimp pink; Golden Frills and
Little Gold; Massasoit, crimson; Atom, vermillion with white picotee;
Starlit and Snow Baby, white; Pint Size, lavender.

GLORIOSA

Can gloriosas be grown out of doors in summer? Yes. Plant
strong tubers in pots of light, humusy soil in March or April.
Transfer started plants to sunny border after all danger of frost has
passed. Place stakes or brushwood for support. Dig up tubers in
fall and store in dry sand or peatmoss through winter, in temperature
between 50° and 60° F.

HAEMANTHUS

Are haemanthus adapted for growing indoors? They are both
interesting and beautiful as house plants or greenhouse plants. Some
of the best are *katharinae, coccineus, multiflorus,* and *albiflos.*

How should I care for Bloodlilies (haemanthus)? Water freely
when leaves are in evidence; keep dry at other times. Give full sunshine, well-drained soil, and repot every 3 or 4 years at beginning of
growing season. Feed when in active leaf growth. Temperature 50°
to 60° F.

HEDYCHIUM (GINGERLILY)

**Is the Gingerlily (hedychium) adaptable for growing outdoors in
the North?** Only in sheltered, warm situations, and then the roots
must be lifted in fall and stored in sand in a frostproof cellar over
winter. Plant outdoors after all danger of frost has passed, and give
abundance of water when growing.

HYDROSME (SNAKEPALM)

Can snakepalm—the one that has a flower like a big purplish callalily, and a huge, finely cut umbrella leaf—be grown outdoors in summer? Yes, and its foliage is both distinctive and decorative. Plant in good soil in sun or light shade and it will quickly grow. Its name is *Hydrosme rivieri.*

ISMENE (PERUVIAN-DAFFODIL)

How can I raise Ismene calathina? Plant out after ground is warm, weather is settled, and all danger of frost has passed, in sunny, well-drained border in fertile soil. Cover to depth of 3 times the diameter of the bulb. Dig after first frost; remove foliage and store *with fleshy basal roots intact* at a temperature of about 60 degrees.

I planted Peruvian-daffodils—bulbs as large as those of amaryllis. On taking up this November, the bulbs were very much smaller. Why was this? Unsatisfactory cultural conditions. Soil perhaps too heavy, or not fertile. They probably will not bloom so well next year.

Should Ismene calathina (Peruvian-daffodil) be stored in dry sand over winter, or left spread out? Either way is satisfactory. It should be kept in temperature of at least 50° F.

IXIAS

Will you give me cultural directions for ixias and sparaxis? Read answers under "Freesia." Ixias and sparaxis need exactly the same treatment.

LACHENALIA (CAPECOWSLIP)

Will you give me the detailed cultural needs of lachenalias (Cape-cowslips)? Plant bulbs close together in early fall, in pots or hanging baskets containing light soil. Treat same as freesias.

Which varieties of lachenalias would you recommend to a beginner? *Pendula* (red and yellow); *tricolor* (red, yellow, and green); *tricolor nelsoni* (yellow); and *roodeae* (blue).

LEUCOCORYNE (GLORY-OF-THE-SUN)

What is Glory-of-the-sun, and how is it grown? A tender, bulbous plant from the uplands of Chile named *Leucocoryne ixioides odorata.* It is handled indoors like freesias. Avoid high temperatures and grow in sunny, airy situation. Blooms late winter and spring.

LYCORIS RADIATA

I have 3 bulbs of Lycoris radiata in a pot in the house. They have been potted since September. Why haven't they bloomed? Is there anything I can do to encourage bloom? *Lycoris radiata* often passes its bloom season. July and August are best months to plant these. Work a tablespoonful of bone meal for each bulb into the surface soil.

MONTBRETIAS

Will you describe culture of montbretias?   They need essentially the same care as gladioli. They are, however, rather hardier, and in favored places may be left in ground over winter if given a very heavy mulch.

OXALIS

How should one grow the tender kinds of oxalis bulbs?   Pot during August in light, fertile soil. Space bulbs 2 or 3 ins. apart just below surface. Water carefully at first; freely when growth has developed. Give plenty of sunshine; temperature of 50° to 60° F. Feed when pots are filled with roots. After flowering, gradually reduce water, and finally dry completely and rest.

POLIANTHES (TUBEROSE)

Will you give me some information on tuberoses? (Washington, D.C.)   Purchase good bulbs of tuberose (*Polianthes tuberosa*), plant outdoors in light soil that is fertile, after ground has warmed up. Lift in fall, and store dry in temperature of 60° F.

RANUNCULUS

Ranunculus bulbs sent from California arrived after ground was frozen. Can I successfully plant them in spring? How should I treat them during winter?   Store in dry sand or peatmoss in cool but frostproof cellar or shed. Plant 2 ins. deep, 6 ins. apart, as soon as ground can be worked in spring. Make soil friable with plenty of leafmold and sand. Position should be moist and lightly shaded. Tuberous-rooted varieties are dug and stored through winter.

SCHIZOSTYLIS (KAFIRLILY)

Will you give me instructions for growing the Kafirlily (schizostylis) in New Jersey?   Plant in spring in well-prepared, light, fertile soil in a deep cold frame. Keep sash off in summer, but protect in fall and winter. Water freely during growing season.

SPREKELIA (JACOBEANLILY)

In California I saw a lily called Jacobeanlily that looked like a curious crimson orchid. What is it? How can one grow it?   *Sprekelia formosissima* (sometimes sold as *Amaryllis formosissima*). Plant bulbs 6 ins. deep in light, fertile loam, in a sunny position. Water freely when foliage is above ground. In cold climates mulch heavily; or lift and store bulbs through winter; remove tops, but *leave roots on.*

I bought Amaryllis formosissima bulbs that bloomed well the first year. The next 2 years I planted some in semi-shade, and in sun, yet they don't bloom. I take them up every winter and store them in a cool place. Bulbs look good. Why don't they bloom? They need a very fertile soil. When you dig them in fall, remove tops but leave roots on. Leave in ground until after first frost.

TIGRIDIA

What soil and situation do tigerflowers (tigridias) prefer? A warm, well-drained soil and a sunny situation. Plant same time as gladioli. Take up and store in same way.

OTHER BULBS

I understand there are a number of South African bulbs that need very much the same treatment as freesias. Will you please list some of these? Ixia, sparaxis, babiana, antholyza, tritonia, crocosmia, lape-irousia, ornithogalum, and lachenalia.

What is the best way of propagating ixias, sparaxis, tritonias, and similar South African or "Cape" bulbs? They all multiply quickly by offsets. These can be removed and planted in bulb pans, about an inch apart, at potting time. They are also very readily raised from seed.

Roses

INTRODUCTION

BY F. F. ROCKWELL

ROSES ARE so closely associated with the painting, literature, music, and even the politics of the world that they have for many centuries been an integral part of our culture. The rose is the very symbol of beauty and loveliness. Since the dawn of history it has been admired, appreciated, and linked with all kinds of human activities. It would be difficult to find an individual who could not recognize a rose—the best known and most loved of all our cultivated plants, and truly the "queen of flowers." Its majestic form, gorgeous colorings, and delightful perfume are unsurpassed. Even the thorns command respect. It is the standard of perfection by which all other flowers are judged.

More than 200 species of wild roses have been described and named by botanists. They are distributed from the Arctic Circle to the equator, and there are types that will thrive in any climate. Few flowers have received so much attention by plant breeders and few have exhibited such potentialities for development. The number of varieties that have been introduced is almost limitless; in the United States alone nearly 5,000 different species and varieties are available.

Contrary to widely held opinions, roses are not difficult to grow. Their presence around long-deserted houses is evidence of their tenacity. A judicious selection of types and varieties and an understanding of their cultural requirements will enable anyone to grow roses successfully.

Many new home owners harbor the mistaken idea that roses are specialists' plants, and that the beginning gardener, with very limited space at his disposal, would do well not to attempt growing them—except of course, for the ubiquitous Climber or two at the front door or along a fence.

It is quite true that such roses are better than none at all, but no true flower lover will—or should—be content until he has in his garden at least a half dozen or so of the modern bush roses to provide flowers for enjoyment both in the garden and as cut flower decoration indoors.

The often-heard argument that roses "require so much care" scarcely seems to hold when one considers that the modern garden varieties give flowers almost continuously from late May into October or November, while most other hardy flowers are in bloom for little more than two or three weeks. And many of the splendid new varieties developed during the last decade or two, especially in Floribunda and the new Grandiflora groups, have remarkable vigor and hardiness. The development of improved "all-purpose" controls for insect pests and diseases has greatly simplified rose culture for the amateur and gone far to assure success even to the least experienced beginner, so we have really reached the day when there should be roses in *every* garden.

SELECTING PLANTS

What are the main types or classes of roses?   1, tea; 2, hybrid tea; 3, hybrid perpetual; 4, polyantha; 5, hybrid or large-flowered polyantha (floribunda); 6, grandiflora; 7, baby (miniature); 8, climber; 9, shrub.

What do the abbreviations HT., HP., etc. used after rose varieties mean?   They indicate the class to which the variety belongs: HT.— hybrid tea; HP.—hybrid perpetual; Pol. (Poly)—polyantha; HPol. —hybrid polyantha (floribunda); Cl—climber; R.—rambler; CHT. —climbing hybrid tea; T.—tea.

What are the standard rose grades?   No. 1. Three or more strong canes 18 ins. or more long; No. 1½. Two or more strong canes at least 14 ins. long; No. 2. Two or more canes at least 12 ins. long; No. 3. One cane with few or no branches.

What age plants should be purchased?   Two-year-old field-grown plants are best for planting in the garden. The actual age, however, is of less importance than the size. The largest plants, known as the No. 1 grade, usually give the best results.

Is it advantageous to buy climbing roses that are 5 or 6 years old? No. In fact, a younger plant, 1 to 2 years old, becomes established sooner and is more successful.

Are cheap roses offered by nurseries a good investment?   Usually not. They are likely to be undersized plants, held too long in storage; or they may be "bench" roses from a greenhouse which have been forced for a year or more. As with everything else, you get what you pay for.

Should one buy budded or own-root stock when planting a rose garden? Approximately 99 per cent of the rose plants sold are budded stock. Good own-root plants are more difficult to obtain, and they are slower to become established. A few varieties may prove more satisfactory on their own roots.

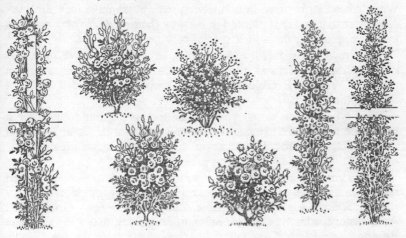

Types of roses: left, Climbing Hybrid Tea; center top, Hybrid Perpetual and Polyantha; center bottom, Hybrid Tea and Floribunda; right, Large-flowered Climber and Rambler.

Are Southern-grown rose plants as hardy as those grown in the North? In general, yes. Northern-grown plants can usually be planted earlier in the fall than those from the South, and therefore have a little better chance to become established.

PLANNING

What roses will be satisfactory in semi-shade? Roses need at least 8 hours of full sunlight per day. The hybrid teas, polyanthas, and floribundas do well in semi-shade; in fact, are better if they have a little shade during the hot part of the day.

Will a climbing rose do well on the northeast corner of a house? Such a situation would be unfavorable. It would be better to use a clematis, honeysuckle, or other vine that can get along with less sunlight.

Should rose plants be grouped together, or placed in separate parts of the yard? The best effects will be achieved if grouped, or, better still, planted in beds. The large shrub roses may be planted with other flowering shrubs. The climbing varieties need the support of fences, arbors, walls, or posts.

What flowers can be combined with roses in a rose garden?   Lilies, delphiniums, pansies, peonies, irises, tulips, daffodils, forget-me-nots, etc., can be used. A border of low growing flowers like pansies or sweet alyssum, edging the rose beds, is often the most satisfactory use of other flowers in combination with roses.

Will it be satisfactory to transplant some old rosebushes to a corner of a perennial garden, or should they be set in a separate rose garden? While roses can be used in connection with perennials, they are usually easier to care for if planted in beds by themselves. Where space is available, planting them in a special rose garden is ideal.

What rose is satisfactory for planting as a ground cover on a terrace?   *Rosa wichuraiana,* the Wichuriania Rose; Max Graf, a rugosa hybrid; Creeping Everbloom; Coral Creeper; Mermaid (south of Philadephia).

What type of rose would you recommend as a ground cover for a bank with a southern exposure?   If the area is large, Creeping Everbloom; Magic Carpet; Clymenestra. For a small space, *Rosa wichuraiana.*

Which rose is best to border a walk?   Tall (4 to 6 feet): *Rosa rugosa* and its many fine hybrids like Flamingo; Grootendorst, cherry red; Sir Thomas Lipton, white. Low: Baby Blaze; Pygmy Gold; Carol Ann, orange-salmon; Cameo, salmon-pink; Pink Rosette; Crimson Rosette.

I have a low rock retaining wall in front of my house that is 175 ft. long. Should roses be planted on the inside, which is on a level with the yard, or on the outside, so they would have the wall for support? Plant on the inside so the rose stems may overhang the wall.

What rose varieties would you suggest for a low rock retaining wall? (Kansas.)   *Rosa wichuraiana* and Max Graf, *Rosa rugosa repens alba.*

What type of roses are best for a week-end summer home?   Shrub roses like Fruehling's Gold, Mabelle Stearns, The Fairy; Belinda; Lipstick, Flamingo, Nearly Wild and Harison's Yellow. These are all iron-hardy and resistant to neglect and plant troubles.

Can I have Climbers which bloom every month like Hybrid Teas? (Northern New York)   Climbing Hybrid Teas are not hardy with you. Among newer, hardy everblooming climbers are Golden Showers; Dr. Nicholas, pink; Inspiration, pink; Parade, rose-red.

What roses are suitable for the rock garden?   Any of the Miniature or Baby Roses which are tiny Hybrid Teas growing only a few inches tall. For the large rock garden, Charlie McCarthy, China Doll, Carol Ann and Pinkie, all 18 inches.

What roses can I plant for very early bloom? *Rosa hugonis* and *R. rugosa* hybrid Sir Thomas Lipton.

SOIL

What type of soil is best suited to roses?   While any productive garden soil can be improved to grow good roses, the ideal type is a well-aerated, slightly acid, medium heavy loam containing an abundance of organic matter.

What kind of soil is best for climbing roses?   Climbing roses do well in a wide variety of soils. The ideal type is a moderately rich, well-drained garden loam that is high in organic matter and slightly acid in reaction.

Is it necessary to have a clay soil for success with roses?   Not at all. Some of the best rose gardens are found in regions where the soil is light and sandy. Almost any type of soil may be improved for roses by proper treatment.

Can roses be grown in light, sandy soil if clay is added?   The clay will have very little beneficial effect. The sandy soil may be improved by adding some form of organic matter, such as peatmoss, well-rotted manure, or leafmold.

What special treatments do roses growing in a sandy soil require?   Working into the soil an abundance of organic material; watering during dry periods; and 2 or 3 applications of a mixed commercial fertilizer during the growing season.

What is the treatment for roses when soil is alkaline? (Texas.)   Roses require a slightly acid soil—pH 5.5 to 6.5. Sulfur and alum are used to acidify soils, and the amounts required will vary with the free lime present. Apply 5 lbs. of sulfur per 100 sq. ft., *and check the* pH after 2 or 3 months. As much as 30 lbs. of sulfur per 100 sq. ft. *may* be needed; 10 to 20 lbs. is more frequently required in very alkaline soil.

Is a gravel soil good for roses?   While it is not an ideal type it can be made satisfactory by incorporating organic material.

Do roses like wet or dry feet?   Roses require good drainage. If water tends to stand around the plants, they should be moved to another location, or tile drains installed, if the condition is very serious. However, wet areas can oftentimes be improved by breaking up the subsoil, mixing coarse cinders with it, raising the level of the bed, and —if the soil is heavy on top—mixing in screened cinders to ⅓ the volume of soil.

Do old rose beds wear out?   This is a serious problem and the answer is not well understood. It is often observed that roses planted in virgin soil do much better than in old beds. Just why is not known, but there may be a number of contributing factors, such as disease infestation, changes in the chemical and biological composition of the soil, etc.

PREPARING THE SOIL

How deep should the soil be prepared for a rose bed? Experiments have shown that the deeper the soil is prepared the more vigorous the growth and the greater the production of flowers. However, it is questionable whether preparing the soil deeper than 18 ins. is worth while. Twelve ins. is considered the minimum.

What method should be followed in preparing a soil mixture for roses? When a new bed is being prepared, dig the soil out to a depth of approximately 18 ins., keeping the topsoil and subsoil separate. Next put back a 6-in. layer of the topsoil in the bottom of the bed. Add 3 ins. old manure, peatmoss, or other type of organic material; fork it in thoroughly. Shovel in another 6-in. layer, and work in more organic matter; last, fill the bed with the subsoil mixed with more organic matter.

How may one prepare the soil for individual plants set in to fill out a bed? Dig a hole large enough to accommodate the plant. Mix the required amount of peatmoss with the soil that was removed, and use the mixture to fill in around the plant.

Can the soil be made too rich for roses? Yes. For example, too much nitrogen may be harmful and injure the roots; too much potash may cause a hard, stunted type of growth.

What is meant by "trenching" in connection with rose planting? Trenching is the term used for the practice of digging a trench (a bed) 18 ins. or more deep and filling it in with especially prepared soil in which the rose plants are set.

Should lime be used on roses? Only if the soil test shows the need for it. (See Soil Testing.)

How much lime should be used to correct an acid soil? If a test shows that the soil has a pH value of 5 or lower, lime should be incorporated. Ground limestone (not hydrated lime) is best for the average garden because there is less danger of applying too much. Use the ground limestone; or common agricultural lime, at the rate of 3 to 6 lbs. per 100 sq. ft. of ground area, depending upon the degree of acidity.

Do roses want acid soil? A slightly acid soil is considered optimum. Roses will tolerate a somewhat wider range of reaction if the soil contains a high percentage of organic material. Roses do best if pH value of the soil is 5.5 to 6.5.

Why will roses not do well in a sweet or alkaline soil? The iron in an alkaline soil is insoluble, and thus is unavailable to the plants.

All garden plants require iron to form chlorophyll (the green coloring matter in the leaves); absorption of iron is interfered with in a highly alkaline soil.

What is the appearance of rose plants when the soil is too sweet or alkaline? The veins of the leaves become dark green and the areas between mottled with yellow. In severe cases, the leaves may become almost pure white.

If the soil is sweet (alkaline), what can be done to make it slightly acid? Such a soil may be made slightly acid by mixing in finely powdered sulfur. If the pH value is 8, use 6 lbs. per 100 sq. ft.; pH 7.5, 3 lbs.; pH 7, 1 lb. Have the soil tested after 2 months to make sure it has become slightly acid.

Is peatmoss useful for acidifying soil? Peatmoss, if used in large enough quantities, will temporarily increase the acidity of the soil. Its effect, however, is not permanent, since the peatmoss-soil mixture gradually returns to nearly the pH value of the original soil. If the soil is neutral, or only slightly acid, the use of peatmoss will be found very satisfactory. It improves the mechanical condition of the soil as well.

Can aluminum sulfate be used to acidify soil for roses? Aluminum sulfate is less desirable than powdered sulfur. It is more expensive, less easy to obtain, and more has to be used. If large quantities are applied, there is danger of the aluminum being harmful.

Is it a good idea to put tile under a rose bed for subirrigation? If the subsoil is heavy, the method usually works satisfactorily; if the subsoil is porous, it will not work. Four-in. tile is used and is laid 12 ins. below the surface.

IMPROVING SOILS

How should a hard-packed soil be treated? A soil that packs very hard is usually the heavy type. Working in organic material, especially peatmoss, will make it more friable.

How can a very loose, porous soil be improved? Such soils are often lacking in nutrients and require additional fertilizer. Watering during dry periods will improve the growth and quality of the flowers. Permanent improvement can only be brought about by incorporating plenty of organic matter.

What should be done to soil that does not hold enough moisture? Add organic material. Peatmoss is the best, but leafmold and well-rotted manure may be used. Water beds thoroughly during dry periods.

How can a red clay soil be improved for roses? (Georgia.) Incorporating Georgia Peat, or a combination of the peat and well-rotted manure will improve such a soil.

FERTILIZER

When is the best time to fertilize roses?   Fertilizer is most effective if applied in the early spring, when the new growth is about 4 ins. long.

How often do roses need fertilizer?   If the soil has been well prepared, 1 to 2 applications yearly are usually sufficient. If the soil is light, low in organic matter, and not very fertile, 3 to 4 applications, at monthly intervals, are desirable. In wet seasons more fertilization is needed than in dry ones.

Is fertilizer put in the hole when setting out a rose plant?   Additional fertilizer is not necessary if the soil has been previously well prepared. Where the soil is poor, a mixture of commercial 5–10–5 fertilizer, or a similar grade, may be mixed with the soil used to fill in around the plant. Not over 1 teacupful to each bushel of soil should be used.

Should any fertilizer be added at the time the soil is prepared?   Incorporating 3 lbs. of superphosphate and ½ lb. of muriate of potash for each 100 sq. ft. is desirable. A mixed commercial fertilizer may be substituted, in which case 4 lbs. of the 5–10–5 may be used for each 100 sq. ft.

How can one tell when roses need fertilizer?   The leaves are a uniform light yellowish green; plants fail to make lush, vigorous growth.

Are commercial fertilizers good for roses?   Almost any fertilizer that contains an appreciable quantity of plant nutrients is satisfactory. A mixed commercial fertilizer, 5–10–5 or comparable grade, can be used at the rate of 4 lbs. per 100 sq. ft.

What can be done if roses have been overfertilized?   Very heavy watering on several days in succession will leach out some of the excess nutrients. Working in peatmoss, chopped straw, or shredded sugar cane will also help.

How do roses look when they are overfertilized?   Usually the growth is stunted, the stems short, and the flowers small. New shoots fail to develop promptly after the first blooming period. The midsummer and fall bloom is reduced. The tips of the feeding roots, normally white, appear brown.

Can manure be used as a fertilizer?   Well-rotted manure is a satisfactory form of fertilizer and should be used at the rate of 3 to 5 bu. for each 100 sq. ft., applied in either early spring or late fall.

Should manure be mixed with the soil for roses?   If the manure is well rotted, it is an excellent form of organic material. Fresh manure may do more harm than good.

How much manure may be mixed with the soil?   Ten per cent by volume, or 1 bu. of well-rotted manure to 9 bu. of soil is satisfactory.

Should hen manure be used on roses? If so, when? Hen manure is a satisfactory fertilizer if it has been allowed to rot somewhat before using. It is advisable to put it on in the late fall or very early spring.

How much hen manure can be used on roses? One bu. for each 100 sq. ft. can be used with safety.

Is horse manure satisfactory for roses? If well rotted, it is nearly as good as cow manure.

Is peatmoss good for roses? Peatmoss is an excellent soil amender for roses, especially if the soil is heavy.

What is the value of peatmoss in a rose soil? It increases the organic matter content, aeration is improved, the water-holding capacity is increased, and the soil reaction (pH) may be made more favorable for growth.

How much peatmoss should be used? On very heavy clay soils as much as 50 per cent by volume may be incorporated. Ordinarily 25 per cent by volume is satisfactory. This means 1 bu. of peat to each 3 bu. of soil.

How should peatmoss be used in preparing the soil for roses? It is best to mix it thoroughly with the soil if a new bed is being prepared. Where individual plants are set in to replace those that have died, mix the peatmoss with the soil that is used to fill in around the plant.

Should the peatmoss be moistened before it is mixed with the soil? It is not necessary.

What kind of peatmoss is best? Any of the commonly available brands of peatmoss (sphagnum moss peat) are satisfactory. It should be fibrous, clean, free from sticks and other debris, and thoroughly granulated. The more thoroughly decomposed sedge and muck peats are less beneficial.

Will peatmoss improve a light, sandy soil? While the benefit of peatmoss is most striking in a heavy soil, it also greatly improves light, sandy soil.

Can both peatmoss and manure be used? Yes, they make an excellent combination. A mixture of 1 bu. of manure, 2 bu. of peatmoss, and 10 bu. of soil is ideal.

What kinds of organic material can be used in preparing rose soil, other than peatmoss and manure? Leafmold is satisfactory and may be used at the rate of 1 bu. to 5 bu. of soil. Compost, muck, and various commercial organic materials can be used.

Is bone meal better on one type of soil than on another? It is most satisfactory on medium acid or strongly acid soils.

Is there any danger in using bone meal on roses? Bone meal contains a large proportion of lime, which tends to sweeten the soil.

If the soil is already neutral or alkaline, the addition of bone meal may make it too sweet for the best growth of roses.

Is it desirable to put bones beneath rose plants? This practice is a very ineffective way to supply fertilizer and is not recommended. It does neither harm nor good. Raw ground bone, however, makes a good fertilizer, with the exceptions noted above.

Is there anything better than bone meal as a fertilizer for roses? Superphosphate is cheaper and more effective as a source of phosphorus. It should be used at the rate of 3 lbs. per 100 sq. ft.

Are wood ashes good for roses? Wood ashes are satisfactory in regions where the soil is acid (pH 5.5 or below). Where the soil is near the neutral point, wood ashes may make it too sweet or alkaline because of the lime they contain.

Can cottonseed meal be used as a rose fertilizer without danger of making the soil acid? While it's a comparatively expensive type of fertilizer for roses, cottonseed meal is effective. It should be used at the rate of 5 to 10 lbs. per 100 sq. ft. There is little danger of the material making the soil too acid unless it already is near the danger point.

PLANTING AND TRANSPLANTING

Should rose plants be pruned before setting out? All small, slender, weak, dead shoots should be cut back to approximately 9 ins. above the union between the understock and scion. Bruised or broken roots should be removed just back of the point of injury. Some nurserymen send out pre-pruned plants ready for planting.

Should roses be pruned when they are transplanted? Unless they are moved with a large ball of earth, they should be pruned like plants obtained from a nursery. (See preceding question.) Even when transplanted with a ball of soil, it is advisable to remove the weak canes and branches, and cut back moderately the strong canes.

What is the best time to plant roses? Fall is the best season to plant roses throughout most of the United States. In the extremely cold regions, where the ground freezes before plants can be delivered by nurserymen, spring planting is preferred.

Can roses be planted in the spring? While late fall is the preferred season, roses can be planted in spring with good success. It is very important, however, that the planting be done just as early as the ground can be worked.

Will spring-planted roses bloom the first year? All the bush or bedding types of roses bloom well the first year. The climbing and shrub varieties seldom bloom to any extent the first season because most of the flowering wood has been removed to facilitate shipping.

Are potted roses satisfactory and how late in the season can they

be planted? Rose plants grown in large tarpaper pots or gallon metal cans are now available from many rose growers and at wayside garden stands the country over. Though more expensive to buy than dormant plants, these are perfectly satisfactory. If correctly planted in a well prepared and enriched hole and adequately watered, a potted rose may be transplanted at any time. They are of particular value to those who have late losses in the rose garden which must be replaced after the leaves are out, and to those who are trying, for one reason or another, to establish a garden late in the season.

How deep should roses be planted? The union between the bud and the understock should be about 1 in. below the ground level.

How far apart should roses be planted? The planting distance depends somewhat on the growth the plants are expected to make. In very favorable climates they may be planted much farther apart than in regions where they do not make vigorous growth. The average planting distance for the hybrid perpetual varieties is 24 to 30 ins.; for hybrid tea, polyantha, and floribunda varieties, it is 18 to 24 ins. Climbers should be spaced 6 to 8 ft. apart.

How large a hole should be dug for a rose plant? The dimensions will depend upon the size of the root system. In all events, it should be big enough to accommodate the roots without cramping or bending them. Usually it will need to be about 18 ins. across and about 12 ins. deep.

Should the roots be placed straight downward or spread out horizontally? Rose roots tend to grow more or less horizontally and should be so placed in the hole. They should not overlap one another, nor be forced into too small a space.

Is it necessary to firm the soil when planting rosebushes? The soil should be very carefully firmed as the hole is filled in. It is best to do this with the fingers to make certain that every root is in close contact with the soil, and that there is no air space under the center of the plant. Where the soil is loose or somewhat dry, it may be firmed by tramping around the plant just before the hole is completely filled. This should not be done if the soil is wet.

In planting roses, the soil should be thoroughly firmed about the roots.

Should rose plants be watered when first planted? Where the soil is loose or dry, watering is always necessary. A space should be left and filled with water 2 or 3 times before the remainder of the soil is put in.

Can roses be planted in midsummer? Not unless potted plants are available. These may be obtained from roadside nursery stands and from a few nurseries which specialize in them.

Can hybrid tea roses which are 4 or 5 years old be successfully moved to a different location? If moved carefully and pruned back severely, they are not likely to suffer.

Can old rosebushes be transplanted? Transplanting old rosebushes (10 to 15 years) is advisable only on a limited scale. Very old plants do not send out new roots readily, and it may take them several years to become re-established. The transplanting is best done in the fall, and the plants should be moved with as much soil as possible.

Should rosebushes be moved periodically? No. Once a rose plant is established, it is best not to move it.

How can I move a large climbing rose without danger of losing it? Do not try to move the plant without first pruning it. Transplanting should be done in the fall. Cut out all but 4 or 5 young, vigorous canes. Lift the plant carefully with a ball of soil.

When is the best time to transplant a large Dr. Van Fleet rose? The fall is the best season for transplanting roses.

How should potted roses be planted? It is best not to break the soil-ball any more than is necessary. Merely remove the pot and place the root-ball in the hole. Be sure the hole is large enough to accommodate the plant. If the ball of roots looks dry, immerse the whole ball in a pail of water until it is thoroughly soaked. Be careful that no air pockets are left between the root-ball and the walls of the hole when the soil is filled in. If the ground is at all dry, the plants should be watered frequently for a period of at least 3 weeks. Shading the plants during the hot part of the day helps in getting them established.

Is it better to try to move an old rosebush than to buy new ones? Old roses often do not move well. It is usually better to obtain new plants.

Can roses be transplanted after the ground begins to freeze, or should they be stored over winter in the basement in case it is necessary to move them? It is best to move them to the new location even though the ground is frozen a little. If the necessity for moving them can be anticipated, the ground in the new location may be mulched with 6 ins. of straw to keep it from freezing. After transplanting, soil should be mounded as high as possible around the bases of the plants, and it is well to prune the tops as for new plants. Move the plants with as much soil as possible.

Can rosebushes be taken up in the fall and stored until spring? It is possible, but seldom practical in the average home garden. If they must be kept over, pack close together in a deep trench, and mulch heavily after soil freezes.

When one has to move to a new house in midwinter, is it possible to dig roses and store them in burlap bags in the cellar? It is possible, but not usually practical, unless the cellar is cold and the air is not extremely dry. While the root-ball may be wrapped in burlap, it is much better to remove the soil and pack the roots in moist peatmoss. Some of the tops should be removed to facilitate handling. The important thing is to store them where the temperature is 35° to 40° F., and watch the canes to see that they do not dry out or shrivel.

Is it true that roses sold in the spring are dug in the fall, and kept in cold storage over winter? This is the usual method and the most practical one for the nurseryman. It enables him to supply plants in the very early spring.

Should rose plants be "heeled-in" if they cannot be planted immediately? If it is necessary to keep rose plants for more than a week before they can be planted, they should be heeled-in. To do this, dig a trench about 12 ins. deep. Remove the plants from the package and pack them closely in the trench, placing them at an angle of about 45°. Cover the root system and several ins. of the tops with soil. They should be set out in their permanent location within 3 weeks.

How may roses be kept if they arrive before planting time? Most nurserymen try to deliver rose plants at the proper planting time and it is best to set them out immediately. The plants will keep satisfactorily for 5 to 7 days in the package in which they arrive if kept cold (33° to 40° F.). Always open and make certain that the packing material is moist, but not soaked. Water if dry.

How shall I care for the rose plants during the operation of planting? Do not let the plants lie around in wind and sun with their roots exposed, for even a few minutes. Take the wrapped packages to the planting bed and unwrap only when you are ready to begin planting. While pruning roots and broken branches of one plant in a package, keep the others wrapped in damp sphagnum moss, or plunge the roots in a bucket of water.

Will the roots of fall-planted roses take hold before freezing? Many experiments give evidence that rose roots grow as long as the soil temperature is above freezing. The fact that some root growth takes place, enabling the plants to become established in the soil, is one of the important reasons for fall planting.

GENERAL CULTURE

PROBLEMS

Is there a rose on the market that does not require any attention? No. In fact, taking care of plants is part of the fun of having them.

Rugosas, the species (wild) roses, and the brier roses need very little care.

Why don't rosebushes grow after giving them the best of care? There is often a great difference between what roses like and what human beings think is good for them. As many plants are killed by improper care as by neglect. It is necessary to understand their basic requirements and then to provide for them. No treatment should be given unless there is a reason. Much is to be gained by letting well enough alone where the plants are making satisfactory growth.

Why do my roses fail to bloom even though they make some growth? There are many possible reasons: shoots produced by the understock, incorrect pruning, insect infestation—especially rose midge—severe winter killing, too many flowers picked, and presence of diseases are a few.

What makes rosebushes gradually die out? Poor location, poor drainage, diseases, winter injury, too much lime, too much fertilizer, not enough moisture, too severe pruning.

Why is it many of our roses have no fine feeding roots? Often the feeding roots are so fine that they are lost when the plant is dug. Certain understocks do not tend to produce many fine roots.

How long after spring planting before fibrous roots will develop? In properly prepared soil they will start in about 1 week. If the soil is too sweet or alkaline, contains too much fertilizer, or is too dry, the fine roots will not develop for some time.

Should rosebushes be taken up and the roots treated? There is nothing to be gained by such a practice under ordinary circumstances, and many of the plants may fail to recover from such a treatment.

Will competition from tree roots prevent roses from flourishing? Roses will not stand such competition. The beds should be located far enough from trees or other large plants to prevent the roots from entering the bed and exhausting the moisture and nutrients of the soil.

How can tree roots be kept out of rose beds? About the only way is to put a concrete or metal barrier between the tree and the bed. Such a barrier should extend about 3 ft. down into the ground.

Why should our climbing rose fail to bloom? Some varieties are naturally shy bloomers. If the canes are killed back to the ground level each year there will be no bloom. The variety may have reverted to the understock. Improper pruning will discourage flowering. It may be in too shady a location.

What is the matter with my New Dawn when it produces only pure white flowers? The variety was probably mislabeled in the nursery, because New Dawn always has light-pink flowers.

Is the fact that my climbing roses fail to grow due to the soil? Most likely not. Lack of success with climbing roses is usually due to some factor other than the soil. Poor drainage, unfavorable location, disease and insect pests, improper winter protection, etc., are more common causes of failure.

What is the trouble with a climbing rose that never gets taller than 5 ft.? The variety may not be a true climber. Perhaps more careful winter protection would prevent losing part of the canes from freezing.

What can be done to keep hybrid tea roses blooming and their foliage perfect, and not inclined to drop from the branches during hot weather? Many of the Pernetiana roses (the orange, bronze, and yellow sorts) have the inherent habit of dropping their foliage in summer, and no cultural treatment will stop it. Black spot (see Diseases) will defoliate roses, some varieties being more susceptible than others. It will not be easy to keep hybrid teas in full bloom in summer heat. Feeding, watering, removal of spent flowers, and a regular weekly all-purpose spray or dust program from the time the leaves develop until frost, will retain vitality and assure a good display during late summer.

Is it true that more can be expected from new rose plants than established ones? It is true of the weaker varieties, which are best the first year or two after planting. The more vigorous ones, however, usually are much better when well established.

How can one grow climbing roses in Vermont? Set the plants in as protected a place as possible. Remove the canes from the trellis, fence, or other support late each fall, after a few frosts have ripened the canes; pin them close to the ground and cover with soil. Put them back on the trellis in the spring. This method of winter protection prevents severe killing of the canes. Do not bend the canes while they are in a frozen condition.

CULTIVATING

Should the soil in a rose bed be stirred or worked every few days? Keeping the surface of the soil stirred by very shallow hoeing is beneficial. Deep cultivation should not be practiced except possibly in the very early spring or late fall.

Is it better to hoe or mulch rose beds? Mulching is preferable because it reduces the amount of labor, helps to retain soil moisture, keeps the soil cool, and does not disturb the roots.

WATERING

Is it a good plan to water roses in dry weather? Roses like plenty of water. They will make more growth and produce more flowers if thoroughly watered during dry periods.

What is the best way to water roses? It is essential to soak the soil to a depth of at least 5 or 6 ins. A light sprinkling on top does more harm than good. It is best not to wet the foliage, because this helps to spread the black-spot disease.

How can roses be watered without wetting the foliage? There are several devices on the market that are practical. The Soil-soaker Hose, Water-Wand, and others are satisfactory. Or the water may simply be allowed to run from the hose onto the bed.

What is the best method of watering standard or tree roses? Allow the open hose to run near the base of each plant until the soil is thoroughly soaked. Place a board under it so the soil will not wash.

SUMMER MULCHING

Should roses be mulched during the summer? Mulching is a good practice. It helps to keep down weeds, conserves moisture, and keeps the soil cool.

What materials are best for mulching rose beds? Peatmoss is ideal because it looks well, is easy to apply, stays in place, improves the soil as it decomposes, and becomes incorporated with it. Buckwheat hulls, sawdust, ground corn cobs, shredded sugar cane and similar waste materials are satisfactory in regions where they are available. Rice hulls make a good mulch, but their light straw color is less attractive. Partially decayed leaves may also be used. Straw and similar materials are usually unattractive and contain weed seeds.

How can one keep a peatmoss mulch from blowing away? Soak it and spread it on the bed damp. After it is in place, sprinkle it lightly with a hose or watering can. When it dries out, it will form a crust and that will hold it in place.

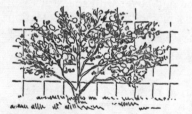

Trellis support for climbing and semi-climbing (pillar) roses.

SUPPORTS

How can I support my climbing roses? With a trellis bought or made for the purpose; over an arch; or on cedar posts with crossbars added for extra support (the later method is especially suited to pillar-type roses).

How can an overgrown rambler be attached to the side of a house? The plant should be properly pruned, by cutting off, at the ground level, all but the new basal shoots. These may be trained as desired by tying them with soft twine to nails driven into the side of the house, or to a lattice attached to the wall.

Are climbing roses satisfactory if attached to the side of a house? While they will grow satisfactorily, the wall of a house is not an ideal form of support. They interfere with painting and other types of maintenance work and are difficult to support on the flat wall without some form of latticework, which should be held out from the wall itself at least 6 inches, and preferably a foot.

DISBUDDING

Should roses be disbudded? Stems that are to be cut for use indoors or for exhibition purposes should be disbudded.

What good does disbudding do? It eliminates competition between the main and the secondary flower buds for nutrients, food, and water. The main or terminal bud of the cluster develops into a larger, more perfectly formed, and better-colored flower.

When should disbudding be done? Just as soon as the secondary buds become visible.

How does one disbud roses? Most varieties produce 3 to 7 buds in a cluster. All the secondary buds should be picked off, leaving the largest one to develop into a flower.

What types of roses should be disbudded? The hybrid teas, hybrid perpetuals, and some varieties of climbers that bear well-formed flowers in small clusters that are useful for cutting.

How can the number of flowers and length of stems be increased? Select free-blooming, vigorous varieties. Plant in a favorable location. Prepare the soil properly. Give adequate fertilizer. Supply plenty of water. Do not disbud.

How many blooms should a standard (tree) hybrid tea variety give the second year after planting? The number will vary widely according to the variety. The average will be around 50 flowers.

CUTTING AND EXHIBITION

What time of day should roses be picked? In the early morning, or late in the afternoon.

Is it best to cut all the flowers? No, unless the plant is large it is best not to cut more than 3 or 4 flowers from a single plant at each season of bloom.

Should a rose bloom be cut at the second bud above where the stem joins the main cane? It is better if it is cut higher up. Robbing the plant of foliage tends to weaken it.

At what stage should roses be picked for best keeping quality? Roses will keep longer if picked when the bud is just starting to unfurl. If picked at too early a stage, the bud may not open. Mature flowers are likely to wilt or drop their petals in a short time.

How long a stem should be taken with roses? Only as long as will actually be needed for a vase or in an arrangement. The less foliage is removed from the plant, the better.

What treatment should be given newly cut roses to make them last

longer? Immediately after cutting, place in a deep container of water in a cool room for 3 to 6 hours before arranging. Keep out of drafts and bright light.

Why do hybrid tea roses lose their petals as soon as they are brought into the house? The blooms were too far developed when cut. Try cutting them in the bud stage and placing them in a dark, cool room in deep water for a few hours before using them.

Are the flower preservatives, like Floralife and Bloomlife, sold by florists, satisfactory for keeping roses? Some of them are quite effective in prolonging the life of cut roses, as they supply essential nutrients.

Why do roses have weak necks? Weakness of the stem just below the flower is characteristic of some varieties in certain localities. Nothing can be done about it except to grow stiffer-stemmed varieties.

CUT POINTED BUDS WHEN FAIRLY TIGHT   GLOBULAR VARIETIES WHEN PARTLY OPEN   2 LEAVES AND EYES LEFT ON STEM   TO DEVELOP NEW BUDS

How to cut a rose.

What causes rosebuds to open before they are fully grown? High temperature is the most important factor.

When should roses wanted for exhibition be cut? Cut the roses if possible the night before; immerse the stems ⅔ their length in cold water; stand in a cool cellar over night.

What precautions should be taken when cutting roses for exhibition? Select those with good stems. Cut when the buds are slightly open. Avoid stems with injured or spray-spotted foliage. Cut several more than are needed. Set the stems in water as soon as possible, and handle them with extreme care. If they must be transported, wrap each bud in waxed paper, and pack very carefully.

When should roses be disbudded for exhibition? When the buds are very small. Bend them over, and the little stem will part at the axil of the leaf and leave no stub. A bud stem in the axil of the leaf is a mark against the rose.

What are the most important things to keep in mind when exhibiting cut roses? The things that count most are length and firmness of stem and sound, unblemished foliage. The flower must be held well up and not have a weak neck. Have the rose ⅓ open when put on the stage. The flower should have no blemishes. When arranging several roses, do not force them into a container so that they are clustered together. Let each rose stand out as an individual.

SUCKERS

What is a sucker? A sucker is a rose shoot arising from the understock of a budded or grafted plant.

How can one tell the suckers from the variety? Usually the foliage and habit of growth of the sucker will be quite different from the variety and invariably the suckers spring from below the swollen "bud" or graft at the base of the plant. The presence of 7 leaflets to a leaf is an indication that the shoot comes from the understock, but it must be remembered that many varieties, especially climbers, also have 7 leaflets. It is much safer to look for differences in size and shape of leaves and leaflets, texture of the foliage, size, shape, and number of thorns, and similar characteristics.

How can you prevent suckers coming up from the root? There is nothing to do but repeatedly cut them off below the surface of the soil.

Can salt be used to stop suckers from coming up? It is not safe. The suckers are growing from the same root as the variety. To eliminate the suckers you must kill the root which would, of course, kill the plant. Keep cutting them off.

Why do the shoots that start from below the ground on my rose-bushes never produce blooms? They are suckers coming up from the understock and sometimes produce blooms characteristic of the stock on which the variety was budded.

REVERSION

Can you prevent roses from turning back to the wild form? Reversion of a plant occurs only when the bud has died or suckers from the understock have crowded it out. Protect the plants from winter injury and keep any suckers cut off *below* the surface of the soil.

Are hybrid teas getting ready to revert to the original stock when 7 instead of 5 leaflets appear on the stems? No. Reversion is the result of suckers coming from the understock. Many hybrid teas produce leaves with 7 leaflets, especially late in the season.

What makes a rosebush grow very tall and bushy without blooming? Probably the bud has died out and the understock has developed.

Should I keep tree roses on which the top has died out but which are sending up new shoots from the base? These basal shoots are coming from the understock. The plants are worthless and should be discarded after the top has died.

CHANGE OF COLOR

What causes roses to be lighter colored at some seasons than at others? The more foliage on the plant the brighter and more intense the coloring. Cool weather increases the color because less of the food from which the pigment is manufactured is used up in respiration.

Will the blossoms of very light climbing roses be darker if iron is added to the soil? No. The color is pretty largely controlled by the genetical make-up of the plant. Iron is rarely lacking in the soil, but it may be insoluble and therefore unavailable to the plants when the soil is sweet or alkaline. Increasing the acidity will increase the availability of the iron.

Will iron or rusty cans have any effect in changing the color or shading of a rose? None whatever.

Will sulfur or yellow ochre make yellow roses darker? Such materials affect flower color only in so far as they improve or hamper growth. Neither of these materials will alter the color.

Why are my Talisman roses pale yellow instead of their real color? Perhaps the plant was incorrectly labeled. Talisman is seldom as brilliant out of doors as in the greenhouse. Too-bright sun causes colors to fade. Flowers on plants defoliated by disease are lighter colored.

GROWING IN GREENHOUSE, TUBS, AND POTS

Is it possible to grow hybrid tea roses in a greenhouse? Yes, but you should use plants budded on *Rosa manetti,* which is an understock better suited to greenhouse conditions.

How do you grow roses in a small greenhouse? Plant in bench in good soil. Keep moist, but not soaked. Keep the temperature as near 60° F. at night and 68° F. during the day as possible. Use plants propagated for greenhouse work rather than those used out of doors, because they are budded on *Rosa manetti* understock and are better adapted for growing in a greenhouse.

Can I grow roses in tubs? If so, how? The chief difficulty will be carrying them through the winter. Fill the tub with well-prepared soil (see rose soil preparation) and set in the plants. They will need to be watched carefully during the summer to see that they do not dry out. They should be brought inside and stored, where the temperature is below 40° F., for the winter.

How shall I treat a rosebush that has been kept outside all summer in a large pot? Must I bring it indoors? Your best plan will be to leave the plant outside all winter. When all the foliage has been shed, dig a trench in the soil and bury the entire plant, still in its pot, on its side. Before really severe weather comes, put extra covering on the soil over the pot to prevent the soil from freezing, which might cause pot to break.

How large a box would be necessary to grow a Paul's Scarlet plant?

A strong box 2 ft. square and 18 ins. deep would be large enough to accommodate the roots for several years.

Is it possible to grow a climbing rose plant in a large box? (Maine.) It is possible, and practical, if one wishes to go to the trouble of handling such a plant.

MATERIALS FOR WINTER PROTECTION

Should tar-paper collars be placed around rose plants to hold the soil higher around the stems? The results of some experiments carried out at Cornell University demonstrated that a tar-paper collar filled with soil is harmful rather than beneficial.

Is manure satisfactory for mounding around roses? It is not quite so good as soil, because it does not conduct heat as rapidly. Horse manure is the best type.

Can coal ashes be used to form a mound around rose plants? Coal ashes are not so desirable as soil, because they do not conduct heat as well. They also tend to make the soil sweet or alkaline.

Is it all right to use peatmoss around roses for winter protection? It is better as a summer mulch. For winter protection it is not so effective as soil, because it is a poor conductor of heat.

Are leaves and grass good for covering roses? While they are reasonably satisfactory, salt hay or clean wheat straw is preferable.

Are oak leaves satisfactory for protecting roses? In general leaves are less satisfactory than straw, because they hold too much moisture. When they are used, soil should first be mounded around the base of the plants.

Are leaves, especially maple leaves, useful as a mulch for roses? Leaves will not take the place of a soil mound. Neither are they as good as straw for a mulch. They tend to hold too much water.

Does wrapping sheets of newspaper around rose plants and covering them with burlap do any good? Such a method affords little protection. If the temperature drops much below the killing point, 0° F., it is quite likely that canes so protected will not survive.

Is it all right to cover rosebushes with peach baskets during the winter? Such a treatment offers some protection, but it will not keep the tops alive if the temperature goes very low. Soil should be mounded around the base of the plant before the peach basket is put on.

WINTER INJURY

What kills rose canes during the winter—cold, or drying out? Experiments conducted at Cornell University under the auspices of the American Rose Society have shown that low temperature is the chief factor. Under some conditions drying out may cause injury.

Why do my roses die back each year after I cover them? Merely covering the plant is no guarantee that the temperature of the canes will remain above the critical point in very cold weather. They should be protected with a soil mound; this conducts heat from the lower layers of soil.

Does it hurt roses to be killed back to the ground level? It does them no good, because the plants will be weakened, due to the loss of stored food. If vigorous varieties are selected, they will make sufficient growth during the summer even if they kill back each winter.

How does one keep roses from freezing back of the graft? Mounding or hilling soil around the base of the plant is a reliable method.

How can a Doubloons climbing rose be kept from winter killing? Take the canes from their support and pin them close to the ground. (See Winter Protection.)

Why did the new shoots wither and die when the canes looked green and healthy when I pruned them in the spring? This is an effect of winter injury. The outer bark is the most cold-resistant tissue of the stem. Often shoots will begin to grow but soon die because the inner tissues have been killed even though the outer bark looks perfectly healthy in the early spring.

Why did the rosebushes I planted fail to come up in the spring? Winter killing, poor drainage, improper protection, poor-quality plants, improper planting—any of these might have caused their death.

HILLING AND WINTER MULCHING

What is meant by mounding or hilling? The practice of placing, or hoeing, soil up around the base of rose plants as a winter-protection measure.

Is it good practice to mound soil up around the base of plants, as some growers recommend? Yes. Where plants are set out in the fall, it serves as winter protection; with spring-planted stock it keeps the canes from drying out until buds have begun to develop. Soil should be mounded as high as possible. Usually enough can be obtained from between the plants without exposing the root system; otherwise it should be brought from another part of the garden. If plants are planted in the fall, the mound should remain all winter; when set out in spring, it should be leveled out 2 or 3 weeks after planting, or when the buds on the canes show signs of making growth.

Which is more successful: hilling the plants, or digging them and burying them for the winter, and replanting in the spring? Mounding or hilling the soil around the plants is the simplest and generally the most reliable method.

How does a soil mound protect the base and crown of a rose plant? Soil, even though frozen, conducts heat from the lower layers of warmer soil and keeps the temperature above the killing point.

Is it all right to cut monthly roses (hybrid teas) to about 8 ins. from the ground before protecting for the winter? Yes. This facilitates mounding up the soil. Even pruning them back to 8 ins. will not eliminate the necessity for spring pruning, because some of the remaining wood is likely to be injured.

When should the soil be hilled or mounded around the base of rose plants? After frost but before the ground freezes. After the soil settles or washes away, more should be mounded up. For this reason the first hilling should be done during early October.

Is there any particular date on which hybrid tea roses should be hilled and protected for winter? Hill before the ground freezes and while soil is in good workable condition. Usually the mulch is not put on until after cold weather arrives.

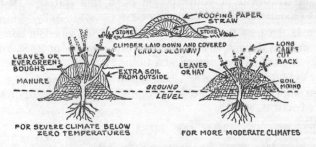

Protecting roses for the winter. Manure, unless very thoroughly rotted, should not be allowed to come in contact with the stems.

How is the soil mounded around the base of a rose plant? Usually it can be hoed from between the plants, but care should be taken not to expose any of the roots. Where plants are large and close together, it may be necessary to bring additional soil from some other part of the garden. This will have to be taken off again in the spring.

How high should the soil be hilled or mounded? As high as possible. Usually to a height of 6 ins. above the soil level.

How are newly set rose plants protected during the first winter? Mound soil over the plant, covering as much of the canes as possible. Later a straw mulch may be put on.

Is it necessary to hill up soil around hybrid tea roses? (Nebraska.) Yes, in your climate to a depth of 12 ins. Cover with 10-in. to 12-in. straw or hay mulch after ground freezes.

Will you give information on covering and uncovering roses? First tie the stems in with soft string, then hill up around the base as described above. When soil freezes, fill the hollows with manure if possible. Later on, if the situation is much exposed, place evergreen boughs among plants to help protect them from the fierce combination of bright sun and cold wind in March. When this period is past, remove the top cover during dull or showery weather. A few days later break down the mounds of soil to cover the manure.

Where a straw mulch is used, when is it put on? When freezing weather arrives. If put on too early, it encourages mice and other rodents, which chew the stems.

Should a straw mulch be put over the soil mound? A straw mulch is of little value in keeping the stems above the soil mound from being killed. In very cold climates, it does help to prevent loss of heat from the surface of the soil and thereby insures a higher temperature in the soil around the stems and roots.

Is it necessary to straw-mulch tea roses in the winter in Illinois and Indiana? A straw mulch alone affords little protection for tea roses. The right treatment in your section is to pile soil over the entire plant as recommended above for newly set roses.

When is the best time to uncover hybrid tea roses in the spring? Just as soon as danger of low temperature (20° F. or lower) is past; when frost is out of the ground and tulips and daffodils begin to come up.

When should the soil be leveled out? In the spring when the weather becomes settled.

WINTER PROTECTION OF TREE ROSES

How may tree roses be protected in cold climates? Lay them down on the ground and cover with soil.

How does one lay down a tree rose? Remove the stake, and, if the trunk cannot be bent down without danger of breaking, lift one side of the root-ball so that it will. Cover the top, trunk, and exposed roots with soil, and later mulch with straw.

Is wrapping with burlap sufficient protection for tree roses in New York State? Not unless the winter is very mild and the plants are in a very sheltered situation. The only safe way is to lay them down and cover as described above.

Why did my tree rose die—even though the buds had started to grow—when it was straightened up in the spring? The trunk may have been infected with the stem canker disease, or a portion may have been winter killed.

WINTER PROTECTION OF CLIMBING ROSES

What protection can be given climbing roses to keep them from freezing if too big to lay on the ground? Nothing can be done except to reduce the size of the plants by pruning so that they can be laid down.

What can be done to prevent climbing roses from freezing out during the winter months? (Illinois.) They must be laid down and covered with soil to protect them from low temperatures. Few climbing roses are winter hardy in Illinois (without careful protection). Lay the canes on the ground (growing them on a hinged trellis is an advantage). Cover canes with at least an inch or more of soil and then cover with branches. Uncover in spring before growth starts.

How should climbing roses be protected? When the temperature does not drop below 0° F., no protection is needed for the hardy varieties. Where temperatures between zero and 10° below may be experienced, mound soil over the base of the plants. In more severe climates remove the canes from their support and pin close to the ground. They may be covered lightly with straw, soil, or leaves, but if so, they must be protected from mice.

What can be done to prevent climbing roses, after being uncovered in spring, from dying back to within 2 to 3 ft. of the ground? Buds are on canes, yet canes die back. Canes were wrapped with marsh hay and waterproof paper. (Minnesota.) Such protection is insufficient. Pin canes close to ground and then cover each cane with 2 ins. of soil; lay branches on top. Uncover *gradually* in spring and before growth starts underneath cover. Lower parts of the canes are more resistant to low temperatures. Developing buds die because inner tissues of stems suffered winter injury.

PRUNING

Is it necessary to prune roses each year? Yes, if the best quality plants and flowers are to be obtained.

What happens if roses are not pruned? The plants become masses of brambles which are very unattractive. Disease and insect pests are encouraged. Flowers will be of inferior quality.

Should roses that were planted in the fall be pruned the following spring? Usually it is unnecessary if they were pruned (as they should be) before planting. Sometimes the tops will be killed back a little above the soil mound; if so, the dead portion should be removed.

Are all types of roses pruned at the same time and in the same manner? No. The different types or classes are pruned at different seasons because of variations in their habit of growth and flowering. While the basic principles involved in pruning all classes of roses are essentially the same, the details of the practice vary.

When is the best time to give the different classes or types of roses major pruning? Hybrid teas (monthly roses)—early spring; hybrid perpetuals (June roses)—early spring; polyanthas (Baby Ramblers)—early spring; floribundas (large-flowered polyanthas)—early spring; climbers—immediately after flowering; shrub roses—continuous blooming types—early spring; others immediately after flowering.

Should roses be pruned in the fall before winter protection is given?
If the plants are large and tall, it is often advisable to partially prune
them by cutting back the long canes. It prevents them from whipping
in the wind and makes it easier to hill and mulch the plants.

**How heavily shall I prune roses in fall that were set out in the
spring?** Hybrid teas may be cut back to 18 ins. above ground before mulching.

Should one cut off the new shoots that develop in the fall? If one
has the time and patience, it is a good thing to do, since the young
shoots are prevented from using up the stored food in the stem. From
a practical point of view it is questionable whether the practice
warrants the effort.

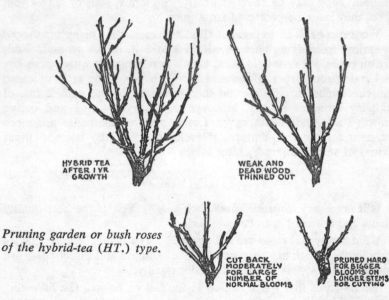

*Pruning garden or bush roses
of the hybrid-tea (HT.) type.*

Is it desirable to pinch out the tips of rosebushes? With shrub
roses it may be done to make a denser, more bushy plant. With
bedding types (hybrid teas, etc.) it tends to delay flowering, but
is sometimes practiced to encourage more continuous blooming.

**How should roses be pruned to produce more buds and longer
stems?** Experiments have shown that the less pruning the more
flowers will be produced. Contrary to the popular idea, pruning has
very little effect upon the length of rose stems. Proper soil preparation,
fertilization, and watering are much more important.

Does severe pruning cause more vigorous plants? No. On the
contrary, severe pruning, especially in climates where winter killing
occurs, tends to reduce vigor. Removing more healthy, vigorous wood

than is necessary only robs the plant of stored food. The stored food insures a vigorous plant with large, well-developed flowers.

How can you prevent roses from coming up between the branches with short stems (2 ins.)? Prune out all weak shoots in the spring.

How can you control the spreading shoots of roses? Cut them off.

When pruning roses, how far above a bud should the cut be made? About ¼ in.

Is it always necessary to make the cut where a bud points outward? It is not necessary, but it is desirable wherever practical. The branches will be better spaced, so that sunlight will strike all the leaves. The practice is thought to decrease disease, and it certainly produces a better-appearing plant.

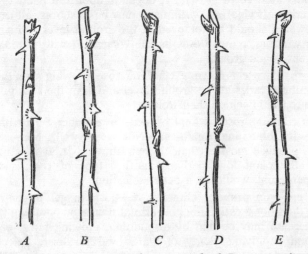

How to prune a rose. A – ragged cut, won't heal. B – cut too far above bud. C – cut too close to bud. D – cut too slanting, comes below bud. E – Right! Slight slant about ¼ inch above bud.

How can one prune roses without getting scratched by the thorns? Protect the hands by wearing heavy leather gloves of the gauntlet type.

Should roses be pruned with a knife, or pruning shears? A good pair of sharp pruning shears will greatly simplify the work and enable one to do a better job.

PRUNING CLIMBING ROSES

Are the large-flowered climbers pruned any differently from the ramblers? As a group the large-flowered climbers do not send up so many new basal shoots each year. For the most part, only the old flower clusters are removed, back to the first well-developed vegetative bud. This is usually where the first normal leaf joins the branch. As new shoots come from the base, the older canes should be cut out. (See illustration, page 506.)

Is it better to prune climbing roses in the fall or spring—or both? The best time is immediately after flowering. Occasionally a little pruning may be necessary in the spring to remove wood that has been winter killed.

How should an everblooming climbing rose be pruned? Very little real pruning is necessary. Merely remove the withered flower clusters back to the first well-developed shoot bud. When growth becomes too thick, cut out a few of the old main canes at the ground.

Should all old wood be pruned out of climbing roses, and just the new shoots allowed to grow? It depends upon the habit of growth of the variety. If vigorous, with many new basal shoots, all canes that have flowered should be removed at the ground level. With weaker-growing varieties, remove only as many canes as will be replaced by the current year's growth.

How shall we cut down a climbing rose growing over an arch? Cut off all old canes at the ground level and save the new ones from the base to train back on their trellises.

Can a climbing rose be kept pruned down under 5 ft. without destroying its blooming qualities? Not very well, because many climbers produce most of their flowers above 3 ft. If it is necessary to keep the plant low, perhaps another type of rose, such as a hybrid perpetual, would be a better selection.

How can you prune a climbing rosebush to get larger blooms? Pruning does not greatly affect the size of flower on climbing varieties. Some increase may be had by disbudding, growing fewer canes per plant, and supplying plenty of water and fertilizer. Select large-flowering varieties.

Should I prune out all branches that have leaves with 7 leaflets because they are throwbacks to the original stock? Definitely no. Practically all climbing roses have 7 leaflets. They often vary from 5 to 9 on the same shoot.

How should an American Beauty climbing rose be pruned? This variety is moderately vigorous; several new shoots come from the base each year. When the plant is as large as desired, remove the older canes to the ground as new shoots come up to replace them.

Should the climbing rose Blaze be pruned? Blaze tends to flower a second time during the summer. Only the withered flowers and seed pods should be cut off. As new shoots grow from the base, the oldest canes may be cut off at the soil level.

How should a Climbing Cecile Brunner be pruned? Each summer, after the blooming period is past, cut out the oldest canes if new shoots are developing from the base to replace them. Otherwise, remove only the withered flower clusters.

Why would a Dr. Van Fleet die after pruning in the fall? Pruning would not kill a climbing rose plant. Its death must have been caused by some other factor, possibly winter killing.

How should one prune Golden Climber (Mrs. Arthur Curtiss James) to make it flower more freely? This is naturally a shy bloomer in most situations. Train the canes horizontally so that more blooming shoots will be produced. Remove only the dead flowers. When it becomes too thick and tangled, cut off some of the fine, whiskery shoots which it often produces.

How many clusters of flowers can be expected on a Paul's Scarlet Climber the summer following planting? Probably not more than 3 or 4 on each cane, because they are usually pruned back before shipping.

How does one prune a Climbing President Hoover? As with other climbing hybrid tea varieties, keep old flowers removed. When the plant becomes too thick, take out a few of the oldest canes at the soil surface.

How do you prune a Silver Moon Rose? This variety is an extremely rank grower. It must be pruned at least once a year, and sometimes oftener, in order to keep it under control. Cut out canes that have flowered. Remove as many of the new slender side shoots as are necessary to maintain neat growth.

How should my Climbing Souv. de Claudius Pernet, which doesn't bloom more than once a year, be pruned? Climbing sports of hybrid teas seldom bloom as continuously as the original varieties. Keep withered flowers and seed pods picked off and prune only as necessary to prevent growth from becoming too thick.

Should Climbing Talisman and Flame be pruned back to 6 ins. from the ground every year? No. As much vigorous wood as possible should be left on Climbing Talisman. With Flame, remove only the shoots that have flowered, cutting them off at the surface of the soil after blooming. Pruning this variety back to 6 ins. will prevent it from flowering.

How and when should I prune the climbing rose Tausendschon, commonly called Thousand Beauty Thornless? Prune back to ground all old canes after it has ceased blooming. Keep the best of the new canes for following year's flowers.

PRUNING RAMBLERS

When, and how often, are rambler roses pruned? The main pruning is done each year immediately after flowering. Sometimes it is necessary to cut out in the spring wood that was killed during the winter.

How do you prune vigorous ramblers that send up many new canes from the base each year? Cut off at the ground level all canes that have produced a crop of flowers.

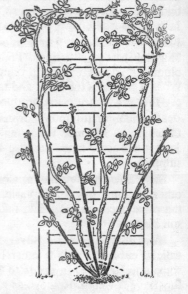

Climbing roses of the rambler type, which flower on new wood of the current season's growth, are pruned, just after flowering, by cutting old canes back to the ground (as indicated by dotted lines in sketch), thus leaving room for the husky new canes.

How many of the new canes should be left on a rambler rose? From 5 to 12.

What pruning is done to ramblers if no shoots grow from the base? Only the withered flower clusters, and any weak growths, are removed.

How and when can an overgrown rambler be pruned? Immediately after flowering cut out at the surface of the ground all but the new vigorous shoots that arise from the base of the plant. These may be trained as desired. Each year remove the old canes that have flowered, and save the new canes.

How can we get a Dorothy Perkins that has not been pruned for years back into condition? After it has completed flowering, cut out at the ground level all old canes. Leave only new canes that are growing from the base.

PRUNING FLORIBUNDAS AND HUGONIS

How are the large-flowered polyantha (floribunda) varieties pruned? This type is pruned in the same manner as hybrid teas and polyanthas.

Is it possible to transplant a large Rosa hugonis (7 ft.) without pruning it? Even if the plant is moved with a large ball of soil and well watered after planting, some pruning will have to be done. Remove about ⅓ of the canes; head the remainder back to 5 ft. Move in the fall.

How and when should Austrian Copper and Hugonis roses be pruned?   Austrian Copper and Hugonis should require little or no trimming except to remove very old or dead wood. If they get too large and coarse, they may be cut back to the ground immediately after flowering. Fall or early spring is the proper time for ordinary pruning.

PRUNING HYBRID PERPETUALS

How are hybrid perpetuals pruned?   In early spring cut out all dead, weak, or injured wood and leave 4 to 8 well-spaced, vigorous canes on each plant. Where plants have not suffered any winter injury, the strong canes should be cut back to about 2 ft. above the ground.

Should June roses that are 6 or 7 ft. tall be cut back?   Unless they are attractive at this height, cut them back in the early spring. (See previous question.) Take out all weak shoots to the ground level and cut back strong canes to the desired height (2 to 4 ft.).

To what height should hybrid perpetual roses, that grow 6 to 7 ft. tall, be cut back?   Two to 3 ft. is a good height.

Are hybrid perpetuals ever cut back during the summer?   Ordinarily, only when their growth needs to be restricted for the sake of the appearance of the plant.

Should roses such as Frau Karl Druschki and Else Poulson be pruned like everblooming roses?   Frau Karl Druschki belongs to the hybrid perpetual class. (See preceding questions.) Else Poulson is a large-flowered polyantha or floribunda and should be pruned in the same manner as other varieties of that class.

PRUNING HYBRID TEAS

How close to the ground should hybrid tea or other bedding roses be pruned?   The exact height above the ground is not important. In cold climates, where plants suffer from winter killing, leave as much of the vigorous, healthy wood as possible. Usually all wood above 4 to 8 ins. from the ground is killed, and must be removed. Where there is little winter injury, the canes are cut back to 12 or 18 ins. to develop uniform and free-flowering plants.

What type of pruning can be done to encourage more continuous bloom in hybrid tea varieties?   Pinching out the tips of a few shoots on each plant will force them to send out new branches. While a few of the first crop of flowers is sacrificed, these new shoots will bloom later and in between the main crops of flowers.

Is it advisable to prune hybrid tea roses after the first bloom in

June? Pruning in the true sense of the word is unnecessary and undesirable at this time. However, withered flowers should be removed.

How should hybrid tea roses be pruned in climates where the canes are killed back in winter? As early in the spring as possible remove all dead, weak, or injured wood. Cut back the strong, vigorous canes to just below where injury is evident.

How much should hybrid teas be cut back in mild climates where there is little or no winter injury? All dead, weak, or unhealthy wood should be cut out. Strong canes should be cut back no farther than necessary to produce an attractive plant. Eighteen ins. above ground is about right to insure vigorous, productive plants.

How much of the stem should be removed when old flowers and seed heads are cut from hybrid teas and other everblooming roses? Cut off the withered flowers and seed heads just above the uppermost 5-leaflet leaf, or where a plump, well-developed bud appears in the leaf axil.

PRUNING OLD-FASHIONED, POLYANTHA, AND SHRUB ROSES

How are moss roses pruned? Cut out a few of the oldest canes each spring; shorten the tops of the remainder.

Should old-fashioned roses like Rosa centifolia be pruned? Keep plants rejuvenated by removing a few of the very old canes to the base of plant; shorten back the long canes.

How are polyantha or baby-rambler roses pruned? Essentially the same as hybrid teas, but less severely. In cold climates, where winter injury is severe, remove in the early spring only the dead, weak, or injured wood. If not injured during the winter, trim back the strong canes to 12 to 18 ins. above ground.

Should new long shoots on the Cecile Brunner variety be trimmed back? Ordinarily Cecile Brunner does not produce long shoots. The variety is a hybrid or large-flowered polyantha and the shoots always terminate in a cluster of flowers. It is probable that the long shoots are suckers from the understock and should be cut off *below* surface of the soil.

When is the best time to prune rugosa roses? Rugosas bloom more or less continuously during the summer and are therefore pruned to the best advantage in the early spring.

What is the correct way to trim rugosa roses planted on a bank? It is important to keep plants rejuvenated and to prevent them from becoming "leggy." Each spring remove a few of the oldest canes to the ground level. Thin tops by cutting out some of the branches.

How can one make a hedge 4 to 5 ft. high of the rugosa variety

F. J. Grootendorst? The bushes are 2 ft. apart. Prune back to the ground level each spring several of the older canes of each plant. Cut new canes at the desired height, if they grow too tall. Keep plants well fertilized.

How should shrub roses be pruned? A few of the older canes should be cut back to the ground each spring to encourage the growth of basal shoots. This helps rejuvenate the plants. If growth becomes thick, remove some of the upper branches to thin out the plant.

How can the shrub and old-fashioned roses be pruned so that foliage will be produced on the lower part of the plants? Cut off the top of young shoots when they are about 18 ins. tall, thus forcing the canes to branch. Cut a few of the outside canes back to 2 or 3 ft. in spring.

PRUNING TREE ROSES

Just how are tree roses pruned? Remove all weak or dead wood from the top, and cut back the main canes to about 6 or 8 ins. from the crown. Take off all suckers that start to develop on the trunk, or from the base.

To what extent can tree roses be pruned? The top of a tree rose is pruned as though it were on the ground instead of on the tall trunk or stem.

PROPAGATION

What different methods can be used to propagate roses? Rose varieties may be propagated by budding, grafting, cuttings, and layering.

Are own-root rose plants propagated at home as satisfactory as budded stock? They are much slower in getting started, but will usually develop into equally good plants. Some gardeners consider them longer-lived and more productive.

What is the "union" of a rose plant? The place where the bud of the desired variety was inserted on the understock in the propagation of the plant. It can usually be seen as a jointlike swollen area 2 or 3 ins. above the roots. It is just below the region from which all main branches of the plant arise.

BUDDING

Are roses propagated by budding, or grafting? Most outdoor roses are budded.

What is meant by budding? Budding is a method of vegetative propagation. It means to graft by inserting a bud of one variety into the bark of another. (See Section II—Budding and Grafting.)

Why are outdoor roses budded instead of grafted? It is the simpler method for large-scale production and requires less greenhouse space and equipment.

What is the best time to bud roses? Usually in July and early August, but it can be done at any time when the bark slips readily.

How do you bud roses? Grow or procure an understock of *Rosa multiflora* or some similar species. Make a T-shaped slit in the bark just at the ground level. From the stem of the desired variety cut out a well-developed bud with the petiole of the leaf attached. Pick out the wood attached to the bark. Open the slit on the understock and insert the bud so that the bark fits close to the wood of the understock. Wrap firmly with raffia or soft twine, but be careful not to injure the shoot bud. After 3 or 4 weeks remove the binding.

Should an amateur gardener try to bud roses? Yes. It is fun to do. Do not be discouraged if unsuccessful at the first attempt. Do not try to produce all your own roses in this way at first. Try budding as an experiment.

CUTTINGS

Can roses be grown from cuttings or slips? Yes.

When is the best time to root rose cuttings? Rose stems will root best about the time the petals fall.

Where can one find the best cuttings on a rosebush? The flower stems make the best cuttings.

How long should a rose cutting be? Four to 5 ins. is the right length. It should contain 3 nodes.

Will a slip from a grafted plant be like the variety or the understock? It will be the same as the variety.

Will all varieties of roses root readily? The hybrid teas, polyanthas, floribundas, and most of the climbers will root easily. Hybrid perpetuals and many of the shrub and species roses do not root so well.

Should the leaves be removed from rose cuttings? Leaves that will be below the surface of the rooting medium (usually sand) in which the cuttings are placed should be removed; others should be left on.

Should the blossom be left on a rose cutting? Never. The middle and lower part of the stem make better cuttings.

What is the best material for rooting rose cuttings? Clean, sharp, medium coarse sand or a mixture of sand and peatmoss.

What conditions are necessary for rooting rose cuttings? Keep the rooting medium moist. Shade during first few days with newspaper or cheesecloth. Take out any cuttings that appear to be rotting, and any leaves that fall off.

Are root-growth substances helpful in rooting roses?   Yes. They usually cause cuttings to root more quickly and to produce a better root system.

Can rose cuttings be rooted in soil under a glass jar?   Yes, if only a few plants are needed.

What special precautions need to be taken in rooting cuttings under a fruit jar?   Select a place where the jar is shaded during the hot part of the day. Keep soil moist at all times. Do not put more than 3 cuttings under a single jar.

How long before cuttings rooted under a jar can be moved?   If the cuttings are taken early in the summer, they are usually large enough to move by fall. They will need to be protected by mounding soil over them.

How does one go about removing the glass jar?   Don't let too much growth develop before removing it. Select a cloudy day. Remove the jar. If the sun comes out, shade the cuttings with newspaper for a few days.

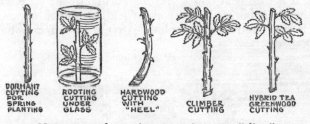

DORMANT CUTTING FOR SPRING PLANTING   ROOTING CUTTING UNDER GLASS   HARDWOOD CUTTING WITH "HEEL"   CLIMBER CUTTING   HYBRID TEA GREENWOOD CUTTING

New rose plants from cuttings or "slips."

Can cuttings be rooted in a cold frame?   Yes. The soil should be removed and clean, sharp, medium coarse sand put in to a depth of 4 ins. or so. It may be necessary to keep the cuttings shaded with cheesecloth.

Can seed flats filled with sand be used for rooting rose cuttings?   Yes, but they must be watched very carefully to make sure the sand doesn't dry out.

Will spring rose cuttings withstand the winter if left in the garden?   Yes, if completely covered with soil and if they are in a place where the drainage is good.

How should rose cuttings rooted during the winter be cared for?   Plant out of doors in the early spring in good soil. Keep them well watered.

Where should one transplant rose slips (cuttings) after they are rooted? They may be planted in their permanent location, or in a nursery bed or cold frame.

How long before a cutting from a climbing rose will bloom? Ordinarily some flowers can be expected the second year after the cutting was rooted.

Can a new shoot which has come up about a foot from the original plant of variety Blaze be moved? If possible, this shoot should be allowed to bloom before it is transplanted to make certain it is the same variety and not a sucker from the understock. Cut the root connection between it and the main plant the spring before it is moved. It will then develop a good root system of its own and will transplant easily.

GRAFTING

What does grafting mean? Grafting is a method of vegetative propagation by which a piece of the stem of the variety is made to grow on another plant. (See Section III—Grafting.)

LAYERING

How are roses layered? A branch is cut a little more than halfway through. It is then bent down, and the portion of the stem where the cut was made is buried in the soil. When the branch appears to be rooted, it is severed from the plant. After a year it may be moved where desired.

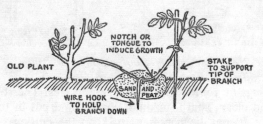

Propagating a rose by layering. New plants of many climbers can readily be obtained by this method.

SEEDS

Do roses come true from seed? Only wild species. Named varieties are hybrid plants, and every seedling will be different.

How may roses be made to set seeds? Some varieties are comparatively sterile and will set little or no seed. Try putting pollen from other varieties on the stigmas.

How does one germinate rose seed? Place the seed in small, un-stoppered bottles in moist peatmoss and store in a refrigerator for 3 months at 41° F. Plant seeds in soil containing ⅓ peatmoss, ⅓ sand, and ⅓ soil. Keep moist and at a temperature of about 68° F. Sometimes seed planted in a protected cold frame in the fall will germinate the following spring and summer.

HYBRIDIZING

How do you "cross" roses? While the flower is still in the bud stage carefully remove all stamens before the pollen is shed. Cover emasculated flower with a cellophane or paper bag. When stigmas have developed, place some pollen of the plant selected for the male parent on them. It is desirable to repeat the pollination on several successive days. Remove the paper bag when the seed pod starts to develop.

UNDERSTOCKS

What is meant by a rose understock? Garden roses are not grown on their own roots but are budded on the stem of a wild rose grown for the purpose. The stem, upon which the rose is budded or grafted, is called the understock. (See Budding and Grafting.)

How can one propagate his own understocks? Make hardwood cuttings 6 to 8 ins. long of smooth 1-year-old shoots of *Rosa multiflora* or other species. Remove the 2 lower eyes to prevent suckering. Callus in moist peatmoss or sand at 45° F. Plant out of doors in the early spring, or root inside and plant out later. Bud during July or early August.

Where may understocks be obtained? Few rose growers offer them except in large quantities. Try rose-growing concerns.

What understocks are used for tree roses? *Rosa rugosa, Rosa canina,* and occasionally *Rosa multiflora.*

PESTS AND DISEASES

What are the main pests, insects, and diseases that trouble roses? See Section VIII—Insects and Diseases.

What are the most common and harmful diseases of roses? What treatment should be used? How often? If a regular spray program is adhered to in the treatment of roses, using Triogen or some similar all-purpose spray, pests and diseases will be kept under control. Aphids, plant lice, leaf hoppers, rose bugs, Japanese beetles, leaf rollers, etc., attack roses, while black spot and mildew are the most destructive diseases.

How can mice be controlled in the rose garden? Poisoned grain should be placed under the mulch, at frequent intervals, in small open containers that protect it from becoming wet. A jelly tumbler laid on its side and covered by a piece of board serves the purpose.

BLACK SPOT   MILDEW   COMMON CANKER   OLD BARK WOUND   BROWN CANKER

Some common diseases of roses.

What causes roses to bloom one-sided?   Usually insect injury from aphids, rose slugs, thrips, or weevil, which see.

I read an article on roses which said they should be sprayed with a 4–4–50 Bordeaux mixture. What is that?   Four lbs. of copper sulfate, 4 lbs. of lime, 50 gals. of water. The copper sulfate and the lime should be dissolved separately in a small amount of water, and then added to the rest of the water.

Does spraying give better control of rose pests than dusting? Either method will give good control if a regular control program is adhered to. With either method it is most important to cover the undersides of leaves.

Why does my baby-rambler rose fail to bloom? I have never been able to clean the plant of mildew. As soon as the clusters form they wither and die.   Start spraying early in the season, or dust with fine dusting sulfur. (See Mildew.)

TYPES AND VARIETIES

AUSTRIAN BRIAR

Are Austrian Briars old-fashioned roses?   Yes. They are hardy and bright-colored; some are shrub types, some climbers. Some varieties are Austrian Copper, single; Austrian Yellow; Parkfeuer, single scarlet.

BLACK ROSE

Is the so-called "Black Rose" really black? Where did it originate? There are several roses for which claims have been made for their black color. Among these are: Zulu Queen, Matador, and Nigrette. The color is not black but dark red to dark maroon.

CABBAGE

Can you give me any information about the Cabbage Rose. Is it suitable for the garden?   The Cabbage Rose (*Rosa centifolia*) is one of the oldest roses to be cultivated. It is an excellent garden plant, being fragrant, hardy and producing quantities of bloom during June.

CLIMBING

What is the difference between a rambler and a large-flowered climber? Any tall-growing rose that requires the support of an arbor, trellis, or similar structure, or can be trained to one, may be classed as a climbing rose. A rambler is one type of climber and is distinguished by its very long, slender canes and dense clusters of small flowers. The variety Dorothy Perkins is a good example of the rambler type.

Are there everblooming climbing roses? For the milder climates, the climbing forms of hybrid teas and polyantha varieties are satisfactory. They are not hardy enough, however, for general use in regions colder than Virginia. For the North, a number of hardy, everblooming Large-flowered Climbers have been recently introduced. Dream Girl, Inspiration, Temptation, Golden Showers, Parade and Coral Dawn are among those which produce flowers every month during the growing season.

What Large-flowered Climbers are especially hardy? All of the standard varieties have similar degrees of cold resistance. See previous question for recommended varieties.

What are some of the best ramblers? Chevy Chase, rose-red; American Pillar, single pink, white center; Hiawatha, crimson, white eye; Minnie Dawson, pure white; Ghislaine de Feligonde, yellow buds, creamy flowers; Dorothy Perkins, pink.

What climbing roses are best to plant on a steep bank with Hall's Honeysuckle? Almost any of the ramblers, such as Dorothy Perkins, Evangeline, Hiawatha, and Minnehaha are satisfactory in such a situation. Coral Creeper, Creeping Everbloom, Little Compton Creeper are large-flowered varieties for such use.

What is the red climbing rose, somewhat like Paul's Scarlet Climber, that blooms in the fall? The variety Blaze.

Are the climbing forms of World's Fair, Pinocchio and Summer Snow really everblooming? None of the climbing sports of dwarf varieties seems to bloom as freely as the original varieties. These 3, however, produce flowers more or less continually through the summer, although never in the quantity they do in June.

What climbing roses are recommended for northern Vermont? Any of the hardier varieties are satisfactory if properly protected by removing the canes from their support and pinning them close to the ground for the winter. Dorothy Perkins, Chevy Chase, American Pillar, New Dawn, Mary Wallace, and Purity should be tried with the suggested method of protection.

What climbing rose would be best for the arch on my garden gate? **(Kansas.)**   Blaze, red; Inspiration, pink; Summer Snow, white; Dream Girl, salmon-pink.

DAMASK

Can you give me some information on the Damask Rose?   The Damask Rose (*Rosa damascena*) is native to southeastern Europe, where it is used for making the celebrated attar of roses. It is one of the oldest roses in cultivation and is second only to the Cabbage Rose in the strength of its perfume. It makes a good garden shrub which is hardy. The real *Rosa damascena* has double rose-pink flowers. There are also many varieties, such as Damas officinalis, Kazanlik, and Marie Louise.

How tall does the rose of Damascus (Rosa damascena) grow, and is it hardy?   The Damask Rose is one of the hardiest species. It grows to a height of about 5 ft.

FLORIBUNDA

What are floribunda roses?   Technically they are hybrid or large-flowered polyanthas. They originated through hybridizing polyanthas with hybrid teas. The flowers are larger than those of the polyantha group, but in growth and flowering habit are much like them.

What are some good Floribunda Roses?   Anne Poulsen, scarlet-crimson; Poulsen's Bedder, pink; Gruss an Aachen, soft salmon-pink; Golden Fleece; Gold Cup; Spartan, orange-coral; White Bouquet; Glacier; Corcorico, and Frencham, red; Fashion, salmon; Vogue, cherry-coral; Betsy McCall, pink.

FRENCH

Will you please name some French old-fashioned roses?   Cardinal de Richelieu, dark purplish-red; Duc de Valny, large, double red to rose pink; *Rosa gallica,* large single, dark pink; *Rosa mundi,* semi-double, white to pale pink, striped red (also incorrectly called York-and-Lancaster).

GRANDIFLORA

What are Grandiflora Roses? Please name a few.   A new class of very large flowered Floribundas. Outstanding varieties are Queen Elizabeth, rose-pink; and Buccaneer, yellow.

GREEN ROSE

I have been told that there is a rose called the Green Rose. What is it like?   The Green Rose (*Rosa chinensis viridiflora*) has been cultivated for a long time. The petals are just narrow green leaves. The flower is very disappointing and not attractive. Sometimes used in flower arrangement before the buds open, as the foliage has a tint of bronze.

Is the Green Rose a climber? No. It belongs to the group of China roses. Aside from its interest as a curiosity, it is of no garden value.

HYBRID PERPETUAL

How do hybrid perpetuals differ from hybrid teas? The hybrid perpetuals were the progenitors of the hybrid teas and in their heyday ranked first in popularity. They have a decided Victorian quality in the largeness, fullness, and boldness of their blooms, but lack the refinement in form of the hybrid teas. The colors include purest white, deepest crimson, and the innumerable hues linking these two extremes. The plants are vigorous, rather coarse, and quite hardy. Most varieties bloom but twice during the season.

What are a few of the best hybrid perpetual varieties? Frau Karl Druschki, white; Henry Nevard, velvety scarlet; J. B. Clark, red; Mme. Albert Barbier, clear salmon-pink, almost yellow; Mrs. John Laing, clear pink; General Jacqueminot, crimson.

HYBRID TEA

What are hybrid tea roses? As a class they are moderately vigorous and with protection sufficiently hardy. Their chief merit is their frequency of bloom, a character that has given them the common name "monthly roses." In the variety, richness, and delicacy of their coloring, and in their perfection of form and pleasing fragrance, they are unequaled by any other type.

What is the difference between hybrid tea and a monthly rose? They are one and the same thing.

What are some of the best of the newer hybrid teas? Chrysler Imperial, President Eisenhower, Konrad Adenhauer, red; Confidence, Show Girl, Linda Porter, Helen Traubel, pink; White Swan, Sleigh Bells, white; Mojave, orange-red; Chief Seattle, apricot-buff.

What are some of the leading older pink hybrid teas? Betty Uprichard, Dame Edith Helen, Margaret McGredy, Miss Rowena Thom, Mrs. Henry Bowles, Radiance.

What are a few good red hybrid teas? Ami Quinard, Charles K. Douglas, Etoile de Hollande, Red Radiance, Heart's Desire. See previous question.

What are some of the most popular yellow hybrid teas? Golden Scepter, Golden Masterpiece, Lowell Thomas, Peace.

What white hybrid teas are satisfactory? Kaiserin Auguste Viktoria, McGredy's Ivory, Mme. Jules Bouche, Neige Parfume, Pedralbes, White Swan, Rex Anderson, Sleigh Bells.

What are a few of the best bicolor or two-toned hybrid tea varieties?

Pageant, coral-rose and gold; Forty-niner, crimson and creamy yellow; Huntsman, red and orange-yellow; Contesa de Sastago, copper and gold.

What single varieties of hybrid teas are worth while?   Cecil, pale yellow; Dainty Bess, ruffled soft pink; Innocence, white; Isobel, flaming orange-pink, Irish Fireflame, buff, flame; Lulu, salmon; Vesuvius, crimson.

Are the new varieties of hybrid teas as hardy and strong as the older ones?   With a few exceptions, yes. In fact, there is evidence that in general the new varieties are somewhat more hardy than those introduced 20 years ago. Old varieties grown today are a rather select group that have stood the test of time. It is likely that a larger percentage of the newer ones will stand the test, and of course it is quite probable that varieties much hardier than any we have today will be produced.

Are roses which win All America Rose Awards sure to give good results?   No rose can be guaranteed to do well in any one individual garden. Roses honored by the A.A.R. Selections Committee have been tested in special test gardens in many parts of the United States. Their behavior, disease-resistance, bloom quantity and quality, foliage, etc. have been closely observed and on this basis they have received enough points for excellence from qualified judges to merit an award. Therefore they should give good results and will do so unless climate, soil or some other local condition is unfavorable; or unless they are poorly handled by their owner.

What types of roses do you recommend for the rank amateur? Hybrid Teas; Floribundas; Large-flowered Climbers; Shrub Roses.

I know nothing about hybrid tea roses, but wish to have a rose garden. What are the best varieties to purchase, as a beginner? (Nebraska.)   The best roses for you are shrub types like *Rosa rugosa* and its hybrids; Harison's Yellow; Rosa hugonis; Belinda; Fruehling's Gold and the roses produced by Dr. Hansen of Brookings, South Dakota (Alika, red; Lillian Gibson, pink; Sioux City, red). If you live farther south, try the following Hybrid Teas, giving heavy winter protection. Red: Crimson Glory, Christopher Stone; Pink: Pink Radiance, Mme. Butterfly, Numa Fay; Yellow: Eclipse, Peace; bicolor: Pres. Herbert Hoover, Countess Vandal, Condesa de Sastago.

I have only a few hours a week to spend in my garden, but I want some roses. Can I grow hybrid teas?   Why not? Get a few of the well-established varieties. Only plant what you can conveniently take care of. Or if you prefer less work, plant only iron-hardy, disease-resistant Shrub Roses like Mabelle Stearns, The Fairy, Flamingo, Lipstick, etc.

MINIATURE

What are "Fairy Roses"?   "Fairy Roses" is another name for the miniature roses which are forms of *Rosa chinensis minima.*

What are miniature roses?   They are very tiny forms of *Rosa chinensis* var. *minima,* or hybrids between this and other species and varieties. The plants are seldom more than 6 to 9 ins. tall, with the flowers proportionately small.

Are there many varieties of miniature roses?   Yes, quite a large number. Some of the best are: Tom Thumb, Red Imp, Oakington Ruby, Dwarfking, red; Tinker Bell, Bo Peep, Rouletti, Sweet Fairy, Cutie, pink; Pixie, Twinkles, white; Baby Masquerade, bicolor; Baby Gold Star.

MOSS

What are moss roses?   A type of the Cabbage Rose, *Rosa centi folia.* The bud of the flower is enclosed in a mossy envelope. Much of the great fragrance comes from the mossy glands. Moss roses are very old, having been in cultivation for centuries. Many kinds are still to be had from nurseries. Among them are Crested Moss (found on a convent wall in Switzerland in 1827), Blanche Moreau, Comtesse Doria, Eugene Verdier.

Is there a reliable old-fashioned moss rose?   The variety Communis, sometimes called Old Pink Moss or Common Moss, is one of the best. Others are Capitaine John Ingram, dark red, and La Neige, pure white.

PILLAR

What is a pillar rose?   The term "pillar" refers more to a method of support than to an actual type of rose. Varieties adapted to a post or pillar are called pillar roses. Certain climbing varieties that do not develop excessively long canes (such as Paul Scarlet climber) are classed as pillar roses. Some of the tall-growing hybrid perpetual varieties which lend themselves to being supported by posts are included in this group.

POLYANTHA

What are polyantha roses?   The term "polyantha" (meaning many flowers) well describes the class. The plants are dwarf, and give a continuous profusion of small flowers in large clusters. They are especially hardy, but less adapted for cutting than other types. For garden display they are unequaled. They were formerly called "baby ramblers" because the flower clusters were similar to those produced by the older varieties of ramblers.

What varieties of polyanthas are worth while?   Cameo, salmon; Katharina Zeimet, white; Mlle. Cecile Brunner, light pink; Chatillon

Rose, vivid pink; Ellen Poulsen, soft rose-pink; Gloria Mundi, orange-scarlet; George Elger, yellow; Ideal, red; Marie Pavic, blush (fragrant); Triomphe Orleanais, crimson.

RUGOSA

Will you tell me something about Rugosa Roses? This hardy species and its many fine hybrids are among the toughest and most long-lived of all roses. They are suitable for planting at the seashore where they make themselves thoroughly at home; in the very cold sections of the West where few roses can survive; and as large shrubs or hedges anywhere that there is room for them. The species is deep rose or white. For some of the best hybrids, see the second question under Shrub Roses.

SCOTCH

What are Scotch roses? A strain of old-fashioned roses with fine foliage and spiny growth. Hardy, disease resistant. Can be planted with shrubs or as specimens. Harison's Yellow, 6 to 8 ft., is semi-double; Stanwell Perpetual, pink, constant bloomer. Scotch roses are varieties or hybrids of *Rosa spinosissima*.

SHRUB

What are shrub roses? They are shrubs of varying heights and dimensions and in the garden are used as any flowering shrub. As a group they contain many beautiful plants, usually blooming in early summer. Some, such as *Rosa rugosa*, have stiff prickles and are used as barriers. Others, such as *Rosa hugonis*, for their beauty of bloom. The group is a large one, embracing many species and varieties, most of which are perfectly hardy.

Would you please give a list of some good shrub roses with their colors? *Rosa hugonis*, pale yellow; Harison's Yellow, golden yellow; *Rosa rugosa*, red, pink or white: (Agnes, yellow; Conrad Ferdinand Meyer, pink, and Mme. Plantier, white; Sanguinaire, red; F. J. Grootendorst, red; Pink Grootendorst;) *Rosa spinosissima, white, R. spinosissima fulgens*, pink; Stanwell Perpetual, pink.

SPECIES

What are species roses? Please name some. The species are the wild roses from which cultivated types have been bred. Some of those most suitable for the garden are *Rosa alba* or York Rose, white, semi-double; *Rosa hugonis*, yellow, early, 6 to 8 ft.; *Rosa setigera*, (Prairie Rose) large, single, pink, 6 to 8 ft.; *Rosa multiflora* (Thunberg), small white flowers in large trusses, red hips which attract birds, *Rosa rugosa*, red or white single. Others are *Rosa centifolia, Rosa chinensis, Rosa foetida, Rosa gallica, Rosa spinosissima, Rosa damascena*.

SWEETBRIER HYBRIDS

What are the hybrid sweetbriers?   They are hybrids of *Rosa rubiginosa*, or Eglantine, having scented foliage, single or semi-double flowers on arching canes, and are strong growers. Lady Penzance, copper; Lord Penzance, fawn colored; Eglanteria (*R. rubiginosa*) pink, small clusters.

TEA

Why are varieties of roses called "tea roses"?   The term refers to the true tea roses. They are not widely grown in American gardens, especially in the North. The flower odor is suggestive of the odor of fresh tea leaves. Harry Kirk, Lady Hillington, Maman Cochet and Bon Silene are members of this tea rose group. They are remontant (repeat bloomers), with well-formed, high centered buds and fine flowers but are tender.

Where did the "tea" in tea rose originate?   Varieties allied to a Chinese species, *Rosa odorata*, are called tea roses. The odor of the flowers was thought to smell like fresh green tea leaves (not the beverage). At one time this species was called *Rosa thea*.

What is the difference between the tea rose and a hybrid tea? The hybrid tea rose is descended from the tea, the tea being one of the parents of the hybrid tea. In appearance the tea and hybrid tea look alike, but the hybrid tea is more vigorous and hardy, and has a wider adaptation. The true tea rose is seldom grown except in the South.

TREE ROSE

What is a tree (standard) rose?   Instead of the bud being inserted close to the ground (as is done in propagating other types), tree roses are budded near the top of a tall understock cane. The plant that develops from the bud is therefore on a trunk or standard.

What is the difference between a standard and a tree rose?   They are the same thing.

Can tree roses be grown in cold climates?   They are difficult to grow in cold regions because they are hard to winter. In regions where the temperature does not drop below 10° F. they are usually satisfactory.

SECTION III-D

Perennials

What is a hardy herbaceous perennial? A plant which lives for several years, whose tops die in winter, but are renewed, from the same roots, each spring.

What is the average age of perennial plants sold by leading nurseries? About 1 to 2 years old.

WHAT TO GROW

Can you suggest a selection of 24 perennials of easy culture, for succession of bloom? Spring: lily-of-the-valley, forget-me-not, coralbell, violet, bleedingheart (tall and dwarf), dwarf iris, mertensia, *Phlox divaricata*, ajuga. Summer: *Campanula carpatica, C. carpatica alba, C. lactiflora*, and *C. persicifolia;* astilbe, coreopsis, eupatorium, gaillardia, hemerocallis, bearded iris (tall), rosemallow, plantainlily, platycodon, hollyhock. Late summer and fall: plumbago, rudbeckia, chrysanthemum, hardy aster, helenium.

What are some of the more colorful perennials? Balloonflower, Carpathian bellflower, chrysanthemum, columbine, coreopsis, dianthus, *Erigeron speciosus*, gaillardia, perennial flax, rudbeckia. *Heliopsis scabra incomparabilis.*

What bright-colored perennials can I use on the north side of my red brick house, to make an attractive rear terrace? Aquilegia hybrids, *Anchusa myosotidiflora, Monarda fistulosa, Anemone hupehensis* and *A. magellanica, Dianthus deltoides* and *D. arenarius, Phlox subulata* varieties, *Plumbago larpentiae, Veronica incana.*

Can you list a few perennials that will bloom well with little or no care, and that will not look unkempt before and after blooming? Any variety of hosta (funkia), any of the numerous hemerocallis, peonies, phlox, *Eupatorium rugosum, Aster novae-angliae,* ajuga, artemisia, baptisia, thermopsis, coreopsis, echinops, *Iris sibirica, Rudbeckia speciosa, Sedum spectabile.*

Will you give the names of the most suitable and inexpensive perennials for one quite busy on a farm? *Silene maritima, Dictamnus* *fraxinella, Linum perenne, Papaver orientale* varieties, peonies, dianthus, Physostegia Vivid, *Platycodon grandiflorum,* heliopsis; gaillardia, coreopsis, *Helenium autumnale.* New varieties of these will cost more than the old established ones. The price, too, will vary with the nursery.

What would be an interesting layout for a perennial bed that is backed with shrubbery? First set out groups of delphiniums—3 or 4 to a group—spaced at irregular intervals over the bed 8 to 12 ft. apart, depending upon size of bed. Then set out hollyhocks in same manner—2 to 3 plants in each group. Intersperse in the same way varieties of summer phlox, then various hardy asters. This will give distribution of bloom. If spaces are left, fill in with Oriental Poppy, achillea, aconitum, *Anemone japonica, Campanula persicifolia,* cushion chrysanthemums, dianthus species and varieties, gaillardia, Gypsophila Bristol Fairy, heleniums, heliopsis. These will lend support to the 4 main kinds at different parts of the season. The principle is to weave the pattern back and forth across the border.

What are good combinations of ordinary perennials in border? The over-all border plan should be based upon the distribution of bloom over the planting and over the season. Color combinations, although effective at the moment, leave gaps in the planting unless planned to be followed up with other plants. Some good color combinations are lupines, Anthemis Moonlight and *Oenothera missouriensis;* Poppy Mrs. Perry, Shasta daisy, and *Linum perenne;* purple iris and *Aquilegia chrysantha;* delphinium hybrids, *Thermopsis caroliniana* and pyrethrum. These are but a few of the countless combinations possible. Be sure that all flowers selected for a combination bloom at the same time, as usually their season is short.

I have a collection of 24 varieties of hemerocallis for continuous bloom during the season. They are all in shades of cream and yellow. Which hardy perennials do you suggest for harmonizing bloom from early spring to fall in a border? Siberian iris, bearded iris, astilbe, cimicifuga, delphinium, *Salvia azurea,* Regal Lily, Veronica Blue Spires, goatsbeard, (*Aruncus sylvester*), *Platycodon grandiflorum,* liatris.

FOR SPECIAL PURPOSES

Which perennials can be planted around Oriental Poppies, to cover their unsightly fading foliage? *Anemone japonica, Gypsophila paniculata* Bristol Fairy, *Thalictrum aquilegifolium,* hardy chrysanthemums, *Eupatorium coelestinum.* This latter perennial starts very late in spring and bushes out by midsummer.

My yard is made up of rock and ashes. Which perennials will grow well here? Everything seems to burn up from heat of sun. *Euphorbia myrsinites, Tunica saxifraga, Sedum acre, Silene maritima, Saponaria* *ocymoides, Nepeta mussini, Lathyrus latifolius, Coronilla cappadocica, Echinops ritro.*

What makes the best plant or flower (perennial) for cemeteries? For shade: *Ajuga reptans, Dicentra eximia,* Vinca Bowles variety. For sun: *Dianthus plumarius, Sedum spectabile, Sedum acre.*

Which perennial can I grow in a small bed bordering my porch? The porch faces north, and I want something at least 1 ft. high. *Dicentra eximia* or *Phlox laphami.*

Which are the best perennials to grow in a border along an active cedar hedge? If there is at least a half day of sun: hardy asters; *Eupatorium coelestinum,* helenium, *Heliopsis scabra, Nepeta mussini, Ophiopogon jaburan, Oenothera youngi, Phlox arendsi* hybrids, and summer phlox are some of the most satisfactory.

Which perennial flowers can be satisfactorily grown in a city back-yard garden where there is practically no sunlight? *Ajuga reptans* and *A. genevensis, Dicentra eximia, Mertensia virginica,* hemerocallis, *Pulmonaria saccharata,* and *P. angustifolia azurea, Phlox arendsi* Hilda, and *Phlox divaricata.*

Can you suggest perennials for small plot of ground facing the east? House is the background. Violets and lily-of-the-valley not successful. Aquilegia, anemone, *Phlox arendsi* and *P. divaricata,* anchusa, epimedium, monarda, *Hosta (Funkia) sieboldi* and *H. coerulea.*

What are some easily grown blue-flowered perennials? Veronica Blue Spires, *Veronica longifolia subsessilis,* Delphinium Belladonna, Tradescantia James Stratton, *Plumbago larpentiae, Platycodon grandiflorum, Campanula persicifolia grandiflora.*

What should one plant on north, east, and south fences to act as a screen, and also as a background for perennial borders? *Clematis montana rubens, Lathyrus latifolius, Polygonum auberti,* Bignonia Mme. Galen.

Will you name some very hardy perennials? Achillea, ajuga, aquilegia, artemisia, coreopsis, dicentra (bleedingheart), eupatorium, hemerocallis, lythrum, mertensia, *Nepeta mussini,* peony, platycodon.

I am interested in perennial flowers that require little work, after once being started, and are also good for cutting. Will you name a few? Bearded iris, hardy chrysanthemum, *Helenium autumnale, Coreopsis grandiflora,* peonies, hardy asters, *Gypsophila paniculata* Bristol Fairy, lily-of-the-valley, *Platycodon grandiflorum,* gaillardia.

Am interested in a small flower garden, including some for cutting. Which flowers would you recommend as of easy culture, and hardy? Any good varieties of bearded iris, any good varieties of hardy phlox, *Heliopsis scabra* Incomparabilis, *Gypsophila paniculata, Helenium peregrina* and *H. autumnale,* delphinium belladonna and delphinium hybrids, *Dianthus plumarius, Dicentra eximia* and *D. spectabilis.*

Are there any shade-tolerant perennials? Aconite, ajuga, anemone, aquilegia, astilbe, aubrietia, bleedingheart, bugbane, Carpathian-bluebell, daylily, doronicum, eupatorium, lily-of-the-valley, *Lobelia cardinalis* and *L. siphilitica,* mertensia, *Monarda didyma,* phlox, plantainlily, plumbago, primula, thalictrum, vinca, and viola.

What are the best types of hardy flowers for a sunny, dry place? *Alyssum saxatile, Veronica incana, Cerastium tomentosum, Plumbago larpentiae, Aethionema grandiflorum, Arenaria montana, Arabis albida (alpina),* Linum perenne, dictamnus, heliopsis, iris (bearded), hemerocallis, *Oenothera fruticosa* (sundrops).

Can you give me the names of some low-growing perennials that can be used for a border? *Iberis sempervirens, Alyssum saxatile compactum, Plumbago larpentiae, Aster novi-belgi* dwarf varieties, polyanthus, primrose, *Sedum hybridum* and *S. sieboldi, Veronica incana.*

What low-growing, neat, easy perennials with good foliage can be used for edging? Ajuga, either with deep green foliage, or variety Metallica, with bronze leaves, is a good choice; it has blue flowers in the spring, husky foliage all season, spreads rapidly, and stands shade and city conditions. Several varieties of sedum may be used for edging, if controlled from spreading too much.

Will you name some bushy edging perennial plants for along walks? *Epimedium rubrum,* best in part shade; *Plumbago larpentiae, Campanula carpatica, Lamium maculatum, Iberis sempervirens, Aegopodium podagraria variegatum,* hosta (various kinds), *Lirope muscari* and its striped variety, *variegata; Sedum hybridum, S. spurium* and *S. sieboldi.*

Can you give a list of low perennials to be grown in beds along a flagstone-walk? *Achillea tomentosa, Ajuga genevensis, Alyssum saxatile citrinum, Anemone japonica,* Aster Countess of Dudley, *Campanula carpatica,* cushion chrysanthemums, dianthus, various species and varieties, *Nepeta mussini, Phlox subulata* varieties, *Plumbago larpentiae,* pyrethrum varieties, *Veronica incana.*

Will you name some perennials for planting along the front of the border? *Alyssum saxatile compactum, Dianthus plumarius, Statice longifolia, Plumbago larpentiae,* dwarf asters, *Veronica spicata nana, Arabis alpina, Silene maritima, Tunica saxifraga, Veronica rupestris, Nepeta mussini.*

What are some medium-height perennials for the center of the border? *Campanula persicifolia* varieties, Artemisia Silver King, *Achillea ptarmica, Aquilegia coerulea, Paradisea liliastrum major, Dicentra eximia, Eupatorium coelestinum, Veronica longifolia subsessilis, Gypsophila paniculata compacta.*

Which are the best tall-growing perennials for a border? *Bocconia* *cordata, Thalictrum aquilegifolium, Phlox paniculata* hybrids, *Helenium autumnale, Rudbeckia purpurea,* delphinium hybrids, asters (tall named varieties), *Cimicifuga racemosa, Campanula pyramidalis.*

Will you give list of plants for a small perennial border, with succession of bloom as long as possible and no plants which are difficult to obtain? *Arabis albida fl. pl., Phlox subulata,* bearded iris, Veronica Blue Spire, hemerocallis, heuchera, dianthus, Phlox Miss Lingard, Shastadaisy, *Nepeta mussini,* delphinium belladonna, hardy asters, coreopsis, gaillardia, *Heliopsis scabra,* helenium varieties, cushion chrysanthemums.

Can you give me a list of perennials to use in a border 2 to 3 ft. wide and 50 ft. long, that would keep it looking well all season? *Anchusa myosotidiflora, Dicentra eximia,* delphinium belladonna, *Dianthus caesius,* gaillardia, geum, *Gypsophila repens* Bodger, *Nepeta mussini,* pyrethrum, summer phlox, *Heliopsis scabra, Eupatorium coelestinum,* hardy asters (novae-angliae and novi-belgi types), cushion chrysanthemums. Constant color can be secured only by introducing annuals for later summer bloom.

Will you suggest varieties for a perennial bed 30 × 10 ft., so as to have continuous bloom from early spring to late fall? Make a selection from the following: March: crocus, snowdrop, squill, winter aconite. April: rockcress, goldentuft, hepatica, moss phlox, marshmarigold. May: perennial candytuft, columbine, globeflower, iris, Virginia cowslip, bleedingheart, polyanthus primrose. June: Japanese iris, early phlox, Shastadaisy, painted daisy, pinks, coralbells, Oriental Poppy, hybrid columbines, lemonlily, delphinium, hollyhock. July: babysbreath, false dragonhead, butterflyweed, loosestrike, Carpathian bluebell, perennial sunflower, balloonflower. August: plantainlily, rosemallow, sneezeweed, coneflower, cardinalflower, hardy asters, sea lavender. September: Japanese anemone, hardy asters, perennial sunflowers, goldenrod, showy stonecrop, hardy chrysanthemums. October: monkshood, hardy asters, leadwort (ceratostigma), hardy chrysanthemums, helianthus, *Salvia pitcheri.*

Is there a perennial that blooms nearly all summer? *Heliopsis scabra, Gaillardia aristata, Nepeta mussini,* and *Dicentra eximea* all come very near it.

Which perennials should I plant to provide flowers all summer? *Anchusa azurea* Dropmore, *Phlox suffruticosa* and *P. paniculata* varieties, *Penstemon heterophyllus,* gaillardia varieties, *Dianthus plumarius* hybrids, delphinium belladonna, Veronica Blue Spires, *Coreopsis grandiflora, Heliopsis scabra, Nepeta mussini.* (See also preceding questions.)

Which dwarf border plants bloom over the longest period of time? *Silene maritima, Dianthus deltoides* Brilliant, Viola Jersey Gem, *Tunica saxifraga florepleno, Nepeta mussini.*

SOIL PREPARATION

How deep should soil be prepared for new border?   For best results, the soil should be dug and prepared not less than 18 ins., and preferably 24 ins., deep.

How shall I prepare new ground for perennials?   Dig the ground to a depth of at least 18 ins., mixing in well-rotted cow manure, leafmold, peatmoss, or old compost, with bone meal 5 to 7 lbs. to 100 sq. ft.

DEEP DIGGING FOR BIG CROP

(1) Soil is removed, a spade deep, from first section of garden plot. (2) Manure is spread on bottom of trench and forked in. (3) Next strip is measured off. (4) Soil removed from second section is thrown over into first trench. Operation is repeated to end of plot, when soil from first trench is used to fill the last one.

In preparing a border, should all stones be removed? Should soil be screened?   For perennials, annuals, and shrubs, stones the size of a lemon or smaller may be left in the soil. Only for seedbeds should soil be screened through ½-in. mesh screen.

Is sand or clay better subsoil for perennial border?   If sand is too loose and porous, drainage will be excessive; if clay is hard packed, drainage will be stopped. Generally speaking, a sandy subsoil is preferable. Hard clay should be broken up and lightened with coal ashes, gravel, or sand.

What element is lacking in the soil when perennials have good color and flower well but lack sufficient strength to stand upright and spread all over the beds?   Possibly insufficient phosphorus and potash; but crowded planting, too much watering, and overfeeding with nitrogenous manures will cause weak stems. However, many perennials need support either by staking or using brush.

For 20 years we have had a perennial border. The last 5 years it has deteriorated; replacements, fertilizer, etc., have not solved the problem. Maple and elm trees grow near; sunshine is one hour a day. Can any soil be improved to overcome lack of sunshine?   Nothing can be done to improve the soil so that it will overcome the lack of sunshine and greedy tree roots.

Why don't my plants near cedar trees thrive? Are there any perennials that will grow fairly well in the shade of cedar trees?   The soil may be "poisoned" by accumulation of years of dead cedar foliage. Try removing this periodically. Give the surface a light application of slaked lime and a generous supply of rotted manure or leafmold. Work till the ground is in good "tilth." Most shade plants, especially the "woodsy" ones, will grow well if soil is friable and not super-acid. Some are ferns, dicentra, *Mahonia repens*, *Vinca minor*, hepatica, *Pachysandra terminalis*, primula, *Plumbago larpentiae*, *Phlox divaricata*, *P. carolina* and *P. ovata*, aquilegia.

FERTILIZERS

Which is the better time to put fertilizer on perennials—spring or fall?   Apply manure or bone meal in the fall. Chemical fertilizer is best put on when plants are actively growing.

Will fresh sheep manure hurt perennials?   No; providing it is not put on too heavily, and is not allowed to come in contact with the roots. Use 1 lb. to 10 sq. ft. and cultivate into surface soil.

What is a good fertilizer for asters, larkspur, peonies, and delphiniums?   Well-rotted barnyard manure, supplemented during the growing season by a balanced commercial fertilizer. A little lime may be needed if the soil is acid.

Is there anything to be gained by fertilizing perennials during the growing season?   In some cases, yes. Many kinds—phlox, delphinium, chrysanthemums, etc.—are helped by supplementary feedings of liquid manure or quick-acting commercial fertilizer, applied when flowers are about to be formed. Whether or not this is necessary depends on character of soil, the initial preparation of the border, and annual routine practices to maintain its fertility.

How do you prepare and fertilize perennial beds in the spring so as

not to disturb the plants? By forking in the manure or fertilizer lightly.

Do all flowers of hardy varieties need lime? My soil is cleared-off pine woodland. Most garden flowers need a soil near the neutral point. (See Lists, pH—Section I.) Your county agricultural agent probably would be glad to advise you on how much lime to apply to your soil.

PLANTING AND TRANSPLANTING

What is the method of planting perennials? Make a hole of sufficient size, with spade or trowel (depending on the size of the root system), to accommodate the roots without crowding. Put plant in hole no deeper than it grew in nursery. Work soil between and over the roots, and pack *firmly* with hands, feet, or tamping stick. Soak with water if soil is on dry side.

Is it all right to plant perennials when soil is sopping wet? No. Soil structure may be harmed as a result. Wait until soil is crumbly but still moist.

When is the best time to remake perennial border? September and early October. Early spring is also good, but early-blooming plants should be replanted in the fall, except for those on the border line of hardiness in the region.

Is August a good month to revamp borders? Definitely not. It is the hottest and driest month as a rule, and newly transplanted stock (with the exceptions noted below) is likely to suffer.

Which perennials should be moved in midsummer or early fall? Bearded iris can be moved in July and August; bleedingheart, Christmasrose, narcissi, peonies in late August and September; Oriental poppies in August; Madonna Lilies as soon as tops wither.

Should all perennials be cut back either after replanting or transplanting in fall? Tall perennials are better if cut back before being moved. Whatever foliage remains down near the soil matters little in the fall.

How can one transplant perennials without harming their growth? By taking proper care in lifting, and transplanting at the proper time. For most kinds this is autumn or early spring.

What is the time for dividing and transplanting old-fashioned perennials in northern Maine: fall, or spring? Fall, if it can be done at least 4 weeks before heavy freezing. It can be done in spring, too; but as early as possible.

In making over perennial borders, which plants should not be disturbed in the fall? What can I do about them? None of the late-blooming ones, such as chrysanthemums, hardy asters, toadlilies, etc. Replant all early and midsummer bloomers, except those likely to suffer winter injury. Dig around others without disturbing them; transplant in the spring.

Should flowers be planted in straight rows or staggered? The effect is better in a staggered planting. When they are grown for cut flowers only, it is more convenient to have them in rows.

When is the correct time to plant perennials in the spring? Will they bloom the same year? Plant as early as the soil can be worked. Plants, if large enough, will flower the same season.

CULTURE

What constitutes good year-round care of a perennial border? In spring (when frost has left the ground) remove winter mulch. If manure or partly rotted leaves were used, leave finer portions and lightly fork into soil, along with top-dressing of complete fertilizer. Reset any plants heaved out of ground by frost. Hoe throughout season to kill weeds and prevent formation of surface crust. Support those plants which need it. Water thoroughly when necessary. Put on winter mulch after first severe frost.

What is the best way to keep down weeds in a border of perennials? Use a narrow scuffle hoe frequently to chop off weeds before they attain much size. Run the hoe through the soil about an inch below the surface. Weeds among the flowers must be pulled out by hand. Certain mulching materials also help to keep down weeds.

How close and how deep shall I keep soil worked around different plants, etc.? Depth depends on the type of plants; shallow-rooted plants need shallow cultivation; deep-rooted plants will take deeper cultivation. All can be worked close, but with care not to cut stems.

Will straw mulch help in weed control and hold moisture? If not, what will help besides pulling and hoeing? A straw mulch or any like material helps in summer to keep down weeds and hold moisture.

Which flowers should be pinched back to become bushy? Can poppies or lilies be so treated? Chrysanthemums, hardy asters, helenium, some tall-growing veronicas and penstemons. Most plants that tend to send shoots from the axils of the leaves can be pinched. Poppies and lilies may not be pinched.

When is best time to cut back perennials; and how far? This may be done in the late autumn, when the herbaceous stems have died down. Cut down to within an inch of the soil for most plants. Some plants have a clump or rosette of green leaves which should not be cut off; just cut the old flower stems. Some good gardeners prefer to wait until spring before cutting off the tops of the perennials. Their argument is that it helps to prevent winter injury because snow and tree leaves are held by the stems.

Why do hardy perennials die off after 1 or 2 luxuriant seasons?

Most perennials need dividing and transplanting after 2 or 3 years. Many are short-lived. Some do not overwinter very well; still others succumb to diseases or insects. Stick to those that are dependable.

How often should perennials be watered?   No definite time can be set; the kind of soil, the needs of the various plants, as well as other factors, have an influence. See that at all times during the growing season the soil is kept moist. This is the safest rule in mixed plantings.

Can plants be watered too much to bloom? I have some shade from maple trees and my soil gets hard if I don't water often. I have very little bloom on my perennials and roses. Iris do quite well.   Shade, rather than too much water, is responsible for lack of bloom. Use shade-tolerant plants. Improve soil by adding humus-forming materials.

Is it true that water should not touch leaves of perennials?   There is scant danger from water on the leaves doing any harm.

Do you have to water perennial flowers in the winter, or do you just cover them?   No watering is then needed, there being no activity. Merely cover them after the ground is frozen.

WINTER PROTECTION

What is the theory back of covering plants for the winter?   The theory varies with the kind of plant. Plants that are not hardy are covered *before* hard freezing to protect them from low temperatures which would destroy the cells and thus kill the plant. Truly hardy plants are covered *after* the ground freezes; not to protect them from cold, but to keep them cold. The theory here is to prevent fluctuation of ground temperature, resulting in alternate freezing and thawing, which cause the injury. A mild spell in late winter followed by a sudden hard freeze is dangerous. In some cases merely shading plants from the winter sun is sufficient. Most winter killing occurs in late winter or early spring.

Shall or shall we not let Mother Nature blanket our border garden with maple and locust leaves and if so, when shall we remove the leaves?   This is not the best way of protecting most garden perennials. Maple leaves tend to make a sodden mass and smother to death any but the more robust plants. Light, litterlike material, through which air can circulate, is best. Covering should be removed gradually when signs of pushing growth are observed underneath. Take off the final covering on a dull day.

Is it necessary to protect newly planted perennials for the winter? What is best method?   It is advisable, in colder regions, to protect plants for the first winter. Salt hay, peatmoss, evergreen branches, or cornstalks can be used. Lay loosely, so as not to smother plants; do not put on until after first hard freeze.

I planted perennial seeds in my cold frame in July. They have made good growth. Can I leave them in the frame until the spring? Should I put a mulch in the frame after December?   A mulch will help. You may want to cover them earlier than December, depending on when you get heavy freezing. Seedlings from seed sown in July ought to make strong plants by late fall, particularly if planted out in a bed. If they are hardy perennials and are well grown, they do not need cold frame protection.

How much winter coverage is needed on established perennial beds of iris, phlox, tulips, and various small plants? How early should this be put on? What is best type? (New York.)   A covering of about 3 ins. is sufficient for the average planting of perennials. Wait until the ground has frozen before putting it on. Use some litterlike material that will not pack down, such as salt hay, pine needles, or cranberry tops.

Is peatmoss a good winter covering for my garden of peonies, iris, hollyhocks, delphiniums, nicotiana, dicentra?   Peonies and bearded iris should not be covered in winter. This favors rot. Delphiniums are better if covered with several inches of coarse ashes. Nicotiana is treated as a half-hardy annual. Hollyhocks and dicentra are the only ones that might benefit from the peatmoss.

Is it advisable to use littery material as a winter cover for plants near the house?   In general, no. The appearance is untidy, and there is some risk of fire. Not all cigarette smokers are careful about the discards. Half-rotted manure or leafmold can be used on the ground, and evergreen branches for top cover.

In mulching plants and shrubs, do you wait till the ground is frozen?   As a rule it is best to wait until the ground has frozen before putting on a protective mulch. Delay up to this point helps to harden the plants somewhat and also encourages rodents to find winter quarters elsewhere.

Should perennials be carefully covered in very changeable climates in the fall? It seems that we always cover or uncover at wrong times, and plants are more tender.   It is really the changeable conditions in winter that make covering advisable. The covering is not to keep out cold but to protect against bad effect of alternate spells of freezing and thawing. Delay it as long as possible in the fall; at least until the ground freezes. With the approach of spring, partially remove the covering; watch the plants and the weather; complete it on a dull day if possible.

Which perennials need a winter mulch, and which prefer none? And what kind of mulch?   Most perennials—except those with heavy green tops like tritoma—are the better for a winter mulch, particularly in regions of alternate freezing and thawing. Leafmold, salt hay, and evergreen boughs are some of the better materials. Light covering is to be strictly observed.

PROPAGATION OF PERENNIALS

SEED

When is the best time to sow perennials under glass?   In late February or early March, in a greenhouse of moderate temperature. With most kinds seedlings will soon be large enough to be transplanted into flats, from which they can be set outside in a nursery bed in May. In this way only the usual summer cultivation is required and strong plants will be available for fall planting in the border if need be.

Can perennials be raised successfully from fall-sown seed?   Where winter is severe and a cold frame is available, seeds of perennials could be sown as winter starts, so as to remain dormant for an earlier start in spring than would be obtained from spring sowing under similar conditions. Losses would be great in trying to carry small seedlings over winter.

Can you provide specific list of best planting dates for popular perennials from seed?   If greenhouse space is available, in March; if only a cold frame, in April; if no glass protection, outdoors in May. Some growers prefer to sow in August, thus securing the advantage of fresh seed of the current season; but sowing in the first half of the year insures huskier young plants, better able to face their first winter.

What is the latest date for planting perennial seeds for bloom in following spring?   Possibly in early August; but May sowing is better.

If you have no sunny window available, can you start perennial seedlings indoors?   Perennial seedlings could be started indoors without a sunny window, but they would be a forlorn-looking lot. Better wait and sow outdoors in May.

Is it advisable to sow seeds of perennials in the open ground?   Fair results could be expected if a special seedbed was made by mixing in fine leafmold and sand in the top 3 or 4 ins. of soil. Sow as early in May as possible and keep the soil nicely moist. A good method would be to sow in seed pans or flats, bury these to the rims in sand or coal ashes, and cover with panes of glass until germination.

Can any perennials be grown from seed by simply scattering the seeds where they are to bloom?   There is no doubt it could be done with certain kinds; but it is not the best, nor, in the long run, the easiest method.

Should perennial seedlings be transplanted?   If the seeds were sown during the summer, transplant when they have developed their first true leaves. Water immediately, and if possible provide light shade for a few days. Cultivate and water when necessary to promote growth.

Why do seeds I save come up so well, while seeds I buy, especially perennial, do so poorly? Because, being home-grown, they are fresh; and they may be sown soon after ripening if need be. Buy only from a reliable dealer.

Which perennials grow from seed easiest? Aquilegia hybrids, *Campanula persicifolia* in variety, Chrysanthemum "September Jewels," delphinium hybrids, *Coreopsis grandiflora,* erigeron, *Gaillardia grandiflora,* heliopsis, *Heuchera sanguinea, Lilium regale,* and *Lupinus polyphyllus* hybrids.

Can Thalictrum dipterocarpum seeds be planted in late fall or early winter? Will they bloom the following season? Yes, under glass; but they probably would not be strong enough to flower the following season.

What is the best method of raising thermopsis from seed? Sow the seed when ripe in a flat of sandy soil, and keep it in a cold frame over winter. If seed is at hand in March, sow in a greenhouse then, first placing it in hot water to soak overnight.

How can I raise trollius from seed? Sow the seed when ripe in a flat of rather porous soil. Keep it in a shaded cold frame, and as far as may be possible maintain cool, moist conditions. It will probably not germinate until the second year.

CUTTINGS

How are perennials propagated by cuttings? Cut off young shoots in spring when they are about 3 ins. long, making the cut below ground if possible. Insert in sand in hotbed, or in propagating case in cool greenhouse. Also, by non-flowering shoots in summer.

Will you tell me how to start slips in sand—such as chrysanthemum, carnation, and hydrangea? Use a box about 10 ins. deep; make drainage holes in the bottom; put in 1-in. layer of coarse cinders, and cover this with moss; add 3 ins. sand, tamped firm. Cover the box with a sheet of glass, and keep it where there is good light but out of sun. Chrysanthemum cuttings are taken from the base of old plants in spring; carnations may be rooted in August; hydrangeas either in spring or in August.

DIVISION

What is the best way to divide perennials? Dig up the plants and pry the rootstock apart into pieces of suitable size with the help of *two* digging forks; or hand forks if the plant is small.

When should perennials be divided?   Early bloomers in early fall, late bloomers in spring. Bearded irises and Oriental poppies in summer.

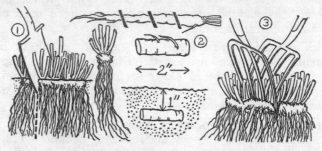

PROPAGATING HARDY PERENNIALS

Clumps or crowns can be cut apart with knife or spade (1); or torn apart with two digging forks (3). Root cuttings (2) of some subjects (Oriental poppy, phlox, platycodon), buried about an inch deep, quickly form new plants.

HYBRIDIZING

How are flowers crossed by hand?   Remove anthers from the flowers you want for the seed bearer before the pollen is ripe. Cover flower with transparent bag. When stigma is ripe (or sticky), put on the ripe pollen from the male parent, return the bag, and tie securely.

How does one go about producing a new color in a perennial? By taking the pollen from the flower of one species or variety and placing it upon the stigma of another. Both should belong to the same genus.

SPECIFIC PERENNIAL PLANTS

ALYSSUM

What soil is needed to raise Alyssum saxatile compactum?   It grows best in a light, porous soil with good drainage.

Alyssum saxatile lives but one year for me. Why is this?   It needs a well-drained soil and full sun in order to live from year to year.

Does Alyssum saxatile compactum need full sun for growing?   It does best in full sun; will grow in part shade but not flower so freely, nor live so long.

How do you make cuttings of Alyssum saxatile that will root and grow?   Take cuttings soon after plants have flowered. Make them about 3 ins. long, or more, with about 1 in. of bare stem below the leaves; cut just below a leaf scar. Put in sand; water; keep shaded for a few days.

Will you explain how Alyssum saxatile compactum is raised from seed? I have had no luck with it. It may be raised from seed sown in summer and wintered over in a frame or bed and planted out in spring; also, sow in spring and plant out early in fall.

ANCHUSA

Will you please give cultural care of Anchusa Dropmore variety? Good garden loam, with fair moisture and full sun. Divide roots every 3 years.

Is Anchusa italica Dropmore a true perennial, or should it be treated as an annual? Is it hardy in Massachusetts? It is a perennial and should be hardy in Massachusetts. However, it is not a long-lived perennial.

ASTERS

When should hardy aster seeds be planted? May be sown in a greenhouse in March; cold frame in April; or outdoors in May.

When is best time to put out hardy asters? In spring before they have more than an inch or two of growth.

How can I keep wild aster (Michaelmas daisies) from growing too high? Pinching them back in early summer should help them stay dwarf and bushy.

Will you please name some red and pink perennial asters? Red: Beechwood Beacon, Red Rover. Pink: Harrington's Pink, Survivor.

Which are good white hardy asters? Mount Rainier, Mount Everest.

Which are good purple hardy asters? Amethyst, Violetta.

Will you name several kinds of dwarf hardy asters? Lady Henry Maddocks, Niobe, Constance, Ronald, and Blue Bouquet.

Which is a strong-growing hardy aster—preferably blue? Climax grows to 6 ft. or more, with lavender-blue flowers up to 3 ins. in diameter under favorable conditions.

BABYSBREATH (GYPSOPHILA)

How do you care for the soil when growing perennial babysbreath? It will grow in any reasonably good soil; it does not have to be rich, but should be well drained and deep, and not more than slightly acid.

Can perennial gypsophila be successfully transplanted? Yes, if care is taken not to break the fleshy roots. It is best done in the spring.

What's wrong when gypsophila petals are so small you can barely see them? Probably you have a poor seedling or another plant, *Galium aristatum,* which is sometimes sold as babysbreath which it resembles.

I have a Bristol Fairy Babysbreath that grows beautifully but never blooms. Can anything be done to make it bloom? Some do not bloom when planted in too rich a soil. Try transplanting it (being careful not to break the long roots), and lime the soil.

How is Gypsophila Bristol Fairy propagated? Propagation is done by division, by cuttings, or by grafting on pieces of roots.

Does Gypsophila Bristol Fairy come true from seed? No.

BLEEDINGHEART (DICENTRA)

I had a large bleedingheart die last winter; was this because I covered it with leaves? Probably you used too many leaves and smothered the plant; or perhaps you covered it too early. Wait until the soil is frozen, then cover lightly. Remove gradually in spring.

My bleedingheart plants grew to large, healthy bushes but would not bloom. Why? Probably planted in too dense shade, or in too wet a soil.

When is the best time to move bleedinghearts? In early autumn, or very early spring.

When is the correct time to divide bleedingheart? September.

CANDYTUFT

How can I propagate Iberis sempervirens (evergreen candytuft)? By seeds sown in spring; by dividing the old plants in autumn or spring; or by cuttings made in summer of the young growth inserted in a cold frame.

What is the best way to get a quantity of evergreen iberis for edging, from seed? Sow in an outdoor bed in May or June. Transplant seedlings to nursery beds, allowing 6 to 8 ins. between plants. Set in flowering quarters in fall, or following spring.

Will you give me proper culture for iberis? Mine is all dying. Iberis usually grows satisfactorily in any well-drained garden soil not too acid, and needs no special care. There are perennial and annual iberis. The perennial kind sometimes does better when plants are cut back to within a couple of inches of the crown after they have flowered. (See also Rock Garden.)

CARNATIONS (DIANTHUS)

Is it possible to grow the English border carnation in the Eastern states? The heat of our summers is not favorable to their culture, and they are not winter hardy here. Some success can be attained by sowing seeds in a greenhouse in February, potting the seedlings, and planting out in May in as cool a spot as possible; a little shade in July and August will help. Pinch them several times to make them branch; give some support to keep the plants from sprawling. Keep nearly all the buds removed until late summer, and let them flower in fall. Summer flowers are inferior.

What kind of fertilizer is best for carnations? The basic need is for some kind of humus; rotted manure is the best. Peatmoss, compost, or leafmold may be substituted, but to these lime and fertilizer must be added. To a bushel of any of the above add ½ lb. of pulverized limestone and 1 lb. of complete fertilizer. Mix thoroughly and spread this 3 ins. deep and mix with the soil. When plants begin to bloom, feed with pulverized sheep manure, dried blood, or tankage, ½ lb. per sq. yd.

The soil here is sandy. Water supply very limited. Will Chabaud Carnations get along on natural rainfall? It will not be possible to get the best returns under these conditions. Set the plants out as early as possible, while the weather is cool. In July put on old leaves, grass clippings, or weeds as a mulch, and maintain it. This will assist in keeping the roots cool. Don't let the plants exhaust themselves by overflowering. Remove most of the buds until cool weather sets in.

Will you give the culture of hardy carnations? Fertilizer needs, etc.? Sow seeds indoors in March in a soil mixture containing equal parts of loam, sand and leafmold. Transplant the seedlings into flats 2 ins. apart. Plant outside in May, about 12 ins. apart. Prepare the bed by forking in leafmold or peat; add 10 lbs. dried cow or sheep manure to 100 sq. ft. Water after planting; pinch out the tips to induce branching. Keep the soil stirred until the end of June, then mulch with old leaves or grass. Keep the plants watered; disbud for larger blooms.

What is the follow-up care of carnation seedlings; also winter care as far North as Pennsylvania? After hardening off the seedlings in a cold frame, set them out in the open in May in a well-prepared bed. (See previous questions.)

How can I grow pinks and carnations in upright clumps instead of spreading all over the ground? Pinks and carnations have a tendency to spread, although some of the improved Marguerite strain are less inclined than others. Insert small pieces of twiggy brush among the plants while they are still small. This will tend to hold them upright. A little tying here and there will keep them tidy.

I am able to raise most all kinds of flowers except hardy carnations. Just what do they need to do well? They need a well-drained soil. The plants should be set out early to become well developed before hot weather. Give them plenty of moisture during hot weather. Some believe in keeping the buds removed until late summer because they flower best in cool weather. Select a good strain like the hardy border, Improved Marguerite.

Why do my carnations have thin stems? The flowers are large, but the stems are so small they will not stand up. Try applying superphosphate to the soil, 4 oz. per sq. yd. Look to the variety; this sometimes is a vital fault that no amount of care will eliminate.

I have 2 choice carnation plants now 2 years old, one is full of buds and blooms, the other has not even a bud. Why? The fault in the non-blooming plant is in the way it was propagated—hard growth from non-blooming stock. Discard it, and propagate from the plant that blooms.

I read in a magazine that if you take cuttings from perennial pinks in October they would grow indoors. Did this, but they are not thriving. Why? What the article probably meant was to take the cuttings in October and winter the young plants over in the house and plant out in spring. They are not house plants. They need full sun, and bloom only in summer. In any case, cuttings are better if taken in August.

Our pinks formed large plants their second year but did not blossom. In the same soil sweetwilliams did very well. What do you suggest? The soil may be a little too rich or too wet, or lacking in lime. A well-drained soil, full sun, and the chance to ripen off in fall are necessary. Do not feed or water after August.

Which dianthus species are dependably hardy? *Dianthus arenarius, arvernensis, plumarius* (Cottage Pink), *deltoides* (Maiden Pink), *petraeus, caesius* (Cheddar Pink).

Which kind of pinks are perennial? Is it better to sow new seed every spring? The most important perennial pink in the garden is *Dianthus plumarius,* of which several varieties, both single and double, are grown. *D. alpinus, D. caesius, D. deltoides, D. knappi,* and *D. neglectus* may be grown in rock gardens. It should not be necessary to sow seed every spring. Named varieties of *D. plumarius* are propagated from cuttings or divisions.

The Scotch or dwarf pink in its usual form is too straggly. Can you name a dwarf compact variety that is better in this respect? *Dianthus deltoides* "Brilliant," *D. arvernensis, D. subacaulis, D. caesius.*

CHRISTMASROSE (HELLEBORE)

What is the botanical name of the Christmasrose? *Helleborus niger.*

How should I start a bed of Christmasroses? Select a position in partial shade where the soil is rich and moist; dig in some well-rotted manure or leafmold. Obtain young plants from dealers and set out in early spring.

I have a Christmasrose that I have had for 3 or 4 years, and last February was the first time it bloomed. Now I would like to move it. Will that set it back again for 3 or 4 years? The Christmasrose does not like to be disturbed, and if you move it again it will in all probability set it back for a few years. Moving carefully with a very large soil-ball would help.

What location should I transplant my Christmasrose to? It doesn't do anything on the south side of the house. The southerly aspect is too warm. Put in a cooler spot, and let it get established. Never allow it to become dry. See preceding answer.

Do Christmasroses need much sun? Christmasroses do best in partial shade, where they are not subject to being dried out in summer.

What makes my Christmasrose die down, then get new leaves, but no bloom? Has not bloomed this year. The plant failed to set flower buds due to some factor like drying out in summer, or poor soil. It may have been disturbed during cultural operations.

Will you tell me how to divide a Christmasrose? Mine is doing wonderfully well, but I would like to give some away. Best divided in late summer or autumn by taking a spading fork and lifting the side shoots without disturbing the main plant. It resents any disturbance, and when well established should be left alone.

I planted a Christmasrose in spring a year ago. It seems to be showing no signs of buds; in fact, no new shoots have come up this fall. It is in a well-drained spot, partially shaded, and covered with a box, one side of which is glass. What is the proper care? How early shall I cover it? What kind of fertilizer? Put fertilizer on in spring. Do not cover the plant at all. A few leaves drifting in among the stems is enough covering. Let the plant become well established, and avoid all disturbance. (See answers to preceding questions.)

How can I start Christmasroses from seed? Sow, as soon as ripe, in a mixture of soil, leafmold, and sand in cold frame, and keep moist. They are slow to germinate, and will probably take from 3 to 5 years to reach flowering size.

CHRYSANTHEMUM

The garden chrysanthemum, originally an oriental plant, has been so changed through centuries of cultivation that it scarcely resembles the species from which it was derived. In the year 1750 it was introduced into English gardens but at that time created very little interest. About a century later it was brought to America, and for years was grown only as a greenhouse plant. Within the last quarter of a century it has become a prominent garden flower—a result of the successful development of hardier and earlier-flowering types and varieties.

Chrysanthemums in the garden give a profusion of bloom in bright autumn colors as a grand finale to the gardening season. Light frosts do little damage to either the flowers or the foliage. If planted in protected spots, they will often remain attractive until mid-November in the latitude of New York State. Farther South, and in other milder climates, they are even better adapted, and a much larger selection of varieties can be used.

While hardy mums are comparatively easy to grow, they will not stand neglect. They need to be divided and reset every second or third year, and kept well fertilized and free of disease and insect pests. Considerable care should be given to the selection of varieties for outdoor planting. There are thousands of kinds in the trade, but only relatively few of these bloom early enough in the fall, or are sufficiently hardy where winters are severe, to be dependable garden plants.

Soil Preparation

What type of soil is best for hardy chrysanthemums? Any friable, free-working soil is satisfactory. It should be well drained yet reasonably retentive of moisture and of goodly depth.

How should a bed for chrysanthemums be prepared and fertilized? Spade it deeply (without bringing up large quantities of unkind subsoil), incorporate a 3- or 4-in. layer of rotted manure and a dressing of superphosphate. If manure is not available, substitute compost and commercial fertilizer. Lime, if necessary, to keep soil approximately neutral.

How shall I prepare a bed for chrysanthemums? My ground is quite low and has a heavy clay subsoil. Spade or plow in fall, adding manure, compost, or leafmold. In early spring apply a dressing of lime, and a week or so before plants are set out, fork in a light application of complete fertilizer. Chrysanthemums will not succeed in waterlogged soil.

Fertilizer

Do hardy chrysanthemums like lime or limestone in the soil? They prefer pH 6 to 7. They have much the same requirements in this respect as the general run of garden vegetables.

What should chrysanthemums, carried over in a cold frame for winter be fed? And when? Do not feed while in cold frame. Add manure and bone meal, or complete fertilizer, to outdoor beds prior to planting; possibly a light side dressing of complete fertilizer when half grown. Liquid manure applied in late summer and early fall works wonders.

What are "azaleamums"? This is merely a trade name for a dwarf bushy type of chrysanthemums, more accurately termed cushion chrysanthemums.

How may manure be used on azaleamums? How freely? Around second-year plants work a 2-in. covering well into the soil together with some bone meal and a dusting of wood ashes. When preparing soil for new plantings, manure and fertilize as for other hardy chrysanthemums.

Do azaleamums need summer feeding? No. Not if soil is fairly good.

Planting; Transplanting

When should one plant chrysanthemums? As soon as the ground can be worked in spring.

Where should mums be planted? Any location that receives sunshine at least ⅔ of the day, providing soil and air circulation are good. Avoid overhanging eaves, walls, and stuffy corners. Don't crowd them among other plants.

What is the best way to plant hardy chrysanthemums? In well-prepared soil make a hole with a trowel or spade, of ample size to accommodate roots. Set plant in position; spread out roots; work soil in among them and press soil firm with fingers. Do not plant when soil is wet and sticky. Water after planting if soil is at all dry.

How often should chrysanthemums be replanted? Strong-growing mums should be divided every year; moderate-growing kinds every second year.

Would it be advisable to divide and reset chrysanthemums in fall after they have finished blooming? No. It is safer to do this in spring. (See following questions.)

When is best time to divide hardy chrysanthemums? How? Early spring, as soon as shoots are 3 to 4 ins. high. Dig up clump; discard old center portion; separate young offshoots; plant as single divisions, 10 or 12 ins. apart, in carefully prepared soil.

Is spring or fall the best time to transplant chrysanthemums that are in a too-shady place? Spring is best, but if necessary they can be moved any time during the growing season if thoroughly watered first and carefully lifted with a good ball of soil.

Can hardy border chrysanthemums be moved when in bloom? Yes. Be sure soil is moist; take up clump with a good root-ball; replant immediately. Firm soil around roots; shade for 2 or 3 days; and *don't neglect watering.*

When is the proper time to plant azaleamums? In spring, just as new growth appears.

Should azaleamums be transplanted every year? Divide and reset them every 2 or 3 years.

How often should Northland Daisies be lifted and divided?   Every second year, in early spring when young growth is appearing.

Winter Care

What is the best way to store early chrysanthemums during winter in Washington?   Lift plants and place in cold frame. If left in garden, cover lightly with evergreen branches, leaves, or similar protection.

What is the best way to care for chrysanthemums after they stop blooming in fall?   Cut stems back close to ground. If brown foliage appeared during summer, burn stems and all dropped leaves—they harbor insects. Cover lightly with evergreen branches and dry leaves.

Should mums be wintered outdoors or in a cold frame? (New Jersey.)   They should overwinter in New Jersey with a blanket of evergreen branches intermingled with leaves. Covering should be light.

What is winter care for chrysanthemums, without a cold frame, in southern Vermont?   A blanket of evergreen branches intermingled with leaves would make best covering. Apply when soil is slightly frozen. Good soil drainage is an important factor.

Can well-rotted manure be placed on top of chrysanthemums as a winter mulch?   Yes, but not close to the crowns. Pack dry leaves immediately around the plants themselves.

When should hardy chrysanthemums be covered, before or after frost?   After the first killing frost and when the soil is slightly frozen.

Will azaleamums thrive in a northern exposure?   Yes, if winter protection is provided. They must have full sun for at least ⅔ of the day.

How can I keep a cushion chrysanthemum over winter? (Minnesota.)   Cushion chrysanthemums should winter over in Minnesota with a light blanket of evergreen branches and dry leaves applied when ground is lightly frozen.

How may I protect large-flowering chrysanthemum blooms in the outdoor garden?   A double-thick cheesecloth covering stretched over a framework affords considerable protection. Avoid growing varieties that are late in flowering.

Will Northland Daisies winter satisfactorily in the East without protection?   They are hardy, but benefit by light protection.

Can you take a non-hardy chrysanthemum, cut it off a few inches from the ground, keep it inside until spring, and then set it out?   Yes, if you pot the roots and carry the plant over in a cool, well-lighted cellar or sun porch. Soil must be kept slightly moist. There are, of course, many reliable hardy chrysanthemums that do not require this attention.

Is December 1 too late to put a chrysanthemum plant outdoors that has been in bloom in the house for about 4 weeks?   Too late for sure results. If planted in a sheltered corner and covered lightly, it has a fifty-fifty chance.

Would semi-hardy chrysanthemums winter in dirt in a barn cellar? Should the cellar be dark or light? A well-lighted barn cellar that is cool should do. Be careful that soil does not dry out.

Culture

Just how do you care for azaleamums? I know they are heavy feeders and I care for them very well, but why do they bloom one year and not the next? Divide every second year. Water copiously, but only when needed during dry periods. Reasonable feeding should be sufficient. Tarnished plant bug and other insect injury may prevent flowering.

How should chrysanthemums (cushion type) be cared for to bloom freely so they look like pictures in the catalogues? Choose sunny location. Don't crowd together or among other plants. Dig in barnyard manure, bone meal, and leafmold to a depth of 15 ins. under your plants. Cultivate frequently but lightly and water copiously when needed. Divide plants every other year.

What is correct care of English-type mums out of doors? They respond to same treatment as other types, but should be overwintered in a cold frame or given careful protection.

Will you give me information on how to grow large chrysanthemums out of doors? Use greenhouse varieties. Grow 1 to 2 stems only to each plant; remove all side buds. Shading with black sateen cloth to hasten blooming, or special protection, will be necessary.

Have read that covering chrysanthemums with black cloth for a certain time during the day brings them into bloom earlier. Will you give me detailed instructions for its use? There is a special black sateen cloth made for this purpose. Starting in mid-July, completely darken the plants from 5 P.M. until 7 A.M. Discontinue when the buds show color.

Can the blooms of large, exhibition chrysanthemums grown outside in the garden be hastened by enclosing them in darkened frames? If so, when should these frames be applied? I am an amateur but sell quite a few flowers to florists. Yes. Build framework of wood and cover with black cloth so as to be as nearly light-proof as possible. (See reply to previous question.)

What care should be given exhibition chrysanthemums? They require careful attention to all details of cultivation, such as propagating, soil preparation, watering, staking, disbudding, etc. When buds appear, apply liquid manure every week or 10 days until the flowers begin to open.

How do you care for Korean hybrid mums? Exactly as for other hardy chrysanthemums, but as they are more vigorous and inclined to spread more than older sorts, they should be divided every year. Light winter protection is advisable.

Will you please give culture on pompon chrysanthemums? Pompons are easily grown in the garden. Good rich soil, thorough watering when needed, and frequent cultivation are the essentials. Only tallest varieties require pinching.

How should I care for chrysanthemums in the spring? Divide and replant if they have been growing 2 years in same place; if possible give them a different location. Otherwise fork some manure or fertilizer into surface soil.

My chrysanthemums have been in 3 years and are large clumps. Should they be thinned out? Into what size clumps? Strong-growing mums should be divided every year; moderate-growing kinds every 2 years. Do this in early spring, leaving each division with 1 or 2 shoots.

How do florists manage to keep the foliage on chrysanthemums green down to the ground? By starting with young plants, taking care that they are never allowed to dry out, but are not overwatered. Most florists do not spray with water but use a rotenone mixture, spraying the plants every 10 days so that insects cannot get a start. (See Section VIII.)

How can I grow many-branched chrysanthemums? Keep plants young by frequent division and pinch them back 2 or 3 times during growing season. Keep staked up; and watered during dry periods.

What is the correct way to disbud chrysanthemums? Many garden mums produce larger flowers if just 1 (the terminal) bud remains on each branch. Remove unwanted buds by rubbing them out with thumb and finger when they are ⅛ in. or so in diameter.

When should chrysanthemums be pinched back? Tall-growing types, at intervals during spring and early summer. Give first pinch when 9 to 12 ins. high, second when about 15 ins. high, and possibly a third in late July. Cushion-type varieties require no pinching.

Should I pinch every shoot on a fall chrysanthemum, or just the center one? All strong shoots are pinched early in season to cause low, bushy growth.

What is the proper method to use for pinching back chrysanthemum plants? Pinch off an inch or so from the tip of strong shoots, using the finger and thumb.

How late in the season should azaleamum plants be pinched back? Azaleamums branch naturally and require little or no pinching.

Should cushion and pompon mums be pinched back in spring? All cushions and many pompons branch naturally and do not require pinching. A few of the taller pompon varieties should be pinched.

What is the best method of pruning and disbudding hardy mums?
"Pruning" consists of pinching out the tips of the shoots when plants
are 9 ins. high, and the tips of all subsequent side branches when they
are 6 ins. long. This practice is discontinued in late July. Disbudding
consists of removing many of the young flower buds so that the one
or more allowed to remain on each stem will develop into especially
fine blooms.

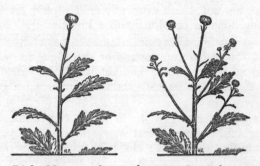

Disbudding a chrysanthemum. In order to
secure a flower of large size, the top terminal
bud (of the several which form) only is left.

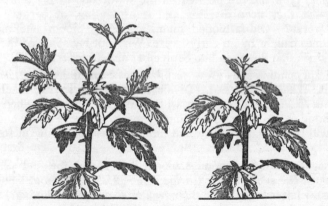

Pruning or "pinching" a chrysanthemum. In order
to throw the plant's strength to the terminal bud,
or a crown bud, side shoots or laterals are removed.

Do Northland Daisies require pinching back?   Pinch once or twice,
as needed, before end of June.

**What is the proper way to tie up garden chrysanthemums? Each
year the weight of mine bends over the stems.**   Wooden or bamboo
stakes may be pushed into the ground near the plants and the stems
neatly tied to these. Place supports *before they begin to flower*, and

try to preserve the natural habit of plant. Avoid tying so that plant is bunched together like a shock of corn. Brushwood pea stakes inserted so that shoots grow up through the sticks are also very satisfactory.

Problems

Are hardy mums reliably hardy throughout the United States? Most varieties are not where extremely cold winters are experienced. Work is being done to develop hardier kinds.

How do you encourage chrysanthemums to have larger blooms, and stand up until blooming time instead of spreading out and laying on ground? Avoid overcrowding and shade. Provide neat stakes and tie plants to them. Grow large-flowering varieties. Give good cultural treatment.

Is there anything one can do to make chrysanthemums bloom earlier in the fall? I had several new varieties this year and they budded so late that they didn't bloom at all. Newly planted mums are apt to flower late the first season. Try them 1 more year without disturbing. When selecting new varieties choose early-flowering kinds.

Why didn't my chrysanthemums bloom this fall? They are the old-fashioned type and are planted on the south side of my house. Was it because they need dividing and transplanting, or because of an early freeze? Old-fashioned mums naturally bloom late and are sometimes caught by an early freeze. Why not try some of the many good kinds that flower in late September and October?

My chrysanthemums grow very tall but have weak stems and few blooms. What shall I do? Divide them in the spring; pinch back (nip out tips of growing shoots with thumbnail), starting when plants are about 6 ins. tall and continuing every 2 weeks until mid-July. This will make plants bushy and more floriferous. Grow in full sunlight.

If seedling chrysanthemums bloom in October the first year and in August the second year (in the same place and about same conditions), what is likely to be their regular season of blooming? From mid-September on if your plants are divided and reset every second year, as they should be.

What makes my hardy mums bloom so early (while summer flowers are still in bloom) that in the fall they are done? I have several varieties. (Pennsylvania.) You must have only early-flowering varieties. Obtain later-blooming kinds. Or hasten blooming by shading during part of the day. (See Culture)

Two chrysanthemums, full of buds that seemed ready to burst several weeks prior to freezing weather, did not bloom. Can their blooming season be hastened in any way? Your varieties are too late for your particular locality. Try earlier kinds. The *buds* of some varieties are not frost hardy, even though the flowers may be.

How can I keep chrysanthemums from growing out of bounds? Both hardy and exhibiton types are 5 to 6 ft. tall. Use phosphates rather than nitrates for fertilizing. Grow in full sun and do not crowd. Pinch back vigorous shoots during May, June, and July.

Are azaleamums hardy? Yes.

Do azaleamums bloom constantly? Reasonably so, from July on.

Our azaleamums have very few blossoms. This is their second year. What is wrong? Azaleamums should be at their best in their second year. Don't crowd. Prepare soil deeply and water copiously whenever needed during summer. They do best in full sun. Tarnished plant bug may prevent flowering.

Why do my azaleamums get taller than a lot of others I have seen? Perhaps the soil is too rich in nitrogen; plants too crowded or lack sunlight. Are you sure you have the true type?

Azaleamums, when originally planted, bloomed during late summer and were of proper color. During second year plants bloomed intermittently all summer and flowers were of mixed shades. Is there any special reason for this? Azaleamums are usually at their best in their second year. Poor soil or dry conditions will cause light and irregular coloring. Frequent cultivation and copious watering when needed will help. Divide plants every other year.

I had a fine collection of Korean chrysanthemums, but each blooming season I find that I have more bronze colors and less yellows, reds, etc. Do they revert? Chrysanthemums do sometimes exhibit the phenomenon known as mutation; but more probably self-sown seeds have germinated and reverted to other colors. The bronze varieties are especially vigorous, and would take the lead.

Do different chrysanthemums mix and change color if planted closely together? (Louisiana.) No. But seedlings which differ in color may spring up among the parent plants. This would be very likely in your climate.

Propagation

How can I best increase choice chrysanthemums? If hotbed or greenhouse facilities are available, take cuttings (in February or March) from stock plants kept over winter in a cold frame. Root in sand, transplant to pots or flats of soil, and set outdoors in April. Plants wintered outdoors can be taken up and divided in early spring.

What is the method of splitting or dividing an azaleamum plant? Same as any hardy chrysanthemum. (See previous and following replies.)

Will you please tell me how to divide or thin out chrysanthemum plants? Lift just as new growth appears in spring. With hands, knife, or a small hand fork pry off from outsides of old clumps small divisions, each consisting of 2 or 3 shoots, with roots attached. Plant divisions 1½ to 2 ft. apart in well-prepared soil.

Is it better to start new chrysanthemums from slips, or to divide old plants? Slips or small healthy divisions give equally good results. The former are better, however, if stock plants are infested with nematodes.

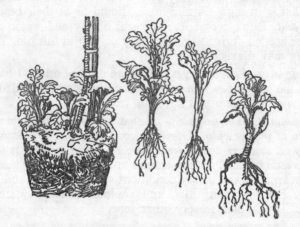

Old chrysanthemum plant, and young growths with roots removed to provide new plants.

Will chrysanthemums grow from cuttings made from tips of shoots that are removed when plants are pinched back? Yes.

When is the proper time to start to root mum cuttings for best results? For large plants, cuttings should be started indoors in late February and the cuttings taken in March. Cuttings taken in April and May are quite satisfactory, but plants are smaller.

How can I graft several colors on a single chrysanthemum plant? Grow a strong, early-started, young plant to a single stem. At the desired height, say 2½ ft., pinch the tip out to promote side branches. On these insert the grafts. A humid atmosphere should be maintained after grafting and the grafts should be kept sealed with polythene plastic film until they have formed a good union.

How can chrysanthemum seeds be saved? Early varieties may produce seeds in the garden. Better results are obtained from pot-grown plants kept under glass from late September on. This is the only satisfactory way of securing seeds from late-flowering varieties.

Can one buy seeds of the large-flowering type chrysanthemums?

They are seldom catalogued. One of the large seed concerns might be able to get them for you.

How can I grow chrysanthemums from seeds to get blooms first year? Start seeds indoors during March. Transplant once to flats or a cold frame before planting in outdoor garden.

Pests and Diseases

What insects and diseases commonly attack hardy chrysanthemums? See Chrysanthemums—Section VIII.

Why didn't my hardy chrysanthemums bloom this year? The leaves turned like dusty-miller leaves. Evidently the plants were badly mildewed. Do not plant too closely together or in shade. Dust with dusting sulfur or mildex, at first sign of appearance of mildew.

What spray do you recommend for black aphids on outdoor chrysanthemums? Use Bordeaux mixture to which Black Leaf 40 is added at rate of 1½ teaspoonfuls to each gallon. This spray, used at frequent intervals, kills aphids, controls certain fungous diseases, and repels the leaf nematode. Systox is a new control.

How can I control chrysanthemum leaf-spot disease? First be sure you have this disease. The effects of leaf nematodes are often mistaken for it. Leaf-spot produces in the diseased areas masses of white spores which are easily seen with a hand lens. To control, pick off and burn infected leaves; spray with Bordeaux mixture or with Ziram; avoid wetting leaves when watering.

What is care of fall-blooming chrysanthemums? Mine die down every fall, lose their leaves (which turn black or brown), and flower very late. They are probably infested with leaf nematodes (eelworms). After blooming, cut back close to ground. Remove and burn all stems and leaves, which harbor this pest over winter. In spring propagate from tip cuttings and set plants in new location in good soil, or in soil disinfected with formaldehyde, chloropicrin or systox.

My chrysanthemum blooms turn brown before fully opening. Why? Foliage is in good condition. Send a few affected leaves to your State Agricultural Experiment Station to be checked for leaf nematodes. (See previous reply.)

Varieties

Will you name the best double early-flowering varieties of garden chrysanthemums which are hardy and which will flower in September? Eugene A. Wander and Algonquin are good early yellows; Seminole, a small early white; Dean Ladd, bronze, My Lady, orange; Canary yellow.

Will you suggest outdoor chrysanthemums to have bloom from earliest to latest date? Try the azaleamums and the cushion pompons, Summertime, September Bronze and September Gold, for early flowering. Any varieties dated in the catalogues to bloom by October 5 will be good for later flowering.

I want a collection of really hardy chrysanthemums—improved plants of the old-fashioned sorts. Can you tell me what to ask for? (Virginia.) Granny Scovill, Jean Treadway, Vivid, and the double Korean hybrids, King Midas, Lavender Lady, and Mrs. Pierre S. du Pont III should be hardy in Virginia.

Which variety or type of chrysanthemum is hardiest? Cushion-type varieties (such as Amelia, King Cushion, and Dean Kay) are both early and hardy. The newer varieties originated by the University of Chicago are good.

What varieties of mums are hardy? We dug and stored some and they died, and those we tried to protect didn't thrive. For the many hardy varieties now available read other replies and consult catalogues of firms specializing in these plants. In severe climates they can be wintered in a cold frame if covered with dry leaves after the soil is lightly frozen. The glass should be shaded or covered with a wooden shutter.

What are the best large-flowering chrysanthemums—both hardy and tender? (Kentucky.) The early-flowering, large commercial mums, such as Betsy Ross, Detroit News, Golden Bronze, Mrs. H. E. Kidder, and Sunglow should do well in Kentucky. For hardy decorative varieties, try Avalanche, Lavender Lady, Mrs. Pierre S. du Pont III, King Midas, Granny Scovill, and Burgundy; or you could make a selection from the "Bird" varieties.

What chrysanthemums are best for our location? (Idaho.) There are many good early kinds available. Try the cushion varieties, such as Dean Kay, King Cushion, September Bronze, and September Gold. For larger varieties, Eugene A. Wander, My Lady, and Early Wonder. It would be a good idea to consult a local authority if possible.

What are the best early-blooming yellow chrysanthemums? Algonquin, Eugene A. Wander, King Midas, and the pompon, September Gold.

Is Astrid correct in denoting a class of chrysanthemums? No. The variety Astrid was the forerunner of the named *arcticum* hybrids, such as Good Morning, and also of the Northland Daisies. The name "astermum" has been used in connection with a type that has aster-like flowers.

Is there any chrysanthemum that is low-growing and spreading, that could be used along the top of a wall? Yes; Golden Carpet, which grows about 18 inches tall, and spreads to 3 feet or more.

Azaleamums and astermums—what is the difference, if any? Give colors. Azaleamums are a class of the cushion type, and may be had in white, yellow, pink, and bronze. All are low-growing and early. Some mums having aster-like flowers have been described as aster-mums, but they do not form a recognized type.

What are the names and where can I get large-flowering ball-type mums? Varieties such as Pink Chief, Silver Sheen, Alameda, and others could doubtless be furnished by your local florist who grows indoor mums, or you could purchase them from chrysanthemum specialists.

What are the best types of cushion mums to provide a good color range? Amelia, King Cushion, Golden Cushion, and Marjorie Mills.

What are Northland Daisies? Where did they originate? What is their history? Originated by Mr. and Mrs. J. Franklin Styer. They are descendants from Astrid, which is either a seedling or sport of *C. arcticum*. Pollen from other types has also been used.

COLUMBINE (AQUILEGIA)

My columbines never grow into healthy plants, as I have seen others do. They have full sun, and the other plants around the columbines grow very well. Why? They need a well-drained sandy loam, neutral or slightly acid. Prepare ground at least a foot deep; incorporate a 2-in. layer of rotted manure; space plants at least 9 ins. apart.

What is the best location for columbines? What fertilizer? Most any location except a hot, dry, windy one; light shade, too, is beneficial. Top-dressing of leafmold, with well-rotted manure or bone meal, in early spring, is good.

What is the proper way to plant columbines? I planted them in rich woods dirt in a spot that got sun in the morning, shade later in the day, fairly well drained. They never came up. The soil and position should be all right. You probably planted them too deeply, and the crowns rotted. They are subject to a soft rot.

From a planting of 15 columbines only 2 bloomed. Could you supply any information as to their culture? See preceding answers. When established, the others probably will bloom.

Can columbine seedlings, coming from seed planted in August, be transplanted next spring? Yes.

Is it possible to transplant old columbine plants? When? Yes. Best done in early spring. Water until established. Don't plant too deeply.

How shall I divide columbines? Lift the clumps, shake off the soil, and gently pull the plant apart, taking care not to break the roots.

DAYLILY (HEMEROCALLIS)

When is best time to plant lemonlily? How? Either autumn or spring planting is all right. Dig soil deeply, adding well-rotted cow manure; dig holes deep enough when planting so that roots are not crowded, and set plants with crown just level with soil.

Do daylilies have to be planted in the shade?   No. Daylilies will grow in full sun if the soil is rich and moist, but otherwise do better in partial shade.

Can hemerocallis be successfully grown planted among other perennials in a border?   Yes, providing you give them space enough to grow.

What is the cause of hemerocallis failing to blossom?   Failure to bloom is most commonly due to too-dense shade, or plants being overcrowded and the soil exhausted.

How can I get lemonlilies to bloom?   Divide and replant in full sun in soil that has been dug deeply (18 ins.) and enriched with a 3-in. layer of rotted manure, plus bone meal at the rate of 6 oz. per sq. yd.

How shall I divide hemerocallis, especially Hyperion?   Hemerocallis sometimes are hard to divide, especially old clumps. The best method is to first dig up clumps, then push two spading forks through the clump, back to back, and pry the clump apart.

Can you give me the name of an exquisite, dainty, lemon-yellow lily, which blooms profusely in early spring, then on and off through summer? Foliage same as dark daylily, only light and much daintier.   In all probability the lemonlily, *Hemerocallis flava*. This species is fragrant.

Will you name some good varieties of hemerocallis that will give a succession of bloom, from the earliest to the latest?   Hyperion, July to August; Mikado, June to August; Waubun, June to July; Theron, July to September; Bagdad, July; Midas, June to July; Tangouni, May to June.

I am interested in hemerocallis. Will you name some of the most popular ones?   Below are listed the first 25 of 100 in the latest list poll—1956—conducted by the American Hemerocallis Society. The numbers in parentheses is the number of votes received by each variety. The names on the right are those of the introducers. 1. Evelyn Claar (150), Kraus; 2. High Noon (126), Milliken; 3. Prima Donna (124), Taylor; 4. Salmon Sheen (122), Taylor; 5. Naranja (119), Wheelor; 6. Garnet Robe (118), Milliken; 7. Painted Lady (112), Russell; 8. Pink Damask (112), Stevens; 9. Pink Dream (110), Childs; 10. Cibola (109), Hill; 11. Colonial Dame (102), Milliken; 12. Jack Frost (97), Lester; 13. Pink Prelude (96), Nesmith; 14. Ruffled Pinafore (92), Milliken; 15. Potentate (86), Nesmith; 16. Dauntless (85), Stout; 17. Show Girl (84), Wheelor; 18. Georgia (79), Stout; 19. Revolute (77), Sass, H. P.; 20. Caballero (73), Stout; 21. Brocade (70), Taylor; 22. Neyron Rose (68), Kraus; 23.

Colonel Joe (67), Lester; 24. Picture (67), Lester; 25. Summer Love (65), Milliken.

Is there such a thing as a double daylily? I have one and thought maybe it was a freak. Yes, there is a double daylily, *Hemerocallis fulva* variety Kwanso.

Can you tell me how to hybridize hemerocallis? The flowers which are to be used as the seed bearer should be emasculated (remove anthers) and enclosed in a waxed or cellophane bag; when the stigma becomes sticky, the ripe pollen from another variety is transferred to it.

What is the best time of day to hybridize the hemerocallis? From about 12 noon until 2 P.M., as the pollen will be dryest at that time.

DELPHINIUM

The modern delphinium is one of the most spectacular and valuable of our garden flowers. The common garden hybrids are tall-growing, and are best used toward the back of a mixed border where they create strong vertical lines and accent points. While the clear blue colors are most highly prized, sparkling whites, rich violets, and soft, pleasing mauves are available. Some species have yellow or red flowers, but they are not so easy to grow in the average garden; nor are the flower spikes as showy as those of the more common types.

The geographic distribution of delphinium species is more or less limited to the Northern Hemisphere, but they are used in gardens on every continent. While their culture varies in different regions, they are grown successfully throughout the United States and Canada. Much of the horticultural development has occurred within the last 20 years, and improved colors and forms are rapidly replacing the earlier introductions.

Delpiniums are ideal as background plants for the mixed-flower border.

There are 4 main types of delphiniums. The erect and tall-growing elatum or garden hybrids bear single or double flowers in dense spikes.

The belladonna and bellamosum strains are dwarfer, with more finely cut foliage and looser spikes. The two are essentially much alike in habit of growth, but the belladonnas have light-blue or white flowers, while in the bellamosum type the flowers are dark blue. The Chinese delphinium is comparartively dwarf, seldom attaining a height of more than 3 ft. The foliage is finely cut and the clear blue or white flowers are borne in a loose, informal arrangement. They are the easiest to grow, and especially valuable for cutting, to be used with other flowers in mixed bouquets or arrangements. There are also several annual species which are well adapted to many regions.

Soil and Fertilizer

What kind of soil is desirable for delphiniums?   A rich, friable loam containing a high percentage of organic matter.

How can one increase the amount of organic matter in the soil for delphiniums?   Experiments have shown that thoroughly decomposed leafmold is the best organic matter to use. Oak leafmold is less desirable than other types. Mix the leafmold with soil at the rate of 8 to 10 bu. per 100 sq. ft.; or 1 bu. of leafmold to 8 bu. of soil.

Is peatmoss good for delphiniums?   In some experiments carried out to determine the best type of organic matter, peatmoss was found to be less desirable than leafmold.

What soil mixture is best for starting delphinium seeds?   A mixture of 1 part good garden loam, 1 part sand, and 1 part leafmold is satisfactory. Sift through a sieve having ¼-in. mesh.

Can manure be used on delphiniums?   Manure, if well rotted, is excellent. It may be mixed with the soil at the time it is prepared or it may be used as a top-dressing. Apply about 5 bu. per 100 sq. ft.

Do delphiniums need fertilizer?   Yes. They require an abundance of nutrients. They have a higher nitrogen requirement than almost any other garden flower. Unless the soil is already very rich they should be fertilized at least twice a year with a complete commercial fertilizer.

When should delphiniums be fertilized?   Make the first application in spring when the new shoots are about 4 in. tall. A second application may be made at the time the plants are cut back following the first blooming period.

Do delphiniums require lime?   They do best in a slightly acid soil (pH 6.8). If the organic matter content is very high, they will do well over a much wider range of pH values (pH 5.5 to 7.2). Lime is required only when a pH test shows that the reaction is pH 6.5 or below. (See Acidity—Section I.)

What type of lime should be used for delphiniums; and how should it be applied?   Ground limestone is best. Where soil is very acid or very heavy, hydrated lime may be used. Spread it evenly over soil surface and work it into the top 3 or 4 ins.

Should lime be applied to delphiniums every year?   No, only when a soil test indicates it is necessary.

How can one tell by observing the plants when the soil is too sweet for delphiniums?   The leaves appear mottled with yellow or, in severe cases, with white. The veins usually retain their dark-green color. A pH test of the soil will confirm the plant symptoms.

Planting and Replanting

In what situation should delphiniums be planted?   In full sun or very light shade and, if possible, with some protection from strong winds.

How far apart should delphiniums be planted?   In perennial borders, 2 to 3 ft. each way. In cut-flower garden, 3 to 4 ft. between rows and 2 ft. between plants in rows.

When should delphiniums be transplanted?   Very early spring is best, but they may be transplanted with success in fall, or immediately after their first period of bloom.

When should full-grown delphiniums be moved?   In very early spring, if possible before growth starts. Move with a large ball of soil.

Culture

How can I keep my delphiniums healthy?   Give them a rich, well-drained soil. Cover the crowns in winter with leached coal ashes to discourage crown-rot. Fertilize occasionally.

How can delphiniums be made to bloom in the fall as well as during their regular season?   By cutting the flowering stems back to the ground as soon as possible after they have finished blooming. New shoots will then come up and flower in the early fall.

How can delphiniums be staked?   Begin when the plant is about 3 ft. high, and place 3 6-ft. stakes in the form of a triangle around it. Tie a band of raffia or soft twine around the stakes about 1 ft. above the ground. As the plant grows, tie additional bands around the stakes. If desired, individual stakes can be used for large-flowering spikes. This latter method is to be preferred in decorative plantings.

Should delphiniums be watered?   Delphiniums require large quantities of water, especially during, and just prior to, the flowering period. They will be improved by thorough watering when the weather is dry.

Is there any advantage in spreading coal ashes around delphinium plants in the fall?   Many successful delphinium growers follow the practice with good results. Just what the benefits are has never been scientifically studied.

What winter care should be given delphinium seedlings started in a cold frame in August? Cover with about 2 ins. of medium-coarse clean sand. Later mulch with straw or salt hay. Put sash on the frame to keep out snow and rain.

Should young delphinium plants, set out in the fall, be mulched? It is always well to protect seedlings transplanted in the fall from heaving. Covering the plants with about 2 ins. of sand, and later mulching lightly with salt hay or straw, will give the necessary protection.

Should established delphiniums be covered over winter? In all but the coldest climates this is unnecessary. Delphiniums are more likely to be killed by poor drainage, smothering, or diseases than by low temperatures.

Problems

Should an amateur buy delphinium plants or start them from seeds? Either is satisfactory, but most delphinium growers prefer to start their own plants. Purchase only the best plants or seeds. Inferior strains are unsatisfactory.

Do seeds from hybrid delphiniums produce desirable plants? If seeds are saved from superior plants they will probably be satisfactory. It is usually best to buy seeds from reliable growers who have taken special pains in producing them.

Why have my delphiniums failed since I moved them and replanted them 1 foot from a hedge where they get south sun? Probably the moving is responsible. They may do better when they become re-established. However, you have set them too near the hedge. They should be at least 2 or 3 ft. away and kept well fertilized and watered.

How can I prevent my delphiniums from growing tall and having brittle stems even though I withhold nitrogen? Vigorous delphiniums are likely to be brittle and to break off during wind- and rain-storms. Withholding nitrogen will not make the stems less brittle; in fact, it may make them more so. (See Nitrogen—Section I.) Nothing can be done except to stake the plants adequately.

Can delphiniums have their tops pinched out, like zinnias, to make them branch? No, the shoots that arise from the bases of the plants terminate in flower spikes. When the growing point is removed, the lateral buds do not develop as they do with zinnias.

How can I keep delphiniums alive during the hot summer months? They may be grown in light shade or cloth houses. In the open keep them well watered and free of crown-rot diseases.

Why do delphiniums freeze out in winter? Delphiniums are really very hardy plants. It is seldom that they are killed by low temperatures. They are more likely to be smothered by snow, ice, or water.

Diseases, especially crown-rot, may develop during the fall, winter, or early spring, and kill the plants. Heaving is another hazard.

How long will delphiniums live?   Where the crown-rot diseases are not serious, they live indefinitely. However, since these organisms are widespread over much of the United States, from 3 to 5 years is the expected life of the ordinary plant.

How can Delphinium cardinale be wintered in cold climates?   It can't. This species is tender and will not stand freezing. It can be carried over winter only in a greenhouse, and even then it is not very successful.

Is there any reason why good delphiniums cannot be grown in Connecticut?   No. In fact some of the best delphiniums in the country have been grown in Ridgefield, Connecticut, by a former president of the American Delphinium Society.

How can delphiniums be grown in a warm climate, such as Florida?   Grow them as annuals by sowing seeds early each spring. The plants are not usually successfully carried over a second year.

Is there a truly perennial delphinium?   In their native habitats many species persist for years, but under garden conditions they are more subject to diseases and are less long-lived.

Why do some delphiniums live longer than others?   Natural variation in vigor, disease resistance, etc., account for the difference in longevity.

Propagation

What is the best temperature for germinating delphinium seeds?   The optimum is 55° F.

What is the best way to raise delphiniums from seed?   Many different methods are successful; it is difficult to state which is best. Where many plants are needed, sow in well-prepared soil in a cold frame in August. Leave the seedlings in the frame over winter and transplant to the garden in spring.

What conditions are necessary for growing delphinium seedlings?   Good light, plenty of moisture (but the soil must not be kept soaked), and a temperature of 55° to 60° F.

Can delphinium seeds be sown in the open ground?   Yes. If you do so, prepare a bed with special care where the tiny seedlings can be protected. It is really better, however, to sow in a cold frame or in seed flats.

When should delphiniums be started indoors?   Seeds may be sown any time between February 1 and May 1. If started early, many of the plants will bloom the first year.

How thick should delphinium seeds be sown and how deep should they be covered?   Sow in rows spaced about 2 ins. apart. The seeds in the rows should be about ¼ in. apart. Cover so that seeds are barely out of sight.

Should delphinium seeds be disinfected? And how? Disinfecting is desirable, especially where the soil is not sterilized. The use of Semesan or a similar product is satisfactory. Merely place a pinch of the powder in the seed package and shake until seeds are evenly covered.

Is it necessary to sterilize soil in which delphinium seeds are sown? Not necessary, but it is good insurance. Measure out 2½ tablespoonfuls of formaldehyde (40 per cent strength) for each bushel of prepared soil; dilute with 4 or 5 times its volume of water; add to soil, and mix very thoroughly. Place soil in seed boxes, saving a little for covering the seed; stack the boxes one above the other to confine the fumes for a day or two, then uncover them. When the odor is no longer perceptible it is safe to sow the seeds. Soil-fume caps will destroy nematodes in garden beds.

Will delphinium seeds sown indoors in spring produce flowers in summer? If sown indoors before April 1 most of the plants will bloom in late August or early September.

Should delphinium seedlings grown indoors be transplanted, or may one wait until they can be planted outdoors? Transplant to flats as soon as big enough to handle conveniently. Use a soil mixture of 1 part leafmold, 2 parts garden loam, and ½ part sand. Good drainage must be provided so that soil never remains soggy.

Is it wise to divide delphiniums that have grown to a large size; and how often should this be done? Ordinarily it is better to start new plants from seeds, but old clumps can be divided if they have become too large; this will usually not be until they are at least 3 years old.

How are delphiniums divided; and how large should the divisions be? Dig the plants, shake off the soil, and cut the clumps apart with a strong knife. Replant immediately in well-prepared soil. Each division should contain 3 to 5 shoots.

Diseases and Pests

My delphiniums suffer from "blacks"; they are deformed and stunted and marked with black streaks and blotches. What is wrong? This "disease" is caused by an infestation of an exceedingly minute pest—the cyclamen mite. Cut off and burn badly infected shoots. Spray from early spring to flowering time with rotenone or nicotine spray or, use a miticide such as Dimite about once a week. Avoid planting delphiniums near strawberries, which are also host to this mite.

What is a cure for crown-rot of delphiniums? Crown-rot is really a name for a group of diseases. All are very difficult to control. Sterilization of the soil with formaldehyde or chloropicrin is the surest method. In small gardens destroy infested plants, drench the soil with Semesan solution or mercury bichloride (1 to 1,000 parts of water). When possible, plant delphiniums on new ground.

I planted out some delphiniums but several were eaten off by cutworms. How can I prevent a recurrence? See Cutworms—Section VIII.

Is mildew on delphiniums caused by the soil? No. Mildew is a fungous disease that infects the leaves. It is controlled by keeping the plants dusted with sulfur. Avoid setting plants too closely together. (See Mildew.)

Types and Varieties

How many colors of delphiniums are there? If all the species are considered, they cover an unusually wide range. The garden hybrids (*Delphinium elatum*), the belladonna, bellamosum, and Chinese types contain white and tones of blue, violet, and mauve. *Delphinium nudicaule* is orange and red; *D. cardinale* is clear red; *D. sulphureum* and *D. zalil* are yellow.

Is there a true pink perennial delphinium? The variety Pink Sensation comes nearest to this description.

What delphiniums are bred especially for hardiness? Giant Northern Hybrids. They can be had in light blue, lavender, violet, white, blue, and pink-lavender, in named varieties.

How can I get the colors I want by growing my own delphiniums from seed? The Pacific Giant Hybrids can be had in blue and light blue, violet and dark blue, white, and in pastel and mixed shades.

EREMURUS

When is the best time to plant eremurus (foxtaillily), spring or fall? Will 2- or 3-year-old plants bloom the first season after planting, or must they be older? (Wyoming.) Plant in fall, since top growth begins early in spring. Usually plants younger than 4 years bloom little, if at all. For first season results 4-year-old plants are set out. They will require a winter mulch (10 or 12 ins. of coal ashes) to protect the roots from too-severe freezing in Wyoming.

Does eremurus (foxtaillily) require a special kind of culture? It is best to give it a deep, well-prepared soil but see that it is well drained. Work in some fine bone meal each fall.

How do you plant foxtaillily (eremurus)? Do you spread the roots out or do you plant with the roots down, like Oriental poppy? They should be planted with the roots spread out flat. The roots will snap off if bent when planting.

How deep should 4-year-old eremurus roots be planted?   Plant so that the crown is about 2 ins. below the soil surface. Too-deep planting is apt to cause the crown to rot, especially in a heavy soil.

I have some 3-year-old eremurus in a lining-out bed. What care do they require; and do they prefer light or heavy soil?   Plant in sheltered position in rich, well-drained soil, in full sun, with the fleshy roots spread out and the bud 2 ins. under the soil. Plant in late September, and cover before winter with leached coal ashes 6 ins. to a foot deep.

Can eremurus be divided, and when?   They may be divided only with difficulty, unless they make offsets freely. Early fall is the best time. Each division must have a bud, or eye.

Can eremurus be raised from seed? When and how long until bloom?   May be raised from seed sown in flats or pots in late autumn or spring. Will bloom from seed in about 4 to 6 years.

EUPATORIUM (HARDY "AGERATUM")

How deep should the hardy ageratum be planted?   It is shallow rooting; plant about 2 ins. deep. The roots are stringy; merely spread them out and cover.

When should hardy ageratum be moved?   It is best done in spring before growth starts.

How often do you have to move hardy ageratum?   Probably best lifted and transplanted every year or two, as it grows into quite a mat which usually dies out in the center.

HARDY FUCHSIA

Is hardy fuchsia a shrub, or can it be included among herbaceous perennials?   It is really a low-growing shrub, but in Northern climates it is often killed down to ground line by the winter, making it in effect an herbaceous perennial.

In what kind of soil should a hardy fuchsia be planted? I had no luck with mine.   A light, well-drained garden loam with some leaf-mold added. It is often planted in rock gardens. Keep it out of exposed situations, and try a light winter cover.

What might cause the buds of a hardy fuchsia to drop off before opening? The plant seemed healthy and many buds formed, but all failed to develop.   If spring planted, the exposure probably was too hot and dry. Fuchsias as a whole are not good garden plants in the East or Midwest, and the so-called hardy sort is far from being so under winter conditions.

Will Fuchsia riccartoni (or the variety Scarlet Beauty) live through

the winter in south central part of Maine? Don't believe all you hear about the hardiness of this fuchsia. Even in the neighborhood of New York its survival is exceptional. At 15° F. it will kill to the ground; and in Maine, unless buried deeply in snow, it's 100 to 1 against the roots surviving.

GERBERIA

What care does gerberia require—including cultivation, pests, and diseases? (New York.) This South African perennial is not hardy, although it may be grown outside in sheltered situations if given winter protection, or lifted in fall and wintered over in a cold frame. More commonly grown as greenhouse plant. Grow in well-drained, fairly rich soil; keep crowns just above soil level. Fertilize in spring with liquid manure. Propagate from seeds (slow to germinate) or, better, by cuttings of side shoots. Spray for leaf roller and green fly, two of its worst enemies. (See Section VIII.)

What garden soil, exposure, moisture, food, for gerberia? (They are hardy here.) (Delaware.) Best in well-drained soil in full sun. Water only in dry weather. Apply weak manure water in spring and early summer.

I have some gerberia roots. I have them in a box 18 ins. underground covered with leaves and dirt. Will they smother, or will I have to install an air vent pipe? The covering is too deep. Tender plants cannot be wintered over by burying them. Without a cold frame or like protection it is difficult to winter gerberias over. An air vent would be of little help. Plant them next to a building; erect a wooden frame around them. Cover with hay and give air in mild weather.

How can I grow gerberia outside? Should be grown in full sun in well-drained soil. Plant only in spring and give cold frame protection for the winter. They are not hardy in Northern gardens.

Do gerberia roots need dividing; and when? They do not require dividing very often; but when the clumps get large and begin to fail, divide in spring.

HELIOPSIS

Where should heliopsis be planted? In what type of soil? Plant in full sun, in any garden soil. Will probably flower better in a fairly dry situation.

HOLLYHOCKS

Do hollyhocks take an excessive amount of moisture away from surrounding plants? Not enough to harm near-by plants. The ground around hollyhocks usually looks dry because their large leaves shed a lot of rain.

IRISES

Like roses, irises have been a part of our historical and legendary heritage. Because of their delicate texture and sparkling hues it is appropriate that they should have been named in honor of the Goddess of the Rainbow, the messenger of Zeus and Hera. In medieval times the fleur-de-lis became the emblem of France. Its abstract form has been widely used as a motif in many forms of art.

Irises have always been popular as garden flowers. The many species are distributed throughout the Temperate Zone and are therefore adapted to culture in most of the civilized world. While some iris species have not responded to the efforts of plant breeders as readily as many other kinds of plants, considerable development has taken place, particularly in the tall-bearded iris group. The size, coloring, and garden value have been greatly improved. Many of the different species used in American gardens are the same as they appear in nature. They have not needed to be improved to make them worth-while garden subjects.

Most of the species and varieties bloom through early and late spring. They are especially useful in the flower border, in the rock garden, and in association with pools and streams.

Soils

Do irises grow better in low, moist ground, or in dry soil? In sun or shade? Bearded irises require sharp drainage. Beardless kinds (such as Japanese varieties) need plenty of moisture but not waterlogged soil. The Yellow Flag of Europe and our native *Iris versicolor* succeed even in swamp conditions. Most do best in full sun.

What is the correct soil for bearded irises? Any good garden soil. Add bone meal and gypsum when remaking the beds. If heavy, lighten with sand or ashes. They require good drainage.

Do Japanese irises require acid soil? Yes, or at least a soil that is not alkaline.

For Japanese and Siberian irises, what soil preparation is required? Spade deeply; incorporate plenty of humus—old rotted manure, leafmold, peatmoss, or compost. Also, if the soil is somewhat poor, add a dressing of cottonseed meal, pulverized sheep manure, or general fertilizer. Do not use lime or gypsum.

What kind of soil is good for Dutch irises? Any fertile, well-drained garden soil other than heavy clay. This is true for all bulbous irises.

Fertilizer

Is manure good for irises? Animal manure should not be used on bearded irises, but the beardless species (including the Japanese and Siberian irises) appreciate well-rotted manure.

What is the best time of year to feed ordinary bearded irises; and how? It is usually better not to feed established plantings, but to rely rather upon fertilizer that is dug in when beds are made. However, if additional fertilizer is applied, use any good garden type of low-nitrogen content in early spring.

Should beds of bearded irises be fertilized each spring? Not if ground was well prepared and fertilized at planting time.

What fertilizer do you recommend for ordinary (German) irises? Bone meal and unleached wood ashes together with a commercial fertilizer low in nitrogen. Mix with soil when beds are made.

Do bearded irises require lime? Only if the soil is decidedly acid.

What is the best fertilizer to use on Japanese irises? Rotted cow manure (or if this is not available leafmold or peatmoss fortified with a light dressing of complete fertilizer). Apply as a mulch in May or early June. In fall, mulch with manure, leaves, or peatmoss.

Planting

Are irises more attractive planted together or scattered in clumps throughout the garden? By themselves they are not attractive over the greater part of the year. Clumps of one variety in front of evergreens are very effective. Many people interplant irises with daylilies.

When, where, and how do you plant German (bearded) irises? In June or July, in good garden soil. Plant rhizomes level with surface in well-drained, sunny beds. Buy your stock from a reliable dealer so that you will recieve good, healthy rhizomes.

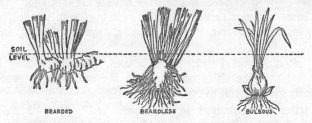

Planting depth for bearded, beardless, and bulbous irises.

Should irises be planted so as to cover up the rhizomes; or should they be left exposed? In light, sandy soil the rhizomes may be covered an inch or so; but in heavy soils they should be left with the tops exposed.

What distances should be allowed between irises when planting? Tall-bearded, 9 to 18 ins.; dwarf-bearded, 6 to 9 ins.; Japanese and Siberian, 18 to 24 ins.; bulbous, 4 to 5 ins. with 12 ins. between rows.

At what distance apart should purchased divisions of German irises be set? For a substantial effect the first year after planting, 8 or 9 ins. A better spacing is 16 or 18 ins., but this takes 2 years to produce a good display.

Should iris rhizomes be dried out before replanting? Not unless diseased, because if the feeding roots are dried no new growth results until new ones develop. Irises may be divided and transplanted without much setback providing their roots are kept out of the sun and they are replanted immediately.

I have been told that bearded irises can be planted only in June. Is this true? No. Many growers favor June, but entirely successful planting can be done in fall, or even in early spring. June planting (just after flowering) has the advantage of affording the divisions the longest time to recuperate before the next blooming season.

Will irises bloom if they are moved early in spring? The Japanese and Siberians usually do; the tall-bearded sometimes (but with short bloom stalks). If possible, avoid moving bearded irises until after the blooming season.

How late can bearded irises be planted in northern Virginia and still have good spring bloom? September. They must have sufficient time to make new growth and become established. Planting in July or early August is recommended.

When and how deep should Japanese irises be planted? Early spring, before growth starts, or late August. Crowns should be set 2 ins. below the surface.

Culture

Can we grow irises successfully? We have a lot of shade. Ordinary garden irises will not thrive in shade. Certain wild species, such as *cristata, gracilipes, verna,* and *foetidissima,* are satisfactory in partial shade.

How often should I transplant irises? Whenever they become so crowded that the rhizomes are growing over one another. This will usually mean about every 3 years.

Can irises be replanted in the same bed? Yes, if redug and fertilized. If disease is present, soil should first be sterilized.

Should irises be thinned out if not blooming freely? If lack of bloom is due to crowding, lift and replant. If some other cause, get diagnosis and be guided accordingly.

What culture do Japanese irises require? Bed must be well drained (it is fatal to select a location where water stands during winter). Enrich soil with leafmold, well-decayed manure, or garden compost. Plant in August; replant every 3 years. They like plenty of water before and during blooming season.

What are the conditions favorable to the growth of Siberian irises? Plenty of sunshine, well-drained, rich, slightly acid soil. They like plenty of rotted manure, also plenty of moisture from spring until blooming is over.

Do the Dutch, English, and Spanish irises all get same culture? In general, yes. Plant bulbs 4 to 5 ins. deep, October to November, in sunny location and in good, well-drained loam. Let remain for 2 years, then lift and replant in a new location. They are gross feeders and deplete the soil very quickly. In severe climates a winter mulch is beneficial.

How are bulbous irises handled in the South? Dutch, English, and Spanish irises are dug after blooming and are stored in a cool shed until late fall, when they are replanted. This because they make fall growth, and if left in ground the flower stalks are usually killed by a freeze in late winter. When lifted and replanted in late fall, stalks do not develop until spring.

Do Dutch irises have to be dug up each year? Not unless they have suffered winter losses. In that case try planting as late in autumn as weather permits. The following year dig the bulbs when the foliage dies down, and store in a cool location until autumn. In extreme climates a winter mulch is beneficial.

When is best time to move Dutch irises? As soon as the foliage has died down. In the South many people lift them at this time and store in airy containers in a cool shed until late fall.

What is correct culture of oncocyclus irises? These natives of the Near and Middle East require a dormant season, without moisture. Grow them in pots or cold frames so that they are kept dry from mid-June to mid-December.

When do you divide and replant Siberian irises? Late August or September.

I have a large garden of Japanese irises set 4 years. When should I divide and reset? They seem to be getting crowded. Immediately after blooming season, in September, or just before growth starts in spring.

How much watering and cultivating do irises need? Bearded irises ordinarily need no watering. Japanese and other beardless types need plenty of moisture until flowering is through. Cultivate shallowly and sufficiently often to keep surface loose and free of weeds.

What care should be given iris rhizomes after the blooming season? If overcrowded, divide them. Remove flower stalks immediately after flowering, and be on the alert for signs of borers or rots. Keep all dead foliage cleaned off.

Does it injure iris plants to take green foliage off in the late fall? Leaves turning brown should always be removed promptly. Green foliage should not be removed nor cut back in late fall because this may adversely affect next year's bloom.

When leaves are forbidden as protection for bearded irises, what can be used? No protection is necessary unless rhizomes have been planted in late fall. Evergreen boughs then make the best protection. Salt hay or excelsior may also be used.

Would you cover iris roots? I have over 400 different kinds and it would be quite a task to cover them all. No. They only need protection if planted in late fall, and then only because their root growth will not be sufficient to keep them from heaving. A few irises of Californian origin need to be planted in sheltered spots.

Problems

How can I transport irises to shows? Obtain large florists' boxes. String tape across them in several places so that stalks can be suspended without blooms touching bottoms or sides. Keep boxes level; or if this is impossible, then tie each stalk to the tapes.

How should I prepare irises for exhibition at my local garden-club shows? Bloom stalks should have at least 2 open flowers. Three would be better. These should be the first blooms. After cutting, stand in water for 30 minutes or longer. Foliage should be displayed with flower stalks. Dead or torn blooms count heavily against you. Varieties should be correctly labeled.

What colors of irises look best in the garden? This is a matter of personal taste. Soft colors usually fit best into general garden schemes. In large plantings, deep purples (such as Sable) and reds (such as Red Gleam) may be scattered in small clumps as accent points. Brassy yellows are sometimes difficult.

Is there any special organization of iris growers? Yes. The American Iris Society. Each member receives the society's well-illustrated bulletins. The address of the secretary of the Society is 2237 Tower Grove Blvd., St. Louis 10, Mo.

I have tried for many years to raise red and pink irises, but can't make them live over winter. What is the reason? Try planting earlier in summer, so that plants become established before winter. China Maid and Miss California (pinks of Californian origin) are sometimes tender. Try Angelus, a pink that originated in the Middle West. Christabel (red) is extremely vigorous, and should do well.

Why won't Japanese irises bloom for me? Too much shade? Alkaline soil? Dry soil? Water settling around crowns in winter? Any of the above may be responsible.

My bearded irises grow and look well, but bloom rarely. What is the reason? They have been established more than 2 years. They get full sun at least half a day. Most likely they are overcrowded and need dividing. Some varieties of tall-bearded irises require dividing every year for good bloom.

Are all bearded irises robust growers? No. Certain varieties, especially dark-colored ones, are less vigorous than others. Some that have originated in southern California are tender, and do not do well in cold parts of the country.

Do irises change colors from year to year? No. But in different gardens the same iris may vary somewhat in color intensity, due to cultural and environmental conditions. Slight variations may occur in different locations in the same garden.

After a few years does a mixed planting of irises gradually lose color and turn white? No. What sometimes happens is that the faster growers crowd out slower-growing varieties.

Why do irises stop blooming after being separated, even though carefully taken apart at right season? They are free of pests and were planted at right depth. Perhaps soil is deficient or exhausted. Try remaking beds and adding bone meal and perhaps gypsum. Sunshine is important.

I planted irises two years ago, half of them grew to enormous size and bloomed, but the others remained small and spindly. How can I make these perk up and bloom? Robust varieties produce a representative bloom stalk the first year after planting, others take 2 years to become established. Furthermore, varieties vary in height; it may be that you have some of the intermediate varieties growing together with tall-bearded sorts.

My irises (early dwarfs and Siberians) bloomed the first year but not the following 2 years. What is wrong? Perhaps they do not get enough sunshine, or they may be too crowded, and in need of dividing. Siberians are gross feeders; they require plenty of fertilizer.

My irises do not do well; they have decreased in size and stopped blooming. The soil is stiff clay. What would you advise? Perhaps your soil is so heavy that just enough feeding roots develop to keep your plants alive, but not enough to build strong plants. Lift, divide, and replant in well-drained beds improved by addition of coal cinders or sand, bone meal, and a dressing of gypsum or agricultural lime if soil test shows need of it. Incorporate organic matter.

What is the difference between the Dykes Medal and Dykes Memorial Medal? No difference. The complete name is the Dykes Memorial Medal, but it is generally spoken of as the Dykes Medal.

Propagation

How should I divide tall bearded irises? After flowering cut the leaves back halfway, lift the clumps, then with a sharp knife cut the rhizomes into pieces so that each has one (or, if preferred, 2 or

3) strong fan of leaves attached. Be sure divisions are disease-free before replanting. Divide every 3 or 4 years.

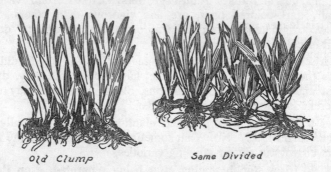

Old Clump   Same Divided

A clump of bearded iris, divided for replanting.

How are Japanese irises divided? When?   It is quite a job if the clumps are large. A heavy-bladed knife or billhook is the best tool. Cut the leaves halfway back and then chop the rootstock into pieces each having 3 or 4 growths. Discard old, lifeless material. Save only young, vigorous portions. Do this work in September, in shade, and keep the roots from drying out.

Should iris seeds picked in fall be planted fall or spring?   In fall; if planted in spring they will not germinate until following year. Plant in open ground or in a cold frame—the latter preferred. In a cold frame they start coming up in late February, and should be transplanted in late June to nursery beds.

Typical divisions of tall-bearded, dwarf-bearded, and beardless irises.

How do you grow irises from seed?   After seed is harvested plant immediately in a cold frame, or save until late fall and plant in open ground. If sown earlier outdoors, young seedlings come up and are heaved out during winter. Be sure soil is well prepared and on light side. Transplant the seedlings, in late June, to a nursery bed, spacing at least a foot apart each way. Nearly all should bloom the following year.

Diseases and Pests (See also Section VIII)

My iris leaves are spotted. What shall I do? This is leaf-spot disease. Cut back diseased foliage and burn it. If this is not done, it will spread disease through garden. Be sure and keep all dead leaves picked off, and in 2 years you will have eliminated disease.

Are irises subject to virus disease? Iris mosaic disease attacks both bearded and bulbous kinds, causing mottling or yellow striping of leaves, and lack of vigor. Destroy all infected plants.

My iris roots have rotted, and watery streaks appear on the leaves. What is the cause? Bacterial soft rot. It often gains entrance through wounds made by the iris borer. Dig and destroy rotted plants; sterilize soil by soaking with 1 oz. Semesan to 1 gal. water. Avoid planting diseased rhizomes. Sterilize knives and tools with Semesan solution, as disease is spread by these. Clean off and burn dead leaves and rubbish in fall.

How can I control thrips on Japanese irises? By spraying or dusting with DDT, lindane or dieldrin.

Grayish plant lice have attacked my iris roots underground. What control measures shall I take? Root aphids are destroyed by soaking the soil with nicotine sulfate, 2 teaspoonfuls to 1 gal. water; or by the use of malathion (follow directions on the package.)

What controls are recommended for iris borers? Clean up and burn all old leaves and debris in fall, and if winter covering has been used burn this in early spring. In severe infestations spray with dieldrin or lead arsenate ¼ lb. to 6 gals. water with a little wheat flour added as a sticker.

Varieties

How are irises classified? Into 3 groups. Group 1: bearded irises (Pogoniris) are derived from species native to southern Europe and Asia Minor. Distinguishing characteristics are a conspicuous beard on the lower petals and thick, fleshy rhizomes. Group 2: beardless irises (Apogon) are derived from species from Europe, Asia, and America; with thin rhizomes and grasslike leaves; they include *fulva, kaempferi* (Japanese), *sibirica* (Siberian), and *spuria*. Group 3: bulbous and miscellaneous, including English, Spanish, and Dutch irises.

Which group of irises is most useful in the home garden? Undoubtedly the tall-bearded (often miscalled German irises). The Japanese and Siberian groups are also very useful.

Which is better, cheap collections with many irises or a few good new varieties? Not always are high-priced varieties better than older, inexpensive kinds. Unless immediate effect is imperative, there is no doubt that a few good irises are to be preferred to a lot of poor ones. They soon multiply.

What are the "best" irises to date?   Below are the first 25 of the 100 listed by members of the American Iris Society in the Iris popularity poll. The numbers after each name indicate the votes received. Truly Yours (928); Ola Kala (742); Happy Birthday (726); Mary Randall (683); Palomino (662); Argus Pheasant (627); Chivalry (625); Elmohr (621); Blue Rhythm (552); New Snow (547); Lady Mohr (541); Pierre Menard (537); Pinnacle (526); Blue Shimmer (487); Desert Song (455); Sable Night (427); Minnie Colquitt (420); Snow Flurry (416); Blue Sapphire (414); Limelight (405); Amandine (403); Char Maize (389); Inca Chief (384); First Violet (375); Helen McGregor (367).

Which are the most popular white irises?   New Snow, Snow Flurry, Spanish Peaks, Winter Carnival, Samite, White Wings.

Will you give me a selection of good yellow irises?   Truly Yours, Ola Kala, Pinnacle (white and yellow), Spun Gold, Mohr Beauty.

Is the bulbous iris Juno known by any other name? Can I obtain hybrids in the Juno group?   No. It and other species of the Juno group are rare in American gardens. They are only suited for skilled growers and comparatively mild climates.

Which are the 12 best varieties of Japanese irises?   Probably unobtainable, even if it were possible for 2 persons to agree on the "12 best." Following are good: Aspasie, Betty F. Holmes, Elbrus, Fanny Hamlet Childs, Goldbound, Koki-no-iro, La Favorite, Light-in-the-Opal, Mahongany, Pluton, Satsuki-bare, Violet Beauty. The "Marhigo" series of seedlings (judging from the colored pictures in the Walter Marx catalog) are as good as any of these named varieties.

LUPINE

What can I use to build up soil for lupines?   They need a well-drained and medium soil. Use sand, leafmold, and well-rotted manure. Lime should not be used on lupines.

One authority says acid soil, another a lime soil for perennial lupines. What is your opinion?   Most lupines seem to do better in an acid or neutral soil.

What should I use to fertilize lupines?   Well-rotted compost, cow manure, or any general garden fertilizer.

Will you give soil and cultural direction for Russell Lupines?   Russell Lupines thrive in any good garden soil in full sun. Seed should be planted in August, about ½ in. deep, and soon after it has ripened. The spikes do not grow so large here as in England.

It is, however, one of our finest perennials. Lupines are short-lived and may not persist after the first year. Give adequate winter protection.

What is the best way of raising the improved types of perennial lupine from seed indoors? I have had poor germination. Sow individual seeds in small pots of sandy soil, first nicking the hard seed coat with the point of a knife. Sown in March and started in a greenhouse the seedlings will show in a week and be ready to plant outdoors, without the roots being disturbed, in May. Or nick the seed or place in hot water for an overnight soak, and sow thinly outdoors in April if the soil is in friable condition.

Will lupine seeds "stratified" come up following year? They should. If kept over winter in a seed container germination is aided by making a nick in seed coat with a sharp knife.

Can lupines be transplanted? Do they last many years? Old plants do not like to be disturbed and are very hard to transplant. Young plants can be transplanted in very early spring if care is used to protect the roots. Lupines are short-lived. For a constant supply sow seed each year.

MONKSHOOD (ACONITUM)

How often should aconitum be divided? These plants flower very freely when they are in established clumps, and may be left undisturbed for years.

How deep shall I plant aconitum, and in what kind of soil? They are best planted with the crown about one inch down, in rich, moist soil, neutral or slightly acid.

Do aconitums need winter protection? They are hardy but should be protected for the first and second winter after planting.

When should I sow seed of monkshood? In late autumn, using fresh seed.

What soil and site do monkshood need? They require a rich, moist soil, and do best in partial shade.

Will you name several kinds of monkshood that would be successful? *Aconitum fischeri, A. napellus* Sparks Variety, *A. wilsoni,* and *A. uncinatum.*

Is it advisable to plant monkshood? I have heard it is poisonous. Monkshood does contain poison. It is said to have been mistaken for horse-radish on occasions and eaten with fatal results. But it is widely grown in gardens.

PENTSTEMONS

I have several pentstemon plants which stayed green long after frost. Is it hardy? You may have plants of the bedding pentstemon, which is not hardy but which stay green until late. The other kinds are hardy, and, with the exception of the alpine sorts, are treated like ordinary perennials. Many of them remain green until long after frost.

How do you trim and care for large pentstemons?   They need no trimming. The wiry stems of the tall kinds need support, best supplied by using twiggy brush inserted among the plants when they are about a foot tall. Growing up through this, with loose stems tied up and the tops of the brush cut away when flower buds form, they will be held neatly and securely. Cut the stems after flowering, and top-dress with bone meal.

How is it best to divide pentstemon plants?   Lift the plants in early spring, pull them gently apart, and replant.

PEONIES

The modern peony is the achievement of years of steadfast devotion and effort on the part of plant breeders. For more than 2,000 years the peony has been cultivated in China, not alone for its highly prized flowers, but for its roots, which in early times were used for food and medicinal purposes. It was named in honor of Paeon, the physician of the gods, who—according to mythology—received the first peony on Mt. Olympus from the hands of Leto.

Present-day gardeners are inclined to take the peony for granted because it has become so common. The very fact that it is common only serves to emphasize its many worth-while qualities. Hardiness, permanence, ease of culture, and freedom from pests are but a few of its merits. Diversity in flower form, attractive colors, clean habit of growth, and deep-green foliage combine to produce a plant of exceptional value for mass plantings or for the mixed border. Peonies rank high as cut flowers because of their extraordinary keeping qualities. They are primarily plants for the North, for they require the low temperatures of winter to break the dormancy of the buds before spring growth will take place.

Some horticulturists consider that the interest in peonies is on the wane; that their potentiality for further improvement is exhausted. This does not seem to be the case, however, for within the last few years several new varieties have been introduced that eclipse all previous originations in perfection of form and color. They have always been garden favorites and will continue to be so.

Soil; Fertilizers

What type of soil is best for peonies?   They grow well in a wide range of soil types. Any rich, friable garden soil is satisfactory.

Is a very heavy soil satisfactory for peonies?   Yes, providing it is well-drained. Some form of organic material, such as well-rotted manure, peatmoss, or leafmold, should be added to make it more friable.

Will peonies thrive in a sandy soil?   Sandy soil is well suited to peony growing if its fertility is maintained. Well-rotted manure and commercial fertilizer should be used.

What is the proper method of preparing the soil for peonies? Spade it to a depth of 12 to 18 ins. Thoroughly work in some well-rotted manure or other form of organic material at the rate of 4 bu. per 100 sq. ft. Incorporate 3 lbs. of superphosphate to each 100 sq. ft. If the soil is acid apply lime (5 lbs. per 100 sq. ft.) several weeks before planting.

How deep should peony soil be prepared?   Because they may remain in one spot for many years, it is desirable to thoroughly prepare the soil to a depth of from 12 to 24 ins.

Do peonies need lime?   Peonies grow best in a slightly acid soil (pH 5.5 to 6.5). If the soil is very acid (below pH 5), the addition of lime is beneficial.

What kind of lime and how much should be used for peonies? If a soil test shows a pH value below 5, apply ground limestone or ordinary agricultural lime at the rate of 5 lbs. per 100 sq. ft.

What kind and how much fertilizer should I use for peonies? A mixed commercial fertilizer of 4–12–4 or 5–10–5 analysis is satisfactory. Use 4 lbs. for each 100 sq. ft. Well-rotted manure is also satisfactory. Avoid the use of fresh manure.

When peonies are planted in the fall should they be fertilized then, or the following spring?   Work fertilizer thoroughly into the soil before planting. No additional fertilizer will be needed the spring following; but each succeeding spring use a mixed commercial fertilizer.

Do peonies need fertilizer; and when should it be applied?   Yes. Apply commercial fertilizer in spring. When growth is about 4 ins. high work it into the soil around the plants. Rotted manure makes a good fertilizer to put on in the fall.

Planting

Should peonies be planted in full sun?   The best results are obtained when the plants are exposed to full sunlight. It is desirable, however, to put them where they are somewhat protected from strong winds.

Can peonies be grown in partial shade?   While they do best in full sun, they will grow satisfactorily in partial shade. They require at least 6 hours a day of direct sunlight for good results.

Does the peony plant need to be kept away from other flowers in the beds?   Providing they are properly spaced and cultural conditions are right, other plants exert no influence whatever on the blooming of peonies. They are often used in mixed perennial borders, and are excellent for the purpose.

When should peonies be planted?   September 15 to November 1.

How deep do peonies need to be planted?   The crown, from which the buds arise, should be only 1 to 2 ins. below the soil level.

Does it matter whether the eye of a peony is 1 in. or 2 ins. below the surface?   No. It is important, however, not to exceed 2 ins. If planted too shallowly, there is danger of the roots being heaved out during winter.

I planted peonies the last of November; was it too late?   Planting may be done any time until the ground freezes, but the ideal months are September and October. This gives them an opportunity to become partially established before winter.

I planted peonies in a temporary location in late November. When and how should I transplant them to their permanent place?   It would be desirable to leave them where they are until October, when moving would be much easier. However, if you feel you must move them in spring, dig them with a large ball of soil as soon as the ground has thawed, and replant immediately.

Can peonies be shipped and planted in spring?   It is not recommended as a general practice, because the results are seldom satisfactory. Only in special instances should this be done.

If I move peony plants in spring will they bloom the same year?   Yes, if moved *very* early, before growth starts. The soil must be kept moist at all times. (See previous question.)

Will peony roots, which have been kept in the cellar all winter, grow satisfactorily?   It is never advisable to treat them in this manner. However, if they have not dried out, and appear to be in good condition, they will survive. It may take 3 or 4 years before they regain their full vigor.

Will peonies bloom the first summer after transplanting?   Usually; if the plants are vigorous and were not divided into small pieces; and if the transplanting was done at the right time. The blooms may not be so large and perfect as those produced in succeeding years.

Why does it take peonies so long to bloom after dividing?   Dividing the clumps is a severe operation; it results in the loss of roots in which food is stored. Dividing at an improper time causes recovery to be especially slow. If the divisions are very small, it may take 2 to 3 years before the plants are sufficiently vigorous to bloom.

How do you recognize healthy peony roots suitable for planting?   They should be approximately 1 in. in diameter, smooth, free from bruises, and each containing at least 1 plump bud and several smaller ones. No decay should be evident near the cut surface.

Culture

How can you bring an old peony border back into bloom?   If the plants are very old, it is advisable to divide the clumps and replant them in well-prepared soil. Keeping the bed free of weeds by shallow cultivation, and applying fertilizer in the spring, will increase the quality and quantity of the flowers.

Is it necessary to dig up peony roots every year and break them up to obtain more blossoms?   No. It is best not to divide and transplant peonies any oftener than is necessary to maintain vigorous growth. Ordinarily every 5 to 8 years is often enough. Better-quality blooms may be had by fertilizing and making certain that the plants do not lack moisture at the time they come into flower.

Should peonies be disbudded?   Size and quality of flowers are improved by disbudding. The practice is advisable if blooms are to be used for cut flowers, or for exhibition purposes. In the garden, where mass color effects are desirable, it is not important.

When should peonies be disbudded?   The earlier the better. Ordinarily it can be done when the plants are about 18 ins. tall. Just as soon as the secondary buds become visible they should be removed.

How are peonies disbudded?   A peony stem usually has from 3 to 7 buds. The main or terminal one produces the largest and most perfect flower. All of the buds except the terminal one should be picked off, leaving but 1 on each stem.

Disbudding peonies.

Should the flower buds of newly planted or transplanted peonies be removed the first year?   Some growers do this to help the plants recover from shock, but it is not absolutely necessary. Most gardeners allow their plants to bloom even though the flowers are not so large and perfect as they will be later.

Do peonies need to be cultivated?   Very little cultivation is necessary except to remove weeds. The best time to destroy weeds is very early in the spring before the plants have made much growth, or late in the fall after the tops have been cut off. During summer the top 2 ins. of soil should be kept loose by shallow hoeing.

Do peonies require much moisture?   A moderately moist soil is suitable. In spring when the flowers are developing, if the natural rainfall is not abundant, thorough watering increases the size and quality of the flowers.

Does irrigating peonies when in bud bring the flowers on sooner, or does it hold them back?   It tends to hasten flowering. If the soil is very dry, irrigation also greatly improves the size and quality of the blooms.

How can I keep the stems of peonies from falling over?   Support with special, circular wire "peony stakes," or use individual stakes to each stem. Good growers shake the water out of peony heads after each rain. Planting in a location sheltered from wind helps to prevent damage.

Is there any way to make the stems of peonies stronger?   Some otherwise fine varieties naturally have weak stems. There is little that can be done except to give them artificial support. It is also well to plant them in full sunlight and, if possible, where they are protected from strong winds.

In picking peony flowers, should the stems be cut at ground level?   Do not take more stem than is actually required for the arrangement. It is advisable to leave at least 2 or 3 leaves below the point where the stem is cut. These leaves will produce food for the production of the succeeding year's flowers.

Should the old flowers and seed pods of peonies be removed?   During the flowering season old blossoms should be picked off before the petals fall since this helps to control the botrytis blight disease. Seed pods compete with the roots for the food produced in the leaves. Do not remove leaves when picking off the old flowers and seed pods.

Should the foliage on peonies be cut back after the blooming season?   No. The foliage should not be cut until it has been killed by hard frosts. The food manufactured in the foliage is stored in the roots, and thus helps produce flowers the following year. If the foliage is cut back shortly after blooming, the plants are deprived of their next year's food supply.

Should the dried foliage of peonies be cut off to the ground in the fall, or left on until spring?   In fall. Its removal helps to prevent the spread of disease.

When is the proper time to cut down a peony? After the foliage has been killed by frost. The autumn coloring of peony foliage is usually quite attractive.

Problems

Should peonies be protected in winter? Peonies should be mulched the first year after planting to prevent heaving. After they are well established, no protection is necessary.

Will peonies do well in warm climates such as Florida? No, they require low temperatures to complete their rest period.

Are peonies hardy in cold climates? They are among the hardiest of garden flowers.

Why do peonies, several years old, fail to bloom? The following conditions may prevent blooming: too deep planting; too shady a situation; poor drainage; plants need dividing; disease, especially of the roots; botrytis blight disease; roots infested with nematodes; lack of fertilizer; lack of moisture; lack of sunlight; injury to buds due to late frosts.

I have peonies, about 12 yrs. old, that only have a blossom or two a year. The soil is black, sandy loam. They are not planted too deep. Are they too old, or what can be the trouble? An application of complete fertilizer at the rate of 4 lbs. per 100 sq. ft. may correct the trouble. Nematodes also may cause failure to bloom. If infested with nematodes, the best thing to do is to discard roots.

Is there any way to tell the color of peonies from the roots or from the buds on the roots? No. Experienced growers can recognize certain varieties by root and bud coloring, but there is no general rule to follow.

What would you do with peonies that have been in the ground for many years and are not doing well? Dig and divide them during October. Replant them in well-prepared soil in a good sunny location.

What can I do to make peonies bloom as they did for the first 5 years? They were divided 4 years ago and are growing in a sunny situation in well-drained clay soil. Try fertilizing them each spring with a mixed commercial fertilizer.

I have some very old peonies. Last summer the flowers were almost single, and many did not bloom well. Why? Old plants often fail to produce perfect flowers. They should be dug, divided, and replanted in well-prepared soil.

When should peony flowers be cut for use indoors? Preferably in the early morning. Select, for cutting, buds that have just started to open.

How are peonies scored or rated? On a scale of 10. A rating of 10 represents the highest possible excellence, or absolute perfection, in both plant and bloom. Varieties rated at 9 or above are very high in quality. Between 8 and 9 they are considered good. Few varieties are grown that rate less than 7.5.

Propagation

Can peony roots be divided in spring with as much success as in fall?   No, *early* fall is the best time.

How are peony plants divided?   Dig the clumps carefully so as not to injure or bruise the roots. Wash off all soil. With a heavy, sharp knife cut each clump, through the crown, into several pieces. Each division should have several plump buds, which in the fall are approximately ½ in. long. Roots without such buds rarely produce plants.

Would it be advisable to separate a peony root with a spade, leaving part in the ground and removing part?   This method can be used and has the advantage of not interrupting the bloom of the portion that is left in place. However, it is usually better to dig the entire plant and divide it carefully. Before replanting there is an opportunity to prepare the soil to improve growing conditions.

Can peonies be raised from seeds?   Yes, but this method is used only for the production of new varieties; it is slow and tedious.

How should seeds of peonies be sown?   Collect when ripe. Keep in damp moss until November. Sow in a cold frame or protected bed. Cover the seeds to their own depth, and mulch with peatmoss the following spring. Keep the bed shaded and reasonably moist. They usually take 2 years to germinate.

How long does it take peonies to bloom from seeds?   They ordinarily germinate 2 years after sowing. After 3 years' growth, a few flowers may be expected. This means 5 or more years from seed-sowing to bloom.

Diseases and Pests

What can I do to control ants that are eating the flower buds of my peonies?   Ants do not eat peony buds; they feed on the sweet, syrupy material secreted by the developing buds. They do no harm to the peonies except, possibly, to spread botrytis blight disease. (See Ants—Section VIII.)

Why do peony buds dry up without developing into blossoms? The plant seems disease-free. The leaves do not dry nor is there any sign of bud rot.   Probably botrytis blight. This may be prevented by carefully cleaning the bed in the fall and by keeping it clean of dead leaves all seasons. Spraying with Bordeaux mixture every 10 days from the time the leaves show until the flowers open is a good control measure. Late frosts in spring may kill buds.

Is there something lacking in the soil when peony leaves turn brown at the edges early in July? Usually this is the result of drought, or of infection with some root disease.

Varieties

What are the names of the different types of peony flowers? The most distinct are single, Japanese, anemone, and double.

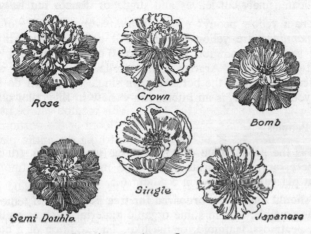

Peonies—various flower types.

What is the difference between single peonies and the Japanese type? Singles have 5, or possibly a few more, true petals around a center of showy, fertile stamens. Japanese types have a single row of large petals, but the center consists of much enlarged stamens which bear very little, or no, pollen.

What is the anemone type of peony? It somewhat resembles the Japanese but the centers of the flowers are composed of much enlarged, petallike stamens which bear no pollen whatever. These center petals are long and narrow, more or less incurved, and imbricated.

What varieties of anemone-flowered peonies are desirable? Aureolin, rose-pink; Golden Dawn, ivory; Red Bird, dark red; Laura Dessert, pale pink.

What are a few good single peonies? L'Etincelant, pink; Le Jour, white; Pride of Langport, pink; Scarf Dance, light pink; and Verdun, crimson.

Which are some popular varieties of the Japanese type? Alma, pink; Ama-No-Sode, rose-pink; Charm, dark red; Hakodate, white; Mikado, crimson; and Prairie Afire, cream-rose.

Which are a few of the best double peonies? A. B. Franklin, white; Baroness Schroeder, white; Cherry Hill, red-maroon; Cornelia

Shaylor, pale rose; E. J. Shaylor, deep rose; Festiva Maxima, white; Hansina Brand, pink; James Boyd, flesh pink; Karl Rosenfield, red-crimson; La France, light pink; Longfellow, red; President Wilson, rose; Reine Hortense, rose; Sarah Bernhardt, deep rose; Therese, pale rose; and Walter Faxon, pink.

Which peony flowers 2 weeks before the common ones? The Fernleaf Peony (*Paeonia tenuifolia*) is a very early-flowering species with delicate, finely cut leaves and single or double red flowers.

Is there a yellow peony? *Paeonia mlokosewitschi, P. lutea,* and *P. wittmanniana* are yellow-flowered. All are early-flowering, low-growing sorts not common in gardens. There are several yellow-flowered tree peonies. Argosy, Chromatella, La Lorraine, and L'-Esperance are some of the better-known singles. Souvenir de Maxine Cornu, yellow-orange, is an interesting variety in this color class.

Tree Peonies

What is the proper type of soil for tree peonies? A friable rich soil is necessary. Incorporate well-rotted manure or leafmold. The optimum pH value is between 5.5 and 6.5.

How should the soil be prepared for tree peonies? By spading as deeply as possible. Mix in some organic material, such as well-rotted manure, peatmoss, leafmold, or the like. The addition of a complete commercial fertilizer is also desirable. If a 5–10–5 or some similar grade is available, use it at the rate of 4 lbs. per 100 sq. ft.

Can tree peonies be planted in spring? While October is the best season, success may be had from *very* early-spring planting.

How old do tree peonies need to be before they will flower? Tree peonies are often slow to begin blooming. Normally, however, they produce a few blooms the second or third year after planting.

How can I propagate tree peonies? The usual method is by grafting in August or September. The scion should have at least 2 eyes. Its base is cut wedge-shaped and is inserted in a piece of root about ½ in. in diameter, and 3 or 4 ins. long, taken from an herbaceous peony plant. The scion is held in place with raffia or with a rubber band. The grafted roots are placed in good soil, in a cold frame, where they can be protected during winter. If a cold greenhouse is available, the grafts may be placed in a deep pot and kept indoors over winter. One of the eyes of the scion should be below soil surface. Tree peonies may also be propagated by layering, division, and by seeds.

Which are some of the best tree-peony varieties? Carolina d'-Italie, flesh-pink; Madame Stuart-Low, salmon-red; Blanche De-chateau Futu, white; and Reine Elizabeth, salmon and copper; Oriflame, cherry-red; Osirus, chestnut-brown.

PERENNIAL PEA (LATHYRUS LATIFOLIUS)

How do you start what is called "wild sweetpea"? I have tried planting seeds and roots without success. The perennial pea (*Lathyrus latifolius*) is best started from seeds sown in autumn, preferably where they are to grow permanently. The plant has long, fleshy roots and resents disturbance.

What is the best way to plant and care for everlasting peas? If by "everlasting" peas you mean the perennial kind, they rarely need special soil preparation or care. A sunny location and average good garden soil that is not acid are about all they require.

I have a well-established perennial sweetpea, which failed to bloom last year. What can I do to it, to produce bloom? The perennial pea usually flowers freely when established, even in poor soil. Try mixing superphosphate with the soil, 6 oz. per sq. yd.

Should hardy sweetpeas be cut back in the fall? How far? They may be cut back to just above the ground level any time after the tops have dried up.

Is the perennial pea a good plant for a large lattice fence? Yes, if the slats are not too large for the tendrils to grasp. It will grow to a height of about 8 ft.

PHLOX

How is soil prepared for phlox? Soil should be dug to a depth of 1 ft. to 18 ins. and mixed with a 3-in. layer of rotted manure.

When is the best time to plant garden phlox? Either in early fall or early spring. If fall planting is practiced, the plants should be mulched with a 3-in. layer of rough litter, hay or straw, to prevent possible heaving as a result of freezing.

What is the best exposure for phlox? They thrive in full sun, but will grow in partial shade. A minimum of 3 to 4 hours of full sunshine is desirable.

What are some good varieties of garden phlox? Red: Leo Schlageter, Africa, Colorado, and B. Comte. Pink: Daily Sketch, Nordlicht, Elizabeth Campbell, Jules Sandeau, and Painted Lady. White: Snowcap, Mary Louise, and Tapis Blanc. Other colors: Count Zeppelin, George Stipp, Silvertone, and Widar.

Can you name 6 varieties of phlox for continuous bloom? Miss Lingard, Leo Schlageter, Columbia, Atlanta, Charles Curtis, and Cheerfulness.

How far apart should phlox be planted? Set them 15 ins. apart and allow 3 or 4 shoots to grow from each plant.

Do phlox require much water? They need plenty of water during the growing season, but the soil must be well drained.

Do phlox require summer feeding? If the bed was well prepared by deep digging and the incorporation of manure, it may not be necessary; but they do respond to side dressings of fertilizer or to applications of liquid manure when flower buds are about to form.

How can I handle phlox to get more perfectly shaped heads of blossoms? They now grow ill shaped. Probably your plants are old and need lifting, dividing, and replanting. Good trusses are obtained by thinning out the shoots that appear in spring, leaving several inches between those left. Apply a mulch of grass clippings around the plants, and give liquid manure weekly. Perhaps you have a poor variety.

Would appreciate some tips on raising phlox. Is it advisable to reset plants, and how? Phlox grow best in a well-drained rich soil; need a fair amount of water. Lift, divide, and replant about every 3 years. Cut off old flowers. They are subject to mildew; spray or dust regularly. (See Section VIII.)

In transplanting phlox, how deep should they be set? Is bone meal and peatmoss good for them? Phlox should not be planted deeper than 1 to 2 ins. Bone meal and peatmoss are all right for phlox; mix them thoroughly with the soil when planting, or work in around plants in early spring if established.

How deep should phlox crowns be planted? Just about one inch below the ground surface.

Do you spread out the roots when planting phlox, or leave them straight? Phlox roots should be planted straight down, so dig the holes deep and give them plenty of space.

My yard is on a slope. I have trouble with hardy phlox. They don't seem to bloom as they should. Is the soil the cause? May be. Phlox need a rich, moist, but well-drained soil. It might be the variety— some are poor bloomers. Disease or a pest like red spider may be responsible. It might be due to drying out of the roots, which are close to the surface.

Why don't my phlox thrive? Foliage is sometimes whitish looking, turning to brown, lower leaves drop off, and blooms are poor. (New York City.) Phlox are subject to red spider mite infestation, which causes a whitish appearance at first, then leaves turn brown; also mildew and a disease which causes the lower leaves to drop. Deep, rich, moist, but well-drained soil and periodic dusting with sulfur will help. Phlox is extremely difficult to grow in the city.

Do phlox run out? Yes. Phlox will deteriorate if not lifted, split up, and replanted in good soil every 3 or 4 years.

Should phlox be pinched back, thus preventing top-heavy plants while in bloom? Pinching would induce branching, resulting in smaller heads of flowers.

Could I plant hardy phlox at the base of poplar trees to follow

tulips? Phlox may do there all right, especially the arendsi hybrids, which grow very well in part shade. The regular summer phlox will have too much competition from the tree roots.

What is the procedure in propagating perennial phlox by cutting up the roots into small sections? When is best time to do this? The plants are dug in September, and the roots cut into lengths of 1 to 2 ins. They are scattered in a cold frame and covered, ½ in. deep, with a half-and-half mixture of sand and soil. The young growths are kept in the frame until spring, and are then planted out in nursery-bed rows.

How should I start the better varieties of phlox? Mine always die. Phlox is propagated by lifting and dividing in the fall. Choose the new divisions from the outer edge of the clump, and discard the old center, which is too woody for good growth.

Why did my phlox change color? Many plants which were white, salmon, or deep red, are now a sickly magenta. You probably allowed seeds to ripen and self-sow. Unfortunately, self-seeded phlox revert to their ancestral purplish color; and, as they are usually exceptionally vigorous, they crowd out the desirable but less sturdy varieties. Weed out seedlings and do not permit plants to go to seed.

Should the seed heads be cut off the new hardy phlox? Yes, because that will help the plant conserve its energies and also prevent seedlings from self-sown seeds, which may smother the original plants.

I have been told that unless phlox seed heads are kept cut off they will revert back to the original lavender. Is it possible for roots of any plant to change like that? The reason for the so-called reversion is self seeding. The seedlings are always different in color, are very vigorous, and in time will displace the original variety. The original roots normally do not change. Cut off faded flowers to prevent reseeding.

Does dwarf phlox reseed itself? Please name a few kinds. Yes, some of the dwarf phlox seed themselves but will probably not be the same color as the original plant. *Phlox subulata* varieties alba, rosea, lilacina; *P. stolonifera*, *P. divaricata*, and *P. d. laphami*.

PLATYCODON

Do platycodons need a rich soil? No; any garden soil will suit them in the open.

When should platycodon plants be set out? In the spring.

How do you keep platycodon in bloom? Keeping the old flowers pinched off to prevent seed formation will help.

Should platycodon be pinched back? It is not necessary, but permissible if a more bushy plant is desired. It must be done when the plants are about 6 ins. tall.

Do platycodons need winter protection? They are perfectly hardy and need no protection.

How is platycodon propagated? By division, in spring; or by seed, sown in fall or spring.

PLUMBAGO

What perennial of easy culture has blue flowers late in the season? *Plumbago larpentiae* (*Ceratostigma plumbaginoides*). It is tolerant of city conditions, thrives in sun or shade, and blooms until frost.

POPPIES

What fertilizer for perennial poppies? Any balanced one will give good results. Take your pick of the several special garden fertilizers offered by responsible supply houses, or a farmer's 4–8–4 or similar formula.

Will you give full planting instructions and care of Oriental poppies? Should be planted out in August or September, making the hole big enough so that the fleshy roots are not broken or twisted upward; water well if weather is dry; protect in winter with salt hay or dry leaves to prevent crown rot.

How shall I care for Oriental poppies? (Maryland.) They don't need much attention. Cut off flowers as they wither; keep the soil around them constantly raked shallow; occasionally work in side dressings of balanced fertilizer. A mulch of manure or leaves after first heavy frost in autumn would prevent bursts of growth in winter, which may happen in your locality and would not be helpful to the plants.

My Oriental poppies come up and grow well, but never bloom. They get afternoon sun. Should they be in a different place? Transplant in April or August into a sunnier spot.

When is the best time to plant or transplant Oriental poppies? In August, after the leaves have withered, and early in spring before growth commences. They dislike being transplanted, so injure the roots as little as possible; don't keep them out of the ground long, and water in thoroughly. If you grow them from seed, transfer the seedlings from flowerpots with the ball of soil intact.

When is the best time to thin out plants such as Oriental poppies? Thin out seedlings whenever the young plants tend to crowd. In growing practically all plants, thin out so carefully and continually that seedlings do not touch each other. If you mean dividing the roots of large plants, August is the time.

Will Oriental poppies planted in the spring bloom the same year? Yes, but you should buy large established plants. Plant them in March or early April, give them good care, and you are quite likely to get some flowers.

Can I sow Oriental poppy seed in May, to bloom next year? Yes, if the plants are given good care. Transplant seedlings into individual pots to avoid root disturbance when they are planted in their flowering positions.

How do you protect Oriental poppies in winter? I have lost 3 different settings. They may be set out in very early spring, but the best time is in August, when they are dormant. Is the soil well drained or waterlogged in winter? They resent the latter. Little protection is needed. A light covering of salt hay or coarse ashes over the crown will suffice.

Is it necessary in this section to mulch fall-planted Oriental poppy before December? (South Dakota.) Tuck excelsior around the crown beneath the leaves; then mulch them with rotted manure or compost after the soil freezes.

Is there any danger of Oriental poppy plants mixing if they are planted close together? Occasionally parent plants will mix, and after a few seasons you can hardly help having in your group of plants some which are self-sown from seed dropped from the parents. These will be mixed.

PRIMROSE

What kind of soil do primroses need? A fairly rich and moist but well-drained soil; the addition of leafmold is good. Should be planted in partial shade. Some, such as *P. japonica* and *P. rosea,* will grow in full sun where the soil is constantly wet.

Do primroses need fertilizer? Yes, they need a fairly rich soil. Well-rotted cow manure is probably the best.

What do you advise as a fertilizer for cowslips? (Virginia.) Well-rotted cow manure. Maintain the soil near neutral point by applications of pulverized limestone, if necessary.

What summer care and winter protection do primroses need? (Virginia.) Should be given shade and not allowed to dry out in summer. They are hardy and should not require any winter protection in Virginia.

What time of year is best for splitting up primulas? After they have finished flowering in late spring.

Are primroses easily raised from seed? When is seed sown? Primroses come readily from seed sown in spring. Use fresh seed. Protect the seedlings in summer by shading.

PYRETHRUM

How do you separate pyrethrums? Should be divided after they have finished flowering. The clumps are dug up and pulled apart, or pried apart with two spading forks.

ROSEMALLOW (HIBISCUS)

How shall I treat hibiscus (mallow) before and after flowering? In spring dig in some old rotted leafmold and bone meal. Cut off faded flowers, and prune back to the ground in the fall after frost.

Should rosemallow be left in ground all winter? Yes; the roots are perfectly hardy.

How can hibiscus (mallow) be grown successfully from seeds—how many years before plant will be large enough to bloom? Hibiscus seeds are best sown, 2 in a pot, and then planted out from the pot in permanent position. Will take about 3 years to bloom.

Rosemallows are beautiful plants, but attract Japanese beetles in droves. Are there any means of keeping the beetles off them? Use a spray especially designed to repel Japanese beetles. (See Section VIII.)

SALVIA

What extra care would you advise for salvias? *Salvia pitcheri* grows well in good garden soil with a reasonable amount of moisture, and in full sun. Lift and divide the plants about every 3 or 4 years.

Are there any perennial salvias? Yes; there are many. The ones usually found in gardens are *Salvia farinacea, S. officinalis, S. pitcheri, S. pratensis,* and *S. nemorosa. S. farinacea* is often treated as an annual in Northern gardens.

SCABIOSA

When and how do I divide my scabiosa roots, grown from seed planted last spring? Your plants would hardly have grown enough from seed last spring to be divided now; plants 2 or 3 years old may be divided by cutting or pulling the plants apart in early spring and replanting.

FLOWERING SPURGE (EUPHORBIA COROLLATA)

When should Flowering Spurge (Euphorbia corollata) be planted? Spring or fall? Best in spring.

SHASTADAISY

What is the best way to protect Shastadaisy plants in the winter? Cover with salt hay after ground is well frozen, and gradually uncover in spring.

How should Shastadaisies be divided? By digging up, in early spring, the outside rooted shoots either singly or in clumps. Shastadaisies are usually short-lived in the North and should be divided every year or two.

TRADESCANTIA

What is the botanical name of "widows' tears"? *Tradescantia virginiana*. It is also known as common spiderwort and snake-grass.

TRITOMA

Can you grow tritomas from seed in the winter and transplant in the spring? Yes; transplant the seedlings into 2½-in. pots, and plant out in early May.

Should tritoma be cut down to the ground after blooming? Just the flowering stems should be cut away after blooming. The foliage usually persists through the winter and affords some protection to the crown.

Do tritomas have to be taken up, or can they be left out in the open all winter? In very cold sections it is better to lift them. Pack the roots in earth and store in a tight frame or in cellar until early spring.

How do you prepare tritomas for winter along the north Jersey coast? When is the best time to separate tritomas? Give winter protection with salt hay or some other suitable material; do not cut off their leaves until spring. Separate tritomas in spring only.

Is it possible to divide tritomas? How should it be done? Divide them in spring only. It may be done by division of the roots, but much easier to dig up the offsets which come on the side of the main crown. See that these have roots.

VERONICA

The crowns of my veronica are rising above the surface. Can I remedy this? Veronicas tend to raise their crowns if left in the same spot for some time. Dig up and replant every 2 or 3 years.

Why does my veronica, variety Blue Spires, sprawl instead of growing upright as the spicata and subsessilis varieties do? I have it from 3 different nurseries and all plants do it. It is characteristic of this variety to have weak stems. Little can be done to overcome this, other than to support the stems. This is best done by sticking twigs in the soil around the plants before the shoots begin to sprawl. Try variety Blue Peter.

VIOLA

What is the proper time to plant viola seed for spring blossom? In latter half of August, or early September.

Will you discuss culture of violas? I planted good plants last year, but blossoms didn't form till frost. Nearly all violas need cool conditions, moisture, and partial shade. Hot, exposed locations are not conducive to good results. Provide a moist soil containing plenty of leafmold and the above conditions.

Does Viola pedata bicolor prefer sun or shade?   Grows naturally in full sun and in an acid, sandy soil.

VIOLETS

Is the wood violet a perennial? I grow it as a house plant.   It is difficult to say which violet you have, as several are known in different regions as the wood violet. All of these are perennials.

I am very much interested in growing English violets. Have a cold frame, and yet don't seem to have any success; had good roots and thrifty leaves; flowers very small and few. Will you give me some information?   Remove sash, and shade the frame with lath screens in summer to keep plants cool; cut off all runners as they appear; feed and water to build up vigorous plants for late fall. Ventilate freely in fall, winter, and spring whenever temperature is above 35° to 40° F.

What is the proper method to water English violets?   Water only when foliage can dry off before night. They need plenty of water during their growing period, but the soil must be well drained so that water does not collect in pools.

Should the runners be clipped off violet plants? Why do the plants grow up out of the soil instead of staying in it? How may large blooms and long stems be secured?   In commercial culture the runners are cut off as fast as they appear in order to build up the plants for flowering. The plants root at the surface, with the crown above; as they develop, the crown rises still higher above the soil. Young plants give the best bloom, hence a number of these must be kept coming along. Long stems and good flowers are produced on young, well-developed plants in a rich but well-drained soil. Thin out old plants in spring.

Why do English violets, growing for 3 years, refuse to bloom? These are planted on west side of house.   Violets need moist conditions and some shade from a hot sun. If you can supply these and keep the soil covered with a mulch of old compost, peatmoss, or grass clippings, they may bloom. They should be watered when necessary, and fed liquid manure. Renew part of the planting annually with strong, rooted runners. Our hot climate is not the best for violets.

My English violets produce seeds, but I never see any blooms; or maybe they bloom without petals, for they never come out of the ground like a flower, but develop into seed pods. Can you explain?   Violets produce cleistogamous flowers, which are mostly on or under the ground. These are small, self-fertilizing flowers which never open.

YUCCA

How old must a yucca plant (from seed) be to blossom? Will it

bloom frequently?   About 4 to 5 years old; then the clump should bloom every year or at least every second year after that.

Is it necessary to mulch a yucca plant?   No; the common yucca is very hardy and prefers a dry, sandy soil.

What is the preferred time for moving yuccas?   Best done in early spring, when plant is dormant.

Have several yucca plants that were on the place when we moved here 5 years ago; why don't they bloom?   Probably planted in shade, or too heavy a soil. They prefer a light, sandy soil, good drainage, and full sun.

When can I separate yucca?   Detach young suckers in early spring; or divide old clumps immediately after flowering, or in the spring.

SECTION III-E

Annuals and Biennials

INTRODUCTION

BY F. F. ROCKWELL

AND ESTHER C. GRAYSON

THERE HAS BEEN a tendency on the part of many gardeners during recent years to look down their noses a bit when annuals are mentioned. The fact remains that annuals offer the beginning gardener the means— when it comes to beautifying his or her new home with flowers—of getting the fastest and the mostest, for the leastest.

By no means, however, should annuals be considered merely as stop-gap plants, to be used for temporary results until one can obtain something better. For many purposes, and for many special effects, there *is* nothing better. Many of the famous gardens of England make lavish use of annuals to obtain the breath-taking color displays for which they are noted.

While most annuals are so easily grown that they present no great challenge to the gardener's skill as a grower, they do test his skill— and offer him endless opportunities—in the employment of color and design in ways that will give his place individuality as well as beauty. And they do possess the great advantage of *flexibility*. Shrubs and perennials, once established, become more or less permanent fixtures. Annuals, used to supplement them, make it possible to shift the emphasis as one wishes, from year to year, or even during one season, and thus to obtain a series of interesting focal points not otherwise possible.

The flower arranger too, will find that some annuals are almost indispensable in enabling her to maintain a really constant supply of blooms for cutting, and for supplementary foliage.

So in planning the all around garden, annuals should never be eliminated from the picture. There is no necessity of selecting only the usual kinds, such as zinnias, marigolds and petunias. Any gardener who feels that he has outgrown annuals should try some of the kinds with which he is not familiar. He will find some amazingly interesting subjects.

ANNUALS; AND PLANTS COMMONLY TREATED AS SUCH

What is an annual? An annual is a plant that lives but one season from seed sowing to flowering, setting of seed, and death.

What is meant by a hardy annual? A half-hardy annual? A tender annual? Hardy annuals are those the seeds of which can be planted in fall or very early spring. Half-hardy annuals are cold resistant, and seeds of these can be planted early in spring. Tender annuals are easily injured by frost and must be planted only after the ground has warmed up and all danger of frost is past.

WHAT TO GROW

Can you give me a list of a few annuals (flowers) that will stand early planting in the spring? (Vermont.) Sweet alyssum, scabiosa, candytuft, sweetpeas, cosmos, cornflowers, larkspur, shirley poppy, pricklypoppy (argemone).

Will you give list of annuals requiring least care for home gardens? Marigold, verbena, gaillardia, cosmos, spiderflower (cleome), calliopsis, petunia, zinnia, salvia, scabiosa, annual phlox.

What annual flower would you recommend for planting in a completely shaded area? There are no annual flowers that will grow well in *total* shade. A perennial ground cover such as *Pachysandra terminalis,* English Ivy, *Ajuga reptans,* and periwinkle (*Vinca minor*) would be more suitable for such conditions. Your best choices, if you want to try annuals, would be cleome, cornflower, godetia, lobelia, nasturtium, nicotiana, wishbone-flower (*Torenia fournieri*), and balsam.

Which annual flowers are best for flower beds—along sidewalks and on side of house? Ageratum (dwarf forms); *Begonia semperflorens* varieties; dustymiller (*Centaurea cineraria*); *Lobelia erinus;* marigolds (Tagetes) dwarf varieties; petunia (dwarf varieties); sweet alyssum.

Which are the easiest annuals to grow in a sunken garden? Fragrant species preferred. Ageratum, alyssum,* calendula, centaurea, dianthus,* iberis,* lobelia, dwarf marigold, matthiola,* mirabilis,* nicotiana,* petunia,* phlox,* portulaca, torenia, nasturtium,* viola, dwarf zinnias, if low-growing plants are desired, otherwise any variety.

Will you give me the names of a few unusual annuals, their heights, blooming dates and uses? Bells of Ireland (*Molucella laevis*), green, 24 inches; late summer; flower arrangements. Nemesia, various (ex-

*Fragrant

cept blues), 18 inches; edging, bedding. Nierembergia, lavender-blue, 12 inches; window boxes, edging.

TRANSPLANTING

When should flat-raised seedlings be transplanted? How many times? First transplanting should be done when seedlings have formed their first true leaves. Many plants benefit from a second transplanting, when 2 or 3 ins. high, to individual pots, before they are moved outdoors.

What is the best mixture of soil for transplanting seedlings from flats to pots, or to the cold frame? Sandy loam mixed with ¼ well-rotted manure (or dried manure or rich compost), and 4-in. potful of a complete fertilizer to a wheelbarrowful.

What annuals to you recommend as foliage plants for use in arrangements? Castor bean; sideritis, gray; coleus, variegated; prickly-poppy, white-veined foliage; *Amaranthus tricolor,* variegated.

What are the best tall annuals for background planting? Celosia, cleome, cosmos, datura, hollyhock, larkspur, marigolds (tall varieties), salvia, tithonia, snapdragons (tall varieties), zinnias, (tall varieties).

I have difficulty in removing annuals from flats without ruining their root systems. Any pointers? Water thoroughly a few hours before transplanting. With an old knife, or a small mason's trowel, cut soil into squares, each with a plant in the center. The plants can easily be removed with root system almost intact.

What is the right technique in setting out annual plants? Remove plants from flats with as little root disturbance as possible. Stab trowel in soil, pull toward you, set plant in hole, remove trowel, push soil around roots, *press soil* down firmly, and leave a slight depression around stem to facilitate watering.

How does one "thin out" seedlings? Choose cloudy weather when soil is moist, and spread operation over 2 or 3 weeks. Pull up weakest seedlings before they crowd each other, leaving 2 to 6 ins. between those remaining, according to their ultimate size. When those left begin to touch, again remove the weakest, leaving the remainder standing at the required distance apart.

How much space should be given annuals, when thinning them, or planting them out? Distance varies according to variety and habit of growth. A rough rule is a distance equal to ½ their mature height. Swanriverdaisy, Virginia stock, and similar weak growers, 4 ins.; marigolds, Shirley poppies, etc., 1 ft.; strong growers, such as spiderflower and sunflower, 2 to 3 ft.

When can seedlings raised indoors be transplanted into the open?
Hardy annuals, as soon as large enough. Tender annuals, when all
danger of frost is past. First harden them off by placing them in a
cold frame or protected spot for several days.

*Steps in transplanting. Plants in flats or in plant bands (as shown)
are kept moist by watering from the bottom. When setting out
(preferably on a cloudy day) dig holes, apply water and after
it has soaked away insert plant and pack soil firmly about roots.
If soil is dry apply more water at surface.*

CULTURE

**Is it wrong to plant the same kind of annuals in the same space,
year after year?**   So long as the soil is well dug each year and the
humus content maintained there is nothing wrong with the practice.
China asters, snapdragons, and marigolds may well be changed each
year.

What type of soil, and what fertilizing program, is best for annuals?
Most annual flowers do best in a well-drained, rather light soil in full
sun. Unless it is really run-down and deficient in plant nutrients, only
a light annual application of rotted manure, plus some standard commercial fertilizer, is advisable.

What is the best fertilizer for the annual and perennial flower beds?
For most annuals and perennials a 4–12–4 or 5–10–5 fertilizer is
recommended. For perennials with fleshy roots a 2–10–10 fertilizer
may be substituted.

How deep should the soil be prepared for annuals?   Nine ins. for
good results. Some growers go twice this depth to assure maximum
growth.

Do popular annuals have decided preferences for acid or alkaline soil? Most popular garden flowers tolerate either a slight acid or alkaline condition and thrive in a neutral soil. (See lists under pH, Section I.)

My 3-year-old garden is on a slight slope, with sun all day. The first year, cosmos and pinks did fine. Now everything dwindles and dies. Even petunias won't grow. What can I do? Dig deeply and add 3-in. layer of well-rotted manure or leafmold. Set the plants as early as you can, depending upon your conditions. Sloping site and a hot sun are not conducive to good growth because of the moisture conditions. Get moisture down around the roots of the plants; keep a heavy mulch of partly decayed leaves or grass clippings over the soil in summer.

How shall I top annuals to make them bushy? What does one do, pinch them or cut them with a knife or scissor? Pinch out no more than the growing point with thumbnail, if possible, so as to avoid wasted energy on the part of the plant.

Exactly what is meant by "pinching back"? Pinching back is the removal of the tip of a growing shoot to induce branching.

Which annuals, and at what stage, should be pinched back for better growth and more flowers? These annuals may be pinched to advantage when from 2 to 4 ins. high: ageratum, antirrhinum, carnation, cosmos, nemesia, petunia, phlox, salvia, schizanthus, tagetes, and verbena. Straggly plants of sweet alyssum may be sheared back in midsummer for better growth and to induce flowering later in the season.

Is it true that if flowers are picked they bloom better? On plants that continue to make flowering growth it is best to pick off flowers as soon as they fade, to prevent the formation of seed, which is a drain on the plant's energy.

What would cause annuals to grow well but come into bud so late in the summer they are of little use? Seed was planted late in April. Most annuals are blooming at midsummer from April-sown seed. Lobelia, scarlet sage, torenia, and tithonia are examples that should be sown under glass in March for good results. The late, older varieties of cosmos usually do not have time to flower in the North, even if sown early under glass.

Why do I have to tie up so many plants—zinnia, marigold, and other common plants? They grow fine, bloom generously, yet if not tied do not stay erect. May be insufficient phosphorus in soil; or perhaps they are exposed to too much wind; or heavy rains may have beaten them down.

Most of our annuals pass out about August, leaving few flowers for fall. Is there any way we could renew our plantings so that flowers

are available until late in the season? There are numerous annuals which, sown in summer, will provide bloom right up to frost. These are *Browallia americana (elata),* calendula, candytuft, celosia, globe-flower, the little fine-leaved marigold (*Tagetes signata pumila*), *Phlox drummondi,* sweet alyssum *Torenia fournieri,* verbena and all types of zinnias. The dates for sowing must be closely adhered to. These apply to the vicinity of New York City and would suit a rather large region. The date of the first killing frost in fall must be allowed for in the more northerly sections. With care, seeds can be sown out-doors and seedlings transplanted direct to their flowering quarters, or potted up and held over, and used as needed. The latter plan is better for torenia and browallia. Sow these the first week in June; trans-plant to 3-in. pots. At the same time sow celosia, nicotiana, dwarf scabiosa, and tall marigolds. Third week in June, sow California Poppy (sow where to bloom or in pots), globeflower, candytuft, *Phlox drummondi,* and tagetes. None of the above will grow to the size of spring-sown plants. Last week in June to first week in July sow calendulas, sweet alyssum, and zinnias of all types, including Haageana hybrids and Z. *linearis.* Alyssum and calendula and verbena will survive light frosts.

How long from planting of seed to cutting of flowers on asters, stock, snapdragons? (California.) The length of time required will vary somewhat according to the type and variety, the time of year, and conditions under which grown. Early varieties of either might be ready in 14 to 16 weeks. Snapdragons will be bushier if pinched when about 3 ins. high, but pinching delays flowering.

How can I save the seed from annual flowers? Select healthy plants of the best type, allow the seeds to mature on the plant, but gather before they are shed, then dry in an airy, rainproof place safe from mice.

Will seed from hybrid annuals flower the following year; if so, will they come true? Seeds of the so-called annual hybrids saved one year should give flowers the next. They would most likely come pretty true, but some variation could be expected.

I have looked and looked for the answer to this question and haven't found it yet. When different shades of the same flower are planted together, which ones may I save seeds from and have them come true to their parent? Which ones not? You have not much chance of getting seed which would come true from any of them.

Do the following come up without replanting? Bergamot, ageratum, ladyslippers, four-o'clocks, sweet alyssum, morningglories, moon-flowers. Of this group only bergamot is a perennial; this will come up each year. All the others are annuals. They come up from the seeds dropped from the plants the previous year. However, to be on the safe side it is best to sow seeds each spring.

PROPAGATION (INDOORS)

Is one seed disinfectant satisfactory for use on all seeds? No. There are special disinfectants for certain seeds. (See Section VIII.) For annual seeds use semesan or rootone.

Seeds of many vegetables and flowers are benefited by being dusted with a disinfectant before planting. The operation is simple—a mere thorough shaking up with a pinch of the dust. The cost is infinitesimal.

What is a flat? A shallow, topless box (usually about 3 ins. deep) with holes in the bottom to allow for drainage of water from soil. It is used for sowing seeds, inserting cuttings, etc.

Is there any rule about the dimensions of flats? There is great variety in flat sizes. Usually they should be not less than 2½ ins., nor more than 4 ins. deep. If more than 14 × 20 ins., they are likely to be too heavy to carry with comfort.

Can cigar boxes and cheeseboxes be used instead of flats for starting seeds indoors? Usually cigar boxes are too shallow. Cheeseboxes are all right when only a few seedlings are to be raised and they can be accommodated on narrow window sills. Bore small holes in the bottom for drainage.

What soil mixture is preferable for seeds sown indoors? One part good garden loam, 1 part leafmold or peatmoss, and 1 part sand, screened through ¼-in. mesh screen; or half sand and half peatmoss; or pure fine sand, or vermiculite, watered with nutrient solution.

For starting seeds, rooting cuttings, potting seedlings or small plants, soil or compost should be sifted through screen of ¼-in. mesh.

What is the procedure in raising seedlings in sand, with the aid of nutrient solutions? Take a flat 3 to 4 ins. deep, with provision for drainage. Place a piece of burlap or sphagnum moss over the holes and fill with clean sand. Soak it with water, then with the nutrient solution diluted 1 part to 5 parts water. Sow seeds thinly; cover with sand; firm well. Keep the sand moist with the dilute solution. When the seedlings have made true leaves, use equal parts nutrient solution and water.

Can ready-to-use nutrient solutions be purchased, or must the separate chemicals be obtained and mixed at home?   Ready-mixed nutrient solutions are obtainable from garden supply houses, and should do for raising seedlings. For more extensive use, chemicals may be purchased and dissolved to make solutions according to tables recommended in books on the subject, or obtainable from State Experiment Stations. (See also Soilless Gardening—Section I.)

How do I go about sowing seeds of annuals indoors?   Cover drainage holes in containers with moss or pieces of broken flowerpot; follow with an inch of "rough stuff"—flaky leafmold, moss, or screenings; fill with screened soil mixutre (¼-in. mesh); press down level, and sow seeds.

How deep should seeds be planted in flats and pots indoors? How deep in rows outdoors?   Indoors, very small seeds are merely firmly pressed into soil with a tamper, or covered with a dusting of fine soil or sand; medium-sized seeds covered ⅛ to ¼ in.; large seeds about 3 times their diameter. Outdoors, seeds are customarily covered a little deeper—half as much again.

What is a tamper?   An oblong piece of board with a handle attached (similar to a mason's float) for tamping soil firm in flats. For use in pots or bulb pans the base of a tumbler or flowerpot can be used.

Is it better to scatter the seeds, or to sow them in rows?   When flats are used, it is preferable to sow in rows. You can judge germination better, cultivate lightly without danger of harming seedlings, and transplant with more ease. When pots are used, seeds are generally scattered evenly and thinly.

How can very small seeds be sown evenly?   Mix thoroughly with sand before sowing. Use of a small gadget known as the sow-rite seed sower also helps.

When starting seeds in the house in the winter, what do you put in the soil, so that the plants will be short and stocky and not tall and spindly?   No treatment of the soil will prevent this. Good light, moderate temperature, and avoidance of overcrowding are the preventives. Turn pots daily to keep the plants from "drawing" to the light.

When would seeds for annuals be planted in seed flats in spring?   Mid-March usually is soon enough, in the North especially, if raised under space limitations. Allow from 6 to 8 weeks before it is safe to plant the seedlings outside.

STARTING SEEDS INDOORS

Compost is sifted, ready to go into flat, with cracks (for drainage) in bottom.

Sifted compost is placed in flat, pressed down in corners, and leveled off.

It is then pressed down firmly and thin layer of fine soil sifted over surface. Small seeds are barely covered from sight.

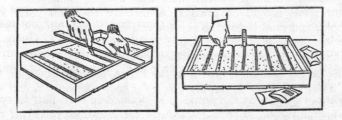

Rows are marked off (2 to 3 ins. apart) with label or pencil, and seeds sown thinly.

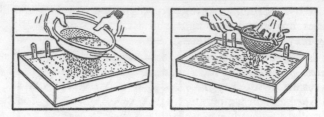

Rows (carefully labeled) are covered with sifted compost, sand, or sifted sphagnum moss.

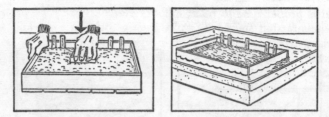

Surface is pressed down firm and flat watered (from beneath) by placing in tray or sink, until moisture shows on surface.

How should seed flats be watered after the seed is sown? Water thoroughly after seeding with a fine overhead spray from watering can until soil is saturated. Subsequently, water when surface soil shows signs of dryness. Do not overwater, nor permit flat to dry out. (See following question.)

Can seed flats be watered by standing them in a vessel of water? Yes, if more convenient. Do not leave in water any longer than is necessary for moisture to show on the surface. Do not submerge flat; place in water about 1 in. deep. Many growers prefer this method to watering the surface, as there is less danger of washing out fine seeds.

I have tried starting annuals indoors but without much success. Is there some trick about watering, or soil, that I should know? I've always used ordinary wooden flats and bought good seeds. The soil for seeds should be porous. A mixture of equal parts loam, leafmold, and sand is good. Keep the soil just moist, but not sodden. Sometimes poor germination comes from covering seeds too deeply. Sow them no deeper than twice their diameter.

Why do my seedlings, grown in the house, grow to about an inch, bend over, and die? Damping off, a fungous disease. Prevent it by disinfecting seeds with semesan or rootone, thin seeding, not overwatering, and giving seedlings fresh air without drafts. In severe cases, disinfecting soil or sand is advisable.

The seedlings in my seed flat get very tall and leggy, and very light

in color. Why? Seedlings in this condition are said to be "drawn." The causes are insufficient light and too-high temperature. Overcrowding may result in insufficient light.

What is the best germinating temperature for annual nicotiana and annual gaillardias? I have planted both late in the spring with dubious results. Must they have a cooler temperature to start? Indoors in April a night temperature between 50° and 55° F. is suitable. Annual gaillardia germinates well outside in late May or early June. Self-sown nicotianas often germinate in early June, but are a bit late for best effect.

What is proper time to plant indoors seeds of pansy, petunia, and other annuals, that should be started early, but not too soon, as we often have frost here in May? (New Hampshire.) Pansy may be sown inside in January, but the best plants for spring display come from seed sown in August. The pansy can stand some frost; March or April is a good time to sow petunias for good plants to set out as soon as the weather is warm enough.

How can I start seedlings indoors to prevent too-rapid growth and decay? When shall I plant outdoors? Too-high temperatures and too early a start often account for conditions described. Few plants need starting indoors around New York before late March. Most of these are ready for planting outdoors in late April or early in May.

How do you make new plants blossom early in spring? There is not much that can be done to make them bloom early unless they are forced in a greenhouse. Most plants have to reach a certain age before they will flower.

PROPAGATION (OUTDOORS)

What should the temperature be before planting annuals in the garden? (New York.) There can be no set temperature figure. Hardy annuals may be seeded as soon as the ground is ready to work; half-hardy annuals about 4 weeks later; tender ones when all danger of frost is past for the region. In and about New York this is usually during the second week in May.

How early may annuals be planted in the Philadelphia, Pennsylvania, area? Hardy annuals late March to April 1; half-hardy kinds mid-April to end; tender kinds from first week in May to end of month.

What does this mean: "Sow seeds when the maple leaves are expanding"? The unfolding of the maple leaves in the spring indicates that the season has sufficiently advanced for the gardener to sow certain of his hardier seeds outdoors.

How does one sow seeds for annuals in patches outdoors? Rake surface soil to break lumps and remove large stones. If seeds are small (alyssum, petunia, portulaca), scatter evenly, and pat down soil. For medium-sized seeds, rake soil again lightly *after* sowing, and pat down. For seeds which have to be covered ¼ in. or more, scrape off soil to required depth, sow seeds, and return soil removed.

English sparrows take dust baths in my newly planted seed patches. How can I prevent this? Lay pieces of burlap or of fine brush over the seeded areas. Remove when seeds have germinated. Keep seedbed constantly moist.

What is the best method of insuring germination of small flower seeds in heavy clay soil, which consists mostly of subsoil, due to excavation for house? It grows plants very well once they get started. Hoe out rows 2 ins. wide and deep, fill with good screened compost, and sow the seeds in that. Before sowing work in a generous amount of peatmoss, sifted compost, or old manure, if possible, to improve the general texture of the soil.

Which annual seeds are suitable for autumn planting? Larkspur, poppy, gilia, sweetpea, portulaca, nicotiana, salvia, celosia, cleome, alyssum, centaurea, petunia (robust kinds), coreopsis, kochia, euphorbia, cosmos, candytuft. They must be sown sufficiently late, so they will *not* germinate before freezing weather.

Which seeds can be sown out of doors, not later than November, to germinate next spring? (Ohio.) Annual poppies, balsam, California Poppies, cornflower, portulaca.

Can larkspur, centaurea, and other seeds which are recommended for planting in the fall, be planted in February? (Maryland.) Seeds of these plants can be sown outdoors just as soon as the soil is dry enough to work in the spring. For a broad naturalistic effect the seed could be scattered in February even if the ground was not fit to rake.

Is it advisable to sow seeds of annuals, such as cosmos, zinnias, and marigolds, in late autumn, so that they can germinate the first warm days of spring? Cosmos is the only one of these likely to come up if sown outdoors in autumn, and there is nothing to be gained by this for early flowering, if seed can be sown in a cold frame in April.

How late is "late" when we are told to plant seed in late autumn? Usually about the average time of killing frost for your locality. Consult zone map in back of book. Some seeds (sweetpeas and other hardy annuals) may be sown after frost, provided the ground is not frozen.

Is it necessary to prepare the soil for seed planted in the fall? Yes. Soil should be just as carefully dug, fertilized, raked, and graded for fall planting as for spring planting.

Which flower seeds should be sown where they are to grow because

of difficulty in transplanting? Poppies, annual larkspur, calendulas, nasturtiums, dwarf lupines, portulaca, mignonette, Virginia stocks.

If such plants as petunias, phlox, etc., are permitted to self-seed, is there a true-to-color reproduction? Not usually.

PROPAGATION-CUTTINGS

How are plants like snapdragon, petunia, verbena, and other annuals started as slips from the original plant? These may be rooted if short side shoots, 3 to 4 ins. long, are placed in sand in a

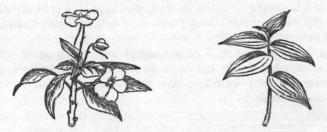

Cutting of patience-plant, with leaves trimmed from base, ready for insertion in rooting medium. Cutting of tradescantia or wanderingjew.

closed container, in July and August. If the slips have flower buds, these should be pinched off. (See Cuttings.)

Why does coleus wilt so badly when I try to start new cuttings in soil? The air about the cuttings is too dry. Cover them with a bell-jar, battery-jar, or preserving jar until they have formed roots. Trim large leaves back one half.

How are geranium slips rooted? Geranium slips may be rooted in sand at almost any time of year indoors during cold weather. The cuttings should be about 4 ins. long, and about ⅓ of the stem should be in the sand. Make the basal cut ¼ in. below leaf attachment. They can be rooted readily out of doors in September. Keep sand moist but not soggy.

What is the best method of handling lantana cuttings—our cuttings this year rooted well and got off to a good start after potting, but after a short time wilted and died. We kept them on the dry side, and shaded. After potting them, water thoroughly and keep in a closed, shaded propagating case for a week or two. Then gradually admit more air and remove the shade.

SPECIFIC ANNUAL PLANTS

AGERATUM

How is ageratum started for outdoor planting? Sow seeds in a protected cold frame in early April, or outdoors early in May when danger from frost is past. The best method is to sow them in seed pans or small pots of fine-screened soil. Sow on a level surface and press the seeds in. Set pan in water until moisture shows on the surface; cover with glass and shade; remove when germinated; transplant 2 ins. apart when first true leaves show.

Can I sow seeds of Ageratum Irwin's Beauty or how are the plants raised?   Ageratum Irwin's Beauty does not come true from seeds. It is propagated by cuttings. These are usually taken from outdoor plants in late summer, rooted in sand, and kept in a cool greenhouse during the winter. From these plants cuttings are taken in spring to furnish material for outdoor planting.

What is the proper care of ageratums over the winter?   Young plants, started late in the season, may flower as house plants during late winter. Cuttings are taken from the young growth in September and rooted in sand.

ALYSSUM

Why does white sweet alyssum come up year after year when yellow and purple don't?   The white alyssum reseeds itself; the purple will not, as the seeds do not live over the winter; both of these are annuals. The yellow is a perennial and probably is winter killed.

ARCTOTIS

Would appreciate instructions for success with African-daisies (arctotis). Mine achieve the bud stage, but never blossom, falling off at that point. Can it be too much water, or are they perhaps pot-bound? (Kentucky.)   Dropping of buds can be caused by extremes. Too much moisture around the roots or their drying out; warm, humid conditions or a sudden chill. Use fine bone meal for fertilizer; have the soil open and well drained. Don't plant in very large pots.

ASTER

How can I grow annual asters?   Select wilt-resisting seed. Plant indoors in flats or pots in late March or April; transplant into the open when danger of frost is past. Or sow seed outdoors in May. Select "early," "midseason," and "late" varieties for continuous bloom. If in a region where aster "yellows" are prevalent, grow under cheesecloth screens.

What culture do asters require?   The types best suited for sowing outdoors are American Beauty, American Branching, California Sunshine, Giants of California. Get wilt-resistant varieties of these types. Prepare seedbed by forking over the soil and working in peatmoss or leafmold. Draw drills 2 to 3 ins. apart and ¼ in. deep; sow seeds

6 or 8 to the inch about mid-May. Cover with a half-soil, half-sand mixture, and water with a fine spray. A light covering with hay or strips of burlap will help retain moisture until germination; then remove *immediately*. Keep the soil stirred between the rows and keep the seedlings watered. Transplant when seedlings have formed their first true leaves. Soak the soil a few hours before, lift seedlings with all roots, and keep them wet. If wanted for cut flowers, set in rows 18 ins. apart, the plants 9 to 12 ins. apart in the rows. Set the seedling in the soil so that the bottom leaves are resting on the surface. Give a good watering; keep soil cultivated until plants get large. Enrich the soil prior to planting by digging in 3 ins. rotted manure; or use compost or peatmoss mixed with dried cow or sheep manure —6 lbs. manure to 1 bu. of compost or peatmoss. When flowers show, feed liquid manure weekly.

Will you please give information on the raising of asters in New Jersey? Early Branching and Queen of the Market types for early flowering (July) should be sown toward the end of March, either in the greenhouse or a protected cold frame. The later-flowering kinds (Sunshine, Giants of California, Late Branching, Crego, and American Beauty) can be sown directly outdoors early in May. (See preceding question.)

Which are the best annual asters for cutting, for a small garden that does not recieve more than the average amount of care? The soil is reasonably good. Varieties of American Branching, Burpeeana, Giants of California, and California Sunshine.

Which are the best varieties of winter asters? (Illinois.) You are probably referring to the practice of forcing the annual aster by growing the seedlings under light in January. The types used are Early Branching and Ball Branching. Any of the varieties within these 2 types are suitable.

We have China asters. Do they reseed themselves? (New York.) Yes, occasionally, especially the single-flowered kinds. However, it is better to raise new plants under controlled conditions annually.

Can't asters be planted in the same spot each year? Better not. They are subject to several diseases that collect in the soil, making it desirable to select a new site each year unless special precautions are taken. (See next question.) The ground, of course, can be used for other plants.

Is it true that asters cannot be planted in the same space a second year? No—not literally. Asters can be grown in the same spot by using disease-resistant strains, by disinfecting the seeds, by mixing tobacco powder with the soil to discourage root aphis, and by screening with cheesecloth to keep out leaf hoppers which transmit the virus disease known as aster yellows.

What is the best procedure in disbudding asters? Should the top be pinched out when they are young to make them branch? Asters usually are self-branching, producing a number of branches, and do not need pinching. Each branch will bear a terminal flower, together with numerous other buds on small side shoots. All these must be removed, retaining the main bud only.

Do annual asters come true from seed collected from a flower bed? If several varieties were growing together, variation could be expected.

BALSAM

Is Balsam worth growing? Yes, especially for positions in part shade. Try the new camellia-flowered double strains on bushy, branching plants.

BELLS OF IRELAND

How are the seeds of Bells of Ireland germinated? Mine don't come up. Sow in a carefully prepared seed frame in May when soil has warmed up. Keep constantly moist until germination. Transplant to garden beds in late June.

My Bells of Ireland don't look like the ones in the flower show arrangements. Why? Flowering stems are "groomed" by removing all the foliage, leaving only the bell-like bracts with the little flower "clappers" in the center of each.

BROWALLIA

When should browallia be sown for outdoor flowers? Which varieties should I use? For early flowering, sow in late March indoors, or in a cold frame after mid-April. Outdoor sowing can be done about mid-May. These dates apply in the vicinity of New York City; farther North it would be 7 to 12 days later and correspondingly earlier farther South. *Browallia americana* (*elata*) and *B. speciosa major* are the best for summer.

What is the method of growing browallia for the house; and what is the best variety to choose for this? Sow seeds in August; transplant into 2½-in. pots; as the plants grow, shift to 4-in. then perhaps to 5-in. pots, but don't overpot; water sparingly after November. Sow again in January for early-spring bloom. Use *Browallia speciosa major*.

CALCEOLARIA

Some years ago I saw a hardy annual about 6 ins. high, with lemon-yellow blossoms about the size of a fingernail, shaped like the calceolaria. Leaves were quite lacy and fernlike. What is its name? It may have been an annual calceolaria. The species *mexicana*, *scabiosaefolia,* and *pinnata* all more or less agree with your description.

CAMPANULA

Are annual Canterbury bells easy to raise from seed? Yes, annual types bloom in less than six months from seed. Colors are the same as in biennial strains.

CANDYTUFT

My annual candytuft only bloomed a short time, then died. Why? Annual candytuft blooms very quickly from seed but only for a short time. Plant seeds at 2 or 3 week intervals for constant bloom during cool spring and fall weather. Candytuft does not do well in the heat of summer.

CLEOME

I have seen lovely pink and white spider plants. Are they something special? Pink Queen is a fine variety which won a silver medal for excellence. Helen Campbell is a pure white. If your plants self-seed, pull up all purplish-red volunteers.

CASTORBEAN

I always grow a few castorbean plants and am interested in them. Can you tell me more about them, their cultivation, and if there is a market for the bean? (Ohio.) Castorbean plants grow best in a rich, well-drained loam soil. Seeds may be planted in May where they are to grow, or started earlier indoors and then set out later. There is a market for the seeds, of course, but it is well supplied by commercial growers. The commercial crop is produced in the South, where a long season allows for maximum production.

Is it advisable to plant castor-oil-bean seeds around the lawns to prevent molehills and mole runs? Castorbean plants have very little if any effect on the mole population.

Is there anything poisonous about the castorbean plant? The seeds contain a poisonous principle called ricin. They are best planted where children cannot get at and eat the beans. Fatalities have been reported from eating as few as three seeds.

CORNFLOWER (CENTAUREA)

Why do our bachelor buttons or cornflowers show retarded growth, with feeble flower stalks? Sow the seeds on a finely prepared soil in the fall or as soon as you can work the soil in spring. Sow thinly; cover about ¼ in. Thin out the seedlings to 9 ins. apart when large enough. Yours probably were too crowded.

What treatment do you prescribe for bachelor-buttons for large blossoms and long period of bloom? If by bachelor-buttons you mean the annual cornflower (centaurea), you should get excellent results by giving them a moderately rich, well-drained soil and extra watering during dry weather. Keep faded flowers picked off. (See preceding answer.)

COSMOS

When should early cosmos be started from seeds?   Sow in a cold frame in early April and transplant directly to the place to flower, or sow outdoors in late April.

I like and grow cosmos. Pink plant blossomed in early July—very unusual to me. Why should this happen? The rest of my plants blossomed in fall as usual. I know of the yellow early bloomer.   There are several forms of early-flowering cosmos, including pink varieties. The Sensation type blooms in 8 weeks after the seed is sown. You probably have an early kind.

DAHLIA

Is it true that some dahlias flower the first year from seed?   Yes, especially the dwarf bedding dahlias like Unwin Dwarfs and Coltness Hybrids. See Dahlias, page 451.

DIANTHUS

What are the best annual pinks?   Double: Chinensis; Fringed. Single: Westwood Beauty; Heddensis.

DIMORPHOTHECA

How long can dimorphotheca be expected to stay in bloom? The plants I had last summer bloomed from about June 1 to July 15 and then died.   Six weeks of bloom is about all you could expect, though the time might be lenthened somewhat by snipping off all withered blossoms to prevent seed formation. It is a good plan to make a second sowing of seed 4 to 6 weeks or so after the first, to provide blooming plants for the second half of the summer.

What are the requirements for African-daisy (dimorphotheca)? It just never comes up. Can it be planted early? I buy good seed. (Washington.)   Sow the seed outdoors in spring when the ground has warmed up, or indoors 4 to 6 weeks earlier. Give the plants light, well-drained, and not specially enriched soil. Be sure they get plenty of sun.

EVERLASTINGS

I want to grow some everlastings for winter bouquets. What shall I select?   Acroclinium; globe amaranth; helichrysum; statice; honesty; xeranthemum.

FOUR-O'CLOCK (MIRABILIS)

I have been told you get larger bushes and greater amount of flowers from four-o'clock roots the second season. Are they to be left in the ground, or dug up and dried like certain bulbs? (Missouri.) Mostly used as annuals; the roots would be very unlikely to live through winter outdoors in your region. The large, tuberous roots can be lifted before hard frost and stored indoors for the winter, like dahlias. It is the prevailing opinion that they will flower earlier and produce better bloom. Try it, but sow some seeds outdoors in May to be sure of a crop of flowers.

GODETIA

I have no luck with satin flower. Can you help me? These lovely, bushy, 18 inch annuals with their masses of hollyhock-like salmon, orange, pink, red and lavender flowers, prefer part shade and a cool, moist location. They thrive on Cape Cod in a well watered garden but cannot stand areas where nights are hot and humid.

KOCHIA

I have heard of an annual which can be used instead of a real hedge. What is it? Burning Bush or Kochia. The rounded plants, like sheared evergreens, grow 3 feet tall. During hot weather the foliage is light green but in autumn it turns a rich red.

LARKSPUR

How early should larkspur be planted? (Virginia.) As early in the spring as the ground becomes workable, or in late fall about November.

What month is best to plant larkspur and raggedrobin? (Virginia.) Larkspur and raggedrobin (lychnis) can be sown in November for spring bloom, or as early in spring as possible.

Will larkspur do well if transplanted? It transplants very poorly; sow the seeds where the plants will flower, and thin out the seedlings to 9 ins.

When shall I transplant annual larkspur? Only when the seedlings are small—just large enough to handle; large plants do not transplant successfully. Better to sow where they are to bloom and thin them.

What is the secret for successful larkspur? Ours start well, but fade away before flowering. Sow seeds in well-drained, moderately fertile soil, in full sun or light shade. Thin seedlings to stand 9 ins. apart. (See preceding answers.)

LOBELIA

Will lobelia grow in part shade? Yes, the low-growing varieties are ideal for window and porch boxes or hanging baskets as well as for partly shaded edgings. Choose Gracilis Blue for boxes and dwarf varieties for edgings.

MARIGOLD

What types of marigolds do you suggest for a garden of annuals? African (tall, double including carnation-flowered, chrysanthemum-flowered, dahlia-flowered, peony-flowered; French Single; French Double; Dwarf Signet (*Tagetes signata pumila*).

What marigolds shall I grow for variety in color? Man-in-the-moon, very pale yellow; Glitters, canary yellow; Fluffy Ruffles, gold; Limelight, lime-yellow; Mayling, primrose yellow; Tetra, deep orange. Dwarf: Butterball, yellow; Lemon Drop, lemon; Red Head, gold and maroon; Cupid, yellow.

Would you kindly tell me why my marigolds didn't blossom well last summer? Could it be the fault of the ground? It may have been any one, or several, of a number of reasons: too late sowing; too much rain; too heavy or too-rich soil; insufficient sun; overfeeding or over-watering.

Are seeds good which have not been picked until after a killing frost, such as marigolds? The first killing frost would probably not be severe enough to harm the seeds.

NASTURTIUMS

What nasturtiums shall I grow to produce seeds for pickles and salads? What shall I do to keep them free of the little black bugs? The old-fashioned singles, either dwarf or tall. The much more beautiful and attractive sweet scented doubles produce few seeds. Keep young plants sprayed with Black Leaf 40 to keep off aphids.

NICOTIANA

I have seen flowering tobacco in mixed colors. What variety is this? The Affinis Hybrids or Sensation Mixed. Crimson Bedder is deep red. All are delightfully fragrant, and will grow in part shade.

NIEREMBERGIA

How shall I grow nierembergia from seed? Start indoors in March for early bloom. Purple Robe is a fine violet-blue variety.

PERIWINKLE

How and where shall I plant the annual periwinkle? Periwinkle (*Vinca rosea*) is a native of the tropics and practically everblooming. Sow seeds in January in a warm temperature. The seeds are sometimes difficult to germinate, and at first the seedlings are slow of growth. Have the soil well drained and don't overwater. When these seedlings produce the first true leaves, transplant to 2¼-in. pots, later on to 3-in. pots. From these transplant to the open ground when all danger of cold weather is past. Provide a fairly rich soil. Once established they need little care beyond watering occasionally.

PETUNIAS

Can petunias be grown successfully with only 4 hours of afternoon sun? Yes, provided other conditions are suitable.

How can I prepare seedbed for petunias? When shall I plant in St. Louis area? (Missouri.) Have the soil well drained, moderately rich, and very thoroughly cultivated, so that its texture is fine and light. Sow thinly in spring when soil is in good workable condition.

When is the best time to plant petunias? In what soil? (New York.) The new Hybrid F₁ and F₂, Fringed Giant, Ruffled, Double and other improved petunias are best started indoors in March in the vicinity of New York. See Propagation Indoors, this section.

When is the best time, and what is the best way, to plant petunia seed? (Alabama.) In your region, outdoor sowing of petunia seed is likely to be the most satisfactory. It may be done as soon as the soil has warmed up in spring. Have the soil very well and finely prepared, and barely cover the seed.

Can petunias be sown in the fall? (Ohio.) Fall-planted petunia seed sometimes comes through the winter and germinates in the spring—this depends chiefly on climate, location, and the character of the winter. Spring sowing is preferable in middle and northern sections of the country.

How long does it take petunia seeds to germinate, and when should one transplant them? Good petunia seeds sown on prepared soil, only lightly covered, and kept at greenhouse temperature, should germinate in from 8 to 12 days. Transplant when the first *true* leaves appear. (The leaves that show at germination are only seed leaves.) This might be approximately 10 to 14 days after germination.

Should petunias always be transplanted, or will they bloom well where originally planted? If the soil and other conditions are favorable, they should do well where originally planted. But thin the seedlings to 6 ins. or so apart if they come up thickly.

Set out petunias in bed with partial shade when they had just begun to bloom; plants withered and died until 90 per cent were gone. Soil analysis said nothing was wrong. Gladioli did well in same bed. What was wrong? Probably root injury when transplanting, plus too much water. Petunias will stand some shade but not too much.

I'd like a mass of petunias for borders but have no success growing from seed. How can this be done? How early to start, etc.? (Connecticut.) Petunia seed for a mass planting is best sown as soon as the soil has warmed up. Have the soil very thoroughly pulverized, and barely cover the seed. Keep watered, and thin out plants to 6 or 8 ins. apart when they are a couple of inches tall. For earlier bloom, start seed in flats indoors in March, and transplant outdoors early in May.

Is there any way to prevent petunias growing lank during late summer? I keep seed pods picked off pretty well, still they look straggly by August. This tendency is hard to prevent in some varieties unless the flowers are cut quite often; prune back the longer stems to encourage stockiness. Use compact-growing kinds.

Why can't I raise petunias? They are the only plants I have a complete failure with. I buy good seed, but the plants that do grow just get tall (leggy), with very small bloom, if any. A hard question to answer without more information. The plants may be too crowded, or the soil may be too heavy and shaded. Try careful thinning and pinching back young plants.

Why can't I raise any petunias? They come up but die. Perhaps the soil is too heavy and claylike, or it may be too wet. A light, well-drained soil in practically full sun is best, and it should be only moderately rich.

What makes petunia plants turn yellow, especially if grown 2 years in succession in the same soil? Petunias are subject to several virus diseases that discolor the leaves. The condition may also be due to a highly alkaline soil. Dig in peat or leafmold, change the location, and prepare the soil deeply.

Why do petunia plants grow large but have no blooms? Soil probably too rich, thereby forcing excessive stem and leaf growth at the expense of blooms. Try them in another place where the soil is poorer. Don't overwater.

Can you explain just how to snip off a petunia plant (brought in from outdoors) so that it will have many blooms instead of spindly stems? Cut back about half of the stems to 4 or 5 ins. When these have developed new growth, cut back the remaining stems in the same way.

How can I force petunia (giant and ruffle types) under average conditions as to light and heat found in a home? Your chances of raising petunias under home conditions are slight. In greenhouses, cuttings are taken in September from summer plants, the young growths being used. These are rooted in sand and then potted up in small pots. They do not bloom much in the winter but begin about February. Seeds can be sown in January and February for early flowering. Petunias need plenty of light and a fairly even temperature—about 55° F. at night. You might try digging up old plants in fall, cutting them back, and planting in pots.

Will petunias reseed successfully? (Indiana.) Sometimes they will; it depends on conditions. The more common kinds reseed freely, but the colors will be unsatisfactory. For good petunias secure good seed each year.

How can I root cuttings from double petunias? If the plants are growing outdoors, take the cuttings in August or September. Select young growths about 2 ins. in length that grow from the older stems. Trim off the bottom leaves and insert them ½ to 1 in. deep in pure, moist sand in a cold frame in a warm atmosphere. Shade and keep the sash on for about a week. Give light when they are rooting; this will be indicated by the foliage remaining erect. Keep the sand moist.

Dwarf, compact-growing annuals (such as the Gem Petunias) are used for the foreground of mixed borders and for edging.

How can I root petunia cuttings in winter? About February take young side growths, trim off the lower leaves, and set them firmly in moist sand. (See previous question.)

Which kind of petunias shall I get to grow against a small white fence? Something not tall, but rather bushy. F_1 Hybrids like Ballerina, Comanche, Prima Donna, Red Satin, Flamingo. Dwarfs: Cheerful, Blue Bird, Peach Red, Improved Rosy Morn and Snowball. Doubles, like Burpee's Salmon, White, Orchid, and Mrs. Dwight D. Eisenhower; the F_2 Hybrids, in mixed colors; Balconies, Salmon, Black Prince, etc.

What type of petunia is best for garden work—for all summer beauty? The regular "bedding" and "balcony" types are generally the most satisfactory.

POINSETTIA

What is the best treatment for annual poinsettias? Have some, but they appear weak, and are having a hard time. Not very easy to germinate the seeds outdoors. Suggest you sow in a small pot or seed pan indoors last of April. Use a soil mixed with sand and leafmold or peatmoss screened through ¼-in. mesh. Cover with glass and shade but remove when seed germinates; give all light and air possible; transplant outdoors when first true leaves appear.

POPPY

Do California and Shirley Poppies reseed themselves? Yes, usually; but much digging of the soil in the spot where reseeding took place will bury the seed so deep it may not germinate.

When is best time to plant the (annual) peony-flowered poppy? Can it be successfully planted on top of the snow? (Kansas.) If in your region the poppy usually reseeds itself, and plants come voluntarily the following spring, you can very well sow on the snow. Otherwise sow just as early as you can get on the soil.

When is the correct time to plant poppy seed? How is it best sown? Just as early as you can work the ground in spring. Rake the soil as fine as possible; make level and firm it slightly; scatter the seeds thinly, press them firmly into the soil but don't cover. Thin out the seedlings when 2 ins. high, spacing 3 ins. apart. Two weeks later thin again to 6 or 9 ins. apart.

PORTULACA

How can I make portulaca catch and grow? Portulaca is usually easy to grow from seed sown outdoors in either October or early spring. It should have a well-drained, light, and not rich soil, in full sun.

SALPIGLOSSIS

How can I grow large, healthy salpiglossis plants? (New Jersey.) Sow seeds in a well-prepared bed in May. Work peatmoss or leafmold into the surface, sow the seeds thinly in rows 2 ins. apart. Cover them not more than ⅛ in. deep. Transplant 12 ins. apart in soil deeply dug and enriched with old manure or compost; or with peatmoss mixed with dried cow or sheep manure, 10 lbs. to a bushel of peat, plus ½ lb. of ground limestone. Spread an inch deep and dig in. Do not soak the soil until the plants are steadily growing and have some size. Cultivate frequently. When flower stalks form, feed with liquid manure; or apply sheep manure, about 1 lb. per 40 sq. ft.; hoe and water in; repeat every 2 weeks during bloom.

SALVIA

How do you start red salvia seeds? (South Dakota.) The seed should be sown indoors in a warm temperature, about the latter part of March or beginning of April, in small pots or seed pans. Cover seeds ⅛ in., and set pot or pan in water until moisture shows on surface. Cover with glass and newspaper, but remove as soon as seed germinates.

Are there other colors of bedding salvia besides the red and blue? Yes, the so-called Welwyn Salvias, and others, can be had in white, salmon-pink, purple, mahogany, and lilac.

SCABIOSA

What is the best method of culture for scabiosa? (New Jersey.) Sow seeds outdoors about April 15 or indoors in March. Give the plants a sunny position where the soil is rather light in texture, moderately rich, and in full sun. Do not cover the seeds deeply; not more than ⅛ in. Transplant when the seedlings have made their first true leaves, setting them in the soil so that the lower leaves are resting on the surface. Set 9 ins. apart each way.

SNAPDRAGONS (ANTIRRHINUM)

Do snapdragons require a rich, shady place? (Idaho.) They should have full sun and a light, well-drained soil that is only moderately enriched. Early planting is desirable for best bloom.

What is the best fertilizer for snapdragons? Rotted manure or leafmold when preparing the soil, which should be neutral or slightly alkaline. Feed liquid manure when coming into flower, or give a dressing of complete chemical fertilizer.

Can snapdragon be sown in the fall? (Kentucky.) Yes, in your part of the country but it must be done sufficiently early to provide young plants which will be large enough to withstand the winter with protection. Sow in August.

When shall I plant snapdragons? (Wisconsin.) The best time to set young plants out is in the spring when the ground has begun to warm up. Seeds should be started indoors in March.

When is the best time to set out snapdragon plants? (North Carolina.) Early in spring, when the ground has really started to warm up.

Are snapdragons strictly annuals? Mine bloomed after several frosts and continued in leaf. (Virginia.) No; in the South they are often treated as biennials. Generally speaking, they are handled as hardy annuals (more cold resistant than most). Botanically they are perennials.

Must snapdragons be supported by stakes at planting time? Mine were all in curlicues, and staking them after 8 or 10 ins. tall didn't help at all. It is a good idea to put in the stakes at the time the young plants are set out, and start tying as soon as signs of flopping over begin. A better plan is to use twiggy brush and insert pieces 18 ins. long among the plants. The growths will work up among the twigs. In an open situation, with proper care of soil, they ought not to need much support.

Can you tell me how to grow snapdragons? I buy the plants and they bloom a little while, then die. (Mississippi.) Perhaps the soil is too rich, too heavy and claylike, or poorly drained. Or there may be too much shade. Snapdragons like an open situation, light soil, and not too much feeding. They dislike a hot situation and bloom best in cool weather.

How can I attain many-flowered snapdragons in my summer garden? I get good plants but there are many stems and few blooms to a stem. Thin out weakest shoots, apply superphosphate and pulverized limestone to the soil at the rate of 8 oz. per sq. yd., and scratch into the surface. Full sunshine is necessary. Set out well-developed plants in early May.

Why can't I grow snapdragons from seed? They never come up. (Kentucky.) Sow in late April in well-drained place where the soil is light and only moderately rich and has been raked into fine texture, free of stones and lumps. Cover seed with sand not more than ⅛ in. deep, and do not pack hard. Cover with burlap, which remove as soon as seed shows germination. Water regularly in dry weather. Disinfect the seed with Semesan before sowing.

Can snapdragons be carried over winter in a cold frame? (New York.) Yes, if they are less than 1 year old. Actually, these plants can be considered as biennials in the South, or in the North when frame protection can be given in the winter.

How shall I protect antirrhinum outdoors to survive sub-zero winters? (Kentucky.) Attempts to bring snapdragons through such winter weather outdoors often fail, whatever precautions you take. Try mulching with 3 or 4 ins. of coarse straw or salt meadow hay after ground freezes. A cold frame is about the only safe means of protection.

Can you give best method for protecting snapdragons through winter? Would it do to cover them with one of the glass substitutes? (Georgia.) A mulch of straw or salt meadow hay, 2 or 3 ins. thick, is the best winter protection for snapdragons in the garden. Or the plants could be carried over in a cold frame. A glass substitute, by itself, would not do.

Are there such things as perennial snapdragons? No, from the practical gardening standpoint. Technically, they are perennials, but in the North they are too tender to be treated as such. There are some species grown in rock gardens which are truly perennial in regions that have mild winters.

What are the best snapdragons for the garden? Please name one or two, tall or medium kinds, rust resistant or not. I do not have good luck with "snaps" of late years. By all means get rust-resistant kinds. Good varieties are: Tall: Tetraploid strains. Tip Top varieties; Colossals. Medium: Super Majestics; Extra Early Hybrids; Base-branching varieties. Dwarf: Magic Carpet; Miniature strain.

Could you tell me which are the largest and best snapdragons to plant? Size and quality are strongly influenced by the grower's skill and the cultural conditions he provides. Other things being equal, try the "giant" types listed in the catalogue of any leading seedsman.

STOCKS

What causes stocks to mature without blooming? May have been the common stock (*Matthiola incana*), which acts as a biennial and does not flower until the second year. Ten-weeks Stocks are annual, and flower the first year if conditions are to their liking.

Of 100 Ten-weeks Stock plants in our garden, 20 of the smallest, most puny ones bloomed. The other 80 grew into beautifully thrifty plants from early summer until a hard freeze came, but did not bloom. Why? Ten-weeks Stocks usually fail to bloom if subjected to constantly high temperature—60° and over. Yours were grown under border-line conditions, enabling a few individuals to bloom.

How can I make Ten-weeks Stocks bloom? (New Jersey.) By starting them indoors in March and setting them outside late in April. This enables them to make their growth before hot weather comes.

Can stocks be wintered through? (Kansas.) Yes, if you have the biennial kind, *Matthiola incana*, and a mild, dryish winter climate. For the average gardener, this type is not worth trying or bothering with.

SWEETPEAS

When is the best time to plant sweetpeas? As early as the ground can be worked in the spring; or the seeds may be sown in a cold greenhouse or cold frame a month or more ahead of the time when frost may be expected to be out of the ground, and then transplanted.

When and how shall I plant sweetpeas to insure blooms? If you have a frost-free frame, you can sow the seed in September or October in a flat or in small pots, and in March transplant where they are to flower. Or if you have a coolish porch or window, temperature not above 45° to 50° F., you can sow in February, shift into pots, and, after hardening, plant out in late March. If there are no such facilities, sow where they are to flower as early in March as you can; prepare the ground the preceding fall. (See question on preparation.)

Can sweetpea seeds be sown in the fall, for earlier and stronger plants in the spring? If so, at what time, and how deep? Sweetpeas can be planted in fall just before ground freezes, putting them 4 ins. deep and mulching lightly with straw or litter after hard freezing. It is doubtful, though, whether the plants would be appreciably earlier or finer than if spring-sown as soon as ground can be worked.

Can sweetpeas be planted if the ground softens to a depth of 2 ins.? No. Wait until all the frost is out; otherwise the soil will be too muddy to work.

What is the planting date for sweetpeas in Oklahoma? Sow in November and give protection during the coldest part of winter; or sow in late winter, as soon as it is possible to work the soil.

In our mountain climate, what is the best time to plant sweetpeas? When and how should I prepare the soil? (New York.) As early in the spring as it is possible to work the soil. If the soil could be prepared the previous fall, so much the better. (See previous and following answers.)

How shall I prepare ground for sweetpeas for cut flowers? Dig a trench 1½ ft. wide and deep. Mix with the soil a 3- to 4-in. layer of rotted manure, and bone meal at rate of 1 lb. to 10 to 15 linear ft. If possible, do this in the fall so seeds can be planted without delay early in spring.

I want sweetpeas in clumps in flower border. How do I go about it? Prepare soil as described in previous answer except that instead of a long trench you should make circular planting stations 2 to 3 ft. in diameter. Support the peas on brushwood or a cylinder of chicken-wire netting held up by 4 or 5 stakes. Or you can use a dwarf variety such as Little Sweetheart.

Will you let us know something about the cultivating of sweetpeas? How far apart should the plants be? Should they have commercial fertilizer? See preceding answers for soil preparation. The plants should not be closer together than 4 ins. Commercial fertilizers, used according to manufacturer's directions, are good for application along the sides of the row after the plants are 4 ins. high.

How deep should sweetpea seeds be planted? Usually about 2 ins. Some gardeners prefer to sow them in a trench 6 ins. deep, covering them at first with 2 ins. of soil. As the plants increase in stature, the trench is gradually filled in. This works well in sandy soils.

How early must I place the supports for sweetpea vines? When they are about 4 ins. high. If left until they topple over, they never seem to grow so well as they do when staked early. Twiggy branches stuck in on both sides of the row, or in among the plants if they are grown in clumps, make the best supports, but chicken-wire netting, or strings supported by a frame, will do.

How much sun for sweetpeas? Soil? How to combat lice? General care? Full or nearly full sun is best; some shade is tolerated. Soil should be deep, well drained, rich, and well supplied with humus material. Be sure it is neutral or somewhat alkaline—never acid. Spray with nicotine sulfate for plant lice. Keep weeded and cultivated; water regularly; feed weekly with liquid manure when buds begin to show.

Will sweetpeas do better in part shade? Is it right to plant them in January? (North Carolina.) They are likely to remain in bloom somewhat longer if shaded during the hottest part of the day. Seed can be sown in January if the soil is well drained and free from frost.

How can I raise sweetpeas? Formerly had no trouble, but can't seem to grow them now. Perhaps the soil needs enriching. Sweetpeas need a rich soil. Prepare as described in previous answers, side-dress the row after the plants are 4 ins. high with a complete fertilizer. Feed liquid manure when the plants are in bud. Plant as early as possible.

I have never been successful with sweetpeas, my favorite flower. I get about 3 bouquets, and then they die. Can you help me? I have used a number of methods with no success. (Oklahoma.) Maybe the summer sun is too much for them; try shading with cheesecloth as soon as really hot, dry weather starts. Water thoroughly and regularly. Try preparing the soil and sowing in November, or December, giving a little protection in cold weather. Spring-flowering type is somewhat heat resistant.

Had very healthy-looking sweetpea vines, but no blossoms. Why? Soil may be deficient in phosphorous; or they may have been planted too late for buds to open before hot weather blasted them.

How can the blooming season of outdoor sweetpeas be prolonged? By picking the flowers as fast as they mature and by shading from hot sun with cheesecloth or similar material, plus abundant, regular watering. Usually hot weather limits the season.

Sweetpeas that are planted in November usually make some winter growth or early-spring growth. Will it be advisable to shear this top growth and let the base of the plant start new and tender growth? (Virginia.) Yes, pinch the growth back to where the stem shows signs of sprouting at the base. This later growth produces better flowers.

Is there any way to keep birds from eating my sweetpeas and ranunculus as they come up? (California.) Lay a few pieces of garden hose or rope alongside the rows; birds are afraid of snakes. Or cover with cheesecloth. Strings with white rags hanging from them may also help.

How can I successfully grow sweetpeas in a greenhouse? (Texas.) For your region the seed should be sown in late August. These plants should give a crop the greater part of the winter. Try another sowing in late September. Prepare soil 18 ins. deep, with old manure ¼ the soil volume. Add 1 lb. ground limestone and ½ lb. superphosphate per 20 sq. ft. Sow in rows 36 ins. apart, 1 ounce to 35 linear ft. Thin to 4 plants per linear ft. Support the vines by stretching a wire at ground level along the row, another at 10 to 12 ft. in height. Stretch strands of string between and train the vines up the string. Watering and feeding must be related to growth and flowering. In winter water only when moisture is low, as seen by examining the soil 1 to 2 ins.

below the surface. After flowering begins, feed every 2 weeks with liquid manure. Use only the greenhouse varieties.

Is the Spencer Sweetpea the same as the sweet-smelling variety that had a place in Grandmother's garden? Essentially it is the same, though greatly improved in size, form of blossoms, and range of colors.

Which varieties of sweetpeas are the best for a hot, dry climate? What is best method of planting? (Kansas.) Sweetpeas rarely succeed outdoors in a hot, dry climate unless sown very early. Your best chance is to plant in earliest spring, keep well watered, and shade with cheesecloth from direct sun. There are, so far as known, no varieties especially adapted to your conditions. The giant heat-resistant and spring-flowering types are quite heat resistant but need abundant moisture.

TORENIA

What can I use instead of pansies in late summer? *Torenia fournieri,* an attractive little plant, very bushy with purple, lavender and gold flowers like miniature snapdragons. Foliage turns plum-colored in late autumn. Start the seeds in May in a seed bed as they are very tender.

TITHONIA

My tithonia plants never bloom. Can you tell me why? This Mexican sunflower with its handsome, single, brilliant orange blooms, must be started early indoors to give generous bloom before frost. The variety Torch grows only 4 feet tall as against the type which reaches 6 feet. Torch also blooms earlier. Use it at the back of the border or as a screen plant.

VERBENA

How can I raise verbenas? I have not much luck with them. (Kansas.) Verbenas are not easy unless you have facilities for raising them. The seed is variable in its germination. Requiring a long season, seeds must be sown about March 1 in a temperature of 60° F. at night and 70° to 75° F. during the day. The seedlings are pricked off (transplanted) into flats, after the first true leaf appears, using equal parts loam, sand, leafmold and rotted manure. Keep in same temperature until established (10 days), then harden off the plants in a cold frame before planting outside. Set out in the ground when danger of frost is past.

When is the season to plant verbena? The plants should be set out when warm weather is established. Seeds are best sown indoors 2 months prior to setting out plants. (See previous question.)

ZINNIAS

What soil is best for zinnias? Zinnias appreciate a fairly heavy, rich loam. Additions of rotted cow manure and commercial fertilizer will produce sturdy plants.

We have been unable to grow zinnias. Our soil is rich and well drained. We are able to grow asters, but they attain no height or size. What could be the cause? Maybe soil is too acid. Have it tested, and if below pH 6 bring it up to neutral.

Is the middle of April too early to plant zinnia and marigold seed outdoors in central Pennsylvania? It might be suitable for marigold, but May 1 would be better for zinnia.

Should zinnias be transplanted? Zinnias are very easily transplanted. They may, if desired, however, be sown where they are to grow, and then thinned out.

How should I gather zinnia seeds? Select healthiest plants with the best flowers. During late August or early September allow the flowers to mature on the plant and when the seeds are quite dry and dark, harvest them. Spread on paper in a dry, airy place. When thoroughly dry, discard chaff and place best seeds in sealed envelopes or jars. Label and store until planting time.

Why did seeds from a certain zinnia, when planted the next year, not come true to color? Because it was a variety not capable of transmitting its characteristics by seed, such as the new hybrids; or the flowers were fertilized with pollen from other plants of a different color.

How can I get zinnias which will fit into my color scheme? Buy named varieties like Apricot, Riverside Beauty, azalea-pink; Daffodil; Eskimo, white; Glamour Girls, pastel shades, to name a few.

Which zinnias do you suggest for a small garden? Cut and Come Again varieties; Fantasy; Cupid; Lilliput; Navajo; Mexican; Persian Carpet; *Zinnia linearis*.

BIENNIALS

Biennials—plants which start their life cycle one year, pass the winter in a state of dormancy or "suspended animation", and then grow on to complete their lives in the following year—are comparatively little used by amateur gardeners. Even pansies, best known of the biennials, and one of the easiest of all flowers to be grown from seed, are usually bought in spring as plants in full bloom, instead of being raised from seed—at a fraction of the cost of plants—by the gardener himself.

One of the chief reasons why biennials are not more generally grown by the home gardener is that seed should be sown at a time when he feels that the planting season is over. Biennials sown in May or early June—or, in the case of some of them, such as pansies and Siberian Wallflower (*Chieranthus alloni*), as late as late July—can be transplanted as soon as the true leaves develop. By mid-September or October the little plants are ready to be transferred to their allocated positions in the garden, or (in severe climates) carried over winter in a frame, under a protective covering of straw, rough compost or evergreen boughs, applied after the ground has frozen slightly. Covering with glass sash, except in *very* severe climates, is not necessary.

One of the great advantages of using some biennials in the garden scheme is that they provide very early color out-of-doors, and also cut blooms for bringing indoors, weeks before spring sown annuals will be in flower. They are unsurpassed for "filling in" wherever color may be lacking in the spring garden, for they produce almost immediate results.

When is it best to sow seeds of most biennials?   July and early August are considered the best times. This gives a fairly long season to produce good-sized plants for blooming the following year. Hollyhocks, for extra-heavy plants, are best sown in June; but pansies and forget-me-nots are best sown in August, as very large plants of these may winter kill. Others fare very well from July sowings.

How are the so-called biennials best used in the garden?   They are valuable in the mixed border for early-summer bloom. Solid plantings can be made of such kinds as foxgloves, with early lilies, such as Madonna and Hansoni. Combinations like Canterburybells in different colors, faced down with sweetwilliam, pansies, English daisies, and forget-me-not, are valuable as a ground cover for a bulb bed. The biennials must be followed with annuals to fill the bare spots left when the biennials die. In the mixed border they are best used in small groups near later-blooming perennials that will tend to cover the bare spots left. The later-blooming biennials (like hollyhock) can be given due prominence in a mixed planting.

Will you give a list of biennials, with their time of bloom?   This will include many that are perennial but which in garden practice are grown as biennials. Canterburybells (*Campanula medium*), cup-and-saucer (*C. calycanthema*), steeple-bellflower (*C. pyramidalis*), June and July; English daisy (*Bellis perennis*), April and May; foxglove, June–July; hollyhock, July; honesty (*Lunaria*), May; hornpoppy, July; rosecampion, May to June; pansy, April to June; Siberian-wallflower (*Cheiranthus allioni*), May to June; sweetwilliam (*Dianthus barbatus*), June to July; forget-me-not (*Myosotis alpestris* and *M. dissitiflora*), April to May.

Do any of the biennials self-sow?   Yes, quite a few, such as foxglove, forget-me-not, rosecampion, steeple-bellflower, and hollyhock. But if the soil is too assiduously cultivated, the seedlings may be killed.

Are biennials winter hardy in Northern gardens?   The hardiest are the campions, foxglove, hollyhock, steeple-bellflower, honesty, horn-poppy, sweetwilliam, Siberian wallflower. Most other biennials (see list) need considerable protection, preferably a cold frame.

At what time of year should biennials be planted outdoors?   Plants started the preceding year are set out in very early spring for blooming the same year.

SPECIFIC BIENNIAL PLANTS

CANTERBURYBELLS (CAMPANULA)

What is the best time of year to plant seed of Canterburybells and foxglove?   June is a good time to sow seeds of these plants. If sown later, the plants may not be big enough to flower the next year.

Will Canterburybells grow well in upper New York State? When should the seed be sown?   Yes, they will do very well but must have adequate winter protection. Do not stimulate growth by watering or feeding after mid-August. After a hard freeze, cover with brush over which spread a layer of marsh (or salt) hay or similar covering. Sow seeds in June.

How can I grow Canterburybells and cup-and-saucer?   The cup-and-saucer type (*Campanula calycanthema*) is a variety of the regular Canterburybell (*Campanula medium*). The cup-and-saucer requires the same culture and conditions as the regular Canterburybells.

What is the best winter mulch for Canterburybells? (Wisconsin.) Light, littery material that will not pack to a sodden mass over the leaves. Before covering, remove any bad basal leaves that might rot. Tuck the material in around the plants, and stick a few twigs among them to keep a light covering from lying directly on the leaves.

Why is it that Campanula medium sometimes does not blossom? This spring I had two dozen nice-looking plants, transplanted in fall last year; but none of them blossomed.   Plants of Canterburybells, unless they reach a good size, may fail to bloom the first summer. Many, however, will persist through the second winter and set bloom the second summer. Biennials will occasionally, for some unknown reason, do this.

I planted Canterburybells in July, expecting them to bloom the following season, but they did not. Why?   The plants were old enough to bloom. Did you notice if the crown was attacked by any disease? Sometimes virus diseases will attack the plants, causing mottling of the foliage, and possibly prevent blooming. Root lice also will check development.

FOXGLOVES (DIGITALIS)

Can you give us information on growth of Digitalis purpurea, or references from which it may be obtained? (Michigan.) For details of culture consult *Farmers' Bulletin 663,* "American Medicinal Plants," or *Miscellaneous Circular 77,* "American Medicinal Plants of Commercial Importance." These 2 works are obtainable from Superintendent of Documents, United States Printing Office, Washington, D.C.; *Bulletin 663* is 5 cents; *Circular 77* is 30 cents.

What do you do with foxgloves that do not bloom the second year? Will they bloom the third year if kept on? Yes, they probably will; foxgloves frequently behave in this way.

Should we cover our foxglove plants heavily in winter? (Vermont.) In your region they will need adequate protection. Mulch soil with decayed leaves, lay cherry or birch branches over the crowns, and on top of this spread an inch or two of marsh hay or straw. If covering packs on top of the crowns it will cause rot, hence the branches. Evergreen boughs—not heavy ones—are also valuable. These are used alone.

Will foxglove, if separated in winter, bloom the following year? If you refer to the common foxglove, *Digitalis purpurea,* from seed sown the previous summer—probably no. The perennial kinds may be separated in spring.

What parts of foxglove are poisonous, if any? Probably all parts. The drug digitalis (poisonous in overdoses) is obtained from the second year's young leaves, so presumably the poisonous principle is most abundant in them.

What is the best method of gathering foxglove seed? Gather the lower seed capsules from the stem as soon as they show brown, but before they open to shed the seed. Select from the best type.

PANSIES

What is the best location for pansies, for good bloom? A cool, moist, well-drained soil, in a sunny location.

What is the best soil for pansies? Any soil which contains plenty of humus. Well-rotted manure, peatmoss, or leafmold, mixed with the soil, will help. Neutral or slightly acid reaction is best.

When is pansy seed sown? (Minnesota.) In August, to produce plants large enough, before cold weather, so they can be wintered in a covered cold frame.

What is the best method of growing pansies? (Iowa.) Plant seed in cold frames in August, transplanting 6 × 6 ins. when second set of leaves appear. When freezing weather arrives, cover plants with straw, and keep frames closed. About March 1 remove straw, but keep glass on, and ventilate freely. Remove glass about April 1, and set plants in permanent position between April 1 and May 15. Best soil is a good loam with plenty of humus and moisture.

What conditions are necessary to get pansy seed to germinate? (North Carolina.) First obtain *fresh,* plump seeds. For the seedbed use a mixture of 1 part each of soil, sand, and leafmold or peatmoss, put through a ¼-in. mesh screen. Select as cool a spot as you can—a cold frame that can be heavily shaded is ideal. Level and lightly firm the soil. Broadcast the seed on the surface (or sow in rows 4 or 5 ins. apart), and cover with ⅛ in. of fine soil, press lightly, and shade, but leave space for ventilation. As soon as seeds have germinated remove the shading, except during the hottest part of the day. Give full sun when seedlings are well through.

Would pansy seed sown in the open in April come up and bloom by June 15? Pansy seed sown the first of April might possibly show a few flowers by June 15 if growing conditions were favorable. The finest spring display comes from seed sown in August.

Are pansy seeds, if sown outdoors in September, likely to survive the cold weather during winter and flower next summer? (New York.) No; the seed should be sown early in August. In vicinity of New York City young plants will live outdoors with light covering. Farther North they should be grown in cold frames.

Will you tell me when to transplant pansies? (Texas.) Presuming you mean pansy seedlings, you should plant them in their permanent locations (from seedbeds, flats, or pots) in September or October for bloom during the following spring. Young plants, grown in cold frame or in open beds, may be transplanted in the early spring.

Is it better to purchase pansy plants for autumn planting, or for very early-spring planting, if one desires them for sale purposes around Mother's Day? Purchase seedling plants in September, and grow these on to blooming size.

Why don't pansy plants bloom and grow all summer when planted in spring in full bloom? Mine don't. They bloom best in the cool weather of spring and early summer. In an exposed place they deteriorate in the heat; also the earlier heavy bloom exhausts the plants.

What would be the cause of pansy plants growing long stems and very small flowers? Too much shade, or overcrowding. A good strain of seed, August sowing, winter protection, a good soil, and not too much shade are the prerequisites for good results.

Why do blue pansies often have petals streaked blue and white? The seed strain is not good. Blue pansy seed that comes true to type is offered by reliable seedsmen.

When wintering pansies in a cold frame, should one wait until the soil in the frame has frozen, then close the frame and keep it covered with a mat or leaves until spring? No. Best plan is to give plants light, ventilate whenever frost on glass melts, and cover with mats only on coldest nights. Do not remove snow from frames.

What is considered a foolproof winter mulch for pansies? (Wyoming.) Branches of spruce, fir, or pine; straw or hay held down with chicken wire. If hungry mice or rabbits abound, spray pansies first with aluminum sulfate.

When is the best time to apply winter protection for pansies? (Wyoming.) As soon as the surface inch or two of the ground freezes.

When is it safe to remove the winter covering on pansies? (Wyoming.) When severe freezing is past. It is well to remove this (and all such mulches) on a cloudy or rainy day. Sudden exposure to sun and wind is unkind to leaves and buds.

Last year's pansies did such a wonderful job of self-seeding for this season that the resulting plants are lovelier and stronger than the new ones we grew from seed with great care. Any particular reason? Probably due to some cross-pollinizing which developed strong, healthy plants. However, continuous intercrossing year after year will result in deterioration. To maintain the strain, weed out poor plants and poor colors as soon as flowers open.

What are the best varieties of pansies for fall planting? Use separate colors of the Giant Swiss strain.

What is the name of the really giant pansies (4 ins. across)? Are they grown indoors or out? For indoors in winter, use Don's Winter Flowering strain. For outdoors in spring, Super Swiss Giants in separate colors. These can be obtained from any reliable seed firm.

ROSECAMPION (LYCHNIS)

Will you please give botanical name of mullein pink or rosecampion. *Lychnis coronaria,* of easy culture and hardy.

SWEETWILLIAM (DIANTHUS BARBATUS)

When shall I plant sweetwilliam? What kind of soil is required? In a sunny spot, or in shade? (Missouri.) Set plants out as early in spring as the ground can be worked. They like a well-prepared soil with plenty of humus-forming material (like old manure, leafmold, or peatmoss) in addition to a good dressing of dried sheep or cow manure. They prefer a sunny location.

Can seeds of Dianthus barbatus be planted in late fall or early winter? Will they bloom the following season? This is a biennial normally sown in summer for bloom the following year. There is an annual strain which would blossom the following season if planted under glass.

Sweetwilliam will not live through the summer for me. Why? Sweetwilliam is grown as a biennial. It usually dies after flowering.

Do foxglove and sweetwilliam (Dianthus barbatus) come up a second year? The common foxglove (*Digitalis purpurea*) is a biennial. Sweetwilliam is used as such. Rarely do they appear the second year except from self-sown seedlings. It is best to sow seeds of these kinds every year to insure a supply of plants.

WALLFLOWER

What is the difference between wallflower and Siberian Wallflower? Wallflower, (*Cheiranthus cheiri*), grows to a height of two feet and produces yellow, mahogany and brownish flowers in spring and again in autumn. Siberian Wallflower *Cheiranthus allioni* or *Erysimum asperum* is only about a foot tall and produces fragrant yellow flowers in early spring. Golden Bedder is the best variety.

Can you tell me how to grow wallflowers? Both types of wallflowers require cool nights and moisture in the air during the growing season to thrive. They are supposedly lime-lovers but sometimes grow well in acid soil, as near the seashore, when other conditions suit them. *Cheiranthus cheiri* is quite tender inland, but grows well near the coast in New England. Wallflowers need full sun and a sandy soil. Both are usually grown as biennials.

Lawns and Turf Areas

INTRODUCTION

BY P. J. MCKENNA

AND F. F. ROCKWELL

IT IS THE DESIRE of every homeowner with some ground to have a good lawn. A lawn enhances and improves the whole aspect of the property. It ties together in a common unit the various scattered landscape features, and adds considerably to the keen enjoyment of the home and garden.

Setting about the task of making a lawn brings one face to face with numerous problems. Some of these are local in character, others are general, and apply almost wherever lawns exist. Among the latter are insect pests that annually take a heavy toll of numberless turf areas; diseases that, under the influence of certain weather conditions, suddenly make their appearances; drought periods in summer; unusually cold spells in winter; and weeds like crab grass, plantain, and others that, getting a hold, increase the difficulties of maintaining a lawn.

Basic Requirements

In making a lawn a few basic factors (too often overlooked) must be considered. Every blade of grass is part of a complete plant, each with its own root system, and capable of manufacturing its own food. During the growing season this plant is continually drawing on the soil for the materials necessary to sustain itself. When you consider that in a square foot of good sod there are over 400 of these plants competing for food and moisture, you begin to appreciate that the most important phases of lawn making are, first, to provide the soil conditions necessary for the best growth of the turf; and second, to maintain these conditions thereafter.

Lawns made in the fall are the most successful. Then grass makes its best growth, roots have a chance to become established and to penetrate deeper than is the case with a lawn sown in the spring, when high temperatures force constant top growth. In late fall, even after the grass tops are dormant, root development goes on until the ground is frozen many inches deep.

Types of Turf, and Their Uses

It is well at the outset to realize that there are several kinds of turf, and that success depends largely upon selecting one to fit the soil and the situation. It would be folly to attempt to create a lawn of

An unbroken stretch of lawn, with appropriate planting around the edges, is always more effective and pleasing than when the turf area is broken up by flower beds or trees placed in the center.

Velvet Bent on poor, infertile soil, or to try to form a turf of Kentucky Blue Grass in deep shade, or even on a steep slope. Each situation demands its own treatment, for the problems involved are not the same.

Turf of Creeping Bent, such as is generally used in putting greens, is a high-maintenance type of turf requiring frequent cutting, watering, and top-dressing. It is best suited to good, fertile soils that must be given more than average preparation. The kinds of turf most generally used are the strains of Creeping Bent, Velvet Bent, and Seaside Bent. All have the same growth habit in that they spread by surface stems ("stolons"); hence the need for frequent cutting and for top-dressing to keep the stolons in close contact with the soil.

Kentucky Blue Grass and Merion Blue Grass, two of the best for lawns in temperate regions, also require a good, fertile soil. They grow best in cool, moist weather. The tops will brown in midsummer heat, but come back in fall with renewed vigor as the roots, which spread by underground stems, are uninjured.

The fescues, another group frequently used, are the toughest of the lawn grasses. Most of them possess wirelike tops, making them difficult to mow. However, they will grow on poor, dry soils and are fairly successful in shade. They do not spread much by creeping roots, however, as do the other grasses. The best of the fescues is Chewing's Fescue. Spreading but slowly, it is best used in combination with transient grasses like Red Top and rye grass. When established, it makes a durable sod and is used in mixtures for growing in shade and on terraces. Meadow Fescue grows well in sun or shade and will stand up fairly well under dry conditions. It makes a loose sod, however, and should not be mowed too often.

Of the other grasses used in lawns, Rough-stalked Blue Grass grows well in shade, but requires a good soil well supplied with lime. This grass will not persist under close and frequent mowing. Periodical feeding is necessary, and even then a dry summer may end its career.

Among the few rye grasses (rye grass is often confused with rye for grain), Perennial Rye is the best. Good seed germinates at once. The grass grows fast, but is short-lived, lasting only about two years. It is used in mixtures where it is designed to hold until the more permanent grasses become established. It can be used alone and will create a green sward in a short time—a fact of importance if one is trying to cover a poor soil by sowing in early summer with a view to improving the soil before putting in a permanent lawn later on.

Preparing the Soil for Turf Areas

The most important of all lawn operations is the initial preparation of the soil. At no other time in the life of the lawn is it so easy to create (as far as possible) the conditions necessary for good turf. To be favorable, soil conditions must not only encourage root formation, but also depth of penetration. The rooting depth is influenced by two factors: good drainage and deep working of the soil.

Drainage is the first prerequisite. In wet soils, air—which is very important to roots—is excluded. Under wet conditions lawn grasses will not long survive: either they are winter killed, or crowded out by coarser-growing grasses. Poor drainage is associated with low-lying sites in which the water table is near the surface, and with soils of clay texture through which water moves too slowly. Aeration and the water travel in clay soils are improved by mixing screened cinders, the size of beans or peas, with the top 12 ins. A layer 1 to 3 ins. deep is not too much. Low-lying sites are drained by installing tile pipes, or by raising the grade sufficiently and providing enough pitch for surface drainage.

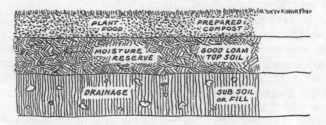

Foundation for a good permanent lawn.

The soil should be worked (dug or plowed) 10 to 12 ins. deep, but the subsoil must not be brought up to the surface or bare spots will result. Organic matter, without which a good lawn is not possible, must be used in some form and incorporated at the time of working the soil. It improves the whole physical condition of the soil, especially its moisture-holding qualities, and promotes root action. There are several sources of humus. Farm manure and good compost contain valuable nutrients, while peatmoss, humus, muck, and leaf-mold contain but little. All, however, improve the soil. The material used is spread on the surface 2 to 4 ins. deep. Bone meal is scattered over this 4 to 6 lbs. per 100 sq. ft. All is then dug or plowed under, or, if the soil has been dug, thoroughly worked into the surface.

This is also the time to get grub-proofing material into the ground to check the beetle grubs, using chlordane 5% dust ½ lb. per 100 sq. ft. For an even covering mix the powder with sand or fine soil, using 10 lbs. to 1 lb. of powder. After the soil has been roughly leveled, spread the material evenly and rake it into the surface. A few weeks before seeding broadcast a combination nitrogenous fertilizer and a weed seed killer such as Lawn and Garden Cyanamid or Aero-cyanamid, carefully following the directions on the package as to when and how to apply it. The area should be fairly even, merely needing a few operations with a rake to finish the grade. Plowing, on the other hand, may leave much unevenness, needing more than raking to level the grade. Soil may have to be moved from high to low spots. Even after this, it is better to roll the area to take out further unevenness. Other things to be considered are trees or areas reserved for beds and borders. The grade should be adjusted to blend with these features.

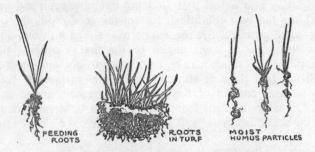

A square foot of turf contains some 400 individual grass plants, each of which must be well fed. An abundance of humus in the surface soil is especially important in maintaining the moisture supply.

Terraces

Terraces present different and sometimes difficult problems. The all-important factor of moisture supply is the main consideration. If the slope is steeper than one foot in three, and with a southerly aspect, the problem of getting a turf started from seed, and then maintaining it, is a particularly difficult one. Here fertile topsoil is even more important than on level ground. Not less than 6 ins., preferably more, of prepared soil, with old rotted manure (or well-dampened peatmoss) constituting ⅓ of its bulk, is used for surfacing. If the slope is long, place strips of sod, 8 to 10 ins. wide. at right angles across the slope at 3-ft. intervals, and seed the lawn grass in between. To prevent washing, cover the seeded area with hay or loosely woven burlap; remove gradually as seed germinates.

Grass Seeds and Turf Mixtures

Good seed is the first consideration. Avoid cheap mixtures. They contain grasses such as timothy, totally unsuited to lawns. Besides, the percentage of germination is poor, and much chaff and weed seed is pretty sure to be present. Deal with seed houses that have a recognized reputation for quality. Many lawn-seed specialists have excellent mixtures designed to fit particular situations.

The rate of seeding will depend upon the kind of grass to be used. For an area of 1,000 sq. ft. (20 × 50 ft.) 5 lbs. of a mixture in which Kentucky Blue Grass predominates is needed. Of the bent grasses (the seeds of which are much smaller), 3 lbs. is ample.

Fescue seeds are larger, and in addition their germination is poorer than that of most other grasses. It is therefore best to use as much as 6 lbs. per 1,000 sq. ft.

Seeding and Sodding

A calm day and a soil that is damp but not wet (and certainly not dry) are the best conditions for sowing seed. Split the quantity into two equal portions. Broadcast one over the plot in one direction, and sow the other at right angles to the first. Covering the seed is accomplished by using a rake, with a light back-and-forth motion that will not pull the soil about. Firming the surface by rolling or tamping assures contact of the seed with the soil, and even germination. On sandy or light loam soils this can be done with the soil slightly moist; on heavy soils, it is better to have the surface perfectly dry.

As soon as the area is seeded, raked and rolled, a thorough watering is given, preferably with an oscillating sprinkler, or one which produces a fine mist spray. The usual rotating type is apt to deliver too much water to some areas and not enough to others. "Puddling" of the surface is almost sure to wash the seed into the low spots, the result being an uneven germination with many bare spaces. The object should be to soak the lawn thoroughly and evenly to a depth of at least 4 inches. To insure even germination, the lawn area must be kept consistently moist until after the seedling grass is well up. If it is permitted to dry out even for a day some of the germinating seedlings may be burned out.

Sodding. The advantages of sodding are that results are immediate, and the work can be done equally well in spring or fall. Its drawbacks are the expense involved and the difficulty of securing weed-free turf to use for sodding. The soil is prepared and leveled as for seeding, the surface inch being kept loose to embed the turves (sods) which, for easy handling, are usually 12 by 12 ins. They are set close together, tamped into place, and loose soil, in which seed is mixed, is worked into the joints. The area is then rolled and, if the weather is dry, watered frequently. Sodding is particularly valuable on terrace slopes because, in addition to the immediate effect, the danger of the soil and seeds being washed out is avoided. Beginning at the base of the slope, the sods are laid as for a lawn, and each sod— or, if the slope is not too steep, each alternate row of sods—is fastened to the slope with wooden pegs. The area is then treated as for the lawn.

Early Care of the New Lawn

The first mowing of a fall-seeded lawn should take place when the grass is about 2 to 3 ins. high, but close cutting should be avoided. Another cutting may be necessary before winter, but it is essential that the lawn go into winter with a good top growth to afford protection to young roots from the drying action of freezing winds. In March, even before the frost is out of the ground, seed down any bare spots that may appear. Later, as growth is beginning, top-dress with sifted soil mixed with turf fertilizer, 3 lbs. to the bushel. Apply a bushel of this to every 100 sq. ft., and with the *back* of a rake work it down among the young grasses. When the surface is dry, firm with a roller.

Begin cutting when the grass is over 2 ins. high but do not cut close the first summer. Rake off all mowings to prevent disease until the dry, hot weather of July and August, when the mowings may be left on. The machine should then be adjusted to cut at a height of at least 2 ins.

How to Maintain Good Turf

Feeding. Keeping the turf thrifty is the first step in lawn management. This means supplying nutrients in abundance and at the right time. The only period during the growing season when nutrients are useful is when there is plenty of moisture in the soil. Spring and fall are the two best seasons for feeding. Although fertilizer supplies the nutrients that grass needs, the best form of spring feeding is a top-dressing of compost. This is especially important on lawns of Creeping Bent. (A mixture of soil with ¼ its bulk of rotted manure, peatmoss, or leafmold will do.) One cubic yard will cover 1,200 sq. ft. With this quantity mix 30 lbs. of grass fertilizer, of a 5–10–5 analysis, if it can be obtained. The top-dressing is spread evenly with a shovel, worked into the grass with a wooden rake, and the area is then rolled.

Mowing at 1½ ins. should be frequent in early summer, the cut grass being removed. In July and August the mower should be adjusted to cut at about 2 ins., depending upon the kind of grass. Creeping Bent lawns will have to be kept below the 1½ ins.

Watering—an important factor in maintenance—will depend upon the kind of soil and the exposure. For best results, water must not be withheld until the soil is completely dry, for then it is difficult to raise the moisture content. Examine the soil *beneath* the turf, and if after 4 or 5 days of hot sun it is showing a tendency to become dry, water immediately, *giving a thorough soaking*. Sandy soils will dry out much sooner than loam soils that are well supplied with organic matter, and a lawn that has been cut at about 1½ to 2 ins. will not dry out so quickly in midsummer as one that is kept shorter.

Weeds and How to Control Them

The maintenance of a dense, thrifty turf is the best insurance against weeds. If any appear, they should be eradicated at once. Allowed to secure a hold, their elimination is difficult. Deep-rooting weeds, like dandelion, if not too numerous, are best dug up. Merely cutting out the crown will not kill them. Dandelion spreads by roots and by seeds. Constant close cutting to prevent flowering will, after a time, reduce their numbers, gradually weakening the old roots.

Large-scale eradication is best done with chemicals, spraying with iron sulfate (copperas), 1½ lbs. in 2 gals. of water. (This will cover 350 sq. ft. of area.) It will also kill plantain, chickweed, and others. Several applications will be necessary at 2- to 3-week intervals during the season. Iron sulfate will blacken the grass, but this will disappear in a few days, especially after the grass is cut. This chemical will also stain stone, cement, metals, and clothes. A stronger solution (3 lbs. to 2 gals.) squirted into the heart of dandelion and plantain with a pressure oilcan, or applied with a pointed stick dipped in the solution, is also effective.

Crab Grass. The most insidious weed of all is Crab Grass. The pest is an annual and dies with the first frost; but the abundantly produced seeds start into growth the following May or June as the weather becomes warm. Crab Grass thrives only in full sunshine. Keeping the grass at 2 ins. high and maintaining a close turf are the best preventives. Young plants must be removed as soon as recognized.

Preventing the formation of seed is important in controlling Crab Grass. Raking the lawn to bring up the creeping stems where the mower can catch them will help. Removing the whole plant is better. Where Crab Grass has become well established, only drastic measures will eradicate it. In this event the lawn may have to be entirely remade. Using a portable kerosene torch about the time the seeds are ripening will consume the plant and scorch any seeds that have fallen on the ground. Good control has also been obtained by using sodium chlorate or sodium arsenite. The latter is a deadly poison; the former, although not poisonous, is highly inflammable. These salts can either be sprayed on, or mixed with sand and spread dry. One pound of the salt mixed with a 2-gal. bucket of sand will treat 1,000 sq. ft. To complete the eradication, two further applications, at double this strength, will be necessary. Apply from the end of July through August, if there is considerable moisture present.

New chemicals now available are most helpful. Several of these, sold under such trade names as Lawn and Garden Cyanamid are calcium cyanamid compounds which may be applied to the bare ground some weeks before seeding, and which kill the ungerminated seeds of crabgrass. In using an herbicide of this sort it is most important to follow exactly the directions on the package.

Other crabgrass killers such as Alanap, Crag 531, PMAS, Scutl and KOCN, kill in the seedling stage.

The growth on a fall-planted lawn is usually dense enough by the following May to prevent the germination of crabgrass seeds which require full sun. This is another good reason for making your lawn in autumn.

Diseases and Insects

Besides the grubs which eat the roots of grasses, and are controlled with chlordane (as advised above, in making a new lawn), the other serious pest is the chinch bug. There are usually two infestations, the first in June, the second in August. Timing the control is important, but this pest can be handled with a single treatment of chlordane dust or spray, applied between June 1st and 15th.

The chinch bug sucks the juices out of the grass stalks, leaving brown, dry, injured areas, circular in outline. The bugs usually are found at the outer edge of the circle working on the live grasses. The insecticide must be forced down into the grass where the pest is working.

Fungous diseases sometimes cause trouble. The worst of these are brown patch and dollar spot, which look much alike. The conditions conducive to an infestation are high temperature, excessive humidity, and a soft, lush growth of grass. Circular brown patches appearing in June, when the grass is wet, are indications of the disease. Mercurial preparations, of which there are several (such as PMAS, Tact-c-lect, Semesan, and Nu-green), are the best controls. A homemade mixture consisting of two parts calomel and one part corrosive sublimate, applied at the rate of 3 ozs. per 1,000 sq. ft., may be used. Mixed with 2 to 3 gals. of water, it is applied as a spray; or it may be mixed with a bucket of sand and spread dry. If the weather remains humid, repeat the treatment every 10 days.

Calendar of Lawn Operations

Late winter (February or March). Sow all bare spots with a lawn-seed mixture and cover with ¼ inch of sifted soil.

Spring. When frost is out of the ground, top-dress with compost, as previously advised, and work in with a rake. Roll, using a roller 150 to 300 lbs. in weight, but not so heavy as to pack sod. Roll when the lawn is *moist but not wet*.

Remove any dandelions or plantains that show, or treat the plants with a spot weed killer.

Mow when 2 to 3 ins. high, maintaining the height at 1½ ins. Remove clippings and put on compost heap.

Summer. In June, if weather is hot and humid, watch for brown patch and treat as advised. If there has been previous injury from chinch bug, or if bent grass predominates in the lawn, dust during the most vulnerable period. Watch now for young Crab-Grass plants, and *remove while small*.

In midsummer raise the cut to 2 ins. Watch the moisture content of the soil and water if needed.

Fall. In August, inspect for chinch bug. Toward the end of August or beginning of September cut the grass close, removing the clippings. Rake the sod with an iron rake to remove weeds. Apply turf fertilizer, 10 to 25 lbs. per 1,000 sq. ft.

Repair all bare or injured patches, digging up if necessary. Seed, and cover with sifted soil. Keep the cut at 1½ ins. and mow regularly. As cold weather approaches, raise the cut to 2 ins. until top growth stops.

LAWNS

GRADING

How should a lawn be graded? What operations are involved? Grading first depends upon the particular site and whether paths or driveways are to be laid out. Existing trees and areas for planting must also be considered. Outline the paths and drives with stakes. Remove the topsoil from these and spread it over the lawn area. If the dwelling is much higher than the street, slope the grade gradually down to meet the lower level. Do not terrace unless the situation demands it. If the dwelling is on a level area, give the lawn a slight pitch from the house to the street.

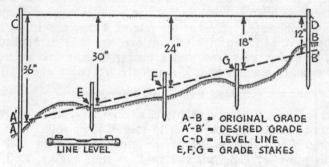

Establishing a grade line where an uneven surface is to be regraded. A–B—original grade; A'–B'—desired new grade; C–D, cord stretched level between two stakes (it is leveled by means of a little instrument known as a "line level"); E, F, G—grade stakes set at equal distances between points A and B. The grade stakes are marked, as indicated, and the soil is cut down or filled in to establish the new grade.

How much pitch must be given a lawn, and how is the pitch determined? A pitch of 1 ft. in 20 ft., or even 30 ft., unless the soil is heavy clay, is sufficient to give surface drainage. The grade can be established by using a line and a line level, and thus determining the difference, in height, between the high and the low points.

If there is much unevenness in the ground, should it be dug or plowed before grading? The soil, of course, will have to be loosened to move it. The practical thing to do is to remove all the topsoil, loosen the subsoil, and do the grading; then finish the grade with the topsoil. This insures an even depth of good soil over the entire area. If the existing topsoil is not sufficient to give about 4 ins. covering, provision should be made for the adding of extra soil.

Our house sets quite a way back from the street and several feet above it. How should the front lawn be graded? A low, sloping terrace, 10 to 15 ft. wide, across the house front will tend to give it a feeling of stability. Work the soil down to a gradual slope from the bottom of the terrace to the street.

What is the procedure to follow if much soil has to be moved around? In large operations the easiest way to move quantities of soil is with a bulldozer, or a team of horses and a drag scoop can be used. In small areas, soil can be loosened with a rototiller and moved in a wheelbarrow.

How is the soil leveled to make it even for seeding? Several rakings are sometimes necessary. Rake first with an iron rake to remove stones, sticks, and other debris, at the same time filling in as many hollows and smoothing down as many hills as possible. Some shoveling may be necessary to get rid of the worst of these. Then rake with close-toothed wooden hay rake to remove smaller stones and break up lumps. Roll lightly. Ridges and depressions will then be apparent and can be leveled off by raking or shoveling. Rake again before seeding.

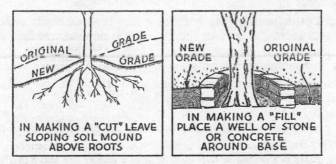

IN MAKING A "CUT" LEAVE SLOPING SOIL MOUND ABOVE ROOTS

IN MAKING A "FILL" PLACE A WELL OF STONE OR CONCRETE AROUND BASE

Grading around an established tree to obtain a properly sloped lawn surface.

We need to fill in to get a good slope for a lawn, but there are large trees in the way. Will the grading injure them? If the grade is to be carried much over the existing level, some protection must be given the trees. It may be necessary to build a dry well of stone around the trunks to allow air and moisture to reach the roots.

How high can the soil be raised around a tree without injuring it? This depends somewhat on the variety of tree. In general however, where the soil is light and well drained, the grade may be raised around trees a foot or two without appreciable injury. If the soil is heavy and not well drained, raising the grade as little as 6 ins. may cause injury.

How large should a tree well be? (Maryland.) Generally speaking, the diameter of a tree well should be four times the diameter of the tree. Deep wells should be provided with tile drains running out laterally from the bottom. They should not be narrowed in at the top, since it may be necessary to get down into them to clean out leaves.

PREPARATIONS FOR SOWING

When is the best time to prepare the soil for a lawn? It should be prepared at least 2 weeks before seeding. This is one of the reasons for fall sowing. Not enough time is available in spring. Much will depend upon the extent of the preparation. Time should be given for a thorough working of the soil and for allowing it to settle.

What is the proper method of making a lawn? See Introduction for directions. Adjust these to the conditions existing in your own locality as to kind of soil, site, and exposure. Consult a seedsman about proper mixture.

Is it necessary to make the soil for a lawn fine, or can it be left rough? The top surface must be made very fine, so that when the seed is planted the earth will come in close contact with it; root action is promoted in well-tilled soil.

Can I get information on building a new lawn on sandy soil? To produce a successful lawn on sandy soil it is necessary to incorporate large quantities of humus-making materials. Humus is the deciding factor in establishing a lawn on a sandy soil. (See Introduction.)

How may I start a new lawn from my old one? It was completely ruined by Jap beetles and severely burned by the sun. Remove all weeds. Dig or plow to a depth of 9 to 12 ins. if the topsoil will permit. Then proceed as outlined in the Introduction concerning grub-proofing, seeding, etc.

Can I get a good lawn on very stony ground? This is a difficult problem. Remove as many of the larger stones as possible. Seed with 1 part each Red Top and Perennial Rye Grass, and 2 parts Chewing's Fescue. Gradually build a new surface by top-dressing with fine soil and compost. Reseed in spring and fall to promote a thick turf. Because of stones, the grass may have to be cut higher than the ordinary lawn (see top-dressing, seed quantity), until a new surface has been established.

How deep must I prepare soil for a lawn which has never been cultivated before? See Introduction. The instructions given there will have to be adjusted to the depth of topsoil and the kinds of plants that now occupy it. Provide, if possible, 4 ins. of topsoil. The initial work is all important.

How much topsoil is needed for a lawn? At least 4 ins. of good topsoil is needed to insure the grass getting a hold. Six to 8 ins. is better.

Should the soil be compacted before seeding? The type of soil and its condition will have to be considered. If the soil is heavy and very damp, it would be better not to compact it. On a light soil, yes, especially if there has been much grading. The compacting will then reveal depressions that can be corrected before seeding.

Preparing surface for sowing grass seed. After grading and raking, the ground is rolled, and again raked to fill in uneven spots. On new or filled-in ground, it may be necessary to repeat these operations two or three times, until a perfectly smooth, even surface is secured.

How should a lawn be treated to discourage weeds before seeding? If the soil has been prepared for seeding, there is little that can be done against weeds before they germinate. Chemicals will have no effect either. If the lawn is to be sown in the fall, a good seeding (as discussed in Introduction) and good fall growth will be a factor in weed control. In spring, little advance control can be attempted. If a season can be devoted to the cover-crop method, this will eliminate many weeds. The best insurance is to stimulate a dense turf.

Our land was once covered with clover hay. To raise a crop of grass (lawn), will it be necessary to plow the ground in order to sow the grass

seed? If the land is properly graded, it is possible to make a lawn without plowing. Perennial weeds, such as thistles, teasles, and plantains should be removed. Use a good seed mixture 3 lbs. per 1,000 sq. ft., and cover with soil. Under constant mowing many of the former grasses and clover will disappear. Reseeding and top-dressing annually will gradually build up a good turf.

How do you supply drainage to a lawn on heavy clay soil? Water stands for hours after a rain. Dig the soil at least 12 ins. deep; incorporate a 4-in. layer of screened cinders; mix thoroughly with the soil. Pitch the grade several inches to facilitate surface flow. If the area needs more extensive treatment, dig trenches 20 to 30 ft. apart, 12 ins. wide and 18 ins. deep and lay agricultural tile, with a pitch of 6″ to 100′, with 1 or 2 ins. gravel or cinders on top. Then fill the trench with soil.

Can I make a temporary lawn? Our season here is short and I do not wish to undertake the work involved in making a permanent one. Yes, a temporary lawn can be made, but some work will have to be done even for a temporary lawn. Dig the area 3 to 4 ins. deep and break the soil down fine. If the soil needs lime, apply 50 lbs. of ground limestone to 1,000 sq. ft. As recommended elsewhere give a dressing of chemical fertilizer or dried manure. Sow Perennial Rye Grass 10 lbs. per 1,000 sq. ft. Make the first cut when the grass is 4 ins. high. Keep the height at 3 ins. if possible.

How soon after sowing the average lawn-seed mixture should we expect to see grass? The purity of seed, the temperature and moisture conditions, and the physical condition of the soil exert much influence on this matter of germination. Given pure seed and with the temperature between 65 and 75°, Perennial Rye Grass, fescue, and Red Top will be up in 5 to 10 days, bent grass in 10 to 20 days, and Kentucky Blue Grass around 14 to 28 days.

Is a layer of topsoil 4 in. deep sufficient on top of a base of ashes to grow a good lawn? Much will depend upon the kind of topsoil. Be sure it contains at least 15 per cent humus. A 2- to 3-in. layer of peatmoss, leafmold, or partly rotted leaves placed over the ashes before putting on the topsoil will further assist the moisture-holding qualities.

Could you tell me how to get a good lawn? Have used the best seed available, also the best fertilizer. Had ground dug up twice, and I still grow mostly all Crab Grass and very coarse grass. Your soil is fully impregnated with weed seeds. Grass has too much competition. Two courses are possible: (1) Allow the weeds to grow in summer and before they seed eliminate by burning them off with a torch, grubbing them out, or treating with chemicals (see Weed Control); the lawn will look unsightly. Late August prepare to remake the lawn. (2) Prepare soil in May. In early June sow a cover crop. (See Cover Crops for directions.) Remake lawn in fall.

GRASS-SEED MIXTURES

What is Mascarene Grass, and what is it used for? Mascarene Grass (*Zoysia tenuifolia*) was found in the Mascarene Islands. It makes a turf much like Red Fescue but produces quantities of short root stalks which in places will force the turf up in ridges. It has been used to some extent in lawns in California and along the Gulf Coast. In the latter region it remains green all winter.

Why are mixtures of several kinds of seed advocated instead of just one kind? Soils differ in their structure and fertility, there are light soils and heavy soils. Growing conditions are always fluctuating, are never stable; at one time they will favor one grass, at another time other grasses are encouraged. Sunny exposures need one mixture, a shady location another. The lawn mixtures put out by reputable seedsmen are the result of experience, study, and trial. The "one-grass" lawn is seldom if ever a success.

What is meant by "nurse grass"? What is it used for? The term "nurse grass" is applied to such quick-growing grasses as Perennial Rye Grass, Red Top and even to such crops as oats and rye. A nurse grass is used in the grass mixture to occupy the ground quickly until the more permanent grasses, which usually are slow, become established. Nurse grasses, too, are short-lived and give way to the more permanent grasses.

Is annual Blue Grass the same as Kentucky Blue Grass? No. Annual Blue Grass (*Poa annua*) is an annual grass starting early in the season and usually going to seed in midsummer. In some places it is a weed. Kentucky Blue Grass (*Poa pratensis*) is a perennial grass that comes up each year from its own roots and is one of our valuable lawn grasses. Merion Blue is an improved variety of Kentucky Blue, the seed of which is more costly. Less is needed to cover however, and the grass is more disease resistant, and makes a better lawn.

Is Timothy Grass suitable for lawns? Timothy is not a lawn grass, although it is found in some of the cheaper lawn mixtures. It is a bunch grass and spreads but little.

I have an area that is damp all season. Is there any grass that will grow here successfully and compete with the weeds? When should it be planted, and how often cut? Sow Meadow Foxtail and Red Top in equal parts, and use 5 lbs. per 1,000 sq. ft. Although these grasses are tolerant of wet soils, it might be better to sow in spring, as winter conditions may injure a new seeding. Allow the grass to grow to 4 to 6 ins. and have it mowed a few times with a scythe or a machine that will leave a high cut.

Is there any ground cover that can actually take the place of grass on an open plot of ground in full sun? There have been reports (notably from California) that such substitutes are available. No satisfactory substitute has yet been found for grass. The claims occasionally made about certain plants as grass substitutes have not been borne out by experience. The latest is a plant called *Dichondra repens* (sold as Dewdrop Grass). This is a low-creeping plant resembling clover, but related to the morningglories. It spreads rapidly, and, once established, is difficult to control. Certain other plants have been offered under the same guise, such as camomile with fern-like leaves and small daisy-like flowers; *Lippia canescens* with gray-green foliage and lavender flowers; lily-turf, (Mondo "grass") (*liriope muscari*) with narrow grass-like leaves; and turfing-daisy, (*matricaria ichihatchewi*). Most of these do best in mild climates. Dwarf Dutch White Clover is probably the best substitute for grass in the north. Some are good ground covers but they are not grass substitutes.

What kind of grass should be used on heavy red clay soil? Two parts Canada Blue Grass and 1 part each of Perennial Rye Grass and Red Top. Use 5 lbs. per 1,000 sq. ft.

What is best grass seed to sow for orchard (small lot) with semi-sandy soil? Use a mixture consisting of equal parts of Red Top and Sheep's Fescue; failing Sheep's Fescue, use Red Fescue, or Perennial Rye Grass. Seed at the rate of 6 lbs. per 1,000 sq. ft.

What kind of grass could be planted in an orchard, that would not have to be cut, and would look like a lawn? There is no grass that will quite fill these requirements. The nearest to it would be Kentucky Blue Grass, and this should be cut at least twice during the season.

What grass can be sown in June on a poor soil and make summer growth? Sow Perennial Rye Grass when the soil is damp.

What is the best mixture of grass seed? (Maryland.) Grass seed should be selected to fit your particular need. Soil condition, moisture and site, as well as the particular region and the kind of lawn desired, govern to a large extent seed selection. For an all-purpose lawn around the average home, use 50% Chewing's Fescue, 35% Merion Blue Grass and 15% Rhode Island Bent. For shade use 50% Chewing's Fescue, 30% Rough Blue Grass, 10% Astoria Bent and 10% Kentucky or Merion Blue Grass.

Why are patches of fine, wiry grass appearing in my lawn? Probably one of the fescue grasses; most likely fine-leaved fescue.

Is fescue a harmful weed and likely to spread? It is not a weed nor does it spread very much, if at all. The fescues tolerate dry soil conditions.

I have a bank in which there are a few rocky outcrops. The soil is sandy. What kind of grass would grow there? After improving the soil with fertilizer, sow a mixture containing 3 parts Chewing's Fescue, 2 parts Colonial Bent, 1 part Perennial Rye, with white clover 1 ounce for every lb. of seed. Sow 6 lbs. per 1,000 sq. ft.

What grass-seed mixtures do you recommend for shady places? There are several standard mixtures on the market. Consult an experienced seedsman about your particular location, as conditions differ. If the soil is good and the trees are the deep-rooting kind, try the following: 3 parts Rough-stalked Meadow Grass, 2 parts Chewing's Fescue, 1 part Rhode Island Bent. Use 6 lbs. per 1,000 sq. ft.

How can I have a nice lawn with poor, sandy soil? It is impossible to get good topsoil. Apply bone meal and tankage in equal parts, 20 to 30 lbs. per 1,000 sq. ft., or one part bone meal and 3 parts dried manure, 30 to 40 pounds per 1,000 square feet, and mix with top 6 ins. Sow a seed mixture of 3 parts Chewing's Fescue; 2 parts Colonial Bent; 1 part Red Top; 1 part Perennial Rye Grass.

Which, in your opinion, is better for a large lawn—blue grass and clover mixture, or bent grass? Bent grasses in general are suited to special conditions and demand greater attention than do other types of grasses. A mixture in which Kentucky Blue Grass predominates would be better. Clover can be used, if desired, at the rate of 1 oz. per lb. of the seed mixture. But sow the clover separately.

What kind of lawn grass shall I plant in places where it is sunny all day? Sow a mixture consisting of 3 parts Kentucky Blue Grass, 1 part Perennial Rye Grass, 2 parts Chewing's Fescue, 1 part Red Top, 1 oz. white clover per lb. of seed. Use 5 lbs. per 1,000 sq. ft.

What grass grows best on sandy soils? A mixture containing 2 parts Chewing's Fescue, 1 part Red Top, 1 part Perennial Rye Grass, and 2 parts Colonial Bent, sown at the rate of 6 lbs. per 1,000 sq. ft. should give a good turf.

What is the best kind of grass for an ordinary lawn? Experience has taught that the planting of one kind of grass in an ordinary lawn is not practical. If the soil is in good condition, sow 2 parts Kentucky Blue Grass, 2 parts Chewing's Fescue, 2 parts Rhode Island Bent, and 1 part each Perennial Rye Grass and Red Top. If white clover is desired, add 1 oz. per lb. of seed. Sow at the rate of 5 lbs. per 1,000 sq. ft.

White Clover

Is a clover or all-grass lawn the more desirable? Most of my neighbors have a clover lawn; they seem to get best results. My lawn

is all grass in spring and summer but in fall it turned brown, while the clover kept green. Will the clover return in spring? It is possible that your lawn is a Crab Grass lawn, which would turn reddish brown as cold kills the grass for the year. Clover would be preferable to this, and a mixture of good lawn seed with 5 per cent white clover added should be satisfactory. Be sure to apply lime every late fall (see lime), and top-dress with compost and bone meal at least once each spring and autumn.

May I use grass and white clover seed purchased in late summer and fall this year for next spring? Yes, but use about ¼ more than the recommended allowance to make up for possible reduction in germination. This would occur mostly in any fescue grass seed that may be in the mixture and which does not live so long as other sorts. The clover will be little affected, assuming that the seed has been kept dry and not too close to a radiator.

Is white clover useful in a lawn? Yes, owing to its withstanding drought and to its being little affected by fungous diseases.

Will white clover grow on most any soil or does it require a rich soil? On almost any soil, but it does best on a rich, *deep, neutral* soil.

How much white clover seed should be used in a seed mixture to insure a good stand of clover in the lawn? Ten per cent by weight will give a thick stand.

What quantity of white clover seed should be used in an average lawn mixture? About one ounce of clover to every pound of grass seed.

Do you recommend the use of white clover in the lawn? The use of white clover in the lawn is a matter of personal preference. Some like it; others dislike it. It will grow in dry weather and often covers areas where the grass has been killed.

What are the objections to the use of white clover in the lawn? It is objected to mostly in turf used for games. Golf balls are lost in it, tennis balls are stained by it, as also are white shoes. White clover is very slippery when crushed, and accidents in football, tennis, and polo are not uncommon on it.

Does white clover become a pest in lawn? In the opinion of some, it does.

I pulled out the Crab Grass, sowed Kentucky Blue Grass, but white clover came up. Does clover remain green all winter? In regions of mild winters, white clover will give occasional bursts of growth as warm spells occur. On a small area, in such regions, a clover turf can be kept very much greener during winter by watering it from time to time. Top-dressing and fertilizing would help too.

HOW AND WHEN TO SOW

Would it be O.K. to sow lawn seed in January or February if the snow leaves the ground clear? (Ohio.) In winter, it is good practice to seed while there is a *little* snow on the ground. On slopes, where the seed might wash in a thaw, it is better to wait until the ground is clear.

Is spring or fall better for lawn seeding? (Illinois.) The best possible time for lawn seeding is in the fall, September 1 to October 15 being the general range. Grass seed germinates well in this period with cold nights and sufficient moisture. Fall-sown grass becomes firmly rooted. There is no weed competition, and the grass has an early start in spring. In spring sowing the danger is that the young grass will not be strong enough to withstand summer droughts because of inadequate roots and fast-growing tops.

When is the best time to sow grass seed? (Indiana.) In the section of the country extending from southern New York west to Omaha the first half of September is the best. Farther southward somewhat later; farther North somewhat earlier.

How early in spring can lawns on Long Island be seeded? As early as the soil can be worked; late March if possible.

Is it advisable to plant grass seed in December? (New York.) If earlier planting is impossible, and there is little danger of the seed washing away, December planting might be tried. The better course would be to wait until late winter and sow just as the ground starts to thaw and is "honeycombed" on the surface. (This assumes, of course, that the soil was prepared in the fall.)

Is it best to wait until warm weather to sow grass seed? (New Jersey.) No, grass seed thrives best during the cool, moist periods of very early spring and early fall.

What practices or methods are generally used to insure sowing seed evenly over the lawn? A calm day is the first requirement. Seed cannot be sown evenly when a wind is blowing. Practices vary from dividing the seed into 2 parts and sowing each part at right angles to the other, to splitting the quantity into 4 parts and sowing it from 4 different angles. Marking off the area to be sown with parallel strings, stretched between small stakes placed at regular intervals of 5 to 10 ft., is helpful. Throwing the seed forward with a circular sweep of the arm aids in getting even distribution. On large areas the seed is usually spread with a machine made for the purpose. This can be adjusted to sow any quantity and give an even distribution.

QUANTITY OF SEED NEEDED

Why is there so much difference in the quantity of seed suggested

for sowing? What factors determine the quantity of seed to use?
The season of the year, the location, whether shady, sunny, or sloping,
and the vitality of the seed have much to do with the matter of
quantity to sow. Not all the seeds sown will germinate and it is
essential that enough be sown to insure a good stand of grass. One
of the factors involved is the size of the seed and number per pound.
Bent grass seed runs from 4,000,000 to 8,000,000 seeds to the
pound; fescues around 500,000; Kentucky Blue Grass 2,000,000 and
rye grass about 250,000. The more seeds per pound, the less the
quantity needed.

SOWING SLOPES AND TERRACES

**What is the best way to grow grass on a bank, near the house, on
the north side? I have found it almost impossible.** Have good
soil, and add limestone if soil is acid. Sow a shade mixture obtained
from a reliable seedsman, or make up a mixture yourself consisting
of 60 per cent Chewing's Fescue, 25 per cent Canada Blue Grass,
10 per cent Red Top, 5 per cent Colonial Bent. Use 5 lbs. per
1,000 sq. ft. Top-dress with sandy soil mixed with fertilizer spring and
autumn. Sow additional seed every spring and autumn also. Do not
mow more often than once a week; water copiously in July and
August; only sparingly rest of the year. Broadcast wood ashes every
spring, up to 25 lbs. per 1,000 sq. ft.

What is the best procedure when seeding slopes? The greatest
danger is from washing out of seed and seedlings. If the slope is
long, lay rows of sod at 3- to 4-ft. intervals across the slope and
seed between the rows. Logs of wood 6 to 8 ins. in diameter laid
along the slope and supported by wooden pegs will do instead of
sod. The interval between the logs must be reduced according to
steepness of the slope. Mix the seed with soil before sowing, or
cover the seed with soil after sowing. Sow when the soil is moist
and roll lightly if practical. If not, the seed should be firmed into
the soil with the back of a spade, or a tamper.

Should any added protection be placed over newly seeded slopes?
Protection should be given until the seed has germinated. Old
burlap may be stretched over the area, or grass clippings, hay, or
straw spread over it. Coverings must be removed after germination.

**The slope of my garden is 1 to 1. Could you suggest a grass, shrub,
or vine to stop erosion? The temperature in winter is occasionally
20 to 30° below zero.** Use the seed mixture recommended for
terraces. But before doing so sow and rake in some rye seed. Use
equal weights of rye and grass seeds; sow rye first and cover about
one inch deep, then sow the grass seed. Mow the rye as soon as it
is long enough for a mower to cut it, and turf will gradually change
from one of rye to one of grass. (For other suggestions see Ground
Covers.)

What is the cheapest and best way to replant a sloping, sunny front lawn? I have reseeded and used new topsoil, but only a part looks good. Unless the soil is good, it is impossible to keep moisture on a slope. Probably your lawn is struggling along on a very thin layer of topsoil. Best procedure would be to remake it in early September, but cheapest scheme would be to renovate it. Open the soil without unduly spoiling what you have; scratch it with a sharp rake, or hold a garden fork vertically and work it up and down, filling soil full of holes. Spread 1 to 2 ins. of good topsoil, smooth with the back of a rake, and sow seed. Do this every April and September, and in addition apply fertilizer twice a year and limestone every year in late fall, unless you are in a section where there is naturally a large supply of lime in the land.

Should the soil for a grass terrace be rich? As rich as you can make it. Terraces and slopes need plenty of humus to hold moisture, as it is a big factor.

What kind of grass is best for a terrace? Get a mixture for the purpose from a reliable seedsman, or make up your own mixture of 35 per cent rye grass and Chewing's Fescue, 20 per cent blue grass, and 10 per cent white clover if you wish.

When should a terrace be planted? (Connecticut.) September 1 and April 15 would be two most desirable dates in your section, weather permitting.

How can I get grass started on a terrace? The degree of slope must first be considered. If the slope is less than 22½°, sow the seeds directly when the soil is moist and conditions are right for quick germination. If between 22½ and 45°, you can also seed it, but before sowing the grass seed sow rye (the grain, not rye grass) and rake it under, completely covering it, then sow the grass seed on top and roll it in or tamp it with a spade. If the slope is over 45°, the grass seed will have to be sown in holes. Make the holes 3 ins. deep, 3 ins. wide, and 10 ins. apart; fill them with a mixture of seed and soil, using 1 part seed to 10 parts soil. There should be at least 4 ins. of good soil on the surface. Until terrace is well established it will be necessary to resow spots washed out by erosion.

How often should the grass on a terrace be cut? At least once a week, unless slope is so severe that mowing is difficult. In this case, as often as you can.

SODDING

I have some old pasture turf I wish to use for sodding but it has stones in it. Do you think it will be all right? Sod that has stones in it cannot be cut evenly nor will the sod hold together. When stripping the sod, the tools are continually being obstructed; when the sod is lifted, the stones fall away, leaving nothing but a mere shred of turf which even with the best of care would hardly resume growth on a terrace.

My terrace was repaired with sod in spring, and now some of the sods are turning brown. What could be the cause? There are several reasons. Sections of the sod may have been very thin with little roots left to help renewed growth; they were uneven and extra soil was not used to imbed them properly, thus leaving air pockets; they were not firmly embedded and tamped into the soil or the watering after the sod was laid was uneven or insufficient.

Establishing a new lawn by means of sodding. The ground is prepared as for seed sowing, and the sods (cut to an even thickness of 1½ ins. or more) are carefully fitted into place, firmed with a tamper or the back of a spade, and kept thoroughly watered until new roots form.

I wish to cut a section of good sod from my lawn to cover a small terrace. How must I go about cutting the sod? How should I sod the terrace so that it will be even? To sod the terrace evenly, the sod must be even in size and thickness. To get an even size, lay a 12-in. board on the turf and, standing on it, cut the turf along both sides of the board. When the whole section has been cut in foot-wide strips, with a lawn edging knife, make another series of 12-in. cuts *across* the strips. This will leave the section cut into 12-in. squares each of which can easily be cut under with a sharp spade. To get an even thickness of sod, proceed as follows: Secure a shallow box 1½ ins. deep and 12 ins. square but with only 3 sides. Slide a sod into the box through the open side, grass side down, and, using an old sickle, the blade of a scythe, or a heavy knife, rest the blade on the sides of the box and slice off any soil that is higher than the 1½-in. sides. Treat each sod the same way. Prepared thus, the sods will be even in width and thickness. With the surface of the terrace level, lay the sod as directed in the Introduction. Have a barrowload of soil handy to fill up uneven spots as sodding proceeds. Slightly overlap each sod as it is laid and vigorously tamp it in with the back of a spade. Spike each sod with a wooden peg and water several times at intervals of 3 to 4 hours, so that plenty of moisture is available to the new roots of the grass.

How do you prepare a lawn plot for transplanting sod? Prepare the soil as advised for a lawn. Remove all stones and adjust the grade and have the surface loose. (See Introduction.)

Will sodding eliminate patches of Crab Grass? Perhaps, if there are only a few patches and the Crab Grass has not seeded. Otherwise it might be a questionable practice. Crab Grass seeds itself beyond the area occupied by the plants.

LAWNS FOR SPECIAL CONDITIONS

Shaded Areas

Can you suggest an aid to sparse lawn around our oak-tree trunks? Perforate the soil to several inches with a spading fork. Top-dress with good soil and fertilizer and sow a standard mixture of shady grasses. (See Fertilizer, Seed Mixtures.)

Does the lawn area close to trees need any special care in order to keep it in good growing condition? Because of the competition of the tree roots, grass near trees requires more fertilizing and watering than in open areas. Also the grass should not be cut so low.

Under a European linden tree on my lawn the grass in early spring and summer grows reasonably well. Toward late summer it thins out. What suggestion would you make to remedy this situation? Soil is slightly acid. Grass under trees needs more maintenance than grass on lawns. To maintain grass under trees a regular program of feeding, top-dressing, and watering must be kept up. Do not cut the grass so low nor so frequently as the regular lawn. (See Applying Fertilizer.) Apply 50 lbs. pulverized limestone per 1,000 sq. ft. in late fall.

Will clover grow under trees, or will it be necessary to plant a special mixture for shady lawn? It is better to plant a shady-lawn mixture. Clover will not survive under trees.

What grass seed do you suggest to make a lawn under maple trees? Grass is not successful under maple trees. Maples are surface-rooting trees, and grass could not compete with the large roots for food and moisture. By midsummer the grass usually disappears.

What type of grass will succeed under elms, hackberry, linden, and other trees with surface-feeding roots? Please state variety, not just shade mixture. A mixture is much more successful than one kind. Failure is not due to a mixture but to inadequate preparation and to the lack of attention that grass in shade requires. The only lone kind that has given results is Rough-stalked Blue Grass, also called Rough-stalked Meadow Grass. Use 5 lbs. per 1,000 sq. ft.

Play Areas

How should the soil for a playground lawn be prepared? More than the average amount of humus is needed to maintain a spongy surface to prevent packing. As much as a ton per 1,200 sq. ft. of old rotted manure, spent hotbed manure, or compost should be worked in by plowing, disking, digging, or by rototiller, to mix it thoroughly with the soil. With the humus use 75 lbs. of ground limestone. If the soil is heavy, incorporate a 3-in. layer of very coarse sand, or screened cinders, about the size of peas, in conjunction with the manure. Failing manure, use a good grade of cultivated peat which must first be dampened down, spread on 4 ins. deep, and then mixed in as advised for manure. In this case 100 lbs. of lime will be needed. With the peat use a 10–6–4 fertilizer, 30 lbs. per 1,000 sq. ft., but a 4–8–4 or something similar is better if manure is the source of the humus. Grading and getting an even, compact surface are essential. These are accomplished by alternate harrowing, or raking, and rolling to eliminate depressions and form a true, even surface.

What grass do you recommend as most durable for a playground? What rate of seeding is necessary to secure a good turf? Because of the conditions of growth and the wear to which grass is subject, the seed mixture and the manner of seeding on a playground are different from those of the ordinary lawn. Consult an experienced grass seedsman about your particular site and the kind of sports for which it is to be used. The following mixture is typical of the kinds used on sports fields: 35 per cent Chewing's Fescue, 25 per cent Kentucky Blue Grass, 20 per cent Red Fescue, 10 per cent Red Top, and 10 per cent Perennial Rye Grass. Sow 6 to 8 lbs. per 1,000 sq. ft.

How should the seed be sown on a playground lawn to get an even covering? Use the wheelbarrow type of seeder or a mechanical grass seed sower. Split the quantity of seed into equal portions and sow the portions at right angles to each other. Cover with a light seed harrow, or by raking and rolling.

How high should the grass be allowed to grow before its first cutting? Allow the grass to grow to 3 ins., then reduce it to 2 ins. Maintain the length of the grass at 2 ins. thereafter.

What are the most important operations concerned with the upkeep of a playground lawn? The maintenance of the right moisture conditions is a critical factor. The soil should not be allowed to dry out; neither must it get soggy through over-watering. By keeping the soil moisture constant, the grass will be kept in continuous growth and all food materials that are applied will be more efficiently used. Top-dress in spring and again in fall. (See Applying Compost.) Reseeding is another important operation. This differs from the practice on the average lawn. Keep the turf constantly supplied with seed. Wash seed in when watering; the seed will be pushed into the soil by treading or by shoe spikes. Grub-proof for beetle grubs as advised in the Introduction. Keep a sharp lookout for fungous diseases, especially during hot, humid weather. (See Diseases.) Avoid the overuse of highly nitrogenous fertilizers or grass will become soft. Do not allow heavy trucks on frozen sod.

Service Areas

The front part of my lawn is subject to much treading down. What kind of grass would stand this wear, and how would I maintain it? The soil, if heavy, must be well supplied with humus combined with coarse sand or screened cinders, to keep the surface from packing. Annual top-dressings and reseedings when traffic is not too bad will also be required. It may be necessary every few years to perforate the surface to encourage aeration. (See Spiking.) Sow with 3 parts Chewing's Fescue, 1 part each of Red Top and Perennial Rye Grass, and 2 parts Kentucky Blue Grass. Seed at 6 lbs. per 1,000 sq. ft.

City Lawns

I have a typical New York City back yard which gets about four hours of sun daily. Grass grows well until August, when it dies out although liberally watered. What is the cause? The fault lies with the soil which, without improvement, is not capable of supporting a stand of grass in summer.

Can I do anything to my soil to help it retain moisture? This is a city lawn. Soil in city lots is often heavy. Incorporate to a depth of 8 ins. a 2-in. layer of dampened peatmoss. Apply 12 lbs. of ground limestone per 100 sq. ft. and rake it into the surface. Use a 5–10–5 fertilizer at the rate of 4 lbs. per 100 sq. ft. and thoroughly mix with the soil before seeding.

Is a single kind of grass better on a city lawn or would you prefer a mixture? A good grass mixture is to be preferred to a single kind. Conditions are not always suited to one kind of grass.

What lawn seed will grow under city conditions? Two parts Chewing's Fescue, 2 parts Colonial Bent, and 1 part each Red Top and Perennial Rye Grass. Add white clover if desired, 1 oz. per lb. of seed. Use 5 lbs. per 1,000 sq. ft.

For a city lawn, when should the seed be sown for best growth? Early September is the best time to get the lawn started to take full advantage of fall growth and assure a good start in spring.

Will a city lawn be permanent after one planting?   No. It will be necessary each fall or spring to reseed. Use half the original quantity over grass; full quantity on bare spots.

How often should the grass on a city lawn be cut?   At least once a week, perhaps more often in early summer. In July and August the cutting must be adjusted to rate of growth.

What height would you leave grass on a city lawn?   It is best kept cut to about 1½ ins. in early summer, increasing to 2½ ins. in midsummer.

How often should a city lawn be watered?   This is the prime cause of much disease, which is more prevalent under city conditions because of poor air circulation. Cut the grass a little shorter before watering. Soak thoroughly and, if possible, choose a windy day. (See Control of Brown Spot.) Avoid constant sprinkling, and do not flood. Water once a week.

My lawn is completely surrounded by concrete, close to a subway with filled-in soil. I have used topsoil, lime, and regular blue grass seed mixture. In spite of conscientious watering, the grass burns up because of the sun beating down all day. Is the grass hardy?   Blue grass is hardy. Although the tops die back in the excessive heat of midsummer, the roots are not so easily injured. Look to the watering practice. Does the water penetrate deeply, or is the water merely sprinkled on, evaporating in the heat and providing ideal conditions for brown patch? Topsoil should be good and at least 4 ins. deep.

BENT LAWNS

Is bent grass lawn expensive to start?   Every new lawn should be on soil prepared with meticulous care; so a bent lawn from seed should cost but little more in preparation, the difference being mostly in the cost of seed. Bent stolons cost more than bent seed, and their preparation and planting are more expensive.

Is a bent grass lawn hard to maintain?   Yes. Don't think of a bent lawn unless you are prepared to take every care of it. Mow twice weekly; watering, when necessary, must be generous; apply fungicides at first sign of brown patch. Fertilizer and top-dressing, should be given spring and autumn. Weeding should be continuous, as bent grass does not crowd out weeds. The holes made when they are removed heal over quickly.

Must the soil for a bent lawn be very rich?   Yes. Bent lawns require a soil rich in humus and high in fertility. Good drainage, too, is very important to a well-aerated condition and root growth.

How early in spring is best to start a new lawn with Creeping Bent grass?   Immediately frost is out of the ground and land is dry. Autumn is another good time. *Late* spring is to be avoided.

Will the treating of bent grass seed with certain chemicals stimulate growth? There is little evidence to prove that these preparations have any effect on growth. Put your emphasis upon obtaining first-grade seed and insuring the conditions for germination by good soil preparation.

How do you sow Creeping Bent lawn seed? The 2 to 4 lbs. of bent seed per 1,000 sq. ft. that you will use may be divided into 2 equal parts. Broadcast ½ over the entire area, and rake once only and in one direction; broadcast the second half over the entire area also, and merely roll, making no attempt to cover it. Select a still day, take half handfuls, and throw them horizontally with a circular motion, stooping as you do so.

Must the soil for a bent lawn be grub-proofed? If the application of arsenate of lead for grub-proofing does not delay your work of preparation, it may be applied before your final raking to prepare the surface for seed. If you are pressed for time, however, broadcast it after the lawn is established and repeat every 3 to 5 years. Allow 10 lbs. per 1,000 sq. ft.

How should I take care of my bent grass in spring? Mow, first with a high-set mower, then gradually lower the adjustment each time you use it, so that at the end of 2 weeks you have it at its normal height. Spread fertilizer and top-dressing.

Should bent grass be rolled? Yes, but not until all frost has gone and the soil has dried. Use as light a roller as you can get results with. (See Rolling.)

Should the first mowings of bent grass be raked off? Yes, if they are long enough to rake together. But aim to mow so frequently there-after that your clippings are short and powdery and you could not rake them up if you wished to.

How often should bent lawns be cut? Twice a week at least. Golf putting greens are often pure bent, and are examples of exquisite turf; at certain times they are mown every day.

I have a bent grass lawn. How short should it be cut? One person says as short as possible; another says 1½ to 2 ins. It is important, first, that you cut it regularly and often. A height of 1½ ins. would be all right. The standard on a golf putting green is ¼ in. Do not cut as short as this.

Would there be any serious effect if the grass on my bent lawn were not cut for a while? Yes. When you *do* get around to mowing it, you will injure it, perhaps permanently, besides encouraging weeds. If the grass gets tall, cut with the mower set as high as you can mow with it, then lower it and use it the next day, continuing until you have *gradually* brought the lawn down to its normal height.

How late in the season can cutting of bent grass be continued?

Right up to winter. Raise mower to maximum height in October, so that the grass is somewhat longer before winter.

Does bent turf require much watering?   Yes. The soil should never be allowed to become dry during the growing period: spring, summer, and autumn.

Is Creeping Bent advisable in the country when water has to be obtained by electric pump?   This should not be an obstacle provided there is a good supply. However, if the water is very cold, better use it as late as possible in the evening or early morning; never in sunlight.

In watering my bent lawn is it all right to flood it?   Avoid flooding; use a nozzle or sprinkler that delivers in small droplets. If the lawn still puddles, turn off the water for half an hour and then sprinkle again.

How often should bent lawns be fed?   At least once in spring and once in autumn. In most sections of the Northern states (bent is rarely successful in the South) an application of limestone in late fall or earliest spring will be desirable also. (See Lime.)

What is the proper kind of fertilizer for bent lawns?   A balanced one, like 3–8–2, 4–8–4, or 5–10–5 is to be preferred; it should be a mixture of organic materials and chemical fertilizers. Acceptable compounds are made up by leading supply houses.

How can I fertilize a thick turf of Creeping Bent without burning it?   Use ½ the quantity that the maker recommends. Give a similar half-rate application a week later. Spread the material at a time when the grass is dry; immediately knock the powder off the grass leaves by drawing the back of a rake across the lawn; water thoroughly. Many turf keepers mix fertilizer with compost or screened soil, thereby lessening the chances of burning. Grass is sensitive in July and August; much less so at other times. Never apply more than 1 lb. of nitrogen per 1,000 sq. ft. at any one time. The first figure of a fertilizer analysis indicates the pounds of nitrogen in a 100-lb. bag of the fertilizer; be guided by this. (See Fertilizer.)

Is a mixture of hardwood ashes and bone meal applied heavily on a bent lawn in February and March good or bad for the grass? How much of each would I use?   Excellent. April 1 to 15 would be better. Two dressings may be given, one in September and one in April, unless you note an increase in clover. If the clover becomes excessive, change to a balanced fertilizer high in nitrogen. Allow 25 lbs. of bone meal and 50 lbs. of ashes per 1,000 sq. ft. at each application.

What about top-dressing bent lawns?   Very helpful. Fertilizer is mixed with screened rich topsoil, and spread. Quantity of soil is as much as possible without hiding the grass, usually about ¼ in. thick, and is raked in. Amount of fertilizer is determined by the nitrogen factor in the analysis. In a 4–8–4 formula the first figure indicates that in 100 lbs. there are 4 lbs. of nitrogen. We do not apply more than 1 lb. of nitrogen per 1,000 sq. ft., otherwise turf will be scalded; so 25 lbs. of this mixture is the most that could be used on 1,000 sq. ft. Instead of screened soil, compost is often used. (See Compost.)

Can bent lawns be top-dressed any time? Yes. But top-dressing is best omitted in July and August.

What is the minimum number of top-dressings that must be applied to a Creeping Bent lawn to keep it healthy? Minimum annual top-dressings would be two: one in spring and one in fall. But aim for four if possible: the first very early in spring, another in June with the others put on in early September and October.

This spring I planted Astoria Bent seed and it came up and grew very well, but there have been no signs of creeping or of stolons. Does this type of bent grass creep, or don't the stolons start the first year? It creeps, but slowly, because the stolons are normally very short. They usually appear the second year.

Does Colonial Bent Grass spread by underground stolons or surface stolons; or both? Its stolons, which are above ground, are short. It spreads so slowly that it may be regarded almost as a non-spreading grass. Strongly creeping kinds for latitudes north of Washington, D.C., are Creeping Bent and Seaside Bent. For points south of Washington, D.C., except where altitude produces conditions similar to the Northern states, the typical creeping grasses are Bermuda and Carpet.

Is it practical to sow Creeping Bent grass seed with regular lawn mixture and let it eventually crowd out ordinary grass? Highly practical. Good grass-seed mixtures put up by reputable supply houses often contain as much as 10 per cent by weight of bent seeds. Whether it crowds out other grasses or not depends upon the treatment given the lawn. Feeding, regular and frequent mowing, and watering when necessary, will encourage the bent; neglect the turf and the bent will disappear.

What quantity of bent grass seed should I use with regular grass mixture to insure a good stand? The 10 per cent usually contained in mixtures may be increased to 25 per cent.

I have a blue grass lawn. Could I convert it to a bent lawn? Yes, but it may take a year or more. Add Seaside Bent to some screened soil, 1 part by measure of the seed to 10 parts of the soil. Broadcast this every spring and fall, allowing ½ lb. of seed to each 100 sq. ft. Spread fertilizer 1 week before or 1 week later.

If I sowed a few pounds of bent grass when fertilizing in spring, would it grow and gradually work into a bent lawn? If the soil is fairly rich and there are not many weeds, this could be accomplished over a period of time (for quantity to use, see previous question). To succeed, you will have to encourage the bent grass to become established by close mowing twice weekly, fertilizing spring and autumn, top-dressing, and watering generously when needed.

I planted Creeping Bent in my front yard, which is quite shaded. I had no luck with it; brown spots appeared, and it doesn't seem to spread. What can I do?   Creeping Bent is not very tolerant of shade; sow instead a shady-lawn seed mixture containing Chewing's Fescue, Velvet Bent, and Canada Blue Grass, or *Poa trivialis,* known as Rough-stalked Blue Grass, if it can be obtained. These four are shade tolerant.

From Stolons

How is the soil prepared for starting Creeping Bent grass from stolons?   Have at least 6 ins. of good topsoil, broadcast 100 lbs. or more of sheep manure or similar desiccated animal fertilizer over 1,000 sq. ft. Work it into the surface and rake the soil smooth. (See Soil Preparation—Introduction.)

How do you estimate the quantity of stolons needed?   One sq. ft. of plants taken from the nursery bed or nursery row will plant 8 to 10 sq. ft. of new lawn.

The bent grasses spread by means of stolons which form new individual plants.

In planting a bent lawn with stolons (instead of seed) the mass of stolons and roots is cut up into short lengths.

When is it best to plant the stolons?   Either in the early spring or late summer.

How are the stolons spread over the ground?   Best way is to cut them into 1-in. lengths, broadcast them by hand, taking care that nowhere is there a space of more than ½ in. between pieces.

Are the stolons covered with soil or rolled in?   Both. Roll them into the surface; cover with ½ in. screened soil; and roll again.

How can stolons be inserted in an old lawn which is being renovated?   Pot-grown stolons are now available together with a cylindrical metal planter which cuts out the turf to exactly the size of the pot-grown plants, which are inserted in the holes, pressed firmly into place, and watered thoroughly.

Should the ground be watered after the stolons are planted? Keep continually moist until young grass shows through. Use a fine nozzle; if soil covering is displaced, add more.

Planting a lawn with stolons. The cut-up pieces are spread over the prepared surface and rolled in; sifted compost is then spread over them to a depth of ½ in., and the surface again is rolled.

How high should the grass from bent stolons be for the first cutting? As soon as a mower, adjusted to cut medium long, can effect a cut; approximately about 2 ins.

Should a bent lawn from stolons have any winter protection? Only if you happen to live in a region where from experience this type of lawn is known to be subject to winter kill; then a few inches of covering may be applied. Tobacco stems held in place with birch or maple branches are sometimes used; so are branches alone.

Weeds and Pests

What do you put on a bent lawn to make ground more acid and thus stop growth of weeds? The standard chemical is ammonium sulfate 3 to 5 lbs. per 1,000 sq. ft. But it can be overdone, so occasionally apply a balanced fertilizer. Liquid manure, made by steeping rotted cow manure in water, discourages many weeds. Aluminum sulfate, too, is sometimes used to make soil acid, also at 3 to 5 lbs. per 1,000 sq. ft. *Ammonium* sulfate stimulates growth; *aluminum* sulfate has little effect on the grass. An application of lead arsenate (for grub-proofing) to some extent discourages weed growth.

How can I get rid of White Clover in a Creeping Bent lawn without killing the bent, or resorting to the laborious backbreaking, hand-pick-

ing method? I have tried aluminum sulfate and frequent dressings of ammonium sulfate, but clover seems to thrive on them.   Try raking quite harshly once a month with an iron rake, with the teeth filed sharp. Continue with applications of aluminum and ammonium sulfate; alternate them with cottonseed meal, castor pumice, or shredded cattle manure. With cow manure made liquid to the color of beer drench the turf every six months. A more drastic way is to scald the turf with a solution of sodium arsenate, 2 ozs. in 4 gals. water per 1,000 sq. ft.; grass is injured temporarily, and clover more seriously; several treatments may eliminate the clover.

What causes, and how can I get rid of, mushrooms and toadstools in a sunny bent lawn?   Usually fragments of manure, and sometimes pieces of rotting wood, are to blame. Fungi of this type do little harm, and the growth may be rubbed away with a rake. If serious, punch a number of holes with a vertically held garden fork; then saturate the soil with Thiosan, 4 ozs. in 10 gals. of water; repeat weekly if necessary.

I have a bent lawn. Last summer we had heavy rains. But from July to late September my grass turned to brown spots and died out. Can you give me information?   If condition showed within 3 days of excessive rain, possible reason (1) is "damping off" or pythium; (2) if in hot spell, probably brown patch, dollar spot, or copper spot; (3) if hot sun followed heavy rain, might be "scald" when water in puddles cooks the plants; (4) if spots were like burns and reddish brown, suspect chinch bugs; (5) if dead grass lifts up readily, like a piecrust, look for May beetle grubs. Also consider wear, dogs, fuel oil. (See Disease and Insect Control.) Dust with chlordane for chinch bug. Correct surface drainage so that no puddles form.

Does Astoria Bent Grass from seed always get brown patch and die out?   If conditions are right, you should have little of this kind of trouble, although all bents are sensitive to fungous injury the first year or so. Possibly your soil lacks porosity and remains wet too long between rains. Also, in grading operations, was subsoil brought to the surface? Did you immediately apply fungicides when you first saw brown patch, continuing with further applications every 10 days? Is the lawn under trees? Astoria Bent is not shade tolerant.

What is the proper yearly care for bent grass lawns? How avoid brown spots?   Broadcast fertilizer and top-dressing twice in spring and twice in autumn; roll in spring; remove weeds as soon as you see them, and water generously in July and August. Try to do without water in spring and autumn, but avoid letting the grass suffer through dryness. Mow twice weekly. (See Disease Control for Brown Patch.) Repeat at 10-day intervals until September 30.

We have bent grass and there is a small gray grubworm eating the roots of it. We have found about 12 in a space of about 5 ins. square.

What remedy will destroy them? These are undoubtedly grubs of the Japanese beetle. (See Grub-proofing—Introduction.)

What shall I do for chinch bug in beautiful large front lawn which is mostly bent grass? It got quite a start before we knew what it was; now we want to prevent its spoiling our lawn another year. See Insect Control—Introduction.

Have started a Creeping Bent lawn from seed this fall. Worms are coming up through it at night causing eruptions in the soil which kill the grass in these spots. What should I do about it? Carefully use a bamboo rake to distribute the material in the worm casts, or drag a flexible steel mat over the grass, or "swish" the surface with a very long bamboo. Never mow until you have first done this. There is a substance sometimes used as a fertilizer called mowrah meal, which usually kills earthworms. Chemical worm killers are also available such as bichloride of mercury (one ounce dissolved in 15 gallons of water will cover 500 square feet). Water in after sprinkling the chemical over the area.

What is the best way to prevent damage to young bent grass by worms? Possibly the sod webworm, the infestation of which is affected by weather conditions. Mix 7 lbs. arsenate of lead with twice its bulk of sand. Spread over 1,000 sq. ft. Work it in with a broom. Water with a hose.

MOSS LAWNS

What is the name of the moss that is used for planting lawns? Will it grow anywhere? Its botanical name is *Sagina subulata,* commonly called Lawn-moss. It is used extensively in the Pacific coast states. It will grow almost anywhere in the United States except the Rio Grande Valley and the region south of Fort Pierce, Florida. In extreme Northern latitudes, it usually winter kills. It is not a true moss.

Does the moss used for lawns need a good soil? It thrives best on a fertile soil, but it has grown well on the "dobe" soils south of San Francisco. Having a shallow root system, it can be surface fed like bent grass.

Is the moss that is used in lawns grown from seed? How is it planted? Lawn-moss is planted from divisions. Two-in. squares are planted 6 ins. apart. A quicker effect can be had by planting them 3 or 4 ins. apart. In planting the roots are well covered and firmed, and the crown (sprig) kept above the surface.

Does moss make a level, green lawn? Lawn-moss does not remain level. Being of very vigorous growth, it rises in small mounds or knots. In order to keep the surface even, these mounds must continually be compressed by rolling. Occasionally the lawn must be cut with a disk harrow and top-dressed.

How many years can I expect a moss lawn to last?   In a climate where no great winter cold occurs, and if rolling, disking, and top-dressing are consistently carried out, Lawn-moss will last for several years. A disease similar to brown patch will at times infect it, destroying areas in the sod. This is controlled by the same agents prescribed for brown patch. The rapid growth of the moss soon covers the bare spots.

Would the fact that moss has flowers add to its value in the lawn?   True, it blooms very prolifically in early summer with tiny flowers on 1-in. stems and it is very pretty. The flowers, however, do not last long.

Will the planting of a moss lawn relieve me of all the work involved in caring for a grass lawn?   There will be little difference in the amount of work involved in the upkeep. You will have to roll a moss lawn as often as you would have to cut a grass lawn, and the danger of the moss dying out is greater than that of grass, especialy if the moss is overfertilized.

REHABILITATION OF OLD LAWNS

Could one gradually create a new surface on an old lawn by top-dressing?   Annual or semi-annual top-dressing of rotted compost would, in a few years, build up a new surface.

What materials would I use for surfacing a lawn?   Surfacing materials are best obtained by composting good garden soil, manure, and old leaves. Build a pile 4 ft. high with the soil, manure, and leaves in alternate layers 6 ins. thick. A sprinkling of chemical fertilizer over each layer and watering to keep materials moist will help decompose the pile more rapidly. Allow at least 6 months before use. For immediate use, make a compost by thoroughly sifting and mixing together 3 parts loam, 1 part pulverized peatmoss and 1 part dried manure.

How and to what depth is compost applied?   Compost must be screened before applying. One cubic yard is needed to add ⅓ in. of surface over 1,000 sq. ft.

Is it possible to renew an old lawn by adding fertilizer and some seed?   Provided the turf has not deteriorated too seriously, a program of this sort coupled with weed eradication consistently kept up would go far to restore an old lawn. Annual dressings of compost would still further improve it.

What is spring and fall treatment for an old lawn, badly run down and grub eaten, as to fertilizer and seed?   Remove weeds and all dead grass; dig bare areas, and break up the soil. While digging, work in arsenate of lead, 10 lbs. to 1,000 sq. ft., and apply a complete fertilizer. Sow 2 parts Chewing's Fescue, 2 parts Colonial Bent, 1 part each Red Top and Perennial Rye Grass; cover, and roll. Fall treatment: Top-dress. (See question on Top-dressing.) Reseed again any spots that are bare or thin.

In reseeding an old, established lawn, is it sufficient to scratch the topsoil? If not, how deep should I dig the ground? If the soil is in poor condition and weeds have taken hold, the mere scratching of the topsoil would hardly suffice. The only permanent course would be to dig up the area, clear out the weeds, and remake the entire lawn.

What fertilization should an old lawn be given between spring and fall? If the turf is good and if there is considerable bent grass present, top-dressing about the end of June might be desirable if sufficient water is also available. On the whole, a good spring and fall feeding should be adequate.

What can I do to improve the appearance of my lawn in winter? (Atlantic City, N.J.) Near the seashore or in the south where no deep freezing of the soil occurs, a program of monthly lawn feeding with a complete plant food (of 10–6–4 formula for sandy soils or 8–6–4 for heavy soils), or with an organic fertilizer such as milorganite or agranite, will go far toward maintaining a handsome lawn through the colder months. Zoysia lawns, for instance can be kept green most of the year in such locations by resorting to winter feeding.

Is it safe to burn grass that has grown tall on a lawn which has been neglected for 2 years? If so, what time of year is best to do burning? If you can find it dry enough in late fall, burning it off then would destroy many insects and weed seeds before they have a chance to get deep into the soil. Burning may be done in early spring also. It will not injure the roots.

What is the best fertilizer for spring for an old lawn of 14,400 sq. ft.? Last fall we spread 330 lbs. of bone meal, 100 lbs. of lime, and 55 lbs. of seed. A nitrogenous fertilizer would be best for early spring growth. Use either dried cow manure or tankage, 30 to 40 lbs. per 1,000 sq. ft.

CARE OF NEW LAWNS

Having no roller last spring we just tamped the soil down. Is that the cause of the holes in the lawn? The uneven firming by tamping may be partly to blame. The condition is more likely the result of poor grading. If hard and soft areas were left, the soft spots would settle.

The fall sowing of my lawn resulted in patchy growth. Can the spots be filled in by spring planting, or should I wait for another year? Early spring patching is usually satisfactory. Loosen the soil, apply seed liberally, and use some nitrogenous fertilizer, such as sheep manure, to give the young grass a quick start.

When is the best time to put manure on a lawn seeded in fall? Apply well-rotted and sifted manure in early spring.

How late can one make a new lawn in fall and still get good results in spring? Lawns should not be planted later than the middle of October. In the East, later plantings sometimes become established enough to winter well, but results are uncertain.

Can a new lawn be made in spring? Yes, although the grass will not have as good a root depth as fall-planted grass.

About 2 years ago I made a new lawn. Each spring it is reseeded. It grows for a while, then it gets full of weeds and looks like a hayfield. I'd like to know what to do. Weeds must first be eradicated. (See Introduction and questions on Weed Control.)

Will spreading a thin layer of black dirt over my new lawn, which is seeded in sand, help to enourage its growth? This will help very much, provided it breaks down easily and will work into the surface and is not just a plastic material that will lie on the top and bake in the hot sun.

Would manure on fall-planted grass seed help to protect grass and fertilize the grass in spring again? If seed was sown late and the grass is very short, a thin layer of manure, if well rotted, would give protection and at the same time add some fertilizer. If the grass was sown early in fall, it would not need manure but an application of complete fertilizer in early spring would be very beneficial.

I am having trouble to get a nice yard—have planted the best of grass seed and fertilizer, and still it dies. What is the trouble? Your seed mixture may not be adapted to your soil requirements. Thorough preparation as outlined in the Introduction is the most important step. Poor drainage, poor soil texture, and lack of humus may be the trouble.

Made a new lawn in spring. Used new topsoil and the best grass seed. Now it is full of Crab Grass and brown spots. What causes this? The Crab Grass seeds were in the topsoil. The brown spots probably were the fungous disease by that name. (See Diseases.)

Have had no results with my lawn after using an expensive mixture of grass seed. What procedure must I follow to insure a better lawn? Should I have the soil tested? If so, please advise where. Expensive grass-seed mixtures alone will never make a lawn unless the seeding has been preceded by adequate soil preparation (as outlined in the Introduction). Except for determining lime requirements, the soil test is of little use. Your Agricultural College will test your soil.

My lawn has small, hard mounds in it. Can I correct this without completely rebuilding the whole lawn? There are two approaches to the problem? (1) Slice the mounds off with a spade and remove enough soil to put the sod back level; or after slicing the mounds off, loosen the soil and sow seed. (2) If the mounds are not too numerous, level up to them with fresh topsoil and reseed the areas.

What causes moundlike humps in a new lawn? Caused by poor grading and sowing the seed before the soil had settled sufficiently to reveal unevenness in the grade; or by mole runs.

MAINTENANCE OF ESTABLISHED LAWNS

How can I make my lawn look nice? It has sun and good soil. Use fertilizer in spring and fall to invigorate the turf. Make a yearly top-dressing of compost. Eradicate weeds before they seed. Adjust the cutting to the season, and supply sufficient moisture before the soil supply is exhausted. Constant reseeding of poor spots and liming will aid.

Areas in my lawn die out each winter; is this because some of the grasses are not hardy? The more permanent of the lawn grasses are winter hardy. The condition may be due to lack of drainage, poorly aerated soil, or Crab Grass. The latter dies after the first frost. (See Crab Grass.) Dig all poor spots, work in humus, and sow seed in late winter.

Why is my lawn, in a sunny location facing south, full of bare spots? Have patched with new seed, but this has not been successful. Probably the soil where the bare spots appear is too shallow or not fertile enough to support a good stand of grass. Remove the soil to a depth of 4 to 6 ins. Fill with good soil, and reseed.

All summer my lawn was beautiful, but this fall it turned brown while other lawns were still green. What is the cause? Probably your soil is shallower than that of your neighbor's. Hence when dry weather comes yours suffers first. Summer watering would help. Top-dressing with humus-making material would be more permanent.

At the point where my lawn touches the sidewalk I have been unable to grow grass. Have you any suggestions? The grass roots were dried out on coming in contact with the concrete in summer. Try putting a layer of peatmoss 1 inch thick next to the sidewalk. Keep it well watered.

Our house has a field of grass on which we look out. We enjoy the daisies and first stand of young grass. After that, when should it be cut, and how often per year, to keep it attractive? It is now full of red bunch grass. Cut the first grass before the seed ripens in the heads. Two more cuttings at monthly intervals during the summer should keep it orderly.

Should grass clippings be removed? Remove in the early part of the season if the grass is long, and especially during wet periods. Short clippings during hot, dry periods can be left on.

Should my lawn be rolled in midsummer? No; this compacts the soil and causes quicker drying out.

Our lawn is full of deep holes. How shall we go about renewing

it this coming spring? The only practical plan is to fill the holes with topsoil, level off with a rake to even the grade, and then reseed. More than one treatment may be required.

Is it advisable to repair bare spots in the lawn in fall? Yes; all bare spots should be repaired in early fall. Inspect them again in spring for reseeding.

Would appreciate some information on the reason for spiking lawns. How is spiking done? Spiking is carried out for the purpose of opening up a heavy soil or very thick turf to permit air, moisture, and plant nutrients to reach the grass roots. The turf is perforated by rolling with a spiked roller on large lawns, or by a hand spiker on small areas. The tines of a digging fork plunged into the turf will answer as well.

Will spiking improve a poor soil? Spiking the soil alone will not improve it. The amount of top-dressing that can be worked in, together with fertilizer, will bring the improvement.

Under what conditions should spiking be done on a lawn? If the turf is thick or compacted through the use of heavy mowers or by rolling, or if the soil is a heavy clay and the grass is being starved even though fertilizer and water are applied, spiking has been found to be beneficial.

Is spiking practical on a small lawn? Yes, if the soil is heavy and the other conditions indicate a need for it.

What is the best time of the year to spike the lawn? As early in spring as it is possible to begin operations and the soil is not wet.

How late in fall can you cut a lawn? This will depend on the region and the severity of the winter. Throughout the East growth slows up in September; close cutting after that should be avoided, especially where winters are severe or lawn is new.

Will grazing the cows on the grass injure it? Grazing late in the fall would be the same as late mowing. It would deprive the grass of a winter top.

Will cows tramping on a lawn in the fall, leaving hoofprints, do any damage? If the sod is thin or the ground wet, the surface will become full of small depressions in which water will lodge, to the detriment of the grass.

Is it good practice to allow tree leaves to remain on the grass all winter? The leaves should be removed from the lawn. An accumulation of wet leaves on the grass in many instances will be harmful.

We are going to lime our lawn in December; in March use lead arsenate for beetle grub; in early May chemical fertilizer. Will this

be all right? This is a sound program. It might be better to apply fertilizer in April, particularly if its nitrogen content is largely organic.

How should a lawn be treated each spring and fall so as to assure a good carpet of green all through the summer months? Spring and fall treatments with fertilizers and humus-forming materials, while they will promote the vigor of the lawn grasses, will not overcome the effects of a long drought. Only a constant supply of moisture can assure this. (See Maintenance; Watering.)

If exceptionally good care is given to a lawn, will it last indefinitely or will it need to be redug and seeded? A well-cared-for lawn will normally last many years.

How do you increase the fertility of an established lawn? By top-dressing with humus-forming materials and fertilizer. (See Top-dressing.)

MOWING LAWNS

I have been told that the reason for my lawn not thriving is that the grass is cut too short. It is kept at 1 in. and sometimes less. Is this too short? What is the proper height at which to cut a lawn? One inch is too short. The food upon which the grass depends for development of root and top is manufactured in the green leaves (tops). In proportion as the grass top is restricted the roots also are restricted. Lawns in general would be in better shape and weeds less a problem were the grass allowed to grow longer; 2 to 2½ ins. is none too high for the average lawn.

How often should a terrace be mowed? This will depend upon the rate of growth. If the grass is kept vigorous through feeding and watering, mowing will be done more often than if grass is thin and is not so vigorous. If the height of the cut is maintained at 2 ins. the grass must be cut when it exceeds 2½ ins. Also, mowing will be more often done in early summer than through midsummer.

Should grass be left cut short for the winter? It would be better to allow 2 to 3 ins. of growth on the average lawn before winter sets in. This, however, would not apply to bent lawns. These are usually top-dressed in late fall.

In mowing a lawn must you use a catcher for the grass? The catcher would avoid the necessity of raking if the grass is heavy early in the season. When the cut is light, as in midsummer, the clippings are just as well left on the lawn.

The lawn was cut in October, and since then the grass has grown quite long. What should I do in spring with the grass? Before growth begins comb out the dead grass with a rake and if possible mow the area to give all possible light to the new grass.

Should grass clippings be saved? Certainly. They should be added

to the compost heap, or used as a mulch under broad-leafed evergreens or shrubs. They are a source of some plant food elements
and good humus.

Lawn Mowers

**I wish to keep the grass on my lawn more than 2 ins. high, but
my machine is not constructed to cut above this height. Is there
any way I can get around the problem?**   Wind a small rope around
the roller, or have special attachments adjusted to the wheels.

**How can you check the height a lawn mower will cut? How is
the cut adjusted?**   Place the machine on a level pavement and with
a rule measure the height from the pavement to the iron plate against
which the revolving blades cut. The height of cut is adjusted by
raising or lowering the roller.

**I seem to have difficulty adjusting my lawn mower to cut evenly.
How can you tell when a mower is properly set?**   The cutting
blades are adjusted by screws which are found on each side of the
reel blades, on the bearings. The adjusting of these screws will adjust
the evenness of cut against the plate at the bottom. The tightening of
one side more than another will after a time wear that side down,
causing an uneven cut. In this case the blades will have to be
ground and set by someone who understands this and who has
the equipment to do it.

Power Mowers

**I have a country place with a large lawn bordered by open wood-
land and pasture. What power mower do you recommend?**   A
rotary type mower, powerful enough to keep blackberry vines, seedling
trees, grapevines etc., from encroaching on the lawn area.

**My home is on the outskirts of town and I have a beautiful rolling
lawn of well-established bent grass. What power mower shall I buy to**

take care of this? By all means purchase a reel-type mower which will do as good a job as a well-sharpened hand mower.

We have a large, general purpose lawn, formerly mowed by hand. This has become too costly. What type of mower should we get? You would find a rotary mower completely satisfactory, and easier to maintain in good condition than the reel-type mower.

WATERING LAWNS

What is the best method of watering the lawn? Should one use a hose or a sprinkler? Should the ground be flooded? I have been given so much conflicting advice that I am confused. Avoid flooding the ground if possible. Flooding compacts the soil and invites disease. There is no doubt that a sprinkler designed to throw a fine spray over a large area is better than a hose. There is a more even distribution of water and this sinks in gradually without flooding. It is not the amount of water that is applied to the surface that helps the grass but that which reaches the roots 4 to 6 ins. below. If when watering the water collects in pools, shut the supply off for a few hours and water again. Once the pores of the soil have been opened the water will penetrate much faster. Flooding will occur when the soil is dry and especially if the water is applied too rapidly, as from a hose.

How can you hit the happy medium in lawn watering to avoid both burning out and scalding out? Watering should be started before the soil becomes dry. This will give better penetration, and food materials will be kept available in the soil. Enough should be given to moisten the soil for several inches deep.

How soon after the grass seed germinates would you water a slope? How often should water be applied in the first stages of growth? Slopes and terraces dry out faster than level areas, especially if the aspect is sunny. The period after germination is a critical one until the roots of the young grass take hold. If the surface looks dry, water with a fine spray. Do not play the water on too long and thus cause washing; just enough to moisten the soil. How often to water will depend upon the weather. If dry, water every 2 or 3 days until the grass is tall enough to shade the roots. Afterward adjust the watering to the weather.

How should a terrace be watered so that the water will soak in? The water I apply just runs off and does not penetrate. The top portion of the terrace will dry out sooner than the lower portion because of the moisture moving downward. Apply the water in a fine spray, moving back and forth with the hose and distributing the water evenly over the whole area. Only enough should be applied to soak in. After a few hours apply some more and repeat until the soil is moist to a depth of 4 ins.

Although watered 2 or 3 times a week my lawn in some places is drying out. Does it need more water? The lawn is not being watered; it is merely being sprinkled. The water it receives remains on the surface and evaporates. The soil down at the root area is always dry. When watering is needed, give the area a good, deep soaking; water again when examination of the soil shows the need for it. Do not wait until the soil is dry.

Is the chlorine in city water harmful to grass? No, not at all.

EDGING

What is the most practical way to edge the lawn along the path and driveway and around shrubbery beds? Mine were left as steps 3 in. or more high and now they are crumbling. High edges around paths and drives are difficult to maintain unless the turf is compact and the soil fairly heavy. If the path and drive are hard surfaced and not loose gravel, remove the sod from a space 3 ft. or more back from the lawn edge and grade the soil down to meet the surface of the path, leaving no step. Make the slope so gradual that the mower, when going over it, will catch all the grass. Turf edge along the beds should be kept about 2 ins. high to prevent the soil from being washed over the grass.

Is there some means of keeping the margins of my lawn neat without always taking a slice from the sod edge? Use edging shears. These are similar to a hedge shears except that they have long handles and the shears instead of being straight are turned at right angles to the handles. They are designed to trim the lawn edgings along paths and beds which a mower cannot catch.

Is there any material I can obtain that will make a permanent edging to the lawn? How about a strip of concrete? Concrete edgings are quite practical and can be stained a dark color to harmonize with the turf. However, unless they are sufficiently reinforced they will crack in winter. Concrete absorbs moisture. If the situation is exposed to full sun, the grass will dry out near the concrete. Wood strips, too, are used, but they must be constantly renewed. The low iron aluminum or asbestos corrugated edging strip, designed to be installed in sections, is a good answer. It is also inconspicuous.

ROLLING

Is the purpose of rolling a lawn to level the bumps? Not at all. Irregularities due to construction should not be corrected by rolling. The purpose is to settle the turf back after the winter action of freezing and thawing and to press the grass roots into contact with the soil.

What weight roller should be used? A light soil can stand a much heavier roller than a heavy soil. A very general rule for a ballast roller is 75 lbs. per foot of width. Better a light roller than a heavy one any time.

Is it best to roll the lawn when it is wet to obtain a good level surface? On a heavy soil that would be fatal, for the surface would dry out hard. Roll when only slightly damp, or even when the lawn is on the dry side.

How frequently should a lawn be rolled? Normally, one rolling in spring to settle the turf after winter freezing is all that is necessary.

COVER CROPS

What is meant by cover cropping? Cover cropping is the planting of a quick-growing, lush vegetation that can be turned under. The purpose is to build up the vital humus content of the soil and to crowd out weeds.

Can you tell me what to use for cover cropping? For very early spring planting rye, rye grass, common vetch. For summer (sown in June), buckwheat, cowpeas, soybeans. For fall, to hold over winter, rye, Rye Grass, Crimson Clover, Alsike Clover.

Is it better to sow lawn seed early in spring on our 100 × 200 ft., or sow buckwheat, soybeans, clover, or rye to combat weeds first and then seed to grass later in fall? Used to be a nursery; soil light, sandy muck. Without a doubt the cover-crop plan is to be preferred for weed control and the supplying of humus.

If you advise a crop to sow first, which would be best and why? It is possible to get two cover crops before fall. Sow rye or rye grass as early as possible in spring, and turn it under about June. Seed again to buckwheat or soybeans; preferably the latter, because it is a legume and will add nitrogen.

Should I use fertilizer? How much? Use fertilizer on summer crop to stimulate a thick growth. A 5–10–5 or similar complete fertilizer, 20 lbs. to 1,000 sq. ft.

How much seed would I need? Use 3 lbs. rye or rye grass seed, 1 to 1½ lbs. buckwheat, or 2 to 2½ lbs. soybeans per 1,000 sq. ft.

When should the crop be turned under? Turn the summer cover crop under about mid-August, approximately, or when it is still green.

Can anything be done to prevent weed seeds from germinating in the new lawn? Yes. After turning under the cover crop, treat the area with Lawn and Garden Cyanamid, a nitrogenous fertilizer which also kills weed seeds. See introduction.

How long after turning it under could I sow the lawn? Two to 3 weeks after turning under the summer cover crop prepare the lawn for seeding.

HUMUS AND PEATMOSS

Would a covering of peatmoss over the grass in summer help to hold the moisture and do away with watering? In actual practice this does not obtain. If the peatmoss becomes dry, it will absorb the moisture from the soil. Besides, the peat may encourage surface rooting unless it is incorporated *in the soil* at the time it is prepared for seeding. Peatmoss does much to retain moisture as it holds sixteen times its own weight in water.

I bought some black material which I was told was a good lawn food, but it did no good. Was this a fertilizer? No, it probably was not fertilizer. A lot of dark materials are being sold as lawn food. Most of them are waste from manufacturing plants and some of them may be injurious. Lawn food materials should be purchased only from reliable firms.

FERTILIZERS

What kind of chemical fertilizer is best for grass? We have part shade and part sunshine in our yard. A chemical fertilizer having 10 per cent nitrogen, 6 per cent phosphorus, and 4 per cent potash (10–6–4). Same for shaded area. Half of the nitrogen should be in organic form.

Is commercial fertilizer good for lawns? Yes, commercial fertilizer is excellent for lawns. The nutrients in it are fairly quick acting.

Can commercial fertilizer be used at any time? It is best applied in early spring or in late fall.

How is commercial fertilizer best applied? In dry form, either by hand or by a spreader. Mixing it with ⅓ its volume of fine soil or sand helps to get even distribution. Water in thoroughly.

What quantity commercial fertilizer should be used over a given area? Thirty lbs. per 1,000 sq. ft. is a good application.

Can you advise me the best top-dressing to use on a very sandy lawn to enrich the soil? Use good, screened topsoil, and add rotted manure, leafmold, or peatmoss—1 bushel to 8 bushels of soil. Broadcast fertilizer, as suggested above.

When and how should top-dressing be applied? Scatter over the lawn in spring as growth is beginning, using 2 bushels per 100 sq. ft.

Would you advise the use of superphosphate on the lawn? Superphosphate will prevent the grass from becoming too soft, a condition inviting disease; it also stimulates root action. Use 2 to 3 lbs. per 100 sq. ft.

When using only bone meal to fertilize the lawn, how much should I use in the spring, and how much in the fall? I want to make 2 applications for 1,000 sq. ft. If it is steamed bone meal (and this is the best), use 15 lbs. in spring and 10 lbs. in fall. For finely ground bone meal, 20 lbs. in spring and 10 lbs. in fall.

May bone meal be put on a lawn without injury to the grass? Yes, at any time.

May superphosphate be used at any time? Although there is little danger of injury from superphosphate, this would be better applied when the lawn is moist in spring to insure its being of value to the grass.

What value is tankage on a lawn? Tankage is valuable for its content of organic nitrogen that becomes gradually available to the grass as it is needed; also for the stimulation of bacterial action.

Are hardwood ashes good or not good for lawns? Hardwood ashes promote growth and hardness of grass stems. Applied as a top-dressing, 5 to 10 lbs. per 100 sq. ft., it is a good grass fertilizer.

When should lime and wood ashes be put on the lawn? It would not be necessary to put both on at the same time. Wood ashes contain a high percentage of lime as well as potash. Apply the lime in late fall and the wood ashes in April.

In applying lime, fertilizer (bone meal), arsenate of lead, and grass seed on lawns, can any two or more be safely applied simultaneously? Soil conditions and temperature exert considerable influence on these materials and their action at the time of application, making it advisable to apply them separately. Suggested procedure: Arsenate of lead followed by fertilizer at a week or 10-day interval; a few days later apply lime. If pulverized limestone is used, the seed may be applied simultaneously with it.

Should you sprinkle fertilizer over snow on lawns, which have bald spots, to restore the grass? Fertilizer will not restore grass if it has died out. Only reseeding would restore the bald spots. The seed may be sown in late winter, even on top of snow. In the South and elsewhere in areas where there is no deep freezing, a monthly application of a 10–6–4 formula complete fertilizer through the winter months will help keep the grass green and healthy.

The soil of our lawn is composed of sand covered thinly with black dirt. This has hardened. Would an application of fertilizer this spring help to open it up? Lime would open it up better than fertilizer. Use 60 lbs. ground limestone per 1,000 sq. ft. Follow some time later with fertilizer. Loosen soil with a spiked tamper, or tines of a fork, before applying.

How is fertilizer best applied to grass under trees? Do the tree roots use it up? The most complete method is first to feed the trees by placing fertilizer down in the root zone. This is done by removing pieces of sod and making holes by plunging a crowbar to a depth of 18 ins., the holes being about 2 ft. apart. Use a funnel and pour about ¼ to ½ lb. of fertilizer into the hole, water well, fill up with soil, and replace sod. Proceed to fertilize the lawn by broadcasting fertilizer in the usual way.

What will promote the growth of fall grass? It is best promoted by using rich, screened topsoil to which has been added the fertilizer suggested in the Introduction. Thoroughly mix the fertilizer at the rate of 1½ lbs. of fertilizer to 1 bushel of soil. At the end of August apply 2 bushels to 100 sq. ft. and, using the back of a rake, work the material down among the grasses. Water thoroughly.

When is the best time to feed the lawn, spring or fall? This depends on the type of fertilizer used. A quick acting one is best for spring use while one which releases nitrogen slowly like Golden Vigoro is best suited to use in fall. Spring *and* fall feeding is advised.

COMPOSTS

Should sifted compost be used to top-dress an established lawn? This is excellent practice. Apply in either spring or fall, first cutting the grass short so that the compost will work down to the roots when broadcast over the lawn surface.

How is compost applied to the lawn for top-dressing? It is usually taken on to the lawn in wheelbarrows and spread roughly with a shovel at first. The final spreading is done by using the blunt teeth of a wooden rake. The back of an iron rake or a coarse broom may be used to spread the compost evenly over the area and at the same time work it down around the base of the grasses.

How is compost prepared before being applied to lawns? The compost, when well rotted down, is first put through a ¼-in. wire screen. In large operations a power-revolving screen is used, but in small areas a section of ¼-in. wire mesh 4 × 3 ft. is nailed to a wooden frame which is tilted at an angle and supported by a prop. The compost is thrown against this to remove all foreign material like pieces of wood, stones, and coarse, unrotted compost. The screened compost is then thoroughly mixed with active fertilizer at the approximate rate of 4 to 5 lbs. of fertilizer per bushel of compost.

MANURES

What proportion organic fertilizer per 1,000 sq. ft.? Apply 30 lbs. of dried poultry manure or 15 to 20 of tankage per 1,000 sq. ft.

To what depth must fertilizer be mixed with the soil? Fork the material in and mix thoroughly with the upper 4 in. of topsoil.

What about the use of chicken manure on grass as a top-dressing? Chicken manure is a good grass stimulant. Use the dried product at the rate of 5 lbs. per 100 sq. ft.

Would you advise using well-rotted cow manure in preparing a lawn? How much on 1,500 sq. ft. of area? Because of its beneficial action on the soil and grass, rotted cow manure is the best of all materials to use in preparing soil for a lawn. If the soil is poor, apply a coating 2 to 3 in. deep.

How is cow manure best applied? Spread over the ground and dug into the soil. If used for top-dressing turf, it should be well pulverized, sifted, and a complete fertilizer added. (See questions on Top-dressing.)

Is mushroom manure for lawns? Mushroom manure, although not too rich in nutrients, is a splendid source of humus for lawns. It gives maximum results when worked into the soil at the time of preparation.

Can cottonseed meal and manure be used together when making a lawn? What proportion of cottonseed meal to manure? Yes, the combination is quite practical. The action of the cottonseed meal may be hastened somewhat by mixing with the manure. 1 part cottonseed meal to 15 parts manure is a good proportion.

Is sheep manure suitable for lawns? When is it best applied? Yes, a good grade of sheep manure makes a fine top-dressing for lawns. It may be applied any time during the season and is particularly valuable when applied early in spring and again in fall.

How much sheep manure should I use for 1,200 sq. ft. of lawn? Sixty lbs. is a good dressing. This is at the rate of 5 lbs. per 100 sq. ft.

I am told that if rotted cow manure is placed on my lawn in the fall I will not have to use commercial fertilizer on it for about 5 years. Is this true? Rotted manure is excellent material, but it should be used on the lawn in fall only after it has been so completely broken down that it can be worked in among the grasses and not merely left on top. One dressing in 5 years without any other fertilizer would not be enough to maintain the lawn. An annual dressing coupled with the use of a complete fertilizer would be better for keeping the turf in vigorous growth.

Do you suggest the use of farm manure for a grass lawn? If it is not fresh and if it spreads easily, farm manure can be applied lightly before the grass gets into very active spring growth. When growth is well under way, the surplus manure should be raked off.

I can get old hotbed manure. Is this good to dig into lawn? See question on mushroom manure. This is the same material.

Should lawns be covered with stable manure in the fall? As an agricultural practice, covering grass with manure in winter is an accepted one. On lawns it is sure to bring in weeds, and may injure the grass. It also makes a spotty lawn.

I have a large pile of gravel to dispose of. If I sift it, how much would I dare use to build up my lawn as a top-dressing and keep from rebuilding it? From the point of view of nutrients, sifted gravel would have no value as a top-dressing for a lawn.

What is the best time to fertilize the lawn with manure and commercial fertilizer? Apply in fall, but only if the manure is well rotted.

LIMING

What is the action of lime on lawn? If the soil is heavy, lime will help to keep it porous, permitting air and moisture to penetrate. Because of many decayed roots, lawns tend to become acid. Lime will correct this tendency and will release plant-food materials for the grasses.

What kind of lime is best to use? Pulverized limestone, also known as ground limestone, is the safest kind to use.

How much lime should be used on the lawn? Fifty lbs. per 1,000 sq. ft. is a maximum application for lawns at any one time. If a test reveals the need for more lime, put it on in two separate applications at an interval of several months.

How often should you lime a lawn? Frequency of liming will be determined by the type of soil, the grasses, and the amount of fertilizing materials used. The most accurate check is a yearly soil test for lime needs.

When is the best time of the year to put lime on the lawn? Late fall is best. When applied at this time, lime penetrates the soil to a greater depth than at any other time of the year.

Can lawns be limed in December satisfactorily? Yes, in fact December is a very good time to apply lime.

Is field lime good for lawns? When is it applied? Field lime is also known as agricultural lime, both being the same as ground or pulverized limestone.

I understand that "liming" an established lawn is ineffective, and may be harmful. Is there any way to correct an acid condition in such cases? Calcium in some form must be used to correct acidity and lime is the best form. Lime is not ineffective on an established lawn. It is needed. (See question on lime.)

DISEASES

What is the best prophylactic program to prevent brown patch or dollar patch? Keep the grass in steady growth, never allowing it to get a check by drying out. Keep regular mowing program with the length of the grass at 1½ to 2 in. If a bent lawn, do not exceed 1 in. Use a balanced fertilizer with a compost. In hot weather, especially when the humidity is high, rake with a wire rake twice a week. Every morning swish off the dew with a long bamboo pole. During June and July, and at other periods when fungus is feared, spray with a disinfectant. (See Introduction.)

What causes brown and dingy spots on our bent lawn grass? This is probably brown patch, a fungous disease that attacks most lawns in hot, humid weather but is more prevalent on bent lawns. The tops are injured, and in severe cases the roots, too, are killed. For control, see Introduction.

What is the best way to repair a lawn damaged with small spots? The grass seems to have died completely. The lawn was treated with arsenate of lead last year and with a combined fertilizer and grub killer this fall. This is probably dollar spot. It is not associated with grub-proofing treatment. Remove top 6 inches of soil and replace with fresh compost. Reseed (see Introduction). Or treat lawn area with crabgrass seedling killer, loosen soil with rototiller, and reseed.

What causes dollar spot, and what is the treatment? A fungus *Sclerotinia homoeocarpa.* See Control for Brown Patch, in the Introduction.

What is snow mold? This is a disease of closely cut turf observed at the edge of melting snowbanks. The disease will spread in high humidity at temperatures below 40° F. without snow. It is more prevalent on bent lawns (control same as brown spot).

Each spring I have a good grass lawn in a semi-shady location until we have a wet humid spell, then algae form and grass dies. Do you know of any treatment to prevent or lessen the damage caused by formation of algae? Algae or scum is usually related to wet-weather conditions or to wet areas in the lawn. Spray the infected spots with one of the preparations recommended in the Introduction. In a day or two rake the area over thoroughly and apply a dressing of sand.

What makes lawn grass turn yellow? We planted our lawn this fall. It came up very green, and now it has turned yellowish in spots. Spots where seeds fall too thickly and where extra fertilizer is concentrated will show this. Yellowing is also common in fall when too much moisture is present, evaporating too slowly from some areas. Run an iron rake through the spots and scatter sand mixed with a disinfectant. (See Introduction.)

What causes the ground to have white moldy spots after sowing grass seed? A common occurrence on newly seeded ground and somewhat related to the moisture conditions and the use of fertilizer. There is no indication that it is harmful. Should it increase before seed germination, sweep it with a broom to disturb it, allowing air to dry the surface. If it persists after germination, comb the spots once with a sharp-toothed rake.

INSECTS

What causes the lawn to have a yellow-brown color in late midsummer, continuing until snow? This is probably due to the action of beetle grubs which hatch out during the latter part of summer and begin feeding upon the grass roots. Dig up some of the brown area about September. If this is the cause, the grubs will be found under the sod. (See Introduction for control.)

While working on my lawn this fall I discovered several beetle grubs working their way into the ground. How can I get rid of them and when is the best time to do it? The best control is to apply arsenate of lead in August or in April to poison the grubs which are hatched from the eggs deposited by the beetles in the sod. (See Introduction.)

Is there any point in watering down arsenate of lead into my lawn if the neighbors do nothing about the beetle grub? The grubs of the Japanese and Asiatic beetles feed on the grass roots. You will be protecting your own lawn from damage through the use of arsenate of lead.

How can I grub-proof my lawn? We have Japanese beetles. See Introduction.

Is there any more effective way to eliminate a bad infestation of chinch bugs, in a beautiful lawn, than tobacco dust, and when is the proper time to combat this pest? A 1 per cent rotenone dust is equally effective, using 25 lbs. per 1,000 sq. ft. for each brood. (See Introduction.)

PESTS

What should be put on lawn full of earthworms? Bumps all over lawn. The use of arsenate of lead (see Grub-proofing) will eliminate worms. If arsenate of lead is not available, try the following: Lime water made by dissolving lime and allowing the liquid to settle and clear poured over the lawn in the evening. This will draw the worms to the surface. They can then be brushed off the following morning.

I was advised to use mowrah meal to poison worms in my grass. What is it, and how should it be used? Is it poisonous to children? Mowrah meal is used in cases where earthworms are injuring young grass seedlings and the use of any other chemical might injure the young grass. Mowrah meal is made from the butternut tree of India. It is an effective worm killer when fresh, but it deteriorates with age, especially if stored in a damp place. Apply it dry at the rate of 15 lbs. per 1,000 sq. ft. and water it in with a hose. It can be handled with safety and is harmless to human beings.

Are ants harmful to a lawn? Yes, in the sense that they form galleries in the soil and disturb the grass roots. Besides, they throw up mounds of soil, covering the young grasses and killing them.

What is a good way to get rid of ants in the lawn? Mix one part of tartar emetic to 10 parts powdered sugar and sprinkle a little around the ant heaps. Repeat for a day or two. If tartar emetic is unavailable, use thallium sulfate or Antrol.

Our lawn is overrun with ground moles. Could you tell us some way to get rid of them? We have tried trapping and gas, but can't seem to get them. Try (1) carbon disulphide, a teaspoonful at points 5 feet apart; (2) household lye a teaspoonful inserted every 20 feet; (3) paradichlorbenzine; drop in the runways every 6 to 10 feet; cover with soil. Apply cyanogas by pumping into mole runs with dust gun made for the purpose by the American Cyanamid Co.

How can I keep the skunks from digging in my lawn? The skunks are looking for the grubs of the common June bug. The grubs which are close to the surface are relished by skunks. (See Control of Grubs.)

WEED CONTROL

I have started a new lawn and used pure seed. I want to keep it free from weeds. Can you outline a program for weed control? Top-dress the lawn each spring (see Top-dressing); fertilize again in fall. Do not mow too close, not below 2½ ins. Repair poor and bare spots immediately and eliminate weeds before they have a chance to become well established and before they seed. Treat for beetle grubs and other insects and be on the alert in June for fungous diseases, especially if the weather is moist and hot. (See Introduction.)

We have an established lawn that is becoming so infested with Crab Grass that eradication by hand is impossible. Can you suggest any method of control? It is known that Crab Grass will not thrive under the slightest shade, therefore allow the grass to grow after the first of June to shade the young seedling Crab Grass. Cut when 6 ins. tall, but only reduce it to 3 ins. Allow grass to grow tall before another cutting and repeat until the end of August, then gradually lower cut. Reseed and top-dress.

Crab Grass has taken my lawn. Grass was planted 2 years ago in about one inch of good soil on top of dirt and shale rock from basement excavation. Can I rebuild lawn successfully without much expense? How? The soil now is probably well supplied with seeds of the Crab Grass that will germinate when the weather is warm. An inch of topsoil is not enough to grow a turf so thick that it will crowd out the Crab Grass. In August treat with Lawn and Garden Cyanamid to kill ungerminated crabgrass seeds. Loosen surface with rototiller or hand cultivator. Add 2 inches of compost to surface. In September reseed with Red Top and Perennial Rye Grass in equal proportions, 4 lbs. to 1,000 sq. ft. These will grow fast. Keep height of grass at 3 ins. If Crab Grass shows up next spring, increase height of grass to 5 ins.

Lawn is patchy, with Crab Grass; very thin layer of topsoil; many stones from excavation of cellar. Topsoil very difficult to obtain. What would you do? (1) Allow Crab Grass to grow in July to form seed heads. Burn with a kerosene torch. Cut lawn, rake prostrate stems, cut again or burn. Repeat when necessary until September. (2) Rake off all stones; prepare for seeding. Seed with mixture for poor soils.

Will frequent reseedings of good lawn seed discourage Crab Grass? A vigorously pursued program of seeding and fertilizing in spring and fall to maintain a dense turf is the best means of controlling Crab Grass.

What method would you suggest for eradicating Crab Grass from a new lawn? Feed in spring to promote vigorous growth. Reseed all bare patches. Watch for seedling Crab Grass in June. Eradicate by hand if possible. Allow grass to grow to 2 ins. in July. Rake the lawn to bring up Crab Grass stems; pull out or cut with a mower. Prevent seeding the first year. Fertilize. Reseed in early September.

My new lawn, made in April, became infested with Crab Grass in July and August. Can anything be done in spring to prevent reappearance? The Crab Grass undoubtedly seeded itself, ready to reappear when warm weather arrives. The best spring preparation to combat Crab Grass is to promote a thick growth of lawn grass by fertilizing and seeding. Do not cut grass below 2 ins.

Why does Crab Grass spread to a healthy Kentucky Blue lawn when the Crab Grass was cut regularly to ½ in. and wasn't given a chance to flower? Crab Grass, when regularly cut, will form seed heads on stems that lie close to the ground, or on stems so short the mower cannot catch them. Hence the advice about raking to bring up the prostrate stems.

Since Crab Grass is perpetuated only from seed, how early in the summer will all of the last season's seed be cropping up? Crab Grass seed germinates when hot weather arrives—approximately about June, but often much earlier. Presumably any seeds that are lying on the surface will then grow. Where conditions are unfavorable, the seed may remain dormant even for a number of years before germinating. Some will spring into growth through the lawn if patches of grass die from dryness, disease, or injury.

Why is it always deemed necessary to remove Crab Grass from lawns? Even though this dies down annually, and is of coarse texture, it provides a thick mat of green all summer, and its removal is some-

times almost impossible. Crab Grass doesn't start to grow until June. This means that the lawn would be bare, or filled with other weeds, until the Crab Grass becomes thick enough to form a carpet. Crab Grass turns an ugly color in fall and with an early frost it disappears again, leaving an unsightly area that exists all winter. Control of Crab Grass is necessary to an orderly place.

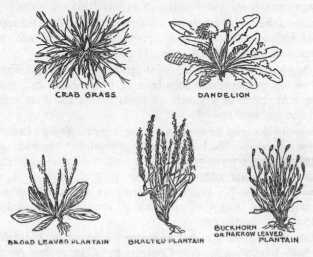

CRAB GRASS   DANDELION

BROAD LEAVED PLANTAIN   BRACTED PLANTAIN   BUCKHORN OR NARROW LEAVED PLANTAIN

SOME COMMON LAWN WEEDS

How is Crab Grass spread? Do you think it is possible that it is spread through the water hydrant? Does it come in grass-seed mixtures? It is spread by birds, and by animals that eat the grass and seeds; by wind, and by surface flooding. One plant is hardly noticed until it has seeded itself. Tests of several water-supply systems gave no indication of the presence of the seeds. New York State Experiment Station by test found it only in a few of the cheap seed mixtures.

What other names are usually applied to Crab Grass? Wire Grass, Summer Grass, Fall Grass, Water Grass.

We were told that White Clover in our lawn would die out the third year, but it's still going strong. Why? White Clover will be reduced when it builds up enough nitrogen in the soil to stimulate the grass, but it will return when the nitrogen supply in the soil is exhausted. This phenomenon has been called the clover grass cycle. (See Clover Control in Bent Lawns.)

How may I eradicate White Clover which is gradually covering my Blue Grass lawn? See Clover Eradication from Bent Lawns.

What other method than mowing can be used to eradicate a troublesome lawn weed which resembles a young pine tree and has deep, stringy, tough mats which have tremendous runners? This probably is

Cypress Spurge, a weed of sandy or gravelly soils. Full control is possible only when the roots are entirely removed from the soil, or crowded out by dense grasses.

Is there any way effectively to get rid of Creeping Jenny from a lawn without digging up the whole lawn and starting afresh? Raise the creeping stems with an iron rake and pull out or mow them close. Improve the surface drainage; this weed likes moisture.

How can I best rid my lawn of dandelions? By cutting top a couple of inches below the soil; applying a chemical adds to the effectiveness of the operation. (See Introduction.)

How do you get rid of devil's paint-brush in the lawn? This weed is found mostly on poor, thin soils because of the lack of competition. Try a tablespoonful of dry salt on each plant. Final answer is to build up the soil and reseed.

How can wild garlic be removed from lawn? Dig or hoe out the little bulbs as soon as the leaves appear. Small patches will succumb to sodium chlorate treatment.

In the lawn, what will kill ground ivy? The use of sodium chlorate, 1 to 2 ozs. per gallon of water over 100 sq. ft. A pressure sprayer is the best means of applying it. It may be applied in late fall without discoloring grass.

What is the easiest way to eradicate Narrow-leaf Plantain from lawn? See Introduction for Control by Chemicals. Apply the chemical about the time the seed stalk is forming.

How does plantain spread? By new shoots from the roots and by seeds. The seeds, coated with a sticky substance, adhere to shoes, clothes, and tools. They are thus carried and disseminated.

Is there any means of controlling quack grass growing on an embankment edging my garden? I haven't been able to keep it under control by hand. The only effective control for quack grass is to smother it out by laying boards over it, spreading tar paper, or heaping soil over it. Several weeks will be necessary to complete the process. Try disodium methyl arsenate.

What is the cause of sow-grass in lawn although calcium content is good? Sow-grass, sour-weed, or sorrel is not related to the alkaline or acid condition of the soil. This weed thrives in acid, alkaline, or neutral soils. Sow-grass commonly thrives on poor soil and in soils low in nitrogen. In good soils it cannot withstand competition with other plants.

How can a lawn be rid of sorrel, sow-grass, and chick-weed? It is too large to remake and it is but 4 years old. Has had some lime and a good fertilizer every year. Spray in June with iron sulfate, 1½ lbs. to 2 gallons of water. A second application may be necessary to complete the job. (See Introduction.)

How can weeds be kept from my lawn? I have 2 vacant lots on each side. (1) Burn the margins of the lots in spring and fall. (2) Cut down the weeds in the lots in June. (3) Maintain a close turf by seeding and fertilizing, so that no spots of bare soil appear.

Is there any method of eliminating weeds from a lawn other than by cutting out each individual root? Cover crops; turf building by top-dressing and seeding. The use of such chemicals as Crag 531, KOCN and PMAS is another means used in the battle to control weeds.

What is the cause of moss on a lawn? Moss is caused by poor drainage that keeps the areas damp; by poor aeration due to a hard, compact soil; and by a lack of fertility. It doesn't always indicate an acid soil.

My lawn does not do well. The soil packs hard and green moss appears on it. We dug it up twice and added peatmoss, fertilizer, and sand. We water and seed it, but no success. What would you advise? Spray the moss with a solution of iron sulfate. (See Introduction.) In a day or two rake off the moss. Dig the area at least 12 ins. deep. If the soil is heavy, work in small screened cinders. Lime, 5 lbs., and tankage or steamed bone meal, 4 lbs. per 100 sq. ft., will improve the soil texture and supply some lasting plant nutrients. If soil is sufficiently moist, do not water when seeding.

There are toadstools growing in my grass plot. What causes them, and how can they be eradicated? They appear in moist, warm weather and are usually associated with soils that are rich in organic matter, especially animal manures. Soak the ground thoroughly with Bordeaux mixture. Perforating the ground with a fork will help the solution to penetrate.

WEED KILLERS

Is there any chemical preparation that will kill weeds in a lawn? When temperature amd moisture conditions are right, iron sulfate has given good results. It is neither inflammable nor poisonous. Others are Crag 531, Scutl, Sodar and PMA. (See Introduction.)

Will the chemicals that are recommended for killing weeds in the lawn also kill the weed seeds? No, these chemicals, although successful under certain conditions in killing the weeds, have no effect on the weed seeds.

Can weed-control chemicals be used on all types of lawns? No, chemicals should not be used on new lawns, on bent lawns, nor on areas where Rough-stalked Blue Grass is growing.

Are weed-control materials dangerous to humans and animals? Sodium chlorate in contact with clothes and shoes becomes a fire hazard. It should not be spilled on wooden floors or other such places. Sodium arsenite, lead arsenate, and calcium arsenate are strong stomach poisons. The person handling them is safe if a dust mask is worn and the hands are thoroughly washed after using them. The treated turf is safe for man and animals after the material has been washed into the soil.

Will the chemical preparations that are used on lawns to kill weeds do so without injury to the grass?   There is bound to be some injury to the grass following the use of chemicals, and if too much is applied, the soil may be made sterile. The moisture conditions of the soil, as well as the temperature prevailing at the time of application, will largely influence the result. There are many factors over which the operator can exert no control. Chemicals, therefore, are not to be entirely depended upon. *When using commercial preparations, adhere strictly to the manufacturer's directions.*